From Rag to Riches & Ruin

My Times at The Salt Lake Tribune
1972-1998 & Beyond

By Diane M. Cole

Cover caricature by Dennis W. Green
Most interior photographs by Timothy L. Kelly and/or from archives of
Timothy Kelly
Dennis Green
Diane M. Cole
The Salt Lake Tribune

Dedication

to Denny for his enduring love and support

FOREWORD

As gray as *The Salt Lake Tribune* was on the outside, on its printed pages, it was colorful on the inside the last three decades of the 20th century. It's that *Tribune* personality that I've tried to capture and preserve in these pages in a typeface and layout reminiscent of *The Tribune.*

During my 25 years there, *The Tribune* made major changes: from hot type to cold type, from letter to offset presses, from newsrooms with old-school, small-time reporters who barely (some didn't) graduated high school, to the new breed of college-educated journalists of any sex who wanted to change the world. Computers were updating the way news stories were researched, written and stored -- and, to a limited degree, delivered to homes. What did not change was the male domination of the newspaper and the tension between *The Salt Lake Tribune* and Church of Jesus Christ of Latter-day Saints.

In the 1970s, '80s and '90s, *The Tribune* stood as the alternate voice to the dominant church that owned our closest competitor, the *Deseret News,* and tacitly ran state government. Since my departure, that church has made *The Tribune's* transition to the digital age all the more painful by obstructing long-time owners and squeezing funding. Despite promises to the contrary, new owners, as members of "the church," are having a hard time maintaining an independent voice.

It would be nice if my memories and observations, augmented by those of my peers and my husband, helped put the era into perspective for students of journalism and Utah's history and for readers in general. Even better would be our ability to generate understanding and a few laughs. I have written this book as a memoir rather than a history to narrow its focus and give myself latitude in the types of details covered. I also wanted to give readers a sense of how staffers' personal experiences affected and were influenced by *The Tribune.*

Though I have tried to be fair and factual, often turning to other sources when in doubt, I make no pretense about my account of events and people being absolutely accurate. My memories, opinions and descriptions are colored by the passing years and my evolving point of view. Some names have been changed to avoid embarrassment to family members and others.

It bothers me that I usually use last names for male staffers and first names and/or nicknames for women. However, I worked at *The Tribune* in sexist times, and this is how I knew most of my peers. On the job, I used first names for many male friends, but in an attempt at consistency and clarity here, I am primarily employing last names.

It took me more than 15 years after leaving *The Salt Lake Tribune* on the Ides of March in 1998 to put my thoughts about it into book form. The process was rewarding because it gave me a chance to revive my skills, relive memorable moments and stay in touch with people I adore. The project also enabled me to record my memories for my own future. As the daughter of parents who died with dementia, I worried if I waited much longer I might forget those stressful but often zany days working on a daily newspaper.

Part I - Breaking from Bountiful

1 - To the Newsroom in 1972

At first blush in 1972, *The Salt Lake Tribune* newsroom intrigued, intimidated and even disgusted me, a knock-kneed 19-year-old long sheltered by the brethren of Bountiful, Utah.

Downtown Salt Lake City, with its grid of big blocks and wide, parallel streets, seemed a world away from home. Ten miles, a wall of stinking oil refineries and suspicion separated my squeaky-clean suburb from the slightly soiled city. In my earliest memories of Utah's capital, sophisticated shoppers in hats and gloves strode between multi-story department stores as I, a tomboy in braids and pedal pushers, waited

Plaque outside the front door of the Tribune Building in the early 1970s.

wide-eyed in my parents' DeSoto in Main Street's parallel parking. At 14, I took Trailways buses to orthodontist appointments on South Temple Street, trips that taught me to turn away from the tattered, reeking riders seeking eye contact or slumped over benches at bus stops. Studio Theatre's high-backed chairs and heavy velvet curtains created a seductive hideaway for my first romantic kiss a year or so later, but the gilded Utah Theater would have been so much better. In high school, a girlfriend and I bought a couple of trendy school outfits at A&E and the Jak's Bridal Arts, both in narrow, carved-stone buildings squeezed between stately business buildings, before sneaking a peek into the dim, smoky

cavern of the Peter Pan to see old men and street-smart kids chalking pool cues.

The Tribune building in the 1960s.

The Tribune Building, smack dab in the middle of all this glamour and grit, impressed this small-town college student. Its ten stories of Art Deco-style brick were faced with glass and marble marked by bronze plaques of the First Amendment and a Pony Express stop. The foyer, with creamy, intricately coffered, two-story ceiling and carved brass and glass mail slot across from the elevators, conveyed elegance and importance. Goosebumps broke out on my arms. Maybe I was just cold in a skirt and jacket too light for winter. If I'd known more about American government and history, I could have attributed the prickles to the prospect of working for an institution that promoted free speech and religion in a state where I held my tongue about my beliefs. I'd been a nonbeliever for as long as I could remember.

My afternoon appointment for a part-time typist position was in the editor's office, I had been told, so I gingerly pressed the elevator button to the second floor. A knot gripped my gut. Dreading another job rejection (I never seemed to have the right connections in the Mormon enclave where I lived) yet wondering whether I was ready for a major change, I gulped in some smoggy air, yanked down the hem of my newest minidress and plunged into the fray. That is, once I figured out which dented, steel-framed glass door led to my future.

A long-haired kid about my age sneered while pointing out the editor's office in the northwest corner of a room twice the size of a basketball court. I had found the newsroom, a dingy, cluttered helter-skelter. Once I reached the laminated counter separating the mess from the editor's office, a secretary with a teased, blond bouffant greeted me warmly and waved me over to a bum-broken, greasy chair while grabbing the phone to announce my arrival. I crossed and uncrossed my spindly legs several times as I blinked through the blue haze drifting over clumps of clunky, disheveled desks strewn with newspapers, mail and marking pens. A four-sided box clock dangled from the yellowing ceiling traversed by a tangle of steel tubes. Musty air infused with acrid tobacco smoke assaulted my sinuses; the din pounded my ears. Phones rang non-stop; names were yelled across the office; machines clacked to a beat in the background.

A mismatched set of middle-aged men identified themselves as Will Fehr and Keith Otteson. They would be talking to me in tandem. Only later did I realize how odd that was. They weren't particularly pals, and they didn't "talk" in the normal sense of the word. More like muttered. Meantime, mole-like creatures either typed, telephone receivers propped against their ears, or leered over half-glasses as the Mutt and Jeff of editors led me across a 1940s-era, cigarette-butt-stained, tan linoleum floor into an absent editorial writer's office where we found three stout oak chairs.

This was Utah's largest newspaper, the winner of a Pulitzer Prize in 1957 for coverage of the worst commercial airline disaster at that point in history. The Grand Canyon crash had killed 128 passengers. To me, an outsider from the fringes of a small, conservative town, it was Timbuktu: foreign yet alluring. My neighbors, who could detect the slightest whiff of exposure, would say the cigarette smoke was sinful. There were many men and few women bustling about in this sooty chaos, so unlike the quiet, orderly offices I knew. With people rushing, slamming down receivers and talking excitedly, it was was clear that something interesting was happening here. Even while doubting I could break into such a different job my second year of college, I had to try.

Since my parents pinched pennies from jobs at Hill Air Force Base and my modest scholarships covered only a fraction of my school expenses, I needed to work somewhere to pay tuition and fees. I was going nowhere at the University of Utah Admissions Office, where bored, dejected women in dull, dead-end jobs picked on part-time clerks lucky enough to go to college like me. For 20 hours a week, I typed details from entrance applications onto paper tape punched full of tiny holes. These were the days before computers talked to one another, so at the end of each shift, I'd roll up my punch tape and take it downstairs to be fed into the administration building's huge computer.

Strange and scary as it seemed, I figured *The Tribune* probably wasn't much more dangerous than the Salt Lake County Sheriff's Office where, fresh from high school, I'd worked graveyard with an overly friendly deputy.

Most importantly, first-hand journalism experience could help me compete for a scarce high school English-teaching job. As an added bonus, I would be working with people outside the usual Utah fold. People whose principles I might understand.

Owned by a family corporation, most of Catholic Irish descent, *The Tribune* provided the alternative voice to the Church of Jesus Christ of Latter-day Saints (LDS) dominating city and state. While the political waters had calmed by my time, the newspaper was furiously anti-Mormon in the beginning. Early editions of the *Salt Lake Daily Tribune* and *Utah Mining Gazette,* first published April 15, 1871, referred to LDS Prophet Brigham Young as a "Satanic" dictator.[1]

With LDS sensitivity and power always simmering beneath the surface, conflict between the church-owned *Deseret News* and *The Tribune* ebbed and flowed through the years until finally bubbling over the top, threatening journalistic independence in Salt Lake City. That part of the story comes later.

I knew next to nothing of the newspaper's institutional history when I ventured into *The Tribune* for the first time that frigid day in February. Journalism was not my dream. I hadn't even considered working on my high school or college newspapers. To me, *The Tribune* was merely my anti-Mormon dad's entertainment, the Sunday Comics and a means to my teaching goal.

Mike Korologos, the guy in charge of promoting *The Tribune* to the public, alerted my University of Utah public-relations class to the job opening. I knew of the Greek with the Muppet mouth and dark-rimmed glasses from "Inquiring Editor," a locally televised contest he hosted for high school students. He also was the front man for the Old-Fashioned Fourth of July at Lagoon amusement park, where kids would stuff themselves with pie and watermelon between races down the Fun House slide and twirls on the Tilt-a-Whirl. Students who read sports news might have recognized his byline from ski stories. When asked how to get journalism work, Korologos told us to get a foot in the door and climb up from the bottom. "We're looking for a typist right now, so come on down and apply."

I called for an interview, the only one to take the bait.

Fehr, a tall, balding and neatly dressed man who talked from the back of his throat -- a theater director would say he didn't project -- started my interview.

"Can you type?"

I leaned forward to hear his soft-spoken words.

"Maybe about 70 words a minute with errors?" My voice quavered.

He handed me a sheet of legal-size paper to prove it after the interview.

Otteson, a Richard-I'm-not-a-crook-Nixon lookalike, squinty eyes, flapping jowls and all, stared at the floor. Or my bony knees, which were exposed. Then, growling from the side of his mouth, he informed me he would be my boss, keeper of my schedule. "You'll type scanner corrections for the Copy Desk on the late shift." Whatever that was.

"When can you start?" Fehr wanted to know.

"I have to give my two-week notice."

"We need you before that. See Shirley Jones [the editor's secretary] about the type test and paperwork."

Keith Otteson

I apparently passed the test, taken at the absent City Desk secretary's typewriter in the midst of newsroom bustle. As I pushed out through the door, I wondered what I was getting into here.

For communications experts, neither Fehr nor Otteson was especially informative. What I knew, I learned from Mrs. Jones, who chatted like she'd known me for years. She gave me appointments to get my picture taken for an identification badge and a physical exam with Dr. White upstairs. I would receive $125 each week, prorated for part-time work (more than I was making at the U.). It was some time later that I learned why we were paid weekly instead of bimonthly like most people: Management didn't want to be bothered by staffers who begged for advances after drinking away their wages within a day or two of payday.

Jeanne Milde, I was told, would show me what to do when I arrived for my 2 o'clock shift Saturday. She would be my immediate supervisor.

Within a week, I discovered I had enlisted in an outfit filled with an odd assortment of characters I eventually would call family. Bountiful became a place to write about, not a place to be.

As Thomas Wolfe would say in his novel of that name, You Can't Go Home Again. Some of the men who inhabited *The Tribune* when I entered the scene resembled the author's 1920s journalists. But there were important differences.

> They were a motley crew, a little shabby and threadbare . . . some of them had the red noses which told of long hours spent in speak-easies . . .
>
> There was something jaded in the eye, something a little worn and tarnished about the whole man, something that got into his face, his tone, the way he walked, the way he smoked a cigarette, even into the hang of his trousers . . .
>
> It was something wearily receptive, wearily cynical, something that said wearily, 'I know, I know. But what's the story? What's the racket?'
>
> And yet it was something that one liked, too, something corrupted but still good, something that had once blazed with hope and aspiration, something that said: Sure. I used to think I had it in me, too, and I'd have given my life to write something good. Now I'm just a

whore. I'd sell my best friend out to get a story. I'd betray your trust, your faith, your friendliness, twist everything you say around until any sincerity, sense or honesty that might be in your words was made to sound like the maunderings of a buffoon or a clown -- if I thought it would make a better story. I don't give a damn for truth, for accuracy, for facts, for telling anything about you people here . . . except insofar as they will help to make a story . . . So there I am, folks, with yellow fingers, weary eyeballs, a ginny breath and what is left of last night's hangover and I wish to God I could get to that telephone to send the story in, so the boss would tell me to go home, and I could step around to Eddy's place for a couple more highballs before I call it another day . . . in my heart I've always wanted to be decent . . . I hate sham and hypocrisy and pretence and fraud and crookedness . . I have a sense of humour, I love gaiety, food, drink, good talk, good companionship, the whole thrilling pageantry of life. . . I'm really not as bad as some of the things I have to do . . .[2]

As cynical, slouchy and even weary as they might be, only a couple of the journalists I knew qualified as liars, cheats and backstabbers who would stoop to the sewers for a story. For the most part, the reporters and photographers at *The Tribune* kept their integrity intact, even if they sometimes could be insensitive to the pain of victims. As a whole, they cared about the people in their stories. I wish I could say the same for some of their successors, whose tales will unfold in time.

---

[1] O.N. Malmquist, The First 100 Years, A History of The Salt Lake Tribune, 1871-1971, copyright 1971, pp. 46-52.

[2] Thomas Wolfe, You Can't Go Home Again, 1940, Chapter 20, p 289.

2- Newsroom Security

The ID cards were a consequence of interlopers in the newsroom. Student anti-war protests led by Kathy Collard, Jeff Fox, Bruce Plenk and Stephen Holbrook, whose family owned Lakewoods Home Furnishings in my hometown, were still simmering on the University of Utah campus, but their causes barely penetrated my goal-oriented consciousness. My nose was too firmly pressed to the grindstone to get involved even if I sympathized. I was just finishing high school May 4, 1970, when Ohio's National Guard shot four unarmed students and wounded nine others at Kent State University, but the horrific incident touched off anti-establishment sentiments and incidents at the U. of U. that fall. A sit-in interrupted business in the Park Building where I worked, an ROTC building was bombed, and an attempt was made to burn the condemned intercultural building. The junior prom died and sororities shriveled from lack of enthusiasm and relevance. The Beatles were singing, "Give peace a chance."[3]

Thirty-four young adults, organized as the United Front to End the War and coordinated by 29-year-old Holbrook, held a prolonged sit-in in *The Tribune* newsroom May 18, 1971 over coverage of the Vietnam War, the local protest movement and environmental issues.[4]

Demonstrators lumped the daily morning *Tribune* and the six-evening-a-week *Deseret News* together in their claim that establishment papers monopolized news coverage through their 1952 joint-operating agreement (JOA) whereby production, circulation and advertising costs, as well as profits, were shared.[5]

Scruffy students sat on the newsroom floor beside crammed-together gun-metal desks as editors, reporters and support staff worked around them. Several staffers loitered outside the circle of bodies, watching and wondering what might happen next, while someone scrambled to track down the boss, Publisher John W. "Jack" Gallivan.

When found at a Westminster College Board of Trustees meeting, Gallivan hustled back to address the protesters, whom he described as "grossly unfair and grossly rude" for refusing to meet with him in a first-floor room set aside for

visitors. After his followers voted to stay put, Holbrook had insisted on remaining in the newsroom where reporters could witness the action. "We are tired of living in a society where all decisions are made in back rooms," he informed the publisher.[6]

Tribune coverage of sit-in.

I would agree that you are nonviolent and fairly gentle and that you are cluttering up my newsroom," Gallivan addressed the group. "We are hard put to meet deadlines every day. Your presence here is interfering with that production. Those who stay are trespassing."[7]

After his retirement decades later, Gallivan remembered the showdown fairly clearly.

I got a call that the hippies had moved in and taken over the newsroom. When I got downstairs, there must have been 20 or 30 of them sitting on the floor, interfering with production. So I told them that they were not accepted here, but if they would come to a conference room we had downstairs, I could hear what they had to say. They refused to do it. They were going to sit there, by God.

So we called the police. The police explained to me that they couldn't arrest anybody on private premises, but I could. So one by one, I arrested them, and then the police took them off and turned them loose when they got down to City Hall. All they did it for was publicity. We made it clear in an editorial after that any demonstrators in *The Tribune* would get no publicity whatsoever. They never came back. Steve [Holbrook] and I became very good friends after that, and he's been a great community servant.[8]

Korologos remembered another version of the story's end. As Gallivan passed by his cubicle after protesters left, he suggested Korologos should have handed out forms for organ donation [a *Tribune* promotion]. Mike retorted, "All you'd have gotten was assholes," to which Gallivan doubled over in laughter.[9]

Some staffers never seemed to forgive Holbook's presumed offense. His later triumphs (such as becoming an influential state legislator at an early age) and trials (his arrest for soliciting sex) evoked equal disdain. If he hadn't invaded their space, *Tribune* newsmen might have been less critical of his long hair and beard. As Utah's more liberal press, they might have appreciated his efforts for peace and social change, including better services for homeless and mentally ill Utahns. As it was, they spit out profanities at the mention of his name, and his 1981 arrest in Salt Lake City for trying to solicit a 17-year-old Job Corps resident provoked snorts of glee.

After the sit-in, most of the public was kept at bay with newsroom door locks and occasional guards.

Ironically, Chicago Charlie (Kyriakos "Carl" Zahos), whose son became Steve Holbrook's surrogate son, always managed to get in by claiming to be Korologos' compatriot. The ripe-smelling tramp in dirty, floppy hat adorned with plastic flowers surreptitiously "traded" pornography for hand soap from the men's lavatory. He brought a human skull into the newsroom one day. "Claimed it was some Turk he'd machine-gunned," according to reporter Mike Carter. "Just sat there and screamed into Korologos' cubicle."[10]

My memory's version of the story: When Greece summoned him to his homeland to celebrate his Audie Murphy-type act of heroism in its war with Bulgaria, Zahos pinpointed a mass grave of enemy soldiers he'd single-handedly gunned down and buried. Zahos then smuggled one skull home in his dirty shorts and gave it to *Tribune* copy editor John O'Connor, whose wife

expelled the souvenir from the house. Another staffer snapped it up and turned it into a *Tribune* icon.

Chicago Charlie

Truth be told, Korologos encouraged his fellow Greek's antics, and he never called *him* an asshole. He would tell inquirers how Zahos immigrated to Chicago, thus his nickname, before heading for a job in Bingham Canyon's copper mine. His wife once had him committed to a mental hospital, where he stayed about a year before given a card certifying his sanity. When anyone accused him of being nuts after that, he pulled out his card and said, "This card says I'm legally sane. Where's yours?"[11]

Another street person to penetrate newsroom security truly was one of the first hippies of the 1960s, Charles "Charlie Brown" Artman.

Charlie Brown, remembered reporter John Keahey, commandeered the Brigham Young monument on Main Street and was "the only guy at the U. who audited every class and NEVER wore shoes, even in winter."[12]

He "looked like Batman or Zorro with a long black cape and a POS 5-speed bike," added staffer Gordon Harman.[13]

This "reincarnated Indian" of the 1960s[14] lost his bid for the Salt Lake City

Commission in 1971. For awhile, he lived in a teepee stowed during the day atop an old bus dubbed The Yellow Submarine[15] and pitched at night atop the hill marked by the university's big "U."

Charlie Brown's mantras were individual freedom, assistance of the poor and rescue of the planet. He smoked marijuana, created a commune on M Street and was arrested repeatedly but never convicted. Years before dying from hepatitis in 1991, he became a Mormon elder.[16]

Among other regular newsroom visitors was Monroe Fleming. Always clad in suit and tie, this African American Mormon collected outdated newspapers for the poor. Born in 1896 in Mississippi, he promoted black musicians in Utah and worked as a busboy, waiter and coat checker at Hotel Utah.[17]

Though denied the LDS priesthood because of his color, he proudly proclaimed Mormon President Spencer W. Kimball his friend and prophet. "I don't bother about it much," he said of his inferior status in the church. "I'll leave it to somebody else . . . My daddy always said, 'It don't matter how you get to the top of the mountain, the view of the moon is the same.'"

Fleming did become one of the first black Mormons admitted to the priesthood, but in my mind, he should have been the very first. Joseph Freeman, a young man my age, got the honor. After Prophet, Seer and Revelator Kimball announced the revelation June 8, 1978, Fleming told *Tribune* reporter Charles Seldin he had "yearned for this day . . . prayed for this day."[18]

Publications across the country picked up Fleming's quote that his Mormonism was no longer like "feeling you're a guest in your father's house."[19]

It goes without saying that women were not given the great blessing then or later.

---

[3] "Give Peace a Chance," John Lennon, 1969.

[4] "34 Protesters Invade Tribune, Police Arrest 13," *The Salt Lake Tribune*, May 19, 1971, Page B-1.

[5] Paul Swenson, "The Daily Double: Deadline in SLC," Utah Holiday, December 5, 1974, p. 4.

[6] *Tribune*, May 19, 1971.

[7] Ibid.

[8] John W. Gallivan interview by Paul Rolly and Dawn House, Snyderville, May 2005, for "Hard news and raucous times," *The Salt Lake Tribune*, May 16, 2005..

[9] Mike Korologos email, January 19, 2014.

[10] Mike Carter to facebook's Tribune group, February 3, 2012.

[11] Mike Korologos email March 20, 2017.

[12] John Keahey to facebook's Tribune group February 2, 2012.

[13] Gordon Harman to facebook's Tribune group. February 2, 2012.

[14] W,J. Rorabaugh, *Berkeley at War: The1960s*, 1989, p.135.

[15] Joseph Bauman, "Charles Artman, Utah's 1st True Hippie, Dies at 52," Deseret News, April 25, 1991.

[16] Ibid., Robert Macri, In Memoriam: Charlie Brown, *Sunstone*, October 1991.

[17] UPI, "Monroe Fleming, One of First Black Mormon Priests, Dies," *The New York Times*, August 4, 1982.

[18] Charles Seldin, "Priesthood of LDS Opened to Blacks, *The Salt Lake Tribune*, June 10, 1978, p. 1.

[19] *Kokomo* (Indiana) *Tribune*, June 11, 1978.

3 - Uncommon Copy Desk Characters and Culture

Tribune Topix, an in-house monthly newsletter prepared by Korologos and patterned after the *New York Times' Winner and Sinners,* which emphasized grammar, editing and good writing,[20] introduced me to the newsroom March 8, 1972, as a "blonde U. coed in journalism."

As Jeanne Milde's assistant, I didn't just start on the bottom rung of *The Tribune* ladder, I toiled beneath it.

Jeanne showed me a legal-size sheet of paper covered with triple-spaced type interspersed with blue, handwritten editing marks. We were to type the blue words, or corrections, between slashes above the typed lines. Then we would pass the edited copies to the slot man (chief copy editor) sitting in the middle of the horseshoe-shaped Copy Desk to be checked and sent up air tubes to the scanner. "What's a scanner?" I asked. She didn't know. "Where's the scanner?" She didn't know. "You just give them to Mr. Halliday," the slot man.

Built like a fireplug in a flowered orange blouse and brown stretch pants with stirrups, my new supervisor sat on a pillow in front of her IBM Selectric typewriter beside the Copy Desk. Her dark-rooted auburn hair was pinned into a bun, and her rhinestone-studded, horn-rimmed glasses half covered heavy blue eye shadow.

The mother of five, who had nabbed her job through welfare services, couldn't understand why her kids couldn't wait for her in the office. She was baffled by our system of typing corrections onto the papers passed back and forth to the Copy Desk. She couldn't imagine how computerized scanners downstairs in the backshop transformed our messy copy into justified type to be pasted onto news pages.

Each evening after his own job preparing used housewares for resale at Deseret Industries, Jeanne's mentally challenged boyfriend Arthur, wearing a crewcut, rolled-up jeans and wide grin, proudly herded his five charges across the newsroom to pick up Mom for dinner. One uncouth member of the Copy Desk crew aped Arthur's happy-go-lucky gait and loud, innocent greetings. "Wanna see the ring he gave me?" Jeanne beamed the first time I met him.

Before many nights on the job, it became clear that certain people on the Copy Desk, no matter how forbidding they seemed, were the ones to consult about my new duties. My superior, Ms. Milde, didn't have a lot of answers, and when she wasn't late for work, she didn't show up at all, leaving me to pick up the slack.

Work turned out to be fairly simple for typists in the era of ATEX and the ECRM autoreader (scanner for setting and justifying type).[21] Between slashes, we typed whatever the copy editors wrote with blue felt-tip pens above the lines of type from reporters. At the top of each story, we typed the headline with size codes.

What was simple for typists wasn't necessarily so for old-time desk editors. They were in the throes of making the transition from penciling corrections onto three-ply typewritten pages pasted together into one long story. The new system could be cumbersome and frustrating because sentences and paragraphs could no longer be ripped from one place in a story and pasted into another. The news copy of certain reporters was so heavily edited, or "dirty," that entire stories had to be retyped, slowing production. Business Editor Robert Woody's stories were notorious for dirty copy.[22]

Copy editors also had to contend with new, unreliable headline counts to fit the new cold-type system that replaced hot lead. The "Borg Count," created by one of their own and widely used in the business, didn't always work. Printers in the backshop "blue room," where the pneumatic tubes spit out copy for the scanner, also were learning the new system and regularly sent page proofs (copies of pages containing pasted-up stories) to the Copy Desk too late for careful proof-reading and corrections before pages went to the presses.

The Copy Desk was dominated by burned-out veteran journalists serving a sentence for misbehavior. One rim rat, as copy editors were known for sitting around the outside of the round desk, sniffed women's chairs after they stood up and declared his wish to be reincarnated as a lesbian. Several kept locked drawers with mini-bottles and pornography to help them through slow nights. The toilet tank in the men's room was a favorite cooler for a flask.

Disgusting or pitiful behavior apparently was the way creative men, in this case, coped with their dead-end status. Each had once been a crack reporter or editor who was washed up or had screwed up, whether by missing too many nights on the job, insulting the editor or getting too creative in print. It was too late for them to leave *The Tribune* but too early to retire.

But even the worst of these guys more than made up for their lack of class with a ton of talent. They knew their business, including grammar, spelling, news style, facts and libel law. They still stood as the last line of defense against mistakes that would undermine *Tribune* credibility.

As staffer Brian Nutting put it, "The Copy Desk was the last refuge of all the burned out guys from the various news desks. Lots of bitterness and cynicism. But some of those guys were real wordsmiths who not only could catch typos and write headlines, they sometimes actually improved on the copy and found embarrassing errors or omissions."[23]

In fact, Brian found himself on the Copy Desk in 1974 after having been a reporter, a move that mystified him. "At the time, I was upset, because being a reporter is so much more fun than sitting in the office. Looking back, I'm glad it happened, because it prepared me for other things later on."[24]

* * *

Allan Dean Halliday

Allen Dean Halliday, also known as Filthy Smith, Filthy McNasty or just plain Deano, usually sat in the desk's slot as chief copy editor. As such, he distributed stories among editors on the rim to be edited for errors and given a headline. He then checked our typed corrections and headlines before rolling and stuffing the pages into capsules that he slipped into vacuum tubes hanging above his head for a quick trip to the composing room.

That task complete, Deano would lift his skinny legs onto the desk, cross his ankles and

lean way back in his tottering, puke-green chair to ash his cigarette up the tube. He'd follow up with a few snide remarks about the story's reporter or lewd comments about the handful of females in the office. Finally, a wicked, nasally chortle wafted across the newsroom.

Nancy Melich, a young writer for *Sunday* magazine, regularly sent copy up the Copy Desk's steel tubes, giving Deano an opportunity to drawl, "Put it where it fits best, Sweetheart."

While Nancy might blush and burn at such tacky treatment, I hardly noticed his noise after awhile. I had grown up with four foul-mouthed brothers and critical parents and could tolerate his kind of flak.

Deano reminded me of a naughty little boy spouting dirty words and caustic criticism for attention. But of course he was hardly a child. With his coloring, lazy-lidded eyes and sonorous, sardonic remarks between puffs on his cigarette, he looked a little like singer Deano Martin.

Born in Salt Lake City, Deano attended the U. of U. before taking a job as managing editor of the *Vernal Express* and then serving in the Korean War. *The Tribune* hired him away from Kennecott Copper Corporation in 1953.

Deano was a good reporter, but occasional binges and mischief got him fired more than once. In one instance, he wrote a fictitious story about the death of a politician's son that embarrassed both the politician and *Tribune* management. Rehired for the Copy Desk, he shared slot duties with nemesis Hank McKee.

Deano was a good editor, too. He "had a habit of sitting low in his chair and looking over the newsroom as if it was his realm," reporter George Raine recalled. "In a way it was, because he was the lord of grammar, and he made us look good when we had lost our way in a sentence."[25]

Deano could write a headline himself -- "Keep Hall Monument? 'Thou Shalt Not'"[26] -- and could be kind, patient and helpful to young people on the Copy Desk.[27] Or not. "The main advice I remember from Dean started with 'f,'" countered staffer Ben Ling.[28]

Ultimately, Deano's penchant for pranks led to his permanent ouster, a rarity for *The Tribune*. One night in 1980, he yanked an electrical component from the tape-punching equipment. Another night he sprayed a wall with a fire extinguisher to demonstrate the newsroom's filth.[29] That dripping streak of grunge -- staffer Gordon Harman called it the "clean streak"[30] --

stayed on that wall, as a thorn in our sides, long after Deano's exit. "That was Deano's last hurrah," Harman noted. "All the drinking and insubordination didn't matter."[31]

The Tribune had employed Deano on and off for 28 years. He landed at Portland's Oregonian, and within a few months of leaving there in 1993, he died of emphysema at 63.[32]

* * *

When sober, **Hank "Crash" McKee**, a handsome World War II pilot from the Lubbock (Texas) *Avalanche-Journal*, showed a little more class than some of his peers on the Copy Desk. He had been city editor, but when I knew him, he worked as night city editor and filled the slot on Deano's days off.

Sporting penny loafers, starched white shirt with rolled-up cuffs, and pressed jeans cinched by a skinny belt and under-turned cuffs, this square-jawed, dimple-chinned cowboy wore his passions on his sleeve. Among them were poker, alcohol, prospects of working at the *Denver Post* (which he eventually did) and a certain attractive reporter, JoAnn "Fifi" Jacobsen. Hank would yank his comb from his rear pocket and slick back his sidewalls before striding the thirty or so feet between his rickety chair and her desk for an editing consultation conducted with crinkled brow over twinkling eyes and a sideways smile.

A couple of Copy Desk grumps slashed JoAnn's news copy mercilessly, bitching and moaning about fluff between her ears. Hank took umbrage at crude, rude remarks tossed around about his favorite girl reporter and more than once, with furrowed brow, sternly warned his co-workers to keep it to themselves.

Yet when JoAnn tried to use Ms. in a story, recalled Gordon Harman, one of my successor typists, Hank bellowed from the Copy Desk barrel (slot): "It's NOT in the style book, so it's NOT getting in!" Jerry Dunton, late city editor, shot back: "Get your head out of your ass and out of the Dark Ages!" Gordon thought they'd go to blows. JoAnn eventually got her way.[33]

JoAnn Jacobsen

Hank was visibly shaken when JoAnn showed an interest in television reporter Sandy Gilmore, who was nearer her age and had created an international incident in 1966 by trying to leave Russia with a bronze bear from his Leningrad hotel. That was during the Cold War, after all, and Utah's congressional delegation had to help get him out of jail.

Hank drove by Gilmore's apartment late one night when JoAnn was there. The phone rang. Hank advised Gilmore JoAnn's father would be displeased if he knew she was there. "Sandy threw a fit, and I went home. That may have been our last date," JoAnn remembered.[34]

Decades later, this is how reporter Brian Nutting remembered Hank:

He was hard to please sometimes, but I think his insistence on fully reporting a story and not guessing about some of the facts really helped me become a better reporter. One of his favorite sayings was 'bull shit' -- except it took him a long time to say those words: buuuuuulllllll shiiiit.[35]

Hank called me Sweetheart in a fatherly, chivalrous sort of way. I suppose that was appropriate, since he was my mother's age.

* * *

John "Shanghai Jack" O'Connor, a nutty but good-hearted ex-sailor with a crew cut, dreamed between nips and headlines of working for the *Boston Globe* back home or moving to San Francisco. Frustrated as hell on the Copy Desk, he stashed mini-bottles in the toilet tanks and locked Chicago Charlie's raunchy magazines in his desk drawer. I understood he had an ailing wife and two daughters he dearly loved.

"He's turned to the bottle and probably is headed further down if he stays at *The Tribune*," I told Mimi, my journal. "He's actually quite intelligent, but . . . "

Claiming he drank so he could write like Ernest Hemingway, Shanghai left me love notes. For my 21st birthday, his card was signed, "Torridly," (double underline) Shanghai." Another playful message told me I was stupendous and ended with, "Don't tell Vandra (Huber, my mentor on the Copy Desk]." I considered his declarations of love diversions from newsroom boredom.

* * *

When I got nervous on the job, copy editor **Edwin "Teddy Bear" Heal** would assure me, "You'll be fine, kid." This seemingly nice old man with the bulbous nose, shaky hands and yellow, overgrown fingernails had begun his *Tribune* career as an errand-running "copy boy" in junior high school, undoubtedly because his father was an editor. He quit to help his brother run the *Murray Eagle*, a Salt Lake County weekly, and then spent several years at other newspapers in Utah and California before landing back on the Copy Desk.

Heal often called in sick, claiming to have broken his arm, and then showed up the next day with arm intact.[36] When his drinking got the best of him, he took Antabuse, a concoction that sent him into convulsions in the newsroom one night. It took Doc White forever to get down from the 8th floor because the elevators were on the blink.[37] Another time, Heal passed out and fell from his chair on the Copy Desk rim. He was fired at least once. He died at home at the relatively young age of 57.

Earl Borg, the roly poly father of the Borg Count that headline-writers used for years at *The Tribune* and far beyond,[38] was a jovial sort whose hands, like Teddy Bear's, shook while writing headlines. Then again, he was 66 and working only part time by my time. Over the years he had worked on various news desks, including the State Desk at the *Deseret News*. Sober or not, he could explain how to make headlines fit perfectly on a page, no matter the size. Police picked him up one night for strolling naked down Main Street. I'm guessing dementia was involved.

Another Copy Desk veteran, **Faye Laley**, could write a good headline -- "This Diet's All Heart, And Easy on Ticker"[39] -- when three sheets to the wind.

* * *

Robert Ellefsen – we called him Elly and Doctor von Lubich – was a short, handsome man of few gravelly words who spent evenings yawning – he'd emit a "Cockamamious!" loud enough for the entire newsroom to hear – while producing impeccable copy and pithy, clever headlines. "And then -- Smoke Gets in Your Sighs" introduced a story on the way cigarettes became emotionally meaningful to some people; it won the staff's May 1972 best headline award. He got a kick out of writing weather headlines that referred to Catholic saints.[40]

Elly had been a crack reporter and editor at the *Chicago Sun Times*, the Ogden *Standard Examiner* and *The Tribune* in his heyday, but even before I met him, he was taking out alcoholic frustrations on Executive Editor Arthur C. Deck. He took a swing at him, yelled out the car window at his house and peed on his front lawn. Not a way to stay in Deck's good graces.

This second generation Norwegian, University of Utah German major and non-Mormon -- yes, we had our heritage and schooling in common -- was raised in Salt Lake City. He joined the Navy in World War II, where he worked in counterintelligence, and began drinking at a young age. At one point he took a job at the *Hartford* (Connecticut) *Courant* but didn't stay sober long enough to keep it.[41] Luckily for him, Art Deck always hired him back after a bender.

When I met him, Elly was on his third marriage, this one to Barbi Fauch Robison Ellefsen, editor of the so-called women's section. According to Barbi, Elly never fell out of love with his first wife, a medical pathologist who moved to California. He had two sons by his second wife and adopted Barbi's daughter, a relationship he retained the rest of his life.

Despite a distaste for travel, Elly took vacations to Southern California's beach front. Perhaps he was still looking for love.

What attracted Barbi to this hard-drinking newspaperman? "He was so

horribly bright and an excellent writer . . . and charming," she said, adding that he was a nonconformist, "devotee of the opera and symphony" and excellent tennis player.[42] If he'd sobered up and put his mind to it, she noted, he could have been a novelist.

Elly never drove, a good thing given his alcoholism. He did drive the day he married Barbi. After reluctantly agreeing to transport his new bride to the end of the block, he turned over the wheel to her. Their marriage dissolved after a few brief years.

Elly spent the last decades of his life -- he survived into his eighties -- drinking and jogging through the Avenues, where he lived alone. He and reporter Anne Wilson, who lived nearby, became friends. Here's her take on the man:

> He was a hopeless romantic, always looking for love. And shy. I think those are among the reasons he used booze . . . he didn't feel like he was enough on his own. He was always bringing me presents, as if I wouldn't like him if he didn't. It made me a little uncomfortable, but he was never anything but sweet to me, even when he was drunk. I never saw him mean.[43]

* * *

Not all the rim rats wrestled with the bottle in the mid-70s. Junior journalists, including young women, sat around the rim to learn the ropes during or after college. A few experienced newsmen worked part time to keep their feet in the door and supplement full-time jobs. Some were Mormons who simply didn't imbibe.

Among the clear-eyed crew was ornery **Ernie Hoff,** who was more than happy to correct me with a scathing cut when he substituted in the slot. A Mormon from Idaho, he had seen better days in the newsroom, having once been city editor and, recently, regional editor. He could be nice and even funny at times, but his painfully swollen feet discolored his mood.

Heber Hart worked late into the odd night after editing Kennecott Copper Corp.'s promotional magazine during the day. Chicago Charlie's sojourns and Shanghai's trips to the lavatory for reinforcements gave this mirthful Mormon a chuckle, and I sometimes suspected he shared in Shanghai's bounty of porn and minibottles. This despite living on Bountiful's squeaky clean east bench -- as opposed to the lower-income flatlands of my youth.

Milt Hollstein, who as head of the University of Utah communications department encouraged me to pursue journalism, sat on the Copy Desk rim occasionally. Like Heber, this Mormon man clearly enjoyed the antics of others on the rim and used the experience as fodder for his classes. It was handy having him nearby when I didn't understand some minor editing issue or needed context for the craziness going on around me.

Wilburn "Willy" Pickett, a former *Deseret News* staffer, kept mostly to himself. In show moments, he rested his well-worn shoes on the rim while eating lunch and reading novels. Many winter days were spent skiing at Alta, where his his wife ran the office and he published *The Alta Powder News* in exchange for season passes.

Pickett " unbridled disgust with most of the copy desk antics,"[44] noted Gordon Harman. When humor columnist Dan Valentine would emerge from his cubicle seeking inspiration for his conclusion, Deano would clang his pica pole (a printer's metal version of a ruler) against a piece of metal beneath the Copy Desk until he withdrew. "This event always pissed Picket off," Gordon said, "but I don't know if it was Dean or Dan he was angry with."

* * *

Jerry Dunton on Regional Desk.

Dunton's *Tribune* history began in the library, also known as Tribune Information, the morgue and archives, where staffers would field questions from the public and file and retrieve background material (mostly news stories on events and individuals in the news) for the writers. If a caller asked a question a librarian couldn't answer, it was the librarian's job to do the research and return the call. When Utah high schools and colleges were having games, the phone rang off the hook. Finally, sports scores were recorded on a separate phone line to free up the Information line for other questions.[45]

* * *

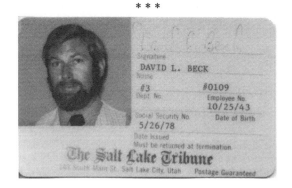

Jerry Dunton, a fairly mainstream copy editor, also worked the regional and late-night make-up shifts. While abrasive on the surface, the plump, inactive Mormon was helpful and friendly -- sometimes too friendly. Fourteen years my senior, raising two adolescent boys and still working on a divorce after three years, Dunton was not for me, and I finally had to spell that out. His favorite pastime being Utah history,

he would yammer for hours with Hal Schindler, *The Trib's* television reviewer and resident history buff/gun nut, and then drive among historical sites on his days off.

David L. Beck, a 30-year-old, arrogant Chicagoan wearing a trim beard and Hush Puppies, often could be found massaging the shoulders of women staffers in the library. He jumped from job to job, sometimes spending a day or two substituting on the Copy Desk. I was his Eliza Doolittle project. When I would answer one of his questions, his quizzical, sardonic smirk would wash me in shame. He assured me I sounded like a hick from Bountiful. "It's not, 'Where's my keys,' but 'Where are my keys?'" he would correct me.

I developed such a crush on him that I signed up for a Jewish writers class at the U., hoping I would better understand big city life and David L. Beck. I went out to dinner with him a couple of times only to be ashamed when he barked orders and then dismissed the waiters. He introduced me to some halfway decent wines, though, and he could keep me entertained with his take on local theater, music and art.

* * *

Gerald "Cuny" Cunningham, an Army veteran from the tiny mining towns of Copperton and Park City, sat on the Copy Desk rim before moving to the nearby Regional Desk and then back to the slot. Born in 1938, Cuny graduated from the University of Utah in journalism and, on the side, published nature photographs in textbooks, magazines and the *Best of Arizona Highways* collection. Though I got along with Cuny, he bullied underlings, especially copy clerks. His days in Germany apparently gave him the kiss-ass, soldier-like quality that contributed to his climb in the ranks and to the publisher's endorsement of his son's application to a military academy.

* * *

Only a handful of women worked on the Copy Desk, and all were young, ambitious and able to tune out distractions from drunks on the rim. Among them was **Vandra Huber**, who caught Korologos' attention when she won *The Tribune's* annual contest for high school journalists. After all, West High alumni stuck together.

This chubby University of Utah graduate with dark, almond-shapped eyes took me under her wing. "If you want to get ahead in the newsroom," Vandra advised, "you need to do something extra to show what you can do."

Usually a tough talker who swaggered to the front of every line, Vandra burst into tears whenever she entered the editor's office to press for a promotion or extra days off. Even so, she worked her way into becoming a prolific, high-profile social services reporter who turned in multiple stories daily. By the late 1970s, she was communications director for the Utah Department of Social Services.

Angelyn Nelson

Mormons **Janice Clark** and **Angelyn Nelson** seemingly belonged at the *Deseret News* but hardly blinked at the wackiness witnessed at *The Tribune*. Janice quietly melted into the background while attending to her editing duties. Angie eventually *did* move to the *Deseret News*, but not before becoming a respected medical writer for *The Trib*.

Blond, sexy Lidia Wasowicz, a faithful Catholic like most of our managers, strode through the newsroom in miniskirts and heels, fluttering her lashes at the vulgarities that greeted her arrival after school. She proudly confided she'd never slept with her fiance, an amazing feat given her flirtatiousness during the sexual revolution. Unlike other newbies on the desk, she always seemed to get holidays off. Her next stop was science reporting for United Press International (UPI) in San Francisco.

* * *

Personal shortcomings aside, some malcontents on the Copy Desk ruthlessly belittled other newsroom personnel, whether for a noun-verb disagreement, unreadable news copy, unpleasant personal habits or a weaving gait on the way to the staffer files. And it didn't take much to divert their attention from the stress and boredom of the job,.

A local beauty queen prancing past the Copy Desk on her way to the photo lab always set off cat calls and wolf howls, embarrassing both the queen and our reporter.

As Ben Ling would tell it, one night the latest Miss Utah entered the newsroom to get her picture taken and give details about herself for a light feature story. The night city editor gave the assignment to tipsy rewrite man Stan Bowman, who groused, "Jesus Christ! When do I get lunch?" and left. The editor searched for another reporter when youngster Mike Carter exclaimed, "Hey, let me get my comb!"[46]

Working the Regional Desk, Jerry Wellman asked Van "Hypo" Porter to take a photograph, but he refused. Whoops and hollers filled the newsroom as the young lady followed Wellman past the copy editors. At the conclusion of this performance, Wellman escorted Miss Utah through the back hall to the *Deseret News,* where the skeleton night crew was polite, professional and prepared. The kicker? She sent *The Trib* a thank-you cake.

Threats between editors to take their differences "out back" sometimes became the evening's entertainment, with the most likely combatants copy editor Hank McKee, News Editor Vard Jones, and Regional Editor Gerry Cunningham.

On his walks around the newsroom, Hank couldn't resist offering unwanted opinions and advice to unreceptive peers. One night, Vard slammed his chair back into Hank's shins, setting off a battle.[47] Another time the pair squared off over whether Richard Nixon was resigning because of the Watergate scandal.[48]

Only once did the antagonists go to blows in my presence, and then bystanders stepped in to break up the fight. As reporter Robert Bryson recalled, it was Otteson who told the two they'd both be fired if they didn't knock it off.

* * *

Rewrite man **Frank Brunsman,** who talked to himself and turned in stories missing key words, naturally became one of the Copy Desk's favorite whipping boys. Other staffers found him memorable as well.

During interviews, Brunsman interrupted and mumbled so much that news sources doubted he understood a word they said. When Mike Carter was a copy boy in the mid-1970s, Brunsman asked him to get a typewriter ribbon, "which he proceeded to unfurl and try to use as a skip rope."[49] In a so-called interview with a federal judge, another staffer recalled, Brunsman put a tape recorder on the judge's desk and announced he'd return later to pick up the answers to his typed questions.[50] Another time, he interviewed someone in the newsroom with no paper in his typewriter. "Maybe he didn't intend to use those notes and was just priming us," Anne Wilson guessed.[51]

His mousy, blunt-cut hair a shorter version of the Little Dutch Boy's, Frank Brunsman grew up on a North Dakota farm, graduated from Minnesota State University and worked for the *Fargo Forum* before joining *The Trib.* After having five children together, he and one of the best teachers at Salt Lake City's South High School split up. Frank then took to cruising local bars and making out in the booths at the dimly lit Manhattan Club. We co-workers wondered how he attracted women when he didn't make sense or eye contact -- his pupils seemed to be dilated -- but he walked into the newsroom more than once with a babe hanging on his arm.

Carter recalled how reporter Jon Ure marveled at Brunsman's second wife, who was "drop-dead beautiful and worked over in federal court. There was endless speculation among Ure, Seldin and others as to why . . ." Carter noted that "of course Ure marveled at most women."

Brunsman still worked at *The Tribune* when John Keahey became business assistant in 1989. "He was always doing byline counts through the ATEX system for everyone in the newsroom." When he was pushed out of the newsroom after 25 years, he received long-term disability with 60 percent of his salary, apparently for a mental ailment.[52]

Brunsman moved to Greenville, S.C., and put his pen to murder mysteries under the pseudonym F. B. Hooker. Excerpts from Crime Times, a self-published novella he presented to me on a visit to the newsroom, says it all:

On her follow-through from booming a Titleist almost three hundred yards straight down the fairway, Linda

Sue Golightly was looking good -- black, buxom and delicious. Her golf attire draped her curvaceous body about as well as a postage stamp covers an envelope.[53]

Brunsman obviously was the main character, Harry:

He could say something like: "Good morning, miss. Looks like it will be a fine, fine day. Tell me, do you play around?" But because of his habit of mumbling, the damsel would mistake Harry's lengthy greeting for mere stomach growlings.[54]

How could you not appreciate such a self-deprecating sense of humor?

Brunsman died suddenly at age 72 in Seattle in 2007. His family described him as nonjudgmental, compassionate and generous to all,[55] worthy traits for a journalist.

That was the year *The Tribune* quit its tradition of granting 8-point obituaries to former staffers, one of the few rewards for service back then. The new rule was that the employees had to have "made an impact on the community."[56] Frank went without.

* * *

Dan Valentine, the google-eyed, gravel-voiced nonsense professional on staff, also was ripe for Copy Desk ridicule.

Readers recognized him as a master of homespun humor and sentimentalism, the "Nothing Serious" humor columnist whose witticisms and bromides were bound into booklets for sale at truck stops and rural cafes throughout the Intermountain West. He and his wife Elaine also were known from a chatty morning show on KALL radio.

Valentine drove newsroom editors crazy by waiting until the deadline to turn in his column. His excuse to cronies was that he didn't want to die right after submitting the column and let Deck get it for free.[57]

In a typical column, Valentine wrote about a variety of subjects, including booze and what he would call the "fairer sex":

A reader wants to know the meaning of a "lame duck" liquor commission.

The answer is simple: The current Utah State Liquor Commission is called a "lame duck" commission because, if the members drink too many liquor samples, they walk like "lame ducks."

Dan Valentine crossing State Street in 1970s.

. . . I was at a social affair the other evening and bumped into a sex-equality female. I'm always bumping into sex-equality babes (I mean persons) at social affairs.

This woman (I mean person) was quite sincere. She said we all have to work harder at the sex equality bit.

"In fact," she says, "I think a law should be passed requiring males to dance backwards half of the time when a couple is on the dance floor.

"Why," she asked with some logic, "is it that the woman always has to dance backward on the dance floor?"

I told her I agreed with her. Personally, I said, "I have never danced with a woman who would dance backwards. I always dance with women who insist on leading."

. . .

This same woman also said she was going to try and get the street department to quit calling those holes in the streets "manholes."

Why not "personholes?"

Why not, indeed?[58]

As a student reading women authors in a class that became part of gender studies on campus, I was hardly amused by this sort of humor. I realized it had to be challenging to churn out keeper columns day after day the way Valentine was expected to do, but give me a break!

In one of the his "favorite" columns re-run during his absence, Valentine recalled some of his high times in the news business:

Like the time I saw Cecil B. DeMille in his nightshirt . . . or the time I peeked at Marlene Dietrich through a keyhole . . . or the time Bing Crosby told me to shut up . . . or the time I tripped over Ernest Hemingway's feet in a hotel lobby . . . (Notice the dot, dot, dots, also known as ellipses.)

I FIRST SAW Cecil B DeMille, the famous movie director, in his nightshirt back in the '50s. He stopped over on a train in Salt Lake for five minutes.

I climbed on the train, knocked on the great man's compartment. He said, "Come in." I went in. He was sitting there bald-headed in his nightshirt. "You DeMille?" I asked. He said "yes." Then the train started to move out of the station. I said, "Goodbye," and he said, "Goodbye." I got off the train.

Marlene Dietrich, the world-famous beauty, came to town and stayed at the Hotel Utah several years ago. I went up for an interview. But she wasn't having any. I knocked on the hotel room door. Somebody said "Scram" in German. But I bent down and looked through the keyhole. All I saw on the other side was an eye looking at me. I don't know whether the eye belonged to Marlene, but I like to think it did.

And on dark winter nights I tell my children about the time their old man and one of the world's most beautiful women saw eye to eye in a hotel hall!

ONE OF THE HIGHLIGHTS of my journalistic career occurred when I met Bing Crosby but Bing Crosby didn't meet me. It was at the Union Pacific Station. Bing and his boys hopped off a train. I said, "Hi, Bing!" He didn't say anything.

I said, "Say, Mr. Crosby, welcome to Salt Lake City." He looked at me like I wasn't there. I said, "Mr. Crosby, are you in town for any special reason?" He took off his hat, his bald head flickered in the morning sun. He said, "Why don't you get lost?" So I did, and *he did, and I've been a Tony Bennett fan ever since.*

Now, we come to Ernest Hemingway. He popped into town where I was working in the late '40s and I was told to meet the great man in the lobby of the local hotel.

I WENT TO THE HOTEL, looked all around for a fellow with a beard. And while I was looking, I tripped over the feet of a fellow with his face buried in a newspaper. The fellow threw down the newspaper, glared at me, and snorted, "You're a clumsy ox." The fellow had a beard. And he might have been Ernest Hemingway. But I'll never know because I sneaked out of the hotel, and ran home, and burned every anthology I owned that contained "The Snows of Kilimanjaro."[59]

Great stuff. The columns often ended with Sam, the sad cynic, saying something like, "The average woman knows what she wants -- but sometimes it's married to another woman!"

Valentine's recipe for bourbon balls was an annual Christmas hit with readers. High balls were high on his own list of favorites.

Brian Nutting, one of his editors, could never understand what readers saw in Valentine.

I once gave him shit about all the ellipses he used ... and he told me that he figured that he used enough to fill up a goodly number of columns throughout the year – and so he didn't have to come up with that much more copy.

He was fond of using the one-to-two-hundred formula (Utah's population was about 1 million and the U.S. was about 200 million, so Utah should have about 1/200th of whatever the country had that he was writing about). I once inserted something like this: The average man in the U.S. is about 69 inches tall so, using the 1/200th formula, the average Utahn is only about two-thirds of an inch tall! Editors were really discouraged from touching Valentine's copy, and he never bothered to read the edited version. But luckily, someone on the Copy Desk caught it.[60]

Even Publisher Jack Gallivan expressed surprise at the great appeal of his columnist, who "used to drive everyone nuts because . . . he would just bleed every call . . . and spent all his time walking up and down in the newsroom."[61] (The dot-dot-dots are in Dan's honor.) He acknowledged, though, that Valentine was funny.

His favorite memory of him dates back the uranium boom:

> Our business editor, Bob Bernick, was invited after the war to speak at the Chamber of Commerce in Moab. Valentine was invited to introduce Bernick. Pretty much all the business community of southern Utah was there. I ran into Bernick in the lobby of the Tribune building and asked, "How was Moab?"
>
> "Well, that damn Valentine took longer telling about himself than the supposed introduction of me and my speech took . . . To make it worse, he . . . defined Mormons as oversexed Baptists. That didn't go over very well.[62]

Midwesterner Valentine attended the University of Chicago and worked as sports editor and columnist for the *South Pacific Daily News* during World War II before becoming editor of the *Rapid City* (S.D.) *Journal* and then moving to *The Salt Lake Telegram* in 1948. During my early days at *The Tribune*, he raised funds for the Utah State Training School and Hogle Zoo. I had to cover more than one birthday for Dan and Elaine, gorillas named in honor of him and his wife. When accused of being a chauvinist, Valentine would respond, "I don't know why women would want to give up complete superiority for mere equality."[63]

Theater critic Nancy Melich learned a lot about writing from the longtime friend of her parents. Although Valentine paced the office for inspiration himself, he advised her, "Don't think, type. Words are like rabbits. Once you put them together, they'll multiply. Once you get a lead, you can always go back and redo it."

The rim rats took bets: first on how long Valentine would wear the same stinking, stained, gray polo shirt without having it washed; next on when he would give up the ghost. Both pools dried up when Shanghai Jack "borrowed" the funds for a bus ticket to San Francisco for vacation.[64] It was 1991 before the second bet might have been settled anyway. Dan died at his son's home in Virginia February 12 at age 73, supposedly after bumping his head in a fall when "distracted by a good-looking blonde."[65]

* * *

Stanley Peter Bowman had been around, he told me, since the 1930s, when film of big basketball games was carried from Provo to Salt Lake by pigeons. In those days, when he

was still a copy boy, some staffers got drunk every night after work in the Chinese slum that gave way to a 14-story parking terrace on Plum Alley.

Stan Bowman on rewrite.

Usually tipsy himself at the beginning of his 3:30 rewrite shift, Stan would stagger across the newsroom in mod flowered shirt with puffy sleeves, Levis and fringed moccasins, jerk open the assignment drawer, fall into his wobbly chair and then gruffly bark into the phone in his baritone. He swore and slammed down the receiver at will. "Go get 'em, Stan!" Deano would shout across the newsroom.

One time, it took Stan 15 minutes just to get the second sheet of paper into the typewriter while taking a story over the phone, and the resulting story was senseless.

The rewrite man made a lasting impression on others besides myself. Almost everyone who worked there offered a story about Stan.

According to Bernie Moss Porter, who had worked as City Desk secretary for awhile, Stan could pound out the weather report in a virtual stupor, and in catastrophes, he could be sharp.[66] Yet one day he drove through a dealer's front window while looking at new cars.

"[Stan's] collection of typos and double entendres was priceless," according to James Ure, who worked at *The Tribune* from 1958 to 1962 before going into advertising. "He had dozens of headlines and articles. I remember a few, but this is a family paper, right?"[67]

"Once Stan, trying to hang up his coat, fell into the coat rack and became entangled like a fish in a net," Ure recalled. "He had to be helped. Then he looked around wild-eyed and went to work, churning out readable stuff, even accurate stuff."

Reporter Jim Woolf recounted the time Stan "was digging for something in the garbage can behind him when he fell in head first. His legs were kicking, and he was cursing as we pulled him out. He had an amazing ability to work while drunk."[68]

Long-time police reporter Mike Carter loved the way Stan would sit and stare at the Secret Witness phone when it rang, hoping it would stop.[69] (*The Tribune* tried for awhile to help the police solve crimes by taking anonymous tips on a dedicated phone line.) He added, Stan's life "must have been like landing on an aircraft carrier in a hurricane every day of his life. Incredible."

Reporter Charlie Seldin used to make his Stan's life miserable with anonymous prank calls from across the desk.[70] Of course all his cohorts would enjoy Stan's show of frustration and belligerence.

Editors like Brian Nutting. who had known Stan since joining *The Trib,* simply worked around the inebriation.

On his first shift on night police, Joe Rolando was told to sit with Stan to learn to do "that &!$%@ weather map" with wire-machine copy, a ruler and a glue stick.

I walked over to his desk and found him fast asleep. When I couldn't raise him by poking him on the shoulder . . . several times, I walked back to Nutting and told him, "Uh, something is wrong with [Stan]." The response? "That's OK, you can learn the weather map another night."[71]

Gordon Harman once fetched Stan, a veteran of both World War II and the Korean Conflict, from the VFW Atomic Post in the old Congress Hotel on State Street after Stan's shift was scheduled to begin. "It was a slow walk back to the newsroom as Stan bounced off of every tree, mail box and parking meter or any other obstacle like a pinball."[72]

John Keahey once watched Dan Valentine, who kept a bottle in his desk and tipped a few too many himself, prop Stan up against the south wall of Walker Bank once while waiting for a cab. "Dan half carried and half drug

Stan to the cab. It took about 10 minutes to get him into the back seat. It was mid-afternoon. Passersby by the dozens walking by."[73]

Stan Bowman working under the influence.

One night at the VFW bar, Stan regaled Keahey and his roommate with stories about his job and personal tragedies. When he was the public relations guy, the wires holding the Main Street Christmas tree snapped, sending the tree into Dupler's Furs. Even worse, the Old-Fashioned Fourth fireworks blasted into a crowd at the Utah State Fairgrounds, injuring several spectators. Then there was the time in the 1950s when a *Telegram*-hired helicopter almost crashed into the stands during a U. of U. football game.

The chopper delivered the homecoming queen to the 50-yard line, where she ceremoniously handed the game ball to the officials. As the chopper lifted off without the queen's weight, the stagnant air currents inside the stadium caused a low drift, and the chopper barely rose above the west stands.[74]

"Stan looked at us, eyes darting from one to the other, and said, 'And you ask me why I drink!'" Keahy recalled.

Jim Ure was on 4:30 p.m. rewrite during the fireworks incident. "With people in flames, [Editor Art] Deck had become more vocal and excited than usual. He had to come into the office past his bedtime. I had to make calls to the city employees who actually touched off the fireworks. Art would bark questions into my ear that in turn I would ask the fireworkers. Then Art would talk to Stan. Then we'd call the hospitals. It went on and on for days. Stan said he wanted his old rewrite job back."[75]

From what Stan told me, he was paid an obnoxiously low wage. It seemed to me he was stuck on rewrite for life, which I didn't expect to last long from the looks of his emaciated body. I was wrong. He retired at 59 in 1981 and lived another decade, during which he dried out.

* * *

Clark Lobb also generated taunts about weird spellings when under the bottle's spell, but his photographic memory, speed, street smarts and good humor kept him in his editors' good stead. He was a "great reporter" who, though short in stature, was City Editor Will Fehr's "designee to handle all the weirdos who walked in the door "[76] -- whether Chicago Charlie, the Worm (a guy who dressed like the devil to wander Main Street) or some ranting reader. He accepted his assignments without complaint, no matter how minor or mundane. He could dictate breaking news off the cuff over the phone and make the most humdrum stories sing.

Lobb probably fit Thomas Wolfe's description of a newspaperman as well as any. Sure, he was slightly cynical, shabby, hung over and even burned out. But over his career, he wrote plenty of big stories, and he could turn a phrase like a pro. If he was jaded, he didn't show it. He seemed sincerely interested in people; in getting the story right and respecting victims. He wasn't the kind of guy to sell out his source or another staffer.

In May 1972, the *Tribune Topix* commended Lobb for his creative treatment of bees lighting on a motorcycle's handle bars. Clark began his story with, "Bees on a Bike: a three-act drama with a happy ending, played before a fairly substantial audience." His conclusion: "It was rated bee, honey." As late as 1980, Lobb's leads continued to receive praise in the in-house organ,

by then renamed *The Tribune Tattler.* One of his stories began: "It seemed so incongruous, so ludicrous that we were sitting on this peaceful patio in suburban Ogden, the warm breeze fresh from the rain the night before, calmly discussing the annihilation of the world." Another about vanity license plates: "Vanity, thy name is motorist." Still another: "When Heber City residents went to Lincoln Rosband's home to persuade him to run for mayor, they made the mistake of calling during a World Series game."

Tribune lore had Lobb writing about "the tattoo man" at the Territorial Prison in Sugar House. When the inmate later led a prison riot that took guards hostage, he refused to negotiate with anyone but Lobb, who talked him into surrendering. [77]

When hiring reporters, Mike Korologos said he wanted deadline-meeters with "street moxy,[78] enthusiasm and excitement who could get the job done at any cost. "I wanted Clark Lobbs without the alcohol." And, possibly, Clark Lobbs without the family drama that often played out in the newsroom as his disgruntled wife and wayward son made appearances between bouts with the law. When liquored up, Lobb's dentures would come loose during dictation, garbling his words beyond recognition. He died in 1981.

* * *

Within a few weeks of joining the staff, I moved into a third-floor, cockroach-infested studio apartment with bed bugs on Third South and Second East, close enough to walk to work and even school if one of the cars Dad salvaged for me broke down. The clutch gave out on my '62 sky-blue Dodge Dart, so he was working on a replacement: an almost neon lime-green '66 Plymouth Duster with black vinyl top.

As much as I appreciated being in the vibrant business district during the day, I was nervous walking to the parking lot in the dark after work. Shopping and restaurants were near, but lots of scruffy characters skulked the sparsely populated streets.

I began taking dinner breaks with part of the motley Copy Desk crew.

"If you're caught up, why don't you come to lunch with us," Vandra piped up. "Aw, come on. Nobody's going to bite ya!"

The most frequent stop was Lamb's Grill, a classic lunch and dining spot for downtown businessmen. Occupying the ground floor of an ornate building constructed in 1905 for *The Salt Lake Herald*, Lamb's offered a polished counter or lacquered wood booths for a quick bite up front. Owner Ted Speros or his daughter Estelle directed the business crowd to linen-covered tables in back.

"Hey, Sweetheart, do you think Daddy could spare another pat of butter over here?" Deano drawled as Estelle strutted our way in her skin-tight jumpsuit and high heels. She tossed a snarky glance over her shoulder, but a starched waitress soon arrived with three more pats. Deano then settled back into the booth, cigarette smoke wafting in front of squinting eyes, to watch the hostess mount an open, narrow stairway to the office. With a sigh, he returned to the   fried eggplant he'd topped with Canadian bacon and drenched with lemon and honey.

The dimly lit Pine Cone across Main Street offered up a large, cheap sandwich. Shanghai Jack and Heber Hart preferred Harry Louie's (King Joy), where they stowed bottles of their special "sauce" behind the counter and ordered ham-fried rice. Ambiance was sorely lacking, but Harry, an avid U. of U. Utes fan, and his wife and kids treated us like long, lost relatives. They   let the news crew charge meals until payday.[79]

Sometimes we'd go out back to Regent Street, the red-light district of years gone by, for a bite at Tampico, the Greek-run Mexican restaurant I called ptomaine palace. It was tough to stomach the cockroaches creeping from beneath the table in the semi-darkness, no matter how cheap or even delectable the enchiladas and beans.

The rim rats initiated me into the world of alcohol with trips to the Swinger and Continental, nearby clubs that served me vodka Collins and screwdrivers before I turned 21, a novelty in a state with such a tight grip on liquor service. They also introduced me to "coffee," a term I use loosely.   The newsroom coffee machine spewed out cardboard-flavored swill for a dime. You got the stuff called "milk" by pushing a button while the slop was being dispensed, but the machine was so scummy, the gunk sometimes came out sour.[80]

On slow nights after my typing and homework were done -- most of my school books were read and papers written on *Tribune* time -- I followed Vandra's advice and accepted shaggy-headed **John Waldo**'s request to clean up stories from his regional correspondents, or stringers.

With an impish grin and gleam in his eye, Waldo bounced on the balls of his feet,

always wearing the same hiking boots and thread-bare tan corduroys, on his way around the faded red pillar between our desks to slyly hand me four or five stories about county fairs, car accidents or new school plans. I couldn't be sure whether the partially deaf young editor, sucking continuously on a stinking pipe, was simply mentoring a new employee or harboring a hidden agenda.

Copy Desk in early 1970s: Unidentified female on A.D. Halliday's lap. Back row, left to right: John Waldo, Gerald Cunningham, Hank McKee, Earl Borg, John O'Connor.

Regardless of his motives, I gained editing and writing experience. Paid by the column inch and seldom schooled in journalism, stringers wrote on and on about such scintillating news as the price of hogs in Delta. (The term "stringer" originated from the days correspondents glued stories together in long strings of copy so a newsroom person could count the inches and send in a pay request for the writer.[81]) Correspondents' tendency to overwrite gave me practice slashing redundancies (Okay, okay, so I could have used more practice). The heavy pounding and ding-ding-ding of the Teletypes, each spewing out national and international news stories at 66 words per minute,[82] along with beeps and whines from the police scanner on the NIPO (night police reporter) desk, helped me concentrate by blocking out the silliness going on around me.

Before long I became immersed in the infectious life of *The Tribune*. Everyone was unique; most endearing. "I Can Never Go Home Again"[83]   became one of my theme songs, because I could never go back to being an innocent Bountiful girl.

Along with the rest of my new family, I peppered my conversations with profanities. I viewed the world from a contrary angle.   I dressed down, avoiding white at all cost, to camouflage inevitable ink smudges on everything that entered the newsroom.

I felt all the more at home when classmates from my university journalism classes started showing up in the newsroom.

Roger Graves, another West High winner of *The Tribune's* high school journalism contest, handsome Charlie Seldin, Gordon-the-Geek Harman, towering Randy Peterson, and equally tall but more adventuresome Brent Curtis began scurrying around the office as "copy boys." Since entry-level girls couldn't be "copy boys," East High classmates Helen Forsberg and Ann Kilbourn took clerk jobs in the library while studying English at the U.

Tom Wharton

Perpetually positive Tom Wharton actually entered the newsroom ahead of me. He began reporting scores and color from high school games while still at Granite High in 1967 and briefly worked for the *Deseret News before* overseeing public information for the Utah Army National Guard for six months. I had been at *The Tribune* just a few months when I attended his marriage to long-time sweetheart, Gayen, whose dour father Max Bennett managed circulation for Newspaper Agency Corp.

Most of my peers and those just ahead of us -- Baby Boomers like Brian Nutting, JoAnn Jacobsen, Barbara Springer, Robbie Bird, Nancy Melich, George Raine and Don Patrick (the red-headed obituary writer who first reported on the new phenomenon of cross-country skiing[84]) --

anticipated exciting careers covering famous people and big events.

I was different. Even after several weeks on the job, including time on the Copy Desk for an advanced editing class, I remained determined to teach English to high school students. Those intentions made it tough to ask formidable Art Deck to approve an internship toward my journalism minor. I doubted he would waste effort on anyone planning to leave.

Cindy Gilchrist

I suppressed my anxiety and got an appointment. Uncharacteristically, I refrained from confessing my plan to quit after graduation. The man of few words shuffled a couple of papers on his polished desk and simply stated, "*The Tribune* doesn't have an internship program anymore."

"Oh, I didn't know that," I sputtered. "Thanks anyway." I retreated to my typing station, tail tucked tightly between my legs.

With no explanation from the front office, I soon was assigned to the Copy Desk full time, and my weekly pay rose to $145. Taking over the typing was freckled, willowy Cindy Gilchrist of the Brillo Pad hair.

* * *

As a copy editor, I was painfully slow and wrote some stilted, idiotic headlines. The one about "Diseased Youth" still makes me cringe.

In my defense, it isn't easy to fit a synopsis into two lines over one column, but I obviously was green. Elly was working the slot that night, and I didn't understand why he tossed the story back to me with a smirk. I guessed "diseased" was the problem and substituted the word "sick." This time he fixed the headline himself, but not before others on the rim got a look at it and laughed. I didn't even think of the word "ill."

That's me on the rim of the Copy Desk and Hank McKee in the Slot.

When Deano worked the slot, he might say, "Take another crack at this one, Sweetheart." If I was lucky, another slotman would say, "It doesn't step." I knew that meant the headline's top line wasn't the longest; the middle line the shortest. But editors often withheld explanations and then ridiculed people for stupid mistakes. I had to bring myself up to speed if I wanted to save face.

I started scouring the newspaper each morning before work to see what was changed the night before so I could divine what I'd done wrong. By overhearing complaints about reporter errors, I learned the difference between robberies and burglaries. I also learned there was more than one way of doing the job. One slot man favored speed and accuracy, another preferred imaginative, punchy headlines, and still another insisted on heads simply paraphrasing the leads. Silly puns and alliteration usually survived inspection. I began to settle in.

Deadlines had become a powerful force in my life.

At first, when down to the last few minutes before edited copy had to be returned to the slot to be checked, rolled up and snapped into a tube for its trip to the blue room, I literally held my breath. I couldn't think. My stomach clenched in waves of pain, meaning I'd soon be rushing to the restroom down the hall. My surging pulse pounded in my ears. The fingers on my free hand furiously stroked strands of hair, breaking off one after the other as the dirges of panic raced through my mind: "Oh, no! This headline doesn't fit! I can't come up with a shorter word. I'll never make it!" I felt like a volcano on the verge of eruption.

Luckily, after enough nights of this misery, late-breaking stories started sharpening instead of clouding my focus, memory and ability to think of the right words. Excitement sometimes shoved aside stress as the motivation to plow through the copy.

Without that transition, I never would have survived six months, let alone 24 years at *The Tribune*. That is not to say the volcano ever went dormant. At any time over the years, panic might surge with a last-minute story, clenching my neck and shoulder muscles into knots. Occasionally, the hysteria resurfaced in my nightmares decades after my *Tribune* departure.

Speaking of stress: One evening Deano slipped me a story by Mr. Deck, who as an officer of the American Society of Newspaper Editors was allowed into Communist China on the heels of President Nixon's historic 1972 visit. It had been 25 years since Americans had visited the repressive behemoth.

I was scared I would screw up the headline and shame myself in an enraged editor's eyes. And why wouldn't I, given my limited vocabulary, life experience and knowledge of news events? After passing my college entrance tests, I hadn't taken a single history or political science course.

Apparently Deano made sure my editing passed muster with the boss, because I kept my job for another day.

My insecurities those early days didn't stop me from criticizing the newspaper in a term paper required for internship credit. I declared that *The Tribune* published too little art, which too often was small and posed instead of spontaneous. There was too little follow-up and in-depth reporting, I said, and reporters failed to search out interesting, thought-provoking, public interest stories. Wire editing was inadequate, I continued, because most of it was done by one editor. Advertising policies, I contended, restricted flexibility in making up pages. If a big story broke near deadline, time and ad space prevented significant changes. My conclusion: "My most valuable lesson from *The Tribune* is that every sentence in the English language has at least two meanings, one of which appeals to Allan Dean Halliday."

Between our first deadline at 7 p.m. and the final at 10 p.m., there was usually enough down time for me to do some homework -- a good thing, since I was working full time and practice-teaching before work most of my senior year. I had a lot of books to read and papers to write. I would slump over the Copy Desk, twirl and break off strands of hair and study, study, study until the copy flow slowed enough for Deano to send me home to my bed bugs. That is, unless it was a Friday or Saturday night, when I might go out with my friends to dance and drink at the Black Bull or some similar pick-up joint down south State Street.

My grades suffered, especially in my Introduction to Mass Communications class, which met at 8:50 a.m. Monday through Friday my last quarter before graduation. I missed two days out of five because I couldn't get going so early in the morning after working and studying -- or whatever -- late into the night. As a working journalist, I didn't take the beginning course seriously. I squeaked by with a C, my worst grade ever.

While I was used to getting A's in other subjects, I rarely earned better than a B in my journalism classes. It was if I'd been pegged as average. Instead of being discouraged, I was determined to prove I could do the job before moving on. It didn't hurt that my proximity to breaking news was enticing.

My year with the Copy Desk was a turbulent time for the country. The drug culture became entrenched. Soldiers were slaughtering and being slaughtered in Vietnam while Richard Nixon's dirty laundry was aired in the news. Watergate further shook young Americans' faith in a government that kept going back on its word to leave Southeast Asia. On May 10, local demonstrators, probably again including Steve Holbrook, demanded prime-time coverage of their anti-war protests, an event that put Clark Lobb, JoAnn Jacobsen, Brian Nutting, Dave Beck and Ernie Ford to work until 2 a.m.[85]

One song or another was always streaming through my head as I daydreamed between the stories tossed my way on the rim. America, the Eagles, Doobie Brothers, Simon and Garfunkle, Led Zeppelin, Seals and Crofts, Chicago and the Moody Blues, among other rock groups, created the mood for these sojourns into fantasyland. Cat Stevens' "Moonshadow" conjured up images of American soldiers flailing away in Southeast Asia as I sat safely in Salt Lake City.

My major concessions to the cultural era were to change from miniskirts and pantsuits to dungarees -- once *The Trib* relaxed its dress code for women, that is -- and to replace my dry, clouded contacts with huge, round glasses. I kinked my long hair and spent a moment or two on "the roof," or bridge over the press rooms between *The Tribune* and *Deseret News*, smoking grass with the staff's male long hairs. If they were doing heavier drugs, I didn't get into it.

Not long after I left the Copy Desk, Paul Wetzel, another non-Mormon from Bountiful, began typing the editors' corrections.

"How in God's name did you tolerate that collection of misogynist misanthropes?" he wanted to know decades later.[86]

Cantankerous and crazy as they could be, those copy editors were characters with a soft side. Their insults and sexist remarks were not much worse than what I'd faced at home from four brothers and belittling parents. In fact, their worst harassment was reserved for staffers outside the Copy Desk. They accepted me as one of their family of cultural outcasts.

---

[20] Korologos, January 19, 2014.

[21] Gordon Harman email to Tribune facebook group, August 29, 2014.

[22] Harman email, October 7, 2015.

[23] Brian Nutting email to Diane Cole, February 14, 2014.

[24] Ibid.

[25] George Raine email, February 16, 2014.

[26] *Tribune Topix*, March 8, 1972.

[27] Joe Rolando to Tribune facebook group, March 1, 2012.

[28] Ben Ling to Tribune facebook group, February 14, 2012.

[29] Joe Rolando to Tribune facebook group, February 14, 2012.

[30] Gordon Harman to Tribune facebook group, February 14, 2012.

[31] Mike Carter to Tribune facebook group, February 15, 2012.

[32] *Deseret News* obituary, February 14, 1994.

[33] Gordon Harman email October 5, 2015.

[34] JoAnn Jacobsen-Wells email, August 2, 2015.

[35] Nutting, February 14, 2014.

[36] Bernie Moss Porter telephone conversation August 26, 2014.

[37] Dennis Green's recollection, 2013.

[38] Raine, February 16, 2014.

[39] *Tribune Topix*, March 8, 1972.

[40] Gordon Harman email, October 9, 2015.

[41] Barbi Robison telephone interview, November 13, 2015.

[42] Robison, November 13, 2015.

[43] Anne Wilson email, November 13, 2015.

[44] Gordon Harman email, October 9, 2015.

[45] Mike Korologos email February 20, 2017.

[46] Ben Ling email to Diane Cole, December 2013.

[47] Robert Bryson email, August 4, 2015.

[48] Paul Wetzel remarks upon retirement, 2012.

[49] Mike Carter to facebook Tribune group November 22, 2013.

[50] Conrad Walters to facebook's Tribune group November 2013.

[51] Anne Wilson, facebook message to Diane Cole, December 31, 2013.

[52] John Keahey to facebook Tribune group November 22, 2013.

[53] F.B. Hooker, "Crime Times," 1994, p. 3.

[54] F.B. Hooker, "Crime Times," 1994, p. 17.

[55] Bonney-Watson online obituary, November 2007.

[56] Keahey, November 22, 2013.

[57] Mike Korologos email, February 25, 2017.

[58] Dan Valentine, *The Salt Lake Tribune*, June 14, 1976, p. 17.

[59] Dan Valentine, "Nothing Serious," *The Salt Lake Tribune*, October 10, 1982, p. B1.

[60] Nutting, February 14, 2014.

[61] Gallivan, May 2005.

[62] Ibid.

[63] "Dan Valentine Dies at 73; Retired Tribune Columnist," *Deseret News*, February 14, 1991.

[64] Gordon Harman email, October 9, 2015.

[65] *Deseret News*, February 14, 1991.

[66] Bernie Moss Porter, telephone conversation August 26, 2014.

[67] James Ure to Tribune facebook group February 8, 2012.

[68] Jim Woolf to facebook's Tribune group February 8, 2012.

[69] Mike Carter to facebook's Tribune group October 4, 2012.

[70] Nutting, February 14, 2014.

[71] Joe Rolando to facebook's Tribune group February 3, 2012.

[72] Gordon Harman to facebook's Tribune group February 8, 2012.

[73] John Keahey to facebook's Tribune group February 8, 2012.

[74] Mike Korologos email, February 23, 2017.

[75] James Ure to facebook's Tribune group February 38, 2012.

[76] Nutting, February 14, 2014.

[77] Paul Rolly and Dawn House interview of John W. Gallivan in Snyderville for "Hard news and raucous times," *The Salt Lake Tribune*, May 16, 2005, p. B4.

[78] Mike Korologos email, January 31, 2014.

[79] Mike Korologos email, February 20, 2017

[80] Nutting, February 14, 2014.

[81] Mike Korologos email, February 20, 2017.

[82] Dave Jonsson, "Computers Revolutionize Tribune," *The Salt Lake Tribune*, July 24, 1988, p. T6.

[83] "I Can Never Go Home Again," We Five, 1965.

[84] *Tribune Topix*, March 8, 1972.

[85] *Tribune Topix*, May 24, 1972.

[86] Paul Wetzel email March 27, 2016.

4- Competence, Kindness and Intimidation

John Francis Fitzpatrick still held sway at the newspaper decades after his 1960 death.

Thomas Kearns, a wealthy Park City miner who bought *The Tribune* about the same time he was elected to the U.S. Senate in 1901, knew Fitzpatrick as secretary for the vice president in charge of the Utah Division of the Denver & Rio Grande Western Railroad, which strung a telegraph line up Parleys Canyon. When Kearns wanted something for his mine up Parleys, he could get it fast if he called Fitzpatrick.[87]

After Fitzpatrick took another railroad job in the Midwest, Kearns sent him a letter in 1913 asking about his availability to become *his* secretary.[88] They met in a Chicago hotel room, where the senator bluntly asked if Fitzpatrick could be in Salt Lake City in two weeks. No small talk, not even about salary.[89] (*Tribune* editors Art Deck and Will Fehr conducted job interviews much the same way.) "By the grace of God, Fitzpatrick got there, because he was the salvation for that [Kearns] family," Jack Gallivan remarked in his latter years.[90]

When Kearns died suddenly in 1918, Fitzpatrick accepted his widow's plea to handle the family business and become publisher in 1924, a position he held 36 years.

Fitzpatrick set high standards for his staff, mostly male. "Fitzpatrick's basic policy in publishing *The Tribune* was to set unreachably high goals, find key *men* [emphasis is mine] who would strive to reach them and then drive himself and his key *men* in their pursuit . . . He was . . . a constant prod to keep his subordinates moving toward the objectives he had set."[91] L.A. Times-Mirror President Harry Chandler described him as a "grand, conscientious publisher."

Fitzpatrick usually lunched at The Alta Club, the men's club downtown where he networked with other movers and shakers of his time, but he also made regular visits to the down-to-earth Mint Cafe to stay grounded with the community.[92]

His reserved, paternalistic management style survived him. As did his reliance on "key men." Don Howard, a longtime *Tribune* employee, described him as a presence "sort of looking over your shoulder to see if you were on the job; and also ready to pick you up if you stubbed your toe."[93] Howard regarded him as fair.

In Fitzpatrick's eulogy at the Cathedral of the Madeleine, Bishop Robert J. Dwyer extolled not only his stewardship, but also his hardness and ruthlessness in contrast to his tender-heartedness, prudence, grasp of reality and self-effacing nature.

Longtime *Tribune* political writer and historian O. N. Malmquist remarked on Fitzpatrick's demand for loyalty among staffers.[94] Employees who questioned the newspaper's integrity might not be fired, but they would never be rehired if they left.

Arthur C. Deck, Fitzpatrick's executive editor for decades, exhibited some of the same shy yet autocratic traits, as did Will Fehr, Deck's successor. Neither was flamboyant, and neither was effusive in their praise of employees. Fair? I'm not so sure. They both had favorites who received more promotions and raises than others. Deck was known to rehire critics, and Fehr would take certain people back. Their habit of skulking about the newsroom obviously was learned. Deck with the clicking pen, Fehr with the jangling change. Malmquist didn't say what Fitzpatrick did to make his presence known.

* * *

Unlike Fitzpatrick, who fell into the job at the insistence of Jennie Kearns, **John W. "Jack" Gallivan** was groomed from the outset to be publisher. But again, it was Jennie Kearns who made the decision. After her half-sister Frances orphaned Jack at age 5, Jennie Kearns adopted her nephew and sent him to all the right schools, including Bellarmine College Prep in

San Jose and the University of Notre Dame, where he studied English. She then insisted he learn all the ropes at *The Tribune*.[95] He worked part-time in the library and circulation department the summers before graduating and following his aunt's order to turn down a writing job at the *Chicago Tribune*.

Jack had "decided to marry Grace Mary Ivers after pushing her into the fountain at the Kearns residence during his fifth birthday party."[96] They both were part of Park City's mining heritage. Grace Mary's grandfather, James Ivers, worked for Silver King Mining Co. in the 1880s, and her father, James Ivers II, was general manager of Silver King when it merged with Judge Mining Properties to become United Park City Mines in 1951. (Her brother, James Ivers III, became president of United Park City Mines and was instrumental, along with Jack Gallivan, in Park City's transition from mining to the ski industry.[97]) Grace Mary and Jack had four children, whom we staffers knew as Champ (John Jr.), Gay (Grace Mary), Mickey and Tim.

John W. Gallivan

Gallivan's full-time career at the newspaper began August 1, 1937 with stints in advertising, circulation, news, the library (morgue) and the Copy Desk while writing a sports column and managing promotions, a job he assumed when L. D. Simmons went to war.

Amid his other chores, he fed the carrier pigeons roosting on the roof of the building.

As one Gallivan story goes, some of those pigeons were released to great fanfare during halftime of a Ute-Aggie (University of Utah vs. Utah State University) football game. The announcer told fans the birds would carry photographic film downtown in time to produce newspapers for sale outside the stadium after the game. Instead of racing back to *The Tribune*, however, the pigeons perched on the north goal post to the roar of fans. Gallivan rushed over waving a broom to dislodge his carriers to no avail.[98]

Telegram General Manager A. L. Fish got the idea for the pigeon system, begun in 1936 and used into the early '40s, from a ship-to-shore picture service used by New York papers. Art Deck was among the managing editors who worked on the project, which put Promotions Director Simmons and his assistant Frank Snow to work for about a year training a flock of 50 or so birds roosted on the newspaper's roof.

Telegram reporter W. H. "Bill" McDougall, Jr. put this predecessor of cell phones and internet into practice transporting news film and copy from isolated areas quickly. In a story for the Nieman Foundation, where he was a fellow, McDougall explained how he got scoops from far-flung airplane crashes, miner strikes, football games and Salt Flat races.[99]

In the winter of 1936, for example, an airliner disappeared en route from Los Angeles to Salt Lake City. It was six months before the plane was discovered high in the mountains, a six-hour trek by foot and pack horse. By pigeon-line, it was "less than 30 miles and about as many minutes" from the *Telegram* roof. McDougall scooped other news reporters by several hours, and his stories appeared on front pages throughout the country.

Out on the road, McDougall would carry a dozen pigeons in a hamper in his car and then stuff four at a time into a fishing creel slung over his shoulder for treks into the countryside. He would release one for each edition of the newspaper, keeping the last for back-up. If an event went on for days, errand boys would drive out to replenish his stock.

McDougall scrawled his dispatches onto 6X8-inch pieces of rice paper and processed miniaturized film blindly in a rubberized, light-proof bag fit with arm sleeves. The story, attached to a pigeon's leg, and the film, carried in an aluminum capsule on its back, were done in duplicate for major stories in case a hawk or poor training thwarted delivery. When attaching the messages, the reporter was careful not to upset or choke the courier or interfere with its tail assembly. The process only worked during daylight, when the birds would fly. A light would blink in the newsroom to announce the arrival of a carrier as it pushed between the bars of its loft.

The quickest, most reliable bird, "News Flight," was somehow "impervious both to hawks and blandishments."[100] Fanciers reported that a few others became distracted by their "lady" pigeons and stayed. To prevent birds from going "stale," McDougall upset hotel chambermaids by letting them stretch their wings in hotel bathrooms at night. When out on a story, he kept creel and hamper close at hand to keep competitors from freeing his flock.

McDougall flew the coop himself, so to speak, but like most of his feathered friends, he eventually found his way home. He left the *Telegram* for the *Japan Times* and United Press in Shanghai before escaping a sinking freighter and spending three years in a Japanese prison camp during World War II. In 1952, he became a Catholic priest and served 20 years as rector of Salt Lake City's Cathedral of the Madeleine before rising to right reverend monsignor in 1963.[101]

Jack Gallivan became one of the monsignor's more active parishioners, leading major restoration campaigns and becoming a knight of the Order of St. Gregory, the church's highest honor for a layman. Long before that, however, Business Manager Tom Mullin gave young Gallivan a job creating and editing an eight-page monthly news section promoting national advertising. When Fitzpatrick died and Newspaper Agency Corp. lost its general manager, Jack moved from the Kearns Building across the street to the Tribune building to assume that role.

Gallivan lapped up the limelight. He relished public speaking and direct community action, and he was liked both inside[102] and outside of *The Tribune*. Public and private promotions came second nature to him. He never underestimated the value of advertising, which represented 25-27 percent of the newspaper's income.[103]

Even before officially becoming publisher September 11, 1960, Gallivan helped Fitzpatrick find ways to expand and diversify Kearns-Tribune assets and to deliver news more

productively. The use of cable and broadcast signals was one such venture.[104]

In its first business partnership with the LDS Church as early as 1925, Fitzpatrick had invested $1,050 in Utah Radio Corp. (KSL). *The Tribune* sold that stock in 1947 to buy into KALL radio with George C. Hatch and Mr. and Mrs. Robert Hinckley. That interest sold in 1954, when *The Tribune* bought half of Channel 2, an investment unloaded in 1970.

Meantime, Gallivan persuaded Fitzpatrick to make a small investment in a microwave-linked cable system in Elko, Nevada, as a way to get the news into that outlying area without expensive truck delivery. Gallivan jump-started TeleMation in 1963, supplying 156 products for the TV industry.

It was time for assistance with all these enterprises, and Gallivan approached Paul G. "Jerry" O'Brien, the personable Associated Press bureau chief who frequently dropped by the newsroom to see if editors were happy with the wire service.[105] "What do you do?" O'Brien asked. "Worry," was Gallivan's response.[106] O'Brien quit AP to help Gallivan "worry."

Jerry O'Brien tips up his sunglasses behind President Kennedy.

One O'Brien contribution was to jury-rig a camera to a Teletype machine to cheaply provide news content 24 hours a day via the Elko cable.[107] By 1964, the scheme merged with Community Television Inc., giving Kearns-Tribune an interest in 10 cable systems. In 1970, Kearns-Tribune held a 15 percent stake in Telecommunications Inc., the nation's largest cable company. That stake eventually would prove momentous for the newspaper and its staff, a topic for later illumination.

Some Gallivan diversification projects put *The Tribune* in the journalistically improper position (in my view) of promoting private interests, even if they simultaneously served a public purpose.

Magnesium Project, later known as MagCorp, is one example. Speaking both as publisher and as president of H-K Company, a joint venture of James E. Hogle Jr. and Kearns-Tribune, Gallivan testified before Utah's Public Service Commission February 6, 1969 in favor of the Bonneville Power Plant as a cheap source of public power for developing Great Salt Lake minerals.[108] He found himself in a similar situation -- lobbying public officials to support a business in which Kearns-Tribune held a financial interest -- as late as 1990 with a supposedly durable highway surfacing product called Syncrete.

Other Gallivan campaigns were more civic-minded, despite indirectly benefitting *The Tribune* and its owners. The Winter Olympic bids, liquor-by-the-drink and the Salt Palace convention center were byproducts of his push for downtown planning and integral to the tourism that would boost economic development for the good of the community as well as private interests.[109] Gallivan also sponsored public-policy referendums for City-County Unification, which never gained acceptance, and urban renewal projects that changed the face of the city.

At a time when Salt Lake City had only three major hotels, including Hotel Utah, Temple Square and the Newhouse, Gallivan and James Hogle organized the privately funded Downtown Planning Association in 1961. That effort spawned ProUtah, Inc., the Utah Ski Association and Travel Utah, all privately funded economic development groups at first, though state government under Gov. Calvin Rampton eventually took over the travel and industrial development functions. Hogle and Gallivan invited 100 leaders from all branches of Utah business and society to constitute the planning association's board of directors, and no one turned them down.

Several members of ProUtah became known as Rampton's Raiders, promoters who flew on an old converted Utah National Guard tanker to big cities across the country drumming up investment in Utah industry. It took "hours and hours to get anywhere," Gallivan recalled later.

Because of poor pressurization, we had to fly very low, and it was rougher than hell. I swear one day I looked out the window and a pelican passed us. We were always exhausted whenever we would arrive at our destination. We would rally and put on a dog-and-pony show for the Chamber of Commerce wherever we were visiting, with invitations to all of the big industries . . . in that town.[110]

The Tribune promoted several bond issues to fund the Salt Palace. Every time an effort to build a community auditorium was announced, Gallivan explained, the Mormon Church would announce plans to build its own conference center as the Tabernacle had become too small. LDS President David O. McKay's pronouncement in the *Deseret News* put the kibosh on the first bond. The tide finally turned when Gallivan used an artist's rendering to show how the Salt Palace could be used during LDS conference 14 days a year. Speeches could be broadcast from the Tabernacle to overflow crowds in the convention arena. McKay not only gave the project his blessing, he offered to lease nine of the 22 designated acres to the county for $1 a year plus 2-3 percent interest. An $18 million bond, "the biggest bond election at that time," passed with a two-thirds majority.[111]

Gallivan embarked on an even rougher road regarding liquor service.

Alcohol consumption and sales were a bone of contention between *The Tribune* and *Deseret News*. In the beginning, the former contended that the church monopolized lax distribution through drug stores like ZCMI; the latter blamed outsiders for drinking problems. While they both supported prohibition in 1917, *The Tribune* took a turn under Fitzpatrick and argued for repeal of the 18th Amendment in the 1930s. Then, despite church opposition, Utah became the deciding state to repeal the law.[112] State liquor laws adopted to fill the void became Gallivan's target for reform.

With political reporter O.N. Malmquist doing the research, *The Tribune* determined that liquor-by-the-drink was the key to attracting big hotels and tourism to Utah. The newspaper proceeded to push the issue not only in editorials but also in news coverage. This was one time, Gallivan conceded, that he failed to use a strong hand and stay in the background as Fitzpatrick had always done. His proposal's supporters were getting "the hell kicked out of them, so I had to go public, so to speak," he said.[113]

Gallivan's 1968 liquor-reform initiative, which would have done away with Utah's quaint brown-bagging policy, died but gave birth to private clubs and the minibottle.[114]   Despite delivering a double punch, mini-bottles somehow were seen by LDS leaders as less likely than a glass of wine or cocktail to corrupt impressionable youth.

With the church's blessing, the state eventually liberalized liquor service for the 2002 Olympics, but it never loosened its tight grip on alcohol sales.   The promise of putting liquor profits into the public schools made controlled alcohol consumption palatable to politicians in power.

Gallivan's promotion of the Winter Olympics was less about the sport -- he was no skier -- than replacing his in-laws' faltering Park City mining business with tourism through skiing. He cleared the transition's first hurdle in 1961 by securing President Kennedy's support for an area redevelopment loan for Park City.[115]   But after two years of trying to promote the new industry, investors headed by brother-in-law James Ivers III were losing their shirts.

"We knew we had the greatest snow on earth, but nobody else did, and we had no money to promote it," Gallivan recounted years later.[116]

While he bemoaned the problem over a bottle of Jack Daniels at Gov. Cal Rampton's ranch residence one night, Gallivan recalled, Utah Adjutant General Max Rich suggested that Utah apply for the 1972 Olympics as a publicity stunt.[117]   Gov. Rampton retorted, "Now wait a goddamn minute! Suppose we win?"   Rich assured the governor the Games wouldn't be back in the United States so soon after being held in Squaw Valley in 1960, so Rampton gave the go ahead to organize an Olympic movement.

With just $27,000 raised by selling OUI pins (Olympics for Utah, Inc.) for $1 apiece, a Utah contingent made a presentation in Rome in 1966 that included a large book mostly prepared by Gallivan's son Mickey.   That book outlined plans to use the grandstand at the Utah State Fairgrounds for opening and closing ceremonies; to freeze over several blocks of Main and State streets downtown for cross-country events, and to flood and freeze the University of Utah football field for ice skating.

"Keeping the promise to the governor," Gallivan recalled, "we lost very handily" . . . to the Japanese.

During the next chapter of the bid process a couple of years later, Mike Korologos worked the 3 p.m.-midnight shift on the Sports Desk when the bell on the Associated Press Teletype ding-ding-dinged incessantly to alert anyone within earshot that something important was coming across the wire.   This is how he remembered it:

I read the bulletin. The United States Olympic Committee had selected Salt Lake City to replace Denver as the bid city to host the Olympic Winter Games of 1976. Denver had won the bid in 1967, beating Seattle, Salt Lake City and Lake Placid.   But after a statewide referendum, Denver withdrew its bid, and the USOC chose Salt Lake City as its replacement.

This was great news for Salt Lake City, especially for Jack Gallivan, Gen. (Ret.) Max Rich, then president of the Salt Lake Chamber of Commerce, and Gov. Calvin L. Rampton, still among the primary promoters of Salt Lake City's bid.   Their efforts still were aimed at garnering publicity for Utah's fledgling skiing industry.

Gallivan had heard the news from other sources, so I hurriedly phoned Rich at the Chamber office.   I was closely associated with him, having served for 10 years as his public information officer while a captain in the Utah National Guard over which Rich presided as Utah Adjutant General.

He took my call right away.

"General. This is Korologos at *The Tribune*. I just read on the wire that Salt Lake City has been named to replace Denver as the U.S. candidate city to host the Olympic Games of 1976!"

Silence.

"General. Denver has pulled out as U.S. host city and Salt Lake has been picked to take its place."

Silence.

"Hello. General Rich . . . are you there? Denver is out and Salt Lake City is the U.S. choice to host the Winter Games of 1976."

"Oh, my god.   What do we do now?"[118]

* * *

Executive Editor Arthur C. Deck

"Competence" was writer Malmquist's one-word description for **Arthur C. Deck**, who started reporting for the afternoon *Telegram* in 1928 and moved to United Press International for a year. Overall, he worked 53 years as a Salt Lake City newspaperman, 30 years of it as *Tribune* executive editor.[119] Malmquist sang his praises:

> *He acquired the skills which enabled him to do anything people working under him were called upon to do, and do them all well . . . Flexible and adjustable, he would have been a competent editor on a* New York Times, *a* Christian Science Monitor, *a* New York Daily News *or a* Chicago Tribune.[120]

Born in Salt Lake City in 1908, Deck graduated from East High and was editor of the University of Utah student newspaper, *The Daily Utah Chronicle*, while studying mining engineering and, according to Copy Desk lore, playing honky-tonk piano at parties. One of his old fraternity brothers occasionally tossed hands full of candy bars around our newsroom, loudly demanding to know where "Ol' Rooster Poop" was hiding.

One of Deck's claims to journalism fame was his response, as managing editor of the *Telegram*, to a strike by Salt Lake Typographical Union No. 115 November 25, 1943. Using his engineering and production ingenuity, he ordered photo-engravers to photograph four pages of typed copy and pictures and send them to the presses. Both the *Telegram* and *Tribune* turned out small and odd-looking, but they offered up the news that way for ten days, until the strike broke.[121]

"We never missed a day's publication," Jack Gallivan said proudly long after his retirement as publisher.[122] In anticipation of the strike, he noted, he and Deck arranged for the three local radio stations to read *Tribune* news stories on the air every hour on the hour in exchange for having their radio program logs published. "It didn't cost us anything." Then when he picked up Art at home to organize the reporting staff to write the radio stories, Art said he had the "great idea."

The editors pasted the masthead of *The Telegram* onto that day's *Tribune,* and reporters typed out three more pages of news to put out a four-page *Telegram*. This went back and forth for the two newspapers, which built up to eight pages. Gallivan further explained:

> We would paste it [the page of stories] up and engrave the whole page and put this thin engraving on the press drums. We were rationing newsprint at the time. The *Chicago Tribune* was struck shortly after this, and they used the same technique. That's what broke the printers union of the *Chicago Tribune*.[123]

By the 1970s, that's pretty much how the newspaper was published. By then, Deck's most creative days were behind him.

The engineering graduate patched failing office equipment with duct tape and put buckets and trash barrels beneath the drips (and waterfalls) that leaked through the newsroom roof during rainstorms. When Lifestyle writer Hazel Parkinson hunched beneath an umbrella while typing out a story, Deck ordered her desk moved.[124]

Malmquist's accolades notwithstanding, the executive editor was not universally admired.

When asked how it was to work with Deck as city editor, longtime city reporter Clarence "Scoop" Williams pointed out that he made $75 a month to Art's $400 during the

Depression. If the photogs gave Deck a photo he didn't like, he would spit on it and throw it in the garbage.[125]

Gallivan described his executive editor as "a very stern disciplinarian . . . He was the editor, by God, get it done on time at *The Tribune*." Still, the publisher added, Deck could be a "gentle, kind and very charitable sort of guy" who never really unwound on social occasions, even with close friends. Deck as a follower, he said, "pretty much a reflection of whomever his immediate superior was . . . He of course did a wonderful job for *The Tribune* because he knew what [longtime Publisher] Fitzpatrick wanted it to be."[126]

At *The Telegram*, the story goes, Deck positioned his desk in the center of his reporters' desks so he could crack the whip. Even so, his reputation for toughness fell short of a predecessor's from the turn of the century. Civil War veteran William "The Colonel" Nelson began his day as editor-in-chief by placing a revolver on his desk within easy reach.[127]

Like immediate predecessor Bert Heal, Art Deck read every word of every story before morning meetings with the publisher and editorial writers, Gallivan noted. But unlike Heal, he slyly added, Deck did not welcome his staffers' children into his office for an all-day sucker.[128]

Gallivan slipped in one more funny aside: Deck once told him that while paying the bills, his "nice, charming" wife Winnifred signed every check, "Love, Win!"

It was neither enjoyable nor enlightening to answer directly to Deck as promotions director, according to Mike Korologos.[129] He regarded Mr. Deck as a manager, not an editor.

The editors were in the newsroom: Hayes Gorey, Bill Smiley, Ernie Hoff, Heber Hart, Bob Ottum, Filthy Smith [Deano Halliday], Elly (Lubich), Bob Williams. Deck didn't edit anything, he just supervised/terrified Otteson and the others to heel to his wishes.

My biggest surprise, disappointment, eye-opener came the day I invited myself into the editorial writers' morning meeting. Prior, I often wondered how Deck would find all the tiniest of tiny errors in the paper that he'd circle and toss to the department heads during the daily 3 p.m. news meetings.

The editorial writers would sit around, go over the paper page by page and point out the errors. Mystery solved.

Not that that was wrong, but he hadn't discovered the errors . . . unless someone called him directly or they were pointed out to him by Gallivan in post-editorial writers' meetings.[130]

When appointed city editor, Brian Nutting avoided eating lunch at Lamb's Grill so he wouldn't run into or be invited to join Deck and his companions (lawyer Dan Berman, Jack Gallivan and other movers and shakers) at their designated booth along the north wall. "Not that there was ever any danger of that," he added.[131]

Though aloof, Deck sometimes surprised employees with caring that fostered a sense of family. Nancy Hobbs was one such employee:

> Deck was scary as hell when I went into his office as a college student and president of the U. Sigma Delta Chi [SDX, Society of Professional Journalists] chapter to ask his help sending me to the national conference, which he generously did. Helped change my view of him; he remains a *Tribune* legend.[132]

An unidentified staffer told *Utah Holiday* Editor Paul Swenson that Deck was not vindictive but "one of the kindest men I have ever known." Employees who took time time off never missed a paycheck. He added:

> *But he's a despot when it comes to deciding what is good and bad for* The Tribune. *As long as he is the editor,* The Trib *will essentially be a one-man operation. He controls everything -- including whether someone will get a raise or whether we will change a comic strip.*[133]

While describing Deck as "a legendary tyrant who was opaque and demanding of staffers," Paul Wetzel noted his kindness "when they landed in rehab . . . [I]t was truly a family newspaper."[134]

Secretary Shirley Jones said her boss was forever having her inquire after the medical condition of staffers' wives. (He apparently didn't ask about the female staffers' husbands during that sexist era.)

Bob Blair, Society editor before managing the editorial pages, played bridge with Art and Winnifred Deck, so he got to know Art in another context as a nice man, if not a back-slapper.[135]   There was a gentle side to the man, he said.

After going to great lengths to prevent layoffs during the Great Depression, Blair related, Deck was forced to fire 40 employees when the *Telegram* shut down in 1952.   One by one, he asked staffers, "Have you got a minute?" -- the cue they faced the chopping block.   At the end of the day, he told Blair he'd had the hardest day of his life.

Perhaps to camouflage his quest, Deck never made a direct approach from his office in the northwest corner of the newsroom to the men's room on the southeast side.

As Mike Korologos would tell it, Deck would stop by political writer Doug Parker's cubicle to ask, "What's up?" Doug would utter something, and Deck would walk away, clicking his pen.   If columnist Dan Valentine was in, he'd do the same at that cubicle, and so on with editors along the way.   His last stop was Sports Editor John Mooney's desk, just outside the lavatory door.

When he'd ask Mooney what was going on, Mooney, never missing a chance to befriend Deck, would regale him with University of Utah athlete stories, a list of buddies coming to town, coach talk, whatever.

Then, lo and behold, Betty Mooney became pregnant.   So when Deck came sauntering by, Mooney couldn't wait to tell him the news.   As usual, Deck stared off into space, grunted, clicked his pen and headed to the restroom.

Every day he was in the office after that, Mooney would give Deck a detailed account of the pregnancy: morning sickness today, doctor appointment,   doctor report, and so on. Each time, Deck said nothing but would click his pen and move on.

Finally it dawned on Mooney that perhaps Deck wasn't paying attention to the pregnancy reports.   To test his hunch, the next time Deck asked, "What's going on?" Mooney responded, "Not much, Art.   We found out today that Betty wasn't pregnant.   She had just swallowed a watermelon seed."

As per the norm, Deck grunted, clicked his pen and marched to the restroom.[136]

Occasionally, Deck slipped onto the scene without detection.   One afternoon Mooney was complaining about him when he emerged silently behind him from the lavatory.   The other sports writers subtly gave him the time-out sign, and Mooney dramatically drew a rubber knife from his desk drawer.   "What's going on?" Deck inquired. "Did you hear what I just said?" Mooney asked nervously.   Receiving a negative response, Mooney breathed a sigh of relief. "Thank God, I almost killed an innocent man!"[137]

I never could warm up to the old guy skulking around the office in half-glasses, wing-tips and vest clicking his pen to let us know he was on the prowl.   I saw him as the ghoul who tossed   lit Chesterfields into the nearest trash barrel, issued seemingly arbitrary directives and ripped down tasteless cartoons, jokes and poetry plastering the Art Department pillar.   My rare interactions with The Man occurred when a copy boy reported that Mr. Deck wanted to see me   in his office.

The scene played out pretty much as Bob Woody put it:

> . . . it was Helen Straub [Shirley Jones' predecessor] who issued those terrible summons: "Mr. Deck wants to see YOU!"
> Rebuke or raise?
> Oh, please, please, please God, let it be the latter.
> "You'll find a little something extra in your check today," followed by a microsecond smile.
> Ohhhh, thank you, kind Sir, thank you, Thank you. Thank you.[138]

Mike Korologos liked to say, "It's good he mentioned it, because I wouldn't have noticed it."   When Mike became ski writer in the 1960s, Deck gave him $200 to buy snow tires, skis, boots, poles and ski clothes.[139]   Even then, $200 didn't begin to cover the costs.

Brian Nutting also experienced Deck's penny-pinching when appointed city editor.   As Nutting prepared to leave for a seminar in Reston, Va., the boss reminded him he was representing *The Tribune* among peer newspapers.   He handed Nutting a twenty-dollar bill to buy a round of drinks.

"Typical," Nutting remarked.   "I was pretty sure $20 wouldn't cover drinks for 35 other editors."[140]

As Korologos recalled, Deck did a better job of representing *The Tribune* as president of the Board of Directors of the American Society of Newspaper Editors from 1973 to 1974.

Each president was expected to out-do his predecessor in picking the most remote site for the group's next annual meeting, and Deck did not disappoint with his choice of Wahweap Lodge and Marina on the south shore of Lake Powell, a relatively new recreational site taking form after completion of Glen Canyon Dam on the Utah-Arizona border in 1966. Korologos went along to help.

Between 25 and 30 newspaper executives and some of their wives, as well as Utah Gov. Calvin L. Rampton, Publisher Jack Gallivan and a high ranking White House staffer who addressed the group. One of my first jobs was to tend bar in one of the lodge suites before dinner in the dining room, where floor-to-ceiling windows looked out on a glorious view of deep blue Lake Powell with its red rock spires and buttes in the distance. It was agreed then and there that Deck had fulfilled his duty of staging the session in the most remote, striking spot. [141]

Long after the wives retired to their rooms, Korologos continued, a handful of editors and guests stuck around embellishing tales of their past year and singing along as one editor pounded out tunes on a small upright piano. They, including Gallivan, Deck and Rampton, had such a good time, they decided the sing-along should continue on the next day's lake tour on houseboats, and it was agreed Mike should get the piano aboard.

A big gulp stuck in my throat, and it wasn't because a martini olive was stuck there. "How am I going to pull that off?" I thought.

Dutifully, after just a couple hours sleep, I found a dining room supervisor, who located a lodge handyman and together we took steps to fulfill the assignment.

While rolling the piano across the small dance floor toward the lodge's back door, where the handyman had parked a pickup truck, Gallivan appeared and asked what was going on. I explained we were doing as all agreed last night – getting the piano onto one of the boats. He wondered aloud what impact the piano's weight would have on the boat's operation and decided it wasn't a very good idea. I did not disagree. Neither did the lodge guy nor the handyman.

Be assured, the absence of a piano did not dampen the desire to reignite the festivities of the night before. What did threaten the party – but only briefly – was the discovery that the catering crew failed to distribute the liquor and mixers evenly when loading the boats. One boat had too much of one and not of the other. And vice versa.

No vodka? No worries!

The boat skippers deftly maneuvered their respective crafts to within 10-15 feet of each other, port-to-starboard, while maintaining their journey up-lake. Guests managed to "equalize" their boats' bar supplies by tossing bottles of mixer and liquor between them. Cheers would erupt with each successful toss and catch. There was plenty of cheering, as not one bottle was lost in the process.

As for the piano, it likely would have never been played.

As for Art Deck, he showed up in tie and blue seersucker sport coat even on a boat in the wilds. His one compromise was to replace his wingtips with tenny runners.

Chief Artist Dennis "Denny" Green called Deck "the worst skinflint I ever knew." Each year, Gallivan would give Deck a budget, and Deck would give half of it back by the end of the year. It took three months of constant haranguing to get a paper-cutter for the Art Department. Then artist Sam Smith broke the thing while trying to slice through an entire ream of paper at once. "I could have killed him."[142]

Tribune photographers and reporters had to hitch rides with other organizations when big news events called for aerial views, whether dam breaks, mudslides or freak accidents. Photographer Tim Kelly couldn't believe his good fortune whenever *The Tribune* popped for a helicopter or small plane.

Later miserliness notwithstanding, Deck had hired a private plane for the story that garnered *The Tribune* a coveted Pulitzer.[143] By repeatedly checking the news wires that day in 1956, he figured out that two missing planes might have collided and ordered reporter Robert F. Alkire and Photographer Jack White to gear up for a trip to the scene before anyone else in the business realized what had happened. [144]

Staffers Barbi Fouch (Robison), Carolyn Monson and Bernie Moss managed to break through Deck's crusty shell to carry on conversations with this man of few words. While most staffers avoided him and some did their best to antagonize him, these three women saw the reserved man in the three-piece suit (even at the annual picnic) as a sensitive, socially withdrawn man.[145]

Again, Woody's description is worth repeating.

It was at the party of parties -- the combined retirement fare-thee-well for Mr. Deck's secretary Helen Straub and Hellenic farewell to Mike Korologos' family home on Fourth South.

We were all there for that one, including The Man [Art Deck], for Helen was his constant and trusted secretary.

The party got frisky. And when I, one of the few brazen and foolish enough to come in toga and wreath -- was frugging and watusi-ing with Patty Fonnesbeck and Melba Ferguson, I see Doug's [Parker] eyes widen with astonishment.

No doubt, this newly named assistant to the newly named business editor [Woody] was wondering whether he had signed up for *The Salt Lake Tribune* or was on a ship of fools bound for Sodom and Gomorrah.

The Man, quite mellowed by the movement, deigned to paternally buss the office lovelies. Among them: Barbara Fouch, who had coquettishly concealed -- and unconcealed -- a fig leaf where classic painters put fig leafs.

"Art, baby," she told The Man as they nuzzled.

It was Black Monday on the Society Desk when The Man came in like cold death. And Carolyn nudged Barbi and said, "Look, Barbara, here comes Art Baby."

No, Barbi was not intimidated by Art Deck nor much else. She sometimes received calls from owner Jane Finn McCarthey, who had promised to get something into the paper for one of her acquaintances. She said:

I'd tell her we don't do that anymore, and she would threaten me with, "When my son becomes publisher, you'll be the first one fired." In a couple of minutes, I'd get a call from the front office. "Gotta minute?" Deck would then tell me he just got a call from Jane, "that poor woman." Yessir, Tom was going to be publisher, and then I was out

on my ear. Deck always thought she was half-swacked.[146]

Carolyn Monson, Bernie Moss and Barbi Robison, left to right.

Some male staffers also enjoyed The Man.

"I just really liked Art Deck," Paul Rolly said of the editor who rewarded him with a raise every time his wife brought another child into the world.

Shy staffer Peter Scarlet also enjoyed Deck, whom he dubbed the Austrian and engaged in one-sided conversations while unfurling the flag outside Deck's office window or cornering him at the staff picnic. Deck may not have listened, but he at least stood still while Peter babbled on about the Crimean war or various leaders of his Mormon faith.

* * *

Will Fehr, the city editor who interviewed me with Otteson my first day, was a defector from the *Deseret News* who found *The Tribune* more compatible.

The son of deaf parents, this Sigma Chi from the University of Utah joined the Navy in World War II and the Air Force during the Korean conflict, when he wrote for Voice of America.[147] He became a *Tribune* copy boy in 1947 and worked on several beats before rising to city editor in 1964. "He was truly objective in reportage of the news," according to Jack Gallivan.[148]

Will Fehr

Unassuming and quiet with a wry sense of humor, Fehr served a supportive role for many staffers who remembered him fondly.

Woody saw the city editor as a buffer against outside forces and the "mandates and moods of The Man."

Will was far more of the newsroom than of the management. Having properly rebuked you and heard explanations, he was at your side when you made that dreadful journey to Don Holbrook's office [*The Tribune's* attorney] to plan a defense against and or draft an apology to the plaintiff who had just laid a million-dollar suit on you and your employers. [149]

When JoAnn "Fifi" Jacobsen joined the staff as a 20-year-old Mormon, Fehr helped her cope with profane newsmen and eased her through her mistakes.[150]

"Will Fehr was my mentor and friend who taught me that to be trusted by readers, a journalist must adhere to the highest standards," she said, adding that he would begin his lectures with a compliment, such as: "You are a nice person and a good writer, but you can't spell worth a damn."[151]

Sometimes Fehr wrote poetry while waiting for a deadline story, she noted.

Fehr had a soft spot for the industrious, eager-to-please young reporter. Despite threats never to rehire quitters, he took Fifi back not once, but twice.

But he had no patience for employees who threatened to quit unless he promoted them. More than one hit a dead-end on City Desk for issuing an ultimatum. Plagiarism was another of Fehr's pet peeves. Anyone who copied another writer's work -- considered an egregious ethics violation -- could expect demotion or dismissal.

Like Fifi, Brian Nutting considered Fehr a friend as much as a boss or colleague. He and Wilf Cannon, Charles Seldin, Tim Kelly and Dennis Green would play tennis on courts across from Fehr's old home in the Avenues. That year, Nutting had the backshop mock up a fake Front Page with the headline "Rocket Fehr Wins Wimbledon" for his birthday.

"Honestly, I can't recall myself thinking I was just sucking up to the boss," Nutting said. "But maybe I was – so subtly that even I didn't notice."

Mike Carter regarded Fehr as a "good editor and man of integrity. He was also shy, unless liquored up, and often just stood there waiting for you to start a conversation."[152]

"He was an idealistic cynic, which might sound like an oxymoron," sports writer Tom Wharton said of Fehr. "He had a great heart and was idealistic about what journalism was all about. He was a passionate newspaperman who never lost his cool."[153]

A case in point was his reaction to the 6.2 earthquake that shook the city at 8:32 p.m. March 27,1975, setting the Tribune building swaying and locking up local phone lines. Fehr calmly assigned reporters to assess the damage and emergency response, and within two hours, a comprehensive story under Vandra (Huber) Webb's byline was ready.[154]

Seldin, George Raine, Jim Woolf and Nancy Funk [Melich] contributed sidebars and follow-ups. Woolf interviewed University of Utah seismologist Kenneth Cook.[155] Raine reported that President Gerald Ford's son, Jack, a Utah State University student in Logan, was rushed from Box Elder High School where he was addressing an assembly.[156] Ellen Marshall, NAC's lunchroom attendant who also ran Hotel Utah's cloak room, told reporters that Skyroom dancers were swinging and swaying more than usual.[157]

Despite a spell early in his career as medical writer for the *Deseret News*, Fehr was no goodie-goodie. He smoked, swore and imbibed as much or more than many on the staff, but he couldn't always hold his liquor. Once he vomited in a downtown gutter after leaving a *Tribune* gathering at our favorite watering hole; another time he retched behind a staffer's couch.

Artist Mark Knudsen recalled the two or three weeks that Fehr tried to quit smoking.

When he couldn't stand it any more, he would come to the Art Department a couple of times a day, put a nickel on Tim Brinton's drawing table and take one of his Marlboros. One time Tim was out of cigarettes, so I offered him one of my Kools.

Fehr said, "I wouldn't take one of those goddamn faggot cigarettes if you paid me!"

The next day, here comes Will. He puts a nickel on Tim's drawing table. I proffer a pack of Kools and say, "Try one of these, Big Boy."

Will: "There goes your Christmas bonus again this year, Knudsen."

Brinton wet his pants.

Fehr showed up to Gordon Harman's wedding in April 1973. While congratulating the newlyweds, he offered advice about their wedding night: "Well, just remember this. It doesn't matter whether you are on top or she is, *The Tribune* comes first."[158]

During a training session years later in California, Gordon could see Fehr's reflection in the computer monitor as he nervously tried to prove he could teach anyone to paginate a news page. More than four hours later, the page was not yet finished, but Will was. He had nodded off who knows how long before. Fortunately -- or not -- he woke up in time for the group's trip to a strip club, where NAC's Jerry Jennings paid an attractive mud wrestler to give the nonplussed editor a lap dance.[159]

"God bless Will's soul," John Keahey said on facebook. "[He was] the man who gambled on a former wire-service reporter who was a burned out flack -- and gave him a 22-year newspaper career.[160]

Thrilled to return to newspapering in 1989 after working PR for Mountain Fuel Supply, Keahey recounted minute details of *The Tribune* decades later.

It was a glorious place, full of wonderfully weird and unique people.[161]

I first walked into that newsroom on the spring of 1964. I was with a college j-school group from Idaho State en route to Provo for a conference. I was overawed at the look and feel of my first "big city" newsroom. We got a tour; a few of us gathered around John Mooney, and he regaled us with lots of stories. A young Will Fehr, who years later became my savior, was sitting across the way. Yelling, thick cigarette smoke, magic.[162]

Not everyone was crazy about Fehr. Rhonda Hailes, an artist who eventually studied psychology, questioned his motives:

Willard [she liked nicknames] would stand over me and others jiggling his change nonstop. I internalized it, thinking if I screwed up, I'd be on the street collecting coins along with my brother. On a psychodynamic level, it might have been a nervous gesture 'cause he felt guilty for paying me and everyone else pitifully low wages. Perhaps he was poor in spirit, so the revved up attention he got made him feel more buoyant?[163] . . . He definitely wasn't Mr. HappyGoLucky."[164]

Fehr was known to overcompensate for his attraction to young women by penalizing some of his favorites. Jamie Tabish, for example, quit in frustration after failing to move up in the ranks from newsroom assistant and cub reporter. Fehr was visibly shaken.

[87] Gallivan, May 2005.

[88] Malmquist, pp. 267-269.

[89] Malmquist, p. 269.

[90] Gallivan, May 2005.

[91] Malmquist, p. 322.

[92] Ibid., 272.

[93] Ibid., p. 271.

[94] Ibid., p. 272.

[95] Malmquist, p. 333.

[96] John William Gallivan obituary, *The Salt Lake Tribune,* October 4, 2012.

[97] "James Ivers dies --- spirit of Park City," *Deseret News*, May 17, 2000.

[98] Mike Korologos email February 21, 2017.

[99] W.H. McDougall, Jr., "News on the Wing: Carrier Pigeons Won Scoops for Salt Lake City Reporter," *Nieman Reports*, July 1947, Vol. 1, Nov. 3.

[100] Ibid.

[101] "Monsignor McDougall, former journalist and adventurer, dies at 79," *Deseret News*, Dec. 9, 1988.

[102] Malmquist, p. 333.

[103] Gallivan, May 2005.

[104] Malmquist., p. 388.

[105] Mike Korologos email, March 24, 2015.

[106] Joan O'Brien email to Diane Cole March 25, 2015.

[107] Korologos, March 24, 2015.

[108] Malmquist, p. 398-99.

[109] Gallivan, May 2005.

[110] Gallivan, May 2005.

[111] Ibid.

[112] Malmquist, pp. 335-342.

[113] Gallivan, May 2005.

[114] Malmquist, p. 343.

[115] "PCMR's history started with Jack Gallivan," Park Record, February 7, 2004.

[116] Gallivan, May 2005.

[117] Ibid. However, Mike Korologos, in a draft Ski Utah promotion September 17, 2015, identified the third person in the room as savings and loan executive Gene Donovan.

[118] Mike Korologos email June 14, 2015.

[119] Gorrell, March 27, 2004.

[120] Malmquist, p. 359.

[121] Malmquist, p. 358.

[122] Gallivan, May 2005.

[123] Ibid.

[124] Nancy Melich interview, March 4, 2014.

[125] Robert Bryson email, August 9, 2015.

[126] Gallivan, May 2005.

[127] Malmquist, p. 245.

[128] Jack Gallivan, "Tribune's Chairman, Reflects on Personalities," *The Salt Lake Tribune,* July 24, 1988, p. T9.

[129] Mike Korologos email, January 19, 2014.

[130] Korologos email, January 20, 2014.

[131] Nutting, February 14, 2014.

[132] Nancy Hobbs email.

[133] Swenson, 1974, p.34.

[134] Paul Wetzel's prepared but undelivered remarks upon 2012 retirement.

[135] Robert Blair conversation, St. George, Utah, Oct. 8, 2013.

[136] Mike Korologos email, January 29, 2014.

[137] Lex Hemphill interview, March 4, 2014.

[138] Robert H. Woody eulogy of Douglas L. Parker August 23, 1995, courtesy of Barbara Woody, April 2014.

[139] Mike Korologos email, January 26, 2014.

[140] Nutting, February 14, 2014.

[141] Mike Korologos email, May 26, 2015.

[142] Dennis Green, May 14, 2015.

[143] "Of All Awards Pulitzer Was the Tops," *The Salt Lake Tribune*, July 24, 1988, p. T5.

[144] Mike Gorrell, "Arthur C. Deck," *The Salt Lake Tribune*, March 27, 2004.

[145] Barbi Robison, Carolyn Monson and Shirley Jones interview with Diane Cole, Salt Lake City, October 7, 2013.

[146] Barbi Robison telephone interview, November 13, 2015.

[147] Paul Rolly, "Former Tribune Editor Will Fehr Dies of Heart Failure," *The Salt Lake Tribune*, November 2, 2010 November 2, 2010.

[148] Ibid.

[149] Woody, August 23, 1995.

[150] Rolly & Wells, *The Salt Lake Tribune*, December 31, 2004; Paul Rolly, "Former Tribune Editor Will Fehr Dies of Heart Failure," *The Salt Lake Tribune*, November 2, 2010.

[151] Rolly, November 2, 2010.

[152] Mike Carter on facebook August 27, 2015.

[153] Paul Rolly, "Former Tribune Editor Will Fehr Dies of Heart Failure," *The Salt Lake Tribune*. November 2, 2010.

[154] Rolly, November 2, 2010.

[155] Jim Woolf, "Expert Says We Must Live with Earthquakes," *The Salt Lake Tribune*, March 29, 1975.

[156] George Raine, "Experts Assess Damage, Results of Earth Tremor," *The Salt Lake Tribune,* March 29, 1975.

[157] Dexter Ellis, *Deseret News*, March 29, 1975.

[158] Gordon Harmon email to Tribune facebook website February 27, 2014.

[159] Gordon Harman email, October 6, 2015.

[160] John Keahey to facebook Tribune Group February 27, 2012.

[161] John Keahey to facebook Tribune group December 18, 2013.

[162] John Keahey to facebook Tribune group February 1, 2012.

[163] Rhonda Hailes Maylett on facebook August 17, 2015.

[164] Rhonda Hailes Maylett on facebook August 19, 2015.

5 - Intemperance on Tap

When it came to describing the newsroom in the 1960s and 1970s, no one could match Bob Woody, who waxed poetic on the subject and appropriately gave liquor a supporting role:

It is not as bosom buddies that most of us knew each other at *The Tribune*, but as colleagues. And we knew each other's values and vanities probably better than our closest and forgiving friends. For *The Tribune* was a cauldron of the comical and the corrosive, deadlines, rebuke and rejection, agony and damned little ecstasy -- where we could see and judge each in a way that really took measure -- people working under pressure . . .

. . . *The Tribune's* blue bible said only it is expected that any employee upon retirement shall be prepared to provide for his own retirement.

Fringes finally come: Pensions, much expanded health and finally -- four-week vacations, the ESOP.

But throughout, the fringe benefit I savored the most was that randy, strident, scurrilous, cynical pack of wretches that were my fellow workers.

Their cynicism and churlishness were understandable. For the pack were in constant conflict with institutional misinformation, hypocrisy and deceit and deception. At the same time the employer that had loosed them to snoop out and provide the scoops, tightened the leash when the snooping and scooping turned uncomfortably toward targets a bit too close to home.

A free press is always an angry press. And when the free press finds its leash restrained by its very own masters, it becomes an even angrier and more cynical press.

When I came on board there were those titans of the newsroom -- the bumptious and booming Bob Bernick, the pious and puckish John Mooney, the sardonic "Nothing Serious" Dan Valentine, the prim and proper Bill Patrick who wrote stories with the precision and care of a surgeon dissecting a cadaver, and the august and grave graduate of the old school of journalism, O. N. Malmquist, confidante of publisher, governor and senators and yet a reporter trusted and esteemed by sources and readers alike -- and who, at age 55, would cheerfully and dutifully take an ordinary obituary over the phone. [Can you see the editor's dilemma in trying to achieve reader-sized sentences while protecting the gems?]

From the goggled Scoop Williams you got the skinny on how Dr. Moormeister had Salt Lake gangsters kidnap and drive a car over his faithless wife in 1928, and how *The Tribune* announced to the nation that prohibition had ended with the final vote of repeal by the Utah Legislature.

The courtly Al Ferguson, pipe jutting from his mouth still tapping out stories of the city beat when he was 75 years old.

From police reporter and our own son of thunder Harold Schindler came spectral and harrowing tales of the misfortunes befallen those misguided and miserable beings who had tried to organize the newsroom. With such forbidding and spectral warnings, we would not utter -- even whisper -- the dreaded word "guild!"

From Bernick came the you-should-have-been-there stories of the days when the *Telegram* fought toe-to-toe with the *Deseret News* and when Deck wiped up the floor with the blood of the staff.

There was the gang of eight: Ross Welser, Frank Porschatis, Carol Reynolds, Van Porter, Earl Conrad, Borge Andersen and a scrawny 17-year-old Lynn Johnson directed by a fastidious little man in a fedora named Brandt Gray: "Just a little smile, please."

And on the Copy Desk: Bill Symons of the Coca-Cola bottle glasses and the anguished bellow: "I can't stand it anymore!" And Dirty Dean Halliday, master of the lewd and lascivious. And there was Stan Bowman staggering in just in time to dot the weather forecast.

At center stage was the erudite and scholarly Hayes Gorey and his editing pencil exacting perfection and professionalism in the newsroom and demanding memos of explanation and expiation for a screw-up or misspelling, or the inadvertent resurrection on Split Page [the first page of state and local news] of a Tooele mayor seven months deceased. If your hair was a bit shaggy, he'd order a haircut; shoes scruffy, a shoeshine.

Watching over the international scene was the wry and lean Bob Ottum, right out of *Esquire* magazine, for whom he incidentally did an occasional freelance piece.

Ernie Hoff coached a gaggle of correspondents from Twin Falls to St. George. Keith Otteson, furrows and frowns for eight or nine hours, would quickly change to beams and gleams the minute he joined us at a late party.

No liquor by the drink yet. It was liquor by the bottle at Bob Johnson's or Bill Simons' places, where we set sail on the Sloop John B. and got in a fight which lasted all night. Robert (E. Lee) Blair, proud reject of two military schools, was still editing regional copy, shortly to enjoy five paradisiacal years as society page editor and face into the sunset as a distinguished chief editorial writer.

With liquor by the drink, the party moved to the Continental Club, where now middle-aged *Tribune* males let down their hair, grew sideburns and Zapata mustaches, pulled on bell-bottoms, unbuttoned their shirts to the navel and adorned their hairy chests with medallions in hopes the 50-cent Continental drinks were the fountain of youth and enlivened libidos.

Among them, the legendary Hank McKee, who had flown C-47s over the Himalayan hump and who could belt out "The Road to Mandalay" like Lawrence Tibbets. But it wasn't the dawn coming up like thunder out of China 'cross the bay. It was the early morning sun rising over the Wasatch, and we had been partying since 7 the evening before.[165]

Drinking among staffers wasn't all fun and games. It often amounted to abuse, and not only among the Copy Desk rim rats and other staff veterans already mentioned.

Rumor had it that the company couldn't find reasonable health insurance because of its astronomically high number of booze-related and psychiatric claims. The alcoholism rate reportedly was 500 percent above average; mental illness 300 percent.[166] If someone fell off the wagon, they usually were welcomed back into the fold once back on their feet.

"Of course there were drinking problems," Brian Nutting noted. "We used to joke that there was a bed on permanent standby at the U hospital for the latest alchy who got too sick."[167]

Reporter Anne Wilson agreed that the drinking "was a little out of control: Stan getting trapped in the filing cabinet and Wilf [Cannon] getting fired on Election Day was evidence of that . . . The newsroom was full of quirky people in those days, and maybe quirky is a nice way of saying drug-addled or addicted or [having] mental health issues."[168]

In 1972, mellow **Wilf Cannon** moved from head copy boy into vital statistics on his way up the ladder to obituaries and the police beat. He was a nice guy whose partying got the best of him. One election night, City Editor Will Fehr found him "shit-faced drunk" in one of the cubicles and sent him home one last time, Brian recalled.[169] "I always will wonder if somehow we couldn't have saved Wilf if we'd gotten into his face about his drinking and made him deal with it earlier."

Liver disease killed him before he reached middle age.

Cannon had told Nutting his drinking problems were genetic, a claim Nutting dismissed as "bullshit."[170] But if Cannon was truly a descendant of leading Mormon pioneers, as I understood, his defense might have been valid. Ex-communicated Mormon Frank Cannon, the son of Apostle George Q. Cannon and writer of some of *The Tribune's* most scathing anti-Mormon diatribes at the turn of the century, was often described as a drunk.[171]

Besides the booze, most staffers smoked, and it wasn't just tobacco. A couple of the long-haired copy boys did a few doobies, joints, jays, bowls, whatever, in the alley or on the roof outside the lunchroom during night shifts. Artist Neil Passey's pupils didn't shrink until halfway through his shift. Prescription drugs like Prozac infiltrated the newsroom as well.

Following Wilf Cannon's path, if a bit more slowly, was inactive Mormon **Jon Ure**.

After replacing Wilf as dayside errand boy, the long-haired Army veteran took pot-smoking and booze breaks and held the job for a record two years. This created a dilemma for his superiors: Do we fire him or promote him so other entry-level staff can rise in the ranks? He was promoted despite his frequent visits to Junior's Tavern and a come-what-may attitude.

Tobacco was the habit of choice among most veteran staffers. The stench settled in my hair and clothes, convincing my parents I'd taken up the disgusting addiction.

Publisher Jack Gallivan puffed up to four packs a day before my time, quitting after medical writer Bill Patrick finally got through to him with countless reports on tobacco's health hazards. Gallivan challenged Patrick to follow suit, but that confirmed smoker only broke it off for a couple of weeks. Even so, according to Gallivan, Patrick lived to "a very advanced age."[172] That is, 83. Gallivan made that observation at age 90, seven years before his own death.

Dennis Green often found himself lighting up a second cigarette while another still smoldered in his ashtray. He wasn't the only one. Ted Heal usually had more than one going at a time. The desk drawers of most veteran staffers were littered with their butts.

Editor Art Deck smoked Chesterfield Kings non-stop. He started countless fires in the office trash barrels by tossing in burning butts. It often was artist Denny Green's job to douse the fires with water used for rinsing his paint brushes, but the copy boys also were called to duty regularly.

"We all got a chance to put out a fire in the wire room trash can because Art had to smoke while reading the wires," reported Gordon Harman. "And forget the fire department! 'Boy!!! Fire in the newsroom!'"[173]

It terrified Brian Nutting, as city editor, when Deck would walk though the newsroom with a long ash hanging from his cigarette because it always seemed to mean bad news.[174]

The Tribune's tolerance for unhealthy habits could be traced to the top, where addiction was a tradition if not a genetic trait.

Copy boy Mike Carter once had to drive a "pissed-drunk Jack Gallivan home from The Alta Club" after being stopped for driving under the influence.[175]

Alcoholism was "a curse of Kearns descendants" who inherited *The Tribune,* according to one of those descendants.[176] Phil McCarthey noted that his great uncle Thomas F. Kearns, the son of the senator, established Utah's chapter of Alcoholics Anonymous. His aunt was known as "Champagne Sheila" because she never went anywhere without a bottle of bubbly tucked into a custom-made violin case." Phil's father and Senator Kearns' oldest grandson Thomas Kearns McCarthey had trouble with liquor.[177]

It sometimes seemed as if *Tribune* staffers were rebelling against or making up for the clean-living culture of the LDS Church. Maybe the imbibers were simply soaking up whatever Mormon teetotalers left on the table. In any case, mood-altering substances helped most of us cope with stresses of the job.

---

[165] Woody, August 23, 1995.

[166] Dennis Green, 2013.

[167] Nutting, February 14, 2014.

[168] Anne Wilson email, December 31, 2013.

[169] Nutting, February 14, 2014.

[170] Brian Nutting email to Diane Cole January 31, 2015.

[171] Kenneth L. Cannon II, "Wives and Other Women: Love, Sex, and marriage in the Lives of John Q. Cannon, Frank J. Cannon, and Abraham H. Cannon, *Dialogue, a journal of mormon thought*, Vol. 42, No. 4, Winter 2010; Cannon, "And Now It Is the Mormons: The Magazine Crusade Against the Mormon Church," 1910-1911, *Dialogue: a journal of mormon thought*, Vol. 46, No. 1, Spring 2013.

[172] Rolly & House, May 2005.

[173] Gordon Harman to facebook's Tribune group February 27, 2014.

[174] Nutting, February 14, 2014.

[175] Mike Carter to Tribune facebook group, September 28, 2015.

[176] Jerry Spangler, "Carrying the torch?" *Deseret News*, June 12, 2001.

[177] Ibid.

6 - Religious Rivalry

From the outset, *The Tribune's* relationship with the Mormon Church was antagonistic. Some called it an "irrepressible conflict."[178] *Tribune* founders, excommunicated converts, expressed outright animosity for the church. In an 1886 history of Salt Lake City, Edward W. Tullidge praised *The Tribune* as a "great newspaper, apart from any anti-Mormon mission."[179] Judge Dennis J. Toohy, who became a shareholder and director of The Tribune Publishing Company, attacked the church on ecclesiastical and moral grounds, contending that "the best blood of Europe has been seduced to come here to Utah, and bow down to a false shrine; all except the people of old Ireland, where the Catholic religion holds them true."[180] Fittingly, Irish Catholics controlled the newspaper most of its existence.

Tribune editorials in the beginning boldly denounced polygamy and LDS President Brigham Young, claiming that "the most graceful act of his life has been his death."[181] The August 30, 1877 editorial announcing his demise described Young in such unsavory terms as a "blarophant" whose religious system was "well nigh Satanic."[182] On May 2, 1880, a *Tribune* editorial writer blasted a counterpart's commentary at the church-owned *Deseret News*: "It emanates from the pen of a three-ply plyg, who, if he had his just desserts, would be keeping company with George Reynolds in the Utah Penitentiary, and instead of writing editorials for the lying Church organ, would be engaged in playing checkers with his nose on the prison bars."[183]

Flamboyant mining magnate **Thomas Kearns**, whose Irish Catholic parents had immigrated from Canada to Nebraska, teamed up with Park City miner David Keith to surreptitiously buy *The Tribune* in 1901 after its editorials blasted his candidacy for the U.S. Senate the previous year. The newspaper had accused Kearns of wangling a deal with Mormon Church President Lorenzo Snow to become the state's second senator[184] after Senator Frank Cannon fell from the church's grace for abandoning the Republican Party in 1896, among other perceived transgressions.[185] Though the son of a Mormon apostle, Cannon made enemies of

other church leaders, and those leaders decided a non-Mormon, non-polygamist would be best received in Washington so soon after the Manifesto outlawing polygamy led to statehood January 4, 1896.[186] There also was talk that Kearns offered the church a land trade for its support.[187]

"With a flick of the finger, the Legislature did the bidding"[188] of President Snow, and Kearns won the national office, which he held through 1904. During his term, there was a lull in the storm between church and *Tribune*, and the church's new president, Joseph F. Smith, cautioned the *Deseret News* against criticizing *The Tribune* and renewing the old "anti-Mormon fight."[189]

But the firestorm exploded when President Smith withheld support for Kearns' re-election and Kearns hired former senator Frank Cannon to write editorials. "Over the next three years, this contest [between church and *Tribune*] was fought publicly in the pages of the *Salt Lake Tribune* and Church-owned *Deseret Evening News*."[190]

The LDS leader testified in a 1904 U.S. Senate hearing that Cannon was not only "a very poor"[191] Mormon but also an anti-Christ.[192] Cannon's apparent offenses, besides quitting the Republican Party, were to frequent brothels, dishonor a housemaid and attempt to make a commission on the sale of church bonds.[193]

In personal letters, President Smith described *The Tribune* as a "malignant sheet" that publishes "filth and impotent slush" and "has been debased below all things previously known as newspaperdum."[194] As his son, Joseph Fielding Smith, put it years later, Cannon had "joined forces with the enemies of the Church in a campaign of bitterness and hate which in some respects surpassed any expression of bitterness ever before manifested against the Church."[195]

Given his descriptions, President Smith believed *Truth*, a lively non-Mormon weekly published from 1901-1908 by John W. Hughes. (Ironically, another non-Mormon John Hughes became *Deseret News* publisher in 1997, when the *News* played tug-of-war with the Kearns family for *The Tribune*.) For example, *Truth's* Hughes accused *The Tribune* of:

> . . . *consummate blackguardism [for policies] conducted by a triumvirate composed of ex-Senator Kearns, Joseph Lippman [Kearns' campaign manager] and ex-Senator Frank J. Cannon. The dastardly and altogether despicable*

methods are conceived by Mr. Lippman, executed by Mr. Cannon and paid for by Mr. Kearns. Such a triumvlrate never before disgraced newspaperdom. When Perry S. Heath, the king of grafters, was manager of the paper it was thought the lowest depths of infamy had been reached by the sheet, but since his flight to other lands, still lower depths have been reached. No man, Gentile or Mormon, who refuses to be a tool and a slave of the owner of the sheet is safe from its calumny and abuse. It not only vilifies individuals, but it blackens the name of the state and the city . . . [196]

The tabloid got personal, libel laws be damned. It claimed "courageous Gentiles" who "despised and loathed him" defeated Tom Kearns for re-election.[197] Calling him one of "the worst specimens of society in the United States," *Truth* asserted that Kearns had come from Nebraska as a "fugitive from justice, not daring to use his own name, but going under an alias [Thomas Williams] to escape the hangman's noose . . . [after H]e killed a man in Nebraska . . . Since he has been here he has established a reputation as a libertine, a despoiler of women" who paid someone to murder a miner who owned ground Kearns wanted.[198] On May 6, 1905, *Truth* alleged Kearns debauched and fathered a child by "a young girl named Eula Wray . . . Notwithstanding his known bad character, his money enabled him to be elected United States senator, although he had not the smallest qualification for that office, densely ignorant, uncouth with all the arrogance of a nouveau riche."[199]

I was born 70 years too late. It must have been great sport to write "news" with no holds barred! Bias? Bring it on! No need to substantiate scandalous accusations. Assassinate character to your heart's content. Make up a few words while you're at it. Wait a minute. Isn't this the role of a gossip columnist?

Kearns and Cannon did not turn the other cheek to the church. Editorials promoted a new American Party of Utah -- derided by detractors as the "Ameri*kearns*" Party[200] -- that would separate church and state.[201] When reporting Smith's Senate testimony, Cannon made this scornful introduction: "Now read his testimony and see whether it sounds like the utterance of an ambassador of Christ the King, or sounds like a cowering, equivocating, fanatical piece of mingled egotism, malice and cowardice."[202] In 1906, *The Tribune* went so far as printing accounts of the church's temple

ceremonies, an affront never even considered during my tenure with the newspaper. In 1909, after spending $60,000 for the information, Kearns' *Tribune* began publishing lists of new polygamous marriages occurring after the LDS Manifesto that forbade them.[203]

While waging a war of words, *The Tribune* and its afternoon *Salt Lake Telegram* also fought a vicious circulation battle against the *Deseret News*. According to legend, the *Deseret News* pumped up its figures by running off thousands more papers than it sold and dumped the extras in the Jordan River west of town.[204] Kearns put Charlie McGillis, a professional boxer from Denver, on the front lines of streets sales. "Nobody but a professional would take the job because you'd get the hell kicked out of you every time you went out on the street to sell *The Tribune*," according to Gallivan, the longtime institutional memory of the paper.[205] McGillis hired a bunch of tough kids as newsies, and they managed to get newspapers into the hands of readers. Afternoons, they fought off *Deseret News* newsies for control of prime corners like Second South and Main streets.

Rumor had it that McGillis, a Jew who changed his name to suit his boxing image, also served as Kearns' bodyguard when necessary and ran a brothel above Felt Electric on Regent Street.[206] His son Dick, a friend of Mike Korologos, started a chain of sports stores known as Sunset Sports.

By 1911, *The Trib* was losing money and sucking profits from Silver King Mine, inspiring the senator's twisted slogan: "It takes a great m-i-n-e to run a newspaper." Kearns and partner Keith sided with solvency and withdrew from their fight against Mormon political involvement -- but not without vowing to remain a vigilant "watchdog against the church intruding on the personal freedoms of anybody," Mormon and Gentile alike.[207]

Now that's a promise worthy of my goosebumps upon entering the Tribune Building.

Ambrose N. McKay, appointed *Tribune* publisher/general manager later that year, supervised an extended recess in the "irrepressible conflict." He and Kearns adopted 10 guidelines pledging independence and impartiality in political and ecclesiastical affairs and "equal opportunity for all deserving citizens not motivated by hatred or intolerance."[208]

The Tribune replaced its meat-ax political commentary with a feather duster.[209] Editorial writers no longer labeled certain political candidates and Mormon leaders (often one and the same) malicious liars and hypocrites. They quit describing the *Deseret News* as "the official organ of the Mormon Church,"[210] "unscrupulous" or having "an element of uncandor and stupidity as well as proneness to blundering."[211] In 1918, when Mormon leaders warned their flock that plural marriage would no longer be tolerated, *Tribune* editorials withheld their earlier sarcasm on the subject.[212]

Paradoxically, Kearns died of a stroke October 18, 1918, eight days after being hit by a Ford at the corner of Main and South Temple streets[213] where a monument of Brigham Young held his hand out to the bank while turning his back to the LDS Temple. It would make a better story to blame the tragedy on alcohol or intrigue, but I don't know the details. All I know is that Kearns' widow turned to his taciturn Irish Catholic secretary, J.F. Fitzpatrick, to run the business until her Irish Catholic nephew, John W. Gallivan, was ready to take the reins.

To ensure *Tribune* independence and mutual prosperity, Fitzpatrick reached an accommodation with the church that set the tone for *The Tribune* for most of the rest of the century.

Fitzpatrick worked with LDS President Heber J. Grant to heal the wounds between their organizations. He conceded Grant's argument that the church, with 70 percent of Utah's population and control of every political office, the schools and "everything else," always would win its battles with *The Tribune*.[214] He accepted Grant's challenge to make Mormons his partners and friends in an effort "cross the gap" between Gentiles and Mormons[215]

Though Fitzpatrick used cooperation and understanding to narrow the gap, he never closed it completely. On matters of paramount importance, he ruled with a strong hand wielded from behind the scenes. Toned-down editorials still promoted certain principles regarding the "Utah problem" [polygamy] but "would have no legitimate complaint on that issue . . . if a genuine effort to suppress the practice of polygamy in violation of law were made."[216] They still opposed a church-dominated economic system, political party and segregated society -- but in reasoned terms. They continued to criticize liquor laws that gave the church a distribution monopoly the previous century.[217] In 1933, *The Tribune* called for repeal of the 18th Amendment contrary to the church's stand, and Utah became the deciding state to end federal Prohibition.

The "irrepressible conflict" resurfaced in the 1940s after someone convinced LDS President David O. McKay the *Deseret News* should have 70 percent of newspaper circulation since Mormons comprised 70 percent of Utah's population.[218] At one point in an ensuing battle for subscribers, a campaign that cost the *News* nearly $10 million between 1947 and 1951, it was rumored *The Tribune* might be sold to the Mormon Church.[219]

The *Deseret News* "lost their shirts during the five-year war" by trying to pump up circulation in outlying areas of the state, according to Jack Gallivan.[220] "Advertising, pure and simple" keeps a newspaper in business. Advertising accounted for about 80 percent of a newspaper's income at that time; circulation about 20 percent, as long it was restricted to the "designated market area," which, for *The Tribune*, included Salt Lake, South Davis, Tooele and Summit counties. Anything outside that area, Gallivan noted, "is just wasted money."

Fitzpatrick's Mormon friendships came to the rescue in the battle for subscriptions.

The publisher had been meeting McKay and ZCMI manager (and future Chamber of Commerce President) Gus Backman for breakfast Tuesday mornings at stately Hotel Utah's coffee shop after the three served together on a 1947 Centennial Commission. When Fitzpatrick convalesced in Holy Cross Hospital with the first of three heart attacks, his two powerful breakfast buddies paid him a visit. McKay went straight to the point: the *Deseret News* would be obliged to cease publication without *The Tribune's* business involvement.[221]

Knowing there always would be some sort of Mormon publication, the ailing Fitzpatrick conceded both papers could be profitable if operated as a single advertising medium. He agreed to pool resources as Newspaper Agency Corp. (NAC) as long as *The Tribune* could control the business affairs of both newspapers -- by naming management -- while leaving each newsroom independent and competitive.[222] The publisher then called his protege, John W. Gallivan, to his bedside and directed him to go with *Deseret News* Editor Mark Peterson to learn from the major joint-operating agreements (JOAs) around the country. Their research led to the 1952 JOA between *The Tribune* and *Deseret News* that combined advertising, publishing and circulation revenues and expenses, while setting certain limits on each, so that both papers could survive with separate editorial voices in the same market.[223]

Gallivan followed Fitzpatrick's peace-keeping lead when he became publisher, ushering the JOA through government red tape in order to preserve *The Tribune* for the benefit of the Kearns family. After all, he had promised his Aunt Jennie the newspaper would remain in the family.[224] At the same time, Gallivan strove tirelessly for church cooperation in creating a cosmopolitan, economically strong community capable of hosting the Olympic Winter Games. That meant, among other things, pumping up tourism by modernizing Utah liquor laws, a tough sell to a church officially opposed to strong drinks.

Management's accommodating attitude toward the LDS church often failed to filter down though the staff, and ultimately, incompatible interests between the competitors would tip the two newspapers' brittle bond off balance.

Whether because her self-assurance or her status as a Catholic protected her from religious tension, staffer Anne Wilson didn't remember any religious tension at *The Tribune* in the 70s and 80s. "No one in our newsroom was Mormon, and we didn't really report on the church, at least not like we do now,"[225] she said in 2013.

But in fact many staffers were Mormons at one time or another in their lives, and if *The Trib* treated the church with kid gloves, it was because of the publishers' efforts to get along.

The Tribune routinely gave prominent, front-page coverage to the LDS semi-annual conference, recognition few reporters and editors rejoiced. When the church reached another membership milestone in the late 1960s, for example, front-page editor Jim Walsh, a recovered Chesterfield smoker from Boston, jubilantly proclaimed: "Ha! There are still more Catholics in Brooklyn than Mormons in the world!"[226]

Some reporters, myself included, returned from the Tabernacle numbed from the "Mo speak" practiced by the brethren and bogged down by page upon page of prepared speeches. Mormons used a serious tone for sing song sentences that would carry listeners slowly up a hill so they could plunge to their point and pause. I considered it a miracle if I could stay awake an entire session.

While working the obituary desk, Ben Ling was responsible for "The Way It Was," featuring a few paragraphs from *The Tribune* 100, 50 and 25 years earlier.

When I scrolled through microfilm of the century-old stuff in the 1870s, I always took paragraphs from the rabidly anti-Mormon stories, even including words like "dirty polygs." The Copy Desk really liked it, but one day Art Deck sauntered up to me at the obit desk and calmly said in his aging voice, "No more Mormon stuff." Message received.[227]

I did the same thing when given the chance. It was impossible to resist. But the editor never said anything to me about it.

Potshots at Mormonism frequently showed up on the Art Department pillar, the place where *Tribune* cartoonists and other staffers displayed not-for-publication jokes and commentary. Wally the German vampire-hunter, for example, could only be defeated by a symbol of the church, which in this case was a Mormon offering him money.[228]

Editorial cartoonist Pat Bagley, LDS himself, pinned up a pillar cartoon portraying a *Deseret News* staffer at an immaculate desk answering the phone with a cheerful, "Good morning, *Deseret News*. May I help you?" In the background, a sign sports the Mormon slogan, "Have you hugged your kid today?" The second panel shows a disheveled guy partially hidden behind a loose stack of papers and a cloud of cigarette smoke, as he barks into a phone, "Ya, *Tribune*."[229]

The Tribune Tattler legitimized the process of venting in-house on the pillar by devoting a page corner to "Pick O' the Pillar" in the 1980s. One "pick" featured Bagley's rendition of the newspapers' JOA, depicted as a two-headed Newspaper Agency Corporation with the besotted *Tribune* (the Odd Couple's Oscar) being lambasted as disgusting by a clean-cut, smiley-faced *Deseret News* (Felix). When resurrected during a JOA conflict decades later, Ben Ling commented, "I hope Felix doesn't murder Oscar."

Sports writer Dick "Rosey" Rosetta wasn't much bothered by Mormon dominance in Utah, but his wife disliked the way their kids were treated at school:

> I was "hustled" along the way (mainly by LDS folks in outlying communities and not all that vociferously) to join the church. But it was never a major issue. I would say to my kids, "be the bigger person and forget it." Pretty simplistic approach, but it worked. I guess. None of my family ever converted, including the three step-daughters I raised. And even though I married a Mormon (not in the Temple!!!), my new in-laws (Mormons all) have not made it an issue.[230]

Some staffers took the religious culture seriously indeed. Reporter George Raine, for example, left the newspaper in 1984 largely to escape Mormon control of politics.

> As journalists, we drilled deep into the culture and the deeper I drilled I saw there was no separation of church and state. An example: Close to the end of my *Tribune* tenure I was covering the State Senate where members were debating a bill to require childhood restraints for kids 5 and under in cars, now the law across the nation. Sen. Verl Asay, a Republican, stood in opposition, and on the Senate floor read a long paragraph from a biography of Joseph Smith on the Mormon doctrine of "free agency" to make his case. I looked around the room and some of the brethren were holding their heads as if to say, "Verl, don't do this." At a break I asked Verl if he realized he had blurred church and state and he looked at me as though I was pigeon shit on his blazer. He said he was doing the people's business.
>
> I did not want to work my entire career in that atmosphere. Even today, 30 years later, the church is much of the Utah story and obscures so much of what is wonderful and to be recommended about the state.[231]

In writing for *American Journalism Review* about Utah Olympics scandals in the late 1990s, NPR ombudsman Alicia C. Shepard noted a kind of self-censorship in the media due to a "quiet sense of not wanting to rock the boat" among Utahns living in the Mormon culture. Shepard pointed out that it was the *Arizona Republic*, rather than any Utah media, that first exposed the church's finances in 1991.[232]

Shepard quoted Mike Carter, who by then covered Utah's Olympics preparations for the Associated Press, to explain the culture:

> *It's very difficult to describe just how insular Utah can be. What you have are a lot of wealthy white Mormon businessmen who watch out for one another. They run the big businesses and they run the state and are indelibly linked to one another through church ties. They call one another "brother." There's an inherent trust among one another.*

Even when reporters uncovered a breach of ethics, according to Carter, whose father was an artist at the *Deseret News*, it might be ignored because of the mutual trust.

In the same article, *Tribune* Editor James E. Shelledy confirmed the influence of the Mormon culture on *Tribune* coverage of issues like Olympics graft:

> *There's too much trust and not enough questioning. What questioning we did and what challenging we did of the organizing committee was considered way out of line. But for me to say we don't get caught up in the culture is a little bit naive.*[233]

Karl Cates, who moved to *The Tribune* from the *Salt Lake Observer* in the late 1990s, also recognized a "certain deference" given to church officials. "You won't see a lot of probing reporting about the church, which is the predominant social, cultural and perhaps economic force," he told Shepard.[234]

---

[178] Malmquist, p. 6.

[179] Malmquist, p. 7.

[180] Malmquist, p. 24.

[181] Malmquist, p. 46.

[182] Wikipedia entry on *The Salt Lake Tribune*.

[183] Malmquist, pp. 42-43.

[184] Malmquist pp. 185-199

[185] Michael Harold Paulos, "Opposing the 'High Ecclesiasts at Washington': Frank J. Cannon's Editorial Fusillades during the Reed Smooth Hearings, 1903-1907," *Journal of Mormon History*, Vol. 37, No. 4, Fall 2011, pp. 13,16, 22.

[186] Paulos, pp. 26-27.

[187] Malmquist, p. 199; Paulos.

[188] Rolly & House, May 2005.

[189] Paulos, pp. 20, 27.

[190] Paulos, p. 5.

[191] Paulos, p. 4.

[192] Paulos, pp. 49-50.

[193] Paulos, pp. 14-15.

[194] Paulos, pp. 53-54, taken from letters from Joseph F. Smith to Heber J. Grant, April 26, 1905, and to Chase Smith, July 23, 1905, Life of Joseph Fielding Smith: Sixth President of The Church of Jesus Christ of Latter-day Saints, 1938.

[195] Paulos, p. 15.

[196] *Truth*, April 15, 1905, Vol. 4, No. 3, p. 1.

[197] *Truth*, April 19, 1905, Vol. 4, No, 4, p. 4.

[198] *Truth*, July 8, 1905, Vol. 4, p. 1.

[199] *Truth*, May 6, 1905, Vol. 4.

[200] "Smoot Laughs at New Party," *Salt Lake Herald*, September 16, 1904, p. 1; *Truth*, .

[201] Malmquist, pp. 231-237.

[202] "President Smith's Testimony," *The Salt Lake Tribune*, February 19, 1905, p6.

[203] Kenneth L. Cannon II, "And Now It Is the Mormons": The Magazine Crusade Against the Mormon Church, 1910-1911," *Dialogue: A Journal of Mormon Thought*, Vol. 46, No. 1, Spring 2013.

[204] Mike Korologos email, February 26, 2017.

[205] Gallivan, May 2005.

[206] Korologos, February 26, 2017.

[207] Gallivan, May 2005.

[208] Malmquist, p. 257.

[209] Malmquist, p. 262.

[210] Malmquist, p. 282.

[211] Malmquist, p. 255.

[212] Malmquist., p. 300.

[213] Malmquist. p. 293.

[214] Gallivan, May 2005.

[215] Malmquist, p. 293.

[216] Malmquist, p. 319.

[217] Mammquist, p. 336.

[218] Gallivan, May 2005.

[219] Malmquist, pp. 362-372.

[220] Gallivan, May 2005.

[221] Gallivan, May 2005.

[222] Ibid.

[223] Malmquist, pp. 375-377.

[224] Gallivan, May 2005.

[225] Anne Wilson email, December 31, 2013.

[226] Mike Korologos email, May 25, 2015.

[227] Ling, December 26, 2013.

[228] Ben Ling email to Diane Cole, December 26, 2013.

[229] Ben Ling, December 26, 2013.

[230] Richard Rosetta email, August 2, 2015.

[231] George Raine email, February 18, 2014.

[232] Alicia C. Shepard, "An Olympian Scandal," *American Journalism Review*, April 1999.

[233] Ibid.

[234] Ibid.

7 - Memorable Gentiles

Mike Korologos was known as a stand-up guy. The guy with the broad, ready smile and stash of politically incorrect jokes loved to tell how he was once fired by his brother Tom Korologos, who then was working the Sports Desk slot.

Mike Korologos, promotions director

Tom didn't like a headline Mike wrote and rewrote several times. Finally, Mike told his older brother in exasperation: "Write the damned thing yourself!" Whereupon, Tom retorted, "You're fired!" When Mike got home early and told their mother Tom had fired him, she freaked out. "You need the money for college! How you going to pay for your school? This is terrible!" The next morning, Mrs. Korologos called Art Deck, who laughed and told her to have Mike report for work the next day.[235]

Mike's parents were Greek immigrants who supported the family with a downtown tavern, the Brown Derby (later The Bomb Shelter) at 4th South and State streets.

Korologos' father, Chris, grew up in a tiny town 150 miles southwest of Athens before emigrating to the United States in 1916 as a 16-year-old boy with a tag on his shirt that said take him to Bingham Canyon, where numerous Greeks found work mining copper.

Mining was not his calling, so Chris Korologos opened a pool hall/bar on the Salt Lake City block now occupied by the Matheson courthouse. He was 34 when Irene Kolendrianos, a flirtatious 17-year-old, caught his eye. They married and had two sons, Mike and his brother, Tom . . . [236]

While attending West High, where he was editor of the student newspaper, Mike met his sweetheart, Myrlene. Between his junior and senior years, he took a job as a copy boy at *The Tribune.*

I started at *The Trib* as a two-to-three-day-a-week copy boy but hung around the office on my "off" days in hopes my fellow copy boys didn't show up or called in sick so I could work their shift. Occasionally, on really busy/newsy nights, the editors would want me to work along with the other two regular copy boys, often including Borge Andersen. One such "newsy" night two planes collided over the Grand Canyon.

I was glad to be around . . . but recall the newsroom being very calm through it all. Don Brooks pulled out one of his numerous maps of Utah to try and pinpoint where the accident occurred. I remember Bob Alkire's lead to this day: "I have witnessed the scene of the nation's worst air disaster in history," or something like that. [Alkire's lead sentences actually were, "I have just come from the scene of the world's worst commercial air disaster. There isn't much left."[237]] For the first time ever, I supposed, *The Tribune's* front page had an aerial photo of the debris in the canyon that ran the full length of the front page.[238]

Television news was up and running by then with Doug Mitchell, Bob Welty, Paul James and Roy Gibson as news anchors, and Mike

Korologos toyed with the idea of getting in on the act. However, "hard-core newspaper types" like Ernie Hoff, Heber Hart, Jim England, Bill Smiley and O.N. Malmquist at *The Tribune* fluffed off the notion that television constituted serious competition for newspapers. Pointing to *Sports Illustrated*, England told him to stick with print because he could do so much more with it on the sports side of journalism.[239]

Like a couple of other West High students he later hired, Mike won a *Tribune* news reporting contest in high school. His came with a $150 scholarship that enabled him to enroll in the University of Utah, where tuition cost $75 a quarter.

Mike Korologos emcees ski race.

Mike subsequently spent several years on the Sports Desk in the early 1960s, culminating in a stint as ski writer. Early on, he would go to "almost any length to get stories and bylines published in *The Tribune*, a formidable task as I was competing for limited sports section space with the older, seasoned writers who were covering the major sports beats."[240] So while helping librarian Jerry Dunton field phone calls about high school basketball scores one Friday evening, an article about Alta caught his eye as he thumbed through a dog-eared book on Utah history.

The article came from the 1870s, when Alta was a gloves-off silver-mining town that boasted some 25 saloons, five breweries, a population of 5,000 and a high murder rate. A bearded person dressed in a burlap robe tied at the waist by a rope-like belt had arrived in town proclaiming he was Jesus Christ. To prove it, he promised to resurrect the dead resting in a cemetery at the base of what is now Rustler Mountain. At first, Alta residents thought the stranger's offer was a good idea, and many were willing pay him $2 per body brought back to life. But when they mulled it over, they realized resurrections would disrupt domestic tranquility. After all, many of those buried at Boot Hill were shot over arguments about mining claims, gambling disagreements or their women. Thus, the town's leaders ruled out resurrections. The stranger insisted, and with each insistence, the town upped the ante for the stranger to get out of town. Eventually, he accepted some $200 and departed, thus preserving domestic tranquility.

Mike wrote a sports story pointing out that Alta wasn't always so tranquil in summer months. Willy Pickett, a Copy Desk staffer who moonlighted as editor of *Alta Powder News* for Alta Ski Lifts Company, asked to reprint the piece. Always eager for another byline, Mike enthusiastically agreed, and the piece went out to season pass-holders and lodge guests. Someone associated with the popular television series *Twilight Zone* saw the article while staying at Rustler Lodge and wanted to use it as the basis for one of the shows. Mike soon received a letter from Rod Serling offering $200 for the TV rights. He jumped at the offer, a bonanza for a ski writer making $90 a week. Before long, *Twilight Zone* aired "Mr. Garrity and The Graves," a segment set in an Arizona mining town where a "stranger" used a well-trained dog to convince the town folk of his supernatural powers. The dog would lie dead still and then "arise" at certain commands. "I didn't care that the program had altered the Alta-based storyline and added the dog," Mike wrote years later. "All I cared about was the $200 and the credits that rolled at the beginning of the nationally aired TV program: 'Based on a story by Mike Korologos.'"[241]

The Korologos brothers were largely responsible for the Utah license plate slogan, "The Greatest Snow on Earth." As Mike's story goes, the circus was in town advertising "The Greatest Show on Earth" when he told his brother, then ski editor, how great the snow was at Alta and Utah's other ski resorts. An idea was born. Tom used the phrase in a headline for *The Trib's Home Magazine* December 4, 1960, and after becoming an account executive at Evans Advertising, he occasionally used it in press releases about the ski industry. Then businessman/friend Emanuel "Manny" Floor made it stick as head of the Travel Council. Barnum and Bailey Circus unsuccessfully challenged the issue in court, enabling Utah to continue using the slogan on license plates and in travel ads.[242] (Tom Korologos later became a powerful national Republican lobbyist, deputy assistant to President Richard Nixon and ambassador to Belgium.)

Mike Korologos molded the newspaper's community image during the latter 1960s through the 1970s as promotions director and chief community representative. He hired most entry-level employees for nearly two decades, oversaw countless *Tribune*-sponsored activities and wrote *Tribune Topix*, the in-house newsletter in which he critiqued the newspaper and attempted to boost staff morale. As if that wasn't enough for him, he conducted readership surveys and opinion polls, supervised the newsroom changeover to computerized printing operations and orchestrated publication of the paper's centennial Famous Pages from the Past and O.N. Malmquist's <u>The First 100 Years</u>, a job that caused the printers' union "great consternation."[243]

The promotions guy also helped with Newspaper in the Classroom publicity, arranged tours of the newspaper plant and speakers for schools, and represented the newspaper at social functions. Plus, he staged social activities for the staff, whether Christmas party or summer picnic.

The way Korologos filled entry-level jobs helped shape the staff. He didn't judge applicants by school grades, he said, because those simply showed an ability to memorize and pass tests. His favorite question of job-seekers, presumed to be future reporters, was: Do you consider yourself creative? Most said yes.

OK, said I, what if I told you we're having a very slow news day and we need a feature story within the next hour or two? What would you write about? That gave me insights into the instincts of people . . . and I had people instincts, being a street kid whose dad owned a bar not too far from *The Tribune*.[244]

Hiring could be frustrating. When recruiting students from the University of Montana's School of Journalism, for example, Korologos was confronted by a professor who demanded to know what he was offering his graduates. When told $75 a week, the amount Editor Arthur C. Deck had authorized, he bellowed: "That's preposterous!"[245] Nevertheless, more than one Montana graduate spent a career at *The Tribune*, including Judy Bea Rollins, the first female to become a deputy editor. But that came much later.

Ambition, tenacity, good timing, sense of humor and ability to tell a story helped carry Korologos through. Those were the days when sexist and ethnic jokes were socially acceptable, so he got away with a lot of off-color and downright offensive humor. But his laughter, generosity and sensitivity always softened whatever comment might otherwise have led to fisticuffs.

Korologos snagged the job with the boast to Editor Art Deck that he could handle it with one hand tied behind his back. In a paper for my 1973 journalism internship, I sarcastically suggested Korologos could do more for the staff he untied his hand. Easy for me to say. Promotions were a big deal at *The Salt Lake Tribune*, which depended on regular readers and advertisers for survival.

"We believed that *The Tribune* had to become a part of every household," Gallivan explained years later. "So we had activities for every member of every household to involve the whole community so that *The Tribune* was the family newspaper."[246]

One of the most successful of the newspaper's 20 ongoing promotions occurred before Korologos' time, in 1951. The Tribune Cooking School co-sponsored by the National Livestock and Meat Board of Chicago attracted busloads of readers to a local theater. Some 2,000 women showed up, probably more for the prizes -- groceries, appliances and a mink stole -- than for the lessons.

After the Meat Board withdrew support, *The Tribune* switched to a spring Home and Garden Show perennially hosted by shriveled garden editor Genevieve Folsom. As many as 200,000 people would congregate at the Salt Palace to admire winning flower arrangements and endure sales pitches from advertisers. It was my "privilege" as a rookie reporter in the late 1970s to cover some of those shows, usually with guidance from rose aficionado Jack Schroeder from the Sports Desk and always with extensive involvement from wizened Genevieve. Born in 1907, her body was withered but her mind fresh.

During the decade of the Depression, *The Tribune* initiated its longest-lived promotion, Sub for Santa. In 1932, the program solicited volunteers to provide Christmas gifts to 4,655 children,[247] and it continued to help low-income families for 60 years.

A "go-go spirit" drove Korologos' promotion of *The Tribune* as an essential part of the community through the 1970s. He assumed, "If I don't act like I believe in a project, no one else will."[248]

He organized and publicized fund-raising birthday parties for Shasta the Liger (a hybrid lion-tiger) and Gorillas Dan and Elaine at Hogle Zoo, a *Tribune* sacred cow given the collaboration of pals Jack Gallivan and Jim Hogle in relocating the zoo from Liberty Park to the mouth of Emigration Canyon.[249] Korologos also supervised the Old-Fashioned Fourth of July at Lagoon amusement park, the garden shows, literary contests and amateur ski and tennis competitions where alcohol ran freely among assisting staffers. Entire towns would compete for *The Tribune's* Tidy Town awards, and Arbor Day became the focus of a statewide tree-planting campaign.

Still other promotions included cosponsorship of the Salt Lake Classic 10K Memorial Day race, an annual J.F. Fitzpatrick lecture, and a luncheon and theological seminar for the Salt Lake Ministerial Association. Maestro Eugene Jelesnik, the small, rodent-nosed violinist who serenaded diners at the Cinegrill Italian restaurant and hosted "Talent Showcase" on KSL Television, conducted the free, *Tribune*-sponsored Labor Day "Music Under the Stars" concert.

Obsessively conscientious but consistently respectful, Jelesnik became an endearing pest to *Tribune* staffers, including artist Dennis Green, who designed his music programs and t-shirt logos. When Jelesnik showed up near deadlines, extra patience was required. But staffer Brian Nutting remembered the maestro as a morale booster for men in the office.

He was in the newsroom all the time. George [Raine] and I developed a code word whenever a good-looking woman (someone with obvious "talent") would come in. We'd say something like, "Jelesnik at 10 o'clock" or "look at that Jelesnik." I know, I know, juvenile

and sexist – but that's youthful newsmen for you.[250]

As a Jew, Jelesnik had escaped the Bolshevik Revolution with his Ukrainian mother and first settled in New York City, where he studied with the New York Philharmonic. This rare Utah gem also did 19 USO tours and was the recipient of several military honors.[251]

For many years, *The Tribune* teamed up with the Salt Lake County Senior Citizen's Recreation Center to stage an antique car show, Concours d'Elegance, at the University of Utah. That event gave Denny Green another chance to exercise his artistic talents with poster illustrations sometimes featuring staffers like me. Denny also was dragged into an annual promotion for the National Conference of Christians and Jews for which Publisher Jerry O'Brien concocted flowery citations penned in Denny's curlicued calligraphy. Myrlene Korologos directed that effort, so there was no getting out of it.

Dennis Green's car poster features himself, me, Will Fehr and Jami Tabish as teens.

And lest we forget, a major part of the promotions job entailed harvest, installation and decoration of a large conifer in front of the Tribune building on Main Street each Christmas. That was the project that drove Stan Bowman to drink before giving Korologos nightmares of his own.

It was a Norman Rockwell scene in the luxurious Korologos livingroom one blustery Christmas Eve in the 1970s as Mike and Myrlene, already well into their Christmas cheer, constructed a large, orange Hot Wheels racetrack that snaked around their holiday tree. Sons Chris and Tony lay dreaming of toys to come. The phone shattered their peace.

"Your damned tree fell down!" the caller growled.

"What?! Who is this?" Korologos inquired (he was *The Tribune's* "inquiring editor," after all).

It was Otteson, night managing editor. Panic wiped out the Christmas cheer.

Korologos raced from his home high in the snowcovered foothills to downtown Salt Lake City to find the 55-foot spruce sprawled across the sidewalk and into Main Street.

It was a sad sight. High winds tunneling up Main Street had taken their toll.

Lacking experience for such a situation, Mike's instincts kicked in. He had to get the tree back up before Christmas morning, not only to avoid disappointing kids in the community but also to protect the newspaper from a black eye. So he called Utah Power & Light, which donated crews and equipment each year to the project. Before long, the tree was dangling from the power company's crane, and Mike had the crew turn the damaged side toward the building. *The Tribune's* own short story about the mishap the next day was the extent of public attention it received.[252]

But there's more to the tree saga. To prevent any more recurrences, UP&L reinforced the tree with cables anchored in the Tribune Building, the Kearns Building across the street and two steel posts imbedded near the gutters along Main Street. The cables did their job for two years, but strong winds again whistled through Main Street, this time earlier in the evening and the season. The force was so great that the longest cable on the Kearns Building snapped, barely missing Executive Editor Art Deck waiting to cross the street on his way to the Kearns Building garage.

Again, Korologos got a call at home. At first he thought it was a prank, because he got a lot of flak from staffers about his "annual erection." But no, when he arrived, people were wending their way around the tree and UP&L crews he'd called, and Dan Valentine, apparently full of holiday cheer, was pacing back and forth in front of the Tribune.

As a KSL-TV reporter approached Valentine for an interview, a furious Korologos jumped in. In his mind, KSL was gleefully preparing to report a news competitor's huge embarrassment, which would be amplified by Valentine's compromised condition. To Valentine's annoyance, Korologos asked what the TV guy wanted to know. With cameras rolling, the reporter asked Korologos' name and title before beginning: "Your tree fell two years ago. That makes the score over the last three years wind two, *Tribune* tree zero, right?"[253]

The company man's sense of humor failed him as he indignantly fired back: "*The Tribune* has been putting up community Christmas trees since 1947. How many has KSL-TV put up!?" The interview ended, and the only footage that aired showed scenes of the tree being placed upright.

In subsequent years, *The Tribune* planted a much smaller live tree as part of the city's Main Street Beautification Project. The first two succumbed their first year to the city's searing summer heat, high winds and snow-melting chemicals. One tree survived several years in the 1980s, once serving as a pulpit for a tattered street person spouting scripture from its higher branches to staffers on the upper floors. Another guy occasionally warbled like a bird through its branches. That tree eventually was removed, too. After serving as the certerpiece of downtown decorations for three decades, Korologos noted, the tree's status was diminished by the LDS Church' holiday lights on Temple Square.

One of Korologos' most memorable assignments in the mid-1960s was to introduce syndicated advice columnist Ann Landers (aka Eppie Lederer) at the LDS Assembly Hall on Temple Square. As he put it, her pithy responses to reader inquiries in those days "held almost gospel-like status among millions of readers across the land."[254]

When Mike and wife Myrlene picked Landers up at Hotel Utah, they still had a lawnmower bound for the repair shop in the backseat of their Ford Galaxy. They assumed Myrlene would sit in back, leaving the front seat for their special guest, who wore "the most elegant, full-length mink coat I'd ever seen . . ."

Myrlene nervously and quite excitedly greeted Ann and proceeded to get into the backseat. Ann would not have any such seating arrangement! She insisted SHE get in the back and leave the front seat to Myrlene.

Horrified and embarrassed, we lost the argument. Ann Landers, a national icon whose column is read by millions of followers, got the backseat . . . to be with the folded up mower, mink coat be damned.

She immediately embraced the scene with grace. "Oh, you've been mowing the lawn," she said half smiling, half laughing. "I wish I could do my lawn more often than I do . . . I seem to always be on the run." Myrlene and I breathed quiet sighs of relief.

At the packed Assembly Hall, I introduced Ann as "an All-American woman" because she was born on the Fourth of July. I was particularly proud of that line.

Upon completion of her talk, Ann quickly was surrounded by hosts from the Church of Jesus Christ of Latter-day Saints who had arranged for her to be a special guest during the weekly Thursday night rehearsals of the Mormon Tabernacle Choir next door in the Tabernacle.

"Come, Ann. We've arranged special seating for you at the choir rehearsals that are about to start. We must hurry."

As I escorted Ann down the stairs and off the stage, a teen-age girl approached Ann and caught her eye. "Hello Ann. I am (name escapes me)," said the shy teen. "I wrote you that my mom is in the hospital, my dad left us, I'll have to get a job, and I don't know if I'll be able to finish school or not."

Immediately, Ann stopped the entourage, acknowledged reading the girl's letter (which I seriously doubt but she assured the girl she had) and embraced her.

"Yes. I'm so glad to see you," Ann graciously told the distraught teen.

"Come, Ann. We must hurry. The choir is waiting," insisted the Mormon hosts.

Ann ignored the demands and spoke to the girl. "Listen, (name), we'll work this out," she assured her. "Do not quit school. Don't worry about money."

"Ann, we must hurry. The choir is waiting," the guide urged more forcefully.

"The choir can wait," snapped Ann. "I'm going to talk with (name). You go ahead and I will catch up with you."

Then turning to the girl still in her arms, Ann said: "Write me another letter and give me more details. You WILL finish school. We will work this out. I will personally see to that. Please . . . promise me you'll write me another letter."

The girl assured Ann she would write another letter. The choir waited.

(We'll never know for certain, but I'm convinced Ann Landers personally helped guide that perplexed young woman through her seemingly hopeless situation . . . and likely well beyond.)[255]

One of Korologos' most satisfying assignments occurred in the early 1970s, when *The Tribune* launched an organ donor program with the University of Utah Medical Center, which was refining kidney and cornea transplantation. According to Korologos, this was a big deal for Utah, where Mormons were reluctant for religious reasons to give up a part of the "whole" body they believed they needed for their afterlife. He would write features about people near death needing transplants, and it was heartening that in many instances, he would get a call in the middle of the night from the U. Medical Center to tell him a donor match had been found.[256] That campaign was submitted for a Pulitzer Prize and resulted in thousands of donors carrying wallet-sized cards to inform emergency responders of their wishes.

Toward the end of Korologos' tenure, he and Myrlene hosted Caribbean cruises promoted in *The Tribune's* travel section to drum up advertising. Two days out of Galveston on one such trip, the ship ran low on ice, an issue of concern for Mike and Myrlene, who were accustomed to drinking their bourbon with ice. Once into port, passengers were prevented from disembarking for several hours, causing many to miss connecting flights. The reason? A male passenger had died and was put on ice in his cabin bathtub until port authorities could determine the death was natural. Mike discovered on that trip that bourbon and water without ice wasn't that bad after all.[257]

* * *

Robert H. Woody, business editor, stogie airbrushed away but gap in teeth added.

Business Editor **Robert H. Woody**'s silliness, spread liberally over a strong mind and wiry body, became a newsroom legend. With his cubicle just inside the newsroom door, he usually was the first to be noticed: for the odor of his smokes and for the shouting across the newsroom. His name was continually hollered as phone call after phone call came in for him. Already taking notes from someone else, Woody would yell back, "Take a number!" Even when the call was for someone else.[258]

Once in the 1970s, according to Korologos, the Shah of Iran was returning Woody's call about a rumor that he might buy Snowbird Ski Resort.[259] Depending on whose version of the story was told, he either responded with his telltale "take a number" or he took the call on the first try for once.

Perched on his wobbly chair with white shirt sleeves rolled up and phone tucked between ear and shoulder, Woody puffed a rank cigar as he typed, driving to distraction Pat McCoy, the former farm girl churning out church news just outside his cubical. The louder her high-pitched wail, the thicker the smoke billowed as others joined the harassment.

A newcomer to the newsroom described Woody this way:

> I'd been hired as an office clerk at *The Trib* in December '74, and I don't think I'd been in the newsroom for five minutes before Woody came roaring out of his cubicle in a starched white shirt, a Santa hat on his head and a cigar clenched between his teeth. He looked me in the eye and started singing, "O h h h h h C o o o o o o o p p p p y BOOOOOOOY! Can you change my ribbon?" at the top of his lungs. Nobody even looked up. And no subsequent meeting with Woody was ever less amazing.[260]

Business Editor Bob Woody's office.

Woody's office looked like a typhoon had blown through, but he claimed to know where everything was. Tattered, browned news pages hid beneath piles of press releases, annual reports and other business propaganda. Taped to his wall was a magazine cover story on a Hercules' Bacchus Works CEO who prided himself on a messy desk.[261] Next to that was a photo of irascible editorial writer Ted Long, stogie jutting from mouth, whom Woody described as a tyrant to young reporters in the 1950s and 60s. Woody became a reporter in 1957.

There was much more to Woody, who replaced Bob Bernick as business editor in 1966, than immediately met the eye, nose and ears. He was a character of contradiction and contrast.

Most lunch hours and sometimes after 5, our rendition of a Rocky Mountain Renaissance man could be found strolling down Main Street in bow tie, flat-top hat and pinstripe blazer or sitting at the counter of Lamb's Grill hobnobbing with this or that bank president. Then he would ride his bicycle or drive his sixties-era Volkswagen bus 12 miles to the middle-class neighborhood where his New England wife and four children awaited him.

Even while rubbing shoulders with captains of the oil, gas and mining industries, Woody championed the environment and helped the homeless. He belonged to St. Ambrose Catholic Parish but also associated with First Unitarian Church.

In his spare time, Woody studied architecture, karate and Renaissance flute. He also starred as Sleazo in "Mondo Sleazo," filmed by *Tribune* photographer Mike Cassidy, who also made the Utah cult classic "The Giant Brine Shrimp."

A Philadelphia native raised in Texas and Massachusetts, Woody was one of the first newsroom veterans to let his hair down and join a circle of relative youngsters smoking pot. Looking (not particularly sounding) a lot like John Denver, he strummed his guitar and sang "Rocky Mountain High."

It was Woody who conducted "Spring Rites," performed in the newsroom May 1st in the 1970s while our gloomy executive editor lunched at Lamb's.

Spring Rites with Marilee Higley, Mary Dickson, Bob Woody, Ann Kilbourn, Michael Dunn, Vickie Sorenson, Denny Green, Helen Forsberg and John Mooney, left to right.

A presumably innocent female employee was chosen queen and adorned with crown and flowers. A couple of male staffers hoisted her in their arms for a parade around the room and then set her before Woody, the "high priest." After expressing a few lofty, philosophical sentiments about rebirth, the high priest sang a folk song. "Where Have All the Flowers Gone?" suited the occasion.

This is how Woody described one of the last such ceremony:

Then came the noon-hour spring rites orchestrated by the high priestess Hazel Parkinson and handmaiden Marilee Higley (cq) with instructions that the high priest [Woody] find, verify and provide the virgin. Ann Kilbourn was the clear winner of the first annual virgin award, but we were never certain about our second year winner, Teeny Bopper [Vickie Sorenson], a mascot of the Sundowners Motorcycle Club. Sadly, the spring rites turned sour the year we resorted to a recycled virgin.[262]

Before it was trendy, Woody raced in local cross-country ski competitions and climbed mountains. After skiing with the 10th Mountain Division in Italy during World War II, he became a peace-nik "adamantly" opposed to war, Vietnam in particular.[263] His best friend and comrade in arms Newcomb Eldredge met Woody at Camp Hale, the training ground for the ski troops, and then shared a room with him at Dartmouth College in New Hampshire before the two found wives and moved to Colorado. "We skied, climbed and enjoyed the out-of-doors," Eldredge said. "Woody was a Renaissance man of many talents -- writer, artist, musician and a great wit."[264]

A kid a heart, Woody was always entertaining at cocktail parties with tongue-in-cheek chatter in which he pretended to be some public figure currently under fire. Both Bob and wife Barbara had a stream-of-consciousness quality to their conversations that had some of us scratching our heads. More than once at work, Woody slithered from his office sticking his tongue in and out and widening his eyes lizard-like.

This is the same professional who expanded the business news at *The Tribune* from its focus on mining and minerals to "mom-and-pop shops," as Mike Korologos put it.[265] Held in high esteem for his integrity and fairness, he could extract information from sources who wouldn't even talk to other reporters. Woody's one-time assistant, Paul Rolly, told the story of being unable to verify a tip that the Mormon church was considering buying property for development on the city's south side. He called Woody, who was under sedation in the hospital a day after major surgery but still able to get the story.[266]

Longtime friend Harry Fuller felt Woody was highly regarded because he was a fine writer, accurate and fair -- "he didn't take advantage of his writing to embarrass anybody unless they deserved it."[267]

Besides managing breaking business news, Woody wrote a column, "Up and Down the Street," and periodically put out the *Empire Edition*, a tabloid promoting businesses willing to buy ads for it. Almost everyone in the newsroom got drafted at one time or another to help with this pain-in-the-ass project, but it was Woody's assistant who carried the real burden of the daily business grind.

Any staffer who could survive more than a year as business assistant deserved a medal of honor, as Woody would bark a few orders and slip out the door before clarification could be had. Lance Gudmundsen was one of those who, while editing his copy, woefully pleaded to the absent man, "A verb, Woody, I need a verb!"[268]

As Woody's "boy," as Woody called it, in the 1970s, Bob Bryson did the weekly portrait, a "self-serving feature on some captain of industry," the weekday stock report, oil drilling log and press-release rewrites. You might say that Bryson was less than enamored of his new boss.

Bob was a gifted man who enjoyed being business editor with its associated perks: free drinks, lunches and, on occasion, trips.

I was assigned to travel to Wendover to cover the rebirth of the airport there where World War II bomber pilots trained, including the plane [Enola Gay] that dropped the first atomic bomb. Bob was not working, so I was surprised to see him there. Lunch was at one of the casinos, and Bob ordered a steak and several drinks. Mid-meal, our hosts announced we were responsible for our own lunch. Bob blanched, turned to me and asked to borrow $5 and reordered a cheeseburger, no drinks. As were were lining up to pay the bill, the casino manager announced he was buying. Bob was miffed, especially when I told him I needed the $5 back.[269]

Each Christmas, Woody's neighbors would witness a bevy of delivery trucks dropping off booze and other goodies from businesses and other well-wishers. Lunch often was on someone's expense account.

One such Christmas, Bob was enjoying lunch at the University Club and returned after work to drink with his new very best friends. The "evening"

ended at 1:30 a.m with Bob setting off to find his car. It was locked up for the night in the building's exclusive parking lot and he had to hitchhike home. [270]

Woody wasn't the only staffer to receive largesse from the people they covered. Beat writers, the travel editor and critics of art and entertainment tended to attract boxes of candy, fruit, books and other gifts at Christmastime in particular. Sometimes bits and pieces of the payola would end up in the hands of less fortunate invisible staffers as the editors decided it was unseemly for supposedly unbiased journalists to encourage gratuities.

Brian Nutting took a turn as Woody's assistant in the mid-1970s. His take on the "portrait" part of the job was a little different than Bryson's.

Virtually anything [Woody] could think of had some kind of business angle. And so the biz pages, instead of being restrictive, were actually liberating.

I guess I was the stable one of the pair. I did the page layout – which helped me later -- and covered the Public Service Commission, where the utilities seemed to be perpetually asking for rate hikes. I usually did the Sunday "business portrait" of some interesting guy in the community.

It was a great learning experience. I discovered that many successful people never set out with a goal of becoming who they eventually became. It seems like so many of them just bounced along from one key experience to another and fate led them to their current circumstance. I also learned to do my homework about these guys first (much easier to do these days with Google, etc.) and then to get them talking about themselves and mostly keep my mouth shut.

Many years later, when I was writing profiles of members of Congress, I think that learning experience at *The Tribune* really helped.

Woody was so flaky, singing and humming and forgetting things and hanging clippings and other things on every available spot on his cubicle.

He was enamored with the phrase "Eurasian petrodollars." I think it had to do with that Saudi Arabian businessman – Adnan Khashoggi– who wanted to develop that plot of land along I-80 west of the airport. He later became infamous as some kind of international arms dealer.[271]

Actually, Khashoggi bought the Salt Lake International Center from Howard Hughes, the reclusive billionaire who surrounded himself with Mormon aides, clean-livers he could trust not to steal from him. Khashoggi, a Muslim, also liked the non-smoking, non-drinking aspect of the Utah culture and established his Triad Company's U.S. base in Salt Lake City.[272]

Joe Rolando, Woody's longest survivor at seven years, initially was unsettled by his title as "Woody's assistant." "I knew what an editor or assistant editor did, but I wondered if I would be some sort of indentured servant. Fortunately, Woody never made me feel that way."

When promoted to the job in 1983, Rolando was told he would be performing tasks Woody either did not know how to do or didn't want to do, including laying out weekday and Sunday business pages and pitching business stories at 4 p.m. department head meetings. Lacking a deep understanding of business and economics, Rolando hoped to learn enough to make business reporting his speciality.

Woody initiated Rolando with a scare.

At first, he assigned stories about companies requiring little knowledge of business. He introduced Rolando to Gil Warner, president of Associated Foods, Utah's wholesale cooperative of grocers, in advance of the groups annual meeting. Woody also assigned several Sunday portraits of business leaders, features focused on the life events that shaped their business savvy. Woody's idea was to humanize the often dry matter-of-factness of business and economics.

A few months into the job, Rolando was feeling fairly comfortable, even finding some of his own stories. But in March of 1984, Woody called me to his desk. "With the concern of a father," he said he wanted Rolando to become familiar with all types of business so that he could confidently fill in for him.

"Don't worry, Joe," he said. "I've set up luncheons for you with my sources who can give you the background you need." As Rolando recalls:

I could not believe a boss would be that thoughtful. For two or three weeks, I met some business experts at high society places such as The Alta Club, the Hotel Utah and the Ambassador Club for lunch, or in their offices -- places requiring ties and jackets. I had only one white shirt and had to buy a couple more.

I met with Fred Ball, president of the Salt Lake Area Chamber of Commerce; a major shareholder in one of the key silver mines in the Tintic Mining District in Juab County; United Steelworkers of America local union officers who represented workers at Geneva Steel, Utah's only integrated steel plant, and Kennecott, Utah's large copper mine.

Bank executives taught me principles, terms and philosophy of finance and economics. I learned the relationship of net income to common stock performance and the definitions of non-performing assets, preferred stock, tender share offers or hostile take-overs and stock splits. This was welcome preparation for what had always been for me a vague world of annual reports, Security and Exchange Commission filings and balance sheets.

More interesting was learning the colorful histories of local institutions, such as First Security Bank, Key Bank, Valley Bank & Trust and Zions Bank. I gained an appreciation of the role of local titans -- Eccles, Huntsman, Hemmingway and Kearns -- in business and community development.

Then Woody hit me with a bomb. He had arranged for my hands-on tutoring so I could fill in for him during an eight-week vacation to England. My training would prepare me to cover annual meetings for all the major lending institutions, Union Pacific Railroad, Tintic mining companies and a number of other less noteworthy local stock companies.

The knowledge also was designed to help me write all the breaking business news while he was out of town, whether about financial institutions, Kennecott, U.S. Steel Corp., Sperry or Hercules Aerospace, all prolific employers in the state.

Woody made clear I must cover all the annual meetings and should not expect any help from City Desk laying out daily and Sunday business pages.[273]

Filling in for Woody was surprisingly exhilarating for Rolando. By each day's end, he was exhausted from covering as many as two or three annual meetings, breaking news, laying out the business pages and attending the daily news budget meeting, He didn't leave for home until after 7 p.m. "Looking back, I am happy I was baptized in business writing by fire. I learned a lot and stayed with Woody for seven years. [274]

A photograph of Woody embracing a group of hair-dyed London punkers hung in his office forever afterward to remind Rolando of that trip and his own business education.

Another memorable Woody moment occurred a cold, snowy night when Bob had car problems. After putting the business section to bed for the night, Woody mentioned his van wasn't working, so Rolando insisted on driving him home to spare Barbara the danger of driving the icy roads to pick him up.

We were only a few miles from his home when he invited me in for a drink. I told him that was nice of him but I did not expect anything for taking him home. "No, no, Joe," he said. "I want you to come in and have a drink with me." Finally, I said, "Bob, that would be nice."

At the door, he had trouble finding the right key. He gave up looking and said he knew there was a spare in the front yard. He looked several places and then grabbed the keys out of his pocket again. He pressed one key into the lock and it fit.

"Barbara, Barbara, Joe's here!" he hollered as he opened the door. "Where's the whiskey?"

When no one answered, he acknowledged she must have not arrived home yet. So, he began a frantic hunt for booze, first in the kitchen cabinets, then out the back door and finally in the utility room. He said, "Sometimes she puts it in the washing machine. But it's not here."

By now, I was growing uneasy and said, "Hey, Bob, don't worry about it. We can do this another time."

He was adamant. "No, No, Joe. It's here. Hey, wait a minute . . . How about some beer instead, Joe?"

When I told him that would be fine, he said, "Wait here. Don't go anywhere. I'm going over to (Jack) Fenton's house next door. He has some beer. I'll be right back."

A few minutes later, Bob opens the front door and announces, "Good old, Fenton. He always has something to drink." Bob handed me one of the two cans of beer and he took the other. We sipped while making small talk, and it wasn't long before the beer was gone.

Bob said, "Joe, how about another beer? I can go get some more from Fenton."

I insisted that Jan was waiting with dinner for me at home. I thanked him and left. But as I replayed the night's experience in my mind, I began laughing so hard I could barely keep my mind on driving. [275]

Then there was the time when Rolando was giving Woody a ride down Main Street when a Jeep CJ-5 turned too fast and flipped over in front of them. Woody grabbed his 35 mm camera and pulled a notebook from his shirt pocket and jumped from Rolando's truck before it even stopped. He snapped pictures of the steaming Jeep and then jotted down comments from a witness as the driver dangled upside down by his seatbelt.

Drawing from my recent experience as a *Tribune* night police reporter, I shouted, "Woody, no need to interview anyone. The driver is OK!" He continued the interview until I nudged him to walk with me back to my truck so I could explain quietly that the accident did not create enough damage or injury to meet *The Tribune's* criteria for coverage.

Still, Woody showed me he was not too important to cover a routine accident story, typically assigned to rookie reporters. His first and foremost interest was covering news – any kind. [276]

As crazy as Woody seemed at times, Rolando discovered he was a gentle man as much at ease interviewing an officer of a Blue Chip corporation about the virtues of capitalism as joining a 1960-style sit-in singing and playing his guitar to protest world population explosion.

Woody was the most eccentric, least pretentious and hardest working editor for whom I worked in my newspaper career. It is more accurate to say I worked with Woody -- not for him. He never played the boss card and was more concerned that he and I -- his only staff initially -- had enough time to write the day's most important business stories with accuracy . . . If either of us fell short on time [on] an important story, the other would step up to do it even if it meant staying after the shift tended. [277]

At work, Woody projected an image of a "stereotypical, Jazz-era newspaperman in a state of anxiety determined to get the day's biggest business story first," Rolando said. "Deadlines and coffee kept his adrenalin surging." Rolando could not recall a time when Woody failed to get the day's most significant business story in the paper before the *Deseret News*, "*The Tribune's* most formidable competition."

Moreover, Woody was a serious news reporter whose last-minute changes to articles and layouts were his attempt to get so many stories right in so little time. He assigned others his editing duties so he could write full time, unusual in daily journalism. "The more stories he wrote the happier he was," Rolando said. "His enthusiasm for journalism would have withered if he would have had to layout pages, edit stories and attend news budget meetings." He added:

> Woody had a keen understanding of national business -- from capitalism to the Federal Funds rate, coal to gold and to copper mining and stock dilution to hostile takeovers. His knowledge of Utah's business scene was encyclopedic. His memory was incredibly accurate and insightful, and he always shared his knowledge with me so that before I covered a story I was adequately prepared.[278]

Rolando pointed out that Woody had a reliable longtime source whose identity he never divulged. The man's physical handicap precluded him from getting out much, but he was somehow privy to accurate information about big local business stories. Woody called him frequently to check out rumors or obtain background information.

Breaking news and weekend portraits were the priorities of the business beat in those days because there was too little time, news space or staff to investigate problems.

"I know Woody was often bitter about City Desk's treatment of him," Rolando said, explaining that the editors expected the two of them to cover too much by themselves. They would work untold hours, each sometimes writing up to four stories to cover the important news of the day. "City Desk forgot we were juggling a Sunday section as well as a daily section with no separate copy desk." Rolando said.

It was common, he continued, for a city or wire editor to ask how many inches a story would be before it was finished. If he or Woody estimated 15 inches and it turned out to be 20, desk editors often lopped off the last five inches, assuming they were the least important. Rolando and Woody, the writers, would then have to deal with the consequences of incomplete statements and angry sources.[279]

An English major in college, Woody did not always adhere to the old inverted pyramid style of news writing that lent itself to a quick trim. Rather, he often switched to a more literary form of journalism, especially for his "Up and Down the Street" column, using one short sentence per paragraph and a metaphor to illustrate the story's significance.

Rolando offered Woody's August 30, 1964 column about the demolition of the Dooly Building as an example of his style:

> *Hang down your head, Tom Dooly*
> *Hang down your head and cry*
> *Hang down your head, Tom Dooly*
> *Cause your building's gone bye and bye.*
>
> *A good building merits something more than the routine account when the death knell is sounded. Let's just call this a wake for the Dooly Building at 109 W. 2nd South.*
> *The designer was Louis Sullivan, famed Chicago architect. His credo – "Form follows function" -- bent the direction of American architecture. His pioneering in use of steel for structural systems gave birth to the skyscraper. His apprentice, Frank Lloyd Wright, carried his own architectural torch in the world.*
> *Mr. Sullivan came West in 1890 as the reputation of his firm was spreading nationwide. He had four western buildings on the boards: the Dooly Building – or Dooly Block as it was called; the Hotel Ontario, which was to have been built just south of the Dooly Bldg., and then Opera House Blocks in Pueblo and Seattle.*
> *The Hotel was never completed. It is said that Sullivan designed the lower part, which is now part of the Terminal Building. The top was someone else's idea. Whatever, it also will be razed with the Dooly Building.*
> *The building was named for John E. Dooly, one of the original owners and developers, a banker and livestock and real estate figure.*

It was *The Tribune's* way to popularize certain department editors, including Woody, Sports Editor John Mooney and Entertainment

Editor Hal Schindler, at the expense of staffers performing the grunt work of their sections, according to Rolando. He saw a method in this management madness.

> Each of these departments was literally managed by those who had no title. We were known to our colleagues as "helpers' and to the reading public as "staff writers."
>
> This paid off for the paper. Not only did the editors remain loyal and hard working, but so did their assistants, who could aspire to their editors' jobs one day.[280]

In fact, the Business Desk became a stepping stone to city editor for some of the dozen reporters who helped Woody over the years. (If I'd only known then what I know now!)

Rolando regarded his work with Woody as advancement enough after working for weekly newspapers and then the requisite rookie beats -- police and general assignment -- at *The Tribune*. "I never entertained the notion of ascending to Woody's job," he said.

> *The Tribune* – with few exceptions -- promoted from the bottom up. The paper really did not count previous experience in the weekly newspaper field – or for that fact experience at another daily newspaper -- as a way to bypass its promotion style, unless the candidate's talent was larger than the newspaper from which he or she came.[281]

Toward the end of Woody's career, the City Desk finally gave him more help. Steven Oberbeck was hired from *The Enterprise*, a weekly Salt Lake business paper, and Lance Gudmundsen took on most of the daily and Sunday section layout duties, freeing up Rolando to write full time.

Even then, the business writers missed deadlines.

When Sunday Business switched to color illustrations, for example, the Art Department designed the Front Page. When stories for that page remained unfinished by deadline, Woody and Rolando simply gave the artists some photographs and estimated story sizes. If they didn't fit, they wrote more at the last minute to fill the space. Tension was inevitable, but not between Woody and Rolando.

> Woody and I got along all the time – and I mean all the time - because we agreed about a very fundamental thing: The story was more important than the procedure of getting it in the paper. The latter could be easily remedied by adjusting space or the story itself. However, getting a story's facts wrong or writing poorly could not be remedied.
>
> True, when we would completely ignore the method of getting the story in the paper, we would draw the ire of the Copy Desk or Wire Editor. But having both of us apologize seemed to lessen the severity of our slight.[282]

Whether interviewing an Eccles from First Security Bank fame or going to lunch at Lamb's restaurant with *Tribune* Editor Will Fehr, Publisher Jack Gallivan and Assistant Publisher Jerry O'Brien, Woody wore a Greek fisherman's hat, the cheesy novelty variable sold at the local Greek Orthodox Church's annual festival downtown, Rolando remembered.

> He didn't take off the hat at work, either inside or outside the office, for a couple of years. It was no joke. He was so impressed with the Greek culture that he was taking Greek language lessons at the University of Utah. He was fascinated when I told him my wife Jan was born in Greece and adopted and raised by a Greek family in Utah.
>
> Bob and his wife Barbara drove two hours to the Assumption Greek Orthodox Church in Price for the baptism of my youngest daughter. When the reception crowd started the Greek line dance, Woody and his wife Barbara jumped right in.[283]

As casual as that Greek hat made Woody look, Rolando stressed, it did not affect his seriousness about his work nor make him a pushover for news sources. Rolando related this anecdote to illustrate his point:

Woody was wearing that hat the day in 1984 that Editor Fehr invited him and Rolando to his office a couple weeks after a fire broke out underground in Utah Power & Light Co.'s Wilberg coal mine in Emery County. The fire killed 27 people.

Fehr introduced the business writers to Neal Savage, owner of Emery Mining, which operated the mine, and Bob Henrie, his public relations practitioner. Savage and Henrie, under criticism for failing to respond to inquiries about the disaster, wanted to make sure *The Tribune* knew they were available to answer all questions. With Wilberg reporter Mike Gorrell out of the office that day, Fehr turned to Rolando and Woody because of their experience covering mining.

Savage ruined any chance of them believing his sincerity when he implied that the news media was to blame for not telling Emery Mining's side of the disaster, Rolando said, continuing:

Woody quickly looked up from his 3 x 4-inch notebook and into Neal Savage's eyes. "OK, Neal, give me both your office and home phone numbers so we can call you when we need a comment."

Savage, taken aback by Woody's directness, said: "Sure. I'll get them for you." But Woody, suspecting a delay tactic, walked across Fehr's large office to Savage, raised his notebook, pulled a pen from his shirt pocket and said, "Neal, what is your home phone number and your direct line at work?"

After jotting down those numbers, Woody turned toward Henrie and asked him the same question. Without delay, Henrie gave Woody his home and work numbers.

Fehr and I looked at each other awestruck. Fehr, always known for his understatement, said, "Well, gentlemen, is that all?" Savage and Henrie walked out.

Over the years, Rolando noted, some have implied that it was easier to bamboozle business writers than other reporters; that business news was the "journalistic playground that many of us regarded sports writing."

"That is not the case," he emphasized. "It was often a very delicate tight rope we had to walk between writing truthfully and risking losing sources," he said. "I like to think we did not gloss over the truth."[284]

After Rolando and new assistant Oberbeck finished stories about difficult business issues, he said, he would review the facts with the people they'd interviewed to ensure accuracy. "We didn't cave on the controversial stuff the source may have said, but the sources appreciated our attempt to get it right. This is a technique I did not have to use when I worked general assignment or night police."

Woody concluded his career with a farewell column Oct. 7, 1990 that ended: "I thank all -- the many hundreds -- who trusted and confided in me. And, yes, who tipped me off. Without them, I would have been so much the lesser."[285]

Rick Spratling, a young reporter in the early 1960s, recounted for his obituary how Bob, noticing Rick's terror when assigned his first feature story, handed him a note.

Like any good reporter, Bob kept a few gems stashed away for slow days. On the note were contacts for scientists experimenting with seeding clouds over Salt Lake City to produce rain. This particular effort had not been reported before, so I had a scoop and a great feature. Bob never told the editors that the inspiration for the story was his; I just filled in the blanks. That first feature led to more success for me at The Trib, and then to a rewarding career in journalism [with the Associated Press]. I've never forgotten Bob's kindness in putting his own interest aside to help a young reporter who was struggling.[286]

When John Keahey inherited Woody's desk in 1993, the middle drawer was still full of his cigar ashes.[287] Randy Peterson suggested that Woody's entire cubicle, with classic Lance photo captions and snuffed-out cigar butts in the top drawer, should have been shipped intact to the Newseum or Smithsonian.[288]

* * *

Younger and older Jack Fenton

Jack Fenton, the rebellious, middle-aged county government reporter who resembled a walrus and loved tweaking elected officials, lived next door to Woody. Like his neighbor, Fenton pushed deadlines, needed extensive editing and qualified as a unique character.

In a favorite bit of *Tribune* lore, Fenton made a big splash when other staffers, at Woody's behest, helped hoist him in his folding chair and fling him into Sports Editor Jack Schroeder's pool. As he sank to the bottom of the deep end, Gordon Harman recalled, Fenton's wife Pat yelled: "He can't swim!" and jumped in after him. Once back deckside, Fenton calmly inquired, "Did I miss anything?" Even after Fenton was dead and buried 30 years later, his wife still fumed about that incident.

Fenton once checked with the City Desk when told by the county attorney to pledge an oath of secrecy over a discussion of the Salt Lake City-County Jail. The editor instructed him to refuse the oath and get the story. "What if I get thrown in jail?" he asked. "Don't worry, we'll get somebody to cover for you," was the response.

Reporter Jim Woolf's description hits the mark:

> Fenton would give Fehr fits by turning in apparently straightforward stories that contained just a word or phrase carefully selected to piss off one of our pompous elected officials. Fehr would review them and decide everything was fine and the next day field calls from furious commissioners. Jack responded with a mischievous smile and a claim that he had no idea what the commissioner was talking about.[289]

Eyes twinkling, Fenton frequently slipped wit and double meanings into his stories and tended to stick up for the "little guy," including new Vietnamese refugees needing language services, in community-oriented stories.[290] At the end of his work day, he would tell his competitor from the *Deseret News* Steve Fidel, "It's time to go help the old farts."[291] He was volunteering at the county senior center, a community commitment that followed him into retirement.

Fenton's interest in journalism began in high school and followed him though into jobs with the Army Hometown News Service in Kansas City and *Ottawa Herald* in Kansas.[292]

The "gruff, blunt interviewer" had a reputation for eating spicy foods, keeping a cappuccino maker in the county newsroom and loving modern jazz.[293] He also enjoyed whipping up -- and drinking -- fancy cocktails. "I drank a lot of his scotch . . . he mostly tolerated me, so he was a pretty good guy in my book," according to Mike Carter.[294]

Reporter Robert Bryson noted that Fenton was a "bit of a gourmet" who recommended the cheeseburgers at Ben's Cafe and the ribs at Ophelia's. One summer afternoon as Bryson passed the City-County Building, he spotted Fenton with *Deseret News* reporter Gordon Kirby at an outdoor concert lunching on steak tartare, complete with blood dripping from his mustache. When told they looked like wolves who'd downed a deer, they howled in unison.[295]

Bart Barker, a former county commissioner, recognized Fenton's grasp of Salt Lake County government:

> He knew Salt Lake County inside and out. He knew it better than a lot of elected officials. He was definitely a classic. Out of all the reporters who covered the county during my tenure [1981-1991], he was the most interesting character, and you kind of grew to love him -- even though I got burned by him a few times. He was no light touch.[296]

Former county spokeswoman Jeri Cartwright, who worked in broadcast news and public relations over the years, described Fenton as an "independent, rebellious kind of guy . . . all mush on the inside . . . He toughened me up and I needed that."[297]

Fenton and editorial writer Harry Fuller were friends who attended the University of Oregon and worked in the newsroom at the same time. When running for the Summit County Library Board decades later, Harry was interviewed by the acting county manager, who'd been a Salt Lake County bureaucrat. Once he realized Harry knew Jack, the manager spent the rest of the interview recalling Jack Fenton exploits.[298]

* * *

Several other memorable non-Mormons at *The Tribune* in the 1970s displayed their talents on the **Sports Desk**, or playpen as it was affectionately known.

Jack Schroeder and John Mooney were co-editors, and filling out the staff were Don Brooks, Marion Dunn (a Mormon), Richard "Rosey" Rosetta and Bill Coltrin, who died at halftime of the BYU-Texas game at the Cotton Bowl September 20, 1971.[299]

Jack Gallivan remembered Bill Coltrin as one of the best writers during his tenure: "He covered mostly high school. He was a very good writer . . . a wonderful person. He became very lame, finally had to have a leg amputated. He always had that big smile."[300]

The playpen was very somber the night Coltrin died, but everyone all his job and even somehow cobbled together a story about the football game, according to Brian Nutting.

Nutting sometimes thought about transferring to sports, which he considered more fun than his night police beat. He and some other cub reporters sometimes spent their free time covering games for the eight cents a mile they received for driving to and from games. Once he was paid just 12 cents for reporting a game at nearby West High School. "We [cub reporters] didn't care. It earned us a byline."[301]

* * *

Sports Editor John Mooney

John Mooney, or Moonbeam as staffer Peter Scarlet called him, was the big kahuna of sports, and I mean that literally and figuratively. The former college boxer hired by the *Salt Lake Telegram* in 1939 was a well-fed, impish Catholic who did a hilarious Hardy imitation to slim photographer Ross Welser's Laurel. He would puff away at a smelly stogie or suck on his favorite pipe while his plump yet nimble index

fingers pecked his keyboard like a woodpecker attacking a tree stump.

Mooney's predecessor, John Derks, had been a tough act to follow. After suffering a massive stroke, Derks was so dedicated to the job that he watched from the rear-view mirror of an ambulance stretcher as the local baseball diamond was named in his honor.[302]

John Mooney at play with photographer Ross Welser.

Nevertheless, Mooney became a Utah sports legend in his own right, covering events small and large, from high school and college contests to international middleweight champ Gene Fullmer. He also wrote a column and became the first sports writer inducted into the Utah Hall of Fame in 1978. He helped pick college Hall of Famers as a member of the National Honors Court, and, like his predecessor, he eventually had his name attached to a sports venue. The University of Utah named the press box at Rice-Eccles football stadium in his honor.

Mooney not only tipped a few, he made a habit of reaching around the backs of women at the Xerox copy machine to pat their breasts. Otherwise, he was lovable in an old-school kind of way. He raised funds for many humanitarian causes and volunteered at Salt Lake City's homeless shelter.

Mooney made a hefty impression on Mike Korologos, particularly after Mike moved up to the Sports Desk from copy boy in the 1950s. Nearly 60 years after the fact, Korologos could recall Mooney jokes and exploits.

For instance, when Brigham Young University President Ernest "Ernie the Attorney" L. Wilkinson fired football coach and former Utah University tackle Tally Stevens, whose win-loss record sagged to 6-16 during the 1959-60 season, Mooney quipped, "I guess that makes Wilkinson a Tally wacker."[303]

Korologos was on hand January 2, 1957 for Mooney's story on Gene "the Cyclone" Fullmer's famous upset against Sugar Ray Robinson, known as the world's best-ever boxer "pound-for-pound" in the 1940s and early '50s.

As a new sports writer, Korologos found himself taking Mooney's dictation of the 15-round fight in Madison Square Garden. Mooney was perturbed that all Sports Desk veterans had gone to dinner, leaving a rookie to take his call. By the whoops and hollers in the background, Korologos could tell Mooney was calling from a victory party where he'd already dipped deep into his schnapps. But true to form, Mooney created the story off the top of his head "quite eloquently, quoting Shakespeare (Mooney was quite an authority on Shakespeare)" and relating how the "ugly duckling" beat the "beautiful swan." Korologos struggled with the copy:

I was typing as fast as I could on the old Royal typewriter as I didn't want to interrupt his train of thought, which flowed nicely and made lots of good copy. The story was quite long, obviously, and the roll of three-ply paper I was typing on draped well down to the floor. When Mooney was finished, I ripped off the copy paper and quickly realized nobody would be able to edit all the typos by hand in the margins and between the double-spaced lines, as was the procedure then, so I completely retyped the story before I gave it to Bob Williams, the slot man who was returning from the backshop. [304]

Even I, who knew next to nothing about sports, remembered "The Cyclone" from my childhood, and I got a little thrill when I caught sight of the local celebrity in the newsroom and at his Midvale restaurant.

Another of Korologos' favorite Mooney memories features Pud the bookie.

Most days around 3 o'clock, local bookies called Mooney for results of horse races back East. Mooney would scour the long strands of copy draped behind the the AP and UPI Teletypes, spot the results and convey them to the callers.

It was also common for Mooney to get the munchies in the afternoon. He then would invite someone nearby for a cup of coffee and slice of Boston cream pie at the Mayflower across Main Street or the Mint Cafe on Regent, a popular "sports bar" of the day (it was always full of Mooney fans).

One summer afternoon in 1957, Pud the bookie called for the pertinent information, and Mooney dutifully put down the phone and headed to the wire machines. Just then, however, another call came in, and he stopped to chat. As he hung up, he called over to me, "Come on, Kid, let's go get some coffee."

The crowd at the Mint greeted Mooney with gusto, and he offered his usual quips and one-liners with a chuckle. Within moments of getting their coffee and cake, though, Mooney nudged me in the ribs and said, "We've got to get back to the office. Let's go. Hurry!" I thought the police were about to raid the place because of the unspoken sports betting that took place there, so I hurriedly gulped down my coffee, took a couple more bites of cake and departed posthaste.

On the hurried walk back to the office up Regent Street and the NAC back stairs, I asked John why we had to leave the Mint so quickly. He said: "He didn't see us, but Pud was on the phone in the back waiting for me to give him the results of the third race at Hialeah."[305]

Mooney's nemesis and arch rival was Hack Miller, the *Deseret News'* "bombastic" sports editor who frequently wrote his column in the first person so he could slip himself into the story, according to Korologos.[306] "Upon reading one especially self-aggrandizing column, Mooney spewed out this gem: 'If the "I" key on Hack's typewriter ever broke, he wouldn't have anything to write about.'"

Chicago Charlie, the former Kennecott miner from Greece who looked and smelled like he lived under the street, also riled the randy Irishman.

Mooney would set traps of pencils and notepads on reporters' desks as easy prey for Charlie's sticky fingers as he headed for the men's room, according to Gordon Harman, a copy boy and typist at the time. Still fast on his feet from his own boxing days, Mooney would pounce, catching Charlie in the act of pilfering. "Charlie would glare through his flowered hat and put the pencils back. Today, Charlie would have Mooney in court for entrapment,"[307] Harman speculated.

Popular columnist Dan Valentine delighted in rankling Mooney as his rival "face" of *The Tribune*. With a cubicle between the two, Korologos watched the drama unfold:

Valentine would "zing" a susceptible Mooney in an oft-repeated ritual Fridays, payday. While Mooney was writing his column, Valentine would saunter past Mooney's office intently examining his check stub. Within earshot of Mooney, he would say to nobody in particular, "Ah, geez! Art gave me another raise!" and continue on his way to the men's room. Mooney would throw a tizzy fit. "God damn it, my column is twice as long as Valentine's, and I cover sports besides!" I doubt he ever caught on to the ruse.[308]

* * *

Mooney gadded about sports venues and churned out his column, **Jack Schroeder** ran the nuts-and-bolts of the Sports Desk. This "egghead of the sports desk" was known for his intellect and "the wailing wall of the newsroom" for patience mentoring new writers.[309]

Jack Schroeder

Dick Rosetta described Schroeder as "sometimes distant, but always a teacher. He taught a lot of young sports scribes -- including myself, Tom Wharton, Steve Rudman and Steve Wilson, a quartet of reasonably successful newspaper professionals. Not to mention that he was instrumental in hiring Lex Hemphill."[310]

He was always here [at the office], from late morning until early morning [according to Mike Gorrell]. Jack was always fun to talk to because he had so many varied interests. He could regale you with tales of covering the 1972 Olympics in Munich, Catholicism, cultivating roses or teaching in Austria.[311]

Some of us thought of him as Gentle Jack, a fatherly figure in whom we could confide. Peter Scarlet called him Cardinal, presumably because of his devout Catholicism.

Schroeder graduated from the University of Iowa, a coincidence that somehow offended Mooney. As Jack would tell it -- I sometimes doubted the veracity of his claims -- he was sports editor of his college newspaper, held graduate degrees and survived the 1944-45 Battle of the Bulge. War injuries caused frequent headaches and incessant sniffing and prevented his pupils from dilating normally.

Schroeder joined the *Salt Lake Telegram* in 1947 at age 24. Over the years he covered big stories like Arnold Palmer's win of the Utah Open and the Munich Summer Games, where he called in not only sports stories but news updates of the terrorist attack on Israel's weight-lifting team.

He never married and loved raising roses, giving rise to speculation about his sexual orientation. Jack's rose-brick house sat around the corner from Denny Green's childhood home, and for unexplained reasons, Denny's younger brother Jerry, after working in *The Tribune* library, had nothing good to say about that neighbor.

Schroeder periodically opened his parents' Holladay home, which sported an extensive bar and backyard swimming pool, for parties that continued into the wee hours of the morning as sports writers trickled in, one by one, after putting their part of the paper to bed.

Although Schroeder was a patient listener, according to Joe Rolando, he made few if any decisions his last years on the job and "ruined many of my dress shirts."

He'd walk through the newsroom looking over the shoulders of reporters with a cigarette in hand. He'd lean over my shoulder and ask me what I was working on. When I arrived home, my wife noticed burn holes on the shoulders and collars of my shirts.[312]

Schroeder had a sense of humor. During the Great American Smokeout, he showed young reporter Ben Ling how the metal buttons promoting the event could be flipped over and used as ashtrays. Ling also remembered Schroeder worrying about the inevitable reader uproar when the pagination department, which used computers to create news pages beginning in the 1980s, misplaced the Star Gazer astrology feature one night. Paginator Gordon Harman found an old Star Gazer, and he and Ben came up with predictions of their own, one of which was, "Have a good day. Pet a dog." No complaints, and Jack was pleased and amused.[313]

* * *

Don Brooks, the gruff and runty "dead fish editor" with occasional teeth who puffed out his chest like a banty chicken, called me Cupcake. Brooksie, as I called him, was a cantankerous softie who toiled on sports part time after everyone else his age (except maybe Art Deck) was retired. It was common to hear Brooksie bellow across the newsroom, "Boooooooyyyyyy! Rush must, get on the ball! This ain't the Murray Eagle!"

Brooks was a wizard with crossword puzzles and, naturally, spelling. When Korologos was a cub writer, Brooks waved his story in the air while growling across the desk: "Korologos, you are the first writer I've ever met who misspells his own byline!"[314]

Also strict with grammar and news style, he gave my college friend Tom Wharton a ration of crap for making errors when calling in high school sports from the hospital room where his wife Gayen was giving birth to their first child. Wharton had worked his butt off getting details from three games before getting the call that Gayen's parents had rushed her into delivery.

Wharton later got even by pointing out that Brooks confused the locations of Lake Powell and Flaming Gorge in print. The headline of Brooks' next column read: "I Don't Never Make No Mistrakes."[315]

After one of many tussles on the Sports Desk, pint-sized Brooksie ended up backside first

in one of the newsroom trash barrels, his arms and legs flailing uselessly.

Tom Wharton is fishy gear.

When the hard-drinking heavy smoker finally quit coming into the office, I visited his subsidized highrise apartment. While regaling me with delightful tales of bootlegging in Montana and the exploits of various *Tribune* personalities, he snarled at his equally tiny wife, "Get the girl a drink!"

As a young buck, Brooksie worked as a bellman at the Moxum Hotel next to the Brown Derby owned by Mike Korologos' parents. Brooksie often slipped into the bar to buy beer and cigarettes for hotel guests. Korologos speculated he "probably bought them liquor too, as my dad did some bootlegging." He added:

> Brooks knew my dad and mom before I was born, which led him to tell me -- when he edited my poor copy in disgust: "Korologos, the best part of you ran down your dad's legs."[316]

* * *

My first memory of upbeat Midwesterner **Richard "Rosey" Rosetta**, a football writer hired in 1963, was the blue, choking cloud of cigar smoke in the newsroom after the birth of his first child. As time went by, I noticed his habit of touting his value and success as a sports writer, editor and columnist, an insecurity possibly tied to his upbringing:

I was the seventh child (the "caboose") of a family whose father was a coal miner and railroad dock worker and whose Mom was a housewife. We lived in a little eastern Kansas community (Osage City, Kansas, population 2,250). When I say I am from humble beginnings, we didn't have indoor plumbing until I was about 12 years old. I give you this information to sort of set the table for who I became.[317]

Rosey had no plans to attend college until "brow-beaten" by his high school drama teacher into submitting applications. He snared a $200 grant-in-aid for Washburn University in Topeka, where he was a "fish out of water" while only 35 miles north of home. His dad, a "throwback, hard-working Italian of immigrant parents," warned him against accepting invitations for rush week. "Now don't go do anything stupid," he advised his son. "Those groups just party, get drunk and cause trouble."

Sure enough, pledging to Alpha Delta, the top academic fraternity, became "one of my better life decisions," Rosey said. When he wasn't studying for average grades, covering sports for the school newspaper or working 50 to 60 hours a week to pay his way, he was cleaning the latrine as punishment for poor table manners.

Rosey said he came out of his shell the summer before his sophomore year, 1960, when appointed Washburn's student sports information director. Among other things, he took student photos and compiled student publications. His senior year, he became editor of the school newspaper and planned to attend law school, but Washburn President Harold E. Sponberg steered him toward journalism.

Rosey told Sponberg he'd been turned down for a Wall Street Journal Newspaper Fund internship, which included three months at one of three newspapers and $500 toward post-graduate study.

Dr. Sponberg roared, in Arthur C. Deck-like exasperation, "I'll check on that!" He then dialed a long-distance number and said, "Paul, this is Hal. I have a young man in my office who says you turned him down for a grant. What do you mean there are none left? This kid needs a job, and he's a helluva writer." There was a pause. "Oh, so you do have one left? Paul, that's great. Thanks a lot, Roomie." Paul Swenson,

director of the WSJ Newspaper Fund project had roomed with Sponberg at Gustavus Adolphus.[318]

Based on broadcasts of the Mormon Tabernacle Choir Sunday mornings, when announcer Richard L. Evans described Salt Lake City as the "crossroads of the West," Rosey chose *The Salt Lake Tribune*. "Sounded exotic to me," he said. So he wrote Art Deck that he would report to duty June 1, 1963, drove the 1,100 miles from Topeka in two days, parked in a lot on Regent Street north of the Flagstone Tavern and Tampico restaurant (venues he visited often in later years), and found *The Tribune* newsroom.

My first interaction was with Keith Otteson.
Me: "I'm Dick Rosetta, the Wall Street Journal Newspaper fund intern."
Mr. Otteson: "Big deal! Can't you see I'm busy?"
Next: Vard Jones.
Me: "Hello, I'm Dick Rosetta, the Wall Street Journal Newspaper Fund intern."
Vard: "What's that? Can't you see I'm busy?"
I thought I'd try the other side of the desk. The guy's nameplate said Hays Gorey.
Me: "Hello . . . " (You know the rest.)
Mr. Gorey: "I don't have time to talk right now."
At least he didn't say, "Can't you see I'm busy?"[319]

After that, the college kid from Kansas just strolled around the smoke-filled room with stars in his eyes. From the view of a 21-year-old, there were lots of old people: Bill Patrick, O.N. Malmquist, Dan Valentine, Bob Bernick.

Over in another corner was a short, pudgy guy with short, wavy hair smoking a cigar and typing kind of funny-like with two fingers . . . like he was hunting and pecking. But he was typing fast while humming and tapping his foot. It was John Mooney. Hell, I was afraid to introduce myself to anyone else.[320]

So he left, found a cheap motel down State Street and returned about 9 a.m. the next day, this time asking secretary Helen Straub for Mr. Deck. The meeting was brief. "You'll be making $75 per week until the summer is over.

Bob Rampton [the promotions guy] will show you around."

Harry Fuller took Rosey under his wing, showing him the ropes on the state government beat and introducing him to "big-wigs" at the Capitol. But then he got the mundane task of taking down corporate licensing applicants from the Secretary of State's office. When Rosey whined about being a Wall Street Journal intern, Harry said, "Big deal. That's just the way it is with new reporters."

The low point of Rosey's initiation occurred the night on general assignment when a kid from Granger reportedly was lost in the foothills above the Capitol. Otteson ordered him to cover the story, so he jumped into his 1962 Mercury Comet and dashed up the hill. About a dozen emergency vehicles, lights flashing, led him to the spot, a muddy mess from the rain.

> I asked a lot of questions and got few answers, but ultimately, one police officer said, "It's over. It's OK. The kid has been reported safe at home. His parents said he was afraid he would be punished, so he basically snuck home, climbed through a window and didn't say anything for awhile." End of story, right? Wrong.
>
> I trudged back to the office muddy as hell, walked over to Mr. Otteson and said, "Everything is OK. The kid is safe at home, yada, yada, yada." Mr. Otteson, sort of a short guy, slowly rose from his chair with a glare, straightened his arm, pointed a long finger at me and bellowed, "Go! Go out to this kid's house and get the God-damned story. And don't come back without it!" Well, the wind from that verbal blast knocked me right out the door and back to my car. I didn't have time to ask, "Where's Granger?" I did get the story, even though the parents wouldn't let me talk to the kid. Oh, I didn't get a byline. [321]

Rosey's first foray into sports, something he knew about, came later in the summer.

> My problem(s) was (were), not necessarily in any order, the guys who were out to prove I DIDN'T KNOW SPORTS: Bob Williams, Bill Coltrin, Mike Korologos, Don Brooks, John Mooney, Jack Schroeder and Marion Dunn. And there was a really quiet, super guy on the desk named Joe

Ribotto, who later that month would join the military, opening up a spot on the Sports Desk.

> In that month of August, 1963, I was grilled, cajoled, verbally flogged and basically dehumanized by the "gang of seven." By not coddling me (Brooks called me the "Kansas Corncob") but rather breaking me much like a cowboy would break a wild horse, the "gang" shaped up the guy "who knew sports." I knew a helluva lot more after that August of 1963. [322]

His internship coming to an end, Rosey prepared to head back back home to law school with his pregnant wife when it occurred to him to ask for Ribotto's job.

> After much teeth-gnashing and rebellion from the "gang," I got the job. And I held it for 39 years, except for three months in 1965 when I left *The Trib* July 2 -- despite Mr. Deck's warning that he was making a mistake -- to go back "home" and work for the *Topeka Daily Capital*. Back in Kansas, I was a miserable sap. I had been promised a job on sports in the fall, but that didn't happen. [323]

When Art Deck called in mid-September with another job offer, Rosey discussed it with his wife, who was pregnant again. The decision wasn't a slam dunk. His parents and siblings were in Kansas; the young parents had just finished moving, and funds were short despite his salary having risen from $90 to $115 a week. So when Deck called again the next afternoon, Rosey stepped up to the plate and said he'd need $130 a week to return. After declaring the sum outrageous and letting the line go silent for "what seemed like an eternity," Deck told him to "just get out here." Click. The line went dead.

> I was overjoyed. I'm not sure my wife was overjoyed, but she was a good sport. In the next 24 hours or so, it became apparent we were going to have to rent a moving van to get us back to SLC. United Van Lines wanted $325. This was going to wreck the plans. It was my turn to make a call.
>
> "Mr. Deck, we've got a small problem. It's going to cost us $325 to hire a moving company."
>
> Silence. A lot of silence.

Mr. Deck: "Hire the van and.tell them to charge it to Arthur C. Deck at *The Tribune*." Click.[324]

By September 30, 1965, Rosey was *Tribune* prep editor. As far as he knew, no other employee had left and been invited to return to *The Tribune* in such a short time.

* * *

Several other sports writers populated the playpen in the 1970s.

Curly headed **Ray Herbat**, clad in white shoes and belt, covered baseball and consistently called me Sweetheart with beer on his breath. He left *The Tribune* to start a business selling baseball cards but ended up clerking at Seven-Eleven after he being cheated by his wife and father-in-law.

Short **Steve Rudman** was a nose-to-the-grindstone sports fan enamored with reporter Jane Cartright. Rudman replaced Jack Schroeder as assistant sports editor before marrying Jane and moving the the Northwest, where he eventually wrote for the *Seattle Post-Intelligencer*, founded The National Sports Review and became director of research at ESPN.

Roger Graves, one of the few Mormons on the sports side, rose from copy boy to sports writer, specializing in golf, before being shifted to the news side for an infraction. **Marion Dunn,** another Mormon, was an all-around nice guy.

My old classmate and prep reporter Tom Wharton tried to line me up with **Steve Wilson**, a tall blond about my age in sports. After I overheard Wilson derisively referring to me as a rabbit (yes, I looked like one with my big glasses and buck teeth), I turned away whenever we found ourselves on the same path. Thirty years later, long after he'd married and moved on to other newspapers, we found ourselves at the same cocktail party, where he apologized. Apparently despondent from his divorce some time later, he took his own life.

Grant Messerly, sporting a sandy mustache, clomped across the newsroom in cowboy boots and jeans to joke with artist Dennis Green about their love of sheep before Grant quit to run a sheep ranch in southern Utah.

What can I say about **R.C. Roberg**? Known for rarely cashing paychecks, possibly because he came from money, he had a comb-over that resembled an old-fashioned leather football helmet. He showed little interest in anything except air travel, which he did often. As the story goes, he built up so many frequent-flyer miles he flew to Honolulu and back

without leaving Hawaii's airport. He was fired once but kept showing up to work until returned to the payroll.

RC Roberg and Grant Messerly at Lamb's Grill

Readers may notice the absence of women from the playpen. At least one female -- Lois Barr -- wrote about skiing in the 1960s, but it wasn't until the late 1980s that **Jill Johnson**, hired as a paginator, swaggered into the old-boys network. Jill came from the ranks of the copy clerks, which was unfortunate, because she wasn't experienced when admitted to the Sports Desk. Though athletic, she needed more time writing and reporting to withstand the pressure of deadlines and critical colleagues.

Sports Desk in 1980s with its first full-time female writer Jill Johnson and Dick Rosetta in the slot.

More women were admitted to Sports in the 1990s, but the first were not always the best. A part-time hire from Los Angeles who knew Hollywood madam Heidi Fleiss as "a very nice person" lacked journalistic ethics. After interviewing a ski contact, for example, she pointed out an expensive jacket she'd just love to have -- and then accepted it.

* * *

Norm and JoAnn Jacobsen-Wells, Doug Parker and Carol Sisco. and Paul and Marjorie Rolly, left to right.

Quiet, professional **Douglas Parker,** who took few notes and wrote comprehensive, straightforward stories from memory, joined *The Tribune* in 1963 after working for papers in Nebraska, Louisiana and Kansas. This balding brother of a non-Mormon clergyman had been a U.S. Navy airman, graduated in journalism from the University of Kansas and received a Stanford Fellowship in 1961.

Parker's first *Tribune* supervisor, Bob Woody, had this to say about him:

> We were called gentlemen of the press. Why, I don't know. I never knew any gentlemen of the press or gentlewomen of the press for that matter -- maybe Donna Lou Morgan. But gentlemen? Doug Parker came closest.
>
> [W]hile we were bombastic, backbiting and bitching, Doug was courtly, civil, cheerful, gracious and never, ever out of control.
>
> *Tribune* employment was empowerment. And for some that was a potion to swell the head, inflate the ego, disease the brains with arrogance and cockiness, and churlishness.
>
> As political editor, Doug was among the most empowered. But of all, he was least enamored or deluded by that empowerment.
>
> Long released from the bondage of the Business Desk, he was natural successor to O.N. Malmquist. Our chief editorial writer Harry Fuller, who worked with him in the early years at the Legislature, notes that Doug was

meticulous and extremely accurate. He did not presume to insinuate his analysis in his stories or indulge in snideness. He did not see himself as the font of wisdom.

And in manner, that summed up Doug's character. He did not preen, primp or fulminate.

As a young reporter, Doug had covered some of the early voting rights trials in Shreveport, La. He not only wrote of civil rights but believed passionately in the efficacy of civil rights.[325]

Carol Sisco noted that her husband wasn't one to tell stories about himself or his work, but:

> I do know he . . . was greatly affected by the braveness and tenacity of people who'd been discriminated against for years but still wanted the right to vote. I also know that he got tear-gassed with [*Chicago Tribune* political columnist] Mike Royko.[326]

That could have been during the 1968 Democratic National Convention in Chicago or the 1972 Republican National Convention in Miami. We're not sure which.

"Mother Jones" told Woody that Parker got into less trouble on the staff than anyone else, the kind of guy school teachers would have loved to have had in class. Lance Gudmundsen added that "Doug Parker gave the Fourth Estate a good name." He speculated there would have been less Prozac taken at *The Tribune* if there had been more Doug Parkers.

While Parker was always welcome at *Tribune* parties, Woody noted, he remained more observer than participant. Perhaps his first foray into the fray taught him a lesson.

As the story goes, new employee Doug Parker sprawled to the floor while attempting to woo features writer Judy Bea Rollins during a Christmas party at Mike Korologos' house on the east bench of the Wasatch Mountains in 1965.

> The drinks flowed. Festivities were at a pitch that only *Tribune* staffers could reach. To give revelers a preview of what the unfinished section would look like, I draped newsprint from Press Room end-rolls floor to ceiling over the wooden 2x4 studs.
>
> Judy quickly caught the eye of Doug Parker, who stationed himself

between Rollins and any return to the bar she might have tried. They found themselves in the soon-to-be hallway in the back of the basement. With drink in one hand, he put the elbow of the other arm against the "wall" and started to suavely lean in.

"So, how long have you been at *The Tri . . .*" he murmured at the cornered cutie as he disappeared through the torn newsprint.[327]

That departure aside, Parker "more than any of us understood self restraint -- and survival," Woody ironically observed.

In my view, the gentleman's low-key ways may have undermined his survival in the cut-throat future of *The Tribune*, but that part of the story is for later.

Meantime, Gordon Harman observed that Parker represented the *Tribune's* "classy" side. "Not that the rest of us were a bunch of slobs, but he's what I think of when I recall *The Tribune* slogan from back then: 'One of America's Great Newspapers.'"[328] Mike Carter also called Parker "a class act,"[329] and Andrea Otanez (Mike's ex-wife by then) said she "learned so much from Doug by example."[330]

"A delightful, no-sweat guy to work with whose cynicism about politicians was even deeper than mine,"[331] added John Keahey, who covered the Utah Legislature with Parker in the early 1990s.

* * *

John Cummins

John Cummins was another balding gentile who qualified as a nice guy. Sporting cowboy boots and silver-clasped bolo tie, this rural Coloradoan took over for respected education reporter Bill Smiley upon retirement. He approached every inquiry and discussion with a positive, laid-back attitude, rarely courting controversy and rarely showing excitement about a news story.

His relaxed attitude was probably the easiest way to handle a beat too vast for comprehensive coverage. He was expected to regularly report on bimonthly school board meetings in at least five public school districts, graduations at dozens of high schools, colleges and universities and all the issues pertinent to private and public education across the state, including tuition hikes, presidential salaries, enrollments, school taxes and spending, student performance and teaching trends. All of which he did reasonably well.

* * *

George Raine, "urbane, with such a strange sense of humor,"[332] began working at *The Tribune* in 1964, the same day as artist Mark Knudsen and just before graduating from Judge Memorial Catholic High School. Having been editor of the *Judgeonian*, Raine was eager to join the pros at *The Tribune*.

Here's how Raine remembered the staff he'd joined:

At the time, there was something of a Catholic pipeline to *The Tribune*, which I am sure was part of a culture created by Jack Gallivan -- at least Catholics who were interested in journalism seemed to be accommodated. Two of my Judge classmates, Dan Tabish and John McGean, were hired as copy boys. Jack Ivers, who was also a Judge product and a year younger, was a librarian. I believe Tom Durkin, who worked on the Copy Desk, was Catholic, too, and, of course, so was Jack Schroeder. Tim Kelly and his photo colleague Lynn Johnson were Catholic as well.[333]

There was a group of young editors at *The Tribune* in the late 60s and early 70s who might be called young guns in today's political vernacular who did much to give shape to the reporting -- Lance Gudmundsen, Ernie Ford, Jerry Dunton among them -- who were just a few years older than my Baby Boomer wave, but we viewed them as relatively grizzled veterans; they also acted the part, wise beyond their years.[334]

Like me, Raine worked his way through college at the University of Utah and spent little non-class time on campus. Unlike me, he was vulnerable to the military draft. So he took the advice of *Tribune* photographer Borge Anderson, an Army Reserve commander, to sign up for six years of Reserve duty while working and going to school part time.

After a couple of years as a copy boy, Raine moved up, as most young male writers did back then, to obituary writer and then reporter, beginning with night police and then City Hall. He graduated from the U in 1971 and started a master's degree in theater. By the time he got it five years later, he'd lost some hair from top of his head, resorting to the dreaded rat's-nest comb-over that Assistant Publisher Jerry O'Brien employed, and worked about three years in *The Trib's* arts section writing about theater, dance and music. He was among the staffers to put out the paper's first Sunday arts section.

Master's studies notwithstanding, Raine missed news and returned to City Desk as a reporter, often covering emerging environmental issues, and as assistant city editor.

George Raine and John Serfustini listen to street singer.

One of his days at the desk, someone jumped from the roof of the Hotel Newhouse. Raine asked the one seasoned reporter in the newsroom to run down to the hotel to check out the story. "I cover [his beat], not people who take headers off hotel roofs," the reporter dead-panned, leaving Raine to call around for the information himself.

The many World War II veterans at the newspaper influenced Raine's approach to reporting.

I learned a lot about true grit from Schroeder, who had been an Army lieutenant in the Battle of the Bulge, and from Gus Sorensen, who had been a Marine. Both, though, as well as other vets on the staff [Bob Woody and Will Fehr among them], had great humanity and benevolence, likely byproducts of their experience.

I saw in them my own dad, who had served in the Navy during the war, and had great regard for them. They taught a valuable lesson -- never give up, get the story. It's true in newspapering and in every other profession.[335]

Raine believed that lesson helped his pursuit of two major stories in his tenure at *The Tribune*: the likelihood that above-ground testing at the Nevada Test Site caused leukemia and other cancers in people downwind, and the Pentagon plan to base the MX Missile system in the western Utah desert.

Both stories had legs [remained newsworthy for a long time] and required perseverance. The cancer story played globally, and Reagan's MX scheme fizzled when opposition was too great to overcome, even in the empty reaches of the desert.

One of the last MX stories I did was about Gov. Scott Matheson taking a helicopter to Trout Creek to be the commencement speaker at the high school graduation for a class of two, Rusty and Susan. Matheson talked about the system's impact on Rusty and Susan as they were coming of age. The tents soon folded.[336]

Over the years, Raine developed strong feelings about Utah's political culture, where power was concentrated in the "narrow band from *The Tribune* north to the Main Street banks to the LDS Church offices and up the hill to the State Capitol."

While lunching with political editor Doug Parker at Lamb's Grill one day in 1976, then-Gov. Cal Rampton stopped by their booth. He told Parker he should get to know and profile Scott Matheson, the politically unknown general counsel at Union Pacific

Railroad. Though not part of the establishment, Matheson obviously was Rampton's choice as his successor. Doug did the story, and the state came to know its future governor.[337]

* * *

Brian Nutting, a raven-haired, spectacled police reporter in 1972, was part of Raine's fun and games who became my lifelong friend.

Nutting had quit a job at the Utah State Liquor Store to write obituaries but moved to night police (NIPO) the next day. Back then, reporters still typed stories on three-ply carbon paper edited with pencils. Until glue sticks came onto the market, paragraphs had to be cut and pasted from messy, toxic-melling pots of glue.

Nutting teased me mercilessly, arguing with almost every word from my mouth. When single, he let piles of uncashed weekly paychecks gather dust on his coffee table and kitchen counter among old newspapers, beer empties and smelly cigar butts. His chintzy economy car, used furniture and cheap cigars also bore testament to his thrift.

Sports columnist John Mooney tried to get him to order quality cigars through catalogs, but Nutting stuck with the budget variety at Jeannie's Smoke Shop on State Street. All the better to stink up the newsroom.

A typical night on NIPO was hardly glamorous and offered few chances for the bylines that made the job worthwhile. Bri, as I usually called him, would begin his beat with a trip to the cop shop to listen to police, sheriff and fire dispatchers. Once he learned the 10 cop codes, he could tune in when something interesting popped up on the radio. He did some ride-alongs and spent many cold nights standing around a 10-50 PI, or fire, waiting to talk to the guy in charge.

The Tribune required all photographers and police reporters, including Gus Sorensen, who drove Car 1, to have radios in their cars so they could keep in touch with City Desk while out in the field. Nutting got one, too, but his was just the radio guts stuffed into a big box in his car trunk. A small microphone was strung through the car and clipped within his reach, near his car radio.

Nutting vividly remembers covering the death of Percy Clark, a cop gunned down outside a market on Third Avenue:

> The cops were staking the place out, and as the guy ran out, Percy stood up and told the guy to stop. The guy shot him and then was shot himself about a million times by the other cops in the stakeout. I wasn't even working that night, but the shooting took place right around the corner from where I was living. I was the first reporter on the scene and talked to lots of emotional cops right afterward. They left the robber's body lying there on the sidewalk for a long time.[338]

Another night, Nutting witnessed a silly incident that also stuck with him for decades. Wolfman Jack, the gravelly voiced disc jockey, drew a crowd in front of The Tribune building. Several enthusiastic fans approached the platform where he stood a few feet above the sidewalk. When he leaned over to give a woman a hug, the crowd grabbed and pulled him onto the sidewalk. "Wolfman dusted himself off and stalked off to parts unknown, cutting his triumphant appearance short."[339]

NIPO included the "added bonus" of calling area hospitals to check on people on the "death watch." That is, gravely ill public persons whose condition deserved news stories. It also was NIPO's job to call hospitals New Year's Eve to find the first baby of the year so *The Tribune* and other businesses could shower it with gifts and "play it" for good publicity.

Another chore was writing a few police-beat "shorts" or "briefs" -- one- or two-paragraph stories taken from police reports on burglaries, DUIs, rapes and accidents -- to plug into holes when other stories came up short in the backshop.

Nutting would get off work at 1:30 or 2 a.m. after helping the night crew edit the final edition of the paper and send down corrections. He then was off to Little America or Bob's Big Boy for breakfast.[340]

When fellow police reporter Wilf Cannon introduced Nutting to Suzanne

Scattergood, a University of Utah student from New Jersey, he triggered events that eventually would put   Nutting in the center of national journalism. But first, Brian and Suzie had to get married.

While occasionally covering the courts, Nutting got to know Utah Supreme Court Justice D. Frank Wilkins, the man he chose to perform his marriage. After pronouncing Brian and Suzie husband and wife, he addressed the crowd, "Everyone, kiss everyone." He refused Nutting's offer to pay but instead accepted a slim book of Kahlil Gibran's writings and a sizable share of the event's liquor supply.   (Judge Wilkins also became a friend and father figure to another *Tribune* police reporter, Peter Scarlet, who much later used his advice to hold onto his job. That episode comes later.)

Once released from NIPO, Nutting spent a year or so on the Copy Desk before joining the swelling ranks of reporters who did time as Woody's business assistant. Then he raced up the ladder to a top spot on City Desk before changing direction. More to come on that.

235 Mike Korologos email, January 19, 2014.

236 Mike Gorrell, "Utahn lends an assist to Athens," *The Salt Lake Tribune*, August 5, 2004, p. C1.

237 Robert F. Alkire, "Wrechage Dots Wall of Canyon," *The Salt Lake Tribune*, July 2, 1956, p. A1.

238 Korologos, March 25, 2015.

239 Mike Korologos email March 24, 2015.

240 Mike Korologos email, March 28, 2015.

241 Ibid.

242 Mike Korologos email, January 31, 2014.

243 Korologos email January 26, 2014.

244 Korologos, January 26, 2014.

245 Korologos, January 19, 2015.

246 Gallivan May 2005.

247 "Tribune's Parade of Popular Promotions," July 22, 1988, p. T12.

248 Mike Korologos interview, 1973.

249 Gallivan, May 2005.

250 Nutting, February 14, 2014.

251 "Obituary, Eugene Jelesnik," *Deseret News*, February 18, 1999.

252 Mike Korologos email, June 8, 2015.

253 Ibid.

254 Mike Korologos email, May 25, 2015.

255 Mike Korologos email, May 25, 2015.

256 Mike Korologos email, January 31, 2014.

257 Mike Korologos email. April 10, 2014.

258 Catherine Reese Newton to Tribune facebook group March 2, 2012.

259 Paul Rolly, *The Salt Lake Tribune*, April 22, 2010.

260 Memories of Bob Woody, *The Salt Lake Tribune* obituary, May 5, 2010.

261 Rolando March 1, 2012.

262 Woody, August 23, 1995.

263 Laura Bryn Sisson, The Dartmouth, April 27, 2010.

264 Memories of Woody, May 5, 2010.

265 Sisson, April 27, 2010.

266 Paul Rolly, The Salt Lake Tribune, April 22, 2010.

267 Laura Bryn Sisson, "Woody, '50, a journalist, dies at 84," *The Dartmouth*, April 27, 2010.

[268] Mike Gorrell to facebook's Tribune group November 11, 2013.

[269] Robert Bryson email, August 4, 2015.

[270] Robert Bryson email, August 9, 2015.

[271] Nutting, Feburary 14, 2014.

[272] Mike Korologos email, March 3, 2017.

[273] Joe Rolando, April 2017.

[274] Joe Rolando, March 1, 2012.

[275] Joe Rolando email, January 21, 2014.

[276] Rolando, April 2017.

[277] Ibid.

[278] Ibid.

[279] Joe Rolando email April 30, 2017.

[280] Ibid.

[281] Ibid.

[282] Ibid.

[283] Ibid.

[284] Joe Rolando email April 2017 regarding a CNN commentator's assertion that President Donald Trump had a harder time dealing with the national press because he couldn't get lies past them they way he did with the "business press on Page B6" when involved in his real estate business.

[285] Paul Rolly, *The Salt Lake Tribune*, April 22, 2010.

[286] Memories of Woody, May 5, 2010.

[287] John Keahey, November 16, 2013.

[288] Randy Peterson to Triibune facebook group February 2, 2012.

[289] Jim Woolf email to Tribune facebook group, November 27, 2011.

[290] Dan Harrie, "Tribune veteran, long-time Salt Lake County reporter Jack Fenton dies," *The Salt Lake Tribune,* November 29, 2011.

[291] Ibid.

[292] Ibid.

[293] Ibid.

[294] Mike Carter to facebook's Tribune group September 20, 2014.

[295] Robert Bryson email to Diane Cole.

[296] Jack D. Fenton obituary, *The Salt Lake Tribune,* November 29, 2011.

[297] Harrie, November 29, 2011.

[298] Harry Fuller email, November 26, 2011.

[299] Tom Wharton, "Bountiful store opened ahead of its time," *The Salt Lake Tribune*, February 18, 2013.

[300] Gallivan, May 2015.

[301] Brian Nutting email, February 14, 2014.

[302] Gallivan, July 24, 1988.

[303] Mike Korologos email, January 5, 2016.

[304] Mike Korologos email May 24, 2015, taken from email to *Tribune* columnist Kurt Kragthorpe April 28, 2015, and based on memo from Mike to Tom Korologos in 1957.

[305] Mike Korolgos email, May 27, 2015.

[306] Mike Korologos email, May 25, 2015.

[307] Gordon Harman to facebook Tribune group February 9, 2012.

[308] Korologos, February 25, 2017.

[309] Jack Schroeder obituary, *The Salt Lake Tribune,* November 7, 2002.

[310] Dick Rosetta email to Diane Cole November 7, 2002.

[311] Jack Schroeder former newsman at *Tribune*, dies, *Deseret News*, November 7, 2002.

[312] Joe Rolando to facebook's Tribune group September 21, 2014.

[313] Ben Ling, December 26, 2013.

[314] Mike Korologos email, January 26, 2014.

[315] Paul Rolly & Dawn House, "Hard news and raucous times," *The Salt Lake Tribune*, May 16, 2015, p. B4.

[316] Mike Korologos email, March 3, 2017.

[317] Richard Rosetta email, August 2, 2015.

[318] Ibid.

[319] Ibid.

[320] Ibid.

[321] Ibid.

[322] Ibid.

[323] Ibid.

[324] Ibid.

[325] Robert H. Woody eulogy of Douglas L. Parker August 23, 1995, courtesy of Barbara Woody, April 2014.

[326] Carol Sisco email, August 1, 2015

[327] Mike Korologos email, June 14, 2015.

[328] Gordon Harman to facebook's Tribune group September 22, 2014.

[329] Mike Carter to facebook's Tribune group September 20, 2014.

[330] Andrea Otanez to facebook's Tribune group September 21, 2014.

[331] John Keahey to facebook's Tribune group September 25, 2014.

[332] Nutting, February 14, 2014.

[333] George Raine email, December 28, 2013.

[334] Raine, February 16, 2014.

[335] Raine, December 28, 2013.

[336] Ibid.

[337] Raine, February 18, 2014

[338] Nutting, February 14, 2014.

[339] Ibid.

[340] Ibid.

8 - Mormons in Our Midst

Toward the end of the century *The Tribune* employed several Mormons, some just as zany as their irreverent peers. Although most LDS staffers resisted the corrupting influences of our worldly office, a few apparently succumbed to temptation.

I considered City Editor Will Fehr a Jack Mormon who believed church tenets without practicing them. Both he and his artist wife Cynthia smoked and drank regularly.

Night Managing Editor **Keith Otteson** was another Mormon who didn't let rigid church rules restrict so-called sinful behavior much at work, where he would swear up a storm, sneak cigarettes and harass his female staff.

The Navy veteran was caught off guard the afternoon his daughter Gina dropped by unexpectedly. As she approached the clump of editors' desks, he shoved his smoldering ashtray into the drawer with his hoarded wire stories. The smoking desk revealed his secret.

Otteson enraged and repulsed me. As my immediate supervisor, he made me scrape and beg for time off, rarely granting my first or second choices of vacation days. When I called in sick, he required a full rundown of symptoms, which often included horrendous cramps.

Even worse, like Biggie Rat from the 1960s King and Odie cartoon, Otteson would regularly slink over to a female staffer at the copy machine or at their desks to mumble something about taking a break out back to neck. Neither I nor Nancy Melich before me dared protest or complain, afraid of losing status as team players.[341]

Writers Babs Springer and Bernie Moss were not so shy. When Otteson creeped up behind their chairs, they elbowed him in the groin, sending him to his knees. Of course they were not beholden to the toad for time off, raises and promotions like I was.

* * *

Vard "Wildflower" Jones, the world and national news editor who put together Page One, was raised in southern Utah's red rock town of Blanding by Kuman Stanley Jones, driver of the first wagon down the Hole in the Rock in 1879. Riding his chair like a horse, this fifty-something guy with Coke-bottle glasses ripped apart stories from the news wire with his steel pica pole, stuck them on vertical spikes around his desk (without looking) and scribbled layout and headline orders so fast heads would spin. His nearly perfect pages rarely required trims in the backshop.

Vard's mentally disabled daughter had three disabled children who looked to Vard for fatherly guidance. Vard cheerfully called the kids at least twice each day from work. His grandson sold glazed donuts in the newsroom, always wearing a big, open smile on his round, pimply face.

While patient with his "children," the perfectionist picked to pieces whatever anyone did to his Front Page, whether it was to write a three-line weather forecast or trim a wire. He was quick to lambaste copy boys who dragged their feet or put a piece of copy in the wrong spot on his desk, which abutted Otteson's.

Vard was naturally wired, fanatical about everything he did, whether golfing, birding, studying wildflowers or rock-hounding.

Whenever someone new came into the newsroom, Vard would sidle up to them and conspiratorially challenge, "Name a wildflower." Huh? was the usual reaction among those who didn't know the common name of even one and didn't care o be pestered. "Any wildflower."

"Sego lily?"

"*Calochortus nuttallii*," he'd announce triumphantly before rattling off a full laundry list of other scientific names and slipping back to his seat, where a fan going broke up the second-hand smoke shrouding his desk. If, by some fluke, he couldn't come up with the scientific name, he'd buy the newcomer a cup of so-called coffee or a flat Coke from the nearby vending machine.

Gordon Harman, one of my contemporaries, remembered hearing this conversation about once a week:

Vard Jones: Name a wildflower!
Jon Ure: Marijuana!
Vard: Cannabis sativa, and it's not a wildflower.
Jon: I think it's pretty wild.[342]

Vard and buddies Walter P. Cottam, the botanist co-founder of Nature Conservancy, and A. H. Ellett, a future Utah Supreme Court justice, spent Thursdays wandering the wilds of Utah identifying flowers, trees and birds and collecting arrowheads and rocks for jewelry. Vard expertly carved the birds he studied and occasionally brought one in for admiration. He also brought me seeds from a Cottam oak, a hybrid now growing alongside my driveway. When things got too quiet in the newsroom, our wire news editor blew into his cupped hands, producing a train whistle mimicking a charging locomotive.

Ben Ling, possibly the first Asian on staff, was working as a corrections typist one afternoon when Vard asked him how to say "hello" in Chinese. Sitting across the desk was Ling's Skyline High classmate Nancy Hobbs, who said "herro" under her breath. Ben liked the idea and repeated it, louder this time. Editors Gerry Cunningham and Keith Otteson burst out laughing, and Vard, "as he sometimes did," laughed so hard he rolled around on the floor beside his desk.[343]

After graduating in journalism from the U. of U., Vard had begun his newspaper career writing for the *Deseret News*. In 1959, he moved to *The Tribune*, where he retired in 1981.[344] When he died from lymphoma July 1, 1993 at 73, his obituary identified Maxine Martz, a *Deseret News* reporter, as his best friend.

* * *

Constant critic **Hal Schindler** -- Harold Moroni Schindler, that is -- was an odd duck, not only because of his status as a non-drinking Mormon but also because the Ichabod Crane-like creature, peering over glasses perched on the end of his nose and strung around his neck from the temple tips, pontificated interminably about gun control, the sorry state of television and anything else that stuck in his craw at the moment.

Obviously, Schindler was someone to avoid near deadlines. His monologues killed other staffers' concentration.

Even so, Schindler's grasp of Utah history could impress. Writer John Keahey's plan to visit Mountain Meadows, the spot where Mormons massacred 120 men, women and children crossing southern Utah from Arkansas in 1857, got Hal going:

He smiled, sat down, leaned back, and put his feet on my desk. He began to tell me . . . why southern Utah Mormons would be behind such a thing, the journey of the Fancher wagon train into Utah and through Salt Lake City and points south. His lesson lasted at least an hour, maybe longer, and it was unforgettable. I can to this day probably recite most of it from memory, it was that vivid.[345]

Hal Schindler

Without graduating from college, Schindler became a recognized historian. He wrote episodes of "Death Valley Days" and "Gunsmoke" and finished a history, <u>Orrin Porter Rockwell: Man of God, Son of Thunder</u>, in 1966 that became the University of Utah Press' best-selling book.[346] Schindler appeared in Ric Burns' public television documentary "The Donner Party" and lent his expertise to Burns' later film, "The American Experience: The Way West."[347]

Toward the end of his career, Schindler used information from pioneer diaries to write a feature series for Utah's sesquicentennial about the Mormon trek to the promised land. Denny Green did the illustrations, as he often did for major feature stories.

"He knew as much about Utah history as anyone I ever knew," Brigham D. Madsen, U. professor emeritus of history, said of Schindler.

"He had a tremendous memory for facts, and was very articulate in expressing them."[348]

Schindler also was known for meticulous writing and editing, mentoring many young writers in the importance of cadence and rhythm,[349] noted Terry Orme, one of those young writers who eventually became *Tribune* publisher.

The product of German immigrants who raised him in "Noo Yawk," as he put it, Schindler was honest, reliable and basically good-hearted. But his sense of humor sometimes fell short. When Ben Ling changed his "Noo Yawk" spelling to "New York" while proof-reading one of his columns, Schindler threw a fit. Editor Will Fehr advised Ling to "stop yanking Schindler's chain," and the Noo Yawka stopped speaking to Ling for about a year.

Ling also offered this memory of the man:

> I always wondered why such a tall, gangly guy would prefer hockey over basketball. I played hockey in high school, so I had a connection with him there, but I didn't hate basketball like Hal. He would grumble about men running around in their underwear and dismiss them with an impatient wave of his lanky arm.[350]

Having started at *The Tribune* in 1945 at age 15, Schindler had worked his way up from "the worst copy boy John Mooney had ever met."[351] He witnessed five executions as a crime reporter and wrote a column for 27 years about television, a medium he disdained. Ultimately, he managed the Sunday magazine and arts news.

Schindler pursued his passion for history until the end, which came in the form of a heart attack while headed for the Utah Historical Society to research the Utah War for yet another book. Always seeking comic relief from sad situations, derisive staffers speculated that the stress of picking up an unexpectedly large bill at a retiree lunch overtaxed the tightwad's heart.

* * *

Equally reliable **George "Gus" Sorensen,** a conservative Mormon and military veteran, covered suburban Salt Lake County. The old-timer was one of *The Tribune's* most trusted reporters, especially at the Utah State Prison.

Raised in Riverton not far from the prison, Gus graduated from nearby Brigham Young University, where he covered sports for the *Daily Universe.* He married in the LDS

Temple and began his 44-year news career at *The Salt Lake Telegram* before moving to the morning paper.[352]

Meantime, the square-built, freckled ex-Marine not only fought in the World War II battle of Iwo Jima but also earned a Purple Heart from the Korean Conflict's battle at Chosin Reservoir. After reaching the rank of major, he became a captain in the Marine Reserve.

Gus Sorensen

While "Gus couldn't write his way out of a paper bag," according to editor Brian Nutting, he was always on call and available to chase a fire or a murder in the south part of the county.

> He was so dedicated that he decided to wait to have his heart attack on the first day or so of a long-awaited vacation. He knew all the cops and firemen, so they would tell him things, and then Gus would be the one to decide how much information needed to be parceled out in the story, and what stuff to keep off the record.[353]

More than once, the big-hearted, perpetually nice guy joined in searches and rescues after calling in his story.[354]

Nancy Melich spent a week with Gus when interning for *The Tribune* in the early 1970s. She learned never to do anything over the phone that she could do in person. It had seemed that Gus was merely going from place to place passing the time of day, but in the process, employees in the various towns would mention things that proved newsworthy. They also were apt to call Gus with tips later on.[355]

George Raine was assigned to fill in during one of Gus' vacations:

I made arrangements to pick up Gus' company car from him that evening out in what may be the sprawl of South Jordan now. While making the car hand-off, a sheriff's department radio call came about a man holding a shotgun on his front lawn. We drove to the address and hid behind cop cars, peeking out at the troubled man. Within a few minutes the man put the shotgun under his chin and blew his head off. We gathered some notes and drove back to the office. We sat for a few minutes gathering our thoughts, and Gus excused himself to go to the bathroom. He was in there for what seemed like a long spell, so I looked in on him. The old Marine was vomiting and sobbing. We wrote the story.[356]

It was Gus who found a new venue -- Draper Park within his beat -- for the staff's annual picnic after Salt Lake City outlawed beer at Washington Park in Parleys Canyon. As Dave Jonsson recalled, Gus was sweating bullets because he had called in a favor with Draper City to allow us to use the park. "He was worried about his reputation, the company's reputation, bad press."[357]

And for good reason. Beer or other strong beverages usually flowed freely when two or more staffers socialized, and they weren't about to let a silly local law douse their fun. At Draper Park, staffers slipped into cars and behind trees to guzzle a few between innings on the softball diamond.

Gus was so active in the LDS church that he was a "high priest" in his ward and served two missions after retirement in 1986. But church work was not his sole contribution. He sat on the Governor's Task Force for Victims Rights and worked as an usher at Utah Jazz basketball games. This all-around good guy died at age 75 from Lou Gehrig's Desease.[358]

* * *

Pat McCoy was an unmarried BYU graduate in charge of Saturday's church page. Sadly for Miss McCoy, her high-pitched, nasally protests over the cigar and cigarette smoke clouding the newsroom exposed her to considerable scorn before she eventually returned to Idaho.

One of McCoy's primary antagonists was Lance Gudmundsen, Woody's razor-witted business assistant whose desk abutted hers. As JoAnn Jacobsen finished her 3:30 rewrite shift late one night, Lance asked if she'd like someone to walk her out. McCoy shrieked, "Why doesn't anyone ever walk me to my car!?"

Gudmundsen deadpanned, "Don't worry, Pat, there's no such thing as a blind rapist."[359]

This apparently followed an earlier conversation between the two when McCoy worked night police. "I have a rape here," she told Gudmundsen over the phone. "What do I do with it?"

Gudmundsen didn't miss a beat: "Cherish it."

* * *

Peter Scarlet and Lance Gudmundsen outside the closet at Halloween.

Lance Gudmundsen, a talented pianist and cat-lover from the conservative bedroom community of Lehi, withstood his share of taunts over his sexuality. The stress of social censure undoubtedly contributed to his reliance on prescription drugs like Prozac.

Like most gays at that time, Gudmundsen hid his private life to keep his job and avoid attacks on the street. When he took days off to tend his sick cat and returned bruised and battered, rumors rippled through the office. Crass copy editors seized the opportunity to mock the man within hearing distance. Vacations to places like New Orleans, where he could be himself and find "roommates," became his refuge.

Writer George Raine regarded Gudmundsen as "an elegant man . . . complex, and a lovely writer as well." He also was impressed that a young Gudmunsen drove an Austin Healy 3000, "the finest sports car to my thinking,[360]

Speaking of elegance, his pet name for me was Panther with the Clap.

Over time, Gudmundsen worked as Robert Woody's business deputy, as assistant city editor and as a features writer. Encouraged by a new executive editor in the 1990s, he wrote openly about gender issues and brought his partner to office parties.

However, it could be said Gudmundsen came out of the closet at our 1985 Halloween party in Summit Park. Adorned in a little prince costume, he got so woozy he fell backward into our so-called cloak room and was hoisted out by other revelers.

* * *

Dave Jonsson departed the "Mormon church and religious belief in general" at the start of his *Tribune* career. "I enjoyed the irreverent and decidedly diverse atmosphere at the paper. I felt I had now found my peeps and I didn't look back."[361]

Dave Jonsson, Capitol reporter

In junior and senior high school in Salt Lake City, Jonsson had been the kid with the camera around his neck shooting for the school newspaper or yearbook. He enrolled in journalism at the University of Utah because it was as close as he could get to photography. One day in the U's Journalism Lab late in 1963, he heard Lynn Johnson was going into the Air Force, leaving an opening in *The Trib's* Photography Department. Jonsson got the job at $60 a week, less than the $75 new reporters were paid, but he was happy. "I would have paid *The Tribune* to work there."

When I started in Photo, photographers who went out on sports assignments had to be strong as oxen if they wanted to get sequence photos. The sequence camera, the Hulcher, was as big as a microwave. It was pressed into service on special game days, like BYU vs. Utah. I remember Brandt Gray carrying that beast and the portable wirephoto machine, and it was a struggle. Plus, of course, the film had to be developed in the field and wired at glacial speed one at a time to a copy boy waiting at the wire machine.

Nowadays, of course, with digital technology, photogs' cameras easily do amazing sequence shots, and with wi-fi cards in their cameras, the images arrive at the Sports Desk within seconds of being taken.[362]

His first year on staff, Jonsson became a reporter. Three years later, after a stint as Gus Sorensen's alter ego on the Davis County beat, he rose to the State Capitol beat, where he covered three governors -- Cal Rampton, Scott Matheson and Mike Leavitt -- over 19 years.

Ensconced in the dingy Capitol press room, sight unseen by the rest of the news staff -- except, that is, for the copy boys who collected his copy -- Jonsson became "kind of a ghost employee."[363] Once he could send stories to the newsroom via Teleram, he became even less conspicuous, but he did remember one newsroom incident years later.

The sports guys were tossing around a ball of the Art Department's rubber cement, which they had poured onto the desk to dry. After idly lighting a cigarette, Bob Williams tossed the match in the direction of the volatile ball, which exploded in flames. He tore a fire extinguisher away from Jonsson to put out the flames[364] and then raced to the restroom to soak his badly burned hands.

Occasionally an editor would complain that Jonsson couldn't be found after lunch, which he sometimes took at home near the Capitol.

Peter Scarlet, both a copy boy and beat reporter then, claimed Jonsson and his *Deseret News* counterpart would jockey for a position on the office couch for an afternoon nap with lights out and door locked.

By then, Capitol coverage consisted primarily of press releases, calendars, meetings and press conferences. Rising star reporter Paul Rolly started digging up dirt on state politicians and bureaucrats to fill the void in investigative reporting, ruffling Jonsson's feathers but spicing up our news pages.

* * *

Robert "Buffalo Bob" Bryson, whose fuzzy-pelted profile resembled that of an albino bison, hailed from California and Idaho, where he worked at several smaller newspapers before joining *The Tribune* in 1969. Also nicknamed Noah for his flood-length bell-bottoms,[365] Bryson covered various beats with little fanfare over the next 30 years.

Bob Bryson on assignment.

He had this to say about his first assignment, 2 p.m. rewrite:

Translated, you got to edit the weather report. I was working with Stan Bowman, who often took his lunch at the VFW Club, where the menu was limited but the drinks flowed. After one such lunch, Stan staggered back into the newsroom, attempted to hang up his coat, lost his balance and fell into the coat rack. He was soon sent home, and I got to do his job as rewrite as well as mine.[366]

Bryson had been on the job just three days, floating from desk to desk, when he found himself next to someone sleeping soundly.

Otteson came by, lifted the guy's head and announced: "Mr Smith, you have been drunk for four days. The limit at *The Tribune* is three. You're fired." and slipped his blue slip under his nose.[367]

Bryson was grateful to learn one of his new employer's rules.

One night after that, he was ordered to track down Roger Porter, another Idahoan hired for rewrite who had gone to the Salt Lake Area Chamber of Commerce's annual party during his "lunch hour." About 10:30 p.m., Bryson called Chamber President Fred Ball and, identifying himself as Art Deck, told Ball to send Porter back to work if he found him. "Roger quickly came back but never forgave me," Bryson recalled.

This Mormon felt comfortable at Utah's non-Mormon newspaper. He had been a Democrat from birth and didn't "grow up as a Mormon boy" in the usual sense because his family "tended to believe in having fun first, despite religious or state laws to the contrary."[368]

Drinking -- by other staffers -- gave this teetotaler cachet in the newsroom. Besides standing in for Stan, staying awake during his shift and tracking down strays, Bryson drove his peers home from nearby D.B. Cooper's Social Club, a basement bar named after the hijacker who got away.

From rewrite, Bryson moved to night police, a job requiring him to sleep during the day so he could work until 2 a.m. His description of his irascible editor Ernie Hoff as a "noted philosopher" who insisted that his writers "keep it tight" illustrates his sense of humor.

With Hoff on City Desk one night, Bryson tracked down a story about a five-car wreck in the Avenues. As he had done for five previous police stories, Hoff asked if Bryson could tell it in two paragraphs. That way Hoff didn't have to remake the slop obit page late at night. (The news hole on that page shrank or expanded according to the number of obituaries coming in.) When Bryson replied in the negative, Hoff turned surly for the rest of the evening.[369]

Bryson's next "promotion"-- "that's what Will Fehr called it" -- was to federal court after his predecessor had an affair with a court clerk who also was Judge Willis Ritter's girlfriend.[370]

The eccentric U.S. district magistrate terrified many a staffer between 1949 and 1978. He was the judge, after all, who ordered the arrest of 24 postal employees for making too much noise outside his office, who played strip spin-the-bottle at the Club Manhattan and who ordered the Ten Commandments to be removed from the Metropolitan Hall of Justice.[371] Since he often lunched and dined with Editor Art Deck, Bryson's stories had to satisfy both.

One story I wrote suggested Ritter had let off easily some miscreants who stole government property. The next day Ritter "invited" me into his chambers.

"Who the hell changed your story?" he demanded.

The man had spent a lifetime listening to bad liars, but I decided to do the same.

"It was those numbskulls on the Copy Desk," I told him.

He bought it, but I never repeated that error.[372]

Bryson next did the first of three stints as Bob Woody's assistant on the Business Desk before returning to rewrite, where it was his duty to take dictation from aging Clarence "Scoop" Williams on the Salt Lake City beat.

Scoop never wrote anything and was, in the terms of the trade, a leg person. Because of that omission, he had no idea what others had written for him. After 20 minutes of note-taking, you could then write a 10-inch story.

In fact, some of us on rewrite doubted if Scoop could even type. If you asked him for background on any story, he would say, "You know, we have had lots of stories about this. You can look them up" [in the morgue]. You had to ask him each time if this was the beginning of a new story or end of the one he was "dictating." He often had no idea.

But Scoop was still a reporter. When I was assigned to learn his beat, he approached one of the city commissioners and asked for some details on a recent council vote.

"Dammit, Scoop, I can't do that now. I am too busy," the commissioner said.

Scoop got the details he needed elsewhere and added this notation: "Commissioner So-and-So, asked about the incident, said he was too busy to talk to *The Tribune*."[373]

As Scoop's assistant, Bryson called the director of Hansen Planetarium about a tip that the organization soon would be seeking tax dollars. After the story appeared and Salt Lake City Council members got complaints about a possible tax increase, the director got reamed and tried to pass the blame to Bryson by telling Will Fehr the phone conversation had been off the record.

"That's bull ----," Fehr said. "Don't lie to me."

"I have never heard . . .," the director began.

"Well, -----, you're hearing it now," Fehr said, hanging up.[374]

A delighted Will Fehr then turned to Bryson: "It's always good to tell an asshole to go straight to hell."[375]

* * *

JoAnn "Fifi" Jacobsen, the petite former Utah State University cheerleader with big bangs and glasses, was the favorite of several newsroom men, not just Hank McKee. Her boss Will Fehr was another, but so was reporter Brian Nutting. In fact, he'd had a crush on her since their teens, when their fathers, both education professors at the U., took them to Ethiopia while helping establish Haile Sallassie University. Another admirer was Don Brooks, the crusty sports writer who dubbed her Fifi, which she considered "a term of endearment by a beloved . . . friend."[376]

With the exception of Shirley Jones, Fifi was friendlier with male editors than other male and female staffers. She sashayed across the newsroom in pumps and form-fitting, stylish dresses and flashed a toothy grin, crinkled her button nose and sweet-talked editors from the side of her mouth, undulating between squeaky baby talk and a breathy, hushed, rushed sort of secrecy. When Korologos featured her in the *Tribune Tattler*, he ran a bikinied caricature as a centerfold. "Such a politically correct time!" she noted decades later.[377]

Fifi's first *Tribune* job was writing obituaries, "one notch higher on *The Tribune* totem pole than a copy boy." For a year she put up with morticians' monotonous jokes about people dying to get into her column[378] and was paid only $90 a week, but the job offered other perks. She felt honored to work in the same newsroom with "legendary journalists" Dan Valentine, John Mooney and Jack Schroeder.

By the time I entered the scene, Fifi had advanced to 3:30 rewrite and 2 p.m. general assignment. It was tempting for me, a gangly, feminist newbie, to dismiss her as a shallow blonde, a Plastic Fantastic who used her sexuality to manipulate male editors and sources. But I was mostly jealous. Fifi worked as hard or harder than anyone else on staff. While men vied for her attention, she kept churning out copy to earn countless bylines.

Her early repertoire did include a silly first-person visit to Planned Parenthood's waiting room -- that's as far as she got -- and a feature on BYU campus fashions. But she moved on to some of the weightiest stories of the era, including the first successful implantation of an artificial heart.

She also did an expose on the University of Utah's purchase of an expensive new house for incoming President David P. Gardner, who wanted more room to entertain than the existing home provided. U. of U. PR guy Ray Haeckel's heavy lobbying failed to get her story killed, but it was moved inside (off Split Page).[379] DJ Tom Barberi had a field day with the issue on KALL radio, and the TV stations ran photos comparing the two houses. Finally, Fifi and Valentine tweaked Gardner with a picture of themselves in the office coat closet captioned, "From our dining room to yours."[380] When I met Gardner a few

years later, he still resented the rude "welcome" he received from that story.

Though friendly and upbeat, Fifi kept some distance from the dysfunctional antics of the newsroom and the heavy off-hours drinking. She devoted much of her free time to her church and family, which, not long after marrying Norman Wells, included two sons adopted from Asia.

> I was an active Mormon, and it [the anti-Mormon atmosphere] didn't bother me. I always saw the need for two newspapers with different views. I did have to be day city editor some Sundays and remember going to church smelling of tobacco, which my mother didn't appreciate.[381]

Even so, Fifi exhibited insecurities, anxieties and stress like the rest of us. Her tinted glasses and bangs camouflaged a childhood eye injury that inspired many stories involving the Utah chapter of the National Society to Prevent Blindness. She drove a sports car and drank "wepsies" (Manischewitz white cream wine mixed with Diet Pepsi)[382] to balance her energy with calm.

Fifi left *The Tribune* three times: to be executive director of the Utah Society to Prevent Blindness in New York, to write the biography of wealthy LDS businessman Robert H. Hinckley, and to be Congressman Dan Marriott's press secretary in Washington. When Will Fehr refused to rehire her a third time, she accepted an offer with the *Deseret News* so she could return to Utah to raise her children. Once Fehr retired, she came back to *The Tribune* in 1991.

* * *

Socially awkward **Peter Scarlet** mumbled almost as badly as Frank Brunsman and playfully dispensed nicknames among the staff. Brunsman was dewey eyes; Mike Korologos Sluggo (from the cartoon "Nancy"). Actually, Mike Cassidy, the kid with the movie camera hired as a copy boy with Scarlet, came up with Sluggo because of Korologos' round head and close-cropped hair, but Scarlet made sure the endearment stuck by using it faithfully. Korologos countered with a story about a sexy staffer's snickering when first introduced to the new employee. It was all in the name, Peter Scarlet.

Scarlet lurked about the office, cigarette in hand and eyes darting furtively beneath protruding brow, to bend the ear of anyone glancing his way. When I came onboard, he was in his mid-twenties and had just moved up from statistics columnist to night police, a job that put him in the company of gruff cops who showed scant interest in his glorification of Napoleonic and Prussian wars and heroes.

Peter Scarlet

Scarlet's nasally, muffled voice could drone on for hours in an archaic dialect developed from reading voluminous history books. Now and again, he'd burst into a jag of giggles brought on by a crazy coincidence of history. His analytic mind could draw uncanny connections between legendary figures and Utah's political and religious leaders. His love for world history ran so deep that he returned to college to get his degree in his 40s.

This garrulous Mormon's LDS anecdotes were better suited for his next assignment: putting out Saturday's Church News. Within the office, he insisted on referring to Gordon B. Hinckley, a counselor in the LDS First Presidency who made it to the top job in 1995, as "Bitner," his middle name.

The peskiness of his "loquaciousness" aside, Scarlet was quite an "affable," intelligent and sensitive "chap" (I'll call his favorite terms Scarletisms). He had time for chatter because he only wrote stories explicitly assigned, and then he banged them out in minutes, seldom proofreading

or tightening his copy. He was neither ambitious nor self-motivated until it came to something he really wanted to do. If anyone "shunned" (ignored) or "spurned" him (more Scarletisms), he would slink away crushed and attach unflattering nicknames to the offenders, retelling their foibles forever after.

When growing up in Rose Park, the affordable west-side community developed for veterans returning from World War II, Scarlet and his pals served LDS Sacrament together. That is, after tearing Wonder Bread into small chunks as the body of Christ, the pre-teen Deacons rolled leftovers into tiny spitballs to toss at one another as speakers bore their testimony of the church's truth.

They also played war in and near the sludge ponds created by oil refineries and other dirty industry in the sulfur swamps dividing the Great Salt Lake from the foothills between Salt Lake and Davis counties. Even into adulthood, these playmates simulated war games with toy soldiers and tanks and then camped out with guns in the desert in western Utah. Yet Peter was not a robust outdoorsman. He was soft and thick around the middle, not the kind to get his hands too dirty. His expensive, pressed shirts and slacks came from Brooks Brothers and Cabelas sportswear.

Because Scarlet lived his early *Tribune* years in a Main Street high-rise a few blocks south of downtown, he often took the bus to work. This helped preserve his first pick-up truck, in addition to a couple of subsequent vehicles, in mint condition as long as he lived.

Scarlet's sentimental streak extended to his "affinity" (Scarletism) for old movies with uplifting themes. Among favorites were "Apartment for Peggy" starring a "youthful William Holden," "Cheers for Miss Bishop" and the Claudette Colbert film "Remember the Day." Among the many notes he wrote me over the years was this:

If you are interested in an upbeat, idealized version of the origins of the insurance business, there's "Lloyd's of London," a great Tyrone Power film with fun characters galore in it. I think I also mentioned "Forever Amber," a book-based film that was banned in Boston for I don't know why as Amber loses out in the end. This film, with Linda Darnell in the title role and Cornel Wilde and George Sanders as a fabulous Charles II, has great dialogue in it. Vale.

Scarlet always ended his notes to me that way.

With no girlfriend or wife to return his affections, Scarlet was especially fond of his extended family, his cat and women on his news beats who took him under their wings. His mother was particularly dear to him, and he greatly admired a liberated Mormon aunt who raised a passel of children in Idaho. He also was close to his younger brothers, three of whom died as young men, and for most of his life, to his sister and niece. His brothers' deaths fostered a fatalism that followed Scarlet through his owned shortened life.

* * *

Soon after I entered the newsroom, Woody's respected assistant **Max Knudson** left *The Tribune* for a five-figure salary with the sleazy *National Enquirer*. After discovering that money was no substitute for honor, he returned to Utah as Business Editor for the *Deseret News*. His experience became a lesson to his peers.

* * *

Food Editor Donna Lou Morgan

Another practicing Mormon, **Donna Lou Morgan,** raised five children while fulfilling the dual role of *Tribune* food editor for "34

wonderful years." Her motto was, "I have many more miles before I sleep."[383]

Writing at first under the byline Bonnie Lake, the shapely University of Utah graduate slept only three or four hours a night. Rising well before dawn, she would whip up "tummy tempting tasty treats" at home before putting on makeup, high heels, stylish dress and a bright smile to sweetly greet everyone she met. Some considered her sweetness insincere, but as cynical as I became, I never saw evidence of that.

Denny Green laid out and illustrated a couple of Donna Lou's cookbooks and countless of her weekly food features. Each Christmas, a box of homemade chocolates expressed her appreciation.

Donna Lou didn't let religious strictures discourage her from participating in -- and preparing food for -- the many parties celebrated with other feature writers. At the same time it recognized her co-workers among her "closest and dearest friends," her obituary would someday identify her "family and her membership in The Church of Jesus Christ of Latter-day Saints" as her "most valued treasures."[384]

* * *

Art Deck's secretaries **Shirley Demke Jones** and **Lucy Bodily** were sometimes referred to as the "Relief Society," the LDS women's group assigned to assist the needy. It was no secret that their religion's reputation for honesty helped Shirley and Lucy get their jobs after Deck's previous secretary was caught skimming from the petty cash.

The pair withstood staff cursing and other "vices" with grace and even learned to make coffee to keep the troops going through Election night. The coffee wasn't much good, but it was a helluva lot better than the swill from the coffee machine.

Dennis Green's rendition of Mother Jones.

Having been rejected for a job with U.S. Steel after returning from an LDS mission to Germany, Shirley was "distraught" when hired by *The Tribune* in 1965. It didn't help that she was still single when most Mormon women her age were well into motherhood. But she accepted her fate and even a date with older, non-Mormon staffer Hank McKee. When a handsome younger man of her own faith came along, however, she jumped at the chance for a temple marriage and children.

Bob Woody described her this way:

... [W]e were joined by Shirley Demke, later to become our beloved Mother Jones, confessor, counselor, hand-holder and endearing and enduring and cheerful secretarial survivor of a reign of three managing editors of varying magnitudes of meanness.

More than any she understood the joys, the follies, the frivolities of that tempestuous and tormented assortment of talents and egos in the newsroom. Most of us, sooner or later, with lips trembling and eyes brimming with tears because of some personal misstep or family tragedy, would seek succor from Mother Jones.[385]

"Mother Jones" was *The Tribune* grapevine, spreading gossip nearly as fast as the internet eventually would. This after she pumped each employee for personal information in hushed tones and then dispensed advice for solving their problems. Though usually sweet, supportive and generous, sometimes slipping young staffers money,[386] she could be insulting and even hypocritical as she gulped Coca Colas contrary to her church's prohibition on caffeine.

Shirley waged a sort of power struggle with me, needling me about sensitive issues, which will be related later, and always making me wait for her attention. When I would approach the counter separating her desk from the rest of us, she invariably grabbed the phone for a last-minute call. A simple request for a new reporter's notebook, pen or glue stick, locked in a closet behind her, could drag on for half an hour, deadlines be damned.

Mike Carter saw a better side of our secretary. As a copy boy, it was his job to supply Shirley with Cokes after taking the boss his morning papers and posting American flags outside his front windows. "I fetched a thousand fountain Cokes for her and would fetch a thousand more," he said.[387] "I love Shirley."[388]

And Shirley loved *The Tribune*.

Every one of the staffers was my best friend. I loved every one of them. I had only one fight.

I addressed an invitation to the Christmas Ball to Mr. and Mrs. Douglas Parker. Carole marched in and said, "I am not Mrs. anybody. I am Carol Sisco!" And she started throwing out all the F-words she could think of.

I said, "If you act like a lady, we'll start to treat you like a lady."[389]

Apparently Shirley forgot I'd gone the rounds with her earlier on that issue.

She just couldn't fathom a wife declining her husband's name. "It hurts his self-esteem," she insisted. So when a staffer kept her maiden name, Shirley took it upon herself to change her employee records and insurance forms regardless of the legal ramifications.

Lucy Bodily

Lucy Bodily could be difficult too. She was not shy about suggesting, in her schoolmarm style, that a staffer's expense report was inflated. A request for reimbursement for two hamburgers at the Burger King for a photographer and reporter on a day-long assignment in Park City became grounds for a reprimand. Staffers knew better than to turn in a time slip that called for overtime pay.

When working with Sub for Santa, Lucy sternly demanded to know why applicants didn't have jobs and needed handouts. Yet she let artist Denny Green get away with sneaking up behind her to plant a kiss on her neck.

At her eventual retirement luncheon at Lamb's, she received a world globe. Lance Gudmundsen quipped: "See, Lucy, I told you it was round." Guffaws erupted.

After she left *The Tribune* and became a widow, Lucy proved to be an upbeat, generous mother and friend who never seemed to age. A happy surprise for me.

* * *

Laurene Sowby was another Relief Society "sister" (the Mormon term for female members) on staff. When we first met, she worked part-time with Lucy during Sub-for-Santa season. Later, she took a job with the Information Desk (morgue), often chatting on the phone about church projects. Although Mr. Deck frowned on anyone doing church work on the job -- an artist was fired for reading the Book of Mormon at work[390] -- Laurene managed to get promoted to head librarian when Leah Beckstead retired.

Marilee Higley, a "sister" gone astray, technically was City Desk secretary. However, this Idaho girl spent most afternoons with Harvey Wallbanger before napping on the women's breakroom couch.

* * *

Editorial cartoonist Pat Bagley

To outsiders, **Patrick Bagley** might have seemed mainstream. In Utah, where Mormons toe the church line, he bordered on radical.

The returned missionary son of the mayor of Oceanside, California, was one of three Brigham Young University graduates who became popular political cartoonists in the late 1970s. Cal Grondahl initially set the standard, doodling at the *Deseret News* before finding more compatible quarters at the *Ogden Standard-Examiner*. Steve Benson, grandson of ultra-conservative LDS Apostle Ezra Taft Benson, made a name for himself as a critic of the Right and won a Pulitzer Prize at the *Arizona Republic*.

Mormonism gave the pens of all three an edge that could skewer members of the local culture in their most sensitive places. All three applied for *The Tribune* job in 1978. Will Fehr asked artist Dennis Green to judge their portfolios. Bagley's sense of humor and drawing style won out. The leprechaun look-alike blended in well with the Irish element at the paper.

Bagley studied political science and history before graduating from BYU in 1978. His first published cartoon -- in BYU's *Daily Universe* and *Time Magazine* -- originated as doodling during finance class.[391] Another college effort lampooned BYU's dress code for women. He was drawing caricatures at Orem Mall when he got *The Tribune's* job offer.[392]

Over time, Bagley grew into his role as the sharp, mischievous thorn in the side of the Mormon culture. He was sought after as a public speaker. He produced several cartoon books, which he worked on at the office, and sold T-shirts and memorabilia.

Sometimes I felt his gag lines were a bit obtuse, but the more liberal he became, the better I understood his commentary. Later in his career, he let his hair and beard grow, intensifying his eye-twinkling, impish persona, and his cartoons became increasingly caustic; his Mormon testimony tenuous.

* * *

Gordon Harman was yet another witty Mormon who lost -- or found -- his way at *The Salt Lake Tribune*. Thankfully," he said, "I started working at *The Trib* just in the nick of time to save me from a terrible fate of continuing my religious practice. Being around Mormons all my life made it easy for me to become an atheist.[393]

While still editing Granger High School's student newspaper, Harman wrote stories for *The Tribune's* weekly IN Section. He took a part-time job in the *Tribune* library in August 1971, and before long became one of Jon Ure's copy-boy cadre. It was some time before Ure moved on so that Harman could fill his full-time slot, however, and it was longer still before he advanced to other newsroom jobs, beginning with my old typist position.

Gordon Harman at Halloween.

As a typist, Harman was the first staffer to touch the Harris 1100 paper tape punching machine. The experience was lasting:

> Both Fehr and Mr. Deck saw me fucking with it. The next thing I know I'm down in the composing room, and Norm Carsey is teaching me how to code headlines and body copy and then punch a paper tape that those guys in composing (the "blue room") would run through the photo-optical typesetting machine.[394]

Harman was on his way to becoming chief newsroom computer nerd, a job he held the rest of his career.

Initially, it was Mike Korologos' duty to move the newsroom into the computer age with the cathode ray tube (a Harris 1100), which converted typed copy into coded punch tapes. A three-day session at MIT had introduced him and Dominic Welch to the Harris and exposed them to

"mostly far-out layout concepts on the computer screen."[395] The machine sat north of the City Desk near Keith Otteson and Vard Jones. The tape came in a variety of colors representing different types of stories, such as yellow for news, green for sports, blue and pink for features and business. The high-speed tape winder could cut copy clerks' fingers "down to the bone."[396]

A natural-born nerd, Harman taught himself whatever he could about personal computers and information technology. He took specialized training from vendors who sold tech equipment to *The Tribune*. He also finished a short course in networking from Utah Technical College. Along the way, he managed the newspaper's transition into the use of desk-top computers and the internet for writing stories and pagination for putting pages together. With John J. Jordan in the 1980s, he created Utah Online "from scratch, and as such, I am the grandfather of sltrib.com."[397]

As late as 2018, a slimmed down Harman still was *Tribune* computer systems editor and information technology director.

* * *

Jerry "Radar" Wellman, a wiry, hunched geek from Casper, Wyoming, was fond of law enforcement, radio communications and, like Gordon Harman, newer forms of electronic communications. When the newsroom acquired computers in the early 1980s, Radar was raring for action.

Armed with mass communications courses and an associate degree in police science, Wellman joined the Copy Desk in 1976 and rose in rank to regional editor in 1980. Sitting on one foot, hiking boot and all, he quietly edited copy with one ear cocked toward the police scanner. His thick eye glasses and mousy hair hardly created the impression of a rescue hero, but he did his part with the Civil Air Patrol, where he volunteered expertise in searches and rescues. His AMC Gremlin looked like a porcupine for all its short-wave antennae. Even his wife worked as a cop before a serious fall landed her in a wheelchair and the couple divorced.

In 1983, Wellman's computer skills put him in charge of the paper's data systems, which at first were linked to Newspaper Agency Corp. and even the *Deseret News*. Early on, emails between staffers of the competing papers were forbidden, and it was Wellman's job to plug leaks of confidential information. When he reported policy breaches to the Fourth Floor, which housed the publisher and his entourage, we staffers felt the snitch had violated our privacy and trust. Before long, Wellman transferred to NAC, where he continued to help Gordon Harman and Ben Ling usher *The Tribune* into the digital age.

As the years went on, Wellman found a new wife through an LDS dating service and became an LDS bishop, public safety chaplain and web editor for the *LDS Church News*.[398]

* * *

I've already mentioned **Jon Ure's** deviation from Mormon Church norms, but there is more to come, as they say in this business. **Denny Green** was another staffer loosely connected to the LDS Church. The art director was baptized as a kid but developed doubts when his Sunday School teacher declared his questions devil-inspired. The last straw was the expectation, at age 10, that he portray an angel in a "road show" in order to be a Boy Scout. Artist **Mark Knudsen's** upbringing also was Mormon.

If there were other LDS members on staff in the 1970s, they flew under my radar. Dawn House, Rhonda Hailes, Peggy Fletcher-Stack, Carol VanWagoner and David Noyce were among the faithful to enter the scene later. Most took their minority status in stride and socialized with an irreverent staff at parties and elsewhere.

VanWagoner, who entered the newsroom in 1986, was not bothered by occasional anti-Mormon sentiments after living and working most of her life outside Utah. At least in the beginning, she noticed a healthy, mostly good-natured competition between *The Tribune* and *Deseret News*, as well as a professional and appropriate interest by *The Tribune* in Mormon Church coverage. However, she sensed an attitude change toward the *LDS*

newspaper by the time she returned to teaching in 2001.[399] More on that shift later.

---

[341] Nancy Melich interview March 5, 2014.

[342] Gordon Harman to facebook Tribune group, February 9, 2012.

[343] Ben Ling email to Diane Cole, December 26, 2013.

[344] *Deseret News* obituary, July 4, 1993.

[345] John Keahey to facebook's Tribune group October 31, 2013.

[346] Terry Orme, "Hal Schindler, Journalist and Historian, Dies," *The Salt Lake Tribune*, December 29, 1998, p. C1

[347] Ibid.

[348] Ibid.

[349] Ibid.

[350] Ling, December 26, 2014.

[351] Will Bagley, "So Long, Old Friend," January 2, 1999.

[352] "Death: George Alden (Gus) Sorensen," *Deseret News*, April 12, 1997.

[353] Nutting, February 14, 2014.

[354] Rolly and House, May 16, 2005.

[355] Melich, March 5, 2014.

[356] Raine, December 28, 2013.

[357] Dave Jonsson email, August 10, 2015.

[358] *Deseret News*, April 12, 1997.

[359] Jacobsen-Wells, August 2, 2015.

[360] Raine email, February 16, 2014.

361 Dave Jonsson email, August 10, 2015.

362 Ibid.

363 Ibid.

364 Ibid.

365 Gordon Harman, October 8, 2015.

366 Robert Bryson email, August 4, 2015.

367 Ibid.

368 Robert Bryson email, July 31, 2015.

369 Robert Bryson email, August 9, 2015.

370 Ibid.

371 Todd Zagorec, "Thunder Over Zion: The Life of Chief Judge Willis W. Ritter by Parker Nielson and Patricia Cowley," Utah State Bar, July 1, 2007.

372 Bryson, August 4, 2015.

373 Ibid.

374 Ibid.

375 Bryson, August 9, 2015.

376 Paul Rolly and JoAnn Jacobsen-Wells, *The Salt Lake Tribune*, December 31, 2004.

377 JoAnn Jacobsen-Wells email, August 2, 2015.

378 Rolly & Wells, *The Salt Lake Tribune*, December 31, 2004.

379 Ibid.

380 Ibid.

381 Ibid.

382 Ibid.

383 Obituary: Donna Lou Archibald Morgan, *Deseret News*, October 16, 2003.

384 Obituary: Donna Lou Archibald Morgan, *Deseret News*, October 16, 2003.

385 Woody, August 23, 1995.

386 Chris Jorgensen to Tribune facebook group March 1, 2012.

387 Mike Carter to Tribune facebook group May 6, 2013.

388 Mike Carter to Tribune facebook group February 16, 2012.

389 Shirley Jones phone interview November 14, 2014.

390 Dennis Green conversation, November 25, 2015.

391 Wikipedia.

392 Ibid.

393 Harman, October 8, 2015.

394 Ibid.

395 Mike Korologos, January 26, 2014.

396 Gordon Harman to Tribune facebook group, February 9, 2012.

397 Ibid.

398 Deseret News website, July 19, 2015.

399 Carol VanWagoner email, August 10, 2015..

9 - Art Department Antics

Dennis Green

Mark Knudsen's drawing of Denny.

Just a few feet from the Copy Desk, behind a grimy, dilapidated vinyl couch, sat scrawny, shaggy-headed **Denny Green**, who became art director at the tender age of 27 in 1970. His blond hair and goatee partially covered the smooth, round face of a youngster.

Denny had been on the brink of quitting for more money painting signs for a grocery chain when his boss, Hans Christian "Chris" Jensen, urged him to stick around long enough to replace him. Denny looked up to Jensen, a kind Mormon who created *Sunday Magazine's* "Sheepherder Sam" cartoon from his days in sheep camps around Ephraim. So he took his advice and got the promotion. He also kept in touch with his mentor, who continued painting, illustrating the LDS *Children's Friend* and demonstrating drawing in public schools before losing most of his sight to macular degeneration. His painting of a snowy field in shadows became one of Denny's prized possessions. Jensen was 93 when he died February 2, 1995.

As featured staffer in *Tribune Topix* March 8, 1972, Denny claimed he got his job in 1963 with Howell and White, a graphics subcontractor absorbed by *The Tribune*, because he couldn't add or spell and there wasn't much else for him to do. Tossing his head to the side to get his scraggly hair out of his eyes, the University of Utah Art School graduate further alleged to have taken just enough journalism classes to "know that wasn't for me." He'd been drawing since age 7, he said, when his rendition of a little neighbor girl melted his crayon. He still enjoyed drawing nudes even though drawings of little kids paid more. Finally, he recounted picking up his wife at Liberty Park and becoming a father a few months later.

This embellisher laid double entendres on any woman venturing into his corner of the newsroom squeezed between the men's restroom, coffee machine, Photography Department and Copy Desk. Sometimes he sneaked nasty or funny drawings into illustrations and cartoons for publication. If readers looked hard and long enough, they might find a copulating couple hidden among vines and tree branches. His staff caricatures often appeared in print, and Brian Nutting, for one, appreciated the effort.

You don't need me to tell you all the strange and wonderful things that the Art Department did. Really, the only official contact with those guys I had was when they were retouching a photo. But all the unofficial things I noticed. It seems they were impervious to all the management decrees and rules. I loved it that they seemed to have such an attitude – caring a lot for their art but not at all for conforming to the big shots' wishes! One of my favorites was when Denny insinuated some weird stuff into his drawing. The drawing was so intricate and involved I don't know if the big cheeses ever spotted his sabotage.[400]

Even though my desk was fewer than 15 feet from Denny's drawing table, I paid him little mind. His banter seemed good-natured enough, but I was wary of perverts on the prowl. If I'd thought twice about it, I would have seen from his family's office visits -- his two blonde daughters crawled all over him with Shirley's suckers sideways in their mouths -- that his raunchy remarks were all a show.

As director, Denny managed three other artists. All four of them laid out cover stories and drew illustrations for the *Sunday Magazine* and the Lifestyle, IN and the Art sections. They also retouched photos and drew maps, charts and cartoons for all departments. Denny did the "grunt work" along with everyone else but at twice the speed.

One of Denny's company Christmas cards.

Newspapering was in Denny's blood. His Uncle Earl Green sold ads for the *Deseret News* in the 1920s, and Aunt Mabel Gibby did secretarial work for Salt Lake Engraving, the contractor that produced hot-metal illustration plates for *The Tribune* and its afternoon counterpart, *The Telegram*, before the two combined in 1952. Salt Lake Engraving hired Denny's father, Harold William "Bill" Green, for

an apprenticeship during World War II, when accounting jobs were scarce for new college graduates like him.

Bill sometimes took home lead Linotype blanks (used for column spacing), which his young son Denny once melted into a toy canon to shoot through a neighbor's garage door. Some of his engravings became Denny's collectibles. When engraving became obsolete in the 1970s, NAC created production quality-control jobs for Bill Green and his buddy John Morgan. That's when I first met the gentlemanly fellow.

Bill Green in engraving.

Though his paternal grandparents were Mormon converts from England, Denny's immediate family had little use for the church. Grandfather William Green had been stuck in England on a mission in 1898 when his first three children sickened and died from small pox, leaving his wife alone to grieve.[401] The tragedy never set well with the subsequent children who survived. In fact, Denny reveled in his aunt's recollections of his grandmother and great-grandmother, as members of the LDS Relief Society, burning bills of lading for booze and tobacco carted across the plains by Mormon pioneers. Mormons employed revisionist history to hide early members' drinking habits, he liked to say.

* * *

Mark Knudsen started as a copy boy at *The Tribune* the same day as George Raine and not long after Denny joined Howell and White in 1963. The hook-nosed, curly-headed guy would bounce in his clogs across the office to happily deliver his work where it was due.

Knudsen saw life from a slightly slanted perspective. His off-the-wall line-drawings came with unexpectedly strange, subtle gags. When asked a question, he would pause, look off into the distance and carefully formulate a response. Having studied English and stayed abreast of current events, he usually could be counted on for a meaningful answer.

Knudsen lived with wife Cathy and precocious son Ollie in a small, tastefully decorated bungalow northeast of Sugarhouse. Depression among relatives, a hearing loss and divorce caused Knudsen anguish over the years, but he always pursued his art with a passion, becoming recognized for his desert landscapes after retiring in 2004 and marrying another artist.

Knudsen herded artist Neil Passey, a talented but troubled product of the Sixties, and photographer Tim Kelly in the prolonged production of <u>Utah: Gateway to Nevada!</u>[402] The silly, cartoony paperback testifies to his satirical wit. His own description:

> We had an absurd little riff on the best places to get a lube job along the Wasatch Front. A photo of [*Tribune* photographer] Paul Fraughton standing in front of an auto repair shop in a tux, brandishing a grease gun illustrated. The text was " . . . and for that late evening after the symphony lube job, it's Scampi's, of course."[403]

It took years for the threesome to finish the book while working full time to support their young families, and it's clear from the content that Knudsen did the heavy lifting. The introduction, "from the desk of j. crawlspace III," promises an off-beat ride:

> *You anxiously scan the pages of your Rand McNally on the seat beside you. Desperate computations and alternative routes are carefully considered before the awful reality sets in: the fastest way to get from Colorado to Nevada takes you through terra incognita -- Utah; and like a modern day Magellan, through Utah you must go. Literally dozens of ill-advised and*

ill-fated travelers yearly reach this inescapable conclusion.[404]

1970s Art Department Dennis Green, Mark Knudsen, Conehead Mike Korologos, Sam Smith and Neil Passey (clockwise from front left).

* * *

Neil Passey, the "most talented artist" Denny Green had ever met, could spontaneously draw an anatomically perfect human figure by starting at the fingertip.

Neil Passey with Anne Wilson on Halloween.

The wiry, ragged artist with dilated pupils resembled Charles Manson, pre-murder fame, but their personalities were nothing alike. Passey was a shy, kind pussy cat to Manson's violent viper.   That didn't stop him from suggesting I pose nude for him, however.   I bristled.

Passey wrote and illustrated his first book, "Crusher the Whale," at age 6,[405] and graduated from Cypress High School as a Sterling Scholar in 1968.   He took art classes at the University of Utah and Utah State University before joining *The Tribune* in 1969. Like me, he was still wet behind the ears.

Unlike me, he inhabited the counterculture, dabbling in drugs and dawdling at his drawing table while still stoned. Yet he had a daughter to support and always held an establishment job. Denny Green helped him keep the one at *The Tribune,* even sometimes attending after-hours hashish sessions at Passey's Finch Gallery apartment near the U.

Passey was notorious for missing freelance deadlines. When swamped or bored, he simply shifted to new projects. His apartment was cluttered with half-finished paintings. Nevertheless, he became a leading poster artist of the period, illustrating advertisements for concerts and calendars for Cosmic Aeroplane, the local head shop and bookstore run by Steve Jones.

Catalyst Magazine's July 2014 cover featured Passey's best-known poster, known as Blue Lady and Cosmic Lady, and described him as "one of the most prolific artists in Salt Lake City from the late 1960s and '70s." His posters featured groups like Frank Zappa and The Doors; his art advertised "hip and counterculture establishments of the day."[406]

Summum, a local "church" featuring wine, pyramids and sex, initially commissioned Blue Lady as a bald, blue woman floating above a spaceship and pyramid. Passey labored over the job, getting his model to strike an especially uncomfortable pose, as church founder Corky Ra (aka Claude R. Knowell) ordered one revision after another.   Deadline after deadline passed until Passey declared, "Fuck it!"   He added flowing hair and replaced the pyramid with a Greek temple.   Cosmic Aeroplane bought the painting, which it called Cosmic Lady, for its 1978 calendar.[407]

Passey left *The Tribune* on positive terms in 1978 to become art director for Salt Lake

County's Hansen Planetarium, and he eventually took a similar job with Griffith Park Observatory. Los Angeles was tough on this diminutive substance abuser.

Neil Passey's best-known poster.

At an ATM one night, two thieves broke his limbs, and the shattered shell of a man withdrew with a bottle to a ghost town in California's Mojave desert.   Ashen like a ghost himself, Passey wobbled with a cane into a retrospective of his work in the early 1990s at Finch Lane Gallery at the Art Barn. Tears percolated from his eyes when he realized so many Utahns still cared about him. In December 1995, his liver burst from cirrhosis as he boarded a plane for home. He was just 45.

* * *

His art director title didn't give Denny Green any say in hiring -- or firing -- **Sam Smith,** his biggest headache.

The   Navy veteran from the Northwest presented himself to Art Deck as a triple play: He could draw, write and take photos.   When it became clear that the gluttonous guy -- he consumed an entire package of Oreos and gallon of ice cream in one sitting -- had oversold himself, Deck prohibited further publication of his illustrations. Photos and reporting never came into play.

So, Smith specialized in the weather map and photo-retouching, menial tasks performed Sundays when no other artists wanted to work. But even that shred of usefulness came into question when City Desk editors found no artist for a breaking story on Sunday and called Denny into work. Denny finally found Sam selling caricatures at Trolley Square on *Tribune* time. Because Deck had done the hiring and *Tribune* higher-ups did little firing, Sam continued to take up space in the Art Department.

* * *

There also was a female artist, **Susan Jacobsen**, who worked part time in the department while attending the University of Utah. Bound for a fine arts career, Susie Sweet Cheeks didn't stick around. However, Denny developed a "soft" spot for her, and the two exchanged their own artistic renditions of the mighty rhinoceros as a token of affection, a token Denny never let go.

* * *

Tim Brinton, left; Mark Knudsen and Rhonda Hailes, right.

After Passey quit *The Tribune*, Denny put **Tim Brinton**, a strawberry blond street tough from West High, to work. "Working?" Brinton said after quitting himself in 1983 to go it lone, "that was a sweet job that never felt like work, and I was foolish to leave it."[408] By then he had moved from Southern California to Texas as an independent illustrator for newspapers, including *The Tribune's* editorial pages in the 1990s.

When replacing Brinton, Denny was drawn to the creative portfolio of **Rhonda Hailes**, a Utah

State University graduate living with her parents in Holladay near Denny's parents. Her drawing table stood just outside the men's lavatory, and on her first day, Denny joked that it was her job to check the men's pants to make sure they were zipped up. Her eyes widened. "Really?!"

Gullible Rhonda had a heart of gold and talent to spare, but there were days when Denny wondered what he'd done by hiring her. Headstrong, she asked a lot of questions about assignments and then argued over his answers. Her perfectionism and dithering often put her up against deadlines, something the short-staffed Art Department could not afford. Her compulsions also led to years of indecision about getting married, so she stayed single longer than the average Mormon girl. Ultimately, she married a Mormon artist from the *Deseret News* and became one of my good friends.

Steve Baker

Given the chance to add a fifth artist to his staff, Denny chose **Steve Baker**, a talented, technically trained designer/illustrator from Arkansas who clerked at a convenience store to get by. Thinking about it years later, he remarked:

> Steve was probably my best hire. He was not only a talented artist, he had a great attitude and was a pleasure to work with. His greatest strength was his sense of graphic design (layout), and his illustrations improved over time. I'd give him an illustration or layout design, and he'd always come up with a better idea than I did.[409]

The downsides? Possibly his playful friendship with photographer Dan Miller, who would race up and down the room giggling like a little girl, and his frequent smoking breaks once the practice finally was banned from the newsroom.

* * *

Decorated by artists and other staffers influenced by the likes of counterculture cartoonist R. Crumb, **The Art Department Pillar** became the bane of humorless Editor Art Deck, who passed it several times a day on his way to and from the men's room. No sooner would Deck rip down and ditch the flippant concoctions in the nearby trash barrel and issue another memo forbidding future postings than a new array of the flotsam materialized.

One of Denny's own submissions had secretary Shirley Jones sitting on the lap of boss Art Deck over the caption: "Me and Mrs. Jones . . . We got a thing goin' on." The gag was that these two, one a Mormon mother and the other a stern, non-Mormon recluse, were as likely to get together as me and Robert Redford.

A series of discarded drawings focused on artist Sam Smith's broken glasses, which in reality were taped at the bridge of his nose. Half sheets of scratch paper showed nails driven through the lenses into his eyes, elaborate engineering structures supporting the glasses from his head and shoulders, screws into his ears.

"We did our best work when it wasn't for publication," according to Denny.[410]

A lofty quote from *Tribune* art critic George Dibble hung on The Pillar for ages, coming out occasionally in conversations for years afterward: "The lack of chiaroscuro leaves little to caprice." Another favorite, from a Utah cheesemaker, opined: "How high you aspire is the limit of your achievement in this country."[411]

Knudsen carried detailed memories of The Pillar in his head well into retirement. He really got going with this treatise on an obviously fond topic:

The large red pillar located in the middle of the Art Department became a bulletin board of the absurd, and a no-holds-barred institution that lasted from the late Sixties until the Art Department moved to the mezzanine -- 20 years or more.

Messages of every sort, usually rendered on a newsprint half-sheet, were posted. Although it was mostly an Art Department thing, everyone was welcome, and dozens of staffers from every department participated. Cartoons, prose, poetry, rants and doctored photography were the staples of The Pillar, but anything could and did pop up there.

An early one then: A promotion photo showing Mike Korologos and a group of seven- and eight-year-olds, all in Indian headgear, shooting pool at a play-size table. The caption reads, "Only a fool would take a white woman into Indian country."

Written as a thank-you note to management for the yearly gift of the *Tribune* ham, the anonymous writer describes how he has carved a pair of shoes for his kid from the ham. A line drawing shows toddler shoes carved from ham.

A mug-shot of Don Brooks, the crusty outdoors editor, was retouched to give him shoulder-length salt and pepper locks. Don noticed it on his way out of the men's room, looked at it for a moment, looked at Denny, Neil, myself, shook his head and said, "Fucking hippies." He walked away trying but failing to conceal his amusement.

Then there was "The East Side of Mexico." It started with a simple cartoon drawing of a donkey, maybe a few cactus in the background. The caption read, "A wise old donkey on the East Side of Mexico." It was a sensation. Everyone got into the act. There were poems, flash fiction, critiques and more cartoons. One that I recall was of a donkey sniffing some golf clubs. The caption: "A pro-shop on the East Side of Mexico."

A two- or three-page cartoon strip began with an ordinary-looking woman driving on a lonely road at night. She sees a sign in large letters that reads, "EAT." She sees another, then another, then pulls into a diner, enters and orders. A cascading orgy of gluttony ensues. Bratwursts, parfaits, a side of pig, corn dogs. She finally escapes, resumes her lonely drive and sees another sign in the same bold letters. It reads, "SEX."

The drawing is of a young woman doing gymnastics on the glass barrier between customers and bank tellers. The caption reads, "The teller is balancing."

"Bun-form Hi-Top Galoshes" was another offering that got a lot of participation from the newsroom. It began as a riff on the old cartoon-style, muscle-building ad that we used to see in places like *Popular Mechanics*. Bullies kick sand in the face of the underdeveloped wimp on the beach. A few panels later, he is back wearing shiny Bun-form Hi-Top Galoshes, surrounded by admiring girls saying things like, "Cool galoshes, guy!" The bullies are sulking in the background. A slick, Mad-Ave take on the theme was, "My car, Aston Martin. My galoshes, Bun-form."

There was a drawing of a garter snake with an Elvis-style pompadour. Near the bottom of the drawing is a small driver's license with a Dick Tracy-style arrow informing us that it is "Fake I.D." The caption reads, "Snake preparing to cruise for burgers."

Lots of poetry found its way to the pillar. The only one that I remember was a bovine tribute:

Of all the folks
  I ever knew,
The very best
  Could only moo.

Bill's Penis was a series of 15 or 16 single-panel cartoons of a nondescript, middle-aged guy, expressionless and facing front. One had a tag that read, "Bill's Penis comments on Man's inhumanity to Man." A thought balloon coming out of the crotch area (Bill's penis speaking) said, "I think we should all be nicer to one another." The idea of a guy whose brain has been completely taken over by his penis seemed to resonate with a lot of *Tribune* women. Andrea Otanez said, "I think it's just perfect!"

There were many limericks. I remember one:

A downbeat and frustrated nomad
Was stuck with the surname of Gonad.
  Embarrassed, confessed he,
  My friends call me Teste,
And sometimes it just makes me so mad.

The only survivor from the palindrome project is, "Did I sit on Otis? I did."

I recall a carefully rendered drawing of the interior of the Lincoln Memorial with Abe looming above. Carved into the marble below in Palatino caps was the phrase, "NOBODY LIKES A SMART-ASS."

In the early days of The Pillar, Art Deck would wander by on his way to the men's room, peruse The Pillar, and often take a few of the offerings down and throw them in the garbage. Passey and I would fly into action and have them re-posted before Art re-emerged. He would peer at The Pillar, notice the restoration, smile sort of, and saunter off, jiggling his keys and peering over his half-glasses.

We were kids. We didn't understand what a generous, large-hearted place *The Salt Lake Tribune* was way back then.

Contributors to this little selection include Dennis Green, Neil Passey, Tim Brinton, Tim Kelly, Robert Triptow, Tom Judd, myself and unknown others.[412]

[400] Nutting, February 14, 2014.

[401] "Laid to Rest," *Deseret News*, February 7, 1898.

[402] Tim Kelly, Neil Passey, Mark Knudsen, Utah: Gateway to Nevada! Dream Garden Press, 1984.

[403] Mark Knudsen email, February 25, 2014.

[404] Tim Kelly, Neil Passey, Mark Knudsen, *UTAH Gateway to Nevada!* 1984.

[405] Neil Passey, saltlakeconcertposters.com.

[406] "On the Cover," *Catalyst Magazine*, July 2014, Vol. 33, No. 7, p4.

[407] Ken Sanders Rare Books, July 11, 2014 website posting,

[408] Tim Brinton on facebook, July 30, 2015.

[409] Dennis Green, August 29, 2015.

[410] Dennis Green's recollections, February 25, 2014.

[411] Mark Knudsen email, March 26, 2016.

[412] Mark Knudsen email to Diane Cole, February 25, 2014.

10 - The Sexual Revolution

When I tiptoed into *The Tribune* in 1972, journalism was evolving from a male-oriented, paternalistic business into an enterprise that grudgingly tolerated women and sometimes even made clumsy attempts to accommodate them. But women remained a distinct minority, lacked respect and endured outright harassment and discrimination. Sex abuse was ignored. Though discouraged, dating occurred between employees. It was understood that if staffers married, the junior member of the pair, the woman, would be looking elsewhere for work. So at first, I kept my attraction to men at work hidden, assuming it would only hurt my future on the job.

The few women writers and editors in the early days worked on the so-called "women's pages," first named the Society and Fashion section, then For Women and finally, Lifestyle.

When the company moved to 143 S. Main in the late 1930s, according to Jack Gallivan, there were just two . . .

. . . *lady members of the news staff. Grace Grether and Beatrice "Mother" McCrea sat in comfortable bright space near the windows at the southwest corner of the newsroom. They produced the pages to be edited of special interest to women. McCrea was society editor, Grether wrote fashion but helped with high society notes.*[413]

The publisher further recalled a gala at Fort Douglas in which Grether quoted a "handsome colonel" regarding the guest of honor's gown: "I haven't seen anything like that since I was weaned." Apparently such a racy quote got into print because the editor was taking one of his rare days off.

Laying on the alliteration, Bob Woody reported joining the staff in 1957 . . .

. . . when Grace Grether dictated the delicacies of prestige, privilege, perquisites and propriety as grand dame of the Society Page, aided by one-time USU cheerleader Hazel Parkinson . . . Carolyn Monson was the office sprite who answered the phone.[414]

If a woman's virtue was tarnished back then, it became legendary.

In the 1960s, for example, an attractive female writer hoping to woo back a boyfriend posed nude for a City Desk cohort who supposedly "wouldn't show them to anyone," Mike Korologos recounted. "Her reputation was cemented."[415] Later, while Korologos napped in the basement vault where old editions of the newspaper and slush (back-up materials for stories) were kept, he witnessed a tryst involving that same "attractive damsel." When a female writer of teen news was caught dancing at a burlesque-type bar busted by the cops, her personal story survived her.[416]

Pregnancy was a constant fear among early women staffers., who would be fired once a pregnancy began to show.[417]

"Mr. Deck was uncomfortable around pregnant women," according to Carolyn Monson. "He was afraid that somehow they would get hurt."

More likely, as elsewhere in society then, the men in charge considered public pregnancy unseemly.

Hazel Parkinson, a former college cheerleader my mother's age who wrote women's features and later covered parties of the local elite, was the first woman to carry her baby full term on the job. Although most of Donna Lou Morgan's work hours were spent in one kitchen or another, she raised five children during 34 years as food editor.

By 1977, *The Tribune's* personnel handbook dictated that hospital maternity benefits covered up to $150 for any one pregnancy and then "only to a married person."[418] Staffers paid a $600 deductible for each delivery.

When Terri Ellefsen and Roger Graves, a *Tribune* couple, had their second child by cesarean section in the early 1980s, the policy had progressed to the point where Graves got three days off with pay while Ellefsen did not. Editor Will Fehr's obviously smart-ass explanation: In the old days, women had their babies and went right back to work. Ellefsen's retort: "If I had lived in the old days, I would have died."[419]

* * *

Barbara "Barbi" Fauch Robison Ellefsen managed "women's news" for decades.

Despite having begun her journalism career writing sports news in Caldwell, Idaho, and LeGrand, Oregon, she couldn't get a sports job at *The Tribune* because Deck claimed there were no women's sports. "Never mind that I was a stringer for men's sports for years!" she scoffed.

Barbi settled for a job writing bridal announcements in 1958 and worked her way up to head of so-called Society news, a job she inherited from a man.[420] That man, Bob Blair, explained years later that it was "the fashion of the day" for men to manage women's pages.[421]

Barbi Robison and Carolyn Monson in 1970s.

Though an unapologetic feminist, Barbi admitted to putting up with some discrimination because she needed work. *The Tribune* earned her loyalty by looking out for its people.

When appointed Society editor in 1970, Mr. Deck directed her, unlike her male predecessor, to report to *Sunday Magazine* editor Roy Hudson rather than to him directly. Barbi agreed but proceeded to go to Deck whenever she needed something. After a year or so, "he got used to it."

Sometimes the sexism was almost comical. A female staffer would receive a rose on her birthday while men got bottles of Jack Daniels. Sometimes the inequity worked in a woman's favor. Deck gave Barbi a year off to work on her marriage. **Carolyn Monson**, the City Desk secretary hired in 1956 and promoted to fashion writer three years later, got the same benefit.

Society news -- bridal, fashion, food and decorating -- was clearly geared to women and was anything but democratic from 1963 to 1970, when **Bob Blair** headed up the the section. He'd field phone calls every Monday from mothers upset at the treatment of their daughters, who normally received a one-column photo.[422] If the bride expected better news play, she had to be a college graduate, a member of a sorority or the relative of a local bigwig or *Tribune* editor -- or she had to hire professional photographers Gill & Lignell.

While women's editor, Blair rented a cheap room at Little Hotel overlooking Main Street where he'd take naps, play bridge and serve his female staff mint juleps.[423] Once when he failed to show up at home as promised, his wife Alice dumped several of their dozen kids on him while he was entertaining his female troops in Little Hotel.[424]

Mrs. Blair liked that room nonetheless. Not only was it a great place for their children to view Christmas and Pioneer Day parades, it gave her a place to escape those kids for an evening. She and Bob would sometimes cook a steak on the balcony and people-watch. Carolyn Monson's husband eventually used the apartment to store clothing samples.

Carolyn credited Bob Blair, who regarded her as his Lorelei, with teaching her to write news by advising her to write a story like she would tell it to a friend. She had panicked when Art Deck assigned her, still a secretary, to interview mine-disaster survivors. Editors often used this sink-or-swim method to see what employees could do.

Barbi and Carolyn broke ground at *The Tribune*. Barbi was the first female to take the company car on a road trip; Carolyn made multiple trips alone to New York City for fashion shows. "But, of course, it was all about advertising," Barbi explained. "Makoff's, Adrian and Emily's and Jak's Bridal Arts did a lot of fashion advertising then." As did ZCMI, the Paris and Auerbach's, dress shops I could better afford.

* * *

Upbeat, easy-going **Judy Bea Rollins**, the Montana graduate who caught Doug Parker's eye, was one of the few women who wrote on the news side before joining the Society "girls." She became the first editor of the IN section designed to lure young readers as circulation sagged. After replacing Barbi as head of that department years later, she eventually became the first female deputy editor.

Judy B. Rollins

Other women on the features side of the newsroom in the mid-1970s were Judy Magid, Hazel Parkinson, Bernie Moss on home decorating, Susan Glassman on *Sunday Magazine*, Nancy Melich on theater arts and Robbie Bird, who replaced Judy Rollins on teen news. After proving they could write, my contemporaries Helen Forsberg and Ann Kilbourn moved from the library into dance and other hobby features.

I've already introduced the handful of my contemporaries who infiltrated the news side of *The Tribune* in the 1970s: Vandra Huber, Angelyn Nelson, Janice Clark, Lidia Wasowicz and Cindy Gilchrist on the Copy Desk; JoAnn Jacobsen and Barbara Springer on City Desk. Irene Jones also reported for City Desk, and before the end of the decade, Terri Ellefsen and Mary Dickson were answering the call of "Boy!" in the newsroom.

* * *

Darlene Galbraith was one of several women who got stories into *The Tribune* by working as stringers paid by the inch. A woman of many talents, from teaching elementary school and writing poetry to playing concert piano and flying airplanes -- she was the first woman to fly a military jet out of Hill Air Force Base[425] -- Darlene took photos and wrote stories part-time from Ogden and Davis counties for 25 years. Her son Ryan followed in her footsteps when he became a full-time staff photographer years later.

Another effective female stringer was **Denise Wheeler** of Evanston, Wyoming. She covered the entire area from Summit County, Utah, to Wyoming and helped me gain access to John Singer when I became a reporter.

* * *

I was so naive and accustomed to chauvinism in Utah by the time I joined the staff in 1972 that I didn't initially perceive how pervasive and entrenched it was at *The Tribune*. In my internship report, I acknowledged that prejudice against women in the newsroom was evident, but I guessed it was because of poor performance on the part of a few bad peaches. I planned, according to my school assignment, to try reporting someday if women were permitted on the desk in greater numbers. If not, I wrote, "I'll use *The Tribune* as a stepping stone to other publications as other young staffers have done."

The Tribune's transition to gender equality was often two steps forward, one back.

Women in the early 1970s were required to wear dresses to work, but with special permission, a pants suit would suffice. *Sunday Magazine's* Susan Glassman introduced mini-skirts to the newsroom, and reporter Barbara "Babs" Springer became the first staffer barred from Brigham Young University's campus for hers. As already noted, men like Deano Halliday made no effort to disguise leers and jeers when a shapely woman entered the newsroom.

Again, Woody weighs in.

The times were a changin', and Herb Price wrote memos trying to define an appropriate length and shape of the pantsuit females were just beginning to wear to the office. But it turned out the dress-code memo had the life cycle of a Roe vs. Wade trimester. To the delight of Mooney and other lusters and leerers such as I, we were joined by such as JoAnn Fifi Jacobsen and Nancy Melich in tight pants or mini-skirts and of course the leggy Barbara Springer in hot pants and the bouncy Helen Forsberg and the irreverent Anne Wilson.[426]

Putting Herb Price, NAC's glad-handing general manager, in charge of the female dress code was a farce. His winning wit and kindness aside, Herb openly ogled young women inside the office and out.

Whether women staffers, comprising just 10 percent of the newsroom, relished or resented their sexist reception from such male personnel, they usually put up with it. They certainly didn't complain to the boss. They so rarely resisted, in fact, that incidents like Babs Springer's jab to Otteson's crotch became legendary.

A tongue-in-cheek *Tribune* editorial about the trend of women wearing pants touched a nerve when I was proof-reading on the Copy Desk one night. I scribbled out my outrage with no intention of actually submitting it to the Editorial Page:

> We women "near the City Desk of this newspaper" (all 12 of us) apparently missed the point of "Pants Play," your editorial of Oct. 12. Our "girlish logic" prevents our seeing the editorial logic to devoting eight wide inches of news space to this provoking piece of pap. Did the "reckless soul" who questioned our "feminist wiles" actually intend to imply that all women don nightgowns and dresses out of comfort and their submission to men -- a role they secretly crave? And that they put on their pants and pajamas to assert their power over men -- only during business hours, of course? We assume the author's snide remarks were meant to be amusing. That assumption, along with the realization he was more intent upon stacking literary cliches than writing for content, leaves us with no hard feelings. We're simply sorry current political issues aren't stimulating enough to merit more concentration.

Supposedly urging sensitivity to sexism, the author of the monthly house organ *Tribune Topix* (Mike Korologos) didn't really get it. In March 1972, *Topix* criticized a Split Page picture of a U.S. postal worker for "uninterestingly" holding up new plastic bags used to speed special delivery mail. It would have been much better, Korologos advised, to have a "cute gal kneeling down among many of the bags" while stuffing mail into one.[427]

Korologos woke up briefly in May, when he tweaked the Sports Desk for failing to run a story on the Dinah Shore Golf Tournament despite the nationally televised event offering the biggest payday ever for women golfers.[428] His

wife Myrlene must have said something about the slight.

In March, *Topix* published this offensive yet ground-breaking note from a staffer:

> *Steve Bond and I (Thom Bluemel), foreseeing the need for another copy boy, have collaborated and decided that, in the interest of this newspaper, the opening should be filled, if at all possible, with one of the fair sex, preferably over 18, intelligent, and in all other respects a compliment to her sex. We feel that this addition to the staff would serve several purposes: a) It would eliminate strife and conflict with the women's liberation movement; b) It would boost copy boy morale; c) It would well illustrate the contemporary thinking of the promotion department; and d) It would show that the Tribune management is well aware of its staff's needs and desires for the utmost in working conditions (to improve our efficiency, of course). By the way, it wouldn't hurt if she were good-looking.*

Then, in an historic step forward two months later, Korologos' newsletter announced the ranks of "office boys" had been "infiltrated" by Bernice Martinez, "a mod, 22-year-old East High grad." Korologos congratulated Bernice on being "the first office girl at *The Tribune* as of 2:30 p.m. May 2, 1972. And we'll have no more bellowing of 'BOY, COPY,' if you please." Lest there be too much progress, Otteson continued to yell "boooyyyy!" without looking up when he needed a "copy clerk," the new politically correct term.

And now for another step backward: The same *Topix* edition noted:

> *Since the once-called Women's section was changed to Lifestyle, the gals in that department have been super sensitive when called the "women's department." How come, then, in Judy Rollins' five-part series on rape, did her byline read: By Judy Rollins, assistant women's editor? Ahha. I gotcha.*[429]

Do I detect a tiny bit of resentment there?

* * *

These were the days leading to the introduction of the Equal Rights Amendment (ERA) to the Utah Legislature in 1973. I was especially excited by the prospect of equal pay for equal work and access to better jobs. But of course the measure was quickly shot down with the help of the Hot Doggers, a group of women from rural Aurora, Utah. When resurrected two years later, the ERA's rejection was even more dramatic, this time spurred by a *Deseret News* editorial.

Yet neither failure compared to the brouhaha of 1977, when Utah held its version of the International Women's Year (IWY) Conference in the Salt Palace. Organizers expected 800 participants, they got 13,000. Most were Mormon women answering the church's call to kill "anti-family" proposals on abortion, day care and working women. It made no difference that 41.4 percent of Utah women held jobs in 1970; 50.4 percent in 1979. Protesters' jaws were set and debates loud and illogical. Every IWY resolution for reform died, but *Network* magazine was born to promote issues important to Utah's working women for years afterward.

Terri Ellefsen

Women regularly slammed into a glass ceiling during my tenure at *The Tribune,* and I later would confront my share of barriers to advancement. **Terri Ellefsen**, hired a couple of years after me, found a way around the company's chauvinism. But change required ambition, determination and time.

When hired in the 70s, editors still hollered "Boy!" to get Ellefsen's attention.

Before she moved onto the typist desk six months later, she was increasingly summoned with, "Copy!" In another three months, Ellefsen was reporting. She discovered right away that:

> Women were, in essence, barred from advancing into the topmost position at the paper because of an unwritten rule: Executive Editor was open to those who served as city editor. That position was likewise open to those who worked the night police job. Women were not allowed to work the NIPO job because of a so-called safety factor.
>
> It was disconcerting to realize that "the good old boys" network at *The Tribune* created an inequity for any woman wanting to advance her career. I believe it was my consternation with that thought that ultimately led me on a journey to find another way to move up into the editor ranks.[430]

Despite Ellefsen's efforts, which eventually would bear fruit, the glass ceiling remained intact for Kathy Kapos, who joined *The Tribune* on her 18th birthday in September 1982. Her first job was clerking in the library, where she answered phones, filed photos and news clippings and indexed information on Rolodexes. Next she typed for the newsroom until invited to write for weekly zoned tabloids, where she wrote for a couple of years. After graduating from the U. of U., she became the first female "zone czar" (editor).

> I had been the editor for at least a year when Will Fehr promoted two different male reporters -- Vince Horiuchi and Jess Gomez -- ahead of me. They were hired after me but went from zones to the night cops . . . a job they didn't want to give me because they didn't want me working late at night. It wasn't until 1989 that I was finally moved to City Desk to be the higher education reporter.[431]

There was a legitimate concern for women -- and even men -- walking outside the *Tribune* building or elsewhere in the city at night. I was regularly approached by beggars on my way to my car after work. At least one rape had occurred in the parking terrace on Regent Street, and the wife of a staffer had been attacked in the alley behind our loading dock.[432] Two punks had tried to mug Gordon Harman and reporter Tom Baldwin in the alley, too, but Baldwin had punched one in the face, making him collapse "like a sack of potatoes."[433]

Maybe male staffers had a better chance of overpowering attackers, but night police was no more dangerous than beats like general assignment, education or arts criticism. Meetings, shows and concerts often stretched past 10 p.m., requiring female reporters to walk the streets in the dark. At least on NIPO, there were cops around for protection.

The Tribune was simply tied to a tradition that treated women differently -- a tradition that bothered some of us more than others.

Anne Wilson poses for an illustration.

Anne Wilson, who entered the newsroom between Ellefsen and Kapos, felt she sidestepped most inequity. She even briefly covered cops.

There was sexism for sure, but it didn't seem worse in the newsroom than anywhere else. In fact, I felt like I was mostly respected. And I was the first woman to cover [LDS] General Conference priesthood meeting, although I had to try four doors before someone let me in the Tabernacle.

Mostly, I remember my first 20 years at *The Tribune* very fondly. I got to cover lots of good beats and stories, I was allowed to work part time when I started a family, and I absolutely loved my colleagues.[434]

Maybe Anne's spunk shielded her from the worst discrimination, such as being fondled or denied promotions because of her gender. But she wasn't the first woman to cover a priesthood meeting, because I got the assignment before she started reporting. Will Fehr was testing my gumption, and I did return with the story.

There was another side of *The Tribune's* sexual revolution that also took its toll on me, especially given my understanding that a newsroom romance threatened my future there.

Coming from Bountiful, where girls like me were either used or ignored by Mormon boys, I didn't know how to handle attention from grown men. In fact, I was overwhelmed. I didn't know how to say no to people at work.

John Waldo, claiming to be getting a divorce, flattered me with praise of my rewrite abilities and took me to lunch and drinks before our friendship faltered. In an eloquent letter, he professed strong feelings for me, but I couldn't get past the fact that he kept returning to his wife. Jerry Dunton, who actually was divorced, pestered me with dinner invitations. David Beck also took me out a couple of times in a relationship stayed mostly platonic. Before the year was out, I was contending with a stalker from the backshop.

It was a easier dealing with staffers nearer my age. I went along with long-hair Brent Curtis on smoking breaks and to a couple of parties in the lower Avenues where Maryjane's perfume wafted from the windows. After a date or two, Brian Nutting became like an argumentative big brother.

There also was a brief, embarrassing encounter with a staffer I'd admired in my journalism classes. Given this fraternity student's relationship with a classy sorority sister, I doubted anything could come of our meeting. Little did, except possibly shame and avoidance. When I saw him absentmindedly picking his nose and eating the crud at his desk, I overcame my share of humiliation.

As it turned out, office romance became a common avenue to marriage at *The Tribune*, but that part of the story is yet to come.

---

[413] Jack Gallivan, July 24, 1988, p. T9.

[414] Woody, August 23, 1995.

[415] Korologos, January 26, 2014.

[416] Mike Korologos, August 9, 2015.

[417] Monson, October 7, 2013.

[418] Employe Benefits Personnel Policies, 1977, p. B-3.

[419] Terri Ellefsen email to Diane Cole February 21, 2014.

[420] Robison, October 7, 2013.

[421] Blair, October 8, 2013.

[422] Blair, October 8, 2013.

[423] Bernie Moss Porter telephone conversation August 26, 2014.

[424] Alice and Robert Blair interview, July 30, 2014.

[425] Ryan Galbraith email July 31, 2014.

[426] Woody, Parker eulogy.

[427] *Tribune Topix*, March 8, 1972.

[428] *Tribune Topix*, May 24, 1972.

[429] *Tribune Topix*, May 24, 1972.

[430] Terri Ellefsen email to Diane Cole February 21, 2014.

[431] Kathy Kapos Stephenson email, May 25, 2016.

[432] Melich, March 5, 2014.

[433] Gordon Harman on Tribune facebook website February 26, 2014.

[434] Anne Wilson email, December 31, 2013.

11 - Intermission -- From Backshop to Hollywood

After getting my bachelor's degree in June 1973, I was "promoted" to make-up editor, a change that gave me a 6 p.m. shift in the composing room and introduced me to another passel of people the likes I'd never known. One of those people, an engraver, had committed suicide by swallowing acid at work.

It was now my duty to put the newspaper to bed at night by delivering the first proofs of the paper to the night copy boy for delivery to the homes of the editor (Art Deck) and publisher (Jack Gallivan). I also approved the full press run and typed up a report of any glitches in the system for Deck and his night managing editor, Keith Otteson. In a crisis, such as big, breaking news or an egregious mistake that could get the paper sued, I might have to stop the presses. The responsibility was frightening for a 21-year-old girl from the suburbs.

Fred "Shakeyspeare" Dodds and Vandra Huber taught me make-up.

Dark, wiry **Dodds** was a 30-something Idahoan who wore black-rimmed glasses and sat on the Copy Desk when not downstairs in the composing room, commonly called the backshop. On slow nights, Dodds toyed with the English language, sometimes at my expense. One night he slipped me this little ditty:

There once lived a girl named Diane
   And she sure wasn't from Siam.
She had long, golden hair
   Which she played with, with an unconscious air.
She took much abuse from the copy desk, that's sure
   But she took it in stride, not letting her fur
Rise in the air and lash all about
   Giving vent to her emotions with a very loud shout.
Now it came to pass one date late in the year
   When she was asked to care for a cat very dear.
And she moved in with this creature
   So the men did talk
What do you do with a cat, take it for a walk?

He was referring to my summer living arrangements, which entailed tending a couple of crotchety old cats in a condominium owned by an acquaintance in my mother's carpool. The pussies rarely came out from the closet or from under the bed, but their dander stirred up allergies I never knew I had.

The first rule of my new job, according to Vandra and Dobbs: Don't forget the door clicker to get back and forth from the newsroom to the backshop. Simple but a major pain if forgotten, because there was no one around to unlock the door that time of night.

I began my shift by checking with engravers at the rear of the shop for Veloxes of the graphics for printing. I'd ensure the back of the Veloxes were marked in blue ink with the correct slug, or story name. According to Vandra and Dobbs, it was my duty to "put pictures in the out-tray and Veloxes on the make-up table where they won't be ruined by spilled coffee."

Next I asked the plate-makers, printers and pressmen whether all equipment was working and reported any problems to the night editor. Then it was time to fix headlines; that is, trim or rewrite anything that slopped outside its columns. When a page was camera ready, I checked the corrections against a page proof from the newsroom.

By this time, loud, hot Linotype machines, where news copy was typed to create lead characters assembled upside down, line by line, column by column, into chases for creating heavy-metal press plates, were largely a thing of the past. Only the oldest printers still wore leather aprons to protect their clothes and to hold Exacto knives and wax rollers, and make-up editors no longer had to read upside down lead type.

Tribune presses in 1970s.

Under the new ATEX computer system, it was the job of the make-up editor to make sure printers correctly followed the dummies from newsroom editors when pasting "cold type" onto pages with wax. When a printer shouted "Trim!", the make-up editor marked the place to cut off the extra type or chose a filler story to close a gap.

So soon after switching from hot type to cold, a change requiring new skills and jeopardizing jobs, union hacks held onto every last shred of power. Diehard printers threatened to chop my wrist with a pica pole when I mistakenly touched the trim point with anything but a blue felt-tip pen invisible to the cameras.

Once everything fit on a page, it was photographed for the creation of a press plate.

The labor-intensive, expensive stereotype process, with enamel-coated zinc engravings etched by acid, mounted on lead or wood blocks and washed with benzene, had given way to simpler offset printing, which worked on the principle of oil and water not mixing. Ink flowed onto a press roller, and the plate, whether stereo or offset, rolled against a rubber drum of ink, picking up ink which clung to the drum and then the newsprint. "Like a bumble bee," the engravers would say, "it's not supposed to fly, but it does." The new offset press process made it easier and cheaper to correct typos and other errors, because it was no longer necessary to go through the entire stereotype process to make new lead plates for the press.[435]

Once the presses rolled, I picked up 15 editions from the pressroom for the top editors, who might order the presses stopped for a chaser (late story) for big news or major mistakes. Presses were seldom stopped, because getting the newspapers into circulation -- on doorsteps by 6 a.m. -- was required to control delivery costs and keep subscribers. If I stopped the presses on my own, I could expect a grilling the next day, an experience I somehow avoided.

My report at the end of the shift, which varied from midnight to 3 a.m., included how close to deadline each edition got off the floor, the times the presses started, the amount of type that was killed in the shop, and the accuracy of classified ad estimates. I delivered unused Veloxes and used pictures to the newsroom, and I left copies of my report for Deck and Otteson, who was more than happy to point out my mistakes.

There was time for fun and games in the backshop for make-up editors, myself included.

The same printers pasted up both *The Tribune* and *Deseret News* as part of the Newspaper Agency Corporation, so one of their duties was to remake the movie ad pages to account for the *News'* refusal to run R-rated movies. I got a kick out of seeing what innocuous movies were left on the table. (Neither newspaper ran liquor or cigarette ads by then.)

On holidays, *The Trib* put little American flags at the top corner of the Front Page. Working make-up one February 1st, Brian Nutting had a printer put in a flag with "Fly the Flag, Groundhog Day" beneath it. About one minute after he sent a page proof upstairs, "KVO [Keith Otteson] was on the horn, shitting bricks."[436] The flag was already gone by then.

Nutting described some of the backshop "guys" -- he apparently overlooked the two or three women -- as "real characters."

They were all working a late shift, which requires a certain type of person right there. One night when there was a huge snowstorm, all the backshop guys were being put up in hotel rooms in town so they wouldn't have to drive home in the middle of the night in a blizzard. One guy, who I think lived in Draper, figured that was a great opportunity for an adventure with the little lady, so he drove all the way home to get her and then drove back to town to stay in the hotel.

A couple of printers were polygamists. One had enough money from his working wives and children to own his own airplane.

Backshop conversations tended less toward politics and more toward cars, pool, houses and hunting, and the younger printers would yell across the composing room to each other in fun. "Hey, Mitchell, heard you got a new bike! Heard it's a pussy!"

They were not quite as crass as some of the Copy Desk crew, but there was no shortage of flirtation on the floor. The Mitchell brothers treated me like a little sister, joking and protecting me from pica poles. Another printer, whom I'll call Randy Handy, started hanging around, showing me samples of his artwork, which was pretty good.

Vandra, who dated and eventually married printer Glenn Webb, encouraged me to go with the backshop bunch to local pool halls like the Twilite Lounge for "lunch" about 7:30 p.m. This wasn't the best idea.

Handy, six years older and me and not bad looking, started treating those lunches at local pool halls like dates, and he took me for a ride on his motorcycle in Bountiful's foothills. What can I say? I was flattered, so I encouraged him. I even introduced him to my parents!

Jerry Dunton from the newsroom warned me to stay away from "that crazy bastard." I suspected jealousy on his part, but when the other printers started giving me the cold shoulder, I tried to cool the relationship. Tried. It took a long time to understand or control Handy.

I looked around to safer companions.

UPI reporter Roger Bennett, the guy who got beat up by bikers when covering Evel Knievel's failed attempt to jump the Snake River, sometimes hung out in the newsroom until my shift ended about midnight. We went out a couple of times, but our relationship never took off.

Ronald Baker, typist

Next I gravitated toward **Ronald Baker**, Cindy Gilchrist's replacement in the City Desk's typing pool. The short, small-town boy stood out in that filthy newsroom his tailored Italian suits. Recently released from an Air Force desk job in Italy, he chain-smoked and flitted among the drinking women in the office, Marilee among them. As a friend, he invited me to avant-garde movies, plays and concerts: Elton John (his lookalike), BB King and Frank Zappa.

Aside from pale complexions, we had little in common. I towered over him and turned up my nose at his overflowing ashtrays. I counted my pennies and lived in a borrowed condo while he spent lavishly on albums and a state-of-the-art stereo system. Having quit Snow College, a glorified high school in rural Utah, he took school and work with a grain of salt; I was serious about my grades and job performance. He'd lived in Europe, a place I only dreamed of seeing.

* * *

Sometimes Ron and City Desk typist **Robert Triptow**, Gordon Harman's friend from high school on Salt Lake County's west side, would visit me and friends at my condo for a few laughs.

Long-haired Triptow was a fast-talking, budding underground cartoonist a la Robert Crumb whose fleet fingers flew across the keyboard at 150 words a minute without errors.[437] He often contributed to the Art Department pillar but stayed just one year in the newsroom before descending into the backshop for higher pay. Five years later, he took off for San Francisco, where he let his pent-up creative juices flow into the gay movement and cartooning.

By 1978, Triptow was assistant to the publisher of the *Advocate*, a gay publication. He not only spoke weekly on the phone to San Francisco Supervisor Harvey Milk, he knew almost everyone in the movie about Milk's gay-rights advocacy and murder. In 1984, Triptow became editor of *Gay Comix,* and in 1989, he published an anthology of gay comics.[438]

Meantime, Triptow managed a weekly paper in Los Angeles, where he befriended Charlene Tilton before she became Lucy Ewing on "Dallas." Through Tilton, he met "half of Hollywood." He also knew gossip columnist Joyce Haber, who invited him to dinner at her house with the "golden age of Hollywood celebrities: Gene Kelly and the like."

Triptow returned to San Francisco's cartooning scene to meet a host of countercultural biggies:

I told Helen Keller jokes to Jerry Garcia. I had lunch with Timothy Leary. Posed with Stan Freberg at the San Diego Comic-Con and gave him the "rabbit ears" in the photo. Trina Robbins (the subject of the Joni Mitchell song "Ladies of the Canyon") is one of my best friends. I'm not telling you this to impress, really, but to share with you how miraculously interesting life can be when you're adventurous.[439]

Triptow married William Blakely on Halloween of 2004. By 2015, he had been featured at San Diego's Comic-Con International and was working toward retirement in a "magnificent" oceanfront house on Hawaii's big island. He credited his year at *The Tribune*, where he was exposed to Neil Passey, Mark Knudsen and The Pillar, with his later cartoon publication.[440] He also confessed having had a crush on me that year. "I think now and thought then that your marriage to the creep [Ron Baker] was a waste of a fabulous woman."[441]

* * *

Yes, I married Ron Baker.

While hanging out with him and Triptow, I could keep Handy at bay. Ron toyed with my affections, one day turning up the charm and the next day withdrawing it. One explanation was that he'd never gotten over the tragic accident that killed his high school sweetheart the night they were supposed to be together.[442] Another was my lack of virginity. Given the sexual revolution under way, I was floored. And heartbroken.

To forget Ron, I focused on finding a teaching job. I sent out countless applications and interviewed for a few openings, but the teacher glut limited my prospects. I took a two-week vacation to Honolulu with a girlfriend to check out opportunities there.

I loved Oahu. For the first time in my life, I decided to risk my future for something new. If I couldn't find a job in education or journalism in Hawaii, I'd wait on tables if necessary to live there. I turned in my two-weeks' notice to Otteson and waited eagerly to be rid of the baggage that came with *The Tribune*.

With just a week left to work and a week left before the new school year started, I got the call: "Our English and journalism teacher has quit. Can you fill our opening at Box Elder High School?" My plans for Hawaii died.

I slapped together lesson plans from my college work to cover five subjects: Freshman English, Sophomore English, Creative Writing, Journalism I and Journalism II. For my first week at school and my last week at *The Tribune*, I drove 60 miles each way between Salt Lake City and Brigham City to do both jobs, staying at the newspaper past midnight each night. Unless I was searching the town for an apartment, I used my preparation period to nap. My students soon caught on and tossed pencils and whatnot against my windows to keep me awake.

Adding insult to injury, Otteson trapped me on the stairs to the backshop my last day at *The Tribune* to plant a goodbye kiss on me, and Handy showed up outside my new classroom after school.

My last night at *The Tribune* was August 30, 1973. My final weekly paycheck was a measly $145 ($104.17 take-home pay). Then again, I stood to earn even less -- under $6,000 a year -- teaching, but I got summers off.

As I took my leave, Fred "Shakeyspeare" Dodds handed me a "final ode to the rebel on the Copy Desk:"

> Brigham City's gain is *The Tribune's* loss
> 'Cause old Chesty gave notice to her boss.
> She said she'd teach in school each day
> As the easiest way to earn her pay.
> But the boys on copy desk number nine
> Didn't forget her, they'll always pine
> For young old Chesty and her willing smile
> At which many a man would gladly walk a mile.

---

[435] Dennis W. Green explanation of the transition from hot type to cold type and engraving.

[436] Nutting, February 14, 2014.

[437] Harman, October 8, 2015.

[438] Robert Triptow, Wikipedia, May 2015.

[439] Robert Triptow email, November 17, 2015.

[440] Ibid.

[441] Robert Triptow email, November 18, 2015.

[442] Think: "Teen Angel, can you hear me?" by Mark Dinning, 1960.

12 - Teaching on My Way Back from 1973 to 1975

The next two and a half years spent teaching, being married to a wannabe filmmaker and kowtowing to Los Angeles investors were mostly demoralizing.

I received no support from other teachers or administrators at Box Elder. Besides getting the classes and after-school activities (student newspaper and literary magazine) no one else wanted, I had to continually cajole the teacher in my carpool into waiting for me after school. Her speed-reading classes didn't require preparation, so she never understood the need to stay past 3 p.m. She almost had a heart attack the extra hour it took a student to return car keys stolen   from my desk.

Part of my problem was that I was only 21 with long, kinky hair and miniskirts in a conservative town. Maybe even worse, I failed to devote $100 of my tiny salary to union dues. The union representative's son, a constant headache, was the kid who lifted my keys.

The principal treated me like a recalcitrant teen-ager, calling me onto the carpet for skipping out on a three-hour awards assembly and tossing beer cans in my trash can. He didn't believe someone had left them outside my window on the weekend.

Making matters worse, Handy stalked my apartment, which was above the sister of a student. I feared a morality claim might get me fired. Ron Baker popped back into the picture and proposed marriage just at the right -- or wrong -- time. I took refuge in his offer, and we moved 25 miles south to the mouth of Ogden Canyon.

Dan Valentine recommended Ron for a reporting job at the *Ogden Standard-Examiner*, and he enrolled in correspondence teaching courses at Weber State College. It was a struggle. He didn't know how to write a news story, and when I offered advice, he told me the Copy Desk had considered me a journalistic joke. He also lacked patience for my classroom complaints; he would be a better teacher than I. If not for a friendly new teacher from Brooklyn and many kind, talented students, including the kid who tried to get me to go sky-diving with him, my first year of teaching my first year of marriage would have been a bust.

As the school year ended, I signed a contract for the next year with Clearfield High, nearer my Bountiful roots, and I agreed to spend the summer in Hollywood so Ron could take classes at UCLA on his way to becoming a film director. It was a summer of rude awakenings.

Thirty-five-cent tacos became our main meal of the day so Ron could add to his record collection and splurge on theater tickets. I spent most of my time alone in our cheap studio apartment embroidering signs of the times -- sun, moon, stars and Tricky Dick in a pensive pose -- on a faded pair of dungarees to the sounds of the Stylistics. The fuzzy-headed children next door played "You Make Me Feel Brand New" incessantly on their stereo. Their dad was going to play backup for Stevie Wonder. Our sleep occasionally was interrupted by another neighbor screeching, "Go ahead, drag me in the dog shit, I don't care" or, "Go ahead, take all my pots and pans!" While searching for pots and pans of my own one day, I found a current copy of *The Advocate* in the broiler. Ron stayed in Los Angeles when I headed home for my second year of teaching.

That school year was easier than the first. I had fewer courses, several prepared lessons and friendlier peers. I knew Linda Larsen through my older brother, and we leaned on each other for moral support. Some of my students declared me their favorite teacher. But again, I supervised the student newspaper, and an artist in my carpool resisted staying after school. And discipline still could be a challenge.

Many students came from lower-income and military families, and my last class of sophomores was the worst. After angrily dismissing them early one day, I found a pile of trash on my desk beneath a hanging skeleton gagging on the foot in its mouth. Another day, a cabal of miscreants set my wastebasket on fire. Almost as exciting was the afternoon a student jumped up and socked a classmate in the mouth for jiggling his chair. I was able to sleep that night only because I'd joined the union for lawsuit protection.

My union membership also came to mind when Principal Gayle Stevenson called me into is office to check out a student's claim I taught without a bra. Rather than ask me to undress, he settled for my argument that I was simply low-busted.

My journalism classes made up for the hassles. I took students on a field trip to *The Tribune* and invited several writers to speak to my classes. The girls were taken with police reporter Wilf Cannon's dark, wavy locks and dreamy eyelashes, but most students were put off with Dave Beck's arrogance. They reported that Brian Nutting, Nancy Melich and Judy Rollins made the news business sound interesting, even exciting.

On long holidays, I drove to LA to visit Ron, who was hanging out with a reportedly upbeat, intelligent woman from his film classes. He insisted he was eager for me to move back in the spring.

* * *

Back in Utah, Linda Larsen and I spent several Friday nights at D.B. Cooper's with Nutting and Paul Rolly, the new guy on obits with the ski-jump nose, who kept me abreast of *Tribune* gossip. They were dismissive of the December 1974 issue of *Utah Holiday* magazine which portrayed the *Deseret News* as Salt Lake City's superior newspaper.

It was no coincidence that the Truman Capotesque author, Paul Swenson, was a former *Deseret News* reporter.

Although the greasy haired Swede criticized both papers, his most biting comments were reserved for my previous employer. "Both papers," he contended, "have failed to elude a reputation for blandness, lack of editorial bite and 'hard news' influence in the community."[443] He depicted the *Deseret News* as a primping, do-gooder Little Orphan Annie hampered by its status as an evening paper steadily losing circulation, and he declared that the "good, gray Trib, dignified in typography and tone, dispenses advice on its editorial pages with the restraint and decorum of a sedate, satisfied dowager -- a Mary Worth, one of the paper's long-time continuity comic strip characters."

While saying *Deseret News* beat reporters consistently demonstrated the most "imagination and initiative," he gave Robert Woody credit for having a "thick file of news sources and contacts" on the business beat. He also commended Jack Fenton's coverage of county government as "usually out in front of the opposition," That opposition, he noted, "has been known to rewrite Fenton's 'dupes' [carbon copies of his stories] rather than cover a story in person."

Swenson undressed arts criticism at both newspapers but acknowledged efforts by David Beck and Nancy Funk [Melich]. He wondered how TV columnist Hal Schindler could spend his entire shift turning out his "minimal but sometimes astute" observations, and he described art critic George Dibble as "obtuse," with seldom a discouraging word for local artists.

Publisher Jack Gallivan, interviewed for the piece, attributed *The Tribune's* heavy use of syndicated reviews on the prohibitive cost of local critics.

Swenson gave *The Tribune* the nod for a vast array of wire services and larger news hole for national and international news, but he gave the *News* a slim lead for commentary, primarily its syndicated columnists. Yet he commended *The Trib*'s "straightforward candor and moral courage with its early call for Nixon's impeachment."

The critic obviously lacked the full story behind a gesture that was more a matter of embarrassment and remorse for backing the crook in the first place.

Having supported Republican presidential candidates since Senator Thomas Kearns bought the newspaper, *The Tribune* endorsed Richard M. Nixon's presidency in 1968. As Gallivan explained it years later, he was raised Republican, Publisher J. F. Fitzpatrick was Republican, and the Kearns family remained staunchly in that camp mostly in memory of Senator Kearns.

> After Fitzpatrick's death, I just automatically endorsed the Republican candidate, who was Richard Nixon . . . When I discovered what a horrible mistake I had made, as long as I was publisher, *The Tribune* would never endorse anybody again. I still don't think a publisher has the right to be a member of either party.[444]

Swenson aimed his sharpest barbs at investigative journalism, or lack of it. He attacked both papers for failing to hire writers with advanced education in such fields as social problems, the arts and politics who might have uncovered scandals in mental retardation facilities and the Boy Scouts of America (for discriminating against blacks). Yet he praised the *News* for having at least one full-time investigative reporter, Robert Mullins, and for publishing incisive pieces on public housing and prison halfway houses.

Slanted though Swenson might have been, he did make valid points about *The*

Tribune's boss mixing roles as private promoter and newsman. Gallivan's defense on this score were not reassuring.

The Associated Press story on the Scouts wasn't published because "it had nothing new to offer," he told Swenson. Investigative journalism? "We will crusade in favor of socially productive causes . . . for example, improvement of the community for the minorities."[445]

Gallivan apparently saw little difference between crusading and uncovering problems in the community. His promotion of tourism, business and the Olympics were part of his definition of "socially productive." As late as 2005, when identifying advertising as the key to a newspaper's success, he said his proudest achievement was the "campaigns we carried on to make tourism Utah's biggest industry," generating more than $5 billion a year by 2005.[446]

Gallivan seemingly had refined his views by then, as he also said a newspaper "must be fair and objective" to be great. He noted that it had been the policy of his predecessor J.F. Fitzpatrick, as well as himself and his successor Jerry O'Brien, to keep the news "as balanced as we possibly could" by presenting both sides of controversial issues within the first three paragraphs of a news story.[447] Yet he still didn't mention the importance of unearthing the controversies in the first place. Nor the temptation to bury them. The power of the press was used more than once in his day to kill stories about driving under the influence (DUI) of alcohol.

Even so, he and assistant O'Brien eventually relaxed some of the old taboos in the news and editorial pages. Editorials became less formal and more forceful. Polygamy and criticism of Gallivan's sacred cows remained sensitive, but some unmentionables became mentionables.[448]

Upon publication of his *Utah Holiday* analysis, Swenson became persona non grata at *The Tribune,* and no staffer with any sense was caught speaking to him. Only with a changing of the guard in the 1990s were his transgressions forgotten and his writing, in the form of a *Tribune* book column, given consideration.

* * *

As my second year of teaching wound down, I sent job inquiries to Los Angeles school districts and newspapers and got a couple of responses, but my lack of a master's degree hurt my prospects. Watts schools were interested, but

given the 1965 riots and TV crime news, I wasn't up for that battle.

Me in Hollywood, 1974.

My return to Hollywood was a mistake. Neil Diamond lyrics notwithstanding, L.A. wasn't fine, and it wasn't home for me.[449]

For three lonesome, frustrating months while Ron attended school mornings and entered medical data afternoons, I scoured the classifieds, went to interviews and sanded our unfinished furniture in a moldy apartment that stank of natural gas and stale cigarettes. Gobs of black gunk devoured plaster patches above the tub.

Local newspapers, advertising offices and middle-class schools weren't hiring, so I accepted $1,000 a month as assistant to an investment secretary on the 21st floor of the Crocker Bank Building downtown. Independence and creativity were not part of the job description.

Requirements included business attire and skills in coffee-making, filing, typing and memorization of countless acronyms. To save time, the company used initials for employees, clients and companies in its investment portfolio. The chairman of the investment group, a pompous jerk from Beverly Hills, demanded I do his filing only when he was out.

My shift began at 7 a.m. when no one was on hand to answer my questions about the buy and sell orders I was assigned to fax to the New York Stock Exchange. Although I was the newest employee and knew virtually nothing about the stock market, it was my duty to make sure the purchases didn't violate the ethics of our clients. I had to refer to a long list of client objections that slowed my ability to place the orders.

With Ron using our VW, I walked three blocks to Hollywood Boulevard to catch the 6 bus to downtown. Frightful forms of human refuse still littered the streets from the night before.

By late October, I finally got the hang of the job but still felt stupid, shallow and homesick, like my life lacked purpose. I wanted something more than 700 vinyl records and tickets to the latest show in town, but a house with full pantry in a safe neighborhood, possibly with children, was beyond my wildest dreams. Ron wasn't interested in my ideas, and I started sulking and whining for the first time in my life. I didn't even have the gumption to order dressing for my salad without his endorsement.

My time in Los Angeles taught me that Mormon dominance wasn't the worst thing in the world. I fantasized about returning to the classroom or becoming city editor of *The Tribune* someday. As Ron nudged me closer to the door, I worked up the courage to write lecherous Keith Otteson about my need for a job. As I packed to leave, I received an offer from the *Los Angeles Herald-Examiner* to interview for the Copy Desk. Too late. I was flying back to my Rocky Mountain home without a husband or an income.

[443]Swenson, 1974, p. 6.

[444] Gallivan, May 2005.

[445] Swenson, 1974, p. 34.

[446] Gallivan, May 2005.

[447] Ibid.

[448] Malmquist, p. 395-6.

[449] Neil Diamond, "I Am ... I Said," 1971.

Part II - Return to Reporting

13 - Dying to Get In, 1975

Demoralized and back with my parents in Bountiful in November of 1975, I got nowhere with Otteson. After our encounter in the hallway, I didn't expect much. As a stopgap for my joblessness, a college friend hooked me up with the State School Office writing vocational education lessons, something out of my realm. My lessons taught furniture-store bed sales.

Thankfully, Brian Nutting tipped off Will Fehr to my plight. He rescued me with a call: "Cole, if you're serious about a career in journalism, come in and see me."

The office playmate?!

I was nervous about working for City Desk, not only because copy editors supposedly had criticized my competence, but also because I had never written news stories of my own. I had worked on Waldo rewrites and taught high school journalism, but there were no bylines to my credit. My writing style, I feared, was dull and inconsistent -- verbose and vague one day and quippy the next. Clear and concise I was not. Even so, I was earning $152 a week as a cub reporter by mid-December.

Some horrific crime news circulated the newsroom once I rejoined. Ted Bundy, briefly a Mormon and a law student at the University of Utah during my time there, was arrested in 1975 by a Utah Highway Patrol officer on suspicion of murdering several young women, including one from my own high school. The disappearance of so many women near my age had frightened me earlier, so his arrest was not only a relief but also a major topic of discussion among staffers. When he escaped from the courthouse in Aspen in June 1977.[450] Colorado officials were derided as buffoons. The sick maniac was back on the streets!

Fallout continued over the Ogden Hi-Fi murders in which Dale Pierre Selby and William Andrews forced five Ogden residents to drink Drano before shooting each in the head, killing three, in 1974. The black Hill Air Force Base airmen kicked a pen into the ear of one man and repeatedly raped a teen-age girl. Selby was still on death row in 1976, changing his name seemingly every other day.

Other news of the day told of Gerald Ford stumbling through the balance of Nixon's nefarious presidency. Southeast Asian refugees were acclimating to our culture, giving the schools bilingual challenges and creating local cravings for Vietnamese cuisine. Salt Lake City continued to be a controversial stop for wild musicians and Broadway touring companies like "Hair" and "Jesus Christ Superstar." If Utah's conservative Mormons were offended by near nudity and a rock music approach to Bible stories then, though, they changed their tune by the 1990s, when one of their own, Donnie Osmond, repeatedly starred in "Joseph and the Amazing Technicolor Dreamcoat."

* * *

Rejected by my husband, I sought male companionship but was determined to avoid another office romance that would complicate my job and life. Jerry Dunton became a confidante of sorts; Dave Beck my writing coach; Brian Nutting my affectionate friend; Paul Rolly a drinking buddy. At the same time, I lacked the confidence to control unwanted male attention.

"Sometimes I feel like the office Playmate," I whined to Mimi, my go-to gal when upset or depressed. "John Mooney always pinches me in the ribs (and sneaks his hand toward my boobs), and Otteson has started sniffing and sidling up to me again . . ." As if that wasn't bad enough, Randy Handy from the backshop discovered I was back in town.

Handy followed me home, cased my new apartment while I hid behind darkened windows, called me all hours of the night and popped up without warning. His wife -- I finally found out he was married with children -- called me at work and begged me to leave him alone. In turn, I begged her to keep him away from me, and I lambasted him for his deceit.

One day Mother Jones made a suggestion from left field: "Why not go out with Denny Green -- not to get involved; just for a good time?"

Denny Green in the 1970s.

I had never considered the idea. After all, he was married with children during my previous *Tribune* stint. He was just the wiry, friendly guy with a beard and long, stringy hair who occasionally threatened to ply me with liquor while I waited for my rot-gut coffee at the machine separating the City Desk from the Art Department.

In late January, I boldly called his bluff. "When are you going to let my ply you with liquor?" he asked. "I'm free after work," I boldly responded. He gulped, but after work he walked me to D.B. Cooper's, still *The Trib's* favorite watering hole. I got to know a funny, kind person whose values mostly reflected mine. That night, the only downside seemed to be his choice of cars: a cheap, dangerous Ford Pinto. Worse problems were further down the road.

By Valentine's Day, I was smitten. Recordings of Melissa Manchester, Stevie Wonder, Joni Mitchell, Ramsey Lewis and "A Man and a Woman" serenaded our evenings of affection at home. A month later, he unceremoniously dumped his hairdresser for me and I did the same with a guy I'd grown up with. Meantime, Denny introduced me to his skinny blonde daughters, who were 8 and 10, when we picked them up from school. Stormy was bubbly and sweet; Lulu held back.

I loved Denny's honesty, devotion to family and sense of responsibility. He paid his bills and spent weekends with his children. He was attracted to me without being possessive, competitive or critical. He made me laugh with cartoon messages on half-sheets. A bulbous-nosed caricature of himself as an inmate confided, "It's break time." He drew himself as a skeleton covered with cobwebs at his drawing table: "Oh, that used to be the *Tribune* art director . . . starved to death waiting to go to lunch."

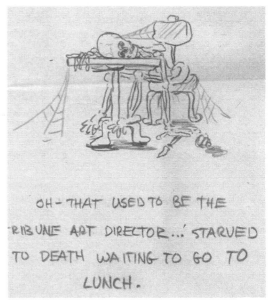

Denny's personalized cartoon in the 1970s.

We had fun on weekends with his daughters, who splashed through brine-fly infested waters around Antelope Island and tickled me until I screamed Sunday mornings. Holidays were festive, with cookie-decorating, Easter-egg hunts and fireworks. Road trips to Disneyland and Elkhorn Hot Springs, where Lulu spent hours fishing, strengthened our bond.

Ordinarily Denny and I met his father, a quality control supervisor for Newspaper Agency Corp., in the dingy cafeteria between *The Tribune* and *Deseret News* for sack lunches of tuna or peanut butter sandwiches prepared by Denny's mother. I would have liked to get out of the ink-and newsprint-clogged air, but I got to know kind Bill Green and enjoyed chatty Mrs. Ellen Marshall, the African-American woman in her late 70s or early 80s who kept the place stocked and cleaned.

Ellen Marshall

Ellen often muttered about lazy people leaving their trash on the formica tables or beside the microwave, but she also entertained us with stories about the higher-ups in the organization or in the dress shops where she bought the expensive outfits she wore under aprons while wiping the tables clean. Mrs. Marshall had dated some dandies in her early days and wore the fanciest hats at the Kentucky Derby she attended each year with the McCarthey family. For me,

Ellen was an education in local diversity and history.

After spending three days sick in bed with me, Denny proposed on April 19, 1976, promising to tie the knot a year later to the day. It wasn't too soon for me, because I felt at 24 I was ready to make a home. Denny moved into my apartment on 13th East, filling the role of the husband I had to claim to qualify for a lease. To the landlord, Denny was Mr. Baker. OK, so he learned to lie a little, but not to me.

We started having trouble with Denny's ex-wife, whom we soon called Swamp Witch, or Swamper for short. When Lulu and Stormy arrived for weekend visits, we had to immediately launder the rancid clothes in their overnight bags scented with cat urine and rabbit pellets. Swamper met Ped O'Fiel from Parents Without Partners, and the Gruesome Twosome began giving us grief about visitation and whatever other conflict they could manufacture. O'Fiel and his three children moved in with Swamper -- before marriage, by the way -- and then threatened to sue Denny for removing his name from their water company account. O'Fiel sanctimoniously sent back an "inappropriate" belly-dancing costume we bought Lulu for her birthday. After living out of wedlock themselves, the Gruesomes refused to let the kids stay with us because we were living in sin.

* * *

I eased into news reporting as one of the last anonymous obituary writers in the newsroom, before the chore was turned over to the advertising department as a money-making function. **Paul Wetzel** was my teacher.

Wetzel's *Tribune* experience synchronized with mine, sometimes dissonantly. The differences stuck in my jealous craw.

The Wally Cox-like character grew up a year behind me in my hometown, but his high school drew students from the upper-crust foothills. He started college out-of-state -- St. John's in Santa Fe -- while I worked full-time to pay school and living expenses. He joined the U.'s Naval ROTC, the kind of structured group that left me cold. I was a boat-rocker; he was patient, cautious and quick to agree with his bosses. I fought for fair treatment -- promotions and raises -- that seemed to fall in his lap.

Korologos had hired Wetzel June 18, 1973 as a copy boy who, like others before and after him, was "harassed and hectored by Vard Jones," the wire editor.[451] By then, I was moving from copy editor to make-up editor and looking for a teaching job. During most of my two-year absence, Wetzel typed corrections for the Copy Desk before moving to City Desk. In his words:

> Jim Woolf trained me on the death beat. (You remember the strange luck that accompanied Rolly and Woolf as they alternated as NIPO. When Rolly worked, nothing happened. When Woolf worked, the cops would crash Eagle One on Ensign Peak or the Congress Hotel would burn down. It drove Rolly nuts.) I spent the next two years on obits, NIPO, and writing city council and police news in Bountiful.[452]

Wetzel showed rare initiative on June 5, 1976, the day the Teton Dam broke outside Rexburg, Idaho, about noon. When he arrived in the newsroom about 2 p.m. for his obituary shift, editors were scrambling and dithering. They hired a small plane to fly George Raine and a photographer over the area that day. The next day, it was Clark Lobb's turn to ride to the site by car with photographer Tim Kelly, and Wetzel jumped into the fray.

> I had the next several days off, so, with Jim Woolf's encouragement, I volunteered to go. In typical pinch-penny fashion, Art Deck told me *The Tribune* could not send me officially, but he couldn't stop me if I wanted to go in my own car with my own camera at my own expense. The Prince of Darkness didn't even offer to pay me. So I drove up in my own car, following Kelly's Toyota SUV.
> We stayed in Idaho Falls. I agreed to stay put and keep tabs on the flood as it bore down on the town while Kelly and Lobb struck out for Rexburg. I landed an interview with a young man who had been fishing in the canyon downstream of the dam when it broke, and, amazingly, survived. He was plucked from a treetop by rescuers in a boat. His fishing companion and his dog both drowned. I interviewed him in the hospital and phoned the story to Angie Nelson on the *Tribune* desk.
> Lobb wrote most of the other coverage, but I contributed reporting, got a joint byline with him on one of the mainbars, and wrote a sidebar on the presumed cause of the dam failure. It was my first reporting on a big story. I think I was gone for three days, and

when I got back, Deck covered my expenses and paid me a $100 bonus.[453]

* * *

Three evenings a week I worked the Obit Desk; the other two I filled in on the Rewrite Desk or 2 p.m. general assignment, where I came up with education features when there were no assignments in my file. I also called area hospitals for the day's birth announcements, careful to avoid errors in names and addresses that obligated us to re-run the announcement. With every inch of print valuable, mistakes earned a slap on the wrist.

I took seriously those months gathering information about the deceased's vital statistics, life achievements, survivors and funeral arrangements. Usually a funeral director called or brought in the information with a faded photograph or blurry snapshot requiring a cropped Polaroid copy, but sometimes I had to contact the family myself. When they declined to give the cause of death, I had to insist as "*Tribune* policy." "Causes incident to age" was the common catch phrase. "Self-inflicted gunshot wound" required special sensitivity unless coming from police reports, when families were forced to suffer the indignity and pain.

For most obits, I settled into a formula when asking for information: "Date of death? Cause of death? Date and place of birth? Parents' names? Did he/she attend college? Was he in the military service? A member of what church and organizations? Did he/she have an occupation? Was he/she married? To whom? Who are the surviving spouse and children, and where do they live? Where and when will services and burial be held? Will there be a viewing? Space limits called for discretion in listing LDS Church positions.

Obituary writing was good training. Besides working fast to meet deadlines while getting the facts straight, I was exposed to emotional and political situations that prepared me for future job pressures. I developed an interest in the lives of people from all walks of life.

"How many obits for State [edition], Sweetheart?" my old friend Jerry Dunton would holler across the newsroom every night about 10 o'clock. The number varied, but it was rarely fewer than a dozen and sometimes more than thirty, a major time challenge.

Carol Landa, a new staffer a few years ahead of me, broke under the stress of too much to do in too little time. She was pounding away at her manual typewriter right up until quitting time when, according to editorial writer Harry Fuller, "yet one more undertaker's assistant dropped his contribution at her work station.

Whereupon Carol burst into sobs, proclaiming she was never going to be able to finish, that "they just keep coming!" Sidling over from my nearby perch, I told her in conspiratorial tones lower than the newsroom din that when 5 o'clock struck, she need only gather her personal belongings and leave; the next shift would finish the leftovers. She took employment elsewhere when the opportunity arrived.[454]

Working the late shift, as I did, afforded me no such option. We finished all the obituaries we received before going home, because they were carefully timed to notify friends and family of the services.

Bereaved relatives, I soon learned, don't need the added distress of errors blemishing their loved one's memory. As a cub reporter, I minced no words with such euphemisms as "passed away" or "left us." Now that I'm older, I'm more aware of the grief the words "die" and "suicide" cause.

As an intern before joining the Sports Desk, Dick Rosetta had a "brief, emergency stint" on obits lasting just one shift.

I had to call a family whose son had ended his life by sticking a shotgun in his mouth. By the time I hung up the phone, I was in shock. I went to some editor and said obits were not a part of my learning curve.[455]

Some survivors assumed their loss deserved special treatment, something more than the formula obituary with sparse facts. If they had the correct pedigree or connections to *Tribune* top dogs, they got what they wanted. Eight-point obits -- those published in the larger type size used in the news pages rather than the agate used in the classified ad section -- routinely were written for doctors, lawyers and business and civic leaders. The disparity irritated my sense of social justice.

I especially resented Mr. Deck's order one night for a full-size news story for a woman of few accomplishments who was merely the mother of an acquaintance. In the first place, the family wasn't ready to turn in the information,

and neither was the mortuary. Fehr insisted I call the family for the information anyway, and "well, it ain't too pleasant calling bereaved families," I whined to my journal, Mimi.

The snobbish son demanded I copy his mother's own version of her life, something never allowed for a nobody. Of course she had omitted the usual details about her cause of death and where she and her children lived. I had to miss my lunch break while sitting around waiting for the son to approve our version of the woman's life. I don't enjoy rocking the boat, but hereafter, I'm going to give nobodies better treatment. If we'll do it for sacred cows [when he could get away with it, the night city editor stamped a haloed cow on the copy], we should do it for others!

Maybe I shouldn't work for a newspaper after all. Terrible hours and salary are bad enough, but sacrificing principles is too much. I foresee blowing my cool one of these nights.

It was *Tribune* policy to treat the deaths of staffers and retirees, no matter how obscure, as news stories. Somehow I didn't object to that perk, probably meant to offset meager monetary rewards.

For longtime staffers and truly deserving community leaders, we kept "advance" obituaries in the "morgue" (library) awaiting the date and manner of death. It was expected that in the slow hours, *Tribune* rewrite staffers would perpetually update these so-called "eight-points" so that late-night deaths would not catch the City Desk empty-handed. They didn't always do their duty.

When education writer Bill Smiley died, George Raine was assigned his obit.

There was little personal information about him in the office, so I called his widow. She was not pleased, saying something like, "He worked there for (who knows how many) years and you are calling me?" I learned diplomacy that instant, it not having been in my tool kit as a 21-year-old, and managed to get her to talk some about Bill and their life together. OJT was part of *The Tribune* protocol.[456]

Ironically, J.F. Fitzpatrick, the man who issued the orders for advance preparation, did his best to undermine his own edict with his sudden heart attack and death September 11, 1960.

Though deserving as the father of responsible journalism in Utah, modest Mr. Fitzpatrick had repeatedly put off reporters seeking details of his life for the morgue. He had forbidden the use of his name in news stories over the years. His death sent reporters scrambling for details. *Time* magazine followed up with a gibe about *The Tribune* publishing a picture of him on Page One in "open defiance" of the "ungregarious" Irishman's longstanding order against such self-aggrandizement.[457]

* * *

The newsroom had changed slightly during my absence. A newsprint shortage forced cutbacks, including the closure of news bureaus in three adjacent states. In a second-floor shuffle, the library moved to the southwest corner defined by the building's front windows. Sports jumped across to the northwest side of the newsroom, and Arts & Entertainment filled the void left along the southeast side. Several staffers were either new to me or held different jobs.

City Desk editors: Jerry Dunton, Angelyn Nelson, Ernie Ford and Lance Gudmundsen, left to right.

As Bob Woody put it, the newsroom by 1975 included "the male cast from 'Hair,' 'Godspell' and 'Jesus Christ Superstar' -- lowly librarian Jim Woolf, copy booyyyyys Con Psarras and Mike Carter, and the lackadaisical Wilf Cannon and Jon Ure who were shortly assigned to the gulag of the police beat. And there was that surly renegade on the obituary desk, Paul Rolly."[458]

Woolf, married to Publisher J.F. Fitzpatrick's granddaughter Maggie since high school, worked in the morgue filing news clippings and answering reader questions on the phone when I first passed through the newsroom a couple of years earlier but now wrote crime news. Psarras was the good-looking Greek godson of Mike Korologos; Carter's dad did

graphics arts for the *Deseret News* during the day and got into stand-up comedy on his own time.

Jim Woolf and Ernie Ford on City Desk in '70s.

Carter, Gordon Harman and Psarras took turns at my old typing desk. They used slow time between deadlines to start a great American novel, taking turns writing paragraphs. "It would have made a great book, but unfilmable," according to Harman.[459]

"Being a correction typist was a fun time, working with Carter, Con, Fred Kempe, Tom Jerman and others," Harman added. "That's when you really got to observe all those old dudes on the Copy Desk."[460]

Like other newspapers in the 1970s, *The Tribune* still was making the transition from the days when most staffers, usually men with limited education, worked up through the ranks of the newsroom, from librarian or copy "boy."

Clark Lobb and Clarence "Scoop" Williams were prominent among that crowd. Several of their peers had finished college, including Art Deck, political writer O.N. Malmquist, editorial writers Robert Blair, Harry Fuller and Wallace Hoffman, business editor Bob Woody, city editor Will Fehr, managing editor Keith Otteson and sports editors John Mooney and Jack Schroeder. It was the editors, it seemed, who held the degrees.

By the time I arrived, college degrees became the norm, though a few of my peers climbed aboard without one. Carter, Harman, Peter Scarlet and Neil Passey were among them, and some never bothered to get the diploma.

Although Harman studied journalism at the University of Utah for five years, his credits fell short of graduation, and he followed the advice of other staffers to forget about it.

Tim Kelly asked me if I was going to get a "reporter" job when I graduated (I'd already been writing for more than a year). Dan Valentine used to tell me that I already had the job, so learning how to do it in school was a waste of time. He also said I should vote for Nixon, which really would have been a waste of time.[461]

Other clerk-level staffers readying themselves for a rise in the ranks were Tim Fitzpatrick, grandson of the former publisher; small, blonde Mary Dickson; brash psychology graduate Anne Wilson; and three former Skyline High journalism students: Ben Ling, Fred Kempe and Nancy Hobbs.

Mary Dickson, a favorite with many men in the newsroom, didn't stay long, instead jumping ship for quicker promotions at the *Deseret News* and then a full career promoting local public television.

Anne Wilson, about my age, spent a few months as a copy clerk before moving up to typist, then obit writer and zone reporter and finally daily news.

It was a true apprenticeship, and I had some pretty good teachers. But there wasn't the emphasis then on investigative reporting that there [was in the 2013]. That's something that requires real determination, persistence and skill with analyzing documents. Back in the old days, we were the only game in town pretty much, and my recollection is that we didn't work all that hard. We sure had fun though![462]

Nancy Hobbs

Athletic animal lover Nancy Hobbs was barely out of high school when she took a job in the library in 1975. Actually, she was still editor of Skyline's student newspaper when she began submitting stories to our IN section for teens. Her brother Lincoln also snared a job at *The Tribune* as a copy boy before going into law. Nancy's relationship with *The Tribune* and me became an enduring one that will unwind later

Fred Kempe, the ambitious son of German immigrants, rapidly moved on to bigger and better things, including the foreign desk of the *Wall Street Journal* and, ultimately, the top spot on the Atlantic Council, from which he gave commentary on global issues for television and radio. He wrote four books, including <u>BERLIN 1961: Kennedy, Khrushchev and the Most Dangerous Place on Earth</u>.

While serving with Kempe on a journalism advisory committee, editorial writer Harry Fuller watched this "lofty thinker" receive a speeding ticket from a Wyoming state trooper who stood by as Fred dropped his check in the mail. Once the trooper left, Fred finagled a postal worker into retrieving his envelope, which he ripped to pieces.[463]

Mike Carter

Mike Carter described his first day of work in December 1974. Under the threat of death from his dad if he didn't show up (Dick Carter had used his connections with his former colleague from the *Deseret News* to get Mike a job), the scruffy, jobless college drop-out got six inches chopped off his mop of blond hair for the interview with Will Fehr. "My first day of work, Jon Ure was at the old Obit Desk with hair so long he could sit on it. Likewise Wilf Cannon, the day cops guy. Hardly what I expected."[464]

Jon Ure

It wasn't long before Carter adapted to the *Tribune* culture, having sex, puking and getting punched in the alley behind the Tribune building, as he put it. Staffers had to be careful when walking from the alley to the sidewalk, he noted, or "you'd get run down by some drunk coming out of D.B.s, I wonder who. I got dozens, if not hundreds, of parking tickets there."[465]

* * *

When I started reporting, Assistant City Editor Ernie Ford still taught at the U. while trying to drag *The Tribune* by his draconian fingernails into more progressive local news coverage and page layout. Tough-talking Bruce Bartley on cops and crusty Hal Spencer, a cowboy-boot clomper covering city government, were two of my favorite additions to City Desk. Roger Graves had quit running errands for City Desk to write sports, where he was gearing up for golf-writing awards. Charlie Seldin was reporting on government. Vandra Huber covered social

services; Angelyn Nelson, health care. Cannon, Ure and Rolly were cubs. Lance Gudmundsen was night city editor, and Nutting had advanced to assistant business editor.

Nutting, Raine and Seldin, a cadre of Fehr's favorite reporters, often enjoyed a good time at work, sometimes at others' expense. Seldin would snatch the ball from Raine's IBM Selectric, for instance, and then expertly feign ignorance.[466] The favorites often tormented Rolly because "he was so easy to tease."[467]

Nutting suggested that I ask Rolly about "the time George took a call for him and left a note saying 'Call Rick ASAP.' In that instance, George wasn't even being funny, but we've never let up on kidding Paul about how he interpreted it."

Rolly had demanded to know, "Who's Rick ASAP? I don't know any Rick ASAP!" Presumably, he called and asked for Paul ASAP, sending witnesses into spasms of laughter.

* * *

Paul Rolly

Paul Rolly was an ambitious but insecure young father five years my senior who had entered the newsroom as a copy boy in 1973 after taking reader complaints in NAC Circulation for three years. The skinny, hunch-shouldered Skyline High School graduate was determined to prove to his stuck-up classmates and a "smug little bureaucrat" that he wasn't a loser.[468] His journalism teacher, Clairann Jacobs, steered him toward newspapers.

OK, so he had trouble getting a date and into sports. Yeah, he skipped a lot of school and barely got a diploma. But he was going to get even with any of the assholes who doubted him. Heh, heh, heh.

I'm just saying it like he would.

The son of active Democrats, Rolly attended his first Democratic Party convention at age 4.[469] He earned a political science degree from the University of Utah, where J.D. Williams, his professor and the first director of the Hinckley Institute of Politics, became his mentor. In 1970, they took a student trip to Europe that helped shape his ambition.

Rolly smoked, drank and was forever losing things and forgetting to put gas in his car. His wife, Marjorie Smith, was an active Mormon who worked hard raising their four kids while Paul worked and stayed late at D.B. Cooper's. Rolly's story-telling talent made for many delightful evenings rehashing news stories in the dark recesses of the bar.

When I first met Rolly, he was moving up from obituaries to NIPO and general assignment. His goal was to write like Clark Lobb or *Chicago Tribune* columnist Mike Royko, shooting from the hip to produce a hard-hitting, accurate story -- with a touch of humor and irony when possible. He eventually achieved that goal.

Breaking up the tedium of a slow night on general assignment not long after my return to *The Tribune*, Rolly took a telephone tip from James D. Peipenberg, owner of the sleazy Broadway Theatre. The public attorney and a judge, then watching what they thought was the theater's only copy of "Deep Throat," were about to seize it for evidence in a porn arrest.

Rolly scooped up a notebook and headed for the door, calling across the room: "Hey, Di, if you want to see 'Deep Throat,' this is probably your last chance." Anticipating a fun reporting lesson, I grabbed my purse and ran to catch up. Reporter Bruce Bartley: "Hey, wait up! I wanna come!"

The three of us half ran the two long blocks up Main and Broadway to the dingy theater. After Rolly got his quotes and the public officials departed, we sat on threadbare seats through a steamy showing of the film the officials didn't know existed. I'd seen porn movies before, after college, and this was just one more. (Post Script: Deep Throat star Harry Reems became a real estate broker in Park City and died at the Salt Lake Veterans Hospital March 19, 2013.)

That was Rolly. Always ready to pounce on a controversial story, especially if it involved elected officials. He became my role model of self-initiated, incisive, investigative journalism. He became my best friend.

Rolly cultivated a host of sources, from secretaries to police officers. Once he put their tips into the paper, his informants stayed on the lookout for more dirt to report. Though a die-hard Democrat, Rolly riled a host of state and local public officials from both parties as they violated ethical or legal codes of conduct.

Rolly was only human. A bulldog in interviews, he expressed certitude and confidence -- some might say zeal and self-righteousness -- even while making a sloppy or callous mistake or two. He cared about accuracy, but he got so excited about his subjects sometimes that he put his story to bed before checking all his facts or giving both sides of an issue fair treatment. Also like many reporters, he was so sensitive to criticism that he carried a grudge.

Salt Lake County Attorney Ted Cannon, a familiar face around the *Tribune* from his 20 years as an NAC printer and proofreader, became a Rolly target when accused of sexually harassing a secretary, Shawna Clark. Until that point in Utah, sexual intimidation in the workplace was rarely if ever publicly acknowledged or prosecuted. Rolly's ground-breaking stories highlighted the hypocrisy of a high-profile prosecutor of pornography carrying on in the workplace.

The soft side of Rolly came out later. In a column July 13, 2009, he recalled the ups and downs of Ted Cannon, from his late start in law to his anti-pornography crusade in county and state attorneys' offices; to the county's successful murder cases against polygamist Ervil LcBaron, forger Mark Hofmann, wanna-be millionaire Frances Schreuder and racist Joseph Paul Franklin; to his fall from grace as county attorney, and, finally, to the bipolar disorder that sent him into obscurity, living on disability payments, before his sad death at age 77.[470]

Rolly's Achilles heel was his penchant for living on the edge. He worked long hours and often drove on gas fumes and a full gut of beer, either resulting from or causing marital problems. Eventually, his foibles caught up with him but didn't necessarily stop him. That story is yet to come.

* * *

Charlie Seldin

Charlie Seldin, from George Raine's point of view, was "far more sophisticated than one might expect" coming from tiny Battle Mountain, Nevada. He did an "excellent job" on big stories like the Gary Gilmore trials and the Mormon revelation that black men could attain the priesthood. "Charlie was a great friend and journalist. He was a natural, always around the ball, to borrow an overused sports phrase, but he found other things to do and quit a few times."[471]

In my mind, Seldin was no poor kid from the sticks. His family had enough money to send him to Wasatch Academy in Mt. Pleasant, an exclusive prep school that undoubtedly polished his style. The University of Utah graduate married a pretty woman and often puffed on a pipe. He quit to work for Saudi financier Adnan Khashoggi in the mid-1980s; to work in advertising and to write books other times. Korologos told me that Seldin was the name his family adopted to avoid anti-Semitism.[472]

* * *

Verdo Thomas in the 1970s.

Upon my return to *The Trib*, U. of U. classmate **Verdo Thomas** was working make-up after replacing me on the Copy Desk in 1973.[473] As the first African American on the desk, he was "ragged unmercifully by the rest of the guys," according to Nutting, who also had worked make-up after I left. "I don't know if it was completely racial, but there was probably some element of that."[474]

Undoubtedly. There was little racial diversity on staff. The first woman "copy clerk," Bernice Martinez, and Fourth Floor receptionist Ramona Gonzalez were Mexican Americans. Ben Ling and Marshall Ding were Asian. That about covers it. Olive-skinned Greeks and Italians were our version of minorities.

Race, as well as religion and gender, posed challenges to old-school editors. As more people demanded to name themselves, editors had to arbitrate, and they didn't always get it right. Do we replace the term Negroes with blacks or African Americans? How about Mexicans . . . or is it Latinos? Hispanics? Indians vs. Native Americans? Which activists prevail in this naming game? editors asked. Should we refer to a person's race or religion at all in news stories? Is it relevant whether a crime suspect is black or Latino? Maybe we should refer to race only for positive stories. How about the first Mexican-American to hold a public office?

Then there was the matter of courtesy titles used on second and subsequent references in news stories. Normally we relied on E. B. White's The Elements of Style or the The AP Stylebook to settle such issues, and we kept a small *Tribune*-devised pamphlet to cover our unique Mormon culture.

Felons didn't merit courtesy titles at all. We used only last names for criminals. That style eventually applied to other men as well -- unless they were big shots like doctors, professors, church leaders and elected officials.

My first bout at the newspaper, women in news stories were treated as appendages of men, always referred to as Miss or Mrs. on second reference. There was no Ms. When that "meaningless" title crashed the party in the late 70s, editors hurled insults at anyone crude enough to consider it acceptable. Even news sources balked, fearing they'd be regarded as feminists or lesbians, which they assumed were one and the same and certainly bad. Change always takes time.

We staffers had to agree on our approach to the Mormon Church, one of our major news topics. Since church leaders regarded "Mormon" as derogatory, we were supposed to first identify their organization as the Church of Jesus Christ of Latter-day Saints, impossible on second reference for a tight news hole. LDS was used then and in headlines. President, prophet, elder, deacon and even sister and brother were titles calling for capitalization. We wrestled with the question of identifying criminals as Mormons. Logically, if we didn't identify the religion of other criminals, we shouldn't do so for Mormons. However, a Mormon's crime often had something to do with religion, so we couldn't avoid it all the time. As when Mormons were molesting kids, bilking money from or even murdering people from their wards (congregations).

* * *

Ben Ling was just a couple of months out of high school in 1976 when he got former classmate Nancy Hobbs' tip about a copy boy opening and Korologos hired him. Ling's first impression of the newsroom was typical:

It reeked of cigarette and cigar smoke and the badly worn signs on the fluorescent lights gave visitors an idea of which open spots among the baskets and stacks of message spikes were the Wire Desk, the State Desk and the News Desk. The main sounds I remember were the clattering of the wire room and Selectric typewriters, ringing phones, and the shouts of editors. Bob Woody: Take a number. Keith Otteson: Boy! Everybody else: Copy![475]

If not for a quirk of fate, Ling's parents might have become Communists or worse. His father was one of 16 Chinese engineering students studying in the United States when Mao marched across the mainland trampling scholars; his mother's family fled to Hong Kong, where she became a nurse. A nurse at St. Mark's Hospital sponsored their move to Salt Lake City, enabling Ling to eventually join *The Tribune's* motley crew. Memories from his first couple of years demonstrate his playful approach to the job:

After about a year I became a corrections typist for the Copy Desk. That's when I first worked with Gordon [Harman]. He showed me how to use the Harris tape punching machine in ways that weren't intended, playing rudimentary games and making tape-punch messages. Around '78, I moved to obits, where I learned that morticians in St. George pronounced "garden" like "Gordon" and vice versa. Yes, there was an obit in which a guy named Gordon liked to work in his garden.[476]

When Ling advanced to night police (NIPO) in 1978, he got a two-way radio installed into his 1976 Corolla.

That big vacuum-tube sucker took up all the leg room in the passenger seat, and Brian Nutting christened me Car 13. I was envious of the photographers and Mike Carter, who had radios with most of the circuitry in the trunks of their cars.

Ben Ling with wife Jeanette after *The Tribune*.

Another Chinese kid, Marshall Ding from Mainland China, was hired as a copy clerk.

I think Schroeder hired him just because his name rhymed with mine. We collaborated on a great *Tribune* Christmas card that year, signed Ding & Ling. Marshall . . . always wore badly worn sneakers and t-shirts and believed that professional wrestling was real. I've heard that he is now an acupuncture doctor in Park City . . . Marshall kind of scared me.[477]

The night beat offered Ling more fun and frivolity.

Wire room machines were replaced with a conference table, which was perfect for a Nerf Pong table. Copy clerk Phil Miller brought in a Nerf Pong set, and the night crew held nightly tournaments until somebody left the set where City Editor Will Fehr found it the next morning. "Fehr put the box in his office," Ling said. "Eventually, Phil took the paddles, net and ball and left the box. I never heard whether Will bothered to check the box again."

Phil Miller, copy clerk and baseball fan.

Ling took away sober memories as well.

He and Tim Fitzpatrick shared the NIPO shift "for what seemed like years." Paul Rolly, night city editor (NICE) at the time, liked to point out that his sons were named Tim and Ben. "I don't know if one of his sons was more lucky than the other, but when Fitz worked NIPO, hardly anything ever happened. When I worked, we had car wrecks, shootings, hostage situations, fires and floods. Fitz used to joke, "If I'd been working when Joseph Paul Franklin was in town, his gun would have jammed."[478]

Franklin was the white supremacist serial killer who gunned down two young African Americans near Liberty Park in 1980 and was executed November 20, 2013.

After first finding the crime beat exciting, Ling finally got sick of the "mayhem:"

It started with the murder of O. Thayne Acord and his wife. I just didn't get excited and curious. Only sick. [Twenty-one years later, Tammy Acord still suffered from panic attacks and severe anxiety over 18-year-old John M. Calhoun's robbery and execution-style shooting of her grandparents.[479]] Then, the last fatal traffic accident I covered was a drunk driver who ran a stop sign and t-boned a family in a station wagon in Magna. The drunk, who had just lost his job at Kennecott (that's why he got drunk), was uninjured. I felt sick

looking at the blanket-covered lumps of dead children.[480]

Ling especially regretted writing two NIPO stories.

One was a "short" (two or three paragraphs) from a Salt Lake City police report about a woman arrested for indecent exposure.

Woolf later told me the woman probably suffered from mental illness, so it didn't help anybody to spotlight her actions. Then Bob Ottum [Valentine's replacement] wrote an attempted funny column that described the woman as a mysterious, attractive flasher. I wonder if that's what inspired that photo of Nancy Melich flashing Seldin. I talked to Ottum about my concern that the woman was mentally ill, but he just launched into a rationalization about some poetic license bullshit.

In the next instance, a Midvale police sergeant who normally told Ling about every little thing going on in his city reported that a guy was shot at for stealing a cold case of beer from a convenience store. The next day, Phil Riesen, who was subbing for Tom Barberi at KALL 910, complained to his radio audience that the shooter should be considered a hero for stopping a beer theft. "I never heard from the sergeant again, and I didn't blame him a bit."[481]

Joe Rolando ignores Charlie Seldin's attempted newsroom distraction in 1980s.

---

[450] Wikipedia.

[451] Wetzel, March 27, 2016.

[452] Ibid.

[453] Paul Wetzel email May 31, 2016.

[454] Harry Fuller email to Diane Cole November 26, 2011.

[455] Richard Rosetta email, August 2, 2015.

[456] Raine, February 16, 2014.

[457] Malmquist, p. 384.

[458] Woody, August 23, 1995.

[459] Gordon Harman, August 29, 2014.

[460] Harman, October 7, 2015.

[461] Harman email, October 8, 2015.

[462] Anne Wilson email, December 31, 2013.

[463] Harry Fuller email, March 26, 2014.

[464] Mike Carter, email to Diane Cole, March 4, 2014.

[465] Mike Carter to facebook Tribune group January 21, 2014.

[466] George Raine to facebook's Tribune group May 7, 2013.

[467] Nutting, February 14, 2014.

[468] Paul Rolly, *The Salt Lake Tribune*, August 2015.

[469] Paul Rolly at *Tribune*-sponsored roast, Gallivan Center, August 19, 2015.

[470] Paul Rolly, "Former prosecutor had highs and lows," *The Salt Lake Tribune*, July 13, 2009.

[471] Raine, February 16, 2014.

[472] Mike Korologos email, March 3, 2017.

[473] Verdo Thomas comments at Tribune "Old Farts" gathering in Salt Lake City, September 20, 2015.

[474] Nutting, February 14, 2014.

[475] Ben Ling email, December 26, 2013.

[476] Ibid.

[477] Ibid.

[478] Ibid.

[479] Derek Jensen, "Victim's kin wants killer kept in prison," *Deseret News*, September 5, 2001.

[480] Ling, December 26, 2014.

[481] Ibid.

14 - Just a Cub in 1976

One of my first assignments outside of obits took me to an abortion protest that became the object of a University of Utah student's assignment to analyze a news story. My story began:

"Society exploits women by abortion . . . legislation to use tax dollars for the slaughter of babies forces us to fight our own tax dollars," declared pro-life spokesman Janet Carroll.

Hundreds of shivering men, women and children gathered on the Utah State Capitol steps Thursday at noon to join in memorial services for unborn children "killed by abortion." Similar groups met throughout the nation and at the United States Capitol to push a pro-life amendment banning abortion. Thursday marked the third anniversary of the Supreme Court's decision to liberalize access to legal abortion.

On January 26, 1976, the student wrote that I used "more style" than most reporters for *The Tribune*. "Her use of color, order, diction and rhetoric are seen throughout the article . . . [the reporter] does not leave the reader with a question in mind . . . The story identifies, defines and explains." The student also described my story as objective; "the reader is not able to tell which side [the reporter] takes.

Prof. Parry D. Sorensen sent me the analysis with the comment: "Jan Bartley chose your story on the abortion memorial service as well-written. I agree and thought you'd be interested in her comments." Well, I WAS interested, even pumped up. I began to think maybe I could make it in this job. But even then, I must have known my lead was clear as mud.

* * *

Considerable anxiety went into my efforts to become a respectable journalist.

Unlike many reporters, I dreaded disasters and other stories that required frenzied phone calls, races to the scene and writing on deadline. On regular news days, I sweated through face-to-face interviews on unfamiliar subjects. I also struggled with phone phobia, the fear of being rejected when I called, something every reporter must face. To get past the paranoia, I'd work on deadline, waiting until the last minute for a necessary comment, so there was no time to talk myself out of making the uncomfortable call.

Going to emergencies was frightening my first few times on general assignment, because there was no one except a photographer there to teach me the ropes, if I was lucky enough to get a helpful one. It took me time to learn to identify an agency spokesmen to approach for the facts at accidents, fires, press conferences and other special events.

Thank goodness new reporters no longer were expected to sleuth downtown hotels and harass celebrities for a scoop. Instead, we were assigned to interview dignitaries at the airport, cover do-gooder organizations' dinners or snag celebrities for impromptu comments at the dedication of a local hospital wing.

At these encounters, my hands turned clammy as I fretted about sticking out in the crowd with my straggly hair, flood-length denim bell-bottoms and boots; about butchering quotes, and about asking stupid questions because of a lack of preparation and knowledge. As an English and education major, I hadn't paid close attention to politics – or current events, for that matter. I felt bereft of the background needed to be any kind of writer, let alone a journalist. But at least I was curious enough about people, events and issues to ask questions.

In a press conference with U.S. Sen. Sam Ervin Jr., for instance, I only half understood the Constitution and his role in Watergate. Naturally, I misspelled his name. Nevertheless, I quoted him accusing Robert Dole of obstructing justice by delaying the Watergate investigation until after the 1972 presidential election. Because of my interests in schools and sex equity, I played up his contention that federal education officials didn't know the difference between a "philosophy and a tadpole" regarding Title IX regulations.[482]

On October 12, 1976, I scribbled in my notebook while waiting to cover a Bonneville Knife and Fork Club at Hotel Utah:

Tonight it's Robert Redford. Last week it was Sam Erwin, ex-senator-turned-lecturer on Watergate, current politics and the Constitution. As usual, I'm perspiring and have cold, clammy hands. There's really no valid reason to be nervous besides the fact there's probably not a single Knife and

Forker in attire worth less than $500. My pants, as usual, are too short, and my maroon purse clashes with my brown scuffed boots. But no one will notice me anyway until I misquote the fair-haired environmentalist/actor.

Now I'm trying to kill a little time in the lobby of Hotel Utah until the knives and forks are finished placing tiny morsels of finely cut crab between the perfectly capped teeth of the guests. Walking toward the ballroom, it occurs to me that my Bic pen looks sort of cheap, so I dig around for the Papermate. After all, if Redford should notice me, I'm not going to be caught redhanded with a Bic, no matter how much better they write.

Damn it! He's not here yet. These celebrities think they have a right to be late. I've gotta have the story done by 10! If he doesn't soon show, I won't even be back to the office by then. Too bad he doesn't trust the press. He could make it so much easier on us all if he'd simply toss me a copy of his speech so I could sit back and drool. Not really. He doesn't excite me. After all, I've heard he's short. Hurry, Bobby Baby, this is a daily, as my boss would say. Should I or shouldn't I go to the restroom while I still have a chance? Before I get past the bannister, I'm met face-to-face with a face I cannot mistake. Not too bad, but he is a lot taller in the movies.

Me interviewing Robert Redford at Primary Children's Hospital.

My story appeared the next morning with the lead: "Redford said it with pictures Tuesday night." Noting his 16 years as a Utah resident, I went on to report his use of slides taken along the Old Outlaw Trail to arouse public interest in preserving the country's heritage. He spoke off the cuff because his prepared statements "are often misinterpreted."[483] Huh?

This was not my sole session with the Sundance Kid. I also tracked him down for a one-on-one promotional piece for Primary Children's Hospital. Photographer Tim Kelly captured my big moment as I tried to be nonchalant but couldn't wait to return to the office to report he was no taller than Denny. I later met the actor on the Fourth Floor, where he chatted with Gallivan and Company about environmental protections.

* * *

It was either feast or famine for reporters on the night shift. Sometimes there was so much to do or the action occurred so late that I had to start writing stories in my notebook during the events or on the way back to the office in a photographer's car. There might be no time left to write a readable story before the 10:30 p.m. deadline. Other times, there was ample lag time to chat with other staffers, work on my own projects or indulge my insecurities.

City Desk kept a basket for in-depth news features and analyses that could be used after slow news days, usually Sundays. Angie Nelson was one of our most prodigious writers, covering health issues. As the daughter of a physician and a mother with chronic health problems, she had an insider's perspective. When she took vacation, the feature basket became frighteningly light.

If there was no breaking news and I didn't have a daily assignment, I did my best to conjure up stories to help fill the basket and justify my existence without treading on other reporters' beats. Even though it was tough to get interviews during my unpredictable afternoon hours, I felt guilty if I sat around with nothing to do for more than a half hour. I often dreamed up feature ideas or leads during the night, in the shower or in the car on the way to work.

While Clark Lobb and even green reporter Paul Rolly could dictate breaking news stories, complete with punctuation and name spellings, off the top of the head, I took prodigious notes and then seemingly spent hours wrestling with a certain phrase. I cast about for a style less dull, mechanical and wordy than mine. But I hesitated to experiment with writing, fearing I'd be laughed out of the newsroom.

Like Rolly, I was touched by the generational cynicism that grew from the Vietnam War, Watergate and corruption in high places. I was suspicious of most public figures and always assumed there was more to a story than I was told. I was curious and eager to learn more, and I became a temperamental self-starter who hated being told what to do or how to cover a subject I felt I understood.

Unlike Rolly, I tried to avoid criticism at all costs. Sometimes I was so cautious that I suffered writer's block. Did I have enough facts to cover the topic thoroughly and fairly? I would ask myself. Am I just another blood-sucking reporter out for a sensational story, consequences to the people be damned? By bending over backwards to cover all the angles, I often wrote stories three times too long for the newspaper.

Even minor mistakes cut deep those first years on the desk. In a story quoting Frances Farley, one of six Democrats and the only woman in Utah's State Senate for 15 years, I spelled her first name Francis. No one on the Copy Desk caught it, and the next day I endured a telephone lecture from her about my stupidity and sloppiness.

Although I admired Farley's politics, which began by serving as campaign manager for Rep. Steve Holbrook of student-protest days and extended to helping people in need, I carried a grudge against her after that diatribe. I expected her to have more grace, especially with one of the few young women reporters in town.

Years later, *Tribune* artist Rhonda Hailes befriended Farley at an Alzheimer's facility and delivered her eulogy. While I focused on Farley's past outburst, Rhonda professed to live by Farley's motto, "One person has power." It was Frances Farley who led opposition to installing MX intercontinental ballistic missiles in Utah deserts. Rhonda praised her as a proud, optimistic humanitarian who gave Rhonda a "brush with greatness."

* * *

Art Deck's skulking in the recesses of the newsroom, peering expressionless over his reading glasses, eroded the confidence and concentration I needed to compose a sensible, intriguing news story. Fehr's coin-jangling while looking over my shoulder hardly calmed my nerves at the typewriter. The newsroom's constant phone-ringing -- our secretary slept in the ladies' lounge instead of answering the damn phones -- didn't sharpen the focus needed for smooth, logical narrative.

Reporters writing on deadline would hold out as long as possible before finally picking up the phone, usually with an impatient growl that put off the readers that Korologos and Gallivan tried so hard to cultivate. Many calls were simply misdirected or one more task reporters couldn't or wouldn't handle.

Already interrupted and assuming it a newsroom duty, I took more than my share of the calls, adding to my frustration. When an arrogant ass like attorney Dan Berman barked, "Rolly!" on the other end, I just barked right back, "Hold on!"

For awhile, *The Tribune* operated a special phone line for readers to report on crimes without identifying themselves to the police. Although yet another nuisance, it compensated as entertainment.

Gordon Harman would answer the Secret Witness line in his "best mysterious voice . . . Seeeeeeeeeecrettttt Witttnessssssss."[484] Joe Rolando overheard another reporter's side of a Secret Witness conversation about a failed newspaper delivery. As the caller argued over the advice to contact NAC, the reporter finally interrupted, "Yes, Ma'am, I understand, but this is not talk radio so I can't stay on the phone any longer. No, no, listen Ma'am. I said this is not talk radio so we can't do this. Thank you, goodbye."[485]

When all else failed, I wrote about education, since I had plenty of ideas and amiable Education Editor John Cummins didn't seem to mind. My interest in the topic stretched back to kindergarten, when I decided to become a teacher, into high school, where I wrote a research paper on school reform, and through college and two years of teaching.

By 1970, more than 300,000 students attended Utah's public schools and well over 65,000 were enrolled in the state's 11 colleges and universities, including LDS-owned Brigham Young University and once-Protestant Westminster College. Relatively few children attended private schools, because there was little need. Most Utah students were Mormons whose tax-funded schools were run mostly by Mormons who ensured they met Mormon standards.

One of my first education stories -- one that was assigned and merited an illustration by chief artist Dennis Green -- dealt with a school class on slavery. Here's how it began:

As more than 30 students feverishly tie knots upon knots in their 12-inch strands of string to the monotonous beat of a Negro slave song, their usually amiable teacher sternly paces the aisles of the classroom with yardstick in hand.

"No smiling and no talking," he demands. "And sit up straight in your chairs with feet flat on the floor! Tie your strings into balls -- tie until you cannot possibly tie another knot."

Where first there were snickers and sneers, the West Jordan Junior High School students soon become serious. Their goal is 1,000 knots for an A -- anything less than 500 is failure. Backs and necks ache and heads begin to pound as the same "there's gwanna be a time when we's gwanna all be free" blares from the class record player.

And to top it off, one of their classmates who poses as an overseer along with their teacher, Jeff G. Lawson, casually sips a soft drink as he patrols the class with his stick and supply of string.

"It's not enough to tell students about the injustices of slavery," according to Mr. Lawson. "They can better understand the slave issue when they experience feelings similar to those felt by Negro slaves," he said. He and Eric D. Johnson have used the simulated slave experience as an introduction to their teaching unit on the Civil War for the past two years. [486]

From experience, I knew certain school classes and sports still were off limits to girls. Grammar lessons had become "irrelevant" in most schools. Disadvantaged students still stood on the sidelines of education. Vocational education and special programs for so-called gifted students were in their infancy.

When the logjam in my brain would break up, I would pound out one story after another just to see them languish in the feature basket for weeks or even months. Extended series were tough to use since they required a space commitment of several days, ordinarily on the front local news page. But I failed to understand that. It bothered me that my in-depth stories took a backseat to more frivolous fare and often ran on Mondays, when readership was lowest.

My stories zeroed in on grade inflation, declining student performance, low high school graduation and college entrance standards,

liberalized discipline, unstructured classrooms and teacher strikes. I waded into school board infighting, school reform, sex education and home schooling among polygamists. I pointed out that Utah taxpayers could hardly keep up with a booming birthrate that crammed the public schools. Utah spending on education, as a percentage of personal income, was third highest in the nation, yet per-pupil spending was lowest.

I wanted to try a first-person account of substitute teaching, for example. "I doubt Fehr would go for it," I confided to Mimi, "but if done right, it could turn out at least as well as his little darling's first-person adventure to Planned Parenthood to pick up assorted pamphlets on birth control." After months of procrastination, I still hadn't started the story, and I had "several garbage features to grind out (upon request), including "a lovely one about a Rotary project as assigned by Jack Gallivan via Arthur C. Oh, joy, I can hardly sit still until I get started on that one." In spite of myself, I ended up enjoying the Rotary assignment. "The guy I interviewed was likable."

That first summer with City Desk I roped Denny into illustrating my five-part series on Title IX, the federal law that promised to change public education by forbidding sex discrimination, especially in sports. With his illustrations, my stories and Assistant City Editor Ernie Ford's encouragement and creative news play, we dominated Split Page.

After the series ran, I received several comments from women who had missed out on opportunities to participate in competitive sports because schools had made no effort to include them in their programs. Claire Davis, a Salt Lake County resident, wrote: "Your article concerning Title IX is very much appreciated. How I wish it had been in existence when I was a young girl in school. It is also dismaying to learn how Utah schools are dragging their feet in implementing it." Dave Robinson, a downtown attorney, slipped me a note June 26, 1976, simply saying: "Please accept my compliments for an excellent reporting job on your Title IX series." One of my sources, former teacher Beth Jarman of the Utah House of Representatives, described the series as "very carefully researched and written very well."

The first part of the series began:

If you are a parent, a student, an educator or a taxpayer, the effects of Title IX will reach you.

But Title IX is embedded in misconception, according to Beth Davis, Title IX coordinator for the State Board of Education.

Some believe the title will force girls and boys to shower and dress together in physical education classes and to use common restrooms. Parents even predict their daughters will be pushed into playing football with their male classmates.[487]

The lead of the fourth part of the series focused on job equality:

Title IX is a godsend as far as some are concerned.

Since this amendment prohibits sex discrimination in education programs, women educators and other employees can lean on the law in obtaining jobs and receiving comparable pay for equal work.

Rosa Wiener, Office of Civil Rights, said 50 percent of complaints made nationally since Title IX's inception deal with employment.

Enid Enniss and Debbie Thomas, coaches at Brighton High School, are suing Jordan School District for back pay. They are charging they have received unequal compensation for coaching sports.

Two women handle 10 girls' teams at Brighton, said Miss Enniss, while nine men coach 13 boys' teams. The school designates $6,000 to the men's coaching staff, $880 to the women.[488]

Ironically, on the same front local page as the second part of the series, *The Tribune* reported on the new Miss Utah, Suzanne McKay, the granddaughter of the late LDS President David O. McKay. In the lead, McKay disagreed with women's rights advocates who labeled a

beauty contest sexist. "I don't think it is at all. It's a marvelous way to grow and share talents and to meet so many nice people." The story went on to say "the brown-eyed blonde, who is 5 feet 6 inches and weights 100 pounds, is not a stranger to beauty pageants."[489]

Not sexist?

The same day, a story about Randy Matthews being crowned Mr. Utah ran on an inside page. There was nothing about his height and weight. There was no quotes from him. Instead, the reporter slipped in this sentence: "Mr. Matthews also walked away with all the special body part awards, except best arms." I could hardly believe the dirty-minded crude Copy Desk left that gem out of the headline.

Grade inflation became another of my split-page stories illustrated with a Denny cartoon August 23, 1976.

Like the cost of coffee, school grades have gone up, up up.

Yet test scores have not followed this trend. While there are more above-average grades among college-bound students now than in 1969, there are also fewer high scores on college entrance tests.

In other words, students aren't any smarter, but they're bringing home better grades. This situation applies both to high school and college students in Utah and around the country.[490]

* * *

Before long, pay became a burr under my saddle. I had lost everything I owned except my VW when I left California, and at *The Tribune*, I earned much less than I had at Capital Guardian & Trust. Even when Denny and I combined resources, we struggled to pay the rent and his child support. He had given his home equity to Swamper.

Salary and vacation time grew drip by drip for lowly reporters. For some, like Paul Rolly, the money faucet was turned up a notch each time he had another kid. I was childless, so I couldn't expect more than meager annual raises. It would be over a year before I could qualify for two weeks off and seven years until my first three-week vacation.

The Tribune's secret for keeping staffers despite lousy pay and scant praise, I soon discovered, was the promise of almighty bylines and a front seat to adrenaline-inducing breaking news. Access to information and seeing our names atop stories gave us a sense of importance and even power. Readers and even some news sources seemed to respect our influence. A story without a byline, on the other hand, became a bothersome burden.

Once I reclaimed my own identity and shed Ron's last name, I vowed never to change my byline again. Public recognition might not pay well, but it gave me cachet.

News scoops and A-1 bylines were intoxicating for buoyant JoAnn Jacobsen.

We worried that if we wandered far from the newsroom, we'd miss out on a big story. So D.B. Cooper's, the bar in the basement of the old Salt Lake Chamber of Commerce on 200 South, became a *Tribune* annex.[491]

Sports writer Dick Rosetta's first byline came from a Mormon youth festival at Ute Stadium the summer of 1963, when he was a summer intern.

It was an incredible sight: hundreds of dancers covering the entire football field. When I returned to the office, Vard Jones said, "Give me 14 inches and don't take all night. We publish every morning." I had no idea how to judge what 14 inches meant. But I gave it the old college try. I had seen how the other reporters would spin the triple-copy paper out of the typewriter, tear it off and pass it to a copy boy.

After a few minutes (it seemed like an eternity), Vard came over and asked, "What's your name?"

I said, "Dick Rosetta."

"No, YOUR REAL NAME!" he bellowed.

I said, "Richard Rosetta."

Vard: "What's your middle initial?"

I said, "R."

Vard: "This is a good review. I'm going to put a byline on it. How did you come up with kaleidoscopic?"

So, I guess using a four-syllable word got me my first byline. I think it was the last four-syllable word I ever used. Let me tell you, a byline on Split Page with a picture of the dancers . . . hey, I was in tall clover.

That summer upbeat Rosey also wrote about the head of the Forest Service for *Home Magazine*. "Another Richard R. Rosetta byline. They were pretty special to a young punk."

Rosey described these as "the good ol' days" when *The Tribune* was hiring, not firing,[492]

and John Keahey added that there were other compensations than salary, such as "a million stories to tell, over and over."[493]

Good ol' Tribune, indeed," countered Mike Carter. "They paid crap, the newsroom was a pit, half the desk was drunk, and they took care of their employees."[494]

* * *

Toward the end of my first year on City Desk, Mother Jones summoned me to Mr. Deck's office. I stood awkwardly -- tremulously -- in front of his desk waiting for acknowledgment. Finally: "You'll notice a small increase in your pay," he murmured without looking up. I feebly mumbled my thanks and left to find a paltry $8 raise, to $160 a week. Within days, though, the real reward came through: I was relieved of obituary duty. I was a full-fledged reporter.

* * *

When I wasn't writing for City Desk, I was churning out copy for the new tabloids inserted into the regular newspaper Thursdays in Davis and Salt Lake counties. Copies of these so-called zones, designed to boost revenue by luring advertisers with localized stories and ads, also were delivered to non-subscribers as wraps for stuffer ads. They sometimes were published on orange or green newsprint.

Walt Schaffer, a Navy veteran from the Copy Desk and make-up, was appointed the first so-called "zone czar," or editor, a job he obviously detested. He frequently muttered and sputtered and slammed his ruler on the desk. As budding reporters, Paul Wetzel, Con Psarras, Anne Wilson and I were among the first assigned part-time to these zones. We shoveled as much copy as we could produce into those pages. In not such a good lesson for cub reporters, we learned to pad -- overwrite -- our stories.

The zones reopened both good and bad chapters from my past, as I often turned to my memory and curiosity for story ideas and sometimes ran into people I knew from Davis County. One was the wounded soldier who threatened me and my little brother -- we were preschoolers at the time -- with a gun when we played in the dirt hills between our properties. Another was a former principal who'd been promoted to school district administration.

On December 18, 1976, Assistant Superintendent Gayle Stevenson, my boss at Clearfield High School, feigned friendliness when we crossed paths in our new roles. Yet whenever he saw me approaching his office, he hid.

My ninth-grade gym teacher and volleyball coach, Nancy Fleming, had become vice principal of a junior high school, so I tracked her down for a story. Here's how it began:

It's fairly uncommon for a principal to be a woman, especially in Utah.

Less than 5 percent of Utah's grade school principals are women -- there may be as many as three women assistant principals in the state's secondary schools. Nationwide, closer to 20 percent of the elementary principals are women.

Despite past explanations for this situation -- women were unwilling or unable to take on the responsibility, not enough women were qualified with administrative certificates, women were not encouraged or welcomed into these areas of education -- women administrators in Davis School District say they have not met with such roadblocks in their careers.

Davis has one of the state's three female assistant principals at Millcreek Junior High School in Bountiful. Nancy Fleming, a psychology graduate, handles the school's discipline problems, an unusual position for a woman.

Rosa Weiner, a representative for the Department of Health, Education and Welfare in Washington, last summer said former physical education coaches usually are hired as vice principals because of the physical clout they bear. Not so with Miss Fleming.

Even though she is a former physical education teacher, she also is a former counselor. She says her size and sex have not been a detriment in her job.[495]

My chat with Fleming's principal, former Bountiful Mayor Matt Galt, made it clear that her move up the ranks was actually quite incredible given doubts among the staff. But she went on to become principal of my old high school, Viewmont, where Almon Flake (his real name) held sway for many years. Incredible for my old home town.

Memories of riding horses in Bountiful's foothills inspired a feature published first in the zones and picked up by the Sunday *Home Magazine*. A horse rancher was using Utah's only Frank Lloyd Wright house as a barn. Here's part of the story:

Utah has a hidden treasure in the mountains east of Bountiful. The rare jewel is a house.

But it's far from the typical house next door. Not only does it lie hidden half a mile up a canyon from the nearest neighbors, but it also bears minimal resemblance to other Utah residences.

It is the only structure in the state truly designed by Frank Lloyd Wright, the father of the international modern school of architecture who died in 1959 after creating nearly 450 designs for buildings around the world.

Its location and the feelings of past and present owners have contributed to the mystery connected with the house. The original owners are heartsick at "losing part of the family" and would rather not be reminded of what they consider a tragedy, and the current owner enjoys his privacy.[496]

One Sunday, a large, dilapidated house on Gentile Street in Kaysville's farmland captured Denny's artistic eye and my curiosity. Our knock produced muffled sounds, but no one opened the door. We imagined polygamists or undocumented workers hiding. Denny snapped a couple of photographs for a drawing, and I followed up with questions of a county librarian.

The result was a feature on self-educated architect William Allen. The London-born brick mason designed Kaysville's Presbyterian Church in 1888, its old public school, a "brutish" Mormon tabernacle[497] and Allen's home on Gentile Street.

In another Kaysville piece, I offended well-known landscape artist LeConte Stewart, as his wife informed me by phone and follow-up letter, with a quote about modern artists.

LeConte was so upset over that statement about the modern artists being nuts -- many of them are among his best friends and in his temperamental upset he wanted me to correct that statement if possible. He truly never never speaks ill of fellow artists. Maybe he did say they were nuts. I don't know, at least he did not mean that. But I understand! He was a bit confused and under a little pressure and he says lots of things sometimes that he should not.

As for the "staffers" who write about things they know little about, in this case, I was referring to us and especially Dad's dislike for modern art.

You do not need to remind me about your husband being a professional artist. I'm sure that is very true, and you will surely learn about art through the years more and more as you go. And God help you to have understanding for him. It will help you both through the years and make you happy -- Please understand my situation. I hope we can be friends.

Sincerely, Zipporah Layton Stewart (over)

Thanks for the article, and please thank the photograph man for the pictures. We are so old and ugly I wonder that he could even want to take our pictures. Mrs. S.

LeConte and Zipporah Layton Stewart at Kaysville home.

At the time, I was so naive and my ego so tender that I didn't fully appreciate the Stewarts' situation. When I had visited their modest, vine-covered cottage in rural Kaysville, LeConte was 86. He had taken me out to the field where he would set up his easel to capture various nuances of the Davis County mountains or sunsets. I was charmed by him, the former head of the University of Utah Art Department, and his wife, the daughter of one of the first settlers of Layton, Utah, and a writer of short stories.

In my defensiveness, all I could hear was an accusation that I had misquoted someone. I didn't understand how Stewart might feel once his words appeared in print; that accuracy didn't require that I report everything he said; that I needed greater sensitivity for my subjects.

Another member of the Layton family in the news around that time was petite Davis County Librarian Jeanne Layton, who gained national notoriety in 1979 for bucking her board's

attempts to ban Don DeLillo's "obscene" *Americana* from her shelves.

Not surprisingly, Morris Swapp, the brazenly conservative mayor of my old hometown, led the charge to fire her. Having made a resounding statement against censorship and suing the Library Board in federal court, Ms. Layton regained her job a year later. The board then denied her a merit raise, a move requiring more backpedaling. Peter Scarlet covered that controversy, complete with its capitulations (a Scarletism), and as was his habit, he developed an abiding admiration for the female protagonist.

My zone duties also led me to Roscoe A. Grover, the host of a kiddie show I watched as a toddler in Rose Park, the post-war neighborhood west of downtown Salt Lake City. Uncle Roscoe, as I knew him, also had emceed a recital at Saltair where I danced to "Micky Mouse's Birthday Party" at age 5. My feature began:

Does Uncle Roscoe's name ring a bell?

Perhaps not, but he loves art. And by sharing his talents, he has kept the love of his life alive through his work and his children.

Many of today's moms and dads remember Uncle Roscoe as the mustachioed man whose dramatic reading brought such children's stories as "Robinson Crusoe" to life on television and radio. He's the one who sketched swans from numbers within seconds and hosted performances by local tiny tots. Uncle Roscoe's Playtime Party broadcast from Hotel Utah more than 20 years ago served as the Romper Room and Sesame Street for yesterday's child in Utah.

Uncle Roscoe's fast-moving shows are a thing of the past. A couple of strokes, some extra pounds and 76 years of life have slowed him down. But even though he walks with a cane and takes longer to get where he's going, he's still going.

"I'm still willing, but I'm slow," the witty liberal artist says. He has retained his dramatic flair, peppering his dialogue with first a Jewish, then a British accent.

Roscoe A. Grover was raised on a Nephi cattle ranch and served his Mormon mission in the Eastern states, where his mission president, breaking with tradition, encouraged him to stay back East to pursue liberal arts rather than returning to the coveralls and pitchfork of Nephi. Once back home, however, he ran a radio station in Cedar City before going to work as chief announcer for KSL Radio in Salt Lake City, where he "got the title in place of the wages."[498]

Low pay apparently was endemic to local journalism.

After an escaped mink ate my pet Mallards and hid behind our washer and dryer, I decided to see how stinking mink farms managed to operate in Salt Lake County residential areas. The farm below our backyard pre-dated our neighborhood, so we were stuck with it. But the hassle was good for something: It filled space in the Salt Lake County zoned edition.

While driving back from a meeting at Salt Lake Vocational College one day, I noticed a Ferris wheel in someone's backyard. I stopped, and another zone story was born.

Dick Brown, the homeowner, enjoyed quarter horse racing and demolition, a job that enabled him to scrounge for Western antiques like Murray Park's old Ferris wheel and train, one-armed bandits, a Wells Fargo safe, pot belly stoves, Indian artifacts and shoe-making equipment from the old North Temple Shoe Shop. He'd snagged Christmas decorations when the downtown Auerbach's department store went under. My news source became a cheap source of antique doors and hardware for my future dream home.

* * *

As my first year as a cub wound down, I yielded to an amateurish urge to mix my reporting position with my private life. Or perhaps it could be argued that a personal problem became the motivation behind a good story.

Swamper had recently landed teaching jobs at two private schools despite her lack of a high school diploma, let alone college credentials. I was indignant at the apparent fraud and self-righteous enough to do something about it. Using my *Tribune* title, I contacted those schools to determine the qualifications required to teach there. One question led to another, and I had the beginning of a comprehensive story on private schooling in Utah. Ernie Ford gave it major display December 13, 1976, with a lead that said:

Education sells.
More Utahns than ever are discovering this and are buying business licenses to open private schools. They

advocate different approaches to education than their major competitor, public education, and more parents are willing to pay at least $1,000 a month per child to get that difference.[499]

Among the schools featured were Carden School, run by fundamentalist Mormons, and Realms of Inquiry, an individualized program that paid Swamper extra for her "vast" experience and education.

Swamper's new husband called me at the office to point out shortcomings in my work. Assuming he was unaware of Swamper's deceit, I sent him a mock story (not planned for publication) about how she had cashed in on a series of tall tales. O'Fiel threatened to contact my publisher and sue me for attempted alienation of affection.

Without a doubt, I'd breached journalistic ethics with a personal vendetta, and when I told Fehr about it, he scolded me about getting involved in Denny's mess. Luckily, Gallivan was not contact; no lawsuit was filed. I didn't learn any lasting lesson about mixing work with family, a topic for later discussion.

By late 1976, I felt more confident on the job and happy at home. Regional VA director Elmer J. Smith wrote a letter to Mr. Deck commending my "comprehensive and realistic" coverage of a Veterans' Day Program in Memory Grove where, ironically, one of my estranged husband's in-laws was recognized as a Congressional Medal of Honor recipient. The *Tribune* staff accepted me as one of the family, and I enjoyed considerable autonomy working at something that potentially offered excitement, recognition and satisfaction. Denny and I, compatible in so many ways, planned to marry and build a home in the mountains. We were in debt but not totally broke. I was content.

---

482 Diane Cole, "Ex-Sen. Ervin Tells Candidates: 'Stick to Presidential Issues,'" *The Salt Lake Tribune*, October 6, 1976, p. B1.

483 Diane Cole, "Robert Redford Recalls Ride on 'Outlaw Trail,'" *The Salt Lake Tribune*, October 13, 1976.

484 Gordon Harman to Tribune facebook group October 2, 2012.

485 Joe Rolando to facebook's Tribune group September 25, 2012.

486 Diane Baker, "First-Hand Feelings: They Learn of Slavery," *The Salt Lake Tribune*.

487 Diane Cole Baker, "Title IX -- Its Effect on All: The Law Against Sex Bias in Schools Frightens Many," *The Salt Lake Tribune*, June 13, 1976, p. B1.

488 Diane Cole Baker, "Title IX -- Its Effect on All: School Administration Open for Women," *The Salt Lake Tribune*, June 16. 1976, p. B1.

489 *The Salt Lake Tribune*, June 14, 1976, p. 17.

490 Diane Cole, "School Grades Inflate With Times," *The Salt Lake Tribune*, August 23, 1976.

491 Rolly & Wells, December 31, 2004.

492 Dick Rosetta to facebook's Tribune group September 13, 2013.

493 John Keahey to facebook's Tribune group September 13, 2013.

494 Mike Carter to facebook's Tribune group September 13, 2013.

495 Diane Cole, "Women School Administrators Cut 'Barriers,'" *The Salt Lake Tribune*, January 27, 1977, p. 6D.

496 Diane Cole, "Bountiful Home: Frank Lloyd Wright in Utah,"*The Salt Lake Tribune Home*, November 27, 1977, p. 4H; "For $4 an Hour, Ride, View Heavenly Sight," *The Salt Lake Tribune*, September 15, 1977, p. 2D.

497 Diane Cole, "First Architect in Kaysville Left Mark on Community," *The Salt Lake Tribune*, October 20, 1977, p. D13.

498 Diane Cole, "Uncle Roscoe Remains on Artistic Course," The Salt Lake Tribune, September 1, 1977, p. 4F.

499 Diane Cole, "Private Schools Popular, But Their Role Stirs Debate Among Some Educators," *The Salt Lake Tribune*, December 13, 1976, p. 21.

15 - Introducing ESOP

Tribune management announced a new profit-sharing plan called ESOP (Employee Stock Ownership Plan). We 100 or so reporters, editors, copy readers, photographers, artists, library personnel, office clerks and news and *Home Magazine*[500] staffers were informed that everyone 25 and older with at least one year of service – I was 25 when I returned to *The Tribune* in late 1975 -- qualified. On January 1, 1976, the company started buying shares of non-voting company stock for each participant. Our employee handbook said:

> *Because the value of your interest in the plan depends on the overall prosperity of the company, the plan should give you incentive to do all that you can to help the company grow and thereby make your career more meaningful and rewarding.*[501]

Staffers with the highest salaries got the most shares. Unless they reached retirement, anyone leaving the company before 10 years forfeited their shares, which were divided among the rest of us. We gained access to our stock within a year after retiring, when we either held onto it or sold it back to the company at its current value.

By December 31, 1977, for example, the company had contributed $196,575 to ESOP in 1976 and $215,666 in 1977, when shares were worth $55 each. At the first of 1978, I had 20.12 shares that grew to 34.9 shares worth $2,094 by the end of the year.

Despite receiving annual statements, few of us staffers paid attention. ESOP was esoteric and remote to those of us who knew nothing about stocks or retirement plans. Ten years was a long time to qualify for ESOP, and retirement was a lifetime away.

Cynic that I was, I didn't expect to see a dime from ESOP because I doubted *The Tribune* doing anything more than necessary for us poor working slobs. I assumed family owners of the newspaper were simply dodging taxes and/or diluting shares of the stock to prevent large share-holders from gutting the company. I knew a Kearns descendant had recently called in his inheritance, forcing the sale of the 10-story Kearns Building across Main Street to buy out his stock.[502]

I wasn't far off the mark, at least on the purpose of ESOP.

After Senator Kearns died without a will in 1918, the family tried to minimize estate taxes.[503] His widow, Jennie Judge Kearns, even moved her legal residence to Reno, Nevada, for tax purposes. Controlling the value of *Tribune* stock was fairly simple when there were just five heirs: Jennie, her three children and John W. Fitzpatrick, who received *Tribune* stock in exchange for his share of the Silver King Mining Co. However, matters became more complicated after the deaths of Mrs. Kearns in 1943 and her daughter Helen a couple years later.

In 1970, Jack Gallivan was anxious about family talk of selling the company. It struck his accountant, Dominic Welch, as unfair that the company's $15-per-share stock had risen to $60 a share but had to be sold at the lower value to support a growing number of heirs with such names as McCarthey, Brophy, Wood, Durkin, Steiner, Stephens and Fitzpatrick. So using a 1969 tax rule shielding the company from taxes on stock appreciation, he devised a plan to buy out John Brophy and Shiela Wood, who held 40 percent of the company and were uninterested in the editorial side of the business. "My plan was greatly appreciated by Gallivan," Welch later recalled. "I could do no wrong in his opinion thereafter, and he supported any financial ideas I proposed."[504]

ESOP was just such an idea.

When the IRS came up with a new Employee Stock Ownership Plan a couple of years later, Welch studied it and submitted an article titled "Going Public Privately" for the Newspaper Controller and Financial Association's monthly magazine. He received $100 for the article "primarily because of Jerry O'Brien's fine editing (I gave Jerry all the credit for the writing, but I kept the check)."

After reading the article, *Tribune* Board Member Colleen Steiner, a soft-spoken granddaughter of Senator Kearns, insisted Welch attend an ESOP conference in San Mateo, California, and develop a plan for *The Tribune*. Which he did. While Gallivan gave it his strong approval, *Tribune* tax attorneys warned that having outside stockholders in a closely held family would be "disastrous."[505] Stockholders approved it anyway. In the end, the attorneys' warning proved partially correct, but that part of the story came much later.

"Colleen cared little about taxes or income, but she had enormous empathy for our employees and poor people in general," according to Welch. "She was my prime supporter on any proposal that helped these people." (Notice how employees qualify as poor people?)

Since Colleen's father, Thomas F. Kearns, had sold all of his *Tribune* stock to the company in 1952, the stock she and her siblings received came from the Jennie Kearns estate. Before she died, Colleen sold half her share to Gallivan's brother-in-law Jim Ivers so she could give the proceeds to charity. The other half, which her husband Richard R. Steiner declined, passed to their three children. "It was a very nice thing for Dick to do, and that's the only kind thing I can say about him," Welch commented.

ESOP's concept was simple, Welch explained. The company could give cash to the plan to buy *Tribune* stock and then take an equal tax deduction for contributing to an employee benefit plan. The plan then could buy *Tribune* stock from shareholders at an appraised price set by Lehman Brothers.

As Welch put it, employees were somewhat right in thinking ESOP was just for tax purposes, but most didn't understand who benefited most. *Tribune* stock rose from $60 a share in 1970 to almost $3,000 in 1997, creating "several dozen millionaires among the low-paid and highly qualified employees."

Until the unimaginable became a reality, we staffers who stayed -- those of us without the gumption to get ahead by leaving our *Tribune* family behind -- had to get by on salaries that lagged behind those of our competitors at the *Deseret News* and in radio and television.

[503] Dominic Welch email, October 12, 2014.

[504] Ibid.

[505] Ibid.

---

[500] Employe Benefits Personnel Policies, 1977.

[501] Employe Benefits Personnel Policies, 1977, p. F-1

[502] Ron Andersen, Historical Salt Lake City Walking Tour, 1998, from Salt Lake City Underfoot, *Utah Historical Quarterly* articles, *Deseret News*, etc., proofread by Randy Dixon, LDS Historical Department. Mormon Trails Association, copyright 1999-2011.

16 - Leaning Left in 1977

Because I worked general assignment Saturday, January 15, 1977, I participated in one of the biggest stories of the day: Gary Mark Gilmore's requested execution by firing squad at the Utah State Prison. He had refused to appeal his death sentence for killing a Provo motel manager. His was the first death by firing squad since 1960 and the first case of capital punishment nationwide in a decade.

Charlie Seldin had reported most of the court proceedings the previous weeks and months. *Tribune* stories had described Gilmore's childhood, girlfriend and attempted suicide. *The Tribune* had crusaded for legislation that would let the media view such executions, arguing that government should never put anyone to death without public scrutiny,[506] but to no avail.

Gus Sorensen, our likable, longtime suburban reporter, was the last to interview the condemned man. One of Brian Nutting's favorite Pat Bagley cartoons showed a nurse waking Gilmore in the hospital above this caption: "Wake up, Mr. Gilmore, it's time for your shot." In the background was a firing-squad rifleman at the ready.

Nutting was night city editor the night before the execution.

What a circus that was! We were getting calls from "news" organizations all over the world looking for some kind of insightful exclusive. One of the TV networks wanted to have a chopper flying above the prison (notwithstanding that the firing squad was indoors). Geraldo Rivera was in town frothing at the mouth and being just as obnoxious as you would think he'd be.[507]

George Raine waited in the freezing cold to cover the warden's remarks and add color to the story that night.

[Photographer] Tim Kelly had the good sense to arrive in a Winnebago that he either rented or borrowed. It had heat, and many reporters, editors, producers, etc., attempted to get in. I only remember Tim allowing one guy in, a photographer he knew from *Time*.
In the morning, when the remarks concluded, there was one very odd scene: Gilmore had been dead for maybe two hours by then, and as we [reporters from around the country] walked along, Geraldo Rivera was shouting into a microphone, "Give me air, give me air (meaning put him on he air), you can hear the shots!" There was a collective groan.

The reporter pool then toured the cannery where the firing squad shot the condemned. We were able to stick our fingers into the bullet holes in the chair on which he sat . . . A columnist from the *Chicago Tribune* wrote in his piece that the execution was so surreal that one reporter actually brought a date to the execution. It was he who had arrived with a date.[508]

All sorts of last-minute legal maneuvers were made to stop the execution. Nutting described the newsroom's reaction:

We'd already gone to press saying he was going to be executed in the morning, but we hustled to get an updated story in for most of the city run saying the execution was off. Unfortunately for us, the state's attorneys immediately got on a plane and flew to Denver to the circuit court of appeals. That court met late at night (or maybe early the next morning) and reinstated the execution, making our headline egregiously wrong – through no fault of ours. In fact, if we hadn't gone the extra mile to get the news of the stay in the paper, we'd have been right.[509]

Along with another relatively new reporter, I wrote a Page One story about the denial of an execution appeal, protests against the execution and Gilmore's life and crimes.[510] It was scary but exhilarating to work on a front-page, national news story.

Writing freelance for Reuters, Mike Korologos submitted several stories on Gilmore, stories that taught him a lot about writing. Articulate, exacting editors with the wire service would ask, "Are you sure that's what happened?" and then they'd tell him, "Describe the gun store (Gallenson's) where the rifles were bought for the execution."[511]

Another big story that month was the death of people vaccinated for swine flu. I didn't get in on that one but instead reported that venereal disease prevention was not being taught in Utah high schools because of Utah's religious conservatism.[512] The story's news play should have been fair warning how a later treatise on sex education might be embraced by my editor. It appeared on the slop obit page despite an illustration by Dennis Green. (I obviously had an inside position to get his help with so many of my stories.)

* * *

Mormon values shaped many of the issues I covered, because the LDS Church dictated much of what happened in Utah's mainstream and influenced the fringes. While conflicted over my desire to shy from the church while shining a light on its flaws, I was forever drawn to the culture's hold on my life. Constant effort was required to keep my reporting impartial.

As a feminist, for example, I was excited to cover parts of the International Women's Year (IWY) convention in Salt Lake as a prelude to a federal equal rights amendment (ERA). It was exhilarating to witness passion and bonding among Utah's thin feminist ranks. However, I was mortified and angry when the Mormon hierarchy urged female members to attend en masse to kill declarations on sex education, abortion and the ERA. The controversy resurrected frustrations from my youth, when sex education was all rumor and birth control inaccessible. As I scribbled notes during the voting sessions, I wanted to publicly declare my beliefs and biases, but as a journalist, I could not.

Recently elected Senator Orrin G. Hatch used the occasion of the IWY to grandstand against anything "anti-family." That is, anything that would give women -- and homosexuals, for that matter -- equality. Three years after the national spectacle, he still bragged about:

> . . . Utah women who stood up and made our concerns heard on such issues as the ERA, indiscriminate abortions on demand, distribution of contraceptive devices to young children without informed consent of parents, advocacy of homosexuality as a legitimate lifestyle . .
> . You will recall that Utah had the largest and most conservative state conference in the nation. And the resolutions passed at that meeting in the Salt Palace were a far cry from the end product finally passed at the IWY National Conference in Houston.[513]

It was partly the $5 million federal expenditure on the conferences held around the country, plus the resulting $3 million White House report, that gave Hatch fuel to raise funds for his own spic-and-span lobby campaign. But he also capitalized on supposedly subversive school programs like federally mandated skills testing and "values clarification," which bordered on "humanism." The kind of programs I favored as a teacher.

Whenever Hatch's favorite conservative women's group, the Utah Association of Women, testified before school boards I covered, I could be counted on to report the representatives' knee-jerk lack of reason. Either I successfully suppressed my bias or readers weren't very perceptive. In 1978, I received a letter of praise from a U.A. of W. board member.:

> I am very impressed with the articles I find in *The Tribune* that you have written. For examples: the one on private schools, the Utah Association of Women and now the Jordan School District.
> As a board member of the U.A. of W., I am concerned as to how we will be portrayed in the news media. When I see you, I know that the *S.L. Tribune* will have a positive story. [Gasp!]
> As parents of four children in the Jordan School District, we have been very concerned with the quality of education our children will be receiving now that we can't afford Carden School [a school run by fundamentalist Mormons] this following school year. . . . An LDS ward in Sandy has ordered a reading course for parents that are concerned because their children can't read.
> Thank you for bringing this problem to the public's attention.

Reader Cloyd Bird sent me a letter about the same time: "I would like to thank you and commend you for the intelligent and fair way you report things. I refer to the Independent American Party meeting last Saturday."

Astonishing.

During a routine school board meeting, I learned that an enclave of polygamists was educating children in a private facility called Oak Hill School. Ever since knowing a girl named Luana in first grade, I'd wondered about Mormon fundamentalists. Smart, shy Luana vanished soon after elementary school and turned up in the local co-op selling jeans and other dry goods. By 14, she was married.

According to my school board notes, Oak Hill was associated with Ronald A. Allred of 16961 S. Camp Williams Road, Riverton[514] and naturopath Rulon C. Allred, who was prophet of the polygamist sect Apostolic United Brethren headquartered in Bluffdale.

Curious, I called the school's headmaster, who agreed to talk to me -- in person. Scared, I recruited Paul Wetzel to tag along on an excursion to the boondocks of Bluffdale for one of my most ambitious early writing efforts involving unique Utah lifestyles.

Packed snow still covered the road to the remote, oversized house we sought, and my Volkswagen Beetle skidded up the driveway. A young man wearing wrist-length underwear answered the door and identified himself only as "head tutor." After talking a few minutes in the cold, he closed off the classrooms and admitted us into a sour-smelling foyer.

Apologizing for giving us the run-around, he explained: "If you knew the hassle we've gone through with the state, you'd understand that publicity is the last thing we want." Zoning and licensing officials had shut down the school of 162 students and 11 instructors, he said, so parents resorted to home-schooling with help from tutors like himself. "What's needed [in education] is a balance in life," he told us, "skill with the mind and skill with the hands, as Utah's Gov. [Brigham] Young advocated."

Subsequent interviews revealed that local school officials ignored the absence of polygamist children for fear of antagonizing Mormon leaders or triggering another Short Creek (Colorado City) incident. The 1953 LDS Church-sanctioned raid on the Utah-Arizona border town led to hundreds of arrests, including Rulon Allred's, and broke up families. (In 2002, Warren Jeffs would become president of the Fundamentalist Church of Jesus Christ of Latter-Day Saints headquartered in Colorado City. He was convicted of child sexual assault in 2011.)

I proudly turned in my story January 20, 1977. It began:

The building has no street number, no house number, no name. No one claims to have heard of what several local educators have described as a "polygamist school" in southwest Salt Lake County . . .

Will Fehr rewrote the lead and buried the story on the slop obituary page, C-23, on February 6, 1977. It then began:

Hundreds of children from polygamous families living along the Wasatch Front attend private schools run by polygamists, which is alright with some public school officials as long as the children receive an adequate education.

OK, so the new lead was less sinister and more to the point, but I had hoped for better news play in either case. I later understood that Fehr and, more importantly, our publisher, hated focusing on polygamists. The reason given was always the same: There's nothing new about it. More likely, my bosses felt polygamy stories offended the Mormon Church when it was more productive to get along.

As far back as the newspaper's founding, the owners occasionally refused to crusade for the "destruction of polygamy."[515] In deference to LDS President Alonzo Snow's support of his election to the U.S. Senate in 1901, owner Thomas Kearns suppressed the topic. That is, until 1904, when a group of Utahns accused such Mormon leaders as Senator Reed Smoot of conniving to break laws against polygamy contrary to pledges made to procure statehood.[516] Then when the new LDS president failed to endorse his reelection, Kearns revived the subject in his outgoing speech March 4, 1905, contending the Mormon "monarchy permits its favorites to enter into polygamy . . . and it protects them from prosecution by its political power."[517] *The Tribune* editorialized: ". . . until Senator Thomas Kearns stood in the Senate . . . and told all, there had never been made an instant and complete picture of the awful situation in this state . . . It was a scene to thrill all humanity who witnessed it . . . "[518]

By my time, the so-called "irrepressible conflict" had quieted again, and Newspaper Agency's employment of more than one polygamist -- in printing and the administrative offices -- might have helped explain why *The Tribune* now ignored the issue. The primary reason remained, of course, Mr. Gallivan's need to work with the dominant force in Utah, which was also his NAC partner, in promoting various causes, including *The Tribune's* financial well-being. Regardless, three months after my home school story appeared, the LeBarons, a rival polygamist group, gunned down Rulon C. Allred on May 10, 1977. All local news outlets gave polygamy prominent play that day and for weeks afterwards. Even *The Tribune* couldn't bury such a sensational story.

During Peter Scarlet's vacations, I got stuck writing and editing the Saturday Church Page. Instead of welcoming the chance to prove I could lay out and oversee page production, I resented the resurrection of childhood memories of religious intolerance in Bountiful. When I was only 5, my playmate's mother said he couldn't play with me because I belonged to Satan. In public school, I was expected to pray "in the name of Jesus Christ" and attend LDS Primary or Mutual after school. My girlfriend's mother labeled me a bad influence because I didn't believe in the "one true church." I worked hard in school so I, the outsider, a faithless Lutheran, could show that the damned weren't stupid. Now *The Tribune*, my refuge from that part of my life, was dredging up the pain.

That aside, the LDS Church's spokesmen treated me well: Don LeFevre promptly returned my phone calls and responded respectfully to my questions and requests for interviews. For the higher ups, I was expected to submit written questions instead of conducting interviews, and I received carefully written responses. LDS Education Commissioner Henry Eyring was gracious and apparently forthcoming for a story about his system. Apostle Neal Maxwell, a member of the State Board of Regents, was friendly.

While handling the dreaded Church Page, I received praise from photographer Van Porter, a Jehovah's Witness, who wrote a letter to the boss commending the respect and sensitivity I showed for an often misunderstood subject.

[506] Paul Rolly and Dawn House, "Hard news and raucous times," *The Salt Lake Tribune*, May 16, 2005, p. B4.

[507] Nutting, February 14, 2014.

[508] Raine, February 16, 2014.

[509] Nutting, February 14, 2014.

[510] Payne Harrison and Diane Cole, "One Plea Denied, A New Appeal on Gilmore Possible," *The Salt Lake Tribune*, January 16, 1977, p. 1.

[511] Korologos, January 26, 2014.

[512] Diane Cole, "Experts Say Better VD Education Needed," *The Salt Lake Tribune*, January 14, 1977.

[513] Orrin Hatch at a "Pro-Family Project" fundraiser, 1980.

[514] Utah State Board of Education Division of General Education, October 20, 1970.

[515] Malmquist, p 6.

[516] Malmquist, p, 226.

[517] Malmquist, p. 240.

[518] Malmquist, p. 241.

17 - Freelancing for Extra Funds

Almost everyone in the newsroom had a stringer or freelance job, tolerated by the boss as long as *The Tribune* got the story first and the work wasn't done on *Tribune* time. If not allowed, according to Denny, employees wouldn't have had a living wage.

Reporter Steve Wayda's new job: Playboy photographer.

One month Denny earned $700 retouching photographs for Brent Herridge and Steve Wayda, the Davis County reporter who took fashion photos for ZCMI ads and eventually became chief photographer for *Playboy*. It took Wayda a few years to pay what he owed Denny, but unlike his partner, he eventually came through.

Will Pickett, a copy editor who produced *Alta Powder News* and performed other public relations for Alta Ski Resort, hired Denny for brochures and a classy 50-year-anniversary poster. Alta tried to pay with an annual lift pass, which Denny refused. He had no time to ski and needed the money, for crying out loud! We kept the poster.

Dan Valentine also hired Denny on the side, to lay out and illustrate his Nothing Serious books. Late into the night, Valentine would pace back and forth between his cubicle and Denny's drawing table, literally breathing down his neck with halitosis rancid from chain-smoking.

There were some memorable times for other *Tribune* freelancers.

Bob Blair, who had many mouths at home to feed, was a stringer for a New York advertising agency that represented Allied Chemical, maker of an antibotulism serum. After an Idaho family was poisoned by home-canned beets (some died), Blair was taking calls at his desk when Deck loomed overhead. "What's going on?" he wanted to know. Deck let Blair off the hook that day.

On his lunch hour for $37 a month, Blair also wrote the editorial content for the *Salt Lake Times*, a business district sheet created as a vehicle for legal ads. On top of all that, he rewrote *Tribune* stories for the *Christian Science Monitor*.

George Raine wrote for nearly 10 years as a stringer for *The New York Times,* a job that often put his byline in the nation's most respected newspaper and led to several job offers, including the one he accepted in 1983 from *Newsweek*.

Bob Ottum was a stringer for *Sports Illustrated* and eventually became its senior writer in New York before returning decades later to write a *Tribune* humor column.

Even I wrote for a Washington-based newsletter, *Education USA*. The job was easy money -- $25 for briefs; $50 for longer reports -- but got in the way *Tribune* deadlines.

Mike Korologos already wrote for ski and travel magazines but welcomed Reuters to the list when Art Deck sought a replacement for O.N. Malmquist, who could no longer be bothered with Reuters when busy with his political beat. The international news agency "was happy to have a continuing relationship with someone in Salt Lake City" who could write about the worldwide activities of the LDS Church and other Utah events.[519]

One day Reuters' London editor called Korologos to see whether he knew of a Utah town called "Wheel-Ard." Misunderstanding her heavy British accent, Korologos asked her to repeat herself several times before she spelled out "Willard." He called the number for M. Dumar in Willard, and his wife answered. When he said he was from Reuters, she screamed: "Melvin, it must be true [that he was named in billionaire Howard Hughes' will]! There's another reporter on the phone!" When Mrs. Dumar calmed down, Korologos asked who had called. She said she had just hung up with CBS.

A breathless, almost speechless Melvin came to the phone. He asked Korologos what he should do. Almost laughing under his breath, Korologos told him, "Man, if it was me, I'd call a lawyer really fast."

Korologos wrote all this down in "a great story to Reuters," but Fehr wouldn't run it, even without the Reuters byline. He used a Clark Lobb story instead, but "he got fewer quotes and none of the excitement and anxiety."[520]

Korologos wrote many Reuters stories on racing at Bonneville Salt Flats, the place where British Sir Malcolm Campbell and his son Sir Donald Campbell sought world land-speed records in the 1940s, '50s and '60s. It was at the Salt Flats where Korologos interviewed Paul Newman in conjunction with the Budweiser rocket car. Newman wore bright green cowboy boots.[521]

Sports writer Marion Dunn covered Bonneville for *The Tribune* when Gary Gabelich was racing for the world land-speed record in the Blue Flame rocket car sponsored by the natural gas industry in 1970.[522] According to Korologos, all the major news agencies were there: *Sports Illustrated, New York Times*, Associated Press and others.[523]

Cell phones had yet to be invented, and the rest-stop phone booth a few miles from the raceway was the nearest landline around. The races were held at dawn, when conditions were best. On his way to the raceway in the wee hours, Dunn unscrewed the mouthpiece on the pay phone. Once Gabelich broke the world record,

"all the big-shot reporters got into their rental cars and raced to the roadside phone" only to find the mouthpiece missing. The next nearest phone was in Wendover, many precious minutes away. "Marion sauntered up to the phone, screwed in the mouthpiece and phoned *The Tribune*, thus scooping the world's biggest news organizations."[524]

Some staffers speculated Korologos' climb up the corporate ladder was impeded by covering a Salt Flats competition for both Reuters and *The Tribune*. Korologos set the record straight:

> I submitted different stories to each news outfit and then turned in an expense report for gas mileage and lunch in Wendover. Deck went bananas, thought I was double-dipping and wouldn't pay the mileage. I was mad, thinking it was very chintzy, but I got over it. Deck never asked me to quit freelancing for Reuters as I continued to do for several years after that.[525]

Korologos doubted the incident had any bearing on his future at *The Tribune*. Rather, he attributed his downfall to the fact he came from sports and promotions. It was customary, he explained, for *Tribune* editors to come from the hard news side of the business.

---

[519] Mike Korologos email, January 26, 2014.

[520] Ibid.

[521] Mike Korologos email, January 27, 2014.

[522] Wikipedia.

[523] Korologos, January 27, 2014.

[524] Ibid.

[525] Ibid.

18 - Personal Troubles as My Guide

In early 1977, Denny and I borrowed a down payment from his dad for a starter home and, at the same time, embarked on the toughest journey of our private lives -- child custody and related domestic conflicts, experiences that influenced my choice of news topics and affected my work performance.

Swamper was neglecting and downright abusing Lulu and Stormy. As an example, she claimed their grandma wanted Stormy's picture but not Lulu's when they brought home their class pictures. It was part of her same old story: Lulu got the brains; Stormy the looks.

More extreme behavior had her breaking infant Lulu's leg while changing her diaper and slamming her through a sliding glass door when she was older. Of course there were always other explanations, such as: Lulu was so spacey she walked through the door.

Swamper also concocted stories about Denny being a drug addict who threw her down the stairs when she was pregnant. She told Denny she couldn't tolerate birth control so he'd have to get a vasectomy. Sick of seeing their children used as weapons in their relationship, he was happy to comply. Then when he received a bill for the removal of Swamper's birth-control device years later, he had the motivation to file for divorce.

It goes without saying that Swamper spent none of Denny's child support on the kids, who needed braces. "It's my prerogative to use the money for whatever I see fit," she would taunt. The Gruesomes Twosome's determination to keep the kids away from us made us worry about their motives.

Although I liked the kids, I wasn't sure how I felt about raising them, especially if it meant foregoing children of my own with the man I loved. Scruffy, scraggly Lulu didn't brush her teeth and told tall tales like her mother. She was standoffish and passively accepted Stormy's so-called "zingers" -- biting insults -- until finally exploding in rage. Perky Stormy was cute but insecure, jealous of any attention going elsewhere. She threw a tantrum at the idea of us having a baby, if by some miracle we could or would get the vasectomy reversed.

I wondered whether the vasectomy was Fate's way of telling me I was better off not having children. With my parents as my guide, I worried I might be too quick to anger and overly critical of children in my care. I discussed the matter with Angie Nelson, the medical reporter who sat next to me and offered insights to myriad personal problems over the years. She referred me to Psychiatrist James Shaka.

"You must back away from Dennis' conflict or you'll be divorced within a year," he told me bluntly. "And you must accept Lulu and Stormy as the only children you'll ever have."

The personality test he gave me indicated I was highly sensitive and reacted strongly to injustice; that I was crushed when rejected or hurt; that I was simultaneously dominant and dependent; that I didn't accept people at face value.

Well, there you have it in a nutshell, so to speak.

My professional judgment apparently was less developed than my sense of fairness, because I permitted Swamper's shenanigans to spawn yet another news story. Some might say I was being a tattletale, a meddler and even a gossip, but I preferred to see myself as a defender of the downtrodden. Either way, the traits ultimately enhanced my career.

Swamper landed yet another job with children. It made me sick that an abusive, neglectful, dishonest woman like her was "taking care" of her own kids, let alone anyone else's. So I again used my reporter role as a pretext for ratting her while simultaneously producing a legitimate news story.

This time the subject was the status of Montessori pre-schools in Utah. Not so coincidentally, two of my news sources had hired Swamper.

Ironically, Dianna Fulton claimed she started her school because she was "horrified" by the quality of public education, that she hired only certified teachers, that "Montessori training without education training can be just as harmful as some traditional teaching methods." I challenged her to explain hiring my husband's ex-wife, who held neither a college diploma nor certification.

Ms. Fulton, who paid Swamper more than anyone else as her top teacher, was flabbergasted. The New Englander had swallowed Swamper's saga of giving birth at age

14 and raising five children while obtaining a doctorate in Montessori from "Vaser." That she neither checked references nor noticed the misspelling of Vassar told me more about her than Swamper. If I reported the situation, Ms. Fulton would have to answer to other employees, clients and licensing officials.

But of course I couldn't write that part of the story after Will Fehr explicitly ordered me to steer clear of Denny's problems. Besides, we rarely focused on staffer families and never quoted employees, and Denny was one of the few who knew the truth in this case. I reined in my biases and left out the juicy details to produce a mundane story that began:

> *Montessori, one of the country's most popular pre-school methods, is suffering some growing pains in the Salt Lake Valley. Operated as learning centers and as an alternative to public education's kindergarten system, Montessori schools can be opened by anyone capable of purchasing appropriate equipment and running a business.* [526]

Further into the story, I noted that "Montessori certificates can be obtained by anyone who completes a one-year correspondence course followed by a workshop." Somehow I doubted Swamper had gone to even that much trouble.

Naturally Swamper lost her job after the Montessori story ran. As Denny and I moved ahead with our wedding plans, she announced that Lulu and Stormy would not be permitted to attend such an event -- not because I told her employer about her fraudulent credentials, mind you, but because I revealed her past marriage to Denny and the fact that she gave birth to just two children, not five.

Our own marriage was solemnized on a Sunday visitation day (instead of April 19 as intended) so Denny's daughters could be there without alerting their hysterical mother. Gathered with us in the living room of a Mormon justice of the peace were our parents and siblings. Even after I had instructed the JP to leave out Mormon prayers and sexism, I found myself indignantly praying in the name of Jesus Christ and pledging to honor and obey Denny. Because the event was nothing like the Gruesome Twosome's recent fancy church wedding, Lulu asked if it was real. When she and Stormy got home, her mother threw a fit and vowed to get even.

Wedding day for Dennis Green and Diane Cole.

Swamper immediately accused Denny of perjury for claiming on our marriage application that he was current with child support. His mistake was applying a portion of the support to mortgage payments to ensure they were paid. It made no difference that he'd given her his share of their $40,000 home equity. Denny had to hire an attorney to argue the point.

Ped O'Fiel got into the act by cutting off Denny's phone access to the girls and erecting more roadblocks to weekend visits. I was forbidden to speak to the children on the phone because I was a "horrible person." To see the kids at all, Denny repeatedly filed complaints against Swamper for visitation violations. More than ever, we questioned Ped O'Fiel's aims.

Back at work, I wrote another story at least partially inspired by Montessori and Swamper's treatment of Lulu and Stormy. My primary motivation, however, sprang from my personal experience as a teacher and from a childhood friend's alleged abuse of elementary school students.

While teaching, I had witnessed ample psychological abuse of students to justify a story. Here's how it began:

> *Child abuse is not unique to parents.* [Now why would I think of parents abusing children at this particular time in my life?]
> *According to several Salt Lake area educators, many teachers psychologically (rather than physically) abuse certain students, and parents are the only ones who can put a stop to it*

"Child abuse goes on for sure in the public schools," a specialist in economically disadvantaged school programs said, "but teachers wouldn't dare use physical abuse anymore. While mental abuse is more subtle, it's just as dangerous."

"Especially hard hit is the child whose parents physically or mentally abuse him," a Salt Lake City District pupil specialist said. If a teacher adds to that abuse, the child is convinced his own low opinion of himself is justified.[527]

This story generated more phone calls and letters of outrage than almost all of my previous articles combined.

J. Richard and Liela Ann Law, a pair of teachers, were "stunned:"

Right now we are so discouraged and genuinely sick of "down on teacher" articles, drastically overcrowded classrooms, the unearned rights of students, the rotten attitude of so many parents and students, that no class or "specialist" could possibly inspire us to humanize anything.

In another letter to the editor, Vic Ashby wrote:

While The Tribune basks in the blessings of freedom of the press, it continues on in the self-destructive practice of "biting the hand that feeds it."

While teachers throughout the state teach and preach a respect for freedom of the press, the press responds to that civic devotion by printing articles extremely damaging to the teachers' images and morale.

Your recent article entitled, "Educator Cites Unwitting Abuse of Pupils" is a most unwitting abuse of teachers' self-concept, exceeded only by the regularity with which it seems to have happened through the years. Please forgive me if I have made a "hasty generalization" or a "sweeping indictment" of your attitude about teachers, but the above mentioned article by Diane Cole is so full of such types of statements that I claim the right to likewise use just a bit of the same technique.

I also received an anonymous personal letter which said:

Please pursue the subject of mental abuse of pupils in Salt Lake Schools by further articles. Often a teacher unwittingly displays her own prejudices at the expense of a small child who cannot combat a narrow mind. Point: Asking a child to stand in a classroom and declare his religious preference if it is not LDS, when all she needs to do is refer to the file of registration cards to find all his shortcomings and not make them public. It is difficult to speak to a good teacher about this problem. She seems completely unaware she has trespassed.

Score! My brothers and I had endured this experience of confessing in elementary school   that we were not Mormons. I had hoped such religious discrimination was a relic of the past by 1977, but not so. I vowed to figure out a way to work that lesson into one of my stories someday.

Steve Hale, information director for the Utah Education Association (UEA), an organization he regularly insisted was NOT a teachers' union, wrote a press release as well as a formal letter of protest to Arthur C. Deck and copied to John Gallivan and Will Fehr.

The press release announced that UEA leaders took "strong exception" to published statements that teachers "psychologically" abuse students. It added that the teachers' code of ethics forbids the kind of abuse implied by the "undocumented generalities made, in some cases, by unnamed persons."

Hale's letter berated the article for failing to permit UEA to respond to claims of abuse, and complained that a later UEA response was misleading and underplayed:

First, I would like to comment on several aspects of the article I consider journalistically unsound.   It is my understanding that three educators were quoted in the story. Diane Cole told me one of them did not wish to be identified. However, this is not mentioned in the story. The reader is left to guess who uttered the statements in several of the article's paragraphs.

Maridell Cockayne's name is misspelled in the article . . .

Now, I direct your attention to the 10th paragraph of the article which states: "Just walk down the halls of some of the schools and listen to the remarks some teachers make to children," said Diana Fulton [sic], a former employe of the local public system. "There really are some wicked teachers." What does this paragraph say? Isn't it a blanket statement that indicts all teachers by implication?

The eleventh paragraph says teachers cheered "in reaction to the passage of a state law allowing teachers to hit kids to defend themselves . . . In that same paragraph it is stated that "many teachers refer to the child as the enemy . . ."

In my more than seven years' association with the UEA, I have never heard of such a reference. I talked to several educators of long experience. Not one had ever heard a colleague refer to children as "the enemy." This leads me to question the validity of this generalization . . .

Diane Cole stated during a telephone conversation that there was a possibility of the Tribune publishing a UEA statement about this matter . . . . we decided to write a release on the subject.

. . . Mr. Deck, I did not write this letter for publication. I wrote it to point out some specific examples of inaccurate, vague and unfair reporting . . . I believe The Tribune has dealt with this matter in uncharacteristic fashion -- a way that does not reflect credit on a newspaper that has established a reputation for fairness. [528]

Well, you get the idea. The tirade went on for more than two full pages, single-spaced. I asked myself: What difference does it make who said it as long as the problem exists? Is UEA going to blackball or harass that person as the Box Elder High School chapter did me when I failed to join UEA there? UEA's paranoid, outraged responses would indicate that the person I quoted should fear for her job, if not her life.

Whether I had hit a chord or unfairly hurt the reputation of good teachers, I didn't doubt the validity of the story. Thankfully, Will Fehr backed me up with a memo to Mr. Deck "concerning UEA and Steve Hale."

Diane Cole has been writing education stories for The Tribune for a year and a half. In all that time, I have never received one complaint from either the UEA or Steve Hale concerning her reporting. She is now being criticized for doing what an education reporter should do and that's talk to teachers about what's going on in the schools. Also, Cole taught school for two years which might give her more expertise about what goes on in a classroom than Steve Hale has.

If the UEA wants to disagree with the teachers Diane interviewed, well and good. But instead of disagreeing with the teachers, the UEA attacks The Tribune.

Diane admits she was too general in identifying Maridell Cockayne's position in the teacher association. Ms. Cockayne is a member of the Salt Lake Teachers Association executive board. She misspelled her name because she apparently could not distinguish between the "B" and "D" when Ms. Cockayne spelled her name for her. How this error negates the thrust of Diane's story eludes me.

As to Hale's comments on Dianna Fulton's statement that there are "some wicked teachers," I can't see how the word "some" constitutes a "blanket statement that indicts all teachers by implication." Besides, Diane is quoting teacher Fulton. Is Hale suggesting that we censor what people say? Hale also criticizes the eleventh paragraph of the story which again involves a quote from Dianna Fulton.

As to being cavalier, The Tribune has printed the UEA statement which criticizes The Tribune and the attached letters to the editor. We even carried a letter from Maridell Cockayne in which she says her views "were intended to focus on a social ill in the hopes that a remedy can be mutually sought by the community, parents and educators."

In my view, this constitutes an attempt by the UEA to intimidate The Tribune's reporters and editors. I don't think we should let the UEA get away with that.

Fehr's support meant a lot. It bolstered confidence in my competence as a reporter. Even better, he said I could write. It aggravated the hell out of me later. though, when he failed to see me as anything BUT a writer when I wanted to be an editor, but that's another part of the story.

* * *

My self-assurance didn't last. Stupid reporting mistakes dominated my dreams. I worked on several stories at a time with few concrete results, fueling doubts about my ability to keep my education beat. It seemed like every time I faced an especially hectic day -- having to be two places at once for stories -- I was rushing to the restroom every half hour to deal with my period. "God, what a curse! It feels like two meat hooks are pulling me down from the inside," I whined to Mimi.

When I wasn't lamenting my inefficiency, I was dissatisfied or bored. As of May 7, 1977, I was making $210 a week. I told Mimi I should return to teaching so I could work on graduate degrees that would qualify me for better paying administrative jobs.

A predictable pay scale seemed an attractive alternative to the "arbitrary raises set by one one senile son of a bitch" at *The Tribune*. "That skinflint is the only boss in the outfit (among Newspaper Agency Corporation, the *Deseret News* and *The Tribune*) who gives hams instead of bonuses at Christmas!"

Paul Rolly, the rising star on the desk, warned me that everyone in the office was sick of my bitching; that I may be passed over because of it.

I had to concede that schools were not clamoring for my services, and reporting could be exciting and rewarding in other ways than pay. It was nice to be recognized as a reporter.

* * *

When Denny and I arrived to pick up Lulu and Stormy for a weekend at the end of the 1977 school year, the Gruesome house was empty. It was weeks before we learned from a secret call from Stormy they were living in Canyon Country, California.

Not-so-sweet Mother Jones twisted the knife by repeatedly asking about the kids and "accidentally" calling me Swamper. When I flinched, she pointed out how fun Swamper was and how much she'd always liked her.

* * *

Walt Schaffer quit as zone editor in the fall. Word reached me that Wetzel might replace him and that I might be assigned to work for him. I was offended, believing that I was better qualified, having been a copy editor, substituted on the Church Page and written more stories. Mimi got an earful:

My nightmare has come true. I still will have to do 2 p.m. general assignment every Saturday or so (I can't stand 2 p.m. general), and my education days will be cut back so I can produce copy for my male superior. And of course such an assignment needn't include a raise. They're bringing in a couple of new reporters who doubtless will earn more than myself.

As far as I can see, they consider me worthless around here whether I work or not, so why bust my ass to produce? And why not keep my eye out for a new job?

I've had it with that demoralizing dump! I wish I could quit now, but Denny and I are so far into debt I can't stand a drop in pay.[529]

On Denny's advice, I wrote a letter to Will about my feelings. I knew I would become too emotional face-to-face.

Beginning by saying I loved my work on City Desk and felt I was dependable and hard-working, I asked for more money and additional education days, fewer general assignment days and no church days. I wanted to say that I'd never again ask for a raise; that I'd quit first, but this is what wrote:

Even when I'm on general assignment, I try to fill in lagging moments with features. I doubt I've ever let down the Davis Tabloid effort, and I've tried to work in as many education features as possible. However, I feel it's physically and practically impossible to do an adequate job with education when I have only two days a week for it (and part of that time is spent in board meetings, etc.). If there's someone in the wings that could handle education (including colleges and public and private schools) any better in two days, I'd like to meet them.

I'll admit that I don't exactly look forward to substituting for Scarlet on church. To tell the truth, I have no interest in or respect for religion, and in most cases I even have contempt for the philosophy. Therefore, it is like pulling teeth for me to drag myself to work during Pete's vacations. Of course I will continue to be his substitute at your behest, but I can't begin to tell you how much I despise it.

I crossed out my complaint about him promoting Wetzel to tabloid chief and then assigning me as his "little helper" instead of letting me at least take charge during vacations. And the part where I contended "I worked on that thing more in one month than he did in a year!"

I feel like a senseless pawn with no continuity or stability to my job! I know

I'm not imagining what's happening to me, because others have actually offered their condolences!

If the past is any indication, I'll soon be wondering why I was passed over on the six-month raise. Since I've had to ask for both of my raises since I came back to *The Tribune* nearly two years ago, I imagine the story will be the same this time.

However, I do appreciate your past efforts in this matter, Will. I realize who holds the purse strings. Shirley has told us all that new employees get six-month raises only for extraordinary performance and that we are not to discuss our salaries. As nosey newsmen, you can bet the subject is discussed. We know who among us makes what and who is getting raises. Considering my experience and efforts in relation to those of my peers, I am underpaid.

I don't want to waste my time worrying about being screwed over or forgotten when the money and promotions are passed out. I'm confused and have a bruised ego. I guess what I really want is a vote of confidence from my superiors.

Thank goodness I never sent the letter. In the back of my mind, I must have remembered hearing about J. F. Fitzpatrick's advice to staffers: Put your anger in writing, put it in your desk overnight and throw it out the next morning.[530]

Even so, I did ask Fehr for more days covering education. When he started calling me "Teach" and "Cole" and gave me another day a week for on education, I knew I'd become a full-fledged member of his team.

I put the extra time to use reporting the end of Utah's five-year-old teacher quota system -- the one that made it so hard for me to land a teaching job. The oversupply of teachers had been controlled,[531] giving secondary teachers one chance in two of getting hired.

Besides profiling folks for the zones once a week or so, I retained my general assignment duties occasionally. One cold day in December I was sent to a small village in the Oquirrh Mountain foothills. This is how my story began:

LARK -- Kennecott Copper Corp. "lowered the boom" on Lark's 650 residents Wednesday night.

Their town will not survive another year, was the short but not-so-sweet

message presented by Soren A. Barrett, a representative of the firm.

"Well, it's a hellava Christmas present!" snorted one of the more than 200 residents packed into Lark Ward's cultural hall.

Mr. Barrett informed residents that KCC, which recently assumed control of the 640 acres of land that make up the town, will not exercise its option to buy the houses built on company-owned land. Neither will it continue to lease or rent the houses it now owns.

"The policy of Kennecott Copper Corp. has been to go out of the housing business," Mr. Barrett said. "It is not in the house or land rental business. Therefore, no leases will be renewed that now are in effect."[532]

Nancy Melich and a couple of other staffers said I'd nailed that one. In fact, Nancy joined a protest of Kennecott's decision, a no-no for purportedly unbiased staffers.

Speaking of bias, on December 5, I got so riled by a quote by Congressman Dan Marriott about the Equal Rights Amendment that I scrawled out a letter that read, in part:

Congressman, you said you oppose ERA partly because it would possibly change child custody laws. Unless you are frightfully naive, you are aware there are some horribly unfit mothers out there dragging their unfortunate offspring through hell. As the courts automatically grant the mothers custody in a divorce suit, regardless how good a father may be -- especially in comparison to certain women -- there is no hope for the hapless child in this case.

My own stepchildren now are living with a paranoid schizophrenic who receives child support yet refuses visitation rights for my husband. The court has little power in the matter as the woman skipped the state to elude bill collectors and others on her trail. The woman has no morals, no ethics, no conscience, but she has the kids. My husband's heart is broken.

As you will see, my raw feelings about custody stuck with me for years on the job, popping up repeatedly in my choice of topics to cover.

After spending much of the previous two years searching the canyons of the Wasatch for property close enough to commute to work, we borrowed $9,000 from Denny's dad for one-third acre of woods in Parleys Canyon. There were no manmade objects in the view we chose for the windows of our future dream home. We would live above the depressing, nauseating inversion that wreaked havoc with our sinuses each winter. This was the sort of uplifting action we needed.

---

526 Diane Cole, "Popular Montessori School Method Suffers S.L. Area Growing Pains," *The Salt Lake Tribune*, March 6, 1977, p. C1.

527 Diane Cole, "Educator Cites 'Unwitting Abuse' of Pupils," *The Salt Lake Tribune*, April 4, 1977, p. 23.

528 Steve Hale letter to Arthur C. Deck April 15, 1977.

529 Diane Cole journal, October 1977.

530 Malmquist, p. 270.

531 Diane Cole, "End Teacher Quotas, Education Official Will Ask," *The Salt Lake Tribune*, November 21, 1977, p. 1C.

532 Diane Cole, "Kennecott Lowers 'Boom' on Lark," *The Salt Lake Tribune*, December 15, 1977, p. B1.

19 - From Zones to Zealotry in 1978

One of our longtime staffers, nice guy Roy Hudson, suffered a stroke in January that sent him into immediate retirement. He could neither walk by himself nor speak to be understood. Sad as it was, I held out hope that the *Sunday Magazine* would improve under Dave Beck's leadership. He was the workhorse on Sunday Arts & Entertainment.

My hopes were dashed when Beck was passed over in favor of longtime TV critic Hal Schindler, but "the goddess of fortune" smiled on Paul Wetzel when Beck resigned and returned to the Copy Desk while looking for another job out of state. Wetzel was invited to write music criticism for Sunday Arts & Entertainment, granting him a "reprieve" from "*Tribune* purgatory putting out the zones"[533]

Apparently I'd dodged a bullet when passed over as zone czar. Wetzel described his sentence as editor as "the longest six months of my life."[534] Gordon Harman replaced him for two years before wangling Ben Ling into a trade for the night police beat. It became Ling's "year of hell." He was nearly fired for "naively and stupidly" telling NAC sales people that the zones "sucked . . . Fehr saved my ass from a furious Jerry O'Brien."[535]

On January 3, 1978, Randy Hatch was introduced around the office. The son of KUTV president George Hatch, Jack Gallivan's friend whose family owned the *Ogden Standard-Examiner*, Randy had recently received a master's degree from Columbia University and was going to learn the ropes of newspapering by working in various departments.

We unconnected staffers were skeptical after Tom McCarthey's arrogance on City Desk. The great-grandson of Senator Thomas Kearns, Tom acted like he owned the place.

OK, he and his relatives *did* own the place. His father, Thomas "Kearns" McCarthey, owned a 40 percent share of the company, but that didn't mean his eldest son had a right to cast aside assignments he didn't like.

Tom got his first *Tribune* job in sports but went home for lunch one day never to return.[536] As a general assignment reporter, he decided which assignments to cover, sometimes leaving events without reporters and Will Fehr

red in the face. What could he do about it, after all?

Kearns McCarthey family.

His father often visited the newsroom from his office in Classified Advertising. Rheumy-eyed in a rumpled suit, the McCarthey patriarch put the touch on John Mooney for sports tips and tickets. He took his family on annual trips to the Kentucky Derby, the Rose Bowl and other games. He also snatched accountant Dominic Welch away from his Fourth Floor office for daytime gambling trips to El Paso or wherever. "Kearns was one of my favorite people in life," Welch noted years later.[537]

"I suppose Randy Hatch started at $150 a week like I did," I cynically conjectured to Mimi.

Ultimately, this newspaper heir earned staffers' respect by respecting us and competently completing whatever tasks he was assigned. He eventually became publisher of Ogden's newspaper.

Meantime, Tom McCarthey moved over to Sunday Arts, where he wrote music reviews and travel stories that included complimentary tickets. In the early 1990s, he would become deputy editor, and by the end of the decade, one of the heirs of a $600 million fortune from the sale of *The Tribune*. Again, that part of the story comes later.

* * *

Will Fehr didn't often tell me what to do, but when he did, I got ticked off. "Get me something on panty raids or whatever else students do these days, Teach," he would say. Translated, I figured he was tired of my boring, in-depth shit on school programs. Ernie Ford validated my suspicion by pointing out that my three-part series on teachers had been sitting in the feature basket for months. "Could it be a hint?" he asked, adding that it was "chicken shit" that Fehr wouldn't tell me why he wouldn't run it.

I grumbled to Mimi January 27, 1978 that I just couldn't be a cutesy feature writer like his pet FiFi. "I'm too boring to spark up some non-event or non-situation so that people will read the garbage."

Denny's homemade greeting cards had a way of buoying my spirits. Consider his Valentine ditty in 1978:

> I've got an ex-wife
>   who definitely sucks
> And our children, it turns out,
>   Are a couple of ducks.
> We bought our dream lot
>   -- it's covered with snow
> And old Uncle Sam
>   has snatched all our dough.
> But through all the hardship,
>   trouble and strife,
> There's one shining moment
>   that's brightened my life.
> And that is the day . . .
>   You became my wife.
> I love you, Diane.

M. Lynn Bennion, Salt Lake City public school superintendent for 24 years and the first administrator of the Utah School Superintendents Association, became the focus of one of my early features. The reserved retiree struck me as an ordinary Mr. Peebles, an image reinforced by his first job teaching seminary in the rural mountain town of Kamas. But his father was the legendary Milton Bennion, the namesake of the U. of U. College of Education I attended for so long, and his humanitarian brother Lowell had spearheaded impressive community service projects at the U. The superintendent's reaction to my profile of him:

You did an excellent job of putting together my rambling remarks . . . I have had many favorable reactions, including one from an influential legislator who said that it was timely and might do some good on Capitol Hill. *The Tribune* is fortunate to have your capable services. I enjoyed our visit and extend warm best wishes for continued success in the important work you are doing.

Susan Keene, an outspoken critic of Salt Lake City's consolidation of schools as enrollments shrank, reacted to the article with a two-page, single-spaced letter castigating the superintendent's control over his school board. Her zeal became a burr under my saddle.

Keene managed to get elected to the board, from which she fought openly and often with administrators, turning two-hour board meetings into four-hour marathons that dragged past my 10:30 p.m. deadline. Since the controversial decisions came last, I never knew until the last minute whether I'd have a story worth reporting. If I did, I raced back to the office to bang out whatever disjointed mess I could muster.

At long last, my first-person account of substitute teaching, with its sidebar on the shortage of substitutes, showed up on Split Page January 30, 1978. I assumed it was a slow news day requiring the city editor to dig deep into the feature file. But once some of my peers started praising the piece, I floated around the newsroom on Cloud 9. My sidebar began:

> *There is no substitute for substitute teaching -- other than being run over by a steamroller, perhaps.*
> *Of course this is only my opinion after having thrown myself to the lions a few times over the past year. I have since talked to other substitute teachers, some of whom actually enjoy the job.*
> *As an education reporter, I felt it was time to put myself back into the classroom with today's youth to see what changes had occurred in education since I was a high school teacher a couple years ago. I also was substituting as a way to pick up a few extra dollars. I have since concluded that money isn't everything.*[538]

"I guess the first-person, semi-humorous stuff can go over after all," I rhapsodized to Mimi. "Of course I didn't even get a grunt from Fehr or a glance from Deck over it."

I received another pick-me-up in the form of a junket to Colorado Springs. Gerald Purdy, Clearfield High's vice principal when I taught there. also served as liaison for the U.S. Air Force Reserve. Noticing my byline, he invited me to tour the Air Force Academy, all expenses paid, and Fehr went for it.

The idea was to interest more students in the academy, and I dutifully gathered information for several features on Utah students and the education program there. The most memorable part, despite my anti-war sentiments, was touring NORAD's eerie, underground control room. The entire experience made me feel more like a professional journalist.

On March 8, I was ecstatic over a $30 weekly raise. My joy soured when I discovered that Wetzel's promotion to music critic came with $280 a week, more than I made. "You'll never be happy if you keep comparing salaries," David Beck advised.[539] I couldn't help myself.

When the new critic pointed out two glaring errors in my Symphony Hall story two weeks later, I petulantly groused to Mimi that people rarely said anything about my work until I screwed up. "I feel competitive with the weasel," I griped. "It ruined my whole day yesterday to discover, with his help, my incompetence. I had the information correct in my notes but screwed up the translation.[540]

Wetzel couldn't have been less concerned about my jealousy that spring. While interviewing Naomi Farr, co-director of Mozart's "The Marriage of Figaro" under production by the University of Utah opera workshop at Kingsbury Hall, he met one of her voice students, red-headed Carol Brain. This is how he described their encounter:

> When I heard Carol sing the role of Susanna, about a week later, I was smitten. Lovely, animated woman with a strikingly supple and beautifully focused soprano voice. Naomi and her husband Lowell, her co-director, subsequently invited me to a party at their home. Carol also was invited. In fact, we were set up. Sounds like a comic opera. We were married Sept. 6, 1980.[541]

* * *

City Desk lost Assistant City Editor Ernie Ford, who took a job as KSL Television's assistant news director. Why, I wanted to know, do all the good ones have to leave? Am I going to have to leave, too, or am I not good enough?

Denny's dad retired from NAC quality control April Fool's Day, bringing to 35 years his time in that toxic facility. Denny and I were on our own for lunch after that, so we were free to frequent our favorite restaurants with Paul Rolly, Brian Nutting. Denny's brother Jerry, who worked as an architect downtown, and my high school classmate Debbie Snider, who worked for Robert Redford's new Sundance Institute. As we strolled the streets of the city, we realized how great it was to work in the heart of the state's capital. We rubbed elbows with movers and shakers and other interesting characters and often stumbled onto an impromptu concert.

Al Church, a Highland High teacher who wrote for *Utah Holiday* on the side, called me at home for inside information about Knight-Ridder buying *The Tribune*. I knew nothing about the rumor and tried to shake him as quickly as I could, because *Tribune* staffers with any sense avoided *Utah Holiday* writers since Paul Swenson's unfavorable comparison of *The Tribune* with the *Deseret News.*[542]

* * *

In a rare move, Fehr spiked outright a story I wrote in April about one of the wives of Alex Joseph, who once had been polygamist leader Rulon Allred's "fair-haired boy." By 1989, he had become a dissident and created his own United Order in Glen Canyon City, a 130-member outpost in the redrock country near Kanab.

Alex Joseph clan.

Carmen calmly told me she was studying law at the University of Utah to help her clan undermine society with violence if necessary. Looking like any other co-ed in a plaid, flannel shirt and dungarees, the self-described revolutionary declared her disdain for her trying, "pinhead" professors and classmates: "They should know I have nothing but contempt for the legal profession and for the obscene democratic system and I intend to use my education to do what damage I can to it." She called Utah Attorney General Robert Hansen "a pig" who refused to arrest the Josephs because he would lose a legal battle over the legality of polygamy. "I say enforce the law or get rid of it!" she said. "But if the polygamy law were struck down tomorrow, every Latter-day Saint would be obligated to practice plural marriage. So the church won't let 'em arrest us."

This is how my unpublished story began:

Attending school hundreds of miles from home isn't Carmen Joseph's idea of a good time. She'd rather be with her own kind in Glen Canyon City, despite its "dumpy, crowded" conditions and frequent controversies.

But to her and her family's "kingdom," her "sacrifice" is necessary.

As one of Alex Joseph's 10 or more wives (depending on who has come or gone since she last was home), the second-year law student is learning "the system's language" so she can communicate effectively in the Josephs' many legal battles.

She is the kingdom's spokesman, Alex is the leader and strategist, she said.

While in Salt Lake City, where she attends the University of Utah College of Law, the 24-year-old student voluntarily leads a limited social life. Alex used to drive up from Kane County on a regular basis, but recently she has been alone or with her brother.

It's not her manner and dress that set Carmen apart from her jean-clad classmates . . . Rather, her philosophy of government -- the system -- gives some cause for pause. "I'm just too much a contradiction of their image of a 'polyg' who wears a long dress and pigtails."

She is quick to note that Mormon fundamentalists reject the Joseph clan and vice versa. "We have nothing in common. They hate us . . . consider us maniac hippies . . . The LDS kids are careful to avoid conversations of any depth. Others look at polygamy as a sort of disease . . . like it would be an insult to ask me about it . . . or they think I'm an absolute raving hippie or lunatic sex maniac."

She gets a kick out of her professors' reaction. "Every once in awhile I think they look at me and think, 'We're educating our enemy.'"

Her family intends to fight the established system with her education, which runs contrary to the usual law student's goal. "I think they should be able to kick this revolutionary out," she said, "but their law says they can't. I'm going to keep taking advantage of that law and beat them over the head with it."

She would like to challenge such laws as the co-habitation statutes that would prevent any of her children from being legitimate. "The attorney general won't have us arrested or even admit there's polygamy in Utah," Carmen complained, "so how can we challenge the law?"

According to Carmen, a University of Montana undergraduate, Alex Joseph's word was law in his southern Utah community, where members voluntarily pledged their allegiance to the ex-Marine and former cop. Voting would only weaken their community, a living demonstration that it works to consecrate everything under one man.

"We love it out there in the desert where the nearest law enforcement is 60 miles away," she said. "I wouldn't trade my relationships with the other girls [wives}for nothin'." One of her sister-wives, Boudicca, worked for NAC upstairs in the Tribune building.

Carmen felt it would be a major honor to bear Alex's children, who would be raised communally by sister-wives so she could work outside the community. The group's children, she said, were being taught to be contemptuous of outside society without showing disrespect. They were expected to respect and cherish their father in the rare moments they spent with him.

While Carmen's mother tried to keep an open mind about her daughter's relationship to Alex, Carmen noted, the parents of some other wives regarded him as the devil, Charlie Manson II.

Alex upset other polygamists by rejecting their authority when he went independent three years earlier, invaded their privacy and mocked their systems, Carmen continued. She claimed Mormon fundamentalist leaders exerted control with a "manipulative but brilliant scheme" for perpetuating the patriarchal system and his "raunchy, underground" business practices.

For example, she explained, leaders of Colorado City (Short Creek) threatened to break up families by publicizing dissidents' names as happened in 1952. So-called prophets declared revelations when dispensing women as wives like commodities on the black market. Men with the most fervor -- and money to contribute to the leader's coffers -- would get the women.

"You can get away with a lot when you're underground . . . like the mafia," Carmen said, adding that Rulon Allred's wives all had nice homes.

Those kinds of comments gave Will Fehr indigestion. Even worse was Carmen's claim that her ultimate goal was to attack the federal government's jugular vein. "I intend to use my education to do what damage I can" to America's system of government, she said matter-of-factly.

Carmen needed a law degree, she told me, to help the community deal with frequent search warrants, land and tax issues, marriage contracts and other legal matters. The group thus far paid no income taxes. Unlike John Singer, the South Summit County dissident who stood alone in his standoff with Utah officials over his children's schooling, Alex had Carmen and her legal expertise to lean on. She considered Alex a "genius" who controlled his family and supported them well -- without paying taxes -- by operating as a religious organization, making knives, selling candles and marketing ginseng.

The audacious spokeswoman left me with two predictions: her "vicious" group would soon have a showdown with government, and Alex Joseph eventually would take a bullet in the back from vigilantes, much as Rulon Allred was shot by members of the LeBaron sect the year before. "We've had Allreds threaten Alex," she noted dispassionately.

Even though she alarmed me, some of Carmen's arguments made sense. I had nightmares about polygamists caressing me and trying to rope me in somehow. But that didn't stop me from whipping up a story as fast as possible. To no avail.

"You're going to get her roughed up, Cole, and it's non-news," Will Fehr said brusquely as he shoved my masterpiece in his drawer never again to see the light of day.

Cathy Free had better luck getting an Alex Joseph story into the paper eight years later, in 1986. Joseph gave her an extensive interview about his beliefs and practices, which by then included 26 marriages. One "wife" had signed a marriage contract with him at age 9 but didn't actually make it legal until age 18. Joseph also

offered our spunky young reporter one of his marriage contracts, a detail she omitted from her news story.[543]

Joseph was not murdered or arrested for his radical ways as Carmen had predicted. Instead, he died from liver cancer at age 62, and Carmen, otherwise known as Elizabeth, turned her attention to the Methodist ministry.[544] Eventually, government attorneys did go after other Utah polygamists for tax and welfare fraud and for sex with under-age girls. The most notorious was Warren Jeffs, the Allred ally who became Colorado City's prophet before moving his clan to Texas, where the treatment of minor children was investigated. He was still stewing in prison in 2018.

* * *

Fehr's snub didn't deter me from putting polygamy into another story that year about the way school officials handled home-schooling by hundreds of fundamentalist families statewide. South Summit School District had singled out John Singer's one-room schoolhouse, High Uintah Academy, for review and found it wanting. I called Singer, an ex-Mormon who had yet to practice his belief in plural marriage.

In a rambling but friendly telephone interview a year before he was shot in the back by deputies, the 47-year-old television repairman explained why he and his wife Vickie were educating their seven children on their 2 1/2-acre farm in mountainous Marion.

Summit School Case Rouses National

Having quit school after eighth grade himself, this member of Hitler's Youth pulled his kids from Kamas public schools in 1974 because of the blasphemous language and morals of the other children, textbooks espousing principles he abhorred, busywork and regimentation. "Not that I'm bragging," Singer said, "but I think I've created a situation that my children like school. It's not boring . . . there's so much variety of things on my place for them to do."

For two or three hours a day, his children studied the three R's, the *Book of Mormon* and the planets, and the rest of the time they learned survival and self-reliance skills, such as building a log cabin, cooking a meal, assisting an animal's birth or tending the garden. Mrs. Singer, who studied elementary education two years in college, said she'd had to teach her children phonics from the beginning because they hadn't learned that spelling method in public school. The three oldest children, Heidi, Susie and Timmy, told me they preferred their parents' school over the public schools because they were free to do what they wanted, whether painting and letter-writing or jumping on the trampoline and swimming in a pool they dug themselves.

Like many fundamentalist Mormons, the Singer family resembled pioneers. The girls wore long dresses and braids, the boys close-cropped hair and sturdy clothes. Singer described his children as friendly and open with visitors and respectful and obedient to their parents. They went about their chores without complaint because they got lots of play time, he said. They didn't sass or question authority.

Denise Wheeler, a *Tribune* correspondent from Evanston, Wyoming, described Singer as affectionate with his family and friendly toward others. "He's not eccentric, tyrannical or a fanatic," she told me. "He's just a devoted family man . . . patriarchal . . . determined to hold his ground, and he will."

Singer let the public schools and even the juvenile court test his children, but when he didn't like the results, he shut them out. School officials had found the children deficient in academics and imposed specific teaching standards. The court's psychologist, Dr. Victor Cline, had concluded that the children had low academic scores and might have trouble coping with society after their isolation, but he also warned the juvenile court against taking the children from their "happy, loving, united home as there would be devastating psychological and emotional consequences."

Even so, in the first case of its kind in Utah, Juvenile Court Judge John Farr Larson cited Singer for child neglect and contempt and ordered his arrest. The Aryan who had been impressed by Nuremberg trial violence vowed to resist violently if necessary.

The arrest order was unenforced for months as various Utahns sought a peaceful resolution to the standoff. Summit County Sheriff Ron Robinson knew Singer would do anything necessary to avoid separation from his family, so he watched and waited for Singer to leave the property to apprehend him.

"Hogwash!" Singer said of the psychologist's isolation claim. His children watched television regularly and met many visitors to the compound since the confrontation. Heidi, then 14, said it was interesting hearing what people had to say about the standoff, but 10-year-old Timmy said even though most visitors were welcome, he was always on the lookout for anybody with notions of taking his father away. "If somebody came snooping around here, I'd go tell my dad." The family "prayed a lot to Heavenly Father that everything will turn out all right," Susie told me over the phone.

Singer insisted his family could hold out indefinitely against the officers waiting outside his compound. "We don't go anywhere. We make most of what we need from scratch, so it doesn't cost us much to live. Whatever happens next is God's will."

He didn't leave his farm in seven months and packed a gun for protection. Friends and supporters -- some from as far away as West Virginia and Tokyo -- sent money or took gifts of food to see the family through the confinement.

Rulon Allred's sister Rhea Allred Kunz, told me that polygamists were watching the Singer case closely because of their fear of a government crackdown on their home schools. "Those I've talked to feel the Singers are fighting a battle for us all . . . it's like when you throw a stone into a pond . . . it will injure all if the state gets the upper hand in the Singer case."

In one of our telephone conversations, Singer chuckled about the "shenanigans of the dirty skunks" who were trying to arrest him and doubted the stalemate would be resolved because the skunks were backed into a corner and "wanted to sacrifice someone else so they could come out smelling like a rose." He saw the education issue as Utah society's smokescreen to get his children away from him, an excommunicated Mormon.

"I'm either 100 years too soon or too late," he said of his quest for religious and social independence. "All I want is for 'the system' to keep its nose out of my business."

Just as the Nazis were subject to a "higher moral law" after committing atrocities, he asserted, so was the American system. He couldn't compromise with authorities, he said, because the conflict came down to a principle of liberty and gospel, or truth, and one compromise would lead to another and then another. "I'd rather be buried in my garden than arrested!"

Excited as I was about my story, I expected Fehr to hold onto it until the showdown blew up, making it moot. To my surprise, he put it on Split Page April 14, 1978.

The standoff dragged into the summer, attracting journalists from around the world to Marion. Brian Nutting referred *The Arizona Republic* to me for a local story about it all. I worked in the office on the freelance job until after 1 a.m. July 26 and then couldn't get to sleep in our sweltering bedroom.

My fatigue impaired my ability to cope with my stepdaughters, who had been permitted to fly to Utah for a month after Denny's extensive legal wrangling with the Gruesome Twosome. Lulu ran off after I'd stayed up all night, requiring us to track her down. I wanted to thrash her.

She and Stormy had both begun ignoring my requests, calling me vulgar names and telling me to shut up. "You're not my mother, you can't tell me what to do," often concluded our conversations. My Mr. Niceguy husband made excuses for them, blaming their disrespect on a horrible home life.

When Swamper threatened to cut the vacation short because Denny and I both worked full time, I was all for putting them on the plane. Instead, we contacted Paul Whitehead, head of psychiatry at Primary Children's Hospital who told us the girls were "moderately abused," depressed, angry and scared of their stepfather.

After the first of the year, Singer got his wish to be buried instead of arrested. In defiance of the law, he had taken another wife, Shirley Black, and refused to release her four children to their father. Law enforcement closed in January 18, 1979 and shot him in the back.

In his inimitable irreverence, Denny made light of the tragedy -- something we journalists often did to release tension -- with one of his little ditties:

Lemme sing you a song 'bout ol' John Singer
One helluva tale, a real hum dinger
Now ol' John said, "I ain't no fool;
None o' my kids goin' ta no damn school.
They teach 'em readin' and writin' and that kind o' stuff
Hell, sewin' and plantin' is more 'n enough.
So none o' you lawmen come 'round my spread
'Cause I got my rifle an' I'll fill ya with lead."
But out to the ranch the sheriff did go
And caught ol' John out in the snow.
Said: "John, your kids ain't in no class,"
Pointed his shotgun and blew off John's ass.
Now it's just to remind you o' that old golden rule:
By God, in Utah, your kids go to school.

The violence did not end with Singer's martyrdom. Addam Swapp married two of Singer's daughters and bombed a Mormon ward house nine years later, sending a storm of state and federal troopers to the farm January 28, 1988. While handling a K-9 dog, SWAT officer Fred House took a bullet from Tim Singer, whose legs had been paralyzed in a farm accident. Though devastated by her brother's death, *Tribune* reporter Dawn House Tracy went to work. Carol VanWagoner, new to *The Tribune* then, witnessed the scene:

> The newsroom was tense. Everyone was listening to the [broadcast] news feed. When Dawn heard the news about her brother, she calmly sat down and started writing a tribute about him. I was transfixed with her poise and courage.[545]

* * *

The Singer saga, on top of the murder of Rulon Allred by followers of rival Ervil LeBarron, amply confirmed Fehr's earlier warning about polygamy fomenting violence. When I later interviewed Anna Lou and Rulon Jeffs_(relatives of future polygamist leader Warren Jeffs) about their fundamentalist private academy in Sugar House, I didn't broach the polygamy issue.

Not until 1999, after Fehr and I had left the newspaper did polygamy become a common news topic for *The Tribune*. Arguments for renewed scrutiny were the exploitation of female children and the hypocrisy of polygamists shunning government involvement in their lives while openly accepting welfare through wives whose marriages were not recognized by the law.

The newspaper submitted Dawn House's series on polygamy to the Pulitzer Foundation that year and eventually devoted specific reporters, photographers and news sections to the fundamentalist Mormons.

In 2001, Tom Green was convicted on four counts of bigamy, one count of criminal non-support and one count of child rape for impregnating his wife when she was 13. Before long, movies and television series brought the lifestyle out of the shadows. Then after becoming FLDS leader in 2002, Warren Jeffs' marriages to teen-agers attracted national attention.

Either I was ahead of my time or I wasn't as persistent and persuasive as House and others who tackled the subject after me. In any case, polygamy was only one of several types of religious zealotry that made reporting from the land of Zion strange.

In August of 1978, a disaffected Mormon calling himself Immanuel David (real name Charles Bruce Longo) gassed himself in Emigration Canyon. Two days later, his wife Rachel (given name Markit Ericsson) coaxed or shoved their seven children from the 11th-story balcony of the International Dunes Hotel before jumping to her own death. Longo had been a Mormon missionary and Brigham Young University student before declaring himself the son of God and creating his own radical sect. Utah's public school system had no record of his children's existence.

Blaring sirens downtown alerted Denny and me to something big as we walked up Second South from our parking place near West Temple after lunch. The newsroom buzzed with activity as we rushed in. "Cole, call LDS Hospital to check on survivors!" Fehr barked.

It was my dubious honor to interview the doctor of the 15-year-old girl who survived with a split pelvis, ruptured spleen, fractured shoulder, mangled legs and head trauma. With resignation, Dr. Terry Clemmer told me:

> We won't know until she's out of anesthesia and shock if there's brain damage. She fell feet first, then hit her face and lower jaw. It looked like she straddled something when she hit. Her larynx and jaw were fractured, but her neck isn't broken, and her head and eyes look good. Her bladder isn't severely damaged, and her kidneys are undamaged. Fifteen surgeons have been performing a colostomy, plastic surgery on her jaw and repairs to her female organs. I have reservations on her survival.

Everyone did his or her part as a team to put the gruesome story together that eerie day. "It's been a shadow on the city all week, with everyone wondering how a mother could do such a thing, or how the children could be brainwashed enough to go along with it," I later told Mimi. "They apparently thought their father was God and they were going to join him."

The story was "a mind-blower" to the writers and editors in New York and London to whom Mike Korologos submitted stories for Reuters. [546]

Dr. Whitehead was widely quoted in the incident, giving Denny and I hope the publicity would add weight and credibility to his testimony in our custody efforts. Meantime, we couldn't help wondering what Lulu and Stormy would do if their crazy mother got it in her head to do something as bizarre as Rachel David.

* * *

Another sensational, non-Mormon story grabbing national attention -- and immortalized in novels and a television movie -- tapped into my worries about my stepdaughters.

Franklin Bradshaw, a seemingly modest owner of a downtown business, Bradshaw Auto Parts, was shot to death by grandson Marc Schreuder at the behest of Bradshaw's daughter. Childhood memories of waiting hours for my father outside the gritty parts store piqued my interest in the crime, but once I learned the details, my imagination ran wild.

Swamper neglected, abused and manipulated her daughters much as Frances Schreuder did her sons Larry and Marc so she would inherit a fortune. Could brow-beaten Lulu or volatile Stormy ever be coerced into killing me or Denny for revenge or money? The Gruesomes obviously felt fine about using the kids, so I had to hope our assets were too trivial for their risk of prison.

Tension intensified at home that summer of 1978. Legal haggling, unexpected taxes and braces for the girls cost money we didn't have. Denny stepped up his photo retouching to help pay the bills, and he often went to bed with cluster headaches. I wasn't giving him the attaboys (positive reinforcement) he craved, because I resented his failure to discipline his daughters and his refusal to try reversing his vasectomy or to explore other ways of having children.

Some days we drove to work in silence before spending all day in the same office without looking each other's way. The guy who used to make me laugh called me a "liberated asshole" one day, a slut the next. Fortunately, we would make up within a day or two and vow to support each other through the stress.

For once we got to take the kids to *The Tribune's* annual picnic at Washington Park in Parleys Canyon without a fuss from the Gruesomes. We had fun, as we usually did at these events.

Washington Park was the staff's favorite picnic site before the state's Dram Shop law put an end to the annual beer bashes. Mr. Deck would soberly stand by in white shirt and bow tie while the rest of us played softball and volleyball and cheered on red-faced youngsters in Korologos' watermelon-eating contest. The threat of the police showing up -- which they did a couple of times -- "was just another excuse to fill our pockets with cans as we left the party," according to Capitol reporter Dave Jonsson.[547]

Soon after we sent the girls on a plane back to California, we opened our front door to find a giggling Lulu. "I'm here visiting Eva," a friend in the neighborhood, she lied. In fact, the Gruesomes had moved back to Utah, waiting just long enough for us to spend money on their airline tickets.

We landed back into a smelly stew of lies, taunts, accusations and punishment.

When we picked up the kids on weekends, Ped O'Fiel required Denny to go to the door so he could heckle him with names like "telephone hero," "wacko," "dumb shit," "loser" and "weasel." He then refused to release the girls until we waited from 20 minutes to two hours, purportedly because we'd returned them home late the previous week.

Since Swamper didn't know me "from Adam," she didn't let me to pick up the kids when Denny worked late. Consequently, we sometimes picked them up after 11 p.m. Somehow, however, Swamper figured out who I was the afternoon I lunged for her throat.

As I held my door and seatback for Lulu to climb into the car, Swamper lumbered across her front yard shrieking for Lulu to get back in the house. She yanked the girl away, wrenching her arm, and I sprang for the bitch, vowing to break her neck. Denny caught me mid-air.

"You shouldn't have done that," Lulu told me when released an hour or so later. "Mom's been waiting for you to lose control so she could use it against you in court." And sure enough, Swamper told a justice of the peace that I'd made terroristic threats against her. Our lawyer got the charge dropped.

On another pick-up incident, Denny was on the verge of attacking Ped O'Fiel when I ran to a neighbor's house to call the police for intervention. As we waited, the neighbor related how Swamper regularly screamed at the kids and threw kitchen knives at Ped O'Fiel's 18-year-old daughter Mary.

Within days of that chat, Mary was kicked out of the house and reported to police as a burglar for taking her belongings. Homeless, she told us about the horrors of the Gruesome household and asked to stay with us.

According to Mary, Swamper beat Stormy and Lulu often and grounded them for weeks at a time for minor infractions. She threatened to flush Stormy's hamster down the toilet and to ring the neck of Lulu's rabbit if they didn't hop to her commands fast enough. When she wasn't taking Valium herself, she was giving it to the kids to keep them quiet.

"My dad is sick," she added.

Aware Ped O'Fiel would accuse us of alienation of affection, kidnap, rape or some other fabrication if we came to Mary's aid, we turned her away, and she moved in with the boyfriend he detested.

* * *

In August 1978, Denny got a $30-a-week raise to $350 a week. My euphoria was deflated by Korologos' failure to invite me to a banquet for zone workers. "Here I was, one of the pioneers, and some participants contributed very little," I whined to Mimi.

Then when Jack Schroeder neglected to tell me and Denny about his party for a new Copy Desk intern, my outsider status was established. "Brian's about the only one who invites us to staffer parties," I told my journal.

Just when I thought my ego couldn't survive another slight, I overheard staffers making fun of me at the State Noodle House, where high partitions hid me from view. David Beck, temporarily back on the Copy Desk, Cindy Gilchrist and the intern mimicked my story about Hogle Zoo's annual birthday celebration for the gorilla couple named after Elaine and Dan Valentine, who used his column to raise funds for their purchase. "I felt like a worthless fool!"[548]

I polished up my resume and made appointments for some teaching interviews.

533 Wetzel, May 31, 2016.

534 Wetzel, March 27, 2016.

535 Ling, December 25, 2014..

536 Barbi Robison interview, November 13, 2015.

537 Jerry Spangler, "McCartheys: Carrying the torch?" *Deseret News*, June 12, 2001.

538 Diane Cole, "Writer Learns Lesson for Survival in Substitute Teaching Experience," *The Salt Lake Tribune*, January 30, 1978, p. 17.

539 Diane Cole journal March 8, 1978.

540 Diane Cole journal March 21, 1978.

541 Wetzel, May 31, 2016.

542 Swenson, 1974, pp. 4-34.

543 Cathy Free on facebook October 15, 2015.

544 Dawn House, "Sister Widows: Wives of dead polygamist rebuild their lives," *Salt Lake Tribune*, November 1, 2006.

545 Carol VanWagoner email, August 10, 2015.

546 Mike Korologos email January 27, 2014.

547 Jonsson, August 10, 2015.

548 Diane's journal, August 9, 1978.

20 - Purposes of PR

By the end of the year, I was waffling about leaving *The Tribune*, not only because my interviews for teaching jobs never panned out, but also because I felt closer to *The Tribune* family. I half-heartedly discussed an option with Mimi:

Maybe I should look into that PR job at the U. of U. It would pay from the mid to upper teens, a nice change from the lower teens. Unfortunately, Ray Haeckle is a bigwig there . . . being able to tolerate him would be a major challenge for me. Let's face it, I'll never be really satisfied.

Being a flack, as we derisively dubbed the public relations people who pestered us for attention and inundated us with press releases, was not something many newshounds aspired to. Hard-bitten reporters and editors regarded flacks as sell-outs, journalists who compromised their ideals and ethics for bigger bucks. Reporters often had to contend with or circumvent a "spokesman" to get to the meat of a story.

For me, Wendell Ashton represented the quintessential flack. On a visit to my PR class at the University of Utah in 1972, the LDS Church's new chief spokesman, who had led efforts to defeat liquor-by-the-drink in 1968 and became publisher of the *Deseret News* in 1978, reeked of cynicism. He essentially told us it was perfectly fine for someone in public relations to stymie, mislead or outright lie to the press and public because his (yes, *his*) first -- and apparently only -- commitment was to the organization he represented.

In fairness, reporters relied on press releases and press conferences for breaking news or on slow news days when we were too lazy to generate our own ideas or follow new leads. Company recognition of people or places helped fill a gaping news hole.

And some flacks were better than others. Ray Haeckle dragged his feet at the University of Utah while By Sims readily responded to our questions at the colleges he represented. J.R. Allred continually griped that Utah State University got less attention than the University of Utah or even Weber State College. He refused to accept my explanation that trips to Logan required a full day for both me and a photographer, something we could not afford every week even if our readers were interested in out-of-town news. His assistant John Flynn was easier going.

BYU's Paul Richards was impressively professional and helpful at the church school, much as most PR people at Mormon headquarters had been when I substituted on the church beat. Jeri Cartright could be counted on to play it straight about Salt Lake County and Utah Transit Authority. After leaving *The Tribune*, Carol Sisco gave reporters the scoop about the state's environmental, social services and health departments. It always helped when information specialists had been reporters themselves.

I became lunching buddies with Janice Keller, public information assistant for Salt Lake City School District, Eileen Rencher from the State School Office and Lee Craig Douglas, who did PR for Westminster College before marrying bombastic legislator Hughes Brockbank and becoming marketing manager for Utah Technical College. Rencher was assisted by a rumpled woman who muddled the answers to my questions, and Douglas was replaced by a fussy guy who drove me crazy with his phone calls and obfuscation.

Having studied journalism herself, Jan Keller understood the kind of information I needed and often provided it before I even asked. She alerted me to positive activities in the school district but also quickly paved my way to the right people when a potentially damaging story was in the works. She also stood up for me, as with this letter to Mr. Deck June 26, 1979:

Some of our board members have been critical recently of some of Diane's reports. I disagree and am sorry she has to encounter this kind of criticism. She maintains her sense of humor through very trying times at our meetings of late, and writes her usual fair report of the meetings.

Those Tuesday night meetings were trying, indeed, as board members or union reps flung insults my way and the meetings dragged on past my 10:30 p.m. deadline. But some of my worst critics came not from Salt Lake City but Granite School District.

More than once, Granite union director Bob Beall yelled at me across a room full of people. He didn't like the "union" word used in print. After greeting me with an insincere, toothy grin, Granite Superintendent John Reed Call cast cutting allusions to media intrusions my way.

Because I sometimes covered more than one board meeting at a time, I heavily depended on PR people for facts about each board's decisions. I would call in a cryptic report of the issues of greatest public interest -- school closures and boundary changes, tax increases and staff firings -- and then follow-up in greater depth the next day.

I was not one of those reporters who could create a masterpiece off the top of my head, so the rewrite person or typist on the other end of the line was in for a challenge. If the flack couldn't provide accurate or complete information, which happened at times, I was sunk.

Once in particular, my friendship with a public information officer backfired, reminding me to keep our relationship professional.

A teacher tipped me off that Darlene Ball, one of the first female assistant superintendents in the state, used a private bank account for district petty cash. During a conversation lasting all afternoon and into the evening, I stupidly told Jan Keller the source of my information and asked her to keep it confidential. She didn't, and Ball prepared to fire my news source. Both Jan and I were stunned by Ball's reaction and rattled by our own lapses of judgment. Fortunately, Jan changed Ball's mind.

21 -Tribune Shooters

In the 1970s, the Photography Department was squeezed into a dim, stifling, closet-like space at the east end of the newsroom. Three tiny darkrooms sufficed for film developing while one slightly larger room contained trays of liquid for developing prints. There was barely enough room in the studio to lay out a nine-foot wide roll of paper.[549] Just outside the studio stood a gun-metal filing cabinet and desk complete with spikes and typewriter for organizing orders. Next to Denny's drawing table was the beat-up yellowish Naugahyde couch where unengaged photographers smoked and chatted between jobs.

By 1978, I'd gotten to know most *Tribune* photographers pretty well. Tim Kelly and Lynn Johnson, in particular, had helped me learn the ropes of reporting fires and other breaking news. Later, they and their peers drove me on feature-writing excursions to public schools, colleges and universities around the state.

Tim Kelly

Besides being a nice, upbeat guy, **Tim Kelly** offered bulk as a bonus. His 6-foot, 5-inch frame, tightly squeezed into and extracted from his yellow VW bug, always made me feel safe, whether I was approaching hostile truckers on strike or walking a sleazy street at night.

I wasn't the only one relying on the gentle giant for security. Paul Rolly often recounted the night in the late 1970s when an irate caller threatened to come to the newsroom to beat the shit out of him. "Bring it on!" Rolly challenged. "Come on down and ask for Tim Kelly!"[550]

Mike Korologos recalled the time Tim Kelly stuffed him into one of the newsroom's huge, green wastebaskets for his over-the-top teasing of the photo lab guys.[551]

Kelly was hired as a copy boy just out of Judge Memorial High School while going door to door down Main Street looking for a job. The loss of an eye in childhood gave him a special perspective that produced award-winning and marketable photography. He became Denny's best friend, leading to years of good times together with his wife Sharon.

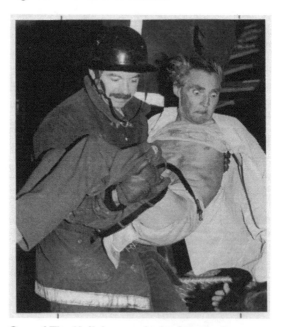

One of Tim Kelly's award-winning photos.

When working as city editor one night, Kelly's former classmate George Raine pushed the button on the City Desk radio. "City Desk to Car One. Tim, it's George. Can you swing by Bill and Nada's? They won the 12th annual Golden

Cup award for the best coffee in town." Tim went, and never lived it down.[552]

Bill and Nada's, the greasy spoon kitty-corner from Liberty Park, would stay open all night and was well-known among late-night staffers for serving eggs and brains.

* * *

Photographers Tim Kelly, Lynn Johnson, Paul Fraughton and John Reynolds, left to right, 1970s.

Lynn R. Johnson, Craig Hansell, Al Hartmann and **Paul Fraughton** were among my other favorite photographers, partly because they took enough care and interest in my stories to produce good illustrations. Unlike some of their pushy, brusque older peers, they were polite to the public and offered me helpful tips about their shots. If we stayed overnight in a motel, they were pleasant company at dinner.

Craig Hansell, left; Al Hartmann, right.

Johnson was just a Mormon kid from a mining town when hired by *The Tribune*. After a stint in the Air Force, he returned to become one of the paper's most reliable shooters, especially for emotional human interest stories. He also became a devout Catholic. Despite his religious conservatism, Johnson willingly covered his

share of shady stories, from brothels to bloodshed.

Hansell was a former military photographer and expert skier and bicyclist whose father Ted worked in the backshop. Skinny environmentalist Hartmann eagerly accepted assignments to Utah's wildlands, especially the desert. Fraughton, a laid-back high school football star with bad knees, excelled with studio shots.

Mike Cassidy in staged photo.

I joined City Desk too late to go on assignment with **Mike Cassidy**, the fun-loving photographer about my age who made independent movies. After leaving *The Tribune* in the mid-1970s to work in animation in San Francisco, he visited the office one day. Shirley Jones asked how he was doing. "I didn't have the heart to tell her I'm sucking cock in the Castro District," he told Denny.

Not all of the photographers left such positive impressions on me.

John Reynolds was a snotty preppy from Salt Lake City's upscale east side who had a special talent for getting under my skin. The twerp often arrived late for shoots because his old Saab broke down, but he missed shots even when he showed up on time.

* * *

Some of the old-school photogs, who more often than not learned their trade in the military, drove me crazy on assignments.

Ross Welser fulfilled his job as head photographer, even if he enjoyed too many toddies after hours. He had taken pictures for the Navy Seabees. By my time, he was easy-going, biding his time until retirement, which he never achieved. At age 64 on December 7, 1982, he stumbled in the office elevator, left work early and collapsed in his Rose Park bathroom. Was it his incessant smoking? Drinking? The chemicals in the photo lab? Who knows?

Frank Porschatis put the photo lab together and then kept it running. He knew the city streets and backroads like the palm of his hand[553] and "knew everyone on Capitol Hill by name and . . . why they were important," according to Tim Kelly.[554]

Porschatis got into photography while working on Granite High's yearbook in 1941 and then snagged a journalism job while fishing. A guy downstream who happened to work for Associated Press asked what kind of fly he was using when Porschatis pulled in fish after fish. By the end of the day, Porschatis had an office job.

He transferred to *The Tribune* a year later but took time off in 1944 to photograph for the Army.

Yoda's look-alike bugged the hell out of me. Though ordinarily impatient, the squirt avoided freeways, stretching a 90-mile drive to Utah State University into three hours and the 50 miles to Brigham Young University into a two-hour crawl. All along the way, he hitched up his pants, rocking back and forth in the driver's seat, excitedly reciting the mistakes of this reporter or that.

Finally reaching our destination, I explained what photos I needed, and Porschatis sauntered off to snap a couple of pictures that may or may not relate to my stories. If he didn't rudely ignore our subjects, he grabbed them by the arm to shove them around. He then hemmed and hawed and cleared his throat throughout my interview, eager to get back to those byways he knew like the back of his hand.

I was as embarrassed then as I was mortified as a teenager when my dad walked outside in his boxers to get the newspaper.

On our way home, Porschatis usually stopped for a takeout hamburger and chucked his crumpled wrappers and cups out the car window. When I failed to follow suit, he stepped up his rocking while glaring at the trash at my feet.

Reporter Cathy Free spent a lot of time with "Pork Chop" a few years later. He usually insisted on going to breakfast after their Davis County assignments.

Frank Porschatis hunts for a shot.

He would order runny eggs, bacon and hash browns, dump a bottle of ketchup over the whole concoction and mix it all together. I was so grossed out the first time this happened that I never ordered anything besides coffee and toast.[555]

One day, Cathy recalled, Porschatis plowed over somebody's mailbox, backed up the car and drove on as though nothing had happened.

He was a genuine character with a soft heart, despite his gruff nature. A few weeks after he passed away, the other photographers cleaned out his locker. Hidden in the back they found several black-and-white glossies of naked young women rollerskating in Liberty Park. Who knew![556]

I did. He had shown me portions of a "porno" film he'd made with Ross Welser. All I saw were a couple of women in bikinis and an especially excited director. But Cathy was right. Porschatis did some endearing traits. He often dispensed fatherly advice with the best intentions, and he was delighted to share his raspberry plants when I was landscaping my yard. He died in 1987 at 64, the same age Welser died.

Gus Sorensen, Van Porter and Tim Kelly, left to right.

Van "Hypo" Porter was so gung-ho for the job in his early years that he equipped his car with all kinds of radio equipment and sometimes slept in the darkroom with his camera tucked under his arm, ready for action.[557] When I knew him, he strode from place to place and made little time for small talk. As an Air Force photographer, he had flown over atomic test sites in the Pacific, exposure that likely contributed to the brain tumor that killed him at 59. Yet another photographer missed out on retirement.

I dreaded seeing **Earl Conrad's** name on my assignment sheet. Reportedly an ambitious shooter in the past, after finishing a tour as a World War II naval photographer, Conrad may or may not meet me at my appointments. Instead of consulting me about the story he was illustrating, the gallant old-timer with slicked-back hair and Errol Flynn mustache took shots willy nilly before tossing me one or two prints that rarely correlated to the event.

Earl Conrad

A Mormon, Conrad was the only *Tribune* photographer of his era to survive into retirement.

Several young photographers started making their way into *The Tribune*, including Steve Griffin, Rick Egan, wild Earth-Firster Dan Miller and Mormon boys Ravell Call and David Allred who later landed at the *Deseret News*.

[549] Tim Kelly, "Tribune Photographers Inhabit Superb New Place," *The Salt Lake Tribune*, July 24, 1988, p. 8T.

[550] Paul Rolly, "Tim Kelly stood tall as a photographer, even taller as a friend," *The Salt Lake Tribune*, January 12, 2015.

[551] Korologos, January 26, 2014.

[552] Raine, December 28, 2013.

[553] *The Salt Lake Tribune*, October 22, 1963, p. 8.

[554] "Frank Porschatis, Tribune Photographer, Dies of Cancer at 64," *The Salt Lake Tribune*, May 8, 1987.

[555] Cathy Free email, June 4, 2015.

[556] Ibid.

[557] *The Salt Lake Tribune*, October 3, 1963, p, 17.

22 - Settling Down in 1979

Denny and I got serious about building our house in Summit Park -- during times of sky-high inflation, of course.

After scouring stacks of home-decorating magazines for months, Denny collaborated with his architect brother on a design that changed from day to day. As usual, I planned to apply my personal experience to a news feature, so I scribbled out my sarcastic thoughts:

We were warned this would be the ultimate test of our marriage. We scoffed . . . until that first argument over the size of our bedroom closet.

Skyrocketing costs meant we could not have every life-long desire built into our dream home. We had to cut, cut, cut! Compromise became our mantra.

My wish for a rock chimney went up in smoke.

We wanted a double-sized bathtub. "Too bad it takes 200 gallons of hot water and two hours to fill," the plumber remarked while pointing to our 40-gallon water heater. Another dream bit the saw (cough) dust. My frozen knees would never join the rest of my body in the warmth of the tub.

So who needs to stand by the sink when the dishwasher door is down? Who says you can't walk around the kitchen table in a 7X7 dining room? Pine is just as nice as oak or cedar, right?

A light socket for less than $100? Forget it! Everything is a least $100, more likely thousands.

To save more money, self-taught handyman Dennis Green is finishing cabinets, walls and shelves while all my furniture is buried under plastic, which is buried under sawdust. We're eating on cardboard boxes.

Adjusting the house plans for the oak bannister we salvaged from a bank demolished for the Crossroads Mall was no picnic. We paid as much to strip these treasures as it cost to buy them in the first place. Sanding, staining and ripping them from their old roosts at least gave us something constructive to do with our copious free time.

When I didn't jump at the chance to shop for garage doors, Denny accused me of sabotaging the project. From then on, I couldn't wait to search the city's warehouses for just the right electrical outlets and plumbing fixtures. Those chimney pipes especially tantalized me, but not far behind were the countless brands of wood stain.

By April, we had applied for a construction loan and put $2,000 into raw materials, including 900 studs procured by artist Tim Brinton for a price we couldn't refuse. We also bought his ancient Ford truck, Thunderbucket, to haul them and adorn our suburban driveway.

Gasoline prices approached $1 a gallon and mortgage rates topped 10.5 percent by August, when Western Mortgage informed us Summit Park lay outside its appraisal area. We were forced to build in phases, out of pocket, which meant postponing the project for another winter.

The good news was that we would save a lot of money in the long run. If we waited another year to pour the foundation and borrowed $20,000 for framing and roofing in 1981, we could be out of debt in just five years!

* * *

Meanwhile, we took time out to remind ourselves why we were a pair. Tim and Sharon Kelly started a brief St. Patrick's Day tradition of Nordic skiing from Park City over Guardsman's Pass to Homestead in Midway. We joined dozens of *Tribune* staffers in a raucous journey that had 300-pound Tim Kelly hurtling down the hill with arms whirring like helicopter blades and Homestead staff blushing.

Trish Brink, a tiny Long Island recruit to the City Desk, was especially rambunctious. Literally cross-eyed drunk, she yowled and laughed so loudly that other diners shrank back into the far reaches of the dining room. Young bloods in our group carried on all night in their rooms. After the third year of our business, Homestead prohibited our return.

By now, a new wave of staffers had entered *The Tribune*, among them Rod and Carrie Pressly, Jamie Tabish, the Kidman brothers, Phil Miller, Guy Boulton, Anne Palmer, Victoria Johnson, Jill Johnson, Ana Daraban, Natalie Mayfield, Adam Kadleck, Anne Mathews, Maureen McCarthey, Joe Baird, Keri Schreiner,

Shia Kapos (sisters Kathy and Trish followed close behind) and Andrea Otanez.

* * *

Prankster Rod Pressly initiated a teen-ager onto the staff with a pitcher of beer at the Dead Goat Saloon. Pert blonde **Cathy Free**, still in high school, had been hired as a copy clerk after submitting stories to the "IN" section in Lifestyle and pestering Korologos relentlessly for a job. "Thankfully, nobody noticed me stumbling around that night because most of the late crew had already had a nip or two from the bottles they didn't bother to hide very well in those old gray battleship desks," she recalled decades later.[558]

Cathy showed more gumption than most as a new staffer. A few weeks into the job, she stood her ground when Keith Otteson stubbornly yelled "Boy!" when he needed a copy clerk.

Keith's face puffed up and his voice became louder as he repeatedly bellowed "Boy!" But I stayed inside the wire room and pretended not to notice. Finally, I heard another shout: "Girl!" And that's what he called me from then on, until I was promoted to a typist position about a year later.[559]

Cathy also made an indelible impression on Capitol reporter Dave Jonsson, who had seen countless copy clerks come and go his 19 years on that job.[560]

Dressed like Stevie Nicks, she ran her *Tribune* errands in a 1977 red Corvette convertible acquired from a neighbor for "a helluva deal."[561]

While delivering a fresh-off-the-press copy of the newspaper to Art Deck about midnight that summer, he caught a glimpse of her roaring up his driveway, T-top down and stereo blasting Fleetwood Mac's "Go Your Own Way." The next day he told Shirley, "I think we're paying the copy kids too much" (about $200 a week).

By the time Cathy became a reporter, "it didn't feel right to show up at a crime scene in a sleek and sexy sports car, especially in neighborhoods where many people didn't own cars and poverty was a way of life," so she reluctantly sold her dream car.[562]

* * *

With some trepidation during this period, I recommended Joy Ross, my best student at Box Elder High School, for a reporting job on City Desk. I knew this LDS woman could write well enough, but I wasn't sure she would fit in. She had been a headstrong loner on my high school newspaper staff. She now wanted to be Woody's business assistant.

She didn't get that far. She bucked her *Tribune* assignments and pissed off her superiors, all the way from Nutting and Fehr to Deck and Gallivan. She went over Deck's head on a story, and he prohibited her from covering one of his sacred cows. When she got to work late one day, he questioned her claim of being at a convention assignment.

I initially blamed the disagreement on Deck's debilitating effect on *The Tribune*, but after the third or fourth time Joy decided a story assignment wasn't worth her time and talents, I woke up. Like Tom McCarthey, she'd become a prima donna who chose which assignments to cover, but unlike McCarthey, she did not own the newspaper. She left *The Tribune* within the year and blamed sex discrimination for her failure to get ahead. I told her inexperience was the culprit.

* * *

My days on general assignment and religion were shrinking, giving me more time as John Cummins' education assistant. I gave Mimi an update May 1, 1979:

I'm still not finished with my feature on Title IX and Sally Brunsman [Frank Brunsman's brainiac daughter at South High School], but what difference will it make now that my other stories have been stewing for weeks in the feature basket? I'm supposed to be dreaming up stories on the juvenile court as part of my education beat, and I haven't put pen to paper after three interviews. On top of that, the guy in charge of staff at the Second District Court is a real dip.

Apparently Judge Regnal W. Garff Jr. (not the dip) didn't share my sentiments:

Just a note to express my appreciation for the manner in which you covered the Juvenile Court and me in your recent series of articles in *The Tribune*. I know you spent a great deal of time getting acquainted with the Juvenile Court and its philosophy and in talking to many people before you wrote the articles, and I think your work product reflected that.

I was pleased with your perceptiveness and the feeling you had for the cases that you observed in court and, also, the ideas I was trying to communicate. I believe that was probably the strength in your articles; that feeling you were able to communicate to the readers.

In other words, what I am trying to say is that I thank you for the professional manner in which you presented the Juvenile Court . . . I have heard many, many comments about the articles, and none of them negative. There were a few tongue-in-cheek comments about the "hanging judge," but I recognize the reason for that headline also.[563]

That summer I also wrote a feature about John Cartan, a student genius from Idaho who strolled the University of Utah campus with staff and robe. Not only did he and his mother enjoy the story, we corresponded occasionally after that. In a letter July 24, 1979, he wrote:

> For one thing, I have been pumping money into my computer, Ariel, as fast I can. She can now talk to me and on occasion serves as a talking alarm clock . . . My next paycheck will purchase a floppy disk drive which is vital to my honor's thesis project. I have been developing a reading package for elementary school children that has good potential. One byproduct of the computer's newfound ability to drill kids on words will be some computer-generated poems and maybe some stories. This will most definitely not be Hemingway stuff, but if I can find the time to make it happen, I may send you some of it. I also have been using my precious spare time to work on maze theory. The gestures of friendship you have made to me are worth more than a thousand newspaper articles.

When I looked up the guy on Google 35 years later, I turned up a software architect for Oracle. On his website, he referred to my article, which he said he tried not to take seriously:

> But it stayed with me, just under the skin, like a faded tattoo.
> For better or worse, this article stamped me for life as a boy with great expectations.
> A wise teacher of mine warned me about this as far back as junior high. In a speech at an award ceremony she said something like this: academic success is usually regarded as a blessing, and so it is. But it comes at a price. As you set forth in life you will be measured against your great expectations. If you fall below this mark, you may be seen as a failure, even if your accomplishments exceed those of the average person. Yet if you meet those expectations, no one will be surprised.
> What she was trying to tell us, and what I have tried to take to heart ever since, is that in order to find any happiness in this life, we have to learn not to measure ourselves against the expectations of others. That can be just as hard to do when those expectations are high as it is when they are low.
> Almost a quarter century has now passed, and the paper on which that article was written has yellowed with age. I am a tad embarrassed by some of the quotations attributed to me (did I really say those things?), but I am proud of it as well, even if I have not yet made many "contributions to mankind." I include it here as part of my family history, because it is a small but telling part of who I was then, and who I am now. You can read it if you like, but take it with a grain of salt. I always did.

* * *

The newsroom's new incentive committee invited me to submit one of my series for a $200 news-writing award and then announced that nothing was up to snuff. Some incentive!

Cash wasn't usually required to get me motivated. My story about in-fighting on the Salt Lake City Board of Education generated a slew of compliments, mostly from outside *The Tribune* but even from a few staffers. I was inspired to follow up with a major analysis. Salt Lake City's school board president sent me this reaction:

> Even before the stories were published, I believe that the concept that an outside third party with a large, believable voice was analyzing the efforts and statements of school board members with the idea of publishing them, caused each board member and many of the administrative people involved to re-evaluate ourselves, trying to bring our actions to a responsible level. I feel that the progress we have made in the last few weeks can be

attributed partly to that effect. [Could you follow that?]

Now that the stories are published, I want to express my appreciation to you and to *The Tribune* for the dedicated, accurate and effective way in which you cover the Salt Lake School District. If I can ever be of assistance to you, please let me know. Cordially, Wayne C. Evans, "the establishment figure."[564]

Charismatic African American evangelist Rosemary "Mama" Cosby grabbed my attention. The high school dropout from Indianapolis asked to rent an empty public school for a private religious program "free from racially prejudiced" educators. Fearing entanglement with a hostile religious zealot like John Singer, Salt Lake City school officials refused.

To flesh out the story, I visited the preacher's ritzy east-side home, complete with white plaster jockeys flanking the driveway. I quoted some of her semi-irrelevant statements because they were so shocking in Utah and suggested the controversy might escalate:

> *Public schools have destroyed our children. We teach 'em not to fight, and they get picked on and get mean . . .*
>
> *[When moving to Salt Lake City] everybody said there was nothing out here but white people and salt . . . I did a lot of prayin' and tryin' to get out of it, but the Lord told me, "If you go, I'll bless you." When I got here, you couldn't get a job even if you were white if you weren't Mormon . . . scrubbing floors wasn't too bad.*
>
> *We've had it hard in America, but I'm glad we come up the way we did. You know, the South lost [the Civil War] 'cause we'd pampered 'em [the whites].*[565]

The school board dodged the bullet by first agreeing to negotiate a lease and then finding another use for the building.

Mama Cosby returned to our news pages even after death in 1997, when her daughter accused Mama's widower, Bishop Robert C. Cosby, of fraudulently diverting funds raised through the Faith Temple Pentecostal Church Mama founded.[566]

* * *

John Cummins won a study grant, and I was rewarded with three solid months of job continuity as his substitute on the school beat. I

had no assistant like he had (me), but I was pleased nonetheless.

Diane Cole, education reporter, 1970s.

One of my first assignments took me on a four-day trip to Blanding and Montezuma Creek to cover state school board meetings..

Throughout the meetings, I sat alongside Kim Peek, the inspiration for Dustin Hoffman's character in "Rain Man." The so-called idiot savant was my age and the son of PR director Fran Peek. Using his undivided, computer-like brain, Kim memorized volumes of names, dates and other facts in a flash. He sometimes burst into giggles when a board members said something that triggered a connection in his massive mind, and Fran quickly ushered him from the room.

Denny, who came along for the ride, was thrilled to see one of his newspaper illustrations in the foyer of White Horse High School on the Navajo Reservation. He took photos of students dancing in Native American regalia for future graphics and spent a couple of days in our motel painting a famous warrior's portrait.

Whether at home or out of town, I frantically checked the newspaper each morning to see how my stories came out. My stomach clenched into a knot as I compared the result with what I'd dictated over the phone or typed at my desk. Each difference gave me heartburn, and I couldn't get over errors until unloading on the editor in charge. You might call me obsessive compulsive. My mea culpa to Mimi September 22:

> I'm not happy with my story on Utah Technical College's Institutional Council meeting Wednesday for several reasons. First, I should have used the juicy quotes about the University of Utah president wining and dining regents in order to gain favoritism. I didn't, but LaVor Chaffin from the *Deseret News* said he did. On top of that, my story was completely reworked and trimmed, indicating I was off base on priorities.
>
> My first school board story was pretty bad, too, I guess. It just doesn't read very smoothly, and it's really kind of hard to grasp from the outsider's view. Damn.
>
> Denny wasn't real thrilled about finding me today's City Edition when I called him, but I'll fret until I see the last piece of shit story. LaVor's wasn't all that great, in my opinion, so maybe it'll pass.

Each fall, Utah schools suspended classes for two days so teachers could attend the annual Utah Education Association (union) convention. I reported that fewer than 1,000 of the state's 14,000 public school teachers attended the opening general session, and a *Tribune* editorial took teachers to task for their poor attendance. In part, it read:

> Approximately 45 percent of Utah's 14,000 or so public school teachers are supposed to attend sessions of the Utah Education Association as a contract obligation.
>
> Last week, at the UEA's opening general session in the Salt Palace, there were an estimated 1,000 teachers on hand...
>
> Taxpayers in Daggett, Davis, Granite, Wayne, Weber, Salt Lake and Logan school districts underwrite attendance at the UEA's annual sessions. In addition, those who also are parents of school-age children often are inconvenienced by the two-day school holiday. They have good reason to resent the teachers' truancy.[567]

UEA responded with an editorial in its own newsletter for teachers:

> One of the prime goals of a daily newspaper is, or should be, accuracy.
>
> With that in mind, let us look for a moment at the activities of the Salt Lake Tribune during and after the recent UEA Convention.
>
> First, that newspaper stated that a general session speaker addressed "about 100 teachers." Then, in an article on another page, that newspaper contradicted itself.
>
> The other article estimated attendance of 1,000 at the general session. It added that "public schools suspended classes Thursday and Friday to allow the state's 14,000 teachers to attend UEA activities, which count as part of their teaching contract."
>
> Of course, that statement isn't true. The two UEA Convention days "count as part of the teaching contract" in only seven of Utah's 50 school districts, which employ 45 percent of the state's teachers.
>
> The Tribune published a partial correction the next day... embarrassing to a news medium that would doubtlessly prefer to be known for accuracy. Still, The Tribune did live up to part of its obligation to the truth. Part? Yes, the correction failed to mention those other thousands of teachers attending other convention activities at the time of the general session.
>
> Maybe that explains why The Tribune goofed seriously in an editorial two mornings later. That editorial went back to its estimate of 1,000 teachers...
>
> All in all, The Tribune demonstrated clumsy handling of the article, the editorial, the correction item and the response. That is sad, because in other instances, The Tribune has shown brilliance in reporting education matters and graciousness in admitting mistakes.

I knew UEA was referring to the brilliance of John Cummins, not myself.

My strained relations with union reps did not extend to Bud Limb, executive director of the Salt Lake Teachers Association. My article about his 1979 retirement made him feel "very good" about his many years in education, he wrote me. "You've got a great career ahead of you with your abilities."

I also got along well with Dave Kadleck, a sports writer before becoming convention specialist for UEA. The happy-go-lucky guy always offered suggestions for upbeat stories while seemingly passing the time of day on passes through the newsroom.

* * *

Our battle with the Gruesomes fired up before fizzling.

When Dr. Whitehead told us the kids wanted to live with us and needed to be removed from their "moderately" abusive home, we filed for custody. Later, Dr. Whitehead said the children had changed their minds and were manipulating us by pitting us against the Gruesome Twosome.

I was upset the girls might have intentionally put us through this conflict, with all the stress, sleep loss and financial drain it caused. I'd even fantasized about divorce! Back to court we went anyway.

We asked the court to move the girls to safe, neutral ground until their living arrangements could be evaluated. The Gruesomes told the kids they were being sent to a foster home because they were delinquents. At least that's how Stormy remembered it. In a treatise to Judge Set-'em-Free Dee, Ped O'Fiel claimed Denny still loved Swamper and was jealously trying to break up her new, happy family. He coached Lulu in a call to the judge in which she dutifully, tearfully begged to stay with the Gruesomes.

Swamper's expert witness, a therapist who'd counseled Denny and Swamper before their divorce, at least provided some comic relief in court. The Gruesomes were model parents, he testified, and Denny was seeking custody to compensate for his impotence with Swamper.

Judge Dee gave no more credence to Dr. Whitehead's credentials than the family counselor's. "All of you are unfit to be parents!" he declared. "You deserve to visit the girls like animals in the zoo." He set an indeterminate recess so the state could decide where the kids belonged.

Suddenly the Gruesomes let us have the kids for a week vacation. Of course they switched the dates several times, wreaking havoc with our work schedules and those of our co-workers. And they had an ulterior motive. The week was spent scoping out houses back East so they could skip town before our case's conclusion.

Swamper got a kick out of the idea of a dejected Denny standing on the doorstep of an abandoned house, 11-year-old Stormy told us when she couldn't keep their secret. She might

miss us, she said, "but we're sure gonna have fun living by the beach. We're gonna be rich! [Ped O'Fiel's] gonna earn $40,000 a year, and I get a sailboat for my birthday!" Lulu added that besides us, the Gruesomes needed to get away from some "big bills."

In September, I called their attorney Roger Sandack for their new address, which he withheld. But he let me know the Gruesomes were no longer his clients, and he apologized for the trouble he'd helped cause us.

Our main consolation, if it could be called that, was that the children had changed their stories about conditions at home and didn't mind losing their father. As an added bonus, we got to save the $350 child support and avoid legal expenses as long as the Gruesomes stayed in hiding. It also was a relief to have our house to ourselves again. I was tired of the kids' messes and drama. We finally could spend some time and money with friends, taking trips, fixing up our tract house for sale and accessorizing our future house.

During our war with Swamper and her sidekick, I'd noticed a lump and ache in my left breast. After two weeks sitting on pins and needles waiting for a diagnosis, my doctor simply told me to cut back on coffee. My mother said her fibrocystic disease gave her symptoms like mine. I relaxed and turned my attention back to work, which had suffered from neglect. Energy usually spent inventing feature stories had gone into fantasies of snuffing Swamper and Ped O'Fiel.

* * *

Surprise! When calling in a story one day, I learned that **Brian Nutting** was our new city editor. Will Fehr and Jack Schroeder were going to share the title "managing editor."

Denny Green and Brian Nutting

I was flabbergasted by Nutting's rapid rise to the top, but there wasn't anyone better for the job. Lance Gudmundsen was capable enough as assistant city editor but kept missing work. He told the boss his cats were sick, but his bruises told a different story. He apparently was recuperating from the latest beating from gay-bashers.

I hoped Nutting's promotion meant he and Suzie would be staying in Salt Lake City for her medical internship. And that our work atmosphere would improve. But what if Nutting demanded too much from us, his peers?

We didn't make it easy on him, as he remembered years later:

> I tried to implement some of the ideas I got from the city editor seminar, but there was lots of resistance from some of the old-timers who'd gotten set in their ways and lazy on the job. It seems like many of them had become apologists for the people they were covering. That's a good reason to keep rotating people around to different jobs -- it's good for their professional development and good for the paper to have fresh eyes on a beat. (Just as long as the rotations aren't too often. In that case, you'd perpetually be learning the job.)[568]

Almost immediately, I started giving Nutting my two cents' worth about the city beats.

"Don't make rash assumptions," he snapped one night at D.B. Cooper's. "You're not one that needs to worry about your work."

I wasn't really worried about my job, but I was never in a better position to have a say about City Desk and took advantage of it. "I guess you can bullshit about work with a co-worker until that co-worker becomes boss," I surmised to Mimi. Within weeks, I feared for our friendship: "Brian always thinks I'm attacking him; I feel left out of things and awkward."

The situation soon improved, and Nutting proved to be a breath of fresh air for City Desk. With his master's degree in journalism and experience as police reporter, copy editor, assistant business editor and night city editor, he had always been competent, but his sarcasm sometimes held him back. Once comfortable in his new position, he was approachable, open, straightforward and even-handed, characteristics too often lacking in our managers. We reporters could be honest with him, and we could count on

him to take our concerns to management. Will Fehr might have done so too, but he rarely explained his or his superiors' decisions.

When Nutting showed up for work one day, actor Ed Asner, who played City Editor Lou Grant on television, was sitting at his desk "being gruff like I wish I could be," he recalled.[569] Truth be told, Nutting could be plenty gruff, but he was usually pretty reasonable and even kind. He wouldn't have fired Stan Bowman, for example, because he "was willing to keep him around for the entertainment factor."[570] At least that's his excuse.

The metal spike, an anachronism by then, became one of Nutting's new tools. Once a story was "spiked," it was as good as gone. A Nutting anecdote:

> When I was on the desk, I learned first-hand about spiking, because there was an actual spike next to the editor. Usually, I could jam the paper right through without even looking. But one time I miscalculated, and I spiked the palm of my hand. It drew blood, but I was more embarrassed than injured.[571]

Paul Rolly, who'd been sniffing out controversial state and local government stories, replaced Nutting as night city editor. The pair then oversaw a strong *Tribune* staff, which included Assistant Business Editor Charles Seldin and gutsy crime reporters Bruce Bartley and Mike Carter. Hal Spencer, Con Psarras and Jim Woolf enhanced the city and county beats anchored by Jack Fenton. Spencer, for example, exposed the so-called Citygate scandal of 1979 in which Commissioners Glen Greener and Jennings Phillips Jr. conspired to give Police Chief Bud Willoughby control of city personnel. Spencer's stories helped trigger the end of the city's commission form of government.[572] Doug Parker, meantime, continued to quietly but capably cover state politics while Dave Jonsson churned out copy from the State Capitol and Bob Bryson covered the courts.

Unfortunately for *The Tribune,* Bartley and Spencer avoided becoming "burned-out shells" in Art Deck's "pool of mediocrity" (*Utah Holiday's* term) by leaving for other news organizations early in my tenure. Bartley went to the wilds of Alaska to report news, eventually becoming an information officer for the Alaska Department of Fish and Game. Spencer, from the tiny mining town of Eureka, also left Salt Lake City for Alaska, where he became Associated

Press bureau chief. Their departure made me doubt my decision to stay in this stinking office in this stifling state.

Hal Spencer

City Desk staffers still made time for fun and games. For instance, Ben Ling described Jim Woolf's "super power."

He can wad up and squeeze a half-sheet of paper into a solid pellet. He explained that you have to put all of your frustration into it. And he has a pretty good arm. We would spend days surreptitiously throwing paper wads at each other. One time, I saved about two days' worth of Woolf paper wads and dumped them on his head. He was always a good sport about it.[573]

Each election day, staffers without assignments worked for extra pay with the Utah Election Service run by Jerry Dunton and Lance Gudmundsen. The job involved calling election judges around the state to check on results throughout the evening and then compiling them for various news media. This obviously was before computers and the internet sped up communications.

While waiting for tallies from the boondocks late into the night, staffers gobbled turkey and roast beef sandwiches and gulped coffee brewed by Mother Jones and Lucy Bodily to stay awake. Unfortunately, I was assigned to interview municipal candidates by phone in 1979,

meaning I worked late but missed out on the extra pay. By then, I preferred money over bylines.

Utah Election Service (staffers) in the 1960s.

Utah Election Service (Tribune staffers) in the 1970s.

* * *

These were the early days of our Halloween parties, drunken bashes that further cemented our connection to the *Tribune* family. By the time our gatherings in the suburbs got under way in the late 1970s, I was usually three sheets to the wind. I started drinking about 7 o'clock, antsy about no one showing up to consume our cold cuts and chip dips. By 9:30 or so, when most people arrived, I was barfing in the sink by the bar. "Hi, Diane," Jon Ure casually said as he mixed himself a drink by my side in 1979. By midnight, I'd passed out on the basement bathroom floor.

That was the year David Beck brought Paul Wetzel's actress sister Anne as his date. The statuesque beauty exchanged her toga for puny Neil Passey's space suit, which purportedly had been worn by Neal Armstrong and displayed at Hansen Planetarium, Passey's new employer. Ms. Wetzel's nipple peaked prettily though the air hose hole. (The next year, Beck brought Deedee Corradini, the future mayor of Salt Lake City.)

My cute but drunk sister-in-law told Beck he was beautiful but "such an ass." That's before she wrestled Paul Rolly to the floor and rubbed his crotch, flattering but scaring the crap out of him. She pestered Suzanne Nutting about getting all the breaks in medical school while she, a nursing student, suffered. Meantime, her inebriated husband sat propped against the wall with a silly grin on his face, unable to walk or talk.

Cindy Gilchrist showed up uninvited, wanting to know why I left her out. Normally the party was open to all staffers, but I certainly didn't go out of my way for someone who'd made fun of me behind my back in a Chinese restaurant.

Tim Kelly, who arrived near midnight after working late, made up for lost time at the bar before shoving me aside in the basement bathroom. He almost walloped Denny for trying to lift his head from the toilet bowl and cover him with a blanket. The next morning, he slipped out the door when his wife Sharon, who had stayed home with their two sons, called looking for him. "Tell her I went to work!" he called over his shoulder. That's when I detected a stench wafting from the upstairs bathroom, where another guest missed the toilet.

* * *

Each year staffers traded off working Thanksgiving Day, Christmas or New Year's. Usually there wasn't much breaking news, aside the year's first birth, which unleashed an avalanche of gifts on the newborn's family. Beat reporters were expected to prepare end-of-the-year wrap-ups ahead of time to fill the paper during these slow news days.

Christmas Eve everyone in the office was treated to a spaghetti lunch at Lamb's Grill. Those stuck working the next day were served a buffet in the newsroom. Artist Sam Smith volunteered to work holidays, not only because his wife was a Jehovah's Witness who didn't celebrate but also because he could scoop up hands full of sliced turkey and beef before other staffers got near the food. I was always happy to miss banquets served in the office filth.

A more popular Christmas perk was the day-time children's party at the Ambassador Club, complete with drinks for the mothers and gifts for the kids from Santa (aka Mother Jones). Employees didn't get in on that one.

Our Christmas bonus consisted of a $25 gift certificate for a ham or turkey from a local grocery store and whatever we might win with raffle tickets earned from United Way donations. Books, candy and other payola from companies

we covered went into the pot. Korologos acted as "jester and master of ceremonies" at these Christmas festivities, and the year that bald Doug Parker won a curling iron for his "hair," even Art Deck cracked a smile.[574]

* * *

At the end of 1979, a couple of compliments helped compensate for UEA's criticism and other school officials' shenanigans.

Superintendent M. Donald Thomas wrote me this letter:

The Board of Education and the Administration of the Salt Lake City School District commend you for your objective news reporting. You have been fair, thorough and unbiased.

We want you to know that we appreciate having you come to our board meetings, covering events in the District, and giving the public accurate and important information. Congratulations!

His assistant, Jan Keller, added a personal note:

Working with you is always a professional and personal pleasure. I appreciate your good news judgment and the help you give me in determining what kind of stories I have that you can use. You are an excellent writer, with a clear and extremely readable style. Your news stories are well done and your feature stories are always delightful, or filled with detail or whatever is appropriate to the subject, showing acute perceptions of school work and people. And, yes, you keep a good perspective.

You are a good journalist and I enjoy working with you.

I answered Thomas' letter with one of my own:

. . . After working with your district nearly four years, it's about time for me to commend you and your personnel, particularly Janice, for your cooperative, open manner of dealing with me as a member of the press.

Janice's information service is especially valuable to me. She not only provides quick, informative and pleasant responses to my questions, but she also offers me countless suggestions for feature articles. Because she isn't pushy or insincere, I feel more comfortable contacting her for ideas than I might some public relations specialists. I can safely say that I've never been ignored or put off when I've contacted district staff. And because it's easy for me to obtain information from Salt Lake City District, I'm more apt to do stories about programs there.

My chumminess with Jan might have compromised my objectivity, making me miss or pass on stories that might embarrass her employer. But at least I was on guard against that happening, and I got information I might otherwise miss.

It was a constant challenge to keep my relationships with public figures and their spokesmen cordial and cooperative yet distant enough to prevent biases in my reporting. We needed one another. While I required tips and accurate information, my contacts wanted the kind of positive press that would enhance their image. If we got too cozy, I might ignore or soften a story, cheating readers.

In my mind, my first obligation was to the public, which relied on me to report how the schools were educating children for future citizenship.

* * *

Many school administrators, Mormons accustomed to conducting business behind closed doors, did not consider attention from me such a good thing. In fact, some made themselves unavailable to my inquiries. Major news releases often were timed for *Deseret News* deadlines, making my stories look tardy.

Supt. Thomas, who came from points East via San Bernardino, had enough moxie and outside experience to use my reporting to his advantage. He fostered my trust by returning my calls and openly speaking his mind, and I gave him the benefit of the doubt when problems flared. By Utah standards, Thomas had chutzpah.

I assumed others favored the *Deseret News* because of their kinship with the newspaper's LDS owners and their acquaintance with long-time education writer LaVor Chaffin. However, my penchant for publicizing problems and using outlandish quotes probably worked against me, too.

I couldn't resist reporting unsophisticated, conservative elected school board members saying or doing ridiculous or hypocritical things that might embarrass Utah's cultural leaders or undermine quality education. Their discussions of sex and "values" education always made good fodder.

Stephen Garrett, a board member who taught English at Cedar City Junior High School after graduating from Brigham Young University, sometimes slipped me humorous, cynical notes to show that some members did "get it."

On December 4, he sent a full-blown letter thanking me for an article I'd written about his teaching methods. As an aside, he noted that two mothers, one of them "a big shot in the local branch of the Utah Association of Women," had their daughters transferred out of his class for teaching "humanism" when discussing a play.

They thought I was a "good" but misguided teacher and they did not want their daughters in my class doing any values clarification types of activities. Board meeting should be interesting with both Planned Parenthood and the U.A. of W. on the agenda. I may even stay awake through this one.

This kindred spirit went on to teach English and journalism at Orem High and before spending two years as principal of tiny Manila High in eastern Utah.

I became a squeaky wheel regarding discrimination against me, as *The Tribune's* representative.

"Why do you always hold press conferences on *Deseret News* time?" I demanded of the schools' PR people.

Eventually, they started giving me a little grease in the form of news tips, exclusive interviews and afternoon announcements. Fran Peek, the state school office's information director, even wrote Art Deck a flattering Christmas letter:

Too often, Art . . . we hear only the negative aspects of news and editorial endeavors.

Several years ago I had the good fortune of working for Dick Harris at his ad agency. One summer I helped your daughter, Stephanie, understand the goings-on inside the agency. She was vacationing from Stanford at the time. Dick taught me that when someone does an especially good job, others should be made aware of it.

This is the purpose of my letter to you.

Since becoming public information officer for the Utah State Office of Education, I've had opportunities to see your education reporters in action. John Cummins has done a great job for education over the years -- still does, but I want to give special thanks and recognition to your very capable Diane Cole who has been substituting for John the past couple of months.

Diane is not only a thorough reporter in what she writes, but she is always on the scene. Always seeks that "little more information" than do most reporters. And, when an item requires followup, Diane's right on top of it.

The Utah Office of Education and the Board of Education appreciate the visibility given our news and activities by The Tribune. Particularly, we appreciate the dedication and professionalism of your education reporters.

Actually, I got along pretty well with Walter D. Talbot, state superintendent of public instruction, my first few reporting years. His chief assistants Rich Kendell and Barnarr Furse were reasonable, down-to-earth guys who were open and honest, comfortable with the press. As was Doug Bates, the school office's legal expert. All three bent over backwards to answer my questions over the years. But after 12 years dealing with underfunded, crowded schools, Talbot resigned in 1982. The state school board didn't do so well replacing him.

For starters, a divided board chose Charles M. Bernardo of Montgomery County, Md., for their new superintendent. After a smear campaign circulated through the Mormon underground, his offer was revoked. Bernardo sued Spectrum Newspapers, Inc., of Bountiful for publishing a column by Susan Roylance of United Families of America.

Roylance's column praised the school board for protecting Utah values from a man who had lived with his second wife (a former nun) out of wedlock and employed someone cited for molesting young boys. Bernardo's $6 million lawsuit accused Roylance and 10 unnamed Maryland and Utah residents of libel and slander. The episode spiced up my job for a few weeks.

Next up: G. Leland Burningham, a good old boy from Weber School District who resented my scrutiny and left the superintendent's office after three years over conflicts of interest and other problems in the state school office. Bernarr Furse filled the 18-month gap between Burningham and another controversial figure, James R. Moss.[575]

Moss was hired in 1986 straight from the Legislature after having taught at Brigham Young University. Reporters complained that his appointment occurred in an illegally closed school board session, so the board perfunctorily made it official in the open.

During his three-year tenure, Moss promoted moral and religious values consistent with the LDS Church and created questionable ties with the private sector. Peter Scarlet followed Moss controversies though to their messy conclusion while I commended his 1990 resignation from a different pulpit. I'll fill you in on that in another chapter.

Tension notwithstanding, I enjoyed bantering with certain players on my beat, sometimes teasing out confidential information that helped me get a big story first. One of President Orville Carnahan's deputies, a future neighbor, leaked that teachers at Salt Lake Technical College were organizing an uprising, for example.

Certain regents let slip their choice of a new college or university president ahead of the official announcement. Schmoozer Kem Gardner, a Democrat and developer who knew "Mother" Jones from their German mission together, gave me a secret or two. He undoubtedly expected something in return, such as an open mind regarding his future runs for governor in 1984 and 1992, but he got little more than an unsolicited review of some of his downtown buildings, including an unconscionably plain box on State Street.

---

558 Cathy Free email, June 4, 2015.

559 Ibid.

560 Jonsson, August 10, 2015.

561 Cathy Free on facebook June 25, 2015.

562 Free, June 25, 2015.

563 Regnal W. Garff Jr. letter to Diane Cole, June 19, 1979.

564 Wayne C. Evans letter to Diane Cole, August 8, 1979.

[565] Diane Cole, "Charismatic Mama Cosby Progresses Toward Opening of Private School," *The Salt Lake Tribune*, October 5, 1979.

[566] Bob Mims, "Late evanelist's estate given $1.2 million in damages," *The Salt Lake Tribune*, January 11, 2005.

[567] "Poor Turnout for UEA Session Spurs Doubt About 'Holiday'", *The Salt Lake Tribune*, October 15, 1979.

[568] Nutting, February 14, 2014.

[569] Nutting, February 14, 2014..

[570] Brian Nutting email, January 31, 2015.

[571] Nutting, February 14, 2014.

[572] Bob Bernick Jr., "Is the end in sight for gang of four?", *Deseret News*, October 13, 1987.

[573] Ben Ling, December 26, 2013.

[574] Woody, August 23, 1995..

[575] Twila Van Leer, *Deseret News*, April 25, 1990, pp A1-2.

23 - Highs and Lows in 1980 Heyday

Denny and I attended Dave Beck's New Year's Eve party, where I bumped into John Waldo from my Copy Desk days. He'd been working for the *Press-Enterprise* in Riverside, California, remarried and returned to Utah to become a lawyer like his father. In place of corduroys and boots, he wore slacks, loafers and a tweed sport coat. I was so uncomfortable around him, you'd have thought there was something between us.

By then, I'd lost interest in teaching and decided I wasn't the outgoing, positive type for public relations. I assumed I couldn't keep up at a news service like Associated Press and wished the *Deseret News* wasn't the only other newspaper game in town.

My lament of the day was too little time to explore the world and too few prospects for advancement. "As it is," I whined to Mimi, "I'm probably not good enough to get ahead much. I'm slow and my deadline stuff usually stinks. I haven't had any real scandals to report."

My salary had risen to $16,120 a year, and I was exhausted from full days covering meetings of school decision-makers. My main challenge was making meetings sound important and even exciting so my editors would publish my stuff. This meant reporting clearly and logically, if not completely, when writing at deadline. I didn't always succeed, so I revisited some issues in detail later, when time permitted.

In a missive to Mimi, I blamed my latest dissatisfaction on Mr. Deck:

I like reporting and associating with some members of the staff, but I despise Art Deck's style of mismanagement. I fear that old, senile asshole. We don't have enough desks, chairs, phones, filing space and clean air to be even remotely satisfied, comfortable or self-confident.

We shuffle from one inadequate typewriter and locked desk to another day in and day out. No one is on City Desk to filter phone calls, so we're all hassled with irrelevant bullshit all day long.

Not even Mr. Nice Guy John Cummins escaped my wrath. In my mind, he wasn't doing enough as education editor, yet he had an entire cubicle for his research materials. I had become attached to his office while he was away. When his study grant ended, I squeezed what files I could into one of his drawers and carried the rest around in a satchel and cardboard boxes.

Although I was blessed with permanent release from the religion page, I returned to zones and general assignment part of the week, leaving less time to follow up on my education ideas. My nerves frayed.

One day, I devoted an entire eight-hour shift to opening mail and making a readable package out of a handicapped transportation conflict. "It's too technical and boring!" I told Mimi. "I've already taken the parent-against-the-system approach before."

Another opus followed public education's swing from the individualized education movement of the 1970s to back-to-basics reform in the early 80s.[576]

"Open classrooms" and flexible schedules had lost favor as grade inflation skyrocketed and employers complained that graduates were functional illiterates. School reform became the mantra of education leaders like Walter D. Talbot, superintendent of public instruction; Terrel H. "Ted" Bell, state commissioner of higher education (soon to become the nation's first cabinet-level Secretary of Education), and Roald F. Campbell, a retired U. of U. professor.

Since I'd researched education reform for high school and college projects before teaching in a liberalized system, I had preconceived notions about the worth of old vs. new school methods. You might even say I was biased. I hoped my reporting came across as fair and fascinating.

I was always antsy about finishing all the stories on my docket and still worried about each one going stale in the feature basket as soon as I turned it in. A short tuft of hair topped my head where I'd twisted and broken off brittle strands while concentrating on my work. I conferred with Mimi about my "weird compulsion:"

I look odd. I can't stop. Whenever I sit down to read or write, my left hand automatically grabs at the stubble left on the top of my head. I've been yanking at my hair or scratching holes in my head since I was about 12 . . .

Why can't I be more relaxed, satisfied and self-assured? The Tribune isn't that important!

Denny Green's caricature of Paul Rolly.

Paul Rolly's lifestyle was bothering me. He would buy a six-pack from a State Street stop-and-go after work and finish it off by the time he pulled into his driveway 10 miles away. It was all about living on the edge: driving with a whisper of gas in the tank, taunting an angry news source or deceiving an incompatible wife from the opposite side of Utah's cultural wall. "If I say anything about it, he'll get pissed, and our friendship will end," I confided to Mimi. "If I were him, I'd be drinking, too, but it's dangerous."

Denny was putting in long hours retouching fashion photos for Wayda and illustrating pamphlets and posters for ambitious Vandra Huber, who had quit *The Tribune* to do PR for the Department of Social Services. We needed about $450 a month from freelance to finance the new house with a credit union loan, but Wayda was five months in arrears.

Denny's deviated septum contributed to sinus infections that caused perpetual headaches non-stop sniffing, especially when he bent over the drawing board and sprayed paint on photos. When not free-lancing, he was paging through old *Architectural Digests* (sniffing), working on kitchen cabinets and bannisters (sniffing) or running errands for the new house (sniffing).

I got the silent treatment for reading the newspaper too much or suggesting drinks at D.B. Cooper's. "Aren't you drinking a lot lately?" Denny asked while rubbing his aching forehead -- and sniffing.

Times like these made me wonder whether my marriage would last. If it didn't, maybe I could have kids after all, I fantasized. But what would happen to my career? *The Tribune* would expect me to quit since Denny worked there longer and held the best position. "He can be very nice and good when he's nice and good," I complained to Mimi, "but what a bastard when he's pissed -- which is more and more often. Sniff, sniff, sniff!"

Meantime, my parents were pulling my family roots from Utah. They sold their house to move to temperate San Diego, requiring me to pack up my childhood memorabilia. Even though I'd often wanted to divorce Bountiful and my past there, I became wistful about ice-skating on Kaysville ponds, sewing my own school clothes and posing with skinny Reed Sorensen in fifth-grade, when we were chosen students of the month.

* * *

Not all was sadness and frustration the first of the year.

I cheered the introduction of legislation to equalize fathers' access to their children in custody cases. Based on our own experience, I hoped child support might hinge on cooperation with visitation.

But that was not part of the proposal, and LDS opposition to the Equal Rights Amendment tempered my optimism. Church officials specifically favored mothers retaining custody and control of children of divorce. They argued the ERA would increase access to abortion, permit same-sex marriage, expose women to military service and make women as financially responsible for families as men.[577] If the church had its way, which it normally did, fair custody laws would be a long time coming to Utah.

The longer the Gruesomes were gone, the greater our financial and emotional footing.

By spring, we'd paid the final $3,000 we owed on our Summit Park property, and we were looking to our parents for building loans. Jerry reworked the house plans again to reflect a variance on the house's setback from the road.

There was a chance the current housing slump would scare up some starving carpenters to work cheap. We had the added advantage of an assumable, 8.5 percent mortgage rate on our house in the suburbs. With most mortgages going for 16 percent, ours should be easier to sell.

* * *

The world stage was unsettled that spring of 1980. Iran still held 52 American hostages snatched November 4, 1979, and Teddy Kennedy pulled out of the presidential race with Jimmy Carter. The president's hostage rescue plan blew up in smoke when a transport plane and helicopter collided in April.

The United States applied sanctions to Iran over the hostages crisis and to Russia for invading Afghanistan. Congress was considering reinstating the draft, even for women for the first time. I didn't oppose women in the military, but I didn't want to be one of them, and I believed military service should be voluntary for both sexes.

Closer to home, Washington's Mount St. Helens spouted May 18, killing 57 people and spewing ash over the West and beyond.

With exceedingly thorough George Raine reporting for *The Tribune*, Utah faced prospects of the Air Force building an MX missile boondoggle in our desert as a multi-billion-dollar defense system. Utah schools were experiencing an unprecedented enrollment boom along with an accompanying budget crisis. Anne Wilson, sometimes teaming up with John Serfustini, was helping with education coverage.

On an even more localized level, redevelopment was changing Salt Lake City. Crossroads Mall went up on Main Street's north end, and new and modernized buildings transformed the old Red Light district on Second South and West Temple. An expanded Salt Palace convention center, apartments and condominiums were planned for Downtown.

* * *

The Tribune evolved with the changing environment.

Its environmental beat, for example, was coming into its own in the 1970s. **Robert "Bob" Halliday**, the lanky gent slumped in front of a typewriter outside Woody's office, was one of the first to cover the subject in Utah. His in-depth analyses seemingly stretched into dissertations.

Bob Halliday of the long sideburns and swooping sidewalls wasn't often in the newsroom my first years there because he was meditating in a cave in Greece, according to another longtime staffer. When present, he kept to himself as well. Unlike some of his cynical peers, he was patient and respectful when I asked for clarification about his voluminous stories.

Robert Halliday, environmental writer

Halliday became one of the few staffers of his era to enjoy a long, relaxing retirement after holding a job he loved for over 40 years:

New experiences every day. As a reporter, I was fortunate to know many of the business, political and academic leaders of my time. As a movie critic for 13 years, privileged to interview most of the film stars of the era. As environmental writer, to realize the fundamental cause of pollution is over-population. And no politician is going to touch that one![578]

In his self-written obituary, Halliday said he lived "87 years of the most exciting, creative period in human history and traveled abroad enough to regain that childlike sense of wonder and personal insignificance." His swan song credited a group of "geriatric dancing fanatics" with giving him "a wealth of warmth, a vigorous way to prolong life and an ideal way to end it . . . dancing all the way to the exit."[579]

I wish I'd known him better.

His proximity to Halliday's desk left Ben Ling with a different impression:

He smoked a pipe. I mainly remember how badly it stunk. One day, I was popping my chewing gum and he said, "Please stop that. It's annoying as hell."

I didn't say anything about his pipe, but later while I was interviewing somebody on the phone, embers from Bob's pipe set a pile of paper on fire between our desks. He also was on the phone and didn't notice the flames. I frantically slapped the flames down. Bob noticed and finished extinguishing the fire.

Oh yeah, gum popping is sooo annoying.[580]

* * *

Newsroom changes included Jerry "Radar" Wellman's move from the Copy Desk to the Regional Desk. Pepper Provenzano, a handsome Italian from the college town of Princeton, replaced him. Jim Smedley, a big guy slightly about my age, also joined the Copy Desk, engaging his pals in games of poker when working late.[581]

Hoping to be promoted to a reporting position, 19-year-old Cathy Free began enterprising stories for the zone editions in her "free" time. Temperamental Vaughn Roche was reporting a variety of topics, and chunky, cantankerous Californian Dan Bates covered Davis County and Ogden. Tim Fitzpatrick finally got to use his physics degree to cover science.

Dan Bates, JoAnn Jacobsen Wells and Paul Rolly, left to right.

Fitzpatrick's brother-in-law Jim Woolf took a trip to Taiwan with city officials. Con Psarras wrote about the "gentleman bandit" while Mike Carter held up the routine crime news. For all his advanced years, Gus Sorensen covered a Holladay hostage crisis. Charlie Seldin focused on the fruitless political proposal to end food taxes.

After entering the newsroom as a copy clerk in 1977, **Terry Orme** hooked up with the Sunday section, writing a feature on longtime *Tribune* art critic George Dibble before launching into reviews of pop music and then movies. An English literature student in college, he was acquainted with the analytical process.

Terry Orme

With his usual home-spun flare, Clark Lobb profiled average Utahns from far-flung reaches of the state. Jack Fenton continued to antagonize Salt Lake County officials, and Angie Nelson still specialized in medicine.

Jon Ure literally floated among beats requiring vacation substitutes.

* * *

Korologos, primed but passed over as Art Deck's heir apparent, quit in disgust for a job at Evans Advertising.

Much as he had loved promotions, Korologos was ambitious. He earlier had told Deck of his aspirations to become editor:

In his loving style he said, "We already have one."

That was the clincher. Mentally, I became divorced from *The Tribune*, a place I loved and worked very hard for many years.

I was 43 years old, looked around and contemplated my future there. I didn't see any place for me to advance to and asked myself, "Is that what/who I want to be the rest of my career here?" The answer was a resounding, "No!" Do I want to spend the next 20 years here putting on birthday parties for gorillas at the zoo, tennis tournaments, ski races, garden shows and July 4th celebrations at Lagoon? Again, "No!"

I didn't want to hang around and get $2.50 weekly raises each birthday for the next 20 years -- the same amount given to Stan Bowman, whose birthday was the day before mine and who most nights spent the entire shift writing a cutline -- as in one -- on the weather map while I was Inquiring Editor TV host/writer/producer, hiring people as personnel director and working my tail off managing promotions for the paper.[582]

When Deck appointed Will Fehr and Jack Schroeder as co-managing editors, the training and testing ground for executive editor, Korologos knew his time was up. He speculated that Deck wanted someone of his own "ilk," rather than a promotions director, to fill his shoes.

In some eyes, I was not a "news" man. Also, I think Deck wanted someone low key, bland, methodical, not someone with enthusiasm, the interest of the staff in mind, new ideas. I'll never forget the meeting where Fehr kept justifying his decision to resolve a controversy by saying, "This is what Art would do." So Deck was running the newsroom from his grave, for Pete's sake.[583]

As soon as he was reimbursed for the repair of a camera he'd damaged while hosting a *Tribune*-sponsored cruise, Korologos submitted his two-week notice of resignation. He received no encouragement to stay. "I wasn't asked why I was leaving, and no raise was offered," he remembered. "In my heart of hearts, I'm glad I left . . . .[584]

Korologos noted that Deck had become so paranoid in his latter years that he would open his mail.[585]

His "proudest take-away" was . . .

. . . hiring so many damned good people for some 15-plus years . . . the likes of Nancy Melich, Paul Rolly, Paul Wetzel, Judy B. Rollins, Nancy Hobbs, Terry Orme, Dave Jonsson, Lynn Johnson, Tim Kelly, Fred Kempe, Craig Hansell,

Shirley Jones, Marilee Higley, Bopper [Vicky Sorenson], Anne Wilson, Con Psarras, Verdo Thomas, Charlie Seldin, Cindy Gilchrist and Peter Scarlet -- all great, longtime employees . . . I hired very few lemons.[586]

His other greatest take-away was the many "lifelong, loving friends" he met at *The Tribune*. He didn't seem to think twice about leaving before being vested in ESOP.

We sent Korologos off with one of Denny's poems and plenty of booze at D.B. Cooper's.

Denny's little ditty was a hit with a staff hungry for a blow-out without the kids for a change. Fehr got so drunk he threw up in a gutter on his way out. His wife Cynthia advised us that night to cover our tails against Deck's capricious decisions.

We kept in touch with Korologos through our Halloween parties, Lake Powell trips and funerals. He also ended up working for Mickey Gallivan and hosting *Tribune* gatherings throughout his life.

Raft trips down the Yampa, Green and Colorado rivers with a company run by "Mother" Jones' handsome husband Richard were the precursors of the Powell excursions. Our so-called River Crew consisted of Mike and Myrlene Korologos as the captain and admiral; photographer Tim and Sharon Kelly; Denny's brother Jerry and whichever *Tribune* staffer he could persuade to accompany him; and staff youngsters Terry Orme and Nancy Hobbs, who'd struck up a romance. Terry's father, a local heart surgeon, had grown up on a ranch in Tooele and passed his love of horses to his son, a trait that played well with Nancy.

We couldn't resist ribbing Richard Jones, whose business was subsidized by his hard-working wife, for his conservative Mormon views. On the bus to the launching dock, Richard sang hymns to ward off evil spirits while he drove and we swore and swilled bloody marys.

Shirley protected her teased buffonte with an umbrella so she could look nice for her man even on the river. Myrlene, who sang at the Jerry Jones Rainbow Randevu (Terrace Ballroom) and Manhattan Club in earlier times, would woo us around the campfire with smoky renditions of "The Lady Is a Tramp" and other nightclub favorites.[587] Our lively conversations invariably involved Utah politics and *Tribune* gossip, penny-pinching and paternalism.

Sharon Kelly, Shirley and Richard Jones, Terry Orme, Nancy Hobbs and Tony Korologos on the Yampa and Green rivers.

For the record, Richard wasn't as squeaky clean as he pretended. While a Mormon bishop years later, he cheated on the faithful wife he'd wed for time and eternity in the LDS Temple. Though shamed into a divorce, Shirley remained confident she would reunite with the father of her children in the hereafter. After all, male Mormons were expected to have more than one wife in the highest kingdom. One of Shirley's best friends, normally placid Peter Scarlet, never let her live it down that she'd hitched her wagon to a "phony."

* * *

By spring, I felt squeezed by work, Denny's prolonged headaches and stress over the new house. It didn't help that we limped along on one car. When reading the newspaper, I was accused of ignoring Denny's pain. If I wasn't ready to leave the office when he wanted to shop for building supplies, I wasn't committed to the project.

Denny twitched and panted in frustration, conjuring up images of crazy Nathan from Sophie's Choice. Fortunately, his fun, sensitive side still showed up often enough to keep us together.

John Cummins replaced Korologos as promotions director, making me education editor.

Denny was upbeat about my new title, buying me flowers and breaking out the wine.

I couldn't wait to get weekends off and my own desk, phone and cubicle along the south wall of the newsroom. By distancing myself from the clamor of the hoi polloi, I expected to compose journalistic masterpieces.

I should have known better. Suddenly the office was rearranged to exclude the education editor from the precious cubicles and make way for Will Fehr, the apparent victor in the race to replace Deck. In my snit, I complained to Mimi:

It's not the first time Deck's had Will shove me out of a desk. Of course I'm supposed to do Cummins' job without Cummins' privileges, and I still haven't had a raise.

I suspect Brian and Will decided I was the logical Cummins replacement, but since it wasn't Deck's idea (he regards women as incompetents), he isn't about to acknowledge it or make it official. I hate that senile old bastard!

I also hated the humiliation of moving out of the cubicle and back into the crowded, cluttered office with no place to put my voluminous education files and books, many inherited from Cummins and his predecessor Bill Smiley, while male staffers stood around cracking jokes.

It wasn't only Deck's fault that a green girl reporter like me was kept from the inner sanctum of cubicles. Years later, Publisher Jack Gallivan put the issue into perspective:

In the new accommodations Bill Patrick occupied one of the forehead-high south wall cubicles which were reserved for *Tribune* stars like O.N. Malmquist, celebrated political writer and author of *The Tribune's* First Hundred Years, and later by Dan Valentine, whose best-read daily column first appeared in the *Telegram*.[588]

Non-star upstarts didn't qualify for the hallowed space. As executive editor, Deck was hog-tied by Fourth Floor traditions. He at least approved Fehr's request to buy a new filing cabinet for my education stuff.

* * *

Jack Schroeder, one of my staff allies, took over *The [Tribune] Tattler,* the in-house newsletter Korologos called *Tribune Topix*, and revised the year-old contest offering cash prizes for outstanding reporting and writing. Helping Schroeder judge the awards were Keith Otteson, Fehr, Brian Nutting, Hal Schindler and Barbi Robinson.

Several months passed without winners. Deck issued this morale-building explanation:

To insure that *The Tribune* will be first and most thorough in the publication of any story of significance to the political or social well-being to the area we serve, we will continue a monthly cash award for enterprise to the individual or team who has exhibited and produced the most significant news story during the preceding month. Cash awards also may be given for excellence in general reporting, art work, photography, headline writing and editing.

If there is no effort deemed worthy of a prize in a given month, awards will be considered during the next monthly period.

In addition *The Tribune* has set up a $1,000 award to be given annually at the end of each year for the most significant example of excellence during the year.

Finally, Jim Woolf spearheaded a series on refugees that got the nod. He received $100 while Angie Nelson, Clark Lobb, Anne Wilson and I split another $100 for our contributions to the effort.

The Tattler kept the good feeling going with praise for Anne Wilson's "scoop on the investigation into certain tampons being responsible for toxic shock syndrome." It added:

> *Con Psarras did a bright and clever story on a 13-month-old baby charged with drunken driving . . . Vaughn wrote an excellent story on the problems of census enumerators . . . Jon Ure got a scoop on the problems facing Jordanelle Dam . . . Bob Halliday added a series on the mysteries of genetic engineering . . . Bob Woody got a substantial scoop on American Express moving their home office to Utah . . . Nancy Funk came up with a light and bright story on Sundance . . . Charles Seldin had the census story a full day before anyone else . . . Jack Fenton followed the Barbershop Quartet convention with a story of some of the group's officials complaining about treatment by hotels. It produced results as local officials began to work more closely with hotels in upcoming conventions.*

* * *

Distractions aside, that spring I submitted a seven-part series about sex education, a controversial topic in a state that swept such issues under the rug. As city editor, Brian Nutting ordered major revisions, and Dave Beck offered to edit and condense it on his own time.

The first part of the series dominated Split Page with an elaborate illustration by Denny. It began:

> *This week more than 100 Utah teens will become pregnant.*
>
> *While the fertility rate -- number of live births -- among American teens has declined by 23 percent during the past 10 years, Utah's has increased by 35 percent. Among 15-year-olds, the increase was 50 percent from 1970 to 1976, while the rate for 18- and 19-year-olds was increasing by only 3 percent.*
>
> *Despite emotional arguments over the cause and prevention of teen-age pregnancy and venereal disease, most Utahns would admit sex-related problems for teenagers are significant . .*
> .
>
> *Is sex education the answer?*
> *Some Utahns insist it leads to promiscuity.*
> *"So much discussion" of sex makes teen-agers want to experiment, according to Erma Christensen, a member of the Utah State Board of Education. "The subject should remain private . . . within the context of marriage."*
>
> *But others believe responsible sex education can improve society.*
> *Ben. F. Mortensen, dean of health occupations at Utah Technical College at Provo with 20 years of clinical experience in mental health, believes if sex education were approached in a rational, factual and gradual manner, the result would be fewer sex-related problems, including rape, incest, child abuse and venereal disease.*
>
> *A common thread among sex offenders is the absence of appropriate sex education, said the former Mormon bishop, adding that most sex offenders he had as patients were from Mormon homes where sex wasn't discussed.*
> *"It was too holy, or too terrible. The men developed a curiosity and put it to work in the form of indecent exposure, voyeurism or molesting children."[589]*

One of my sources was Helen Ure, a former state school board chairman and the mother of *Tribune* staffer Jon Ure. She said school boards were simply scared to give teachers leeway teaching sex education.

After the series started its run, the Fourth Floor declared it way too long. Deck ordered it slashed to four days and hidden deep inside the newspaper. He also dictated the removal of all "dirty words."

We're not talking about the "F" word here. I'd quoted one teenager bragging about having sex as often as he could and admitting his friends regarded dates as "just another piece."[590] A school counselor said, "Girls often feel many of their friends are having sex and that to let a boy enjoy himself is a way to become popular." Pretty racy stuff, eh?

Ben Mortensen wanted to know what happened to the rest of the story. "I somehow have the feeling that your articles were too controversial for Utahns, and someone probably stopped you from publishing your entire essay," he wrote to me May 8, 1980. Good guess.

I told *Network*, a tabloid which reviewed local journalism, not to assume my series was censored; that there were space limitations. Good ol' Keith Otteson blamed the story for being wordy and dreary. Editor Will Fehr lied, telling the journal that we'd run what I'd written.

Fehr rubbed salt in the wound by requiring a comprehensive rewrite of the Planned Parenthood portion within the week. Apparently our leadership was uncomfortable with what I'd written about he Catholic Church's position on sex education and birth control.

The timing was terrible. Mid-May was the education editor's busiest time of year because of high school and college commencements and out-of-town meetings. The Board of Regents' budget session in Ephraim alone had me working from 6 a.m. until past 10 p.m.

Besides being buried in assignments, I was indignant at being told what to do. I'd always chafed against authority, and I doubted I could impartially deal with the Catholic Church's contradictory views. I confided in Mimi:

I'm starting to feel Catholicism is more ridiculous than Mormonism, if such a thing is possible. At least Mormons base their opposition to birth control on a doctrine that they are to procreate to replenish the earth with all the little spirits egging to get their chance on earth.

This is one good reason I shouldn't be doing this damned story. It rubs me the wrong way, and I can't be unbiased about these religious factors.

Fortunately, Angie Nelson offered help with the health side of the story, and we got the thing done. After working on it from 10 a.m. until 4:30 p.m. on a Friday, I spent an hour on a Weber College commencement story before racing the 30 miles to the college to confirm what I'd written. I finished calling in additions by 8:30.

The four-part Planned Parenthood series began June 8, 1980 like this:

Why is the Planned Parenthood Association of Utah under attack?

Family planning specialists believe the controversy is based on misconceptions about their services and goals. Planned Parenthood's local director, Michael Chulada, blames a small, tenacious group for using morality, rumor, distortion and ludicrous accusation to discredit his organization."[591]

Chulada identified a cadre of so-called pro-family, anti-abortion activists who turned up time again in my stories: Joy Beech of Citizens for True Freedom; Margaret Mietchen of Pro-Family Coalition of Utah; Maurine Brimhall of Utah Citizens for Decency; Betty North, Utah Association of Women; Janet B. Carroll, Rosalee Gleed and Connie Pratt of Right to Life of Utah; Dorothea Masur of the Utah Eagle Forum, and Susan Roylance of United Families of America.

These activists' positions revived bitter memories of my teen years in Bountiful, where Planned Parenthood was prohibited once "the pill" became available. I got a prescription for my throbbing menstrual cramps, but a Mormon friend got a tongue-lashing from her doctor and wound up pregnant and needing an abortion -- which she obtained out of state.

I didn't soon forgive my publisher and editors for doing what they had a right to do with reporters. I sulked when Fehr and Nutting asked me to redo my analysis of the state school board's identity crisis as straight news and Nutting chided me for being prejudiced against Mormons. I readily rejected Gallivan's request that staffers "volunteer" for one of his sacred cows.

His April letter said, in part:

There is a bond election on May 20 to decide whether or not the Salt Palace is expanded (more exhibit space, more parking).

This expansion would <u>help our business</u> . . .

In summary, it is an excellent investment . . .

I am anxious to have our organization give full support to this most important community effort. Please don't forget to vote on May 20. A vote for this bond is a vote for our company's future. Please also urge your family and friends to vote FOR this big step forward.

Sincerely yours, J. W. Gallivan, president, *The Salt Lake Tribune*

P.S. Because this issue is so important for our community and our business, it would be most helpful if many of us would volunteer to personally join the campaign. The delivery of a few brochures to your neighbors, or some telephone calls encouraging support, would be very helpful and appreciated. Would you please sign the bottom of this letter (and indicate your home phone number) if you would be willing to assist? Please return it to my attention. Campaign headquarters will mail or phone instructions. Thank you. [592]

This "invitation" resembled the coercive "suggestions" Mormon leaders would give members regarding public policies like the Equal Rights Amendment and school prayer. In my mind, I was choosing between journalistic ethics and job security.

Before long, I stepped in the middle of another Gallivan sacred cowpie.

My probing revealed that Westminster College, the state's only private, non-Mormon liberal arts college, teetered on the brink of bankruptcy and the loss of academic accreditation. This was after James E. "Pete" Petersen, a former labor union leader with no college administrative credentials who directed employee relations for Kennecott Copper Corp., flamboyantly claimed to have solved financial problems as interim president in 1979.

I was the first to report on cutbacks needed to cope with the budget crisis. One of my subsequent stories began:

Several students gathered around Westminster College' s new academic vice president Friday were angry. They wanted to know why they were the last to know about plans to cut back the curriculum.

Douglas W. Steeples, a history scholar who didn't come to the campus until early August, matter-of-factly clarified the college's plans. He stressed that it wasn't his idea but the work of a special consultant and a curriculum committee comprised of faculty and students.

Students referred specifically to reports in The Tribune *and on television Sept. 22. "Usually the administration calls a convocation before releasing this kind of news to the press," one student said. "Why was it necessary to give the interview to* The Tribune *first?"*

Another added, "The article didn't do us any favors. It sounded like we're holding on for dear life."

Dr. Steeples said he expected the story to come out a week or so before students even returned to the campus. "They asked, and I shared." [593]

As Westminster's saga continued, I discovered the new president lied about the school's financial condition. I wrote:

Westminster College officials are still trying to get out from under the debt accumulated during the previous administration, according to D. David Cornell, college president.

"We're paying for the sins of the past," he said in an interview Wednesday.

Last January, Mr. Cornell announced the private, independent college was finally operating in the black. However, he was referring to the operations budget for fiscal 1980 and did not point out that deficits from previous years had accumulated to $1.36 million and the college was $2.2 million in debt.

"It's hard to predict our fiscal condition for 1981," Steve Morgan, college business manager, said. "Development money (donations) is crucial to our survival. We're appealing to the community to help us run a balanced ship." [594]

To get the stories, I'd pressured Westminster's public relations guy, Alan Hanline, and his bosses. I'd have boldly labeled the presidents liars if my own bosses had consented. As it was, I felt pretty proud of my investigative prowess and expected a hearty pat on the back for a scoop that probably would motivate advocates of to rush to its rescue with donations.

For the first time in my journalistic career, I was summoned to the Fourth Floor. A twinge of excitement stirred in my stomach as the elevator opened onto a tasteful, orderly world nothing like the newsroom. I sank into plush carpet as I stepped up to the row of framed Front Pages opposite the elevator doors. The 1969 Apollo 11 lunar moon landing stood out as an exciting memory from my high school years.

The publisher's gray-haired secretary, Marie Briggs, scowled and pointed to an office in the northwest corner. As I slipped into the walnut and studded leather chair in front of Mr. Gallivan's polished desk, I noticed how the heavy drapes framing sparkling windows barely skimmed the floor. (Employees were expected to call the publisher *Mister* Gallivan, never Jack.) What a shame it was, it struck me in a moment of cynicism, that the *Tribune's* decorator had run out of the crinkled, yellowish aluminum blinds we enjoyed so much on the newsroom's grimy windows.

A gruff, agitated voice erupted.

"Do you have any idea what you have done!?" *Mister* Gallivan fulminated, his jaw jutting back and forth while his caterpillar brows slammed together atop his ski-jump nose. "Your timing couldn't have been worse! I don't care how accurate your report may be, the fact is that Westminster is important to this community, and you have virtually guaranteed its failure!"

I was dumbfounded. I had forgotten Gallivan's place on the school's governing board and shot one of his pets in the gut. I shivered in my shoes on my descent to the second floor and tiptoed on eggshells regarding Westminster after that.

It was easy enough to write positive stories on Westminster programs and campus-expanding donations from Bill and Vieve Gore (as in Gore-tex) and Berenice Bradshaw (as in patricide). But it also was necessary to report Pete Petersen's ironic return to reorganize the college, a controversial tactic to crush tenure in order to fire teachers and cut expenses. I couldn't avoid reporting the state's rejection of requests for public funds to prop up the private school's budget.

Years later, on September 15, 1987, a new president, Charles H. Dick, sent me this note:

I wish to thank you for the thoughtful, thought provoking editorial on Westminster College's recovery in today's issue of *The Salt Lake Tribune*. You have witnessed the College's ups and downs from a special position, and your description of its recent history is not only accurate but expertly phrased.

We appreciate your understanding of our situation and thank you for your support.

My support? I felt co-opted and cowed, but what choice did I have?

Other staffers also faced the Fourth Floor's squishy ethics.

Publisher Jerry O'Brien killed a news brief about his heart surgeon's DUI, for example. When police reporter Chris Jorgensen chafed, the boss "gave me the best advice I've ever gotten in newspaper work: 'It's an impure business, Cub. Move on.'"[595] As city editor of the *Billings Gazette* (Montana) decades later, Jorgensen said he gave the same advice to every young reporter he worked with.

Other former *Tribune* reporters Conrad Walters, John Keahey and Mike Carter argued that self-interested censorship undermines newspaper integrity.

"We can't call the impure to account if we behave like hypocrites, especially at the top," Walters said. Carter contended that credibility "is easily lost and rarely recovered." To protect its reputation for honesty, he noted, *The Seattle Times* published embarrassing stories about its owner shooting a neighbor's dog and a columnist plagiarizing. The *Ogden Standard-Examiner* published a story about the managing editor's DUI for the same reason, Keahey added.

Conceding the heart surgeon's story deserved to be published -- it was the only one so blatantly killed his 30 years in the business -- Jorgensen maintained he needed his "young, idealistic eyes opened a little."

---

[576] Diane Cole, "Education's Pendulum Swinging 'Back to the Basics,'" *The Salt Lake Tribune*, March 31, 1980, p. B-1.

[577] The Church and the Proposed Equal Rights Amendment, a Moral Issue, Ensign Magazine, February 1980.

[578] Robert Snow Halliday, *The Salt Lake Tribune*, September 30, 2003.

[579] Ibid.

[580] Ben Ling, December 26, 2013.

[581] Gordon Harman email, October 12, 2015.

[582] Mike Korologos email, January 31, 2014.

[583] Korologos email, January 21, 2014.

[584] Ibid.

[585] Korologos email, January 19, 2014.

[586] Ibid.

[587] Myrlene rounded out her singing career in the 1990s as the "girl singer" for the senior citizens of the Phoenix Jazz & Swing Band, Lance S. Gudmundsen, "Myrlene Korologos: Back Onstage With the Boys," *The Salt Lake Tribune*, October 15, 1995, Page E-2.

[588] Jack Gallivan, July 24,1988, p. T10.

[589] Diane Cole, "Sex Education in Utah Still Hot Issue," *The Salt Lake Tribune*, May 5, 1980, p. B1.

[590] Diane Cole, "Sex in High School? Teens Admit It," *The Salt Lake Tribune*, May 6, 1980, p. B1.

[591] Diane Cole, "Debate Mounts on Family Planning Issue," *The Salt Lake Tribune*, June 8, 1980, p. B1.

[592] John W. Gallivan letter to Tribune staff, April 22, 1980.

[593] Diane Cole, *The Salt Lake Tribune*, September 27, 1980.

[594] Diane Cole, "'Sins of the Past:' Westminster Still Trying to Get Into the Black," *The Salt Lake Tribune*, June 4 1981, p C-1.

[595] Chris Jorgensen, Mike Carter, Conrad Walters, John Keahey, Tribune facebook group, September 28, 2015.

24 - Newsroom Affairs

Until the 1970s, *The Tribune* maintained a nepotism policy that discarded women in office relationships.

Lifestyle Editor Barbi Robison was probably the first female to stay on the job after marrying a staffer. She and Robert "Elly" Ellefsen greased the skids for others by keeping their conflicts out of the newsroom as Barbi promised Deck they would do. No one was the wiser several months after they split.

Who's in charge here?

She is blonde and vivacious and The Tribune's Education Editor.

He is blonde and diligent and The Tribune's Chief Artist.

They're both married — to each other, in fact.

Diane Cole and Dennis Green came to The Tribune by different avenues. She started on the Copy Desk as a summer intern. He came to the Art Department in 1963 and worked full-time while attending the University of Utah.

After Diane completed her education she ventured into the world as an English teacher at Clearfield High School. "I was an idealist about humanistic things and I thought the class would be, too. I gave them lots of home work and that was unpopular. I thought they were there to learn. I liked teaching, but I like this kind of work much better."

Dennis started in the Art Department at the time The Tribune took control of the department. "The Tribune took me from the old regime along with two pieces of furniture."

They had nothing going until after Diane ended her other ventures and returned to The Tribune. "I had looked at him when I was on the Copy Desk and thought he must have been a hippy." (Those were the motorcycle days for Dennis.)

Creative and slightly irreverant, Dennis Green has done some memorable work, especially in the area of Home Magazine. Some of his best efforts were a Thanksgiving cover, a Utah towns cover and, only recently, a view of Williamsburg. He had been a winner in The Tribune's monthly contest for the artwork that accompanied Angelyn Nelson's series on intraocular lenses.

As The Tribune's Education Editor, Diane is harnessed with the task of covering all the major education stories and some take her to various areas of the state.

"Denny is a very creative person," says Diane. "He sends personalized Valentine's Day and anniversary cards. Halloween is his favorite holiday because he likes to dress up and this gives him an opportunity to be really creative."

Dennis has a sense of humor that's always on the surface. "He can get away with a lot because of his sense of humor," muses Ms. Cole.

At home work is divided. Dennis is now a fanatic about equality.

"It wasn't always that way," says Diane. "He likes it because he feels it's better that way. We split things down the middle like mortgage and car payments. This has been a drastic change for him."

"Diane doesn't like housework," says Dennis. "We split that up, too."

They're in the process of starting construction on a new home in Park City. Dennis has built all the cabinets for the kitchen and bathroom. In addition he will supervise the construction.

"Sometimes at night after work we go home and sand the bannisters," says Diane.

So, it's togetherness in the Green-Cole home. Or, is it Cole-Green?

After Denny and I were married, several other staffers struck up a lasting romance as well: reporters Con Psarras and Anne Wilson; reporter Terri Ellefsen and aspiring golf writer Roger Graves; writers Terry Orme and Nancy Hobbs; reporters Doug Parker and Carol Sisco, and theater critic **Nancy Melich** and sports writer **Lex Hemphill**.

The age difference and family status between Melich and Hemphill resembled mine and Denny's, but in reverse. Denny, the parent of two, was nine years my senior. Nancy had two children and several years on Hemphill.

Nancy's father was a prominent Republican lawyer who ran for governor against Cal Rampton in 1964. By taking two University of Utah classes a quarter for seven years, she met her father's challenge of earning a college degree despite becoming the teenage mother.[596] Finding English classes dry, she had switched to journalism when a magazine-writing professor recognized her writing talent. The shift seemed natural since she'd produced a newspaper of her own in 5th grade.

Nancy's first summer after graduation was spent in *The Tribune's* internship program, which exposed her to a different department each week. Having grown up in the gorgeous red-rock community of Moab, she dreamed of writing about the environment afterwards. Told there was no such thing, she applied for an opening in the drama department, where she worked with Roy Hudson, Susan Dudley and George Raine on features, music and movie reviews and the *Sunday* magazine.

It was there, in 1970, that Nancy became "part of the link in the long chain that included the newsroom, Copy Desk, backshop and Circulation Department, all of which depended on early copy production from features to get the rest of the paper to porches on time."[597]

Along the way, Nancy married Tim Funk, a community activist she'd met in college. Inner city poverty and power rates were his primary concerns, and Melich sometimes rallied to the causes with him. Once another news outlet quoted her, a no-no given the perception of bias it created for *The Tribune*. That marriage withered. Nancy's job blossomed when she attended the National Critics Institute at the Eugene O'Neill Theater Center in Waterford, Connecticut, the only place training theater critics.

"It changed my life professionally," she said, explaining that she learned that covering the arts is different than covering a police beat or legislatures. "You need to know something about the craft before you can write about it." (Actually, it helps to know about law enforcement and public policy-making when working those beats, too.)

Nancy Melich

Lex Hemphill

The Sunday Arts section, according to Nancy, cultivated world-class theater, dance and music in Utah. With Hal Schindler as editor, she critiqued theater, Helen Forsberg specialized in dance, Terry Orme reviewed films, Tom McCarthey traveled and reported on pop music, Paul Wetzel covered classical music, and George Dibble analyzed fine arts,.

The section became so attractive that the *Deseret News* tried snatching it up during renegotiation of the joint-operating agreement in 1982. *News* Publisher Wendell Ashton was willing to leave the Travel section with *The Trib*.

Outraged Schindler and Nancy marched up to the Fourth Floor, Nancy's first visit, to alert Mr. Gallivan, who swiveled in his desk chair and dialed Ashton: "Wendell, get your own damned arts section, we're keeping ours!"[598]

Alexander "Lex" Hemphill was working for the *Dover Advance*, a small New Jersey daily, after graduating from a Connecticut prep school and Lafayette College in Easton, Pa. While visiting his sister in Utah the summer of 1975, he dropped off his resume to a few newspapers, including *The Tribune*. His first face-to-face contact was with Jack Schroeder, who enthusiastically took him into Deck.

"Why do you want to work here?" Deck abruptly asked. "When can you start?"[599]

Hemphill naively returned home to wait for a definitive job offer. After several apparently fruitless phone calls, he received a terse letter from Mike Korologos offering $90 a week.

"I knew before I got there that *The Tribune* was weird, sort of dysfunctional," Hemphill remarked years later. "I was caught between two guys competing to be editor [Schroeder and Korologos, who were both assistants to the executive editor], and *The Tribune* didn't pay anything [toward travel for interviews or a move across the country in 1976]."[600]

If Deck had known Hemphill supported the guild movement in New Jersey, he might have left him there. As editor during unionizing attempts mid-century, he considered "guild" a dirty word. Most union members lost their jobs in the 1952 *Telegram-Tribune* merger. (Malmquist gave a more benign account: "After earlier failures, guild supporters organized the circulation, editorial and news departments in 1951, but that union died a natural death from lack of interest three years later."[601])

Hemphill's first years at *The Trib*, sports writers still leaned out the building's second-floor windows with radios to hear the play-by-play of games because there was such poor reception in the newsroom.

He learned quickly that sports took a back seat to news. The most tangible clue? A big deal was made about feeding the editors and reporters who worked late on elections, but nothing special was ever done for sports staffers who worked late every night, often well past eight hours.

When the Jazz professional basketball franchise moved from New Orleans to Salt Lake City in 1979, Hemphill snagged the primo sport. Once the Olympics Games were added to his beat, his life in this unusual, conservative city was pretty good. He covered seven Olympics over the years, including Lillehammer, Norway, in 1994; Nagano, Japan, in 1998; Sydney, Australia, in 2000, and Salt Lake City in 2002.

Fellow sports writer Ace Fibber (not his real name) became a blemish in this otherwise rosy picture.

After infamous Janet Cooke won and lost a Pulitzer in 1981 for creating a fictitious character for a *Washington Post* feature story, Will Fehr warned staffers to keep their notes from sources in their slush in case anyone questioned their stories. Before long, Fibber concocted a bold scam so *The Tribune* would send him across the country for a major sports event normally left to wire services. He supposedly was receiving a special sports-writing award there, and he showed his boss a letter on official stationery to prove it.

When calling in a story on the sports contest, Fibber also dictated a story about his fictitious award. A *Deseret News* sports writer alerted the Sports Desk to the fraud, sending furious writers Hemphill, Steve Luhm and Tom Wharton up the hill to Will Fehr's house with the mortifying news. "If it's true," Fehr said, "we've gotta fire him."

The deception may have been real, but Fibber was back at his desk the next shift as usual. Either he came up with a better story -- "He was always good on his feet," Hemphill noted[602] -- or he threatened to sue or embarrass *The Tribune* in other ways. He had been known to offer promotional news coverage in exchange for favors like property options and freelance jobs in the past. We would wait several more years for his coup de grace.

Meanwhile, new newsroom secretary Ann Poore stepped into Fibber's muck. Sports Editor John Mooney ordered her to send all of Fibber's mail through him. When Fibber caught on to the censure, he accosted Ann in the back hallway. Clutching her coat collar, she said, he pulled her up to his face with menacing eyes and

threatened: "If I don't start getting my mail . . . "[603]

"I told him I took orders from Mooney, not him, and I thought he was going to throttle me," Ann wrote me years later. Sports writer Bob Donohoe encouraged her to take the issue to the top, and she tried, starting with Will Fehr. He told her she would alienate a lot of people, including her immediate supervisor, who was close to Fibber, if she pursued the matter. "I was scared, mostly because Will had been so very cold about it." Ann said.

Over the years, I had seen Fehr handle complaints of sex abuse or harassment much the same way.

Fibber's sleazy stunt was on Nancy Melich's mind one day when walking past Lamb's Grill, nearly bumping into Hemphill going the other way. Although the two had met at one of Jack Schroeder's pool parties, she barely knew him from his trips past her desk, once in bright green slacks on St. Patrick's day, to drop mail down the office's ornate brass mail chute.

Nancy asked how he felt about Fibber's latest antics, and Hemphill blew a fuse, launching into an hour-long ethics tirade. When he paused for air, Nancy suggested they continue the conversation some time, but it was weeks before their evening work schedules permitted it. They finally met for lunch and a drink at Harvey's bar in the Shiloh Inn, beginning a relationship legitimized 11 years later. "So you could say [Fibber] got us together . . . the only good thing he ever did," Nancy said.[604]

Denny naturally put another spin on it: "So you were into Lex's pants from Day 1."

It wasn't always easy working as a couple at *The Tribune*, primarily because no one worked a 9-5 shift. After her day shift, Nancy often covered an evening performance requiring a deadline review. Hemphill would work late covering basketball games.

Of course no one was allowed to acknowledge those extra hours on time slips, affectionately dubbed "cheat sheets." Still, Nancy considered it a great job. "We were lucky to put out a product we'd see the next day and to work with the same group as a family for such a long time," she said.

It must have been even tougher on couples with a spouse outside *The Tribune*. The perks of a front-row parade seat, annual picnic and Christmas ham could hardly compensate for the meager income and missed meals with the family. Spouses put up with partners who often came home late after several stress-suppressing drinks. Conversations at social events were all about *The Tribune*, as if it was the only game in town.

* * *

As a nasty reminder that others had bigger problems than I did, the toddler daughter of a normally easygoing staffer was brutally raped and hospitalized late in 1980. For weeks I couldn't rid my mind of the images of this tiny tot being tortured. And of a good City Desk friend traumatized.

After Craig Hansell's bicycle accident.

We got more startling, tragic news in late September. Photographer **Craig Hansell** slammed into the windshield of a car while bicycling down the steep, winding road through Big Cottonwood Canyon. His left arm and shoulder were mutilated, requiring amputation. As he lay bleeding and broken in the road, someone stole his professional camera gear.

I cried right there in the newsroom at the thought of such a nice guy suffering such severe pain. A collection was taken up to replace his camera. I wondered what he'd do now, with only one arm. How would he sail, bicycle and ski, the sports he loved? This was a guy who snapped photos while skiing down a mountainside!

Once healed, Hansell appropriately transferred to the Sports Desk to cover outdoor sports. Though writing wasn't his forte, he managed to type and take pictures with one hand.

* * *

We endured an especially dreary winter in 1980, with week after week of smog and cold

socking in Salt Lake Valley. Yet I was feeling heat from my beat.

Utah Technical College's president was upset that I quoted his intemperate comments over a no-confidence vote from his faculty. Higher Education Commissioner Ted Bell complained about my story on the Board of Regents' vote to open Provo's technical college to general education students.

My depiction of the decision as a move toward community college status (I could have said university status) undermined Bell's efforts to pacify political forces against higher education expansion during tough budget times. Now I had to worry about his cooperation on other stories.

Accolades showered on LaVar Chaffin, who was retiring as education editor of the *Deseret News* after 45 years as a journalist (and a recent brain tumor diagnosis), made me feel awkward and unappreciated. I knew I would never receive such praise from school officials, and I shouldn't want to if I was doing my job right.

As I wallowed in self-doubt amplified by the depressing weather, I complained about *The Tribune's* filth and half-assed employee benefit plan. I longed for sunny California again even though I knew Denny would never leave this place he called home. I regretted abandoning teaching and summer vacations before qualifying for a reasonable salary. The shocking, senseless shooting of Jon Lennon December 8 deepened my dark mood.

Then the sun came out December 28, 1980, when it was announced that 73-year-old Art Deck, whose wife had died in August from emphysema, would retire after 30 years as executive editor. Will Fehr would take over for him with Jack Schroeder as managing editor.

The change offered hope that I could stay where I belonged, a place whose irreverence helped me cope with Utah's insular, occasionally oppressive culture.

---

[596] Nancy Melich interview, March 5, 2014, Temecula, California.

[597] Ibid.

[598] Ibid.

[599] Lex Hemphill interview, March 5, 2014, Temecula, California.

[600] Ibid.

[601] Malmquist, p. 437.

[602] Hemphill, March 5, 2014.

[603] Ann Poore email, November 17, 2015.

[604] Melich, March 5, 2014.

25 - Deck Departs in 1981

Art Deck died from a heart attack 2 1/2 months after leaving office. The Utah Press Association inducted him into the Utah Newspaper Hall of Fame 24 years later, in 2004.

"Now Will's truly in charge," I told Denny at the conclusion of a bittersweet graveside service.

Within two weeks of the changing of the guard, Stan Bowman took early retirement and went home to sober up.

Sprucing up the newsroom were squares of mousy brown carpet blanketing the burn-splotched tan linoleum Deck had salvaged from a World War II battleship deck. A new coat of beige paint brightened splotchy walls.

With space needed for ATEX system wiring, a false ceiling of fresh acoustic tiles and recessed fluorescents replaced rows of blinking tubes encased in browning plastic below filthy, yellowed paint tinged with greasy specks of ink. The new suspension ceiling hung low enough over the Sports Desk to make a narrow space for five wire-room clocks set to various time zones.

New, intact chairs and relatively streamlined desks appeared. Staffers started using ashtrays instead of tossing butts on the floor. Until coffee and ink stains blemished the carpet a few months into the change, the place looked and sounded almost professional.

Along with physical changes in the newsroom, new efforts were made to improve the product, at least as far as reporting, writing and editing.

Jerry O'Brien's fair-haired boy Gerry Cunningham, slated for night news editor, conducted a survey showing most staffers found headlines clever, clear and accurate but considered writing and editing only fair to good. About a third believed their work was "usually" satisfying and appreciated, yet almost 20 percent seldom felt satisfied and appreciated. While most staffers said photos were used effectively, only half in the Photo and Art departments agreed.

Our monthly motivational prize was granted to the 15-member team, including yours truly, for coverage of a statewide power outage triggered by a fire at the Utah State Prison. Schroeder's *Tattler* described the scenario:

It was Thursday, Jan. 8. Grimy fog gripped the Salt Lake Valley. Day City Editor Lance Gudmundsen began to put together his carefully worded daily Racetrack. That was about 11 a.m.

At 11:24 a.m. the most wide-ranging power outage in the United States struck Utah and surrounding states. Stores closed for the day, schools were let out, people were stranded in elevators and ski lifts. Salt Lake City was all but paralyzed.

City Editor Brian Nutting pondered if it would be a temporary condition. The blackout persisted. Nutting organized his staff and put in motion one of The Tribune's finest performances -- the Great Blackout edition.

Lance Gudmundsen did most of the writing on the main story. Clark Lobb was stationed at the Utah Power & Light Co. headquarters. Con Psarras was stationed in the emergency services bunker. Jon Ure covered the activities of the police.

Angelyn Nelson raced to the hospitals. Diane Cole covered the schools. Pete Scarlet did a history of similar blackouts. Bob Woody contributed two stories on business and industry. Harold Schindler wrapped up the media problems. Barbi Robison did a [roundup of] elevator problems.

Ravell Call and Frank Porschatis took countless pictures. Dennis Green put together a thorough map on the state. Pat Bagley added a wonderful cartoon.

The effort was one of the most unified in years. It was reminiscent of the way newspapers were. And everyone felt proud of the end results.

The list of contributors will share two months' prizes for their efforts recognizing that their real rewards came from a highly praised final product . . .

Did most staffers actually value praise more than pay? More likely, praise eased the pain of a pittance.

That *Tattler* also highlighted *Tribune* performance in the annual contest of Utah Headliners Chapter of the Society of Professional Journalists (SPJ-SDX). Jon Ure, Bob Bryson, Joe Rolando and Steve Saunders won first place in spot news coverage for reporting on the Avalon Apartment fire that killed 12 Vietnamese refugees.

Ravell Call took the pictures that were widely used across the country. Vard Jones laid out the pages, and Brian Nutting directed the operation. It was the first time that most of those involved had been part of a prize-winning effort.

Talk about a back-handed compliment.

Schroeder was impressed with leads by two of his favorite reporters.

First, Lex Hemphill in Sports:

(1) *The Denver Nuggets defaced a masterpiece at the Salt Palace Friday night.*

(2) *NEW YORK -- The Big Apple turned out to be forbidden fruit for the Utah Jazz Tuesday night.*

Next, Woody's latest business assistant, John Serfustini:

(1) *DELTA -- The checks are in the mail. The parts are on order. And IPP is going to wallop this little town with people and money like you've never seen before.*

(2) *LEAMINGTON, Juab County -- Metropolitan Leamington is not what you'd call an eye-catcher. When the Union Pacific train stopped here Thursday, the dignitaries on the side facing the sagebrush asked, "Are we here?"*

The dignitaries on the side facing the massive gray concrete structures of the Martin Marietta Corp. cement plant replied, "Looks like it."

Serf's catchy leads included: "A lot of Israelis are walking around on feet made right in Salt Lake City" and "Anybody want to buy some hot, dirty water?"

* * *

While Denny and I swilled tequila and suffered gastric distress in Mazatlan with the Nuttings January 21, 1981, Ronald Reagan was inaugurated as President, and Iran released its 60-plus American hostages. Though skeptical of the great communicator's prowess as President, we were relieved to avoid all-out war. My subsequent travel feature recounted how Denny got trapped between a gunman and his mark at our Mazatlan hotel's registration desk.

Back home, Denny was sent to court to illustrate the trial of Joseph Paul Franklin, the white supremacist who shot two black kids in a crosswalk near Liberty Park. This was before cameras were allowed in courtrooms, and Denny was excited about this first-time assignment. He came away exhausted each day but was impressed by the circumstantial evidence that neatly proved Franklin's guilt.

Other Utah news had the Army transferring weteye nerve gas bombs to Tooele Army Depot, the public agitated over a nude painting at the airport, and miners threatening to strike in coal country. Harold Schindler wrote an obituary for Fawn Brodie, author of the controversial biography of LDS Church founder Joseph Smith.

* * *

My job was horrendously busy. When not writing fluff about the schooling of child actors in "Annie," I was reporting school lunch price increases, University of Utah budget pressures and conflict at the state workshop for the blind. Plus, it was now my duty each January and February to cover education issues during legislative sessions at the State Capitol.

Of the 10 *Tribune* reporters covering the 1981 Utah Legislature, just two of us were women: me and Angelyn Nelson. Doug Parker took the lead on Capitol Hill as usual, while Vaughn Roche sat in the Senate and Jack Fenton the House. Clark Lobb, Bob Woody, Bob Halliday, Tom Wharton and Dave Jonsson rounded out our team.

For background information and interpretation, I relied heavily on gubernatorial aides and legislative auditors and analysts like Lori Chivers, Mike Christensen, Roger Tew, Bryant Howe, Anna Marie Dunlap and Henry Whiteside. Media hounds like R. Thayne Robson, who regularly issued headline-grabbing dire warnings as director of the University of Utah Bureau of Business and Economic Research, also became part of my routine.

Robson explained complex issues in homespun, common sense ways,[605] but his pronouncements struck me as self-promoting and designed to tell audiences what leaders wanted them to hear. I preferred Christensen's objective research and analysis, because he clearly backed up his conclusions without inserting himself into the headlines.

After Democrat Scott Matheson left the governor's office in 1985, Christensen took charge of Utah Foundation, a privately funded public policy analysis group. Whenever he issued a report, readers could expect a story or editorial from me on his topic because I respected his work and felt comfortable interviewing him.

As much as I appreciated the $45 weekly raise and $200 legislative bonus that came with my new responsibilities, I was working 10 to 12 hours a day.

The education beat had me covering countless state and local education meetings, from pre-school through graduate school. Almost every Tuesday night I worked late because of local board meetings, and almost every Tuesday night all winter it snowed, making my late-night drives especially hellish. School programs, conferences and graduations also demanded my attention, and in between, I worked up stories about education crises, innovations and quirks. I interviewed innumerable students and teachers.

Our traditional method of covering graduations school-by-school had become literally impossible as more than 100 commencements occurred each May and June, many simultaneously. I hated the process, and so did everyone else I recruited to help. I proposed a new approach to Nutting, who agreed.

First I surveyed each high school for information on graduation time, place, number of graduates, speakers and class characteristics. Then I published a list of the details and followed up with features about the Class of 1981 statewide.

Will Fehr's wife Cynthia called the change "interesting" and "useful," almost making the time-consuming effort worthwhile. Unfortunately, it didn't get me out of covering speeches at state's colleges and universities.

I continued to receive hate mail from members of the teachers union. Val Wilcox, a Provo teacher who claimed experience as a society and city news reporter, described my most recent UEA convention coverage as "distorted" and "erroneous . . . evidence of lazy, unprofessional reporting." In her full-page, single-spaced, wide-margined letter, she said I must have been absent the day journalism students were taught not to interview the janitor for facts. Her other observations:

Her article is riddled with inaccuracies . . .

My friend called and spoke with Diane Cole, who, from her comments, apparently did not even attend the event she was supposed to have covered. If there were a question about how to report the attendance, she might have inquired the capacity of Symphony Hall,

but she said, "I didn't know how many were there" . . .

Mr. Slight deserves credit for his help on the planning committee, but he is only one of ten of us, many of whom contributed more time by far. I happen to have been the chairman of this terrific group . . . [Aha! Someone was slighted.]

Is Reporter Cole happy in her assignment as education editor?

As the official education editor, one would suppose that she could manage to include the major session of the most important educational event of the year in her schedule . . .

Perhaps if Diane Cole took time to meet educators she might like us.

I had no desire to meet educators like Val. After obviously failing to read my story herself, she wasted my precious time with this nasty, tedious complaint because she was overlooked. If it meant teaching with people like her, it was best I never returned to the classroom.

Into an already full day, I crammed freelance for *Education USA,* published by the National School Public Relations Association in Washington, D.C. Utah stories became particularly popular when locals led national school reform, such as Alpine School District's attempt to improve productivity by shortening the school day. The state school board's abortive attempt to hire a non-Mormon Easterner as superintendent also attracted the newsletter's attention.

On top of everything else, I idiotically agreed to produce nine personality profiles for Newport Beach publisher Charles Barrett for a paltry $400 apiece and a ridiculous four-month deadline. I was one of a dozen writers contributing to the proposed "Utah Legacy" coffee-table book featuring 115 Utahns influential in the arts, athletics, business, communications, government and law, medicine, religion, science and communities.

The extra workload came at a horrendous time for my personal life. Denny already was fed up with my long hours. With only one car, we were driving back and forth to the suburbs to work, to show our house to prospective buyers and to help my parents clear out theirs. My after-hour interviews and writing binges eroded what little romance was left.

---

[605] "Long-Time Professor/Researcher R. Thayne Robson Dies," U. News Center, May 13, 2002.

26 - The Legacy Project

Desperation, naiveté and pride contributed to my participation in this massive, mostly fruitless task. The book was never published. My main consolations were that my marriage survived and I could apply the interviews to *Tribune* stories.

I also got to know school leaders better, brightening my mostly bland beat a bit.

One was Utah Education Association Director **Daryl J. McCarty**, the pugnacious guy who hated my references to his union. When he announced his retirement, I quickly put together a personality profile that portrayed him as a scrappy defender of teacher rights, a temperamental union man if there ever was one.

McCarty had been UEA's research director and then executive secretary from 1963 through 1982, when the union came of age. During his tenure, teachers began collective bargaining for salaries and job security and went on strike for the first time in May of 1964 and then again in 1989.[606] He wasn't my greatest fan.

Background on T.H. Bell and David P. Gardner gave me a head start when President Reagan pushed them into the national limelight with education reform. Bell became the first cabinet-level education czar, and he appointed Gardner chairman of the National Commission on Excellence in Education that wrote the influential Nation at Risk report.

* * *

Confident Californian **David P. Gardner** wielded power over not only the University of Utah but also the entire State Board of Regents and then articulately spelled out the need for strict national education standards.

The former Army intelligence officer competently led regents around by the nose, commanding the highest salary in state government and the largest budgets for his institution. While Utah's System of Higher Education was required to report the salaries of all its presidents, it kept quiet about Gardner's actual income, which foundations pumped up with trust contributions.

As Gardner put it, his sizable salary and permanent professorships outside Utah gave him the financial independence to take political risks without undermining his family's income.[607] He didn't feel trapped or pushed around at the U., and his salary raised the bar on what he could offer other top educators to join his administration.

Gardner's influence and apparent arrogance got some college presidents hot under the collar. Former businessman Rodney H. Brady, whose white collar always set off a navy blue suit for efficiency's sake, would bluster about improvements at Weber State College deserving recognition. Utah Technical College's Orville Carnahan more timidly made his case for more money. Gardner argued that all boats rose with his.

Like Utah's other public college and university presidents, Gardner came from Mormon stock, his mother and stepmother from Provo, his father from Pine Valley. He remained an active, orthodox Mormon, he said, without having to surround himself with Mormons to feel comfortable.

His life view was affected by growing up in diverse Berkeley, where he was high school student body president, attended lectures by heads of state and Nobel laureates, spent time in the rare books section of the university library and attended cultural events in nearby San Francisco. "That discovery of the Western Civilization's great treasures had a profound influence on my perception of what's important in life and the role of universities, one of civilization's greatest triumphs," he told me. In higher education, he explained, intelligent people and young perspectives keep you alive in a world of ideas.

For years Gardner studied piano and the pipe organ, even considering a musical career. "To play well, the piano requires a measure of concentration and self-discipline that has had an impact on my work," he said. Other factors were Berkeley's rigorous standards and his ability to quickly pick out important parts of a problem to produce and communicate a solution.

His goal at the University of Utah, where he worked 60 to 70 hours a week, was to boost its standing from the the second tier (Number 35) of major universities to Number 20. He expected to get there by raising extra tax dollars, private donations and federal research grants to strengthen his colleges of science, engineering, business, pharmacy and medicine.

During his tenure, he pointed out, the Legislature had quit reducing his budget, federal research grew from $27 million to $60 million, and private fundraising rose from $2 million a year to $11 million. He used the additional money to raise faculty salaries and reduce teaching loads.

Even before his Nation at Risk report came out, Gardner talked of working with public education to better prepare students for college. Soon after the report's release, he accepted the offer to lead California's "elitist" system of higher education.[608]

The only good thing about that news, in my opinion, was that I got the scoop from a loose-lipped regent who also named his replacement: Dr. Chase N. Peterson, another Mormon male and point man for the university's Medical Center expansion and artificial heart development. For once I got an exclusive tidbit.

I liked Gardner. Unlike some movers and shakers in Utah, he treated me with respect and even humor. He recognized that both of us had a job to do that could contribute to public well-being. There was no condescension or time restraints during interviews. In kind, I left him with a "letter of recommendation" July 20, 1983:

> For a decade, you've been the motivating force for many of the improvements in Utah education. Despite your busy schedule, you've answered my inquiries, sometimes taking more time than I could expect, with candor, patience and respect. You even helped me as a writer and reporter by gracefully calling my attention to details and implications I might not have noticed. I developed a healthy respect for you and your office.

His response July 27, 1983:

> Dear Diane:
> Your letter warmed my day. Thank you for your generous, gracious and thoughtful comments regarding my service at the University of Utah. If I can be only partially as fortunate in California as I have been in Utah in establishing mutually respectful and helpful relationships with the press, I shall feel fully rewarded. This is an area of critical importance to any university and especially to the president of the institution. I have always been able to count on fair and accurate reporting by you and on a level of candor and respect that served our mutual responsibilities as well as making our personal relationships pleasant and memorable.
> All the best as you continue your work here or elsewhere. My very best personal good wishes for your further success and happiness. Sincerely, David

Apparently, that mutual respect was lacking in California. In 1992, he resigned from the university system's top post, again with the highest salary in the state. For $243,500 (and undoubtedly more), he had managed a $6.4-billion budget.

Gardner announced he could no longer continue that job without his wife Libby, who served as an unpaid associate to the president until her death from bone cancer and heart failure in 1991.[609] There also had been friction in California over his Mormonism,[610] an irony given his broad perspective of the world.

* * *

President Reagan picked **Terrell H. "Ted" Bell**, Utah's feisty commissioner of higher education, to become the nation's first U.S. Secretary of Education. Another irony, given Reagan's promise to dismantle the federal Office of Education.

The self-described runt of the litter had begun his climb to national notoriety in 1970 as a facilitator of school desegregation while interim of commissioner of the U.S. Office of Education. Later, as President Nixon's commissioner of education, he promoted vocational education and equalized funding of public education for low-income children. In between, he ran Utah's largest school district, Granite, for three years -- an experience he told me he couldn't "think of much to brag about." After becoming Utah's higher education commissioner in the late 1970s, he launched a multi-million-dollar school loan program that sidestepped federal red tape.

Generally self-effacing and cooperative with me as a reporter, Bell described himself and his wife Betty as "hicks." His Idaho father died in a mining accident when Ted was 7, so his mother raised him and his eight older siblings in Lava Hot Springs on laundry income and a $52 weekly workman's compensation check from the mine. "Since I grew up as a runt in a big family, I've had to scratch for my share," he told me.

Bell's high school librarian steered him toward Albion State Normal School for teachers because it charged just $11.50 a quarter for tuition. Before finding a job, he served as a first sergeant and machine-gun instructor in the Pacific during World Ward II. "You had to be more feisty than others to handle that," he said.

Bell climbed education's ranks from teacher-of-all-trades (he led the band, taught science, helped the janitor and substituted as a bus driver in Rockland, Idaho's one-building school system) to head of a $15 billion national bureaucracy. He maintained a wry sense of humor and folksy style, often livening dull meetings with a self-deprecating joke or good-natured jab at one of his peers. Yet he stood his ground and pushed for programs like a bulldog if need be. Perhaps that helps explain Reagan's failure to abolish the federal education office.

* * *

Dallin H. Oaks also added color to my beat and Legacy assignment. The former president of Mormon-owned Brigham Young University sat on the Utah Supreme Court before becoming an LDS apostle in 1984.

While covering BYU's legal battles with the federal government over sex equity in campus housing, I regarded Oaks as an arrogant, stubborn know-it-all. He was someone else behind the scenes.

As a lawyer -- he clerked for conservative U.S. Chief Justice Earl Warren and taught law at the University of Chicago -- Oaks wrote articles and books on abortion and the separation of church and state, espousing positions that left me cold. While BYU president, he legally resisted Title IX, another stance I opposed but could understand. His explanation:

> Title IX has the worthy goal of promoting non-discrimination on the basis of sex, but government overreached its legal power by giving aid to one part of the university, research, and using it as justification for regulating dorm hours . . .
> Title IX infringed on the constitutional rights of the church school to set its own religious standards.[611]

BYU could afford to challenge the law, Oaks noted, because he accepted so little government aid. In the end, a settlement allowed the school to set its own off-campus housing policies regarding same-sex dorms.

As a descendant of Emer Harris, the older brother of the Martin Harris who helped transcribe and publish the original Book of Mormon, Oaks' Mormon roots run deep. (Martin Harris gained notoriety during my time as the purported author of forger Mark Hofmann's white

salamander letter.) Yet Oaks' childhood was far from typical.

Dallin was 8 when his physician father died. Along with two younger siblings, he lived with relatives in rural Payson while their mother, Stella Harris Oaks, earned her masters degree from Columbia University in New York City. Young Dallin voraciously read westerns, science fiction and mysteries, sometimes three or four books a day.

Mormon mothers were not encouraged to work outside the home, but Stella Oaks became director of adult education for Provo Public Schools, a Provo City councilwoman and LDS Stake Relief Society president. She was Dallin's role model, inspiring his work, church and public service ethic. When he proudly told me she helped start social programs like Meals on Wheels for the aging, I saw the softer, likable side of of the man.

Unlike many successful Mormons, Oaks never created a life plan for himself. He considered himself a cooperative team member rather than an individual star.

While other school presidents might be good budget autocrats, Oaks felt his strengths lay elsewhere. He strove to create a "cooperative anarchy" where the most important thing was happening in peoples' minds, the library and the classroom, not in administration. His job, he said, was to keep the campus environment serene so the educators could focus on learning rather than parking, sports or other mundane policies.

* * *

Legacy's publisher sought diversity, ordering interviews of ground-breaking women and minorities in Utah education. **Alberta Henry** filled both requirements as an outspoken, unorthodox supervisor of early minority programs in Salt Lake City School District.

Dr. Henry, as she liked to be called after receiving an honorary doctorate from the University of Utah, did not fit the Utah mold. The exuberant African American was nearly 60 before receiving a bachelor's degree for a job she'd held for nearly a decade. She'd collected accolades from President Nixon, the Elks, the NAACP, The Exchange Club and various Utah colleges and universities for her role in launching the federal Head Start program for disadvantaged children.

But they [awards] don't matter in the long run," she told me. "The Lord deserves all the credit. After all, if I get too many rewards in this life, there'll be nothing left for me in Heaven. What matters is that mothers of every color trusted me with their children at Head Start because of my loving arms."

Dr. Henry was born October 14, 1920 to a Louisiana sharecropper and raised in Topeka, Kansas. Her grandfather, Rev. J.J. Palmer of the non-denominational Church of the Living God, planned to make her into a minister since she was preaching hellfire and damnation so well by age 7. She also was selling newspapers and cleaning up betting on Joe Louis fights.

"I didn't come into womanhood until 17 or 18," she said. "Before that, I was like a boy."

Alberta moved to Utah to recover from near-fatal peritonitis and applied for jobs catering or projecting movies like she'd done in Topeka. She was told colored women were housekeepers in Utah -- a situation she blamed on Mormon denial of the priesthood to blacks -- so she got a job taking care of Wally and Helen Sandack's five children (one of whom became Swamper's lawyer). She also married a Pullman porter and adopted two children.

In 1966, after noticing black kids weren't graduating from high school, she started the Alberta Henry Education Foundation, which helped send more than 150 minority students to college. To prove her students could get an education despite their fears of teacher prejudice, she went to college herself.

In Salt Lake City schools, Dr. Henry organized student trips through an honor society she established in 1972 and eventually became a community relations coordinator who supervised the development of multicultural curriculum.

* * *

Carma Hales, another influential woman featured in the "Legacy" project, flew 615,000 miles between 1970 and 1982 carrying her individualized learning techniques, called the Utah System Approach to Individualized Learning (U-SAIL), to 31 states and nine foreign countries.

Directors of two American Indian programs at Brigham Young University also were highlighted in the book: **Dale Thomas Tingey**, assigned in 1971 to BYU's Indian Services and Research Center, and **John R. Maestas** of the Indian Education Program. Based on the belief that "Lamanites" were special tribes descended from Israel in 600 B.C., these Mormon programs attempted to help Indians live longer, productive lives. Tingey set up agricultural projects at

reservations across the country, while Maestas raised funds for Indian students attending college.

[606] Michael T. McCoy and James B. Eldredge, Evolution of the Utah Education Association into Collective Bargaining in Utah, December 4, 2003, p. 17.

[607] David P. Gardner interview, May 7, 1981.

[608] Ibid.

[609] Laurie Becklund, *Los Angeles Times*, November 20, 1991.

[610] David P. Gardner, Earning My Degree: Memoirs of a an American University President, 2005, p. 154.

[611] Dallin Oaks interview, Utah State Capitol, May 7, 1981.

27 - Back on Staff

When Vandra Huber left *The Tribune*, Will Fehr hired another feisty, salty woman to replace her on the human services beat covering poverty, welfare, mental health, disabilities, abortion, children's issues, Native Americans and prisons.

Carol Sisco, a journalism graduate with a sociology minor from California State in Sacramento, came from the *Ogden Standard-Examiner* by way of Alturus, California, where she worked at one small paper before moving to others in Folsom, California, and Klamath Falls, Oregon. As the only child of a divorced Cajun father and British mother who had met during the war, Sisco was resourceful, changing her own oil and speaking up for herself.

Carol Sisco

"I remember the shock of seeing those blasted typewriters when I arrived," Sisco wrote years after her arrival. "I thought everyone had computers by then."[612]

The Copy Desk was no longer afflicted by burn-outs. David Beck, Tom Baldwin, Cindy Gilchrist, Steve Brown and Kevin Grahman were still bright-eyed and under 40. But Beck was on his way out again.

Between stints at *The Trib*, Beck reported for California's *Press-Enterprise*, and now he was headed for the *Orange County Register* and *San Jose Mercury News,* where he would find a ready-made family. I never would have guessed he'd adapt so well to a wife and teenagers.

Fred "Shakeyspeare" Dodds from my own Copy Desk days wrote me from Lewiston, Idaho, where he worked as economic and community development planner for the Nez Perce Indian Tribe.

I got out of newspaper work because I never did like it, and the pay here is quite a bit better than anything I ever earned as a newsman. And there are no deadlines, no night work, no weekends.
Does the Copy Desk still call you Charles?

Well, that didn't make me feel any better about my working conditions, and I had no idea what he meant by "Charles." So I sought an explanation. His reply:

You must consider the source and the fact the man was deeply in love with you . . .
Shanghai Jack . . . applied it to you as the woman most representative of "Charles," the personal aide to "The Colonel," a man named Tobin in the books written by Alan Caillou . . .
The books were about a soldier of fortune who went to war with his aide and a bottle of Irish whiskey. Need I say more. . . .
[Shanghai] used to get very concerned about your welfare, and he considered you a "15" on the scale of "10."

The Last Supper: Verdo Thomas, Cindy Gilchrist, Tom Baldwin, Gerry Cunningham, John O'Connor, Steve Brown, Bob Ellefsen, Jim Smedley, Ray Brown, Randy Peterson, left to right.

Apparently my working conditions could have been worse -- if I still sat on the Copy Desk. But I was sad when Will Fehr showed Shanghai the door in 1982 for disappearing from the Copy Desk once too often. Something also was said about my old admirer absconding with a betting pool, but I didn't know anything about that.

On March 9, *The Tribune* published Jon Ure's story about marijuana abuse among kids. Michael D. Decaria, director of the Drug Referral Center, was impressed by his excellent conclusions and ability to dispel myths. It probably helped that Ure wrote from experience.

Tragedy struck another Utah journalist whose work appeared on our pages. While AP reporter Jim Boardman was deplaning on assignment, a propellor sliced through his skull and upper body.

Although I didn't know Boardman personally, I relied on his reporting for background material. His severe injuries included brain damage, and he eventually lost his wife, Gov. Scott Matheson's daughter, to divorce. Jo-Ann Wong, an acquaintance from the *Deseret News* and The China Village, her family's downtown restaurant, looked after him for years after the accident.

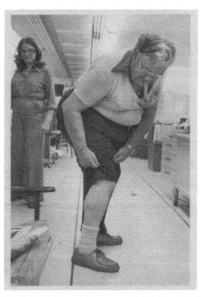

Melinda Sowerby stands behind John Mooney.

Melinda Sowerby, one of our few physically challenged reporters (one side of her body was partially paralyzed), was receiving compliments for her coverage of religion by then. Helen Forsberg was commended for her stories on Ballet West, and Nancy Funk garnered more praise for her theater reviews and features.

In May, Angelyn Nelson began the countdown to her marriage in the LDS Temple to Jerry Hutchison. After so many years as a single woman at *The Tribune,* it was no small feat for

Angie to find a Mormon mate. Not long after the wedding, she moved over to our main competitor, the *Deseret News*, where she became an editor.

Helen Forsberg

* * *

That summer, my personal life took a sharp turn. Ped O'Fiel's daughter Mary told a Rhode Island social worker -- and then Denny -- that her father began using her for his sexual gratification when she reached puberty. She was worried about 13-year-old Stormy, who was having problems in school.

Within hours of that shocking revelation, Denny borrowed $400 from Tim Kelly and left work for the airport. He planned to kidnap the kids if necessary. Thankfully, he didn't have to.

Rhode Island authorities rescued the girls from the Gruesome Twosome just ahead of Denny's arrival, depositing them in a halfway house full of tough teenagers. By week's end, two of the messed-up teens moved in with us.

I hardly recognized the bedraggled young women who walked through the airport gate beside their sheepish father with the forced smile. Their two-year absence had transformed Stormy from a tadpole into a long-legged, big-eyed frog. Lulu had developed curves.

The Rhode Island court had transferred custody to Denny in record time in exchange for paying Swamper six months of child support and letting Ped O'Fiel escape sex-abuse charges. It enraged me the pedophile was free to prey on others, but at least he lost control of his stepdaughters -- our daughters.

We celebrated the Fourth of July at Denny's parents' house as the anniversary of our reunification. Instant, full-time parenthood sent us on a rollercoaster ride that lifted us into the sun one day, when the girls' sweet, spunky nature came out, and plunged us into darkness the next, when their demons emerged.

We still were in the middle of trying to sell our old house and build a new one in Summit Park. Our tiny Honda Civic could hardly contain two gangly teenagers, and we were still spending over an hour a day commuting from 7200 South. We were basically broke.

The kids needed a new wardrobe after the Gruesomes packed rags, rocks and stuffed toys in the "clothing" shipment Swamper's mother arranged -- and financed, she generously reminded us. Lulu's teeth had shifted after her dog chewed up her retainer, so she wanted an operation to realign her jaw. Stormy needed braces, too.

We borrowed another $10,000 from Denny's dad to pay off the Gruesomes, buy school clothes and see an orthodontist.

I still sometimes worked 11 hours a day. After getting up at 6:30 for an early morning session of one education group, I might work past 11 p.m. to finish a local school board meeting that night. My brother called some Friday nights to beg me to type his school papers over the weekend. Now my bored, insecure stepdaughters needed attention, too.

On weekends, Stormy and I squeezed in time baking cookies and learning lyrics to pop songs like Chicago's "Hard to Say I'm Sorry" and Christopher Cross's "Sailing." Lulu danced around the house clanging zills in her revived belly-dancing costume or invited the next-door neighbor into her room to sneak peaks at Denny's *Playboys*.

I sometimes took the girls along on a few reporting trips, which ranged from St. George in Utah's southwestern tip to Utah State University in the north, Trout Creek on the west and Roosevelt to the east. When Board of Education Member Neola Brown complained, I reminded the former teacher that students like Stormy and Lulu were her board's reason for being.

Between meetings, we hiked in Zion National Park and attended Shakespeare plays in Cedar City. A talented actress herself, Lulu enjoyed the plays. Stormy mostly sulked, especially when hiking.

Back home, the panic attacks started. It felt like my heart was breaking through my chest, snagging on my ribs. A prescription for Valium helped but didn't protect me from catching more than my share of colds, compounded by cramps and diarrhea. The upside was that I could hunker down in my bedroom when sick. But not for long.

Our suburban starter finally sold, so we found a Park City condominium so the kids could stay at the same school once the dream house was habitable. The girls had to spend a lot of time alone together after school, where Lulu hooked up with the drama nerds and Stormy hung out with sulky outsiders. By Park City standards, we were trailer trash.

One evening, I got a phone call at work. "Lulu stabbed me!" Stormy screamed.

There were no emergency rooms or clinics nearby then. The father of Stormy's classmate assured us she could hold out until we retrieved her, so we dropped job assignments to race up and back down the canyon to get her severed tendon reattached.

Tim Kelly's VW parked in front of our unfinished Summit Park house.

Five months later, we braved a snowstorm to move our belongings into our unfinished mountain home. In no time, the frigid shell of studs and plywood became a hotbed of lies, tension and vicious battles inflamed by the lack of a dishwasher, countertops, interior walls and carpet.

Lulu smoked cigarettes on the sly, tossing the butts wherever she stood, and refused to lift a finger around the house. Layers of rancid towels and other dirty laundry covered her bedroom floor and spilled into the hall. She dawdled while Stormy shoveled the driveway before we got home, provoking profane outbursts as we pulled up after a long day. To cope, I poured myself a drink as soon as I got through the door. "Lush!" Stormy taunted.

Calls at work became common. "Lulu forgot her key again, and I lost mine!" Stormy announced from the neighbor's house. After rushing through snowstorms to their rescue, the sisters snarled their resentment. That ritual ended when Stormy admitted having her own key all along. She supposedly was teaching Lulu a lesson.

Having no stomach for discipline, Denny took refuge in house construction while his little darlings zapped me with zingers. They called me four-eyes, beaver mouth and a series of vulgarities ending with bitch. When I begged Denny to control his daughters, he accused me of working too much.

We fruitlessly sought professional help. "Nutso," as we called our first counselor, introduced us to the "honey do" jar. Lulu ignored it. Our second counselor advised Denny to set limits and enforce them consistently. He failed. "My folks never told me what to do, and I turned out all right," he asserted. "The kids suffered enough with a Nazi. If they don't start making their own decisions, they'll never learn from their mistakes."

One of their decisions that year was to throw an unauthorized party during our annual Lake Powell trip with the River Crew. We returned to find a slab of gold-swirled marble, which we'd salvaged from The Tribune Building's facade during remodeling, glued in hundreds of pieces to the particle board on the living room floor. Beer bottle shards were embedded in the recently painted drywall outside our bedroom. Partiers had danced on the furniture while dodging an aggressive guest's beer rockets.

When Suzie Nutting announced her first pregnancy, I asked Denny to reconsider having kids together. Forget about it! He had enough kids.

* * *

Fortunately, work offered some comic relief and distractions from stress at home.

After all I'd been through with Steve Hale and his boss Daryl McCarty, UEA bestowed one of its annual "Friend of Education" awards on me during its annual convention at the Salt Palace. Hale wrote this letter of explanation to Mr. Gallivan:

A few years ago I wrote you a letter that sharply criticized an article written by Diane Cole. I would be remiss now if I failed to write you when praise is due Ms. Cole. I had the pleasant duty recently of writing the citation that went with the Utah Education Association's "Honor Roll" award for Diane Cole.

She was cited for distinguished reporting on the complex issues arising these days in education, and for articles on Utah's education scene that "have been lucid, far-reaching in necessary detail, intelligent, readable, and . . . have demonstrated a keen eye for even-handed treatment."

Ms. Cole is a valuable member of the *Tribune* staff, and you have every right to be immensely proud of her and her work.

Mr. Gallivan scrawled a note to me across the top of the letter: "F.Y.I. & congratulations -- a well-earned award."

With my usual cynicism, I suspected union leaders of currying my favor after failing to get rid of me. It seemed I'd received nothing but flack from militant teachers and their lackeys until now. Maybe they intended to stone me during UEA's presentation.

As it turned out, I was ignored amid the chaos of the convention arena. Only Denny, Lulu and Stormy heard what the UEA president said about me. And the kids didn't really care, either.

* * *

Jack Schroeder set up a Peer Review Committee of five staffers from various departments, including me from City Desk, to evaluate an entire month's newspapers. The grueling process required extensive time and effort outside the office when I had none to spare. Somehow I managed to come up with remarks like these about the September 1 edition:

I liked Judy Magid's Monday Musing. Good images: "200 pounds of hysteria . . . How good are you at chewing worms?" I don't believe she cried all night -- too much crying -- she cried last week, too. I like Magid's writing.

Our minimum standard for Page 1 art should be a semi-in-focus shot. This one looks like the punch line for a Polish joke on photographers.

Why so few Forum letters? Aren't they writing them?

Mike Royko: He's a sarcastic s.o.b. but the best editorial columnist in the paper. We should take lessons.

Poland's Labor Tribute -- This editorial flows more smoothly and has fewer writing problems than most recently.

300 Days -- It takes this editorial writer a long time to get to the point, which seems shallow.   Seventh graph seems a rash, unfounded conclusion; almost infantile. Eighth graph -- long, confusing sentence. Tenth graph -- another run-on sentence. Concerning quotes: who is the author quoting?

Toward the end of the year, I wrote a feature about JoAnn's father **Gene Jacobsen**, an occasional candid source of mine as administrator of the Utah High School Activities Association, Society of Utah Superintendents and Utah School Boards Association. Before his education career, he lived through the Bataan Death March to survive 3 1/2 years as a prisoner of war during World War II.[613] And, as noted earlier, he was a colleague of Brian Nutting's father, an education professor at the U.

In a letter to Will Fehr December 16, Jacobsen followed up on my story:

> Never have I enjoyed such popularity! The article about me in yesterday's paper generated dozens of telephone calls, mostly from people wanting the name of my agent.
>
> . . . And, we know well the affection you have for Jo and the care given to her. She is extremely happy in her work.
>
> We share with Bill and Gwen Nutting pride over the progress of Bryan [sic]. He and our son Mike have been close friends for many years, and I even had a small role in his graduate program here at the University.
>
> I wish to extend special appreciation to Diane, not only for the delightful article but for the opportunity to spend two hours with her recently talking about my life as an educator. She is a lovely, talented lady.

So talented that I gave Lifestyle a light-hearted first-person account of my family's struggle to build and adapt to a house in the mountains mid-winter. I made Lulu and Stormy part of the scene:

> Since moving into our unfinished house the week before Christmas, they, like us, have had to cope with reservoirs of dust settling any chance of tidiness, snow nearly choking off our link to city jobs and school and endless troops of stinkbugs crawling from exposed stud walls and insulation to season our meals.[614]

I told the sad tale of shrinking the design and building in phases when costs of building on a steep slope soared and mortgage companies refused to loan in Summit Park, of Denny single-handedly lugging steel beams into place 30 feet above ground, of coping with ice and deep snow without four wheel drive. And of living in rustic conditions.

> We lacked a few amenities, like hot water, a range and oven, home mail delivery and telephone service. Our Mr. Coffee became a major cooking source, and we worried whenever we got off work late, because we couldn't call the children . . . Because we lacked the foresight to string heat wires along the edges of the roof, Denny's had to climb the three stories to the roof to shovel snow and chop away 2-foot-thick icicles to stop the leaks . . .

As was my way, I obsessed about the feature's typos, cliches and strange sentence structure. "My vocabulary and ideas could use some creativity," I moaned to Mimi. Even so, several friends and acquaintances said they enjoyed it.

---

[612] Carol Sisco to facebook's Tribune group February 1, 2012.

[613] Gene Samuel Jacobsen wrote <u>They Refused to Die.</u> He died May 5, 2007.

[614] Diane Cole, "Roughin' It," *The Salt Lake Tribune*, February 12, 1982, P. D1.

28 - Writing About Education in 1982

That January of 1982, I anticipated covering education for several weeks again on Capitol Hill. It was during these annual lawmaking sessions, where I learned a lot about school finance from practical, patient state bureaucrats, that I developed an interest in public policy. The experience gave me confidence in my competence as a journalist.

Down from the Hill, I wrote about "white flight" in Salt Lake City four high schools. The district's open enrollment policy had caused racial imbalances at West and South high schools, raising the prospect of forced integration with cross-town busing.

I submitted stories about South High School's racial diversity and efforts to bolster programs to attract more students. I wrote a feature about Frank Brunsman's ex-wife, a teacher of the year there. But no amount of positive press could stanch the outflow of students, and much to the chagrin of alumni like our own Shirley Jones, the inner-city school would shut down six years later, in 1988.

As aways, I had a backlog of work to do. On March 15, 1982, for instance, my reporter notebooks contained enough information for 10 stories waiting to be written.

The writing process was rarely smooth and easy. It helped to keep files of previous news stories for supplemental facts, because I couldn't count on help from a our chatty librarian, and digital libraries and search engines didn't exist yet. I reviewed my news clips before calling sources on each side of an issue so that I could ask informed questions. Once I had all my answers, I tossed leads and even conclusions around in my head while showering, driving the car and cleaning house.

Then I sat at my typewriter and banged out the lead before wracking my brains for more ideas and words. I struggled to put sentences and paragraphs in logical order amid the distraction of phone calls, gabby peers and the Fehr's jingling change. After moving this sentence or that paragraph around on the page for a few hours and then retyping the package, I was spent. My head throbbed. I needed a release, to relax.

So I headed for D.B. Cooper's to unwind before facing the pressures of home. Over drinks with Paul Rolly, Brian Nutting or anyone else on hand, I'd hash out details of my latest story. During that process, I often realized I'd left a hole in the piece. Or I had second thoughts about a quote or detail that might unnecessarily hurt someone. So I'd rush back to the office or get to a phone to plead with the editor on duty to squeeze in a correction or addition. I never stopped worrying about any one story until it came out in the paper. Even then, I'd circle mistakes and file them for future self-torture.

* * *

Even though school officials fed stories to *Deseret News* reporters LaVar Chaffin, Bobbe Dabling and Vicki Varela at my expense, my relationship with such rivals became a highlight of my job.

It probably would have upset my bosses to know that Chaffin, having covered education more than 30 years, did more to train me than anyone at *The Tribune*. We sometimes shared notes, checked each other's accuracy and filled each other in on information one of us missed. We saved our rivalry for self-generated stories. While on the road, we ate a lot of lunches together. In 1990, years after he retired, Lavor wrote me a note:

> I came across a wonderfully worded get well card from you. That, together with seeing your photo on the *Tribune* editorial page (when you retire the NAC sends you a complimentary subscription to both papers), brought back some pleasant memories. It was both enjoyable and challenging working on the education beat with you.

When Bobbe Dabling was hired out of Ogden, I remarked in my journal on her behavior at the Legislature: "She yaks the whole time with audience members about having the hots for Rep. Roger Rawson and pays little attention to the committee action." I learned to laugh at this character's stories and asides.

Bobbe's departure made way for night reporter Vicki Varela, an attractive Brigham Young University graduate from Denver who'd worked for the Associated Press. In spare moments between assignments, we hiked, skied and lunched together. We even watched a male striptease in San Francisco in 1983 after my one and only Education Writers' Association seminar.

Vicki initially filled a sibling-type void in my life. She was the age my younger sister would have been if she'd survived childhood. Though she really didn't need much mentoring, I tried to help her along and took pride in her ambition and success. I was not her only fan. She caught the attention of an assistant to USU's president, a popular local physician, a reporter at the *News* who would marry her, and countless state officials who wanted her on their team.

As competitors, Vicki and I found ourselves in the middle of a hot story or two, even on the supposedly tepid education beat. At the top of the list was Ted Bell's establishment of the National Commission for Excellence in Education, which produced the reform report that promoted merit pay for teachers and statewide testing of students across the country. We also were kicked out of a meeting together. More on that later.

* * *

Suzanne Scattergood Nutting accepted a residency at the University of Maryland College of Medicine, and our esteemed city editor planned to step down June 1, after the birth of their child. Nutting's non-relationship with Jack Gallivan had weighed on him for some time:

> When I was city editor he called the desk and I answered. He was obviously liquored up -- I think he was at his place in Park City -- and he must have been showing off to his guests, because he told me to gin up a story on something or other, probably a puff piece on somebody's business. It really wasn't a news story and I told him I didn't feel comfortable telling my reporters to do the story. He replied: "They're MY reporters."[615]
>
> I'm not sure he ever knew who I was, even after I was city editor. He was tight with the local business leaders and seemed to be interested in maintaining his "giant in the city" status. That relationship with the movers and shakers started to bother me, and I probably should have quit even if we'd stayed in Salt Lake.[616]

While we suffered without him, Nutting landed at the *Congressional Quarterly* (CQ) in Washington, D.C., in December 1982. Over the next 27 years he was section editor and reporter on the weekly magazine, reporter and editor on the daily newsletter, co-editor of Politics in America for three years and senior editor of reporters covering congressional committee markups.

His *Tribune* experience -- siding with staffers over superiors -- followed him to Washington. A massive layoff of "talented, hard-working folks" got him riled after the *St. Petersburg Times* sold *CQ* to the *Economist*. His impertinent email demanding justification was copied to the entire newsroom and leaked to the outside press, and his embarrassed bosses gave him the choice of quitting or being fired. He chose the latter, which sent him home without severance pay. Then, he took a part-time job with *CQ's* competitor, *Bloomberg Government*.

Nutting fondly remembered his *Tribune* relationships:

> A bunch of us grew up together at *The Tribune*. We not only worked together but played together. I felt closer to them (you included, of course) than any work colleagues I've ever had since. I miss you all a lot – you and Denny and George and Anne and Con (who were two of the best reporters I had -- they both have great news instincts) and many others.[617]

By news instincts, he meant smart, well-informed, naturally curious, able to ask sometimes uncomfortable questions and persistent if they didn't get the answers they wanted the first time. He said he could usually tell whether someone is a good reporter just by overhearing their end of a telephone interview.

Each time I consulted *CQ* for background facts over the years, I thought wistfully of the good ol' days as part of Nutting's team. I wondered what might have become of *The Salt Lake Tribune* had he been treated as the asset he was. He undoubtedly would have become editor someday, a position he would have handled well. He never would have turned staffers against one another, and he probably would have given the LDS Church enough respect to head off a blow-up.

* * *

Nutting's departure put me back on eggshells. He would no longer be on hand to temper Will Fehr, and I faced a new boss I didn't admire. John Serfustini, the strapping Italian who jutted out his chest on long strides across the newsroom as Woody's assistant, had been groomed as his replacement.

Paul Rolly understandably was offended when passed over as city editor and took a job upstairs in the Salt Lake City bureau of UPI.

He'd paid his dues as Woody's assistant and then night city editor. Although I wasn't sure how his drinking and vindictive, reckless tendencies would affect him as city editor, I knew we would miss his sharp memory, sensitivity, courage and story-telling talent.

Losing his cool on City Desk probably hurt his chance for the job.

While substituting as city editor one evening, he went nose-to-nose with Dan Valentine Jr., whose name rather the writing wit enabled him to inherit his father's Split Page humor column. Junior's first foray into the business, a column for *The Trib's* In section for teens, hadn't been a rousing success.

Like his father, Junior waited until deadline to turn in his column. Meantime, the city editor needed to lay out Split Page. When the column came in too long, something had to go, and desk editors removed some the the ellipses (dots) the Valentines often used between topics.

When Junior complained, someone rubbed salt in his wounds with a memo announcing the discovery of the missing dots. A full page of periods was attached. Junior then whined to his mother, who called Will Fehr.

"Keep the elipses," he tersely told Rolly.

Junior later turned in another column late. This time, Rolly whacked off the end, apparently the punchline. When pestered about it the next day, Rolly snarled, "What are you going to do about it, go home and cry to Mommy?"

Somewhere along the line, threats were made to take the dispute out back.

* * *

It wasn't a month into **John Serfustini's** rule as city editor before I seriously regretted Rolly's exit. I told Fehr that Serf didn't like education and I didn't like military rule.

I went into more detail with Mimi: "Serf has a great knack for saying he needs a story for the daily and then not using it. He gets people to work overtime that way, but that trick won't work forever. He makes education assignments without consulting me."

Serfustini was a former Marine and fitness freak from Buffalo, N. Y., who learned Chinese while in Vietnam in 1970. The fan of the *Wall Street Journal* and short sentences graduated from the U.'s journalism school before jumping around Utah journalism and landing with a splash in Woody's department.

John Serfustini strides up Main Street.

After his first news job with the tiny *Wasatch Wave* in Heber City, he had spent two years as editor of the *Sun Advocate,* another small weekly in coal-producing Price, before switching to the *Deseret News* and finally Channel 4 television.

I wasn't the only staffer skeptical of Serf. When he announced the end of grubbies on City Desk, a collective groan rumbled through the office. He used sarcasm to soften the blow:

Grubbies are faded jeans, tennis shorts or cutoffs, Star Wars and soft porn

T-shirts, collarless T-shirts, sneakers and hiking boots. The point, gang, is that when you represent a professional organization, you dress accordingly. Ties are not mandatory.

Free spirits among us found such personal limits hard to endure. Some of us simply hated being told what to do by an upstart. But that was just the beginning.

Serf ordered a "complete operations manual" from all beat reporters by June 5 at 5 p.m. "This includes phone checks and personal contacts (except confidential sources), daily routine and format you use to turn your work in" so that others can "pinch hit" during absences. And he ordered the end of stories with only one source and stories with more than two adds (2 1/2 typed, letter-size pages).

The single-source prohibition made sense to strengthen news credibility and balance, but an arbitrary story size? What if a story entailed a technical new law or court case? "For now, you'll have to sell every inch over 12-wide to the editors," Serf responded.

Serf tried to make me more efficient by forcing me to avoid government meetings and so-called news of record, but I resisted. Many of my follow-up stories were spawned during those often tedious sessions. It seemed to me more efficient to get information on several subjects in one sitting.

It insulted me that the *Deseret News* ran Vicki Varela's stories big while Serf held onto mine several days at a time, sometimes losing them altogether. When I'd try to talk to him about it, he'd bark about long stories and insufficient public interest. When I insisted something was important, he'd tell the night city editor he didn't have anything good that night.

Admittedly, my writing needed improvement. In September, Varela and I covered the State Board of Education's decision to overhaul the school office to save money. Her story, appearing at the top of the local news page with a 60-point headline, began:

The State Office of Education will begin advertising 21 job openings in management Monday because of a State Board of Education vote Friday to reorganize the agency.

My story, on the third local page with a 40-point headline, began:

After meeting with the State Board of Education Friday, G. Leland Burningham, state superintendent of public instruction, altered his agency's reorganization plans. Instead of combining vocational education with other instructional service as intended, the superintendent's plan will give vocational education its own associate superintendent.

Varela's lead obviously packed more punch. It drew readers in with a few short words that clarified the impact of board action. My wordiness was bogged down with jargon and detail that spoke to educators rather than the public. The contrast offers insight into Varela's ability to pass me by.

A better story September 22 about a 6.5 percent tuition hike at Utah colleges and universities also wound up below the fold on Page B-3, unheard of in prior years. Meantime, Valentine's column about llamas took up 15 percent of Split Page (B-1).

Serf didn't reserve his insults for me. He told zone czar Ben Ling to "assure coverage of survival fair; short stories to cidesk, long stories to zone." That is, put long, boring stuff in the zones and save the good, snappy stuff for the daily edition.

Our fearless leader also disparaged women generally by inserting a one-act play, supposedly by Mike Carter, in his Plan of the Day September 8:

COP: Lieutenant, I've got a woman's skull here with a bullet hole between its eyes.
LT: How can you tell it's a woman's skull?
COP: Well, it's empty and its mouth is open. FINIS

Is there any question about the standing of women at *The Salt Lake Tribune* in 1982?

More of Serf's respectful leadership qualities shone forth in his September 27 Plan of the Day:

Special thanks to Frank Brunsman [the mumbler], who made Monday's paper possible. Also to the rest of those who submitted weekenders. As for the rest of you: Regardless of the fact that we will soon be competing on weekends, bear in mind that this is and will be a seven-day-a-week publication. I am well aware of the feast-or-famine nature of the news and am hesitant to make weekenders for all staffers a strict requirement. But I want you to be aware that I don't intend to be caught short on weekends anymore . . . "

It cannot be said that Serf withheld praise. In the Plan of the Day October 28, he called our attention to "ace crime reporter" Mike Carter, "who's not too shabby as a political writer, either." According to Serf, Carter's story on the county attorney race:

. . . not only carried us through the issues but added a sense of presence as well. That sense of presence -- making the reader experience what has happened -- will serve as a marvelous vehicle for getting the "news of record" across.

Offering a sense of presence of my own, Terri Ellefsen that day was covering Davis County news, including crime and oil refinery controversies. Jim Woolf, Joe Rolando and Gus Sorensen were told to see how flooding was affecting the economy, housing and the environment. Jack Fenton's assignment: "Criminal justice folk will discuss the best cheese danish in America." (Sorry, I can't shed any light on that one.) Dave Jonsson was reporting on the state's "zoo strategy" and the swearing in of judges. Walt Schaffer, substituting as city editor, was advised to run Tim Kelly's photo of a school with a wine bottle four columns [big]. Rod Pressly's orders: "Do the definitive story on the Jefferson School, pro and con, along with interviews with transients (bums) to go with the pic on Split Page."

Bums? Really?

* * *

Jon Ure, the happy-go-lucky addict with limited ambition, was substituting as day city editor on his way to becoming night city editor -- a long way from his two years as copy boy and much further along than I ever got on City Desk. JoAnn Jacobsen-Wells, back from her administrative job with the Utah Society to Prevent Blindness, had replaced Angie Nelson as medical writer and was being honored by the Salt Lake County Medical Society for her health-care reporting.

Anne Wilson was working general assignment, while her husband, Con Psarras, was helping out on elections and municipal power issues. Jim Woolf staffed the city news bureau,

waiting in the wings to unearth environmental problems covered by Kevin Graman.

Joe Rolando, another Italian Catholic from Price, filled Serf's wingtips as Woody's business assistant. Beside compact, tightly wound Rolando sat "quick-witted, seasoned journalist"[618] Charles Seldin, who still smoked a pipe and was covering a congressional redistricting brouhaha. Next to Seldin toiled Dan Bates, an "intense journalist" who made every word count on the city beat[619] before taking his quick wit and temper back to California. Steve Oberbeck became Joe's business assistant, with Eric McMullin contributing business copy as well.

On October 29, Serf sent staffers a "note of utmost importance." It was time to implement our "fun" $1.6 million[620] ATEX computer system under the direction of former regional editor Jerry "Radar" Wellman.

Because we'd have more staffers than computer terminals "and the main brain can handle just so much input at any given time," Serf warned us, writers and editors would have to time share. This meant people without deadline stories should process their copy in the mornings and early afternoons. Remote terminals [from news bureaus] would ease the crunch somewhat because "the outposts" would no longer have their stuff delivered during the 4-7 p.m. glut.

"It will take effort to learn [the new system]," Serf rhapsodized, "but take my word for it: You are rewarded every step of the way with an increasing sense of . . . POWER! That makes the learning process enjoyable."

"Power obviously is something Serf appreciates -- as long as it's his own," I muttered.

A case in point. With President Ronald Reagan coming to town, Serf advised political writers George Raine, Doug Parker and Charles Seldin: "Remember, it's not the second coming . . . Short and to the point."

Raine's clearest memory of the special visit was being jostled by a Secret Service agent while waiting with other journalists on the airport tarmac.[621]

Serf gave us another pep talk in his November 1 Plan of the Day:

All this talk about TV being the visual medium is baloney. Print is THE visual medium because all your information comes through your eyes only. That's why layout, typography and, above all, smooth writing, are life and death considerations. When the reader's eye gets tired, you're dead.

Joe Rolando

Joe Rolando was just 16 at Carbon High School when he entered journalism as a backshop printer's devil, press hand and paper jogger at the *Sun-Advocate*, then the state's third largest weekly.[622] The ambitious lad also wrote a weekly high school column before advancing to staff photographer, a job he kept for two years. By 18, he was editor of the *Helper Journal,* a dying, 400-circulation publication that kept him busy 60 hours a week for the two years he attended College of Eastern Utah (CEU). As Joe describes it:

I had only one correspondent who wrote a "Mr. and Mrs. Smith went to Salt Lake over the weekend to shop"-type column and shared a recipe from one of Helper's many good Italian cooks each week. (Of course, I had to take a picture of the lady with her prepared dish for the article.)

I don't know how I managed to pass – let alone attend - my classes at CEU. But I did both, earning a respectable B grade-point average.

The high point of all this is I had increased the circulation of *The Helper Journal* to a little more than 1,000, the population of Helper at the time, won several awards for my photography and front-page layout and was counting the days when I would be able to leave the area and finish my education at the University of Utah, where, for the first time, I would have the opportunity to learn to write from professional news writers.[623]

The plan, Publisher Robert L. Finney promised, was to put Rolando in charge of the *Sun Advocate* once he got his university journalism degree. Instead, Rolando returned home in 1976 to find John Serfustini at that desk. Rolando became one of three reporters churning out local news.

John and I got along famously, even though we were nothing alike. He had spent four years in the U.S. Marine Corp and, of course, had a military demeanor, was graduated from the U. and had excellent writing skills.

Me, well, I was newly out of college and had one advantage: I knew the community and every nook and cranny in Carbon County. I knew when anything happened.

The other two reporters moved on to other jobs within six months, leaving John and I editing and writing -- two newspapers a week. The *Sun Advocate* averaged 20 pages and many times 30 pages a week and came out on Wednesday; the former *Helper Journal*, now renamed *The Sun Journal*, came out on Friday with about 10 pages.[624]

In July 1978, Rolando returned from his honeymoon to discover his mother-in-law had died and Serf had been fired for failing to take pictures at a ribbon-cutting. The day before his mother-in-law's funeral, Joe became editor. He was promised $25 more a week and help with writing and photography. "This publisher was a very deliberate man," Rolando noted. "He didn't ask you, he told you, and I was too young to question him."[625]

Publisher Finney gave Rolando more than 100 resumes of reporters who wanted to work in Price. Then he shot down all of Rolando's choices, including an experienced reporter with a small bump on his back that Finney feared might offend someone. So from July to the end of October, Rolando churned out two issues a week by himself.

"Finally, I reached my emotional breaking point and resigned," Rolando said. After stringing for *The Trib* awhile, Serf hired him. But not before Rolando vowed never again to let someone get the best of him in a job.

* * *

Speaking of emotional breaking points, I teetered on the edge. Still carpooling with Denny, I couldn't work as late or even leave as early as I wanted. Our expenses far exceeded our means. We couldn't afford our property taxes and insurance. We needed cedar for our interior walls (the bathroom was wide open below the stairs to the bedrooms) and clothes, haircuts and root beer for the girls. Yes, root beer. By the gallon.

My stepdaughters were still fighting between themselves and with us, siphoning vodka from our bar and needing rides to and from Park City at odd hours of the day and night.

Denny and Heather Nelson with church check.

Dennis Green's rendition of the First Presidency.

Thank heaven for wholesome **Heather Nelson,** who had broken through *The Tribune's*

sexist barrier against women photographers to throw us a lifeline. In a flash of entrepreneurship, she capitalized on family connections to sell the LDS Church the sketch of the First Presidency that Denny did to illustrate LDS conference stories. The original sold for $5,000, netting Denny $2,500.

"We thank thee, oh God, for a profit," Denny declared. "Now we can pay the taxes!"

Heather went on to study law and join the U.S. attorney's office before marrying Peter Cooke, a Democratic candidate for governor in 2012.

Heather's sale raised Denny's hopes of finding another, less frustrating job. He was feeling overwhelmed by a woefully understaffed Art Department. But his applications to advertising agencies in Salt Lake City and New York didn't pan out. Prospective employers advised him to move to New York to get into that business, something he refused to consider. So he just kept churning out graphics at a furious pace.

* * *

At this stage in Utah history, the state was solidifying its reputation as the fraud capital of the country. Amway, on the scene since the 1960s, had introduced Mormons to a pyramid marketing scheme that appealed to their mutual trust and admiration for financial success. Grant Affleck then used AFCO Enterprises to capitalize on their cultural naiveté in the 1970s.

Affleck sold real estate and then promissory notes by implying he was backed by LDS authorities like Paul H. Dunn, a member of the First Quorum of the Seventy, and the Osmonds (Donnie and Marie and family). Hundreds of Mormon faithful mortgaged their homes to invest in a fund that collapsed in 1982. The next November, a grand jury indicted Affleck, who landed in federal prison.[626]

Paul H. Dunn, by the way, apologized in a 1991 open letter to church members for not always being accurate with war and baseball stories in his church speeches and books.[627] Church authorities put him on emeritus status in 1989.

* * *

Toward the end of the year, the story of the decade fell into JoAnn Jacobsen-Wells' lap.

On December 2, retired dentist Barney Clark received a fist-size plastic mechanical heart, the Jarvik-7, at the University of Utah Medical Center. Dr. William DeVries, the only surgeon authorized by the FDA to do the procedure, made history.

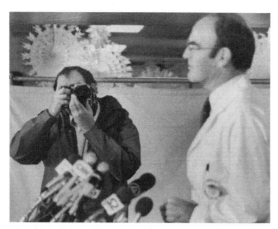

Tim Kelly captures Dr. Chase N. Peterson's press conference.

JoAnn's lead:

A courageous 61-year-old Seattle man, deteriorating rapidly from a failing heart muscle, received a new lease on life Thursday morning when he became the first human recipient of the University of Utah's Jarvik-artificial heart.

The breakthrough became an international sensation. People across the globe waited and watched to see how long the device would keep Clark alive. Dr. Chase N. Peterson, a doctor of medicine who headed university health sciences, explained the process in language the public could understand. *The Tribune* followed the story day by day, running splashy illustrations, photographs and personal profiles.

JoAnn had come a long way from that first-person story about Planned Parenthood's waiting room a decade earlier.

Mike Korologos' renditions of the Barney Clark story, written for Reuters, drove a London rewrite woman to tears. [628]

Scott Rivers remembered the Barney Clark story as one of *The Tribune's* most momentous, possibly because it happened just a month after the shy, pimply faced kid became a copy boy. The Utah floods of a year later also stood out for the movie buff, who quit in 1998 to immerse himself in Los Angeles movie archives.

Mike Korologos dresses as Barney Clark for Halloween.

* * *

On my day off December 6, 1982, Serf's Plan of the Day told staffers not to write another business portrait . . .

. . . or other such personality profile until you have studied Diane Cole's feature on Daryl McCarty [outgoing teacher's union leader] on page B-6 of today's paper. Not only did she get additional sources to define the man with vivid quotes (e.g. "as subtle as a runaway truck"), but she peppered the whole thing with little insightful tidbits about him. The McCarty piece is journalism, not a one-man-testimonial dinner or resume service. It is a standard to compare your work with. The story could've used some portrait-style art, but let's take one thing at a time.

I was floored. A compliment from this city editor? Incredible.

As mentioned earlier, the McCarty piece was extracted from the defunct Legacy project. As was another Serf found noteworthy, my profile of Weber State College President Rodney H. Brady, a man with a lifelong plan and a closet full of identical blue suits.

While I craved the praise, I couldn't help complaining that Serf could have prevented staff resentment with more diplomacy.

On December 9, Serf announced plans for a file of stories . . .

. . . stolen from us by our so-called competition, particularly stories of the weekend variety. Reason: I do not take insults lightly, especially those penned by people who could neither get nor keep a job here. This latest issue of *Journalism Review* is galling because it accuses us of being asleep at the stick while every news organization in the state routinely feeds on the material generated by our staff. As far as I'm concerned, other papers and media are feeding their followers oats that have passed through the horse, and we ought to make that clear.

A metaphor worth remembering.

* * *

Once Serf made **Cathy Free** a bonafide reporter at age 20, she quit college. Her University of Utah classes just couldn't compete with her on-the-job training, and she was "already living the dream."

Serfustini liked the roving features I'd been doing on my days off and asked me to cover the Davis County beat. Never mind that I didn't get a raise to go with the promotion. I was just happy to get out of the newsroom, breathe some fresh air instead of ink and cigar smoke and hit the road to find interesting people to interview, even if they were in Davis County.

When Frank Porschatis, aka "Pork Chop," found out what I was doing, he insisted on accompanying me. I was visiting a different town in Davis County each week, with no idea about who I would be interviewing, and it reminded him of the stories he used to do with Clark Lobb.

We made quite the pair: a 20-year-old with a foul mouth and a "Farrah Fawcett" hairdo and a 60-something photographer with a buzz cut who was always hitching up his pants. Frank was a terrible driver, always twitching in his seat and weaving in and out of his lane on the freeway.

While driving around looking for a story in the small, mostly rural town of Sunset one day, we came across a truck with a large "Mobile Butcher" sign on it. I told Frank to follow it, because it was almost noon and we hadn't found a story yet. We followed, Frank weaving and twitching all the way, and ended up watching Flossy the Cow led to her demise in this van of death. I didn't eat meat for months after that.[629]

Another of the rover's most memorable encounters occurred a year later, when assigned a Robert Redford interview.

I'd gone to Sundance Resort to interview Robert Redford about his new three-mile nature trail. He was 20 minutes late and I was beginning to fear I'd been stood up when he suddenly appeared, splashing across the creek in bright red running shorts and a white T-shirt, which he peeled off to wipe the sweat from his face before shaking my hand. I can't remember exactly what I was thinking, but it was something along the lines of, "If I die right now, my life is complete."

His hair still damp, he walked up the trail with me for a bit through the aspens to point out the wildflowers and plants used by early pioneers and Native Americans. Hiking with Robert Redford on a cool summer morning. Assignments don't come any better than this.[630]

About three months later, Cathy got a freelance job with *People Magazine*, which put her in touch with Redford again and again, but none of the other stories was as fun as the first.

My own meetings with the sexy celebrity over the years were uplifting but less stimulating than Cathy's.

---

[615] Nutting, February 14, 2014.

[616] Nutting, February 14, 2014.

[617] Nutting, February 14, 2014.

[618] Joe Rolando to Tribune facebook group March 2, 2012.

[619] Ibid.

[620] Jonsson, July 24, 1988, p. T4.

[621] Raine, February 18, 2014.

[622] Joe Rolando email November 30, 2015.

[623] Ibid.

[624] Ibid.

[625] Ibid.

[626] U. S. v. Grant C. Affleck, No. 84-2630, U.S. Court of Appeals, 10th Circuit, Nov. 7, 1985.

[627] "Elder Dunn Offers Apology for Errors, Admits Censure," *Deseret News*, October 27, 1991.

[628] Korologos, January 26, 2014.

[629] Free, June 4, 2015.

[630] Cathy Free on facebook June 11, 2015

29 - The Beat Goes On in 1983

As we grew dependent on our computer terminals, JoAnn Jacobsen-Wells wrote about the potentially perilous impact of spending long hours staring at the screens.[631] Her favorite organization, the National Society to Prevent Blindness, issued guidelines few of us followed. We didn't have time for frequent breaks, and our office lighting and furniture would always be substandard.

Barney Clark began having seizures and was expected to die, which he did March 23, 112 days after his implant. JoAnn hadn't taken a day off that entire 112 days.[632] Within two months of the story's end, she announced her departure for Washington, D.C., where she would be Congressman Dan Marriott's press secretary. One of our star reporters was flying the coop, and Fehr warned her she couldn't come back again.

* * *

Keith Otteson retired. The reprobate turned his attention to selling women's shoes and studying Russian and Spanish. I cringed at the thought of his fingers fumbling with women's feet and ankles, but at least I would no longer be exposed to his sexual harassment. In his 2008 obituary, his daughter noted that Otteson "loved editing, and he loved the people who he worked with. A lot of them really loved him, too. He was a friend that not all employers are."[633] A different kind of "friend" indeed.

* * *

I was managing education assignments for Peter Scarlet, Rod Pressly and Doug Clark and receiving crank calls from some geezer who called my stories hypocritical. I speculated to Mimi that it was "the same religious nut" who'd written me the "garbage about 'the truth.'" Those bylines had their downside.

Freelance remained part of my life. *Education USA* paid me $98.75 for two stories. One reported that Salt Lake City schools "closed the door on white flight" by ending their open-enrollment policy. The other, concerning stricter academic standards in Utah, received more space than usual because it highlighted Mormon Church fears that LDS seminary classes were at risk unless school schedules stretched to seven periods.

My salary rose to $475 a week without my having to beg for it, and I got the added bonus of Anne Wilson as my education assistant. Night-time school board meetings became the exception to the rule.

* * *

Home was no haven, largely because we let Lulu demonstrate new decision-making skills.

First she took a night job in a Park City restaurant that required us to pick her up at midnight -- unless she was spending the night with "a friend."

The rancid clothes and towels carpeting her bedroom and bathroom floors grew deeper. When I asked her to do her laundry, she amiably agreed while guzzling root beer and guffawing at Sponge Bob Square Pants. She didn't bother with the wash.

One spring day we received legal papers signed by Lulu demanding that we send her to New York to visit her mother and the pedophile. When we objected, she pointed out it wasn't her idea to leave them in the first place. Although she was still a minor at 17, the prohibition against contact with them was issued in different state.

So off Lulu flew on a round-trip, non-refundable ticket we bought with our meager income. We warned her not to miss her return flight or her mother would have to buy another ticket. "Don't worry about it," she said with a sneer, "I'll be back in two weeks."

She wasn't.

Sweet Swamper offered to take her to Coney Island if she would extend her stay. "I've never been there, and I'm having a great time with Mom!" Lulu chirped on the phone.

At my urging, Denny reminded her to change her airline ticket. "I've already taken care of it," she assured him.

She hadn't.

The day before her senior year started, Lulu called Denny at work to demand another ticket -- the last-minute kind at twice the price.

"We told you this was your responsibility, so now the ball's in your mother's court," Denny matter-of-factly. I was proud of him for finally putting his foot down. Lulu exploded.

"Fuck you! I hate you!" she yelled into the phone. "You owe me $100!" Click.

Huh? We soon received a legal demand for $100, all of Lulu's rainbow geegaws and the cedar chest her mother had sent for her 16th birthday. I didn't know whether to laugh or cry. Denny sulked. I hoped he didn't blame me for leaving Lulu out on a limb.

* * *

On June 2, 1983, sudden hot weather after a long, wet winter sent mudslides hurtling down state mountainsides and water gushing down City Creek Canyon onto State Street. Traffic was blocked, but two walking bridges were built to allow people to cross the street.

I struggled to keep my head above water on my beat. The crush of graduation coverage diverted my attention from a wrap-up on school reform, and before I could get to it, Vicki Varela knocked the wind from my sails with a splashy series of her own in the *Deseret News*. I treaded water with everyday news.

Despite our reporting rivalry, Vicki and I still hiked and dined together while public and higher education officials enjoyed their complimentary tickets to the annual Shakespeare festival in Cedar City. Vicki drove me around town since Denny needed the car at home and I'd taken the bus. It would be a few more months before we finally bought a second car.

Riding the bus was a hassle while toting the heavy "portable" Teleram for transmitting my stories. As clunky as it was, the Teleram was the wave of the future. It reduced the need to dictate over the phone. With afterthoughts as my specialty, however, I repeatedly called the rewrite desk to make corrections anyway.

Vicki and I again found ourselves side-by-side in a dust-up at the State Capitol that summer.

When we showed up for an August 10 meeting of the Governor's Steering Committee on Education Reform, developer/task force chairman Manny Floor (Korologos' old sidekick) declared the meeting closed to the press. We stayed put, knowing the publicly funded group lacked legal grounds for secrecy. We had Utah's Open Meetings Act on our side.

The blowhard puffed up indignantly and suspended discussion of the opinion poll his committee commissioned. Well, I didn't need pollster Dan Jones, a former Bountiful High School teacher, or anyone else to varnish the survey results, which merely proved Utahns wanted major changes in their school system. So I said as much in my story on the subject.

My stand for the public's right to know didn't impress my boss. City Editor Serfustini's interests lay elsewhere.

On June 28, he issued this uplifting order:

New Policy: Absolutely NOBODY goes home without having an editor review your daily stories. Wanna know why? See below for a microcosmic view of an editor's daily grind.

SUBMITTED WITH INTENT TO PUBLISH: (Just a few examples of negligent wordslaughter that city desk got yesterday. You guys want a great newspaper? You make the first move and stop trying to shove garbage into it.)

1 . . . who may have knowledge as to Troy's whereabouts. (Means the same as "who may know where Troy is.")

Serf was more apt to run Peter Scarlet's simplistic, PR-fed stories about Davis County schools than my stuff with statewide reach. I suspected this had a lot to do with timing. Scarlet arrived about 7 each morning and banged out stories from press releases and chats with the district flack, Bonnie Durrance. Many of my stories were filed after 5 p.m., when Serf's patience was paper thin.

On August 23, 1983, newsroom distractions made concentration impossible. I recorded my exasperation in my reporter's notebook:

Three feet to my left rear, Carol either cackles or yawns loud enough to wake the dead. Between us, Will is jingling his coins. Three feet to my right, Joe Rolando grunts, puffs and wiggles around in his squeaky chair while typing. Six feet in front of me, Woody's writing his story aloud. On the other side of the desk, Dan Bates is grousing under his breath while banging out a city government story. This place is always like this. It's driving me nuts!

Monthly attacks of endometriosis compounded my stress. When the pain and mess got unbearable, I stayed home in bed.

It didn't help my case with Serf when, in early September, a junior high school teacher called to criticize the "trite, shallow, insensitive" story I did about her class for a back-to-school feature. Compounding my apparent error, I'd worn Levis to the interview.

Positive reinforcement kept me going. Gary Birdsall, vice president of marketing for Commercial Security Bank, commended my story on the Utah Bank Association's "Your Bank and You" program in the public schools. OK, a long-time friend referred Birdsall to me, undoubtedly affecting his opinion, but I took praise where I could get it. Years later, we became friends through his wife.

A feature-writing opening came up in Lifestyle, and I jumped at the chance to get out from under Serf and the mind-numbing repetition of the education beat. I was no shoo-in. Barbi Robison brought Nancy Hobbs back from a PR job at LDS Hospital instead. The rejection stung, but it was all for the best. When Barbi later coached our women's softball team, I perceived the potential for a power struggle. It bothered me when she left Nancy on the bench too long.

* * *

My peers were changing places.

Jim Woolf in southern Utah.

Jim Woolf replaced George Raine as our full-time environment writer, taking on threats to human health from mine tailings and toxic waste. He highlighted the plight of the Virgin River chub and desert tortoise. He made annual rituals of stories on the peregrine falcons nesting in a Hotel Utah window and the whereabouts of bald eagles.

Sometimes James, as I called him, took me and Denny on eco excursions with his wife Barbara, a radio news reporter. I almost passed out from heat stroke on one such back-packing trip at noon near Mexican Mountain.

Mike Gorrell joined City Desk September 12, 1983 as a night police reporter

after working several years at the *Green Sheet*, a weekly in Salt Lake County. Terri Ellefsen shyly told me she'd had a crush on him in Catholic elementary school.

Mike Gorrell

There was little doubt that Gorrell, a workaholic who enjoyed a drink, would fit in. He was one of the nicest guys in the office, ranking right up there with Tim Kelly, Craig Hansell and Marion Dunn. Like them, he approached people with an open smile.

Gorrell became pals with a new chain-smoking, tightly wound business writer, **Guy Boulton**, whose desk abutted mine. Their friendship served Gorrell well, as he married Boulton's VISTA supervisor, Kathleen Brown, future director of the College of Education Reading Clinic at the University of Utah.

Guy Boulton works Business Desk.

With help from Gorrell and Woolf, who loved to pull his long legs, Boulton honed his writing skills. Like most of us at first, he shoveled all he knew into every story, creating an organizational quagmire. Although I often enjoyed the threesome's camaraderie, the back-and-forth among their desks made it that much tougher for me to write a sensible story.

* * *

City Desk's peer review produced some apt observations about individual staffers and news of the day:

-- Dan Bates sculpts out every word and then is an interested spectator during the editing process.

-- Brian Wilkinson's stories on the borderline poor who are being shoved out of their apartments and rooms by developers, expressed an emotion that brought public response.

-- We've had examples of good stories: Mike Carter's piece on Max Mercier [owner of a local French restaurant accused of sexual misconduct] and Mike Gorrell's on the girl who was shot in the face.

-- Mike Carter wrote a masterful story on the 12-year-old girl who was pinned [by a landslide] in the wreckage of the lodge at Alta. But that also was the time we should have gotten the girl and the paramedic together for a story. Dawn Tracy House did this for Tuesday morning, but we were late on this.

-- Mike Gorrell took us to the mouth of the Wilberg Mine and I, personally, read every word because he was there and I wasn't, but he put me there.

-- When Cathy Free writes a feature she brings her characters to life with skillful use of conversational quotes. You know who these people are and if you read the series on immigrants you had a distinct feeling about each character involved. She has a good ear and listens well.

-- Terry Orme does a great public service in his movie reviews by giving sufficient information without being stuffy or pedantic.

-- Joan O'Brien's story on the woman who wanted to withdraw from her church is another good example.

-- The only interesting story to come out of the LDS conference was provided by Rodd Wagner who discovered that one of the speakers had his speech rewritten.

-- Jim Woolf's coverage of the environmental beat is an indication that stories do not have to be a gray recitation of facts. He has provided news coverage (sometimes on Page One) and well-written news and feature stories.

-- Doug Parker took a proposal about the sales of beer and gasoline not mixing and made it a highly readable story.

-- A good example of how to add additional reading material is visible in the sports section with Steve Luhm's College Notes, the high school tidbits by Joe Baird, Tom Wharton and Patti Auer, the NBA Notes by Lex Hemphill and the Recreation news by Wharton.

-- Lex Hemphill proves that you can be a graceful writer and a sports writer at the same time.

-- Steve Luhm uses short sentences and active verbs to give power to his writing.

-- Utah Journey by Clark Lobb: A good idea. I sometimes wish he could find people a bit more out of the ordinary. The Payson barber seems pretty ordinary. Isn't there somewhere a 95-year-old barber? A barber who collects ears? A bald-headed barber? Anything? Two photos are too many for this, especially when both shots are pretty unimaginative; too similar.

---

[631] JoAnn Jacobsen-Wells, "TV, Computer Screens Can Cause Visual Fatigue," *The Salt Lake Tribune*, January 25, 1983, p. B1.

[632] Jacobsen-Wells, August 2, 2015.

[633] Melinda Rogers, The *Salt Lake Tribune*, June 8, 2008.

Part III - Matters of Opinion

30 - Scratching a Seven-Year Itch

Lulu's absence reduced pressures at home, and Serf's surprise resignation to flack for Utah Power & Light promised to lighten my load at work. (In 2015, Serf was back in Price as the *Sun Advocate's* associate editor.)

"Can I take his place, Will? Please?" I begged only slightly in jest.. After seven years on education, I yearned for a new challenge. I wasn't sure I could manage the job, but I wanted to get on the management track.

Like many staffers, I saw lots of room for improvement at the newspaper. We could have used more art, maybe even with color, on the news pages. We needed to do more to motivate the dead wood to take initiative in covering their beats, perhaps providing detailed feedback on their stories. Specific assignments and production goals might have helped. New blood from papers from outside Utah was an option. Closer editing, with help from additional editors, was required to tighten and liven the news writing. Investigative reporting was a must.

Who was I kidding? I'd never get a chance to fulfill my longtime secret desire to put my ideas to work.

"You haven't worked night city editor, Cole," Fehr answered.

Serf hadn't either, having come directly from the Business Desk. What's more, night work would have been a step down from education editor and undermined whatever family life I had left.

So who got the nod? Walt Schaffer, a part-time Navy information specialist who'd moved from the Copy Desk to zone writer/editor. He had fewer whiskers on City Desk, but he was a male who had substituted as night city editor.

Though disappointed, I assumed I could live with Walt, a seemingly even-tempered sort like Brian Nutting. I considered him a friend. I had a lot to learn.

Meantime, Fehr found a way to keep me off his back while pushing me up the ladder.

On October 19, 1983, he called me into his office. "Hey, Cole, you can write. They need a substitute in Editorial. If you want it, Scarlet can take care of education."

Huh? I knew next to nothing about editorials. In college, I studied education, literature, philosophy and creative writing -- not history, politics or science. The proposal made me nervous. But the first woman on *The Tribune's* Editorial Board? The chance for change, growth and advancement? That was worth considering.

So I gave it a try.

From the outset, the position presented discomfort, dilemmas and disappointments. It meant swapping a large, rough-and-tumble family of reporters for a sequestered cadre of elitists. My productivity and sense of self-worth would suffer for a long time to come.

The other editorial writers saw my appointment as the first step toward fulfilling a dream expressed 20 years earlier by then-Editoral Editor Herb Kretchman for a fourth writer. I started substituting Mondays for Bob Blair, who worked the Saturday shift, in cramped quarters on the 10th floor. Unfortunately, there still were only three writers on hand at any given time, but even three were too many for the work space.

Beginning with the 9:30 Editorial Board meeting on the Fourth Floor, my first day was intimidating and strange.

Large portraits of Newspaper Agency and Kearns-Tribune Corp. board members lined the conference room walls. Alongside Publisher John W. Gallivan were his protege Jerry O'Brien, then Kearns-Tribune director, and descendants of Thomas and Jennie Kearns with last names like Durkin, Steiner, Kearns, McCarthey and Stephens. Thomas S. Monson and Wendell Ashton hung among them as LDS representatives on the NAC board.

After pouring themselves cups from the coffee pot on the sideboard, Gallivan and O'Brien took seats at either end of the walnut conference table and spread the day's newspaper before them. Gallivan, a frown creasing his jutting jaw, wore a full suit while O'Brien arrived without a jacket over his white, rolled up sleeves. He blushed sheepishly beneath the nest of gray, cotton-candy swirls that crowned his head.

Will Fehr, Harry Fuller and Wally Hoffman, all wearing ties and sport jackets, took up seats along the sides. While dragging out an empty chair, I made a mental note to invest in some of Mr. Mac's two-for-one business suits. I was grateful Blair had warned me to bring a copy of the newspaper so that I could lay it out on the table with the others.

A couple of mumbled good mornings and cleared throats broke the silence, after which Gallivan welcomed me to the meeting. My ears blazed. The page-turning began.

Gallivan: "The lead photo is too big. If cut to two columns, we could have put the Reagan strategic defense story above the fold."

With black felt-tip pen, Fehr scrawled a note in his paper's margin.

Everyone turned the page.

Hoffman: "What's happened to all the god-damned proofreaders? I count three typos on Page 3! And this headline doesn't step!"

Fehr scribbled comments on Page 3.

Everyone silently turned another page, then another.

A story on LDS President Ezra Taft Benson's health caught O'Brien's eye.

O'Brien: "Tom says President Benson is spending more time with family." Apparently that was code for his not having long to live. O'Brien's source, Thomas Monson, was second counselor of the LDS First Presidency and a member of NAC's board as chairman of Deseret News Publishing Company.

O'Brien again: "Tom called our coverage of conference first class this year."

Gallivan: "The staff did a bang-up job."

Fehr jotted a reminder on the page.

The conversation brought to mind First Counselor Gordon B. Hinckley's teen morality talk during the recent General Conference. From there, my thoughts turned to Mr. Gallivan's role in truncating my sex-education series. I silently stewed.

More pages turned, several without remarks.

A tall, slender man with dark curly hair strode into the room and poured a cup of coffee. His crooked smile suggesting amusement, he flippantly asked, "What's going on in here? When I'm in charge, you'll be out of here in five minutes." He left without waiting for a reaction.

I had just seen Kearns-Tribune Comptroller Dominic Welch for the first time.

According to Gallivan years later, these daily meetings with the publisher were part of the John F. Fitzpatrick legacy in which editorial writers marched across Main Street to his 10th floor office in the Kearns Building each morning at 10 a.m. to confer for about 30 minutes. "Fitzpatrick's comments on news of the world that required editorial consideration were terse but left no doubt of what *The Tribune's* position was to be," Gallivan wrote, adding that Editor Bert Heal would stay for 10 minutes or so afterwards to fill Fitzpatrick in on news developments. [634]

The routine had changed by 1983. Rare was the meeting that adjourned in less than an hour or resulted in marching orders for the day's commentary. By then the first order of business was the identification of errors for later discussion among news editors. Gruff Wally Hoffman took that role seriously, often ending his litany of complaints with the declaration that City Desk had gone to hell since his time there.

Also high on the board's agenda was the latest prolonged pitch from a visiting politician or lobbyist seeking editorial endorsement. New York Mayor Ed Koch, for example, impressed me as an entertaining egomaniac. And, of course, there was the chitchat.

When we reached the sports pages that first day, O'Brien mentioned talking recently with Jack Stockton from his alma mater, Gonzaga University in Spokane. Having played basketball for the Bulldogs himself, our next publisher was excited that Jack's son was boosting the Catholic school's ranking. (You can imagine his elation when John Stockton became point guard for the Utah Jazz.)

In a later meeting with House Majority Whip Tom Foley, we would learn that he and O'Brien had attended Gonzaga together. In fact, Gonzaga became a common topic of discussion as the university of choice for the McCarthey clan, Gallivan grandchildren and a future *Tribune* editor.

Dialogue done that first day, everyone folded up a newspaper, tucked it under an arm and headed for the door. No decisions had been made about what to write that day. In fact, there was little if any consideration of public issues I expected to write about. The prolonged gathering merely left less time to produce editorials for the next day.

Arriving back at Blair's desk, I didn't know where to start.

Several days into this pattern, I boldly suggested a couple of editorial ideas. They were summarily shot down.

Hoffman dismissed my condemnation of Kennecott Copper's pollution output as out of touch. "Technology has completely cleaned up Salt Lake City's air quality!" he pontificated. No one disagreed.

"We don't want to get into that," Gallivan said about Planned Parenthood, school prayer, the use of eminent domain to force out property owners -- and any number of other topics.

I finally understood the absence of useful discussion. So I began using the morning meetings to read and mine the paper for editorial ideas. I usually kept my mouth shut, turning the pages in unison with the others. It was safer to write something on my own so the publisher was either persuaded by my argument or reluctant to leave a gaping hole to fill late in the day.

My ploy backfired when I castigated the erection of a Christmas creche and Jewish menorah in the downtown plaza named for Gallivan. As cofounder of the Utah Chapter of the National Conference of Christians and Jews, organized in 1967 to foster understanding among Utah's religious groups, my embarrassed boss blew a gasket.

"How the hell did this get into the paper, because I know he (jabbing across the table at Jerry O'Brien) didn't authorize it, and he's in charge of editorial opinion here!" Gallivan fulminated. "This man (still pointing at O'Brien) would never approve this!"

I meekly suggested that this sort of government involvement with religious beliefs led to the kind of discrimination non-Mormons like me felt growing up in Utah.

Gallivan didn't buy it. Neither he nor his children experienced religious problems, he asserted. Conflict-shy O'Brien said nothing.

I chose not to argue that the Gallivans, O'Briens, Fitzpatricks and McCartheys all attended Catholic schools and lived outside the neighborhood wards that dominated most residents' lives. I wanted to keep my job.

This was the year Gallivan became publisher emeritus, officially turning his daily duties over to O'Brien, a Minneapolis native and World War II gunner who'd been his assistant since 1963.

O'Brien loved concocting ways to improve and promote the newspaper.

For example, he commissioned the so-called Belden Study that showed Catholics, Protestants and even 30 percent of Mormons favored *The Tribune* over the *Deseret News*. Local news, Belden found, was the clear priority of readers, primarily retirees, and the average reader spent 33 minutes reading the paper each day.

One of Publisher Jerry O'Brien's promo pictures of the staff in the 1980s.

In spare moments, O'Brien created catchy in-house ads and news-rack signs to extend the paper's appeal. Staffers were asked to pose for several of these feel-good ads.

With both O'Brien and Gallivan heading up editorial meetings, we writers could be caught off guard by O'Brien approving an editorial later killed by Gallivan. It was never the other way around.

When I foundered, not knowing what to write, Harry Fuller suggested, "Write about something you know, like education." So I usually did. Later that afternoon, Harry would rewrite my long, detailed offering, making it longer still.

Choosing and analyzing a topic was not my only challenge.

I had to wait my turn for one of the two computers squeezed into the middle of the 10th floor office housing three editorial writers and political cartoonist Pat Bagley. Concentration in that confined space, the "absolutely worse habitation" [635] possible, was even worse than in the cacophony of the newsroom.

One squeaky chair could disrupt the thinking process. When someone made or answered a phone call, the rest of us had to hear the one-sided conversation. Hoffman's bellow rattled the windows when berating readers wanting to know what happened to their letters to the editor. Afflicted with post-nasal drip, Fuller incessantly cleared his throat. Quiet Bob Blair rarely worked when I did.

Bagley contributed most to my writer's block. Arriving early with his cartoon in mind, he put it to paper while the rest of us turned pages on the Fourth Floor. Upon our return, he showed his creation around the office for reactions. He came to expect my "I just don't get it" and sometimes simplified the gag.

Cartoon in the bag, Bagley spent the balance of his abbreviated work day on the phone analyzing Mormon logic and doctrine with Elbert Peck or Peggy Fletcher of *Sunstone* magazine. He yakked with various readers and other friends, too. Occasionally a girlfriend would drop by for an in-person encounter. Once married to Wendy Winegar, he devoted less discussion to theology and more to family issues while compiling his cartoons into commercial paperbacks for a growing contingent of fans.

* * *

Of the three other writers, I felt most comfortable with Editorial Page Editor **Robert C. Blair**, a droll southern gentleman preparing to retire after 15 years in the department. He opened doors for me.

After reading a few Blair editorials, I realized he was the culprit who wrote the obnoxious women-wearing-pants editorial that riled me my first year at *The Tribune*. On other occasions, he had waxed philosophical on the supposed worthlessness of apricots and zucchini. I forgave him once I learned how hard it could be to fill editorial space on short notice and how amusing his well-turned phrases could be.

The colonel, as people called him, commanded a family of 13 children with his devoutly Catholic wife Alice. After growing up in Virginia and working in a couple of military medical jobs, he had attended colleges a year here and a year there, from Alabama to New Mexico,

before settling on the University of Montana. The allure was the absence of a foreign language requirement, a factor he gleaned from a brochure while recovering from appendicitis in the hospital.

Bob Blair in his 90s.

Blair was kicked out of school more than once, he claimed, [636] for cursing and drinking. Upon his release from Montana, he snagged a spot at *The Tribune* working obits, general assignment and the hotel beat, a "detestable chore" requiring him to check registrations at Hotel Utah and the Newhouse Hotel for famous visitors to interview.

Like a couple of other *Tribune* staffers, Blair and his Realtor wife bought cheap Park City property in the pre-skiing days of the early 1960s. But unlike Bob Woody and Hal Schindler, who got houses for a couple of hundred bucks in back taxes, the Blairs paid a whopping $3,000 for 1119 Park Avenue. Then they sold too soon, missing out on the boom that pushed those properties into the six and seven figures.

Blair's impending retirement would make way for me as a full-time editorial writer and for Harry Fuller as page editor.

* * *

Harry E. Fuller, Jr., an ageless 1955 University of Oregon graduate and 1958 U.S. Army veteran raised by a successful Chicago banker, arrived at *The Tribune* January 30, 1962.

He had driven with a pregnant wife in a dented Volkswagen from The Dalles, Oregon, where was a news editor, sports editor and general assignment reporter.

Harry E. Fuller Jr. in 1970s.

This wry man of many words and phrases entered journalism out of desperation:

Confronting an Eisenhower recession, my job prospects dismal, compelled to determine what it was I could actually sell to a possible employer, it occurred to me that I had, since childhood, been an inveterate story-teller, succeeded in university courses that required writing and therefore, why not newspaper reporting? An equally desperate weekly newspaper owner in really rural Oregon -- Madras to be precise -- took me on. The job's salary was augmented by stipends from being a stringer for the Associated Press, United Press, International Press, *The Portland Oregonian* and a small daily to the south, *The Bend Bulletin.* Thirteen months later I had moved north to The Dalles, where I picked up more newspapering wizardry, a nascent skiing ability and a wife. Exploring a fellow worker's suggestion that I might appreciate Utah skiing, me and the Mrs. motored to Salt Lake City and Brighton up Big Cottonwood Canyon, stopping also in both *The Tribune* and *Deseret News* offices to explore employment possibilities. The keenly prescient Art

Deck instantly saw my potential and hired me away from the unfortunate *Dalles Chronicle.*[637]

There is more to his tale of landing at *The Tribune* and into Editorial's top slot.

Actually, he [Deck] was another desperate newspaper employer facing a personnel vacancy. Hitting the ground running, I was assigned to the City and County Building as a reporter assisting the nonpareil self-taught leg-man Scoop Williams, who, congenially alert to displacement threats, sent me on routine data collection errands around the building. Following this initiation, I did some rewrite duty under the ever strict gaze of regional editor Ernie Hoff before replacing Capitol reporter Jerry Full, who to general amazement and consternation had become press attache for then-U.S.Senator Sherman Lloyd.

Bored and restless after about two years of this, ready to seek some other, more interesting and lucrative employment, I was conveniently asked by then-Gov. Cal Rampton to consider being his press secretary, which prompted me to ask Mr. Deck what exactly was my future at the paper. Well, it seems vacancies were opening there, too, in the Editorial Department -- Herb Kretchman was retiring and Ernie Linford had agreed to be the University of Wyoming's School of Journalism dean. My experience in successfully submitting sub editorials when the guys in that department were absent for prolonged periods evidently led Art to ask if one of those jobs interested me.

I joined Bob Blair in filling the two slots, the best coincidence ever to befall me -- a 30-year career that was more fun than work with, during the concluding years, three bright, insightful, diligent, conscientious and congenial people who were so pleasant to spend office time with it sometimes brings moisture to my eyes realizing how really fortunate my employment decision turned out to be. [He was kindly referring to myself, Paul Wetzel and Lex Hemphill.]

The ESOP distribution did not hurt either.

Fuller stayed in shape by skiing and running up and down the stairs to and from the 10th floor. On the job, he rarely left his office, instead eating lunch from a brown bag at his desk while reading. He took occasional calls from such notables Salt Lake City Mayor Rocky Anderson, who wasted no time being courteous with others.

Fuller loved the writing process so ardently that he studied the dictionary to learn one new, esoteric word each day. These ten-dollar words were worked into pedantic sentences that sometimes wound on and on beyond comprehension.

Even more aggravating was his penchant for editing my copy -- lengthening my words, sentences and paragraphs -- to the point of derailing all train of thought, weakening my premise and conclusions, and leaving gobbledegook I didn't recognize as mine. I wanted clear, forceful editorials, and these mutations failed.

Harry Fuller in 1990s.

Over time, I surmised obfuscation was Fuller's way of avoiding complaints from readers and censure from dual publishers who dispensed unclear or contradictory orders. If people couldn't understand the editorials, they were unlikely to bother us.

Fuller repelled some newsroom staffers by talking down to them or tossing ill-fitting page layouts on their desks at the end of the day, leaving a mess to fix. He never understood that a vertical cartoon couldn't fit into a horizontal hole. Once his wife Lyla left him, however, so did his arrogance. Humility and shyness enhanced his charm.

* * *

Wally Hoffman in his mezzanine office.

Wallace "Wally" D. Hoffman often handled letters to the editor (the Public Forum), giving him ample opportunity to bluster and bark over the phone. Like the rest of us, he also was expected to write an editorial each day, a process he postponed as long as possible. While comfortable expressing knee-jerk opinions out loud, he lacked the knack for putting persuasive words on paper. Consequently, he resorted to regularly "throwing the baby out with the bath water," among other cliches.

The University of Missoula graduate joined *The Tribune* in 1957, when he began stints on City Desk as a copy, make-up, night city and day city editor before moving up to Editorial in 1970.

In every editorial discussion he joined -- that is, any within earshot -- the blowhard made loud claims that sounded like he knew what he was talking about. The louder he got, the less his knowledge could be trusted and the more I avoided his meaningless arguments.

For all his bluster, Hoffman was a good soldier who faithfully followed his superiors' orders. And even though he sometimes berated and humiliated underlings, he could be kind, especially about personal matters. If I was in a pinch, needing time off, he often covered for me. He clearly adored his two children and his wife Shirley, who worked at the University of Utah Bookstore with John Cummins' wife Joan.

* * *

Two months into my new assignment, I wasn't sure I'd made the right decision. I had the sense of purpose, idealism, curiosity and social conscience useful to the job, but I was too timid to take on topics outside education. I hadn't paid close enough attention to current events in the 60s and 70s and was losing sleep over my shallow knowledge of political issues. I knew next to nothing about the judicial system, public health and the environment, subjects of interest to me.

Before writing anything, I researched topics to death, reviewing my copious news files and talking to reporters and outside contacts. Then I wrestled with my sentences and assertions, sometimes working at the computer past 7 o'clock.

But writing was only part of my new job.

Like the others, I fielded phone calls from disgruntled readers. But as the new kid on the block, I also handled local columns, including the Common Carrier, launched in Nov. 29, 1970 to give readers and community leaders a chance to be heard.

Invariably, these writers exceeded the word limit, requiring heavy editing and drawing complaints that stretched my work day beyond Denny's tolerance level. He paced outside my door and then complained of a raging headache on the way home. He would tell people my new job was perfect for me: "She's paid to bitch."

At least my resignation as education editor let in a ray of sunshine of sorts.

Jay Monson, a Utah State University education professor and member of the state school board, wrote a letter December 5 that said, in part:

> . . . I do want you to know that your attendance [at the last board meeting] was missed, and that we will miss you in the future as part of our board meetings.
> You have done a very fine job, Diane, over the years in what I feel has been very accurate reporting of the educational meetings in the State of Utah. I know your talent in this regard is going to be sorely missed. Hopefully we will see you from time to time as you keep tabs on us and the other policy makers in the State.

Undoubtedly prompted by one of his assistants, Superintendent G. Leland Burningham

also commended me for "the excellent service" I had "rendered as a reporter covering the educational issues and the business of the State Board of Education."[638]

The relationship between newsmakers and journalists was something like stroking a snake, with neither side able to let down its guard. As a reporter, I had sometimes fallen short on the sensitivity scale, so I was gratified to receive praise from educators. As much as ever, however, I needed to be impartial, accurate and fair, and compliments like these could compromise that goal. I couldn't let Burningham's sudden kindness, in this case, deter me from criticizing his administration in the future. It was a duty I eventually managed to fulfill.

---

[634] "Jack Gallivan, Tribune's Chairman, Reflects on Personalities," *The Salt Lake Tribune,* July 24, 1988, p. T9.

[635] Harry Fuller email February 10, 2013.

[636] Bob Blair interview October 2013.

[637] Harry Fuller email January 15, 2014.

[638] G. Leland Burningham letter to Diane Cole, December 7, 1983.

31 - Both Sides Now in 1984

After working upstairs one day, I jotted in my journal: "I'd much prefer catching up on my Logan features tomorrow and forgetting about editorial for a change." J.R. Allred had guilted me into another Utah State University visit, and I had several stories stored up.

After another day back down in the newsroom, I sang a different tune. "Once I get Scarlet off my back and shed more of the education duties, I may start to enjoy editorial writing."

Most of my days still were spent in the newsroom, where I stowed notebooks full of school features waiting to be written -- and where Peter Scarlet prattled on about minutia and personalities from my old stomping grounds.

Scarlet's favorite theme was Lucille Stoddard, academic vice president at Utah Technical College in Orem. He was besotted (Scarletism) with the first woman to become president -- even if only temporarily as acting president -- of a public college in Utah. When Stoddard married architect Frank Ferguson, Peter moped (Scarletism) for weeks, but when she continued taking his calls and meeting him for lunch, he perked up.

Because Scarlet's fondest desire was to pontificate from the ivory tower, he often slipped me sketchy mock editorials before beginning his day on City Desk. Besides amusing me, he was living the role of editorial writer through me. Our politics were as far apart as the moon and sun, but some of his ideas wormed their way into my psyche -- and my editorials.

Since I was one of the few in the office to grant him an audience, Scarlet droned on as long as I could stand it. Eventually, I would sternly say, "Leave now, Peter!" Like a faithful hound, he'd slink away, tail between his legs, happily returning for more attention another day.

Scarlet actually became one of my best friends at work. More like a brother. He so resembled my older brother Dick that I sometimes confused the two. Both grew up in Rose Park about the same time and became intelligent social introverts. If born a generation later, they might have been diagnosed with Asperger's autism.

Scarlet and I went to lunch for birthdays -- our own and those of our favorite PR women. He rarely picked up the check, and then only if I curtly reminded him it was his turn.

On the school beat, some still regarded me and Scarlet as a team.

The Utah State PTA, for example, addressed thank-your notes to both of us. Mary Hammond, the group's public relations vice president, wrote that the organization appreciated us attending their open house. "We are thrilled with the editorial you wrote," she said. "Thanks to you and Peter and *The Tribune* for the excellent coverage you've given us."

The PTA later wrote me that its membership increased by more than 6,100 members that year. "We feel that we owe some of this success to the great publicity you have given PTA over the last nine months."

Oops. I didn't intend to provide "publicity" per se, but what can I say?

I eventually got positive feedback for the USU stories as well. Snow College public information officer Doris Larsen applauded my feature on USU's Exceptional Child Center, which was researching ways to prevent and treat mental disabilities. My take on USU's Edith Bowen Laboratory School January 6 pleased its director, Ted R. Williams, as well as Oral L. Ballam, dean of education, and Jay Monson, who said it was good to see me again at a recent school board meeting. "It seemed like old times."

Even some of my editorials drew attention. LaRue Winget, associate superintendent of public instruction, and Kerry Nelson, small schools specialist for the state school office, liked my February 13 editorial on rural schools. "We appreciated the accuracy of the editorial as well as your perception of the problem," their letter said.

I still longed to be some sort of City Desk editor, but with one foot upstairs, that wasn't happening. In fact, my time in the newsroom became increasingly aimless, homeless and friendless.

With no beat of my own, I intruded on other reporters' turf, triggering snarly warnings to back off. Jim Woolf, Charlie Seldin and Con Psarras, who apparently had been interested in the editorial job, quit joking with me. I would arrange my notes on an empty desk just in time for the regular reporter to show up and send me packing. With no set schedule, appointments were tough to make. I was producing far fewer stories than usual and feeling frustrated and guilty about it. So much so that I still had nightmares about being out of the loop 45 years later.

When Will Fehr sauntered by jingling his coins, I dreaded the inevitable "What's up?" After hemming and hawing, I truthfully admitted, "Not much."

* * *

Even worse, my dual role put me in City Editor Walt Schaffer's cross hairs.

Like previous winters, I covered education issues on Capitol Hill. Schaffer complained that I wrote too much about budgets, the Legislature's primary purpose, and that my stories came in too long and late. He wanted stories by 5 p.m., but legislative votes often occurred after that, and then it took time to write up results.

One day Schaffer's carping ticked me off while I was writing on deadline. "Fine!" I retorted. "Forget the story!" I logged off my computer, grabbed by notebook and stormed out the door, fuming all all the way to D.B. Cooper's, where I downed two drinks before heading home.

Next day, Gerry Cunningham calmly explained that he was my editor during the Legislature, and he had been holding space for me in the front section -- space he had to fill at the last minute after I disappeared. I felt like crap about that but still seethed about Schaffer's harangue.

Schaffer and I quit speaking after that, but he didn't let it rest. He told Scarlet how difficult I was to work with and how I missed the mark on the education beat; that he wished I'd stay up in Editorial full-time.

"Rationally," I bellyached to Mimi February 1, "I know Walt's full of shit, but emotionally, I worry about my performance and personality. I also worry about my future at *The Tribune*."

On February 13, Schaffer wrote a "note on discipline" to the staff:

When you are given an assignment, written or oral, you are expected to do it. That means without bitching, moaning or signaling other forms of displeasure. Remember, this is a daily and reporters cover assignments. I don't care whether you have been here 30 years or 30 days. And I don't care whether you don't like the assignment, or whether you don't like me. If you are asked to do an assignment on short notice, carry out the assignment. If that means you have to stay to 6 p.m., you stay. WALT.

Schaffer crammed another memo into staffer files February 22:

I have noticed an increased tendency by staffers to write stories of news value two to three days after the event or meeting. We missed breaking a couple of good NEWS stories just last week. This is a daily newspaper, and from making out the Plan of the Day more than once, I know that no one is overburdened with assignments. And I'll repeat another cliche, this is not a 9 to 5 profession. If you have a story when the meeting or event ends at 4:30, you're expected to return and write it. The papers have been small and we often have trouble getting all the day's events in, but a phone call to the editor on duty will help resolve missing the story, or your time off. WALT.

Reporters could be forgiven for confusion. Not so long ago, the previous city editor had practically outlawed coverage of meetings and routine events.

After cooling off a bit three weeks later, Schaffer called a meeting with me and his superiors, Will Fehr and Jack Schroeder. The four of us settled into Art Deck's old office.

I held my twitching tongue while no-necked mole declared: "I want this prima donna out of my department! You can transfer her to Lifestyle if you want, but I can't work with her!"

Working his jaw, clearing his throat a couple of times and blinking his eyes, Schroeder calmly inquired, "What's the problem, Walt?"

"She writes too many stories, and they're too long," he complained. "She insists on quoting the superintendent, and she's impossible to communicate with. Serf and Brian had the same problem with her."

"How would that runt know?" I grumbled to myself. "He's never been a beat reporter in his life, and he was no friend of Serf's."

I shifted into my out-of-body mode, disengaging my shock to watch the scene from afar. Over the years, this technique had helped me endure insults from my brothers and mother, humiliation from 14-year-old "friends" who dumped me to become more popular, confusion over my first husband's rejection, and rage with my stepdaughters' attacks on me.

I had made false assumptions about Walt Schaffer. While still pals, I had told him about my troubles with Serf, and now he was using my confidence against me. I also had thought he wanted me to take the initiative to cover the education beat as I saw fit. He must have been simmering with resentment all along.

It also occurred to me that Schaffer might be schizophrenic and that I somehow tripped his wire. Perhaps his personal life was a factor. He had trouble with other staffers, too, regularly jumping to negative conclusions and painting everyone with the same broad, dirty brush in his frequent memos. Yet I became the target of his worst explosions, and I was pretty sure it wasn't because of the job I was doing.

Could Schaffer possibly be sexist or insecure about being shorter than me.? I considered. Perhaps he was jealous or suspicious of my friendship with Will Fehr, who often stopped to chat with me. My outward calm during his tirades probably infuriated him as well. I never burst into tears, and he didn't have to worry about me punching him out.

Clearing his throat and blinking again, Schroeder asked: "Are you saying that Diane writes too many stories, Walt?"

"Yes, and they're too damn long!"

Schroeder: "If they're too long, why don't you edit them to fit?"

"I don't have time to deal with all her shit!"

Schroeder: "Diane, what do you have to say about this?"

In earlier years, I would have been crushed and speechless. But I'd seen something like this coming since Schaffer started ignoring me and assigning education stories to other reporters. Fehr knew me better than Schaffer did, so I doubted he would buy this bullshit. I simply responded, "I think I'm doing a good job, and I don't understand what Walt has against me."

Fehr concluded the meeting with: "We're not going to get rid of Cole, so you're going to have to get along."

Afterwards, Schroeder joked, "This is the first time I've heard an editor complain about a reporter doing too much."

Of course Schaffer's personal attack stung. I was used to being a teacher's pet with straight A's -- not a troublemaker. Safe in my bedroom that night, I unloaded on Mimi: "I hate hat creep Walt, and there is no way I'll quit for the sake of an inept city editor! I'd rather bide my time until I'm vested in the stock-sharing plan and then leave if I've taken the shaft."

On April Fool's Day, I gave Mimi an optimistic update:

After his tantrum in Will's office, Walter actually spoke to me twice -- no, thrice -- about stories and said "Hi, Diane" the other day. However, I've heard he's been giving other women in the office some strange messages. I've been in Editorial almost constantly, so I escaped his caprice and irrational invective.

Editorial's growing on me. I'm not quite so self-conscious after working two full weeks, but I know I lack the historical perspective and vocabulary of my colleagues. I've also been too cautious about non-education issues -- maybe realistic is a better way to put it. I just don't have enough background to feel as confident as I need to be. It's been six months since I started this gig. So far I failed to finish editorials two days.

My respite from Schaffer's wrath didn't last. On April 11, he attacked Rod Pressly, my former education assistant, for discussing an assignment with me. I had heard about a tuition surcharge in the University of Utah Department of Engineering and alerted Pressly so we wouldn't duplicate efforts. In early June, Schaffer ran my teacher-surplus story in the state edition only, so most readers missed it. I was mad.

At the end of the month, Schaffer suggested getting a drink together. We chatted about about the Olympic torch being run through town on its way from Greece to the Los Angeles Summer Games. Then he apologized for being an asshole and blamed his frustration on my dual assignment in the newsroom and Editorial and on Fehr's relationship with reporters.

By going behind his back to give assignments directly to writers, he explained, Fehr was undermining his authority as city editor. He was working just four hours a day -- coming in late, taking two-hour lunches and leaving early -- to avoid the aggravation. He was on the verge of resigning.

It was ironic that the guy who violated my confidence and tried to get me fired now wanted my support. I summed up our conversation to Mimi: "He has some pitiful views about his role as city editor. He feels he has no guidance, no help, no authority, no respect. Well, he's lost it all by throwing temper tantrums."

Warmer relations aside, I couldn't help telling Fehr he made Schaffer nervous by talking to reporters; that Schaffer took it out on staffers. That afternoon, Fehr took Charlie Seldin to lunch and offered him Schaffer's job. Charlie declined in favor of his family, so Schaffer kept flailing away.

I managed to stay in the middle of the Memo Man's meltdown to the bitter end, which didn't come for a few more months. When he prohibited reporters from talking directly to Fehr about anything, for example, I slipped a copy to Fehr.

Schaffer's finale began September 10 with one of his more reasonable memos:

Study after study has shown that most readers are quite happy with a 12- to 15-inch story. Lately, I've been receiving stories way too long to cover the subject. Weekenders and features are different. I ask, please that you write news stories tight and accurate.

I am getting swamped each day with answering phone calls. I would like to spend part of my day editing copy, uncovering assignments for the next day and working with new reporters. I can't get this done while on the phone all the time. I ask that each of you only pass personal calls, personnel requests or complaints to me. All other calls go to the ACE [assistant city editor].

The next day (what IS it about September 11?), the city editor snapped.

One day after I put out a memo to aim for 12- to 15-inch stories, I count four 20-inch stories on Split Page -- not knowing how much was trimmed.

Now I realize, that you realize, that Mr. Fehr is still city editor, and that I'm the token or necessary figure to fill a spot and lay out Split Page. And that when you go into his office he will take your side.

However, I'm not going down without a fight on wordy stories. I've got a job to do, and I'm going to do it.

Politely, I will ask that stories be written as tight as possible, unless otherwise requested by editor. Not so politely if people insist on testing the issue. It's going to get ugly.[639]

Naturally my stories were among the offending 20-inchers, some of which were written before the first memo. Why Schaffer and the two editors beneath him failed to trim them, we would never know. Fehr caught wind of this latest rant and called Schaffer into his office.

As often happened when someone deserved to be fired, Schaffer lost rank. For a time he returned to Siberian Davis County, where he verbally attacked a county commissioner. Demoted to night police, he became the target of regular reprimands from his former reporter Rodd Wagner. Then-Business Editor John Keahey, a former Naval Reserve buddy, took him in. Schaffer blew up at Keahey's request for more on his first business story. "I know more about writing than anyone on staff, and I'm not going to be edited by anyone!" he shouted while storming from the newsroom. Next day, he resigned.

After that, simmering Schaffer took a public information post with the Navy Reserve in Washington, retiring in 2011. One day back East, Keahey told me in 2018, Schaffer returned home to find his wife dead on the floor. Ultimately, he added, Schaffer became a skipper on a tourist shuttle on Baltimore Harbor.

* * *

City Desk drama notwithstanding, I still had to conjure up ideas for editorials. One of my early forays outside the field of education involved a health scare sweeping the globe.

The Human Immunodeficiency Virus, identified by Drs. Robert Gallot and Dr. Luc Antoine Montagnier, had killed nearly half of 6,993 infected Americans, mostly gay men in San Francisco and New York City. When told the so-called AIDS virus could spread through saliva and blood, the American public panicked. Religious zealots and others blamed the wrath of God, and gay-bashing escalated. Irrational, discriminatory policies were erupting in communities across the country.

When I voiced my opinion about the epidemic, my colleagues gladly left the touchy topic to me. My editorials called for calm, discouraged discrimination against patients and gays and advised the public to invest in a cure. In a twofer in 1985, for example, I castigated school officials and parents for banishing 13-year-old Ryan White, a hemophiliac infected by blood transfusions before AIDS precautions were common.

I didn't let my frustration with my first husband's sexuality undermine my belief that fairness and humanity required acceptance of everyone's inherent traits. My editorials never subscribed to the popular notion that homosexuality is a choice that harms society.

* * *

With Lulu out of the house, 16-year-old Stormy slipped into her sister's slovenly shoes and left her fun, spunky image behind.

My once sweet stepdaughter snitched vodka from the pantry, refilling our bottles with water, and spiked her coffee with Kalua for the morning trek to the bus stop. A cyclone crashed into her bedroom and bathroom, and she raised hell at school. After smashing her locker partner in the face one day, she called her gym teacher a fucking bitch another.

A job at Burger King's drive-through window did Stormy more harm than good. She met a 22-year-old salesman who winked at me when we met. I later suggested to Denny that the relationship resembled statutory rape. He didn't want to make waves.

Over the next few months, I objected to Winker spending the night at our house and talked to Stormy about preventing a pregnancy. Not that she listened. I would have gladly raised an unplanned child, but the poor kid would have become the rope in Stormy's tug of war for control.

Denny eventually told Stormy her Winker was a loser. She erupted in a torrent of invective before turning on me, the bystander. After slamming the front door, she stalked down the driveway, threatened to beat the shit out of me and hollered for the neighbor dogs to kill our handsome Malamute Hairball.

Winker's retail supervisor and her husband took Stormy in -- for a price. We paid child support, and they corrupted her with drugs they dealt. Of course we didn't know that part of the story until years later.

* * *

Meantime, Denny and I opened our first Individual Retirement Accounts at the Newspaper Employees Credit Union, which withdrew $10 from each of our paychecks. Even better, we inherited $18,000 from Denny's Aunt Thelma, enabling us to buy the lot next door and carpet the house -- just in time to host the May 12 marriage of staffers Doug Parker, 49, and Carol Sisco, 36.

Carol Sisco and Doug Parker sign their marriage license at our house.

Bob Woody described how the two got together:

> One night as Doug and Carol made simultaneous exit of *The Tribune* by the two doors on either side of the library. They chanced in the hall.
>
> He asked if she might give him a ride home.
>
> "Sure," said she.
>
> But no sparks yet.
>
> Later: "I don't suppose you'd like a drink," said he.
>
> "You bet," said she.
>
> And down to the Marriott bar they went. Thus began a one-year courtship unknown to any but Doug's glowering assistant Dan Bates and the library's circumspect Iris Carlquist.
>
> It was a secret so well kept that none of the nosey news hounds at *The Tribune* knew until the couple announced they were to be wed on May 12, 1984. Not even Mother Jones had known.[640]

Sisco had me guess which staffer she was dating, and I went through the entire list of unmarried males -- and even some married ones -- before half-heartedly suggesting Parker. Her eyebrows shot up. I couldn't believe it. Quiet, reserved Parker slipped in and out of the office under the radar. Carol, on the other hand, always made a noisy, aggressive splash. An unlikely pair for sure.

Like Parker, the wedding in our mountain chalet was a modest but proper affair. Carol's parents and Parker's brother flew in for an event featuring champagne and cake.

The two turned out to be attuned to one another. They shared a sense of offense at societal injury and injustice,[641] issues they both covered at the Legislature. But they didn't talk much about work at home, focusing instead on good food, wine, books and travel.

Woody remarked that the Sisco-Parker partnership wrought changes in both:

Certainly he was not a chauvinist. And woe betide him had he been one. For Carol Sisco, who joined us in 1981, was equal in energy, enterprise and outrage to any male who ever worked, cursed, shouted at *The Tribune*, and was perfectly capable of quickly cutting off a chauvinist at the pass. It was as if God had fashioned an unrepentant and unbowed Eve exclusively for an Adam who did not seek dominion over the birds and beasts of the field, much less to be lord and master over women.

Case in point: Doug had covered a political meeting earlier in the day. Carol covered the finale but learned much to her chagrin that the events Doug had reported had been changed by events following. A new congressional candidate confided to Carol he was announcing. Hold the presses!

Carol called Doug at home:

"Hey, everything's changed."

"What's happened?"

"Another candidate . . . Can I rewrite your lead?"

"Sure, go ahead. And add your byline."

With Carol, Doug took a fancy to an obscure Vouvray -- a mild, semi-dry white. That in time led to a taste for even finer wines and a trip to France for sipping champagne in the countryside.

He also cultivated cuisinary [sic] skills so refined that he no longer created by cook book but by instinct.

Housekeeping? No problem. When Carol was busy, he did 90 percent of the work. When he was busy, she did 90 percent. It was an exercise of the marital maxim for happiness. Each gives 90 percent.

Doug's sensibilities extended beyond the sensory to the cerebral. He was a devoted reader: travel and Western history, particularly Wallace Stegner.

Recently, in his non-chauvinistic style, he had begun the works of Shelby Herron, a southern female writer with a certain feminist tinge.

Doug and Carol formerly came and went as independent entities at *Tribune* staff blasts. Now they teamed as Tweedle Dum and Tweedle Dee and as

punk rockers [at Cole-Green Halloween parties].[642]

* * *

Another friend -- my favorite rival from the *Deseret News* -- also staged a wedding that year. Vicki Varela married *Deseret News* reporter Brett DelPorto in a tasteful event at the Salt Lake Art Center. Vicki was on the cusp of leaving the *News* for a public information job with the State Board of Regents at the unfinished Triad Center a few blocks west of downtown.

Triad was financed by Saudi gun merchant Adnan Khashoggi and run by Manny Floor, who lured Charlie Seldin away from our staff to do PR. It became the new site of Utah's annual arts festival, where punkers, cowboys, greasers, professionals, low-enders and average folks had previously wandered among stages and booths on Main Street a few days in June.

* * *

Other ambitious staffers to leave for more opportunity and money that year were Jerry Wellman, who carried his computer skills over to Newspaper Agency Corporation; Con Psarras, who embraced broadcast news, and George Raine, who defected to *Newsweek*.

Con Psarras

Psarras felt he'd hit a dead end at *The Tribune* for pissing off a sacred cow, attorney Don Holbrook. As reporter of electricity rate hearings, Con audaciously asked Holbrook -- in front of our publisher -- whether Holbrook represented *The Tribune* or Utah Power & Light. [643]

Besides being *The Tribune's* attorney, Holbrook sat on the newspaper's Board of Trustees. He had helped Gallivan enact the Newspaper Preservation Act and Joint Operating Agreement in 1952. He also was big in Utah politics, directing Calvin Rampton's campaign for governor, chairing the Utah Democratic Party and running for the U.S. Senate in 1974.

I knew the usually smooth, occasionally short-tempered gentleman from the State Board of Regents, which he led with an iron hand. I would not expect someone of his stature to seek revenge for a reporter's perceived impertinence, yet I had witnessed how embarrassment affected Gallivan. Maybe Psarras was wise to move on.

His self-confidence and journalistic competence gave Psarras options. In August, he became an investigative reporter for KSL Television, where our former assistant city editor Ernie Ford directed news. Despite being a non-Mormon in a Mormon business, Psarras would become news director himself someday.

Money and prestige were not George Raine's primary motivation for accepting *Newsweek's* offer. Even after reporting more than two decades in San Francisco for *Newsweek*, the *Examiner* and the *Chronicle*, he still considered *The Tribune* home. But he didn't want to spend his entire career in a state dominated by the Mormon Church. [644]

Denny and I stayed put, possibly because we lacked ambition and alternatives to move on. Not wanting to return to the bottom rung of teacher salaries, I let my license lapse. Denny quit his search for an illustration job after one too many rejections and the realization he'd need to move to New York or some other big city -- something he never would do.

We were among many to stay on staff, among them Peter Scarlet, Bob Bryson, Dave Jonsson, Mark Knudsen, Sam Smith, Tim Fitzpatrick, Jack Fenton, Ray Herbat, Tim Kelly, Kirk Millson, David Noyce, Doug Parker, Pepper Provenzano, R.D. Roberg, Randy Petersen, Ben Ling, Helen Forsberg, Judy Rollins, Verdo Thomas, Tom Wharton, Jim Woolf, Dawn Tracy, Paul Wetzel, Terry Orme and Gordon Harman.

Verdo Thomas and Ana Daraban in newsroom.

* * *

I hadn't yet given up my dream of someday following in Will Fehr' footsteps to manage newspaper policy for Utah's capital city. But I finally woke up when **Randy Peterson**, the laid-back West High graduate who'd come to *The Tribune* with me from the University of Utah, took over from Schaffer. I didn't have what it took to be an editor at *The Salt Lake Tribune*.

While rising from copy boy to city hall, Peterson never seemed interested or assertive enough to assume the lead. Unlike me, he didn't complain, buck authority or stir up trouble. As it turned out, he calmly and competently took charge of the local news, enabling our News Desk to settle down.

One of Peterson's first decisions answered reporter Cathy Free's prayers. He let her take time from routine news in Davis County to write off-beat human interest features. She loosely based her weekly "On the Job" column on Chicago writer Studs Terkel's 1972 book Working, stories of blue- and white-collar workers in their own voices. As she tells it:

Once a week for the next several years, I did everything from wade through the city sewer system with a pipe inspector to venture deep into a coal mine with third-generation miners and climb to the top of the State Capitol dome with an electrician so he could change the light bulb. Talking to cabdrivers, washroom attendants, gravediggers and secretaries about their hopes, dreams and sorrows, I soon realized that my own job was as rewarding as any that I could write about. Where else could I pull back the curtain to peek at people's lives, capture the essence of their beings and then quietly step away?[645]

To this day, I cannot thank Randy enough for having faith in me and allowing me to rove the state in search of ordinary people and oddball characters to interview. He trusted me to find good stories and I did my best (I hope!) not to let him down.[646]

My partner-in-crime by this time was Lynn Johnson, who was not only an excellent photographer but a fun traveling partner and a good friend [and a future Catholic deacon]. My favorite [road-trip memory with Lynn] had to be the time [in July 1986] we did a story on U.S. Highway 50, which AAA had just named the "Loneliest Road in America."

After finding a religious commune and a Nevada saloon/casino with two slot machines, we headed to Ely, Nevada, determined to find a brothel on U.S. 50. I'll never forget Lynn stopping at the White Pine County Sheriff's Office and asking for directions to the nearest whorehouse on the highway. We strolled into the Green Lantern at about 9 that night, Lynn with his heavy camera bag and me with my tape recorder and notebook. The madame, a heavyset woman named Pat Victor with a silver dollar-sized mole on her cheek, asked what she could do for us. Lynn, not missing a beat, said, "I'm here to shoot some pictures. She's just here to watch."

The ice broken, Pat laughed and called in her "girls" to be photographed and interviewed in their scanty attire as we all sat around the Green Lantern bar. Thankfully, it was a slow night in the middle of the week and no customers

walked through the door. I'm sure they'd have wondered what I was doing there in my khakis and penny loafers alongside these women in their baby doll nighties and spiked heels.

Before Lynn and I left that night, Pat awarded me the distinction of being the first woman to walk through the door who didn't ask for a job. No, I wasn't tempted to switch careers, although these women undoubtedly made more money fulfilling truck drivers' fantasies along a forlorn ribbon of road than I did as a young reporter at The Trib.[647]

Lynn and I roared with laughter all the way back to SLC the next day, wondering what Shirley Jones would say about our "Green Lantern" expense report. It was truly one of the most enjoyable stories of my Tribune career.

In another favorite story with Lynn, I learned that the inventor of the Frisbee was managing a motel in Richfield, keeping the books and filling in as a fry cook and dishwasher. He had lost his millions and had moved to central Utah to start from scratch. We spent two days with him as he regaled us with tales from his past life of luxury and how much fun he'd had going through his piles of money. I was so impressed that he seemed content with the simple life in a dumpy motel.

Stories like this are what drove me to keep going, even though I was making chump change. I loved meeting people and hearing their take on what it meant to be human. It's something I've been doing now every week since 1979![648]

Cathy continued to freelance for *People Magazine*, a job she'd done on the side since 1982 and kept up for over three decades.

* * *

This was the first year our Mike Korologos-led River Crew rented a houseboat on Lake Powell instead of running rivers with Shirley's husband. Korologos' client, Del Webb, provided the boat, leaving me and Denny with a $60 share of the gas and insurance . . . and an implicit obligation to give the company publicity.

These cheap annual outings were great fun -- an opportunity for wild drinking, eating and rehashing *Tribune* mistakes. Myrlene Korologos, our "admiral," oversaw planning and food supplies and always prepared a gourmet Greek meal. Terry Orme and Nancy Hobbs dominated the water skis and created dutch-oven masterpieces. Tim Killy fished; Jerry Green tried and failed. Snores and farts accompanied our sleep atop the boat..

The men of Lake Powell: Mike Korologos crouching; Denny Green, Jerry Green, Terry Orme and Tim Kelly, standing left to right.

We told ourselves our quid pro quo with Del Webb was no worse than *Tribune* owner Tommy McCarthey's junkets as travel editor. But we knew it was unethical. Our employee handbook clearly forbade the acceptance of passes or gratuities: "Under no circumstances is any staff member permitted to solicit passes, free tickets, gifts or emoluments."[649]

My expected story in the Travel Section began:

> Signs of a warm weekend waned as the nine of us shivered in the Sandy Sizzler's parking lot Friday morning, our cars laden with equipment and supplies. Spurred on by 18 months or so of anticipation, including planning parties where Lake Powell was the last topic of conversation, however, we agreed to have fun, come hail or high water.
>
> Both came that mid-October weekend -- just one week after Utahns basked in Indian summer sun. And we did have a memorable vacation.
>
> After driving south six hours from Salt Lake City, we picked up a houseboat and speedboat equipped with waterskis at Bullfrog Resort and Marina in southern Utah. If we'd been paying full price, we'd have spent $1,080 for the 10-person houseboat for four nights, $480 for the speedboat, about $230 to gas up and $69 for insurance. Of course

> those summer season costs don't include what we lugged from home.
>
> Veteran Lake Powell recreationists smiled sardonically as we loaded the houseboat. Having been warned about prices at the lake, we each brought a full ice chest in addition to three or four sacks of groceries, several bottles of wine and various other alcoholic beverages, fishing and camping gear and several unnecessary changes of clothes. The boat settled considerably lower into the calm, clear water.[650]

* * *

On October 19, 1984 I worked 12 hours, beginning with a speech to Salt Lake County supervisors and ending with a catch-up editorial. It was one of these increasingly common days when visitors ate up most of our morning trying to influence the Editorial Board.

This time it was U.S. Senator Orrin Hatch who talked nearly two hours about education, child care, health care and women's rights, topics I knew something about. While this Howdy Doody look-alike seemed reasonable on the surface, I couldn't shake the memory of his self-righteous attack on the Equal Rights Amendment. I didn't trust him.

* * *

It was easy to forget how much *The Tribune* affected people -- until I received note from a reader or someone I'd written about.

Wayne C. Evans, chairman of the Salt Lake City Board of Education mired in conflict during my reporting years, thanked me for defending him against a no-confidence vote: "Thanks! My typewriter won't make an exclamation point large enough to express the feeling." Lorna Matheson, another city school board member, added, "And thanks also for the 'gentle' pat for our board (we needed it)."

In a letter to the publisher, University of Utah President Chase Peterson commended my December 19 editorial, which said, in part:

> Utah college and university students have come up with a magnanimous, sensible solution to the sorry state of school libraries. They're willing to pay a tuition increase well above the inflation rate if the Utah Legislature will triple their money on a one-year, 2-percent surcharge to upgrade the libraries.[651]

If campus libraries weren't in serious trouble, it can be safely assumed students would not be inviting a higher price for their education. The fact is that campus library needs have been deferred the past several years while school officials have responded to other, more pressing financial demands.

That chronic neglect now threatens the viability of higher education in the state. Students simply can't tap the knowledge of past and present scholars unless they have access to old and new publications. State colleges and universities could even lose national accreditation and the ability to attract top scholars if the problem becomes acute.

Last month at the Capitol, the Utah Intercollegiate Assembly adopted a resolution endorsing a 7 percent tuition increase for next school year, plus the surcharge. The students specified, however, that support of the surcharge is contingent upon the Utah Legislature's willingness to add $2.2 million to the students' $1.1 million and to spend the full amount on libraries.

This proposal is a far cry from the '70s and early '80s, when students frequently fought tuition increases regardless of the reasons behind them. It's also unprecedented for Utah students to dictate school spending by attaching strings to tuition.

The conclusion, after a few more paragraphs:

Lawmakers should not only take students up on their offer, but they also should make sure that the one-time revenue supplements, rather than supplants, the basic budget they ordinarily would appropriate for campus libraries.

Dr. Peterson called the editorial "a significant service to Utah education . . . its readability and clarity, particularly the succinct statements of the third paragraph, dispassionately communicate issues that deserve wider understanding."

I'd have felt better if I hadn't sounded so much like a shill for higher education.

I certainly wouldn't have sounded like a shill for the Alta Club if allowed to scrutinize its sexism, but that would have been employment suicide. Gallivan and O'Brien, as members of the elitist male club, dismissed civil rights attorney Brian Barnard as a light-weight gadfly when he claimed in court that a beer license prohibited sexism. All I could do was stand by silently as the sacred dinosaur dug in its heels and quit serving beer.

When it dawned on the good old Alta boys that women would bolster their waning lunch crowd and revenue, they took a more pragmatic approach. They invited Deedee Corradini, a Chamber of Commerce executive and future mayor of Salt Lake City; Genevieve Atwood, Utah State geologist, and Annette P. Cumming, a prominent Democrat, to enter by the front door and sip suds with the gentlemen.

* * *

Later in December, the biggest story of his career caught Mike Gorrell by surprise. This caring reporter's detailed account shows what it was like to be thrown into the middle of a disaster of international proportions.

Awakening December 20 to a TV report about a coal mine fire in central Utah that trapped several men, he wondered whether he might get in on the assignment.

Sure enough, I did. Will [Fehr] told me to go home, get some clothes for a couple of days and head down there. By late morning, I was in the passenger seat of [photographer] Al Hartmann's car, holding a six- or seven-paragraph AP story in my lap that had more information than the TV account, but not much more. The drive to Huntington, where I'd never been before, took quite a bit longer than the 2.5 hours I found it to be after many more trips. A strong winter storm, one that started the previous evening when all was seemingly well at the Wilberg mine, was still dropping snow steadily.

We arrived sometime in the late afternoon. Al dropped me off on Main Street at the old school building that had been converted into the headquarters of Emery Mining Co., which had a controversial cost-plus contract with Utah Power & Light to produce coal for the utility's new power plants, one in the mouth of Huntington Canyon, the other outside of Castle Dale. He then headed toward the mine to see what he might be able to see, which turned out to be not much because the media was kept so far from the site of the out-of-control blaze.

There was a buzz of activity at the building, with mining company people hustling between offices and other clumps of people hanging around in small groups. As I recall, there was a podium of sorts outside of a meeting room where more and more media people were congregating, waiting for the next press conference from the company and the federal Mine Safety and Health Administration (MSHA). I don't think we'd missed more than the first one, maybe two, because everybody was having a hard time making it through the storm to Emery County.

What strikes me now is how informal the setting was. I was able to mix fairly freely with people, coming to recognize that some of them were family members of missing miners – usually not spouses or immediate family, but cousins or best friends – just waiting for word. At some point during the course of the night, which I spent in the meeting room, sleeping on the floor underneath a table, the horrific potential became clear to me. All of those people might be dead or waiting in terror for rescuers to arrive.

We received briefings periodically from Emery Mining's spokesman, Bob Henrie, a level-headed guy who developed a pretty good relationship with the media pack because he seemed to be open with as much information as he could share and kept his cool when confronted with accusatory questions. MSHA had a couple of public information officers there who were around a fair bit, setting up maps of the underground workings and explaining what was going on in really general terms. The more time that passed, the grimmer the feeling became in that building.

By the second day after the disaster, the company had set up a system that directed townsfolk coming to Emery Mining headquarters to provide assistance, such as food for family members gathered in a basement room, to an entrance separate from the news media. But that afternoon, a little old lady mistakenly wandered into the press conference room between briefings and gave the few of us there a wonderful impromptu interview, describing in heart-felt words the anguish that miner mothers feel constantly in not knowing if their children are safe. Her words took on greater meaning later that day when we were informed that rescuers had found the bodies of nine miners. More rescuers were probing deeper in the smoke-filled tunnels to look for the other 18.

A few of the big news organizations, like AP (whose team included Peg McEntee and Bob Mims) and UPI (Paul Rolly), had had phones installed in the meeting room, but that was not the kind of thing *The Tribune* did. So I had to call in information to the desk from a pay phone on the outside wall of the 7-11 convenience store two blocks down the street. At some point in the string of press conferences, the news became grimmer and grimmer with the discoveries of yet more bodies and the intensification of the fire making the rescue operation increasingly dangerous. Because there was competition for the two pay phones at the 7-11 (I believe that was the brand then) and because I had so much adrenaline with the awful new news, I would run the two blocks to get a phone first. It was so cold outside, with temperatures plunging below zero once the storm clouds passed and skies were crystal clear, that my mouth would dry out completely from running and I had a hard time talking. So a couple of times I went into the 7-11 first to buy a beer and to drink it while I gave my information, mostly to Charlie Seldin but also sometimes Dan Bates. They actually wrote the stories that appeared under my byline.

Word that there was no hope for any of the missing miners came at a press conference relatively late on a Saturday night, giving me just enough time to get the desk whatever it needed to get the daily out. I remember going back that night to the room Al had rented in one of a small group of fourplexes on the edge of town heading toward Castle Dale. I just remember how brilliant the night sky was lit up, and the loud crunch of the frozen snow below our feet, as Al and I pondered a bit on what we'd just experienced the past few days. We got up and attended another late morning press conference, where they talked about efforts to shut down the mine to put out the fire, then we went home. It was Dec. 23. Judy Rollins gave me a big hug when I came into the newsroom and I went home, to return to work on Christmas Eve to work my regularly scheduled night cops shift. By this point I was starting to unravel a bit with the impact of being a witness to mass death and I took great comfort that night watching a television special (with

Pepper Provenzano) featuring Two Gentlemen Folk, a class folk-singing duo.

Over the next few months, I spoke almost daily to Bob Henrie, getting updates on the progress of efforts to get back into the mine, find the two miners who had never been located and to recover the 29 bodies, all of which were still sealed in the mine. But my real education into what happened at Wilberg began when MSHA was forced, following legal appeals by the news media, to release the transcripts of interviews that MSHA's disaster investigation team conducted of people who were involved in the firefight, the rescue operation or the operation of the mine. Those transcripts transformed my understanding of and appreciation for the complexities of mining and the true bravery displayed by the would-be rescuers.

I wrote a lot of stories in the year it took to retrieve the bodies and the 2.5 years it took for MSHA to wrap up its investigation, which blamed the company and fined it a lot of money. My coverage continued through a products liability trial that Utah Power and Emery Mining pursued against Ingersoll-Rand, the company that built the air compressor blamed for starting the fire after having been turned on accidentally and left running unattended for days – with a couple of deficient safety parts. It was concluded almost a decade after the fire, a span that gave me the opportunity to get to know some of the victims' survivors for a big five-year retrospective, shot by [photographer] Lynn Johnson. *The Tribune* dedicated lots of space for that, far more than is available today. I wrote a 10-year anniversary piece on Kenny Blake, the one miner who escaped from Wilberg's 5th Right section that deadly night, with the promise I wouldn't bother him again if he agreed to an interview. For the 25-year anniversary, my story – the best one I ever wrote, I think – I laid out the disaster through the eyes of three rescuers who almost died trying to reach their compatriots. My interview with rescuer Gilbert Madrid, who didn't wear a shirt during the kitchen conversation photographed by Ryan Galbraith, was my favorite of all time for its vigor and intensity. Rescuer Kenny Valdez was much more refined, but he was fascinating to talk to as well.

During the course of this story I got to know three men who became heads of MSHA – Dave Lauriski, who directed the rescue operations for Emery Mining; Davitt McAteer, a mine-safety advocate; and Joe Main, a safety representative for the United Mine Workers of America. Wilberg was a union mine. The UMWA's top official in Utah, Mike Dalpiaz, has been a valued source of mine ever since Wilberg, helpful with the coverage of mine-safety issues even though the union now has representation in only one Utah coal mine, Wilberg's sister operation, Deer Creek.

Other prominent contacts on this story were John Serfustini, representing UP&L, and his colleague John Ward, whom I'd covered when he was a Murray High School athlete and I was a reporter at the weekly *Murray Eagle* (*Green Sheet*); Kathy Snyder, who was new in her job at MSHA when Wilberg happened and felt as overwhelmed as Peg and I by its tragedy. I had great help from a woman who worked the desk at the Price motel where MSHA investigators stayed whenever they came to town. She called me and let me know about it all the time.

I took great pride in outperforming my main competitor at the *Deseret News* – Glenn Warchol – who gave me a lot of shit verbally but never could match my copy. I detested Glenn for years until we became colleagues and my attitude softened.

What stands out to me now, after Crandall Canyon and other disasters, is how little coverage we gave to the overall Wilberg disaster. I was the only reporter in Huntington. For Crandall Canyon, we had a whole team of people out there, looking at various aspects of community reaction that I couldn't attempt to do at Wilberg without abandoning the main press center, where you never knew WHEN news might arrive. I don't think we even had live coverage of the funerals a week after the fire, leaving that to stringers. I really cannot believe now that we paid such little attention to the community.[652]

639 Walt Schaffer, Memo to All City Desk Staffers, September 11, 1984.

640Woody, August 23, 1995.

641 Ibid.

642 Ibid.

643 Con Psarras interview August 4, 2014.

644 Raine, February 18, 2014.

645 Cathy Free on facebook, July 30, 2015.

646 Free, June 4, 2015.

647 Cathy Free facebook entry June 28, 2015.

648 Free, June 4, 2015.

649 Employe Benefits Personnel Policies, 1977, p A-8.

650 Diane Cole, "Powell, Great vacation on a houseboat despite weather," *The Salt Lake Tribune*, November 25, 1984, p. T1.

651 "Utah School Library Surcharge Sensible Solution to Problem," *The Salt Lake Tribune*, p. 2D.

652 Mike Gorrell email to Diane Cole, January 27, 2014.

32 - Welcome to 1985

The newsroom ran a brief story January 9 reporting that John Richard Calder was suing *The Tribune* for $150,000 in actual damages to his law practice and $150,000 in punitive damages. He claimed a January 2 editorial "inaccurately" described him as the owner of the Plandome Hotel.

Guess who wrote the editorial? The lawsuit became my baptism by fire in the Editorial Department. Almost like throwing the baby out with the bathwater, but not quite.

Attorney Files Suit Against S.L. Tribune

A bankruptcy court attorney whose name is identical to that of the Plandome Hotel owner has filed suit against The Salt Lake Tribune.

An editorial, published Jan. 2, inaccurately described hotel owner John Richard Calder as a bankruptcy attorney.

Attorney Calder's lawsuit, filed in 3rd District Court, seeks $150,000 in actual damages to his law practice. It asks for another $150,000 in punitive damages.

The Tribune published a correction after the editorial appeared, regretting the error.

My editorial had called upon Calder to clean up his act when the city shut off water to his bankrupt flophouse at 400 South and State Street, creating a health hazard for the 40 or so downtrodden residents. Natural gas had been shut off more than a year earlier, so the seedy hotel had switched to steam to heat, a system that could not work without water.

I based my remarks on three City Desk news stories. In one, published two weeks before the editorial, city personnel identified Calder as a bankruptcy attorney whom they suspected of tapping into the city water line.[653] Since nothing came out to the contrary, I naively assumed these were facts.

As it happens, there were two John Richard Calders. One owned the Plandome; one was a bankruptcy attorney. The latter didn't bother to set the record straight after the news story ran, but he sure as hell was going to make some money off my assault on his reputation with 110,000 readers. *The Tribune* should have consulted government records instead of city officials, he contended in the libel suit served to the Fourth Floor.

Tribune attorney D. Miles Holman ordered me to answer 23 interrogatories in March. I identified each person -- myself, Harry Fuller and Jerry O'Brien -- who approved the editorial. I reported that I'd been writing editorials for 17 months. I explained that most editorial ideas came from news stories discussed in daily Editorial Board meetings; that this one was based on three.[654]

"What a pain in the ass," I bitched to Mimi later at home. "The matter could be explained in one minute, yet I have to play stupid legal games because Brian Wilkinson used erroneous identifying information." I was embarrassed about compounding the error, and I was worried I had irreparably undercut my standing with my Fourth Floor bosses.

While I understood it was expensive to play hardball and fight flimsy claims in court, I feared we would become an easy mark for opportunists if we didn't. The Fourth Floor took its usual route and paid off the ambulance chaser. I never knew how much.

At least for awhile, the lawsuit made me skittish about criticizing individuals based on local stories. It seemed impractical, under our time constraints, to double-check every pertinent detail. Why not write obscure, weak pablum that no one could fault? I could obfuscate myself into oblivion like others did. But I knew readers wanted clear, forceful editorials on local topics, so I had to spend more time consulting reporters and news sources for accuracy and fairness.

Conditions improved during the Legislature, which produced plenty of hot topics with public figures to challenge. Elected officials couldn't get very far with claims of libel.

* * *

There were other matters to keep me on edge, however.

The temperature dropped to 30 degrees below zero at our house February 1, 1985, freezing neighborhood water lines and sending us to work without showers. By February 12, my nose ran faster than I could grab tissues. My contribution to City Desk that day was to rewrite a KUED program on the state of Utah education. Period.

By month's end, my insecurity complex had taken root. I doubted I'd ever make it as an editorial writer. Coming up with opinions loomed as the highest hurdle. In four days, I finished only three editorials -- one for the zoned edition and one just seven inches long.

"Maybe I'll do one on scents for the hell of it," I told Mimi. "I could lament the conflicting odors of deodorants, hand soap, dryer sheets, laundry soap, shampoo, conditioner, makeup, hand lotion, dish soap, aftershave, etc." After all, Bob Blair had successfully tackled similarly weighty subjects, and all those smells did make me sick.

Apparently I'd forgotten how I'd detested Blair's spoofs on office "girls" wearing pants and the burden of autumn leaves, zucchini and apricots.

* * *

At 33, I felt past my prime. I hadn't succeeded in my career, written a book or raised a family. Frown lines furrowed my forehead, and by replacing my huge eyeglasses with soft contact lenses, I'd brought them out into the open.

Bob Ottum

Somehow the success of Bob Ottum, the suave *Tribune* veteran who'd returned from *Sports Illustrated* to write a humor column for Split Page, rankled me. In a missive to Mimi, I complained:

I haven't even tried to write a novel yet, and I probably never will. Bob Ottum's <u>Tuesday Blade</u> made me think, "If he can do it, I can do it -- better." But the truth is, I have no imagination nor memory for detail, so I never will even do it.

Maybe. If I think his book was hokey, I imagine mine would be ponderous and full of spite and self-pity. I'd probably write a factual account of child abuse and family strife in Mormon country . . .

Ottum's dialogue was his own, his perception of people, particularly women, stereotyped. He exploited sex and violence. I especially puked at his comment, purportedly made by a female psychiatrist, that a young woman's sex organs don't wear out.

God, I can hardly stand the guy anymore, and he continues to pat me on the head and kiss me in the office. It's offensive, really. I now understand why Alice Blair thinks he's a creep, but I can't understand Bob's infatuation. I would have thought him more discerning, discriminating.

* * *

In late February, Denny and I met Paul Rolly at DB's to celebrate his appointment as UPI bureau chief. I was late because my "favorite" printer Handy had thrown half our slug lines (story names) away, forcing me to trace the slugs to do corrections on the next day's editorial pages. Rolly's pleasure over his promotion was tempered by concerns about his marriage and family. He was concerned about a friend's widow.

On the way home, sparks flew between me and Denny over the late hours I spent hunched over my computer, forcing him to get home to Stormy as late as 7 o'clock. I yelled back, pointing out that he dragged his feet in the mornings when I needed to read the paper and get to editorial meetings by 9:30 a.m. My normally affectionate, playful husband went ballistic, swatting my arm and spewing a string of four-letter names that ended with "lush."

As I lay awake that night, I imagined a divorce that would give me a chance at motherhood. Denny's difficult daughters would no longer be my problem.

After a few days of the silent treatment, though, we realized our relationship was suffering from several stress factors better endured together. I returned to my role as the straight person for a schtick that made me the butt of his jokes.

Sadly, Denny was no happier with work than I was and wanted to quit. He was sick of handling employee hassles as department manager. Our paychecks barely covered monthly expenses, and we had two years left on his dad's loan and five on the house loan. After "selling" our Honda to Stormy for $500 -- which she made no effort to repay -- we needed another car in order to drive separately to work sometimes, but we couldn't afford one.

Yes, I was slow on the job, partly because my most productive time of day was squandered on long, fruitless board meetings, pesky phone calls from Peter Scarlet and certain readers, and my ongoing obsession with clipping and saving news stories.

I didn't have the time or patience to track down local stories, my main interest, in the *Tribune* library, so I continued to compile a library of my own. When news clippings and press releases stacked up in my out-basket for a month or so, I'd file them in a frenzy late into the evening.

Frequently I started writing after 3 p.m., when I also had to proofread the next day's pages and do the duties of whichever writer was off. If I subbed for Blair or Fuller, I spent hours reviewing and choosing among countless wire-service columns so I could lay out the pages. If I worked for Hoffman, I toiled over letters to the editor requiring substantial editing. If my gut-wrenching cramps were acting up, I wasted precious time lugging myself back and forth to the restroom two floors below.

Photographer Paul Fraughton's invitation to a home-cooked Chinese dinner offered a break from our tension, but I used the occasion to get toasted and throw up through dinner. Terry Orme and wife Nancy Hobbs witnessed the spectacle. The only conversation I remembered afterwards was me calling Orme naive for thinking things could change at *The Tribune*. Of course change occurred eventually, and Orme was in the middle of it as a catalyst and victim. But that story comes years later.

* * *

Gallivan began including Denny -- and me, by extension -- among 20-year staffers invited each year to his Park City home, known as the Pig Farm in honor of Grace Mary Gallivan's porcelain pig collection. I finally got to know the jovial, warm and entertaining side of Gallivan and met his gracious family.

Gallivan's children and grandchildren guided our cars into a pasture where we dodged cow pies on our way to the backyard, where brilliant autumn leaves served as a backdrop for volleyball, storytelling and barbecue. When the sun went down, we gathered in the Cape Cod-style house to chat over an after-dinner drink.

The only downside was the perennial presence of Denny's former neighbor, who played in the Dixieland band, and his wife, Swamper's ally. I had to restrain myself from berating her for ignoring the abuse that occurred under her very nose.

* * *

A seemingly minor change significantly improved working conditions on City Desk. Will Fehr fired mostly absent Marilee Higley, opening the newsroom to someone who took seriously the job of answering phones so that reporters could focus on their assignments.

Ann Poore, while taking "wet newspaper" complaints for NAC for two years, had been badgering Korologos and Fehr for a job in the newsroom. They dragged their feet, apparently wary of her connection to her uncle by marriage, Jack Gallivan.

"I don't care what the hell I do, just as long as it's in the newsroom," she finally told Fehr.[655] When offered Marilee's job as City Desk secretary, however, she hesitated, not wanting to take away anyone's job. Fehr declared it his final offer, and she relented.

It wasn't as if Marilee actually did the job. For years, the good-time girl spent afternoons sleeping off Harvey Wallbanger lunches. Even when sitting at her desk, she missed -- or refused to answer -- most incoming calls,[656] leaving the task to harried reporters. (Sadly, a few years after leaving *The Tribune*, Marilee died at age 48, leaving best friend Helen Forsberg to raise one of her daughters.)

Ann Poore and Jack Gallivan had more than family in common. Gallivan's mother died when he was 5; Ann lost hers, Peggy Ivers Poore, at 3 1/2.[657] Gallivan moved in with his maternal aunt Jennie Judge Kearns; Ann spent 18 months with her maternal aunt Grace Mary Gallivan.

But by 5, Ann's life took a different turn. She became an Army brat and moved from Japan to Germany, Virginia, New York and southern California, where she became president of her junior high school. She skipped high school to start Victor Valley College at age 16. Again, she was elected class president.

Having lived on diverse military bases -- her dad's housekeeper and her 9th-grade date were black -- Ann felt deeply about social equity. She spent one Sunday afternoon sweltering in 90-degree heat in a locked car after refusing to enter a whites-only restaurant in Virginia. She also made grape marches in Salinas with Cesar Chavez and civil rights marches in Monterey and Salinas.

When the Gallivans lured Ann back to Utah to care for her grandfather, James Ivers, she enrolled in the University of Utah, where she helped the school's first African American student body president, Grover Thompson, get elected in 1971. I was there but didn't know Ann, who might have served me as an underage barmaid at the Twilite Lounge my summer as make-up editor, too.

With a bachelor's degree in sociology and English in hand, Ann won a scholarship to study social work for a year. She was particularly interested in social justice, but caseworker experiences let her down. One woman's public subsidy was cut by what she earned ironing shirts at 10 cents apiece. A computer glitch prevented another woman from getting socks for her kids for Christmas.

Still wanting to improve the society, Ann switched to law school. After working as a teaching assistant for the Chicano Law Student Association's program in criminal law, however, she decided to try working her way into a position with impact at NAC.

Sitting between Bob Bryson on the right, Frank Brunsman on the left and Randy Peterson across the desk, Ann controlled 65 or more phone lines on City Desk. With no voicemail, she fielded messages for news writers and editors away from their desks, putting pink message slips into staffer files in the puke-green cabinet on the north wall of the newsroom. "It was onerous," she recalled decades later.[658]

Still, Ann found time to write advance obituaries, mostly for leaders of the LDS Church, staffers and newsworthy locals like Utah Symphony Conductor Maurice Abravanel. Her long interview at the maestro's home gave *The Tribune* a leg up when he received the Presidential Medal of Freedom.

"We had it in the can way ahead of the *DNews*, and their music writer was furious," Ann said. "Front Page. Carolyn Abravanel invited me to the funeral, an honor. I threw a shovelful of dirt on his casket."[659]

She also wrote an obituary for photographer Van Porter. After the funeral, she "got very drunk" on Walker Red with his wife and drove up the canyon in the snow instead of home in the valley.

As Ann worked her way onto the Copy Desk and into writing for Arts and Entertainment, she assumed the secret of her family connection was safe. That is, until Aunt Grace Mary Gallivan identified herself as such in a phone message. What Ann didn't know is that staffers knew the truth early on but didn't mention it.

If we'd gotten acquainted earlier, Ann and I might have become better friends. By the time we met in the '80s, she was too intense, emotional and obtuse for me. And I didn't trust my big mouth with one of the Gallivan clan.

Ann explained her unusual personality:

The thing about skipping high school is that it's a socialization process I missed out on. I've always been a little strange! Especially at things like parties. And I never learned about stuff like makeup or hair or clothes.[660]

I really thought I could make a difference in the world, hippie that I was. And am. I learned the only way I could do that was to be an editorial writer. YOU were the only person who told me that one day I might land there. That was after I made it to the Copy Desk. Anyway, Jay [Shelledy] came along [as editor], and that was the end of my career at the paper. I couldn't bear it.[661]

But that wasn't the end of Ann's involvement with paper. Long after her aunt and uncle departed and *Tribune* survival was at stake, she became part of the newspaper's institutional memory through research for The Newspaper Project. That part of the story is yet to come.

* * *

In mid-May, Paul Rolly lifted our spirits by returning to *The Tribune* rather than accept an offer from the *Deseret News*. Although he'd succeeded as UPI's bureau chief -- indicating, incidentally, that he could have been a good city editor -- the news agency faced bankruptcy. The day he was told not to cash his UPI check because of a budget shortfall, he called Will Fehr, who carried a job application upstairs to him that afternoon.

Rolly soon was covering the Utah Legislature, a job he was born to perform. With more sources than ever, he could uncover political scandals like no one else on staff. He could bang out a more tightly written, accurate blockbuster in record time, with or without notes.

Eventually, UPI reporters Dan Harrie, Cherrill Crosby and Tom Harvey followed their former chief to *The Tribune*.

* * *

Springtime failed to thaw tensions at home.

After living with "horrible pain" for months after damaging knee cartilage on the ski slopes and refusing to wear her brace, Stormy demanded surgery three weeks before high school graduation.

I suggested it might be tough getting across the stage in a cast to pick up her diploma, assuming she had enough credits despite missing so many classes. "I can handle it," she snapped. "And I work in the office, remember? I'll have the credits."

On a brief backpacking break in San Rafael Reef with Jim and Barbara Woolf that weekend, I asked for advice. Like me, Barbara had two teen-age stepchildren.

"I wish Barbara would tell me once in awhile that she appreciates my ability to balance competing interests between her and the kids," Jim offered. Barbara countered that it was tough with Chloe running away and putting out her number as a woman offering callers a good time.

Denny and Diane with Barbara and Jim Woolf hiking in San Rafael Reef.

Not much help there.

Denny and I returned home to a drastically depleted supply of prescription drugs and a teenager screaming about being treated like a child. "You don't even care if I'm in pain!" she howled. "You have no right to tell me what to do!"

Naturally, Stormy got her surgery, and Denny spent the next three weeks driving her to the bus stop and school. He even supplied booze and money for her senior sluff party. Graduation night, she proudly hobbled across the stage on crutches. She looked lovely.

Stormy was less lovely a few days later, when I counted 12 damp, rancid towels on the floor of her bedroom and bathroom.

"We're running out of clean towels," I told her. "You need to do your laundry."

"You fucking bitch!" she snarled. "If you don't stay out of my life, I'm going to kill you!"

Denny didn't have time for our fights. Besides cartooning for Korologos in his spare time that summer, he faced a true deadline on a part-time neighbor's book project. Paleontology Professor Leonard Radinsky from the University of Chicago had hired him to illustrate the book with mechanical dinosaurs. He had to work fast, because Radinsky was dying from stomach cancer.

I took another needed break to visit my parents, who were buying a house in a small ranch town 60 miles north of San Diego, where Mom still worked for the Department of Defense. Rancho California, later known as Temecula, would become family headquarters.

* * *

I returned to bang my head against the wall in Editorial as Fuller edited my work with a heavy hand. My June 2 editorial demonstrates my point. The original version began:

> All's well that ends well. Unfortunately, that platitude only partially applies to G. Leland Burningham's early retirement as state superintendent of public instruction.
>
> Other cliches more precisely characterize the case: The Utah State Board of Education copped out, let the superintendent off the hook and left the public holding the bag.
>
> A board-appointed, fact-finding committee acknowledged the "inescapable fact that there is serious doubt about the suitability" of Dr. Burningham's continued service as the state's chief school officer. The panel's conclusion is largely based on a state audit critical of the superintendent's

handling of state travel reimbursements, sick leave transfers and overtime and bonus payments from his office budget to himself.

A later paragraph said,

As has become his pattern, then, the superintendent worked out a sweet deal that saves his professional reputation, at least on his employment records, and pads his pockets with public money.

Fuller removed "sweet" and changed the last phrase to *"with minimum loss of his publicly paid income."*

Another of my paragraphs said,

Though relatively small, compared to his $65,000 annual salary, the sum [$46,000] symbolizes the school board's inappropriate approach to the unsavory episode.

Fuller changed the last phrase to: *"the sum reflects the school board's timorous approach throughout this entire episode."*

My conclusion:

If board members wouldn't even fire him for good cause -- judgmental lapses unbecoming of a public official -- one wonders what it would take to spur them to action. Or what power the superintendent held over what seem to be spineless elected officials. While state residents are rid of a counterproductive controversy, they're stuck with more bills and the impression that the commander has abandoned a rudderless ship.

Adjustments were warranted, but I was aiming at a hard-hitting, clear and succinct statement. Fuller's wordy changes took readers down a leisurely, winding path that sounded nothing like me and muddled my message. His version:

If board members couldn't exact dismissal for ample cause -- judgment lapses unacceptable from a public official in a position of high and conspicuous responsibility -- what would it take to prompt such occasionally essential action? While state residents are rid of a prolonged, embarrassing and unbecoming controversy, they're

stuck with additional, difficult-to-justify costs. Worse, the impression grows that those chosen to carefully tend the state's public education policies and frugally manage related -- usually scarce -- resources, do so unable to exercise strict personnel discipline, even when that obligation is clearly required.

In the news business, we called this carpentering.

* * *

Bob Blair retired in August after 37 years at *The Tribune*, leaving me his desk, old reference books and peers. My work days in the newsroom were over. I cried myself to sleep that night.

Hoffman, elevated to "senior editorial writer," picked on me incessantly my first week as a full-time member of the 3.5-member staff. He argued with everything I said. Thankfully, Fuller warmed up a little as my new boss. He adored his new title: editorial page editor/chief editorial writer.

It became common for me to work alone Saturdays, mostly an editing exercise that caused stomach pains and a racing pulse the next 24 hours while fretting over my failure to finish an editorial for the Monday shift.

On my recommendation, Jim Woolf replaced me as the part-time editorial writer. Unfortunately, I had to concede to his expertise on environment, one of my favorite topics. Since Hoffman respected Woolf's opinion over mine, he softened his defense of local industries' pollution controls.

With brutal honesty, Woolf let me know I had a reputation for freezing under pressure -- or at least getting a slow start on the work day. He was right, but I didn't like hearing it. Was I the only one requiring peace and quiet to concentrate? When I worked on deadline, there were fewer interruptions and could bang out something quickly, without all the second-guessing and fine-tuning.

Withdrawing from my addiction to the public recognition that came with news story bylines eroded my ego. From now on, I would get little credit or even criticism for my work as an anonymous writer of the publishers' opinions (or my own opinions, as usually was the case). My colleagues offered little praise, and I felt like a nobody -- at least for awhile.

Offsetting the loss of public identity was the behind-the-scenes peek at powerbrokers in action. In Editorial Board meetings, I learned why *The Tribune* rarely altered its staid appearance and approach to the news. Gallivan ordered Fehr to cover certain sacred cows and to quit changing graphics that had "worked just fine" for decades. In other words, if it ain't broke, don't fix it.

In a *Tribune* retrospective July 24, 1988, Gallivan attributed the lack of graphics changes to time-honored tradition:

> *The Tribune's conservative, credible appearance was largely due to [Editor Bert] Heal's expertise in typography and a reflection of his own (and, of course, [Publisher J.F.] Fitzpatrick's) integrity. [Heal] was never fond of the "ugly sister" [Telegram] thrust upon him with its bold, sanseraphed [sic] headline makeup and its overplay of insignificant local news.*[662]

As noted earlier, Fitzpatrick died in 1960.

* * *

Another Editorial perk was membership in the National Conference of Editorial Writers (NCEW). Fuller, Hoffman and I technically took turns attending its annual state-side meeting and an international fact-finding trip. Unfortunately for me, the publisher usually cited budget constraints on my turn to go overseas. Sort of like the time I lost John Cummins' cubicle. Not that I was paranoid.

Not all NCEW activities were fun and games. While preparing for my first convention in Colorado Springs in late September, I critiqued the editorial sections of several other newspapers. I was petrified, because I had no frame of reference for evaluating other newspapers than the *Deseret News*. Even worse, I had no time at work for the laborious task, so I took it home. To Denny's dismay.

The convention helped put my role and performance into context. In touring NORAD and sitting in on discussions of defense programs like Star Wars, I gained greater appreciation for the complexity and importance of the profession. Other newspapers, I learned, handled editorial meetings, guest commentary and letters to the editor much as we did. Their participants criticized our pages as bland, with small illustrations, too few letters to the editor and too many long, confusing editorials.

The social side of the event reminded me of high school and the newsroom. Fewer than 10 percent of participants were women. Some men were on the make. When I shut down a writer from Nebraska, he turned to a woman standing behind him. A drunken Vietnam veteran stalked me in the hotel, provoking me to skip out early.

Back home, I was required to make a formal report to the Editorial Board. After summarizing reviews of our pages and proposing improvements, Gallivan and O'Brien quickly changed the subject, and nothing changed. My final convention task was to write an article for NCEW's journal about the importance of letters to the editor.

* * *

Eventually I regained my sense of identity as a journalist. Community leaders respected the Editorial Board enough to try to sway our opinions. Some readers seemed impressed -- or surprised -- that I was an editorial writer. As if my position were important. Some outside groups, like Planned Parenthood and the American Civil Liberties Union, praised me publicly for editorials.

I perversely enjoyed male movers and shakers looking past me in Editorial Board meetings, assuming I was a secretary, and then squirming or ignoring me when I led interviews about their issues. Some stubbornly directed answers at my male colleagues, who deftly steered them back to me.

* * *

Major international and culturally significant local events attracted our attention in 1985, among them:

-- Ronbo, as I privately referred to the President, sent U.S. jets to apprehend three Palestinians who'd hijacked the cruise ship Achille Lauro. The United States was upset with Egypt for arranging a deal with the hijackers and Italy, which had freed the hijackers' leader.

-- A bomb mailed from Utah injured two people at the University of Michigan, reigniting fears from 1981, when an unexploded bomb was found at the University of Utah, and 1982, when a bomb sent from BYU injured someone at Vanderbilt University.

Utah's connection to the mysterious bombings would continue with another bomb injuring Salt Lake City computer store owner Gary Wright in 1987. Eventually the culprit was identified as reclusive mathematics prodigy Theodore Kaczynski, by then known as the Unabomber. While keeping a house in the Montana woods, he had often worked at odd jobs in Salt Lake City, enabling him to send explosives undetected for years.

-- Ronnie Lee Gardner, who'd killed a Salt Lake City bartender in 1984, was sentenced to death, becoming an historical example of Utah's unique culture. An accomplice had slipped Gardner a gun on his way to the courthouse, and the escapee shot bailiff George Kirk and attorney Michael Burdell.

Because Utah still permitted executions by firing squad in 1984, presumably because Mormon doctrine requires blood atonement for murder, Gardner became one of the last three American inmates to die that way, in 2010. The other two were Gary Gilmore, already mentioned, and John Albert Taylor, who raped and strangled an 11-year-old Ogden girl in 1988 and was executed in 1996.

-- Two Salt Lake City residents died in bombings involving the Mormon Church. I jotted my initial reaction in my journal October 20:

> Some bozo bombed two Mormons, apparently over historical church documents. One of the victims was Kathy Sheets, wife of the actual target Gary Sheets and the favorite aunt of Ann Kilbourn at work. Another was Steven Christensen, a document collector and son of Mac Christensen, the guy in the commercials who sells missionary and two-for-one suits -- the kind I bought for my editorial wardrobe. The suspect, Mark Hofmann, also blew himself up -- or almost. His car was demolished, anyway.

The Tribune's October 17 Page One story, written by Jim Woolf, Mike Carter and Gus Sorensen, identified Hofmann as the bomber. Reporter Dawn House Tracy had been tracking the nerdy Mormon as the master forger who duped the Mormon Church and others, like Christensen, into buying his embarrassing "discoveries" for big bucks and then suppressing them.

The "white salamander" letter, for one, sold for $40,000. The phony letter from early Mormon convert Martin Harris claimed a white salamander, rather than an angel, appeared to Joseph Smith upon discovery of the gold plates translated into the Book of Mormon. Before the murders, Pat Bagley had slipped the cocky creature, depicted with top hat and cane, into his cartoons in the newspaper, books and even on t-shirts. The joke died along with Hofmann's two victims.

Dawn House

Dawn House Tracy, a *Provo Herald* reporter I recommended to Will Fehr in 1983 after covering a Board of Regents meeting with her in Orem, began her *Tribune* years writing features for Lifestyle. Wearing a modest dirndl skirt and short pageboy, this atypical Mormon mother of five could not control her pit-bull nose for scandal for long. When Fehr loosened her leash, she attacked one high-profile, LDS-oriented story after another.

Besides the Hofmann forgeries and her polygamy investigations, she wrote riveting background for the murder trials of Ron and Dan Lafferty, who in the name of God in 1984 slit the throats of their sister-in-law Brenda and her 15-month-old daughter. Ron Lafferty, who had been bishop of Dawn's LDS ward in rural Utah County, blamed Brenda for his break-up with his wife. Like the other stories, this case hinged on religious fanaticism. The Lafferty brothers had become fundamentalist Mormons, fancying themselves prophets.[663]

It would be a few more years before she experienced the horror of her own brother's death at the hands of the son of another zealous Mormon, John Singer.

A 1970 Brigham Young University graduate who dissected her own beliefs to the point of "exiting" the church, Dawn House examined the reasons behind off-beat Mormon events. My early image of her, as a young mother preparing dinner in front of stacks of fruit preserves in a country kitchen, never squared with her aggressive, tenacious reporting style.

She was raised as Darlene House in Azusa, California, by a tough father who died young. Her stepfather was a Mormon she learned to love and respect. Her own marriage to BYU sweetheart Mike Tracy disintegrated during her exiting process, splitting their five children between them and making her available for a future *Tribune* relationship.

* * *

The day after the Hofmann bombings, **Russell Weeks,** wearing mustache, wire-rim glasses and sardonic smile, joined the police beat. All the other crime reporters were chasing down leads, so the Army veteran from small-town Idaho covered a street-corner news conference on the bombings. It was a day to remember in a year that changed his life.

Will Fehr's first question during his job interview was, "So, you know Roger?" Roger Porter, the first newspaper editor to hire Weeks, had worked for Fehr before marrying Lifestyle writer Bernie Moss and taking over his father's newspaper, the *Rexburg Standard Journal.* Porter's nod got Weeks the job.

To Weeks, Salt Lake City "seemed to be one of those places where one could turn a corner and find direction where it was waiting to meet you."[664] Cathy Free was one of those things waiting around the corner.

As a police reporter, Weeks didn't log in a lot of time in the newsroom, but he dropped by at noon so his new boss Randy Peterson could connect a face with the voice on the phone. That was when he and Cathy noticed one another.

Cathy invited Weeks to dinner in Park City, paying with one of her *People Magazine* checks. He drove his new red Fiero because her pink VW was losing its floor and firewall to corrosion. They clicked, and within two years, they married. Many of their days off were spent "finishing up 'weekenders' [non-breaking news stories] and hanging out in the newsroom."[665]

The couple also attended Halloween parties at our house, pool parties at Jack Schroeder's and the annual Christmas "ball" at Fort Douglas "where staffers could smoke as much as they wanted." The common thread of these social events "was the natural friendliness of staffers."[666]

Russell Weeks and Cathy Free pose for 1987 wedding invitation.

Weeks enjoyed working with other police reporters both inside and outside *The Tribune.*

Gus [Sorensen], Hal Schindler and Jennings Phillips [the former city commissioner whose political antics led to structural changes in city government] might disagree, but Mike Carter, and on the TV side Brian Shiffer [briefly a *Tribune* staffer], Ken Connaughton and John Harrington, were the best police reporters I've ever met. I'd add Brent Israelsen when he worked at the *Deseret News* [before *The Tribune*]. He was always sneaky good. I loved his sly smile.

Everyone there could be a pain at times. John Harrington and Vaughn Roche [another short-timer at *The Tribune* who shifted to psychotherapy] punched it out in the police newsroom over a story they disagreed on. But on the whole they were great to know."[667]

Weeks was intrigued by the human element of crime, particularly the ability of sociopaths to get away with tremendous lies.

I saw a pedophile Mormon bishop get a long, long sentence because the *Deseret News* had run a series of articles about how lenient Judge David (Set 'em Free) Dee was . . . I saw a hopeless drunk describe a fight where he killed a man as self defense, and his description of the fight was so chaotic and uncertain that it rang dead true. He was acquitted the day [county attorney] Ted Cannon was convicted of sexual harassment.[668]

Weeks' life changed profoundly when he followed the footsteps of Conrad Walters, Brian Wilkinson and Hal Spencer to the City Hall beat. Decades after leaving *The Tribune*, he still spent his days at City Hall as the City Council's information specialist and public policy analyst. By then he had worked with every mayor and city council member since Palmer DePaulis "midwifed the blue print the city follows to this day."[669]

As Weeks described it, Ted Wilson helped clean up city government, DeeDee Corradini was "the greatest reader of that blue print," and Ralph Becker followed it as a member of the Planning Commission that created it. "Rocky [Anderson] was too caught up in other things to notice the city still followed the footprint."

* * *

Our 1985 Halloween Party was pretty tame, with guests clearing out by 2:30 a.m. To me, that meant the bash was a bust.

As usual, Bob Woody got lost in a snowstorm on his way to Summit Park. A student staffer high on drugs fell into our downstairs stained-glass bathroom door, cracking it, before passing out against the upstairs bathroom door, blocking party-goers urgently needing the toilet.

As Yasser Arafat, Fuller twirled a tipsy Stormy around the living room while his wife Lyla flaunted her belly-dancing garb. Someone dropped a cigarette on our new wool carpet, which Denny's brother doused with scotch. Lance Gudmundsen stumbled into our coat closet. Paul Rolly and Barbara Woolf snoozed on our bed. I searched frantically for Peter Scarlet, fearing he'd frozen in a snowbank, when he was simply bending the ear of my neighbor, Westminster College's current PR representative Dana Tumpowsky.

Next day I stayed home to work on an editorial in peace, but I lacked enthusiasm after Denny told me, supposedly in jest, that my speech was as stilted as my writing. I took a couple of stabs at humor anyway, castigating Christmas catalogs and cologne shoppers. As usual, Fuller rewrote them, but as I told Mimi,

"he didn't ruin them this time, just rewrote the second half. I'm deluding myself into thinking I could ever be a real writer."

Flim-flam Robert H. Woody at Halloween.

Tim Kelly, Steve Brown and Ana Daraban.

Keri Schreiner and Mike Carter.

Nancy Hobbs and Terry Orme.

Tom Harvey, Joan O'Brien and Ann Poore.

Myrlene and Mike Korologos

Paul Rolly and Barbara Woolf before party's end.

Steve Baker and Natalie Mayfield.

Colleen and Herb Price at Halloween.

* * *

There were weightier issues to worry about with Moammar Khadafy and Ronald Reagan exchanging threats of war. Arab nations detested us and Israel even then. Thankfully, the Middle East was Fuller's area of expertise after he met with Yasser Arafat on a recent NCEW trip.

Each of us editorial writers specialized in specific international regions. In addition to the Middle East, Fuller focused on Cuba and South America, two other areas he visited with NCEW. Hoffman always wanted to see the land of his German ancestors and South Africa, so northern Europe and the African continent were his province. NCEW took him both places.

By default, I covered Asia. At least the Vietnam War struck a chord with me because of its influence on my peers and the anti-war movement. The Soviet Empire, Bob Blair's bailiwick, was up for grabs. Though mildly interested, I stood back until someone else filled that void. I needed a lot of self-education before taking that on.

I preferred domestic issues my male colleagues usually skipped: child care, education, public health policy, local laws, political ethics, state and local government and social justice. I advocated separation of church and state, the preparation of women for productive careers and education reform. Before and after Woolf worked with us, I sounded the alarm against turning Utah into a nuclear waste dump.

My September 27 editorial killed several birds -- favorite topics -- with one stone:

Denny Green, Maxine and Neil Passey.

Utahns have been embarrassingly slow to wake up to reality. Indications are that today's girls, who will be tomorrow's working women, still are not preparing for meaningful careers. Consequently, they'll be stuck with the low-level, unskilled jobs that will deprive their children of many of life's opportunities.

The latest college-entrance test scores prove the point. While Utah's college-bound students generally outdo national peers on the American College Test, the state's females tarnish the state's math showing. Local girls scored a 15.5-point average on the math test last year, compared to a 16-point national average for females and an 18.7-point state average for males (the maximum score is 36 points).

Since the male test score is respectable, this state-to-nation deficiency can't be blamed on Utah's dearth of qualified math and science teachers. It's possible, but highly unlikely, that some kind of math psychosis or innate disability afflicts a disproportionate number of females.

A more credible culprit is the community's archaic attitude about women in the workforce. Parents still are not convinced their daughters some day must support themselves and their families, so they aren't steering them toward school subjects that will prepare them for that prospect.

Most Utah women do, indeed, work outside the home, whether they want to or not, according to a recent Utah Department of Employment Security study. Many are unskilled or semi-skilled, single parents whose families depend on substandard wages. One-third of female-headed households lived below the poverty level in 1970.

Unless young women change their orientation, this situation will worsen, economic pressures will force them into the labor market in greater numbers, and they still won't qualify for satisfactory salaries. Meanwhile, the state will support no small number of these women with welfare, and their children will suffer lives of scarcity.

The subjects studied in school affect career choices. Avoiding math, even in high school, restricts job options or at least stalls progress toward the most lucrative. Students cannot enroll in engineering, medicine and business coursework, for example until they have a strong foundation in mathematics.

It just isn't fair, or smart, to send young women into society with misconceptions about their futures. School counseling on the importance of all education, including math, must be stepped up in Utah. Even more critical, though, is the need to rouse parents and community leaders from their dreams of days gone by. [670]

Julia J. Kleinschmidt, director of Westminster College's Women's Career Exploration Program, praised the editorial as "beautifully written and well-stated. This is a message which we struggle to convey through our projects in our Women's Career Exploration Program, but the Prince Charming myth dies hard! We need to keep hammering and chipping away at outdated attitudes and habits, and editorials such as yours make fine nicks and dents!"

My arguments sometimes precipitated change. After haranguing lawmakers for years about Utah's unreasonable child-custody statutes -- statutes the Gruesome Twosome used against Denny and his daughters -- my editorials helped persuade them to equalize responsibility for child support, expand home evaluations in custody decisions and give divorced parents equal access to children. Evelyn Ward, a grandmother whose son faced custody and visitation battles, championed the cause with Utah Parents for Children's Rights. She would call and write me thank-you cards occasionally, and on March 28, I received this note: "Your editorial in this morning's paper is beautiful."

Family pressures and lackluster interest ended Woolf's stint in Editorial, giving his former brother-in-law, Tim Fitzpatrick, a crack at it. As a physics graduate, he was given first dubs on environmental and other subjects involving science.

As a concession to his upstairs rank, Fitz sometimes wore a tie with his rumpled shirt, tousled hair and high-top tennis shoes, but he clearly felt no need to adapt to the Editorial Board's manner of dress. Neither did he devote his full day to the job. Rather, he dashed in and slipped out, sometimes turning in an editorial that day, sometimes not.

I envied his laid-back approach to the job. I supposed his calm self-confidence related to his status as our renowned publisher's grandson. Like Woolf, however, he chose to return to the newsroom.

* * *

For the first time, instead of the annual Christmas Even spaghetti lunch at Lamb's Grill, *The Tribune* threw a staff Christmas party with dinner, drinking and dancing at a nice hotel, the Sheraton. An acquaintance, Joe Muscolino, led the big band music. We cleaned up well, and camaraderie filled the ballroom. It was a morale booster that made us feel like valued employees.

Denny and I also attended a classy Christmas party at Herb and Colleen Price's home in the foothills. Herb, NAC's upbeat but aging general manager, knew how to have a good time. He loved booze and women, including the charming young nurse he'd married. The couple had attended a couple of our Halloween parties.

* * *

By the end of the year, *The Tribune* employed 137 staffers. The 39 women, mostly part-timers, secretaries or clerks, remained a minority, but their ranks had soared since 1972, when I entered the scene. Barbi was still the highest-level female editor. Actually, the only one.

Barbi Robison, top femaie editor in 1980s.

[653] Brian Wilkinson, "Judge Restores Hotel's Water Supply," *The Salt Lake Tribune*, December 15, 1984, p. B1.

[654] Ibid.; Conrad Walters, "Judge Orders Hotel to Pay Water Bill," *The Salt Lake Tribune*, December 19, 1984; Brian Wilkinson, "Trouble-Plagued Hotel Gets Mayor's Reprieve," *The Salt Lake Tribune*, December 27, 1984.

[655] Ann Poore email, August 2, 2014.

[656] Mike Carter to facebook's Tribune group September 27, 2012.

[657] Ann Poore email, November 22, 2014.

[658] Ann Poore email, August 2, 2015.

[659] Poore, August 2, 2015..

[660] Ann Poore, August 10, 2015.

[661] Ann Poore email, November 17, 2015.

[662] Jack Gallivan, July 24, 1988, p. 9T.

[663] Eric S. Peterson, "Blood Brothers," *Salt Lake City Weekly*, July 23, 2014.

[664] Russell Weeks email, June 4, 2015.

[665] Ibid.

[666] Ibid.

[667] Ibid.

[668] Ibid.

[669] Ibid.

[670] "It Adds Up, Women," *The Salt Lake Tribune*, September 27, 1985, p. A18.

33 - Up and Down in 1986

On January 28, the space shuttle Challenger exploded 72 seconds after takeoff. Six astronauts and teacher Christa McAuliffe died in the stunning space program fiasco. As a reporter, I had witnessed the test firing of a solid rocket booster like the one that blew up, somehow making the tragedy more personal for me. I could still feel and hear the colossal power of that huge rocket at Morton Thiokol west of Brigham City.

Predictably, one of our big guns -- not me -- wrote the editorial. As was our habit, we cautioned readers and leaders against rushing to conclusions. When it became known that Thiokol, a company with a major local economic presence, designed the O-rings that failed in freezing temperatures, we soft-pedaled the Utah connection.

Ironically, James Fletcher, president of the University of Utah my freshman year, was reappointed head of the National Aeronautics and Space Administration (NASA) to clean up the public relations disaster. As a Mormon and Pro-Utah booster, he had steered NASA toward Thiokol before his first space agency appointment in 1971. Many heads rolled after the Challenger fiasco, but the shuttle program itself survived until 2013.

Tribune staffers Anne Wilson, Nancy Hobbs and Terri Ellefsen, along with friends Vicki Varela and Suzie Nutting, were having babies, stirring up more discontent over my motherless status. Helen Forsberg, by then our dance critic, and Ann Kilbourn, a Lifestyle features writer, were the only other childless women my age at work. Wilson cut back her *Tribune* hours to spend more time with baby Katie; the others made good use of relatives and babysitters.

That old gnawing in my gut kicked into gear. I noticed signs of aging in the occasional gray hair, wrinkles, dark circles under my eyes, blemishes, flabby rear and poochy stomach. At 34, I was convinced, my time was running out. But as Shaka the Shrink would say, "Don't worry, be happy. You already have the only children you'll ever have."

A television movie, "Choices," with George C. Scott and Jacqueline Bisset, reinforced my poor-me saga. Bisset's character was pregnant at 38. Scott's character, who already had two children from a prior marriage and wanted to spend his latter years in peace with his wife's undivided attention (sound familiar?), insisted she choose between him and the baby. Although this was her only chance for the baby she'd always wanted, Bisset settled on Scott. Then they had the baby after all. I couldn't quit crying over the fantasy, frustration and sadness. A couple of days later, I brought it up with Denny. He declared the subject long closed. Even if he wanted another child, he reminded me, his vasectomy was irreversible.

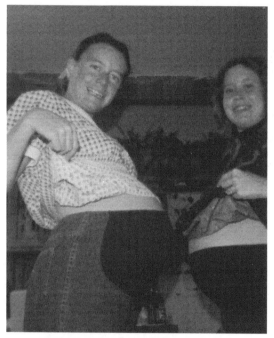

Anne Wilson and Terri Ellefsen show off at baby shower at my house.

* * *

February was particularly stormy. We got home night after night past 9 p.m., sometimes forcing Denny to plow snow past 11 p.m. despite his seemingly endless flu. Without any hints from me, my unadventurous husband planned a getaway to Club Med in Tahiti.

There were good and bad things about the vacation. Tahiti itself was beautiful, as we might have imagined Hawaii 50 years earlier. Snorkeling was outstanding; the sunsets stupendous. We met some interesting people, including a member of the Mafioso Joe Bonanno family.

Some Timely Tips for Tahiti Travel:

Not so nice was the scuba instructor who held my head under water, creating the sensation of drowning. I would have killed him if I could, and I've never put on scuba gear since. The cockroaches in our grass hut were big enough to saddle. The worst part of the trip, however, was the Club Med director's decision to arbitrarily bump us, a working couple with nonrefundable connecting tickets, from an overbooked flight to Los Angeles. He refused to let us trade seats with retirees wanting to stay extra days.

We collaborated on a travel story, complete with Denny's funny illustrations of giant cockroaches and supercilious Frenchmen. Sweet revenge. I exaggerated the negative as a matter of style, motivating one reader to rebut each criticism and conclude: "A trip is what you make it, and from the sound of the article, the writer seems like a very negative person and would not be satisfied anywhere or with anything!"

At that point, the airline offered to take care of our $500 return flight, and a travel agent offered us a free trip to retest Tahiti's waters. We respectfully declined and tried to peddle the story to larger newspapers. It was a laborious process in these pre-digital days because of the need to duplicate and send slides and paper copies. One editor commended our unusual approach as a fun read but not something that would fly in a travel section devoted to advertising.

* * *

After nine months of doctor appointments, Denny's ongoing headaches and tiredness were finally diagnosed as Epstein Barr Virus, later known as chronic fatigue syndrome. We were told it would never go away. His illness brought us closer together.

When I failed to react with obvious alarm, our neighbor Sharon Emerson, clingy and pushy after losing her husband to stomach cancer, insisted I was in denial about our dismal future. Then she Denny about finishing the illustrations for her deceased husband's dinosaur book. I declined her invitation to trade laundry chores for grocery shopping.

Adding to my pain was a longtime teacher friend's criticism of our "off-base" editorials. "It's difficult to lend them any credibility when they're written by people with such a shallow understanding of the subject matter," she opined. Now that slap smarted!

* * *

Denny talked me out of attending Vandra's third wedding June 27. "She's not a good friend," he said. "She only thinks about Vandra."

Actually, Vandra was still one of my Deep Throats at work, feeding me occasional news tips from Utah's Department of Social Services. But she was soon leaving for Washington, where she used *The Tribune's* internal dysfunction for inspiration toward a professorship in human resource management.

I was losing touch with another girlfriend, too. Vicki Varela had quit the *News* to become public affairs officer for the State Board of Regents, a position that put distance between us. She could no longer safely tell me about her job without giving me inside information for editorials. Sometimes it seemed she was lobbying me to support her agency's agenda.

Many Utah powerbrokers were regents, and Vicki had the common sense and ambition to protect and promote them. Ian M. Cumming, the media-shy chairman of Leucadia National Corp., an $8 billion company, would fly her places on his private jet. Mike Leavitt, a successful southern Utah insurance broker, became another mentor. Vicki deftly downplayed the inflammatory comments and cutthroat actions of Doug Foxley, who was on his way to the Legislature and a lobbying business that frequently attracted Paul Rolly's pointed pen.

* * *

Of all people, Gerry Cunningham asked me and Denny to go to dinner with him and his wife Diane that June. Though never friends, we accepted the date on the off-chance he might replace retiring Will Fehr as editor. After all, Jerry O'Brien liked the guy, and it would be unwise to offend him.

Gerry Cunningham, Randy Peterson and onlooker.

Privately, Denny and I discussed how horrible a Cuny promotion would be. "He's such a bully and egomaniac," I said. "God help us."

Our uneventful, stilted dinner turned out to be Cunningham's attempt to find out what we knew about Fehr's replacement and to urge us to put in a good word for him. As if we'd know the publisher's plans. Even if we did have influence, it would hardly be used in Cuny's favor.

* * *

Early that July, Rolly finished five days in jail for driving on a suspended license. He was unjustly punished, he told me, because the judge refused to give him credit for quitting drinking. He wanted to get even by finding a scandal to use against him. Knowing from experience how revenge could warp a journalist's motives, I hoped he'd let the matter drop, but that wouldn't be like Rolly.

* * *

Fuller had become less antagonistic and more complimentary about my editorials, and I controlled my writer's block often enough to leave editorials in the sock most weekends. Just in time to welcome my smug peer from the past, Paul Wetzel, to the department August 5.

By then, Wetzel had been a music critic seven years and had written arts features and laid out the Friday Entertainment section about a year. "I decided that the world would little know nor long remember my opinion of how the Utah Symphony had performed a Beethoven symphony," he said of his decision to move on.[671]

After his first few days as our part-timer, I grudgingly conceded that Wetzel learned fast. "He might be just swell to work with after all," I told Mimi. "He even finished his editorial by 2:30!" As if I, the queen of procrastination, could talk.

Paul Wetzel

* * *

Meantime, **Carol VanWagoner**, a former teacher and divorced Mormon mother of three from California, persuaded Fehr to hire her three days a week to resurrect the Newspaper in Education program. "We can introduce *The Trib* to young readers who will be loyal, paying subscribers someday," she suggested during her interview. "I'll visit classrooms, get teachers onboard, boost circulation and create a kids' page."[672]

VanWagoner didn't realize the paper already had a Newspaper in the Classroom program going at least as far back as Korologos' early days on promotion and kept barely alive by Cummins and then me and Scarlet, as education editors. We didn't do much more than take teachers' orders for a week of newspapers and then line up speakers as requested. But the premise was the same: Snare readers young.

It made sense to hire someone with the time, school experience and ambition to make the program a priority . . someone like Carol.

Her second day on the job, Carol tried to type up a story to introduce her program, but she had never used a computer terminal. There was no carriage return, and she couldn't figure out how to move to the second line.

I coolly resolved my dilemma by hitting the new-paragraph symbol, which stayed visible at the end of every line. I sent the story to Ben [Ling]. He walked over, leaned down, and kindly whispered, "Carol, you just keep typing. It wraps."[673]

Carol VanWagoner

About a year into it, VanWagoner's job became full-time, to which Woody remarked: "Give her an inch and she'll take over the whole damn newsroom. She'll probably have my cubicle before you know it."[674]

In fact, VanWagoner was a self-starter who found promotional projects to keep her busy, like writing a readers' advocate column and running an in-house store featuring shirts and pens with *Tribune* logos and books by cartoonist Bagley and outdoorsman Tom Wharton.

* * *

By now, Stormy and Winker had moved into an apartment together, reducing some of the friction between us. It helped even more that Swamper swooped into town to see Stormy for the first time in six years.

After their brief encounter, Stormy deemed me the best mother she could ever have. She even told me she loved me. I was so shocked I cried.

Later that month, Stormy and Winker acted as if they enjoyed themselves at *The Tribune's* annual picnic. Then they took us to a movie. For weeks, Stormy quit calling me Blubberbutt.

"Maybe their relationship has hope," Denny and I said simultaneously. "Maybe they're growing up."

That is not to say we were fully grown up. A few days before our annual trip to Lake Powell in October, Denny blew his stack when I failed to finish an editorial until 6:45, making us miss a meeting with his cousin. He didn't speak to me for two days, so I announced I wasn't going to Powell. He called my bluff, and I stayed home alone. My reward was a photo of the crew mooning me over the red rocks.

I was not the only Cole with problems. Less than a year after his only real girlfriend -- he fantasized about many -- died of cancer on his birthday, my brother Dick was fired from his job with the Department of Defense, supposedly because of his incriminating audit of the Blackhawk helicopter. Before he could hurt himself -- but not before Jehovah's Witnesses "saved" him -- my mother retrieved him from an Ohio psychiatric hospital to live with her and Dad in California.

About this time, Will Fehr offered to hire my younger brother Tom at $8 an hour in pagination, but Tom didn't want to return to Utah. Maybe that was best, given my poor track record with job recommendations.

When I took Stormy's advice to fly Lulu to Utah for Thanksgiving as a surprise for Denny, old stresses and resentments resurfaced.

Sour-smelling Lulu smoked and bragged incessantly about her military boyfriend and Jesuit school. She further embarrassed Stormy by coming on to Winker's brother. I breathed a fresh sigh of relief when she boarded the plane back to New York.

By Christmas, Stormy and Winker reverted to their obnoxious selves. They bummed expensive lunches off of us and offended Denny's mother, who invited the family to dinner every Thursday. They only came if nothing better turned up, and then they made gagging gestures behind Marge's back as she delivered dishes to the table. Sadly, Marge caught the slight in the mirror above the buffet. Stormy later claimed she threw up her dinner.

---

[671] Wetzel retirement remarks, October 2012.

[672] Carol VanWagoner email, August 10, 2015.

[673] Ibid.

[674] Ibid.

34 - Rolling Merrily Along in 1987

Denny started sculpting for fun, starting with a nice pair of terra-cotta monkeys, while I spent more time skiing around the neighborhood with Hairball. It was an uplifting way to enjoy clear days at the summit while smog from frigid inversions suffocated Salt Lake.

Denny's monkeys

My editorials generated occasional positive feedback, as seen from this Forum letter from Edward P. Itchon, deputy state fire marshal:

Recently you have written two very supportive editorials backing Utah State House Bill 5. The State Fire Marshal's Office wishes to comment on Diane Cole, who wrote both articles. During the interview I asked Diane to make it a point to say that our position was neutral and she said just that.

I have had a lot of contact with both the print and TV news media. I have requested of the reporters certain things such as I did with Diane, and only a few times have they done what I requested.

I'm writing this to commend Diane Cole on her integrity and reporting skills. She has brought respect to your paper with her honesty and ability. Thanks to Ms. Cole I will feel much better when I'm approached by the news media.

Mr. Itchon must have had some awful experiences with the media to mention such a minor matter, but I appreciated him taking the time to thank me.

It wasn't my habit to participate in writing contests, but I was among several staffers placing in the 1987 Utah-Idaho-Spokane Associated Press Association competition. Cathy Free came out on top with first place in light features, second place for columns and third place in serious features. She also was part of the team that took first place in spot news coverage of a January 15 airplane crash over Kearns. Others on her team included Mike Gorrell, Stephen Hunt, Mike Carter, Jim Woolf, Patti Auer and Robert Wood. Tim Kelly's "Reunited" won first in spot news photography, while my editorial, "Sex Education in Utah Schools Needs Facts, Not Indirection," placed second.[675]

Judges for the Utah Society of Professional Journalists (SPJ-SDX) were less impressed with me.

The Tribune Tattler

A Monumental Effort

News is the first rough draft of history. .... Ben Bradlee

It was characterized as a rout. There were some who said the opposition was over-matched.

Regardless of the description The Tribune staff achieved its greatest success in the Utah-Idaho-Spokane Associated Press newspaper competition. The Tribune amassed three first-place awards and a total of eight involving 11 staff members.

Seven reporters combined in a monumental effort to gain first place in the Spot News division with dramatic coverage of a midair collision of a SkyWest Western Express metroliner and a Mooney M-20C. The crash occurred near Kearns on Jan. 15.

The seven-person crew consisted of Mike Gorrell, Stephen Hunt, Mike Carter, Jim Woolf, Patti Auer, Robert H. Woody and Cathy Free.

But Cathy Free didn't stop there. She won a first, second and third in other categories. She took first place in light features, second in columns and third in serious features.

Tim Kelly, The Tribune's chief photographer took first place in the spot news photography category with a photograph of a family that survived a house fire. Staff Photographer Al Hartmann took second place in the feature category with a picture entitled "Serene."

Diane Cole took second place in the editorial category with a winning entry entitled "Sex Education in Utah Schools Needs Facts, Not Indirection."

The Tribune's Outdoor Editor, Tom Wharton, took a third place in the sports feature category.

The judges for the contest were from the Baltimore Sun and other Maryland newspapers. There were more entries this year than ever before and Jerry O'Brien, The Tribune's publisher, was completing his term as president of the organization.

There were many other people involved in the various projects that won awards including department heads, copy editors and desk editors. They share in this glittering moment in The Tribune's history.

My three submissions to that contest called for state action eventually taken by Utah officials. One recommended a combination of tax increases and school program cutbacks, another advocated tighter supervision of publicly subsidized private schools, and the third proposed better sex education. I blamed my poor performance on my measured, pedantic writing style aggravated by heavy editing.

Consider this conclusion on the first one:

Revenue for the public school system simply must be raised sufficiently [Harryism] to avoid a pattern of education problems that would have long-term, negative consequences for the state's economic well-being. Without suitably [Harryism] educated, employable residents, Utah cannot attract the industries and generate the revenue that will make future tax increases less necessary.[676]

Did I really write that rambling mouthful? It was hardly succinct or hard-hitting.

And how about the lead on the second editorial?

Home study has been developing into a new trend for dealing with Utah high school dropouts. As a controversial departure which qualifies for public funding, however, it deserves the closest possible monitoring and evaluation.[677]

Who would know from the lead that I was attacking a former legislator for milking public coffers by "educating" high school dropouts through "independent study" comprised of brief chats with teachers twice a month? I recognize Fuller's hand in there, but enough was mine to claim it.

On to the sex education editorial, one of my favorite hobbyhorses. It was my own style and less restrained than the other two, but it, too, could have been more pointed:

U.S. Surgeon General C. Everett Koop has given this state and nation outstanding advice for dealing with the deadly AIDS virus. It would behoove Utah educators, in particular, to let his recommendations influence public school policy.

Acquired Immune Deficiency Syndrome, the disease without a cure, has already killed about 15,000 of its 26,556 victims in the United States. The death toll will relentlessly rise as the disease spreads.

These grim facts scare people. Many, as seen by the recent decline in national support for legalizing homosexual relations, California's initiative to quarantine AIDS carriers and various lawsuits to keep AIDS-infected children out of the public schools, are striking out in the wrong direction.

Homosexual males are not the only ones spreading AIDS. Although they constitute three-fourths of the AIDS population, more and more intravenous drug users and heterosexuals are contracting the disease.

The quarantine idea is both unnecessary and dangerous. The medical community insists that the virus is spread through sexual contact, using contaminated blood products and sharing needles for intravenous drug abuse, not through casual association in public places. The fear of segregation would only send AIDS carriers underground at the expense of their own health and the public's.

Dr. Koop suggests a more rational approach to the AIDS problem. That is: Instead of attacking people, attack the disease through education.

"Many people -- especially our youth -- are not receiving information that is vital to their future health and well-being because of our reticence in dealing with the subjects of sex, sexual practice and homosexuality," he said the other day. "This silence must end."

The surgeon general, a member of President Reagan's conservative administration, believes sex education courses, starting at home and continuing through all school grades, should teach everyone how to protect themselves against AIDS. This means telling children that engaging in casual sex without condoms increases the risk of infection.

It would be difficult, under current circumstances, for Utah educators to follow Dr. Koop's suggestions. An effective sex education policy has been stymied by its moral implications.

By edict of the Utah State Board of Education, public schools statewide are prohibited from teaching the "intricacies of intercourse," "the acceptance of homosexuality" and "how to do it approaches to contraceptive techniques." Various value-laden interpretations of the timeworn policy have discouraged teachers from even broaching the subjects of intercourse, homosexuality or contraception. They are guided by irrational community fears that such discussion condones promiscuity.

Utahns obviously cannot teach their children how to avoid AIDS infections -- and death -- if they refuse to discuss its causes. The time to reconcile public attitudes and school policy with reality is long overdue in the state's sex education department.

I learned from this failure. For my SPJ-SDX submissions the next year, I loosened my grip on my security blanket -- education -- and struck out in a new direction.

Ollie North's escapades got my juices flowing in the shower July 9, 1987, inspiring me to quickly bang out an editorial that morning. This is what I submitted to the judges, flaws and all:

'Star' of Iran-Contra Hearing Doesn't Deserve Such Status

Lt. Col. Oliver North, the "star" of the Iran-Contra show in Congress this week, qualifies as an articulate and dedicated public servant who unswervingly stands by his convictions. But those convictions, coupled with his perception of the U.S. government and reality, are dangerously askew. [I took some flak for using "askew."]

In short, while Col. North's heart may be in the right place, his head is somewhere else. [Oh, my!] So were the heads of the superiors who unleashed his zeal on U.S. foreign policy.

Instead of simply answering congressional counsel's questions, the decorated Marine has arrogantly tried to convince the public, more than Congress, that his -- and the president's -- cause was just. He must not succeed, because there is no acceptable excuse for circumventing federal law and then covering it up. [I was oh, so naive.]

The U.S. Constitution gives Congress financial clout over foreign policy to prevent just the kind of unilateral decision-making conducted by the Reagan administration through Col. North. And Congress has clearly prohibited both federal military support of the Contras in Nicaragua and the sale of arms to Iran.

The key figure in this fiasco cannot seem to comprehend these concepts. Instead, he sanctimoniously and with matchless conceit subscribes to the notion that the end justifies the means;

that he is above the law; that he, instead of elected members of Congress, knows what's best for the American people and the world-at-large. He even went so far as to scold Congress for its approach to Nicaraguan policy.

Col. North feels he was forced to alter and shred government documents to protect important covert operations from the enemy, including, in his opinion, Congress. In fact, he was protecting the Reagan administration for failing to operate within the confines of the law and such publicly stated policies as refusing to negotiate with terrorists.

Col. North believes he could give a private operator, retired Maj. Gen. Richard Secord, a free hand with profits from the arms sales because it was "the Ayatollah Khomeini's money" and it was necessary to bypass the bureaucracy to get things done. He does not understand that profits belong to the seller, not the buyer. And that the bureaucracy exists to prevent just the kind of unilateral hip-shooting that Col North and his cronies performed.

The colonel continues to contend that he didn't solicit private funds to finance the Contras. Yet he admits to suggesting to private donors that the United States needed certain equipment and that the president would appreciate any contributions.

This week's witness is not simply playing semantics games. He apparently believes what he says makes sense, and top administration officials obviously thought so, too. Otherwise, they would not have indulged his antics on such sensitive foreign policy matters as long as they did.

It's understatement to suggest that this week's revelation about Col. North's nature is not reflecting well on the Reagan administration.[678]

My contest entry, which included criticism of Utah liquor laws and school zoning, took first place in 1988. The judge noted that "topics of public concern are attacked aggressively. While many papers were hailing Col. North, you rightly point out the danger of his taking foreign policy into his own hands and, without histrionics, rightfully put the matter in the president's lap."

The award improved my standing with my superiors. Fuller left more and more of my own wording intact. The encouragement gave me confidence to tackle new topics and to write faster and smoother, without having to weigh every word. All of which made editorial writing more satisfying.

That is not to say, of course, that my crusades could be counted upon to succeed.

Consider this one:

With courage and resolve, I took on the likes of Utah Technology Finance Corporation (UTFC), an outfit run with taxpayer money by the Cannon brothers (Grant, Chris and Joe) for themselves and their friends. That's my take on it anyway. Grant Cannon was founding director of the "agency" that ostensibly made publicly backed loans to high-risk business ventures, including some in which brothers Chris and Joe held a financial stake.

This was at least one time when I could agree with conservative Atty. Gen. David Wilkinson, who declared that UTFC, created in 1983, violated the constitutional ban against using public money for private purposes. Not only was it wrong to spend tax funds this way, there was little public control over the process.

Over the years, I argued repeatedly against state appropriations for UTFC. By the time I left *The Tribune* in 1998, the program still was going strong. I was amazed.

In 1994, *Tribune* reporters Dan Harrie and Tony Semerad found "at least 30 instances in which state officials and university scientists who influence economic-development spending also have had private ties to the companies profiting from the loans."[679] Chris Cannon, former chairman of Geneva Steel (who became a U.S. congressman in 1997) and brother of U.S. Senate candidate Joe Cannon (who became editor of the *Deseret Morning News* in 2006), had received loans worth $390,000. Loans went to other UTFC officers as well.

Not until 1999 did someone sponsor legislation requiring annual audits and prohibiting the agency from loaning money to businesses in which UTFC board members held an interest. The sponsor, Sen. Steven Poulton, a Salt Lake Republican, said: "I personally have tried to kill this agency myself, but it has too many friends. It cannot be killed."

* * *

Thanks partly to a $20,000 inheritance from Denny's Aunt Mabel, we got out of debt. Denny again seriously considered quitting *The Tribune,* this time to reduce our tax load, of all things, and to improve his health. I was worried. Surely we didn't have enough money to live on his freelance and my salary! Instead, we settled

for some unfinished oak furniture and a second honeymoon to San Francisco.

Denny's fun, romantic side was showing more often. The San Francisco trip was meant to surprise me for our 10th anniversary, and it would have worked if I hadn't happened upon the airline tickets while searching his desk drawer for a pencil sharpener. What I didn't anticipate was a new diamond ring to replace the one I'd lost skiing. We stayed in El Cortez Hotel again, listened to The Mamas & the Papas at the Fairmont Hotel and caught "Arsenic and Old Lace" at the Curran Theatre. After jumping some high hurdles, we had landed back in love.

Back home, Fehr agreed Denny could cut his week to three days beginning the next January. I was happy he'd be able to spend more time on his own projects -- and away from the downtown pollution that fostered chronic fatigue.

His first project? A backyard redwood deck for Stormy's upcoming wedding. The one featuring Winker, the self-possessed, immature loser. My goal was to get a healthy garden full of wildflowers going. Denny's next project: a hot tub and exterior paint.

"There's no relaxing for Denny," I told Mimi.

Denny's deck went to waste during the wedding because of snow -- in August. A sign?

Aside from some nasty cracks from Swamper's mother and hints from the groom's family that we'd done it on the cheap ($1,500), the event unfolded nicely. The radiant bride responded with uncharacteristic aplomb to implied criticism, and the handsome groom appeared happy, if a bit tipsy. Uneasy as the union made me, I was somewhat reassured by the apparent sanity of Winker's family, Mormon stock from Utah County.

A few days later at Park West, Denny and I attended our first concert together: the Grateful Dead, a throwback to the late 60s. Denny loved it. On the climb up the hillside, a Dead Head traded Denny his smelly, woven hoodie for enough money for a scalped ticket. The record-size audience buzzed like a beehive, in constant motion, with marijuana fumes wafting among the outside benches. Life was sweet -- for the moment.

Later that month, Stormy acknowledged she'd been abused at the hands of her stepfather and stepbrothers when a pre-teen. Gasp. I had suspected as much, but the girls had always denied it, leading me to conclude their years of insults and beatings -- of powerlessness -- had turned them mean.

Now my old suspicion and anger boiled up inside me, making me regret I'd failed to act on fantasies of sneaking into the Gruesomes' bedroom to blast them to the hell they deserved. I felt deeply sorry for the girls' hurtful childhood and for the mess it created for all of us. I hoped Stormy's revelation might start healing her and our relationship. Already she was more like the affectionate, bubbly girl I'd met in 1975.

* * *

Work waited for nothing and no one. I boldly proposed writing an editorial in favor of executing Dale Selby Pierre, or Pierre Dale Selby as he later called himself.

Normally liberal on justice issues, I favored the death penalty when there was no doubt of guilt in egregious crimes. I believed Selby should die for orchestrating the depraved Ogden Hi-Fi torture and murders that had horrified me as a high school teacher living in Ogden. He and William Andrews were the pair who forced five Ogden residents to drink Drano before shooting them.

In the Editorial Board meeting, Fuller approached my proposal with caution, reminding everyone of *The Tribune's* longstanding opposition to the death penalty. To my utter amazement, Jerry O'Brien, a devout Catholic, announced there were exceptions to the rule, and this was one of them. I wasted no time putting our position on paper and felt fine about it until I saw the next morning's edition.

Suddenly I felt sick about possibly contributing to another human's death, which in this case occurred by lethal injection August 28, 1987. By the time sidekick Andrews was executed June 30, 1992, I had no stomach for the subject. The rationale for my double standard was Andrews' secondary role. He wasn't the brains behind the rampage, even though a detective identified him as the organizer and Selby as the enforcer.

* * *

Occasionally my position as the first woman on the Editorial Board inspired requests for me to speak at schools or to participate in community organizations. The invitation-only Utah Women's Forum -- judges, attorneys, lawmakers and other women in powerful positions -- asked me to join their crusade to promote women in leadership roles, and I proudly accepted.

Among members were legislators Afton Bradshaw, Frances Farley and Karen Shepherd; IRS Director Carol Fay; Associate Higher Education Commissioner Cecelia Foxley; Dr. Mary Beard; state geologist Genevieve Atwood; University of Utah Professor Margaret Battin; Judges Christine Durham, Pam Greenwood, Sharon McCulley and Judith Billings; Salt Lake County Clerk Katie Dixon; Grethe Peterson, wife of University of Utah President Chase N. Peterson; and Norma Matheson, widow of Gov. Scott Matheson. I was flattered to think I belonged with such an array of successful people.

After attending a few Forum meetings, however, I realized this participation compromised my impartiality as an editorial writer. How could I comfortably criticize these women, their decisions or their priorities if I had to face them at the next meeting? Wouldn't my presence chill discussions among members who wouldn't want their views showing up in the newspaper? I also feared I might say too much about my own work situation, angering my bosses. What's more, the meetings took me away from work, requiring me to stay later into the evening.

I submitted my letter of resignation November 14, 1989. My reasons for quitting applied to other group involvement as well, effectively keeping me on society's sidelines. I certainly couldn't consider holding any kind of public office.

Before leaving the Forum, I nominated my old *Deseret News* counterpart Vicki Varela for membership, predicting she someday would be "well recognized for her talents and ideas about public policy." How right I was.

After representing the Board of Regents for six years, with a break in 1989 to sell Utah voters on a Winter Olympics referendum, she joined Gov. Mike Leavitt's inner circle as press secretary and deputy chief of staff. Then she switched to private industry, where as vice president of Kennecott Land she promoted the development of the Daybreak community. Next, she started her own public relations firm and in 2013 was appointed director of Tourism, Film and Global Branding for the Utah Office of Tourism.

Whether Vicki joined the Utah Women's Forum, I never knew. The higher she rose on Utah's political stage, the weaker our friendship grew. We lost touch when she left Leavitt's administration and I quit Editorial, creating the impression she no longer regarded me as an asset or a threat to be handled.

I did support many of the governor's priorities when Vicki was his aide, but I doubt it was in deference to her. At least I hope not. I openly criticized her boss' brainchild, Western Governors University, which I expected to become a diploma mill by giving credit for life experience and online classes. Apparently I was off-base, because the non-profit school still was going strong in 2016, with more than 50,000 students.

* * *

Whiling away one autumn afternoon at home, I contemplated my failure to fulfill my old dream of writing a book. I'd always blamed my youth and inexperience for my lack of a meaningful message, but now I offered Mimi a new excuse.

> I'm probably old enough, nearly 36, and experienced enough, having gone through divorce, step-parenting and 12 years of journalism, but now my memory's so poor I doubt I'd be able to draw much on my past. I've kept some semblance of my past in these journals [Mimi], but they're so focused on internal bitching, I doubt they'd serve the purpose of a memory.

I could have added that my work left me with little time and desire to write more.

With piles of past newspapers to catch up on, I turned away from my self-analysis. By God, I couldn't miss a single local story that might provide background or fodder for editorials. Never mind that story clippings would stew in my out-basket for months before I got around to filing them where I could find them.

This was one of my prolonged periods as editor of the Public Forum, a duty that fell to me about half the time. My dad, who had delivered the *Deseret News* to his Logan neighbors as a kid, thought it was neat that I worked on the Forum, his favorite part of *The Tribune*. He had no idea what a pain the letters could cause an editor like me.

It took me hours to plow through 15 or more letters each day, deciding which ones to use, sending out postcards or making phone calls to verify writers' identities, and then tightening and cleaning up the usable ones without changing their meaning. With space limits, I could publish about half the submissions, and those were restricted to six column inches or so. We wouldn't print more than one letter by any one writer each month, and we rejected cheap shots

and apparently libelous claims. Sometimes we would run several letters on a hot topic, but usually we tried to include a variety of subjects.

No matter how arduous this side job, our five-editorials-a-week quota stayed in place, applying steady pressure to produce, produce, produce. Consequently, I sometimes took letters home to keep up.

In October, I felt pains in chest when I took a deep breath. I blubbered to Mimi:

> It's that damn job, the relentless pressure to produce a statement every day. Sometimes I want to just coast, to chat with other employees like the others do. But no!
> I can't stand the stress, the expectations. I want a break! A big one so I can replenish the empty store of ideas.

To make sure I didn't have a heart attack like all four of my grandparents, I made an appointment with my internist. He concluded I was suffering from anxiety attacks and prescribed Valium to carry around as a prophylactic. I relaxed a little, and the attacks slacked off even without the pills.

Then my blood results came in, and the doctor's office reported that I suffered from Epstein-Barr Virus like Denny. I could expect chronic, as opposed to acute, symptoms of premature aging, sore throats and exhaustion.

It was a good thing I didn't believe it, because when I called for clarification two days later, the lab assistant said I was actually immune to EBV. A good lesson on health care.

That's when asbestos reared its sickening head.

For several weeks, the cancer-causing, fire-resistant insulation was being removed from our floor, stirring up dust and irritating our lungs. We were "protected" by flimsy flaps of plastic hanging in front of the elevator and in doorways. Workers wore white coveralls and simple face masks.

"I'll probably get cancer from it, although Harry and Wally think I'm paranoid," I whined to Mimi. "But they're the ones who don't believe Salt Lake has a pollution problem."

Hoffman still sometimes ranted about so-called misinformation supplied by various scientists and activists concerning Salt Lake Valley air and water. Not only was Kennecott Copper ahead of the game on pollution controls, he would declare, there was nothing to worry about from Dugway Proving Ground, which stored and broke down bombs carrying chemicals and viruses. He probably never bought the argument that Nevada's above-ground nuclear tests caused cancers in Utah, either, and he didn't protest hazardous waste dumps in the desert.

Granted, I was more environmentalist than business champion. I would rather promote a bird sanctuary on Utah Lake than tax credits for Kennecott, for example. But maybe that was because the filth of our air was so obvious, especially during winter inversions. And because big business had a history of valuing profits over public safety. And because public officials, eager for jobs, tax revenue and campaign contributions from big business, could not be trusted to protect us from the health hazards they caused.

Personal knowledge reinforced my cynicism. Denny's grandfather had made a fruitless attempt in the early 1900s to get compensation for dairy cows he lost to Kennecott toxins. As a Hill Air Force Base secretary in the late 1960s, my mother had typed a top-secret report about the death of thousands of sheep in Tooele County. Publicly, Dugway Proving Ground denied biological tests were responsible for the March 13, 1968 incident.[680] Not until 1998 did the federal government admit nerve gas sprayed from a jet 27 miles west of Skull Valley poisoned the sheep.[681]

* * *

For Thanksgiving, I flew to Temecula to celebrate with my family, the original source of my anxiety.

Dad was his old self, badmouthing my brother Tom's new Honda as too expensive and made by "Japs," who were "taking over the world." Used American cars, after all, were the love of his life, having owned a Model T and then spent the rest of his life repairing various models in his garage after work. And he would never get past his part in the war with Japan and Germany.

My oldest brother Bob -- all four of my brothers were still single -- theorized that all women were sluts who wanted to be slapped and ordered around -- unless they wanted to take over the world, that is. All four complained about Affirmative Action putting them at a disadvantage at work.

Mom completed the "Normal" Rockwell scene by stuffing her cheek pouches with dressing before interrupting anyone who tried to talk. After hearing what my brothers had to say, who could blame her?

* * *

On a higher note, Planned Parenthood of Utah gave me a community service award for furthering its goals and principles. "She has addressed [reproductive rights and better sex education] directly and honestly and . . . brought them more into open debate," Mary Carlson, director of community services, said during PPAU's annual awards dinner.

My only problem with the honor -- and I did consider it an honor, given the group's courageous approach to unplanned pregnancy -- was that it portrayed me as biased toward a controversial organization in Utah. Planned Parenthood was blowing my cover, if I even had one after my 1980 teen-pregnancy series.

---

[675] "Tribune Staffers Earn Honors in AP Competition," *The Salt Lake Tribune*, June 23, 1987, Page B1.

[676] "Finance Increases Essential For Utah Public Education," *The Salt Lake Tribune*, September 19, 1986, Page A18.

[677] "State Should Closely Scrutinize Developing Home Study Trend," *The Salt Lake Tribune*, July 27, 1986, Page A12.

[678] "'Star' of Iran-Contra Hearing Doesn't Deserve Such Status," *The Salt Lake Tribune*, July 10, 1987, Page A28.

[679] Dan Harrie and Tony Semerad, "Utah's High-Tech Connection: Private Ties, Public Money," *The Salt Lake Tribune*, January 30, 1994, p. A1.

[680] "Death of 4,500 Sheep Probed in Tooele," *The Salt Lake Tribune*, March 20, 1968, p. B1.

[681] Jim Woolf, "Army: Nerve Agent Near Dead Utah Sheep in '68; Feds Admit Nerve Agent Near Sheep," *The Salt Lake Tribune*, January 1, 1998.

35 - Easier Street in 1988

Denny and I had reached a financial plateau we'd enjoy for years to come. Another of his aunts left him money, enough to buy the vacant lot between us and the next-door neighbor and ensure future open space and quiet. Our beautiful, peaceful house was finished and in the clear. Aside from couches and a chair, we didn't need much new furniture. We added a tax-free bond and certificate of deposit to our slowly growing Individual Retirement Accounts, all of which made me feel secure and free to share with worthy charities. I was happy.

Work? It could have been better if, say, we added a computer terminal to our department and the blowhard bully within our ranks retired. Pat Bagley still distracted me with his phone conversations. Overall, however, my job stress was surmountable. We three editorial writers worked around our equipment shortage by editing letters to the editor by hand for a newsroom typist, making phone calls, researching topics in the *Congressional Quarterly* and other publications, or proofreading pages while awaiting our turn at the two terminals.

The publisher's only daughter, reporter **Joan O'Brien**, walked through Dick Rosetta's plate-glass doors at an office hot-tub party, sending her to the hospital with severed tendons in her hands, arms and legs. While recuperating with crutches, she moved first to Arlington, Virginia, to be with UPI reporter **Tom Harvey**, a quiet guy from Montana her father could hardly abide.

Did the publisher's animosity stem from his years competing with UPI while AP chief? After all, Harvey was a likable, good-natured and competent journalist. More likely, given his agreement to rehire Rolly when UPI's fortunes faltered, O'Brien simply believed no one was good enough for his baby girl.

I had met the smart perfectionist with long, strawberry blonde hair years before, while doing a story about her appointment as editor of the University of Utah *Daily Utah Chronicle*. After graduating, she had waited tables at Lamb's Grill until hired by *The Tribune*.

Joanieo, as some called her, was one of the most generous, brightest, politically savvy people I knew. Given her host of male admirers, she obviously exuded sex appeal. My brother-in-law Jerry, by then a single father, was smitten.

She often went to lunch with me and Denny, Paul Rolly and/or Jerry, who ate almost as slowly as she did. Joanieo compulsively used anti-bacterial wipes on her utensils and beverage rims, chewed each mouthful about 29 times and hated servers to clear other diners' plates before she finished eating.

Over the years, Joan told me a little about her family. Her mother Donna became a nurse after she and her sister ran a small Idaho newspaper as mere children. When her parents separated, Joan stayed with her mother, who died relatively early. The O'Briens had never divorced in the eyes of the church, so Jerry never remarried. His charming girlfriend Louise stood by his side for years.

Joan's three brothers, athletes at Judge Memorial High School, were the apples of their father's eye, leaving less attention for Joan's intellectual ideas and achievements. I assumed there was some male chauvinism -- or at least paternalism -- at play. Eventually I recognized that Joan actually took after her father.

Back East, Joan worked for the Times Journal Company, which she described as progressive compared to *The Tribune*. That is, the Virginia publication paid Christmas bonuses and offered vacation the first year of employment. Yet she missed the *Tribune* people. "The Eastern stereotype of unfriendliness is for the most part true," she wrote in a letter January 29.

In another letter March 28, Joan consoled me for not getting to go on NCEW's South American "junket" even though it was my turn. I was ambivalent about the snub. I doubted whether the publisher's decision was a budgetary necessity, but I was relieved to avoid Peru's Luminoso (Shining Path guerrillas), who were killing people right and left.

Joan also congratulated me on winning the latest SPJ-SDX editorial-writing competition and praised Paul Rolly's Freedom of Information award. She still didn't like her new boss, "Rick the Prick," but she was feeling better about the "fine bunch" of staffers at the *Times Journal*. "But they still can't compare with the *Trib* family," she concluded. "I really miss The Trombone."

She would follow Harvey to Chile, too, before landing a job at the *Fort Worth Star-Telegram* on her way back home.

* * *

Rolly's award cited his commitment to the free flow of information in stories involving Daggett County officials, a Lehi child sex-abuse ring and a grand jury investigation of former Salt Lake County Attorney Ted Cannon. He also was recognized for coordinating a series of forums and seminars among journalists, judges and attorneys on "initiating a better understanding of the relationship between the press and the courts."[682]

This was an especially worthy yet ironic effort in light of Rolly's own sometimes strained relationship with judges and attorneys. A case in point:

After favoring Paul Van Dam, a fellow Democrat, in his 1988 campaign for state attorney general against David Wilkinson, Rolly noticed an unsavory odor wafting through the election and office Van Dam filled for four years.

First, a sleazy operative circulated groundless rumors of embezzlement about Van Dam's Democratic opponent Zane Gill, effectively eliminating him from the race.

Next, the Utah Public Employees Association, headed by Salt Lake County Deputy Sheriff Ron Probert, contributed an outrageous $37,000 to Van Dam's campaign.[683] Outrageous because the A.G.'s office could do nothing for the UPEA, and sums this large were never part of these races in the mid-1980s. By comparison, UPEA donated a pittance to Ted Wilson's gubernatorial campaign, a race that could actually affect state employees.

After Van Dam won, he hired Probert to head his investigative division. Probert lacked the legal qualifications for the job -- a bachelor's degree, so a new position of investigations chief was created for him.

When Rolly wrote a story about the apparent quid pro quo, he started "getting backwards" with Van Dam.[684]

The relationship worsened when Rolly highlighted Van Dam's wasteful lapse of judgment in hiring Joe Tesch as his chief deputy, disqualifying the A.G.'s office from defending Utah's anti-abortion law on appeals. Tesch had worked with the plaintiffs. Van Dam's solution was to retain Jones, Waldo and McDonough (*The Tribune's* attorneys) for the defense at considerable state expense.

Van Dam's excuses for paying for private counsel were a staff shortage and the need to counter claims that a Democrat attorney general could not vigorously defend the conservative law.[685] Unfortunately, the arrangement raised two more conflicts of interest: Van Dam's solicitor general, Jan Graham, had been a partner in the firm, and another of the firm's attorneys had represented an abortion clinic.[686]

So Jones Waldo withdrew from the case. Despite a legislative audit calling for reimbursement of its sizable retainer, Van Dam let it go. Later, Rolly reported, the firm bought paintings from Van Dam's wife and then hired Van Dam once he left office. (More irony: When Graham replaced Van Dam in office, she fired outside counsel on the abortion case.)

That wasn't the end of Van Dam's debacle. He spent another $163,000 of the public's money for outside attorneys to fight Hi-Fi murderer William Andrews' death penalty appeals because Tesch had represented Andrews in court. Then, because David Early had contributed to his election, Van Dam spent still more state funds on private attorneys to take action against David Early Tires.[687]

Rolly filed story after razor-sharp story about these conflicts and monetary missteps, as well as about Van Dam's frequent absences from work. Van Dam apparently was surprised a liberal reporter would pick on a fellow Democrat.

"He never understood that I'm not just a Democrat, I'm a journalist, and if he's going to do sleazy shit, I'm going to report it," Rolly asserted.[688]

And Van Dam was going to get even. His henchman put Rolly under surveillance, catching him in a judgment lapse of his own.

Van Dam learned, apparently from a judge in a social situation, that Rolly's license had been suspended for driving under the influence. Before long, a sheriff's deputy, "who had the reputation of being the dumbest fucking piece of shit in the world," started hanging around Rolly's house in the suburbs. One day he tailgated Rolly's son on his way to school. "This is what cops do -- tailgate people so they'll get nervous and speed up or change lanes without signaling so they can arrest them,"[689] a still-riled Rolly told me years later.

Eventually Rolly was caught driving on a suspended license and hauled off to jail. A deal between lawyer Lonnie Deland and the County Attorney's Office got him released. Then, despite the Van Dam camp's best efforts, charges were dismissed after six months of good behavior.[690]

In subsequent years, Rolly took revenge by portraying Van Dam in a negative light at every turn.

None of this impaired Rolly's wit and sentimentality. He continued to give detail, hilarious accounts of friend and foe alike. He eventually would write moving columns and obituaries about Utahns who made a positive impact on the state despite their foibles. In the end, he became so concerned about hurting the feelings of former *Tribune* staffers, their families and the families of public figures that he declined to repeat for this memoir the many well-worn stories he once told over drinks.[691]

* * *

Elsewhere in the newsroom, Cathy Free's "Freestyle" column successfully helped filled the human-interest void left by the retirement of Dan Valentine and death of Clark Lobb. Her Wednesday "Freestyle" column clearly demonstrated her knack for connecting with people, whether average or unusual.

The Copy Desk had evolved, too. Cindy Gilchrist had become Rose Fryer and left for southeastern Utah to run a motel and gift shop. Gerry Cunningham, Jerry Dunton and Steve Brown took turns at the slot [head copy editor]. The rim, by then adjacent desks with computer terminals instead of a single horseshoe-shaped table, included Ann Poore, Kirk Millson, Jeff Walton, Tom Baldwin, Pepper Provenzano, David Noyce, Tim Fitzpatrick and Andrea Otanez. No alcoholic bad boys.

Brown and Dunton offered entertainment for slow moments: the "Way to Go" files, which told of people dying under crazy circumstances. Cunningham kept a porn story going for years by having each desk editor take a turn adding another vulgar line.[692]

Tom Baldwin at Halloween.

Baldwin, a compact Vietnam veteran from Arkansas whose athletic father worked for the IRS, reminded Ann of Hemingway.[693] I remembered him more as the hunchback who balanced a beer on his hump at our Halloween party, a quiet single guy who enjoyed drinking. According to Ann, he was the culprit who started a fire on the NAC roof, or bridge, between *The Tribune* and *News*.

Along with Ann and others, Baldwin was celebrating on NAC's makeshift "patio" September 9, 1989. While his "famous pozole" (Mexican pork) heated up, the tarred roof started to smoke, sending cockroaches scurrying from beneath the NAC lunchroom where Denny and I sometimes ate. Because highly flammable ink and chemicals were on site, fire crews rushed to the scene. The newsroom was none the wiser until Guy Boulton made a routine call to the fire department. "Anything going on?" he asked. "Yeah, your building's on fire," the dispatcher dead-panned.[694]

No more smoking breaks were permitted on the "patio."

Ann moved up to the Sunday Arts section to edit and write fine arts reviews, as did former copy clerk Scott Rivers. The two clashed to the point of having to be separated, and both eventually were bumped back down to the Copy Desk. Ann had fallen short of a new editor's goals, and Rivers apparently had accepted too much help from his wife on a play review.

* * *

By 1988, *The Tribune* had been computerized for more than a decade. Noisy typewriters and Teletypes and the ATEX copy processing system had given way to word processors and video display terminals in 1982. In 1985, the old make-up process, which used layout dummies to guide the paste-up of news pages, was replaced by pagination, Information International Inc.'s computerized system for creating pages, including headlines, text and graphics.[695]   Once ready, the pages were photographed and transferred to metal printing plates.[696]

Gordon Harman oversaw the early pagination staff, including John Hurst, nephew of artist Steve Baker, and Ben Ling, who eagerly relinquished his title as zone czar. As Ling tells it:

> This was my favorite time at *The Trib* because Gordon ran a loose department.   Sometimes we played computer games like Tetris and some fighter jet simulator, but I also got fast enough on III that I could paginate all five zone sections in one day by myself.[697]

* * *

While Ling and Harman were playing computer games, I was writing an editorial opposing the U.S. attorney's demand that 15-year-old Benjamin Singer be forced to testify against his mother and other relatives in the 1988 bombing of the Mormon Stake building in Kamas.

The Singer story never seemed to die, and neither did my interest in it.   When interviewed for jury duty on the murder trials of Addam and Jonathan Swapp and Timothy Singer, who shot Fred House, I hoped to be chosen. Of course I had no chance. Not only had I interviewed the patriarch of the polygamous clan, I worked with the victim's sister, Dawn House, and read countless news accounts of the saga.

I also wrote an editorial implying that Gov. Norm Bangerter blundered in appointing Roger Livingston to the 5th Circuit Court.[698] Livingston was the deputy county attorney who in 1980 discussed hiring someone to steal and destroy his leased Lincoln Continental because he couldn't afford the payments. I compared his intended insurance fraud with the pot-smoking that derailed Douglas H. Ginsburg's appointment to the U.S. Supreme Court and with the many criminal investigations against U.S. Attorney General Edwin Meese. Livingston not only got his judicial robes anyway, he officiated at Stormy's second wedding at our house.   That's how much influence I had.

Another day, I found myself editorializing about business magnate Jon Hunstman Sr.'s bid to replace Bangerter as the state's Republican governor.   Huntsman was accustomed to managing information about himself, and he was upset with reports of his business practices and activities as a federal administrator and special assistant to President Nixon. Of course he couldn't guard his privacy in public office, and I bluntly told him so on the phone and in print.   As if I could advise a mover-and-shaker.

It fell to me to oppose state and federal laws, including a constitutional amendment, protecting the American flag. Although I was too patriotic to ever burn the flag myself, I couldn't imagine restricting anyone else's right to use the flag as a symbol of free speech.   Even conservative Justice Antonin Scalia, whose decisions I usually deplored, agreed on that.

* * *

By spring, the Editorial Department moved from the cramped, old-fashioned 10th floor to tastefully remodeled offices on the mezzanine between the first and second floors. It might have been nice if the powers-that-be had waited until we vacated to remove the asbestos from our previous quarters, but I let that issue slide as I gleefully embraced a spacious workplace.

Finally, an office of my own, complete with door, window, phone, new carpet, filing cabinets, bookshelves and desk.   It put John Cummins' old cubicle on the second floor to shame. My extension, 237-2020, unintentionally conveyed perceptiveness.

Furnishings were new except for three antique hardwood chairs we asked to keep. We still had just two computers to share but expected a third. For the first time, we had our own conference room for Editorial Board meetings.

Fuller deemed the change "just compensation for crummy exile" from the newsroom before my time.[699]

The Art and Photography departments shared our new home.   Photo's eight shooters inhabited space triple the size of the pitiful, polluted digs on the second floor. The new studio alone was 30 feet wide![700]   The artists were getting a tracing room and cubicles for each.

Along with the new offices, we were promised a receptionist to type our edited Forum letters and to direct calls among departments on our floor. Dominic Welch's daughter Angie first filled the slot but soon quit for motherhood. Trish

Aguayo, a sexy young with a bright smile replaced her.

Trish Aguayo

As with most good things, there were downsides. My office sat between Photo and Art. Nine floors no longer separated me from Denny during work hours. In fact, there were no more than 30 feet from Denny's drawing table to my desk. When he stomped back and forth to the newsroom with an especially infuriating assignment, I felt the tension of his mini-tantrum through the floor vibrations.

YOU WANT IT BY WHEN!?

These disturbances were aggravated by the antics of photographer Dan Miller, the wild environmental activist who ran past my office laughing and yelling while playing games with artists Steve Baker and Rhonda Hailes early evenings. Add to this the loud voice of artist Mark Knudsen, whose cubicle separated me and Denny. Because of his hearing loss, he shouted into the phone when talking to his son Ollie every afternoon.

Mark Knudsen chats with son Ollie.

Another cog in my wheel of good fortune was the mezzanine's ventilation system, or what passed for one. The air intake vent jutted into the alley where diesel trucks idled when dropping off newsprint or replacing the presses. During winter inversions, in particular, we got gassed. Cigarette fumes also filled our hallway as a new smoking room lacked a vent to the outside.

My new office on the mezzanine.

Always one to complain, I sought relief from Fuller and the Fourth Floor. When nothing happened, I called the state Office of

Environmental Protection on the sly, hoping an inspector would pay our building supervisor a visit. Once I realized I couldn't remain anonymous, I lost my nerve and withheld a formal complaint.

After a year or so of choking, I broached the subject to company lawyer Sharon Sonnenreich who, after looking into it, told me to take a walk. Literally. It would cost more than $100,000 to alter the ventilation system, she said, so I should leave the building when bothered by trucks idling in the alley. Denny and I took her up on that, but we paid for it by working later.

* * *

The summer of 1988, *The Tribune* paid tribute to its 50th year in the 10-floor building on Main Street with a special tabloid illustrated with Denny's caricatures of Utahns and other major newsmakers through the decades.

Completed in 1925 for Ezra Thompson, the first non-Mormon mayor of Salt Lake City, the Tribune building was designed in a transitional Beaux Art/Classical Revival style with some Art Deco/Art Moderne thrown in. It stood in the middle of Utah's political center and was wired for every major news-wire service in the free world -- 17 of them -- around the clock.[701]

The Tribune Building in 1990s.

Publisher Jerry O'Brien wrote a column to commemorate the milestone:

The inclination in our profession to seek out newsworthy anniversary years divisible by five and then to make something of it is notably stronger when the number is 50.

Fifty is the Golden One that appears once in a lifetime and demands attention. It especially does if it's family and this grand house of ours is surely that.

The Salt Lake Tribune moved into this place exactly a half century ago, and we now have plans to keep the address indefinitely [ahem] as the news and information hub of the region we serve. Communications has long since gone with the neighborhood.

The Pony Express used to stop out front when the area near our lobby was the Salt Lake headquarters station on the St. Joe to Sacramento run in 1861. Supt. Ben Ficklin had 15 Utah riders taking news both ways with rapid dispatch.

And you can still see where we once had the lofts for our 50 Tribune homing pigeons in the 1930s to deliver news and film from reporters in the field.

Now there's an earth station dish on our roof out back that brings us all the "wire" news at 1,000 words a minutes from the Spacenet III satellite 22,500 miles in the sky.

This special section taking note of our 50th includes some mention of substantial plant improvement that will enhance our ability to serve readers and advertisers.

But as always it's the newspaper people who are The Salt Lake Tribune, the ones who conceive and compose a fresh news and information package every day of the year.

The 141 men and women of The Tribune family include 31 who have been here 20 years or more. (Chairman Jack Gallivan leads the list with 51 years of service, Sports Editor John Mooney has 49.)[702]

Another notable part of the building's past was its location: the site of Salt Lake House, one of the city's oldest hotels. It was here, according to Ron Andersen's historical walking tour,[703] where a member of Cub Johnson's cattle-rustling gang shot outlaw Bill Hickman.

During the Utah War, two "spies" were held at the hotel until shot. *Atlantic Monthly* correspondent Fritz Ludlow interviewed Orrin Porter Rockwell here in 1862.

Cynthia Fehr's watercolor of street in front of Tribune Building.

In 2005, just 17 years after this feature, *The Tribune* abandoned the historic Thompson building to move operations to the new Gateway project on the city's west side. By 2014, a private college had moved in, transforming offices into classrooms and dorm rooms.

* * *

Also that summer, Lulu paid us a visit, as always on our dime, out of "obligation." As she explained it, she didn't know her father anymore and still resented his divorcing Swamper. On the other hand, she added, Ped O'Fiel was "a reasonable guy" who helped her control Swamper.

Reasonable, as we well knew, Ped O'Fiel was not. Perverted and mean he was. When not molesting the girls, he was calling them vulgar, demeaning names and forcing them to sit chair-style (without the chair) against the wall for what Stormy said seemed like hours. That Lulu liked him said a lot about her state of mind.

A few months after, Lulu asked her stranger of a father for airfare to escape Swamper, who evidently shoved her down the stairs. As a family, Denny, Stormy and I agreed it was worth the sacrifice of putting up with her incessant chatter, smoking and slovenliness to give her a chance at a more normal life. Before Denny could send the money, however, Lulu decided to finish her last semester of college first. It would be a year of three false starts, one due to hospitalization for manic depression, before she finished her degree. All while living with Swamper and Ped O'Fiel.

* * *

My second NCEW convention came up in September, this time in economically depressed Fort Worth. While speakers T. Boone Pickens, author Larry King, writer Molly Ivins and politicians Ann Richards, Jim Wright and Phil Gramm addressed public affairs, the Stockyards offered entertainment for younger members. Severals of us danced the nights away, whether or not we knew the Western Swing. My new pals helped me ditch the insecure son-of-a-gun from my first convention who pestered me again in Texas. At dinner, he launched into a diatribe about the Vietnam War that triggered a nasty retort from normally humorous Molly Ivins, who shoved herself back from our table and stomped out the door.

* * *

Jack Schroeder retired September 30 at age 65 and, by his account, began a six-month stint teaching literature at the University of Salzburg. This ended a 41-year career as a newspaperman, including his years as sports writer and executive sports editor, assistant executive editor (with Will Fehr) and then, in 1981, managing editor. For retirement, "the cardinal" (Scarletism) moved into an upscale home on Walker Lane and volunteered at the Catholic Diocese of Salt Lake City.

As the door closed gently behind Jack Schroeder, it swung wider for Gerry Cunningham, who at 50 became night news editor. One more indication he might replace Fehr as executive editor.

* * *

Just before Christmas, Denny accompanied me on a trip to Reston, Virginia, for an editorial seminar. It was a lot of work, even more than NCEW conventions, and I picked up usable editing and writing tips. While visiting the *Washington Post* and *USA Today,* we talked to big-time editors and writers who seemed much like the rest of us. Denny and I also stole away to see our old friend Brian Nutting at home and on the job at *Congressional Quarterly*. Overall, the week nudged me toward more aggressive opinions, but I knew that anything too clear or cutting likely would be toned down to feed our habit of obfuscation. We didn't want to offend anyone, after all.

Vandra's annual holiday letter reported that she was preparing for tenure in the University of Washington's Department of Business Administration, where she was teaching human resources management. "The fact that she was ranked number 2 in the entire business school in productivity out of 100 professors for the last year should help," her letter modestly boasted. Her family, which still included her software engineer husband, had expanded to five dogs showing well in prestigious shows around the country.

The year ended with a wry note from Planned Parenthood spokeswoman Mary Carlson, who thanked me for my "excellent" editorial on abortion. "Maybe someday people will realize that preventing abortion requires preventing pregnancy," she mused. Certain subjects never went away.

—————————————

[682] "Tribune Writer Earns Society's Freedom of Information Award," *The Salt Lake Tribune*, March 26, 1988.

[683] Paul Rolly, "Utah's Sorry Run of A.G.s," *The Salt Lake Tribune*, January 19, 2013.

[684] Paul Rolly interview August 23, 2014, Salt Lake City.

[685] Lisa Riley-Roche, "Does Van Dam Lack Zeal on Legislation?" *Deseret News*, April 12, 1991.

[686] Jerry Spangler, "Lawyers: Who's Representing Utah?" *Deseret News*, September 11, 1994.

[687] Ibid.

[688] Rolly, August 23, 2014.

[689] Ibid.

[690] Paul Rolly email August 31, 2014.

[691] Rolly, August 23, 2014.

[692] Ann Poore email, August 10, 2015.

[693] Ann Poore email, August 25, 2015.

[694] "Tribune Gets Hot News Tip: Its Rooftop Is on Fire," *Deseret News*, September 10, 1989.

[695] Gordon Harman on facebook, August 19, 2015.

[696] Jonsson, July 24, 1988, p. T4.

[697] Ling, December 26, 2014.

[698] "If Only That Simple," *The Salt Lake Tribune*, April 11, 1988, Page A10.

[699] Harry Fuller email February 10, 2013.

[700] Tim Kelly, "Tribune Photographers Inhabit Superb News Place," The Salt Lake Tribune, July 24, 1988, p. 8T.

[701] "The Tribune Building and the Passing Parade," *The Salt Lake Tribune*, July 24, 1988, p. T3.

[702] Jerry O'Brien, "An Anniversary of 50 Years -- a Golden One," *The Salt Lake Tribune*, July 24, 1988, p. T2.

[703] Ron Andersen, 1998.

36 - Stretching My Wings in 1989

In early January, Mom enclosed an article about Alzheimer's disease in one of her letters. She scribbled in the margin: "Since Dad had 33 skull fractures, maybe he's lucky to do as well as he is!" She was referring to a car crash in 1948.

Rather than dwell on Mom's mind-numbing bombshell, I focused on her request to return the clipping "this time." "I just know I'd do the same nitpicking to my own kids if I had any," I told Mimi., "so it's probably best I never had children."

* * *

Mike Carter dropped a bombshell of his own on *The Tribune*. After covering cops longer than most, he hitched up with the Associated Press. Good for Carter; not so good for *The Tribune*. A furious Jerry O'Brien threw a monogrammed pencil at him when he got the news and reamed the AP bureau chief for hiring him away. [704]

As of 2018, Carter still kept that pencil while working as a crack (not the drug) reporter at the *Seattle Times*, where he shared in winning two Pulitzers and was twice a Pulitzer finalist. He gave credit for his successes to "what I learned at *The Tribune* during the Fehr years." [705]

Carter had remarried after splitting with Andrea Otanez, a *Tribune* editor who went into academia when she and Carter moved to the Northwest. "I might be able to ride this old horse out to retirement," he said of journalism.

* * *

NCEW scheduled a fact-finding tour of Southeast Asia, and this time, the Fourth Floor agreed to cover my $5,000 expenses for three weeks in Vietnam, Cambodia, Indonesia and Thailand. I was surprised, excited and nervous.

I had assumed by then the publisher lacked faith in me, a woman, and didn't regard international expertise as essential to our job. Having been on several trips and used the experience to assess international incidents himself, Fuller promoted my participation. The thawing Cold War helped, too, because I would be among the first Americans to see Communist Vietnam since the war that had haunted -- maybe even defined -- my generation.

Thanks to Jim Woolf's favorite restaurant the Orient, French Vietnamese cuisine and culture had become a fascination. Denny and I had volunteered at the Orient when the owner, Dao, sneaked back into South Vietnam to recover valuables he'd buried one step ahead of Communist victors. We washed dishes with his father-in-law, a former security chief in Saigon. Dao's goal was to repay members of the Vietnamese community who had taken his advice to invest in high-return certificates at State Savings & Loan before its collapse. I never knew if he succeeded after two smuggling trips, because he talked in riddles.

For lack of interest, NCEW postponed, if not cancelled, the trip. I resigned myself to missing out again on the biggest perk of my job.

* * *

Whether because I edited op-ed (opinion page opposite the editorial page where columnists appeared) or because I sat at the bottom of the totem pole, I had become the *Tribune* caretaker of **Ernest H. Linford**.

A *Tribune* editorial writer from 1948 until 1967, when he quit to run the University of Wyoming journalism program, Linford still submitted weekly op-ed columns at age 80. His ramblings required a lot of care -- editing, that is. His "ancient typewriter" peppered his pieces with typos.

At O'Brien's behest after a convoluted retrospective erroneously identified Bob Ottum as the author of "Nothing Serious" (Valentine's bailiwick), I wrote the old-timer two letters in 1988. One requested a recent mugshot for his column and the other gave him a limit of 12 to 18 inches of copy, about half his usual. With Jack Goodman also writing features about staffers, I noted, Linford "may be over-indulging in *Tribune* history." (This phrase came from my superiors.) I added that we welcomed more columns about Wyoming history and the environment.

Linford's defensive response reminded us that he was the 1981 recipient of the University of Utah "Service to Journalism" award and that J.F. Fitzpatrick himself granted him the column. He went on:

I presume that the stuff I have previously sent your office and have not seen published is to be assigned to File 13 . . .

I appreciate the friendly interest and help of you and Harry. I got to digging in my old files Sunday. Do you know I have a truck full of stuff I have submitted for my *Tribune* column? Some of it isn't so bad in the eye of the guy who persuaded Art Deck and John Fitzpatrick to let me continue the Trib column even after I departed for the Wyoming wilds . . .

I will be guided by the reaction of the "Ivory Tower" staffers in deciding the subjects for future Linford columns . . . but some weeks it seems little is offered in one particular category and the temptation is to reach out for a subject offering more promise . . .

He concluded that the reduction of one his columns to eight inches made him wonder whether the new guidelines were "just a kind and polite way of letting me down, in effect saying, 'Linford, we don't like your column.'"

I regretted my part in making Linford feel like an irrelevant has-been.

Less than a year later, on February 16, 1989, Lala Linford wrote me and Fuller a letter recounting how her husband had flooded the downstairs on "Friday the 13th" of January before falling and breaking his hip 11 days before he died. Complaining that the "foul-ball bunch" at the IRS had fined her $900 for unreported earnings on Ernie's column in 1986, Lala finished with these words:

Your great cooperation with him to see that his columns appeared was so appreciated. Among those columns he never quite got finished was one on our dear friend Bill McDougall (monsignor), the book Lynn Bennion had just published and the one on the death of Walter Cottam . . .

Thank you both for being so kind and patient with him.

Our restrictions obviously had discouraged Linford from finishing those columns about his old friends. I hoped they didn't add much to the misery of his last days.

I also became the willing editor and go-between for Edward "Ned" McDonough, Gallivan's son-in-law who wrote a law column for laymen. His homespun "Judge Carruthers" laid out legal issues in light-hearted narratives that made me chuckle. Little editing was needed, aside from style changes (capitalization, etc.), and when I had questions, McDonough graciously thanked me for my help. When his sons Edward "Ted" and Michael took jobs as *Tribune* copy

clerks between semesters at Gonzaga, I encouraged their writing aspirations.

* * *

My editorial interests were becoming more diversified and less predictable. Despite our devastating child-custody conflict with the Gruesomes a decade earlier, for example, one of my editorials sided with custodial parents:

Courts Help Fuel Family Feuds

Two recent court decisions, one in Utah and the other in Denver, tear savagely at the fabric of families. For the sake of countless children of divorce, the cases should be used only as the worst examples of American jurisprudence.

Even though Lehi resident Allan B. Hadfield was convicted last year of sexually molesting his two children, two 4th District judges restricted the treatment of the children to a specific therapist who denied their abuse. Consequently the mother cannot obtain appropriate health care for the children in her care without being cited for contempt of court.

The outrageously presumptuous court ruling is both an assault on a responsible parent's rights and a cruel continuation of the children's suffering.

A few hundred miles to the east, a Denver judge threatened to throw a mother in jail for taking her two daughters to a Catholic church. While the mother had been granted physical custody of the children, the father retained so-called "spiritual custody." He insisted the children be raised according to his Jewish faith.

Children's psyches cannot be divvied up between two warring parents without coming apart at the seams. The parent with physical custody of the children must retain ultimate authority for their health, education and religious upbringing. Otherwise, the irreconcilable differences that divided the marriage in the first place can continually get in the way of childhood stability.

Any judge that would support or even tolerate damaging child custody arrangements like those out of Lehi and Denver is inviting additional domestic strife at the expense of hapless children.

Instead of salvaging what's left of broken homes, these kinds of rulings shatter attempts to sensibly [Harryism] restructure families and save children from relentless turmoil.[706]

Keep in mind, I did not naturally assume that a custodial mother should control a child's upbringing. I tried to be fair and reasonable despite my prejudices.

My ongoing commitment to combatting child abuse in editorials was one way I could make something positive out of Lulu and Stormy's suffering. I had shown no mercy when Hadfield was convicted of sodomizing and sexually molesting his two children, and I repeatedly encouraged the State Attorney General's office to prosecute abuses throughout Utah.

I also lashed out at Gov. Norm Bangerter, a man I personally liked yet pummeled on the editorial pages.

Who's the governor kidding? State government has been through good times and bad, but lawmakers even in bygone days didn't issue a blank check for public services.

Gov. Norm Bangerter obviously used his state-of-the-state address Monday to help regain his reputation as a fiscal conservative. The public backlash to the record-high tax increase he proposed in 1986 almost put him out of office last November, and he felt duty-bound to assure constituents he's holding the line on spending.

He simply went too far when he declared "the days of the blank check are over" for government spending. "The level of taxes must not be based on the amount of money government can justify spending," he said. "Rather, the level of taxes must be determined with the full input and support of a majority of those who pay the bills -- the taxpayers."

It's been a long time since state agencies garnered anywhere near as much funding as they could justify. The state did collect more money than it knew what to do with during parts of Gov. Calvin L. Rampton's tenure and managed to cut several taxes. But in 1974, the economy shifted slightly, forcing budget reductions. Gov. Scott Matheson enjoyed an economic rebound of sorts a couple of years, only to initiate a series of budget cuts later in his

administration. The state's rapid population growth, especially among school-age children, simply overwhelmed available resources.

During that period and even since Gov. Bangerter assumed office for the first time in 1984, state agencies have repeatedly reduced spending. Public employees' salaries have been frozen the past three years, to say nothing of several prior years when pay increases lagged behind the inflation rate.

Blank check? Hardly. Insinuating such a thing has existed irresponsibly ratifies critics' contention that spending can be further curtailed without harming public services. It can't be.

If anything, many programs need a budget boost to recover from too many years of insufficient support. They should share in the state's recent revenue revival instead of being sacrificed for additional tax cuts.

Several specific projects loom on the horizon that will add to state government costs. Asbestos must be removed from public schools at a cost of several million dollars. The governor's own pet project, the $12 million West Valley Highway, isn't going to pay for itself. Expansion of Interstate-15 and the construction of a light-rail system to accommodate the Wasatch Front's transportation needs cannot be put off indefinitely. And the collapse of the Quail Creek Reservoir dike will cost the sate something.

It's one thing to say taxes won't be raised anytime soon and that spending increases will be closely scrutinized, but it's quite another to imply state government has been bloated and can operate successfully with fewer funds. Instead of mending fences Monday, the governor may have knocked out more slats.

Take that, Paul Swenson! This was my idea of the kind of "editorial bite" that *Utah Holiday's* news critic said was missing from our pages in 1974.

Domestic violence also grabbed my editorial attention. In January, Bob Terragno, executive director of the Community Counseling Center, thanked me for supporting two house bills:

The editorial accurately reports the facts and thoroughly articulates the rationale for these two important domestic violence bills. (Copies of the editorial were distributed among senators, who passed HB 16 without a dissenting vote.)   We believe these measures will significantly advance the cause of battered women in Utah. Your strong support for this effort is most welcome and deeply appreciated.

My views were not always so highly regarded.

I stepped in a mess when I suggested castigating the state for spending more than $1.5 million -- without going through the proper bid process   -- on Syncrete, the experimental synthetic concrete used to resurface parts of the freeway between 5900 South and 3300 South. Little did I know that one of the project's principals was Jack Gallivan, the entrepreneur still sitting at the head of the boardroom table. He had assured state highway commissioners Syncrete would "work for Utah and the whole world."[707] When Syncrete cracked, buckled and was replaced, I was advised to keep my opinion to myself.

I still worked education into my editorials, of course, and when Gallivan and O'Brien looked the other way, I commended Jordan Board of Education "courage" for discontinuing prayers at high school graduation. The decision was more pragmatic than courageous since a Brighton High School student was suing over denominational commencement prayers, but I was trying to encourage other districts to follow suit. From experience, I knew school prayers in Utah almost exclusively were given with folded arms, began with "Father in Heaven" and ended with "in the name of Jesus Christ, Amen." They were Mormon prayers.

The LDS Church contended that eliminating school prayer "can only be interpreted as an official act of hostility toward religion" forbidden by the Constitution.   A majority of Utahns -- 66 percent -- favored at least silent prayer or meditation in the public schools. But I argued that the Bill of Rights was written with the minority's interests in mind; that government-sanctioned, denominational prayers threatened civil rights, especially in communities dominated by one religion like Utah. "Such prayers tend to elevate the majority's faith at the expense of others . . . Contrary to the U.S. Constitution, they tacitly establish a religion and prohibit 'the free exercise thereof.'"[708]

* * *

Because I still knew most newsroom staffers, I felt comfortable discussing my opinions with most reporters whose stories piqued my interest.   I wanted to avoid rash conclusions, especially after my screw-up regarding John Richard Calder and the Plandome.

Kathy Kapos with Denny.

Upbeat education writer Kathy Kapos became a regular sounding board.   Scarlet, Gorrell, Woody, Boulton and many others also offered friendly advice and background. On the other hand, my old best buddy Rolly brushed aside my inquiries about political conflicts as if I were questioning his reporting. His curt, defensive responses coincided with some personal difficulties, making me wonder whether I'd failed him as a friend.   In any case, my editorials would have benefited from his expertise.

With Tim Fitzpatrick's departure from Editorial, environment fell back into my lap, and Woolf remained my best source on this subject. It confused me when he apparently downplayed the potential for Utah to become a hazardous waste dump.

That's when I learned that Woolf's Deep Throat on the topic was Khosrow "Koz" Semnani, a master manipulator seeking approval for his own business. By tossing Woolf juicy tidbits, he could shape the hazardous waste story and divert attention from his dubious methods and goals.

An Iranian immigrant who'd attended Westminster College, Semnani was Utah's waste-disposal king. When it came out in the mid-1990s that he was pumping money into state political campaigns and pockets of state regulators, he left Woolf looking like a patsy.

At the risk of getting ahead of myself, this is part of that story:

Semnani paid Larry Anderson, director of the Utah Bureau of Radiation Control, $600,000 worth of cash, gold coins and real estate to pave the way for licenses and permits for his Envirocare.[709] When Anderson stupidly sued Semnani for failing to ante up all he was promised, Semnani countersued for extortion.

After leaving office, Gov. Bangerter, Preston Truman, a member of the state Board of Radiation Control, and Senator Steve Rees, chairman of the Senate Health Committee, accepted loans from Semnani. Meantime, the waste king contributed generously to the political campaigns of many legislators and Gov. Mike Leavitt. Not so coincidentally, Envirocare avoided state taxes and significant regulatory fees.

By the time the Envirocare scandal broke, I had offended Woolf for marrying my neighbor -- the one whose husband died from stomach cancer -- creating enough distance between us that I never heard how he felt about his news source's graft.

* * *

Some days in Editorial were worse than others, and April 5 was among the worst. Fuller was on vacation, leaving us understaffed and short of editorials for the weekend. I was working alone that Saturday when at 5:30 p.m., Gallivan killed my editorial on the proposed new Salt Palace arena, a sacred cow. I nearly died while shoveling slop into the gaping news hole.

Wetzel's sluggishness was giving me heartburn. Like I had done for so many years myself, he often deliberated and gave in to distractions until deadlines, forcing the rest of us to bang out something at the last minute to fill the space. We could not afford two procrastinators, after all.

Wetzel offered apt insights upon retirement decades later. In departing remarks to the staff, he described himself as "eccentric, given to crankiness and mania."[710] He put it another way in the speech he never gave:

I am like an ember that burns, day in, day out, to keep the boiler producing steam, occasionally rising to incandescence when events move me . . .

[Editorial writing] is grinding work. An editorial writer writes every single working day, regardless of whether there is news or he has anything to say. It's sort of like monastic discipline . . .

One consequence of working under weak management for so long is that, of necessity, I am virtually self-taught. I had to discover for myself how to be a reporter, a music critic, an editorial writer. That lack of peer training was a weakness of the old *Tribune*, but it also was a strength because I have always had to rely on myself and keep my own counsel. When I made mistakes that should have got me fired, I lived to write another day, chastened and wiser for the experience. And I have learned by watching and reading my colleagues, both at *The Tribune* and in the wider profession.[711]

Yes, we were mostly self-taught in those days. There was no period of apprenticeship in Editorial. We plunged into the job and surmised our mistakes if editorials were changed or killed. No one sat us down and explained what was right or wrong with our work.

* * *

After flying high in the public eye during the media frenzy over the artificial heart, the public image of University of Utah President Chase Peterson plunged in 1989.

Dr. Peterson startled the scientific community in March with a premature press conference announcing that B. Stanley Pons and Martin Fleischmann had solved the mystery of cold fusion. He was so sold on the promise of an inexhaustible supply of cheap energy that he secretly added $500,000 in university research money to $5 million the state provided for project patents and development.

The scientific "discovery" turned out to be a dud that blew up in Dr. Peterson's face several months later.

Upon learning of the $500,000 transfer and seeing how Peterson handled a separate donation to the University Medical Center, the faculty's Academic Senate gave him a no-confidence vote. The usually modest man was criticized for grandstanding.

Dr. Peterson had agreed to name the University Medical Center after businessman James E. Sorenson, who promised to donate $15 million. When other supporters, doctors and students cried foul, the president reneged and Sorenson withdrew his offer.

By June 1990, Dr. Peterson announced his retirement.

I felt sorry for the sensitive, thoughtful doctor and administrator. He had been so gracious when I interviewed him for a personality profile when appointed president in 1983. And he never held my faux pas against me.

The new president had proudly told me he lived in the home of [garble, garble] James at 95 Irving Street while Harvard University provost. Too embarrassed to ask for clarification, I stupidly assumed he was talking about British author Henry James. Some time later, Peterson's wife Grethe subtly mentioned my mistake, giving me good reason for embarrassment. In fact, Henry James' brother William, the philosopher psychologist considered the father of pragmatism, lived at 95 Irving Street. Like Peterson, William James was trained as a physician. He apparently was Peterson's role model.

Dr. Peterson's successor Arthur K. Smith became the first non-Mormon president of the University of Utah. Incredible. The milestone merited mention on the Editorial Page.

* * *

The Utah Chapter of the American Civil Liberties Union bestowed its Cliff Cheney Memorial Journalism Award on the *Tribune* Editorial Board "in recognition of more than 100 years of speaking out in defense of civil liberties and rights of minorities in Utah."

I didn't mind sharing the honor with the rest of the board at Utah ACLU's annual awards banquet. Texas columnist Molly Ivins, who'd covered Utah news early in her career, delivered a rip-roaring speech titled: "'Defend the Bastards!' (Reflections on Being a Civil Libertarian in America in the Late Twentieth Century)."[712] Of course she mentioned polygamy.

That was one of Wally Hoffman's last formal functions as an editorial writer. As he retired, he put his stamp on full-time replacement Paul Wetzel.

* * *

"Temperamentally cautious" Wetzel took seriously Hoffman's admonition that "an editorial writer is the publisher's rewrite man."[713] Consequently, he left to me the bulk of the boat rocking in editorial discussions and commentary.

With Hoffman gone, I grabbed the throttle on mass transit editorials. October 14,

for example, I urged Utahns to take advantage of federal funds to buy up right-of-way for a light-rail system.[714] Citing traffic congestion and increased air pollution as reasons for getting aboard, I wrote: "Congressional leaders have indicated that future federal aid depends on the commitment of Salt Lake area residents who have yet to demonstrate strong support for the project. It's time they did."

Our department picked Lex Hemphill as our part-time substitute for his careful, quality writing and obvious intelligence. This was a different sort of choice, since he came from Sports. But he also led *Tribune* coverage of the Olympics, a valued position given Gallivan's involvement since the '60s and Utah's determination to eventually host the Games.

* * *

The Write Stuff lost every game.

That summer also was memorable for *The Tribune's* agreement to sponsor a women's softball team. Terri Ellefsen Graves gathered a bunch of us together as the Write Stuff for our foray into competitive sports.

Carol VanWagoner played catch; Lifestyle staffer Lori Buttars pitched; Ellefsen and Anne Wilson took spots infield; I fielded flies or covered third when not warming the bench. Sisters and friends filled out ranks that included staffers Andrea Otanez, Ann Palmer and Stephanie Banchero. Good-natured young reporters Dave Clifton and Jess Gomez agreed to coach us.

We ragtag rookies somehow landed in a league with Amazons who'd competed in college. I soon discovered I no longer ran like the wind and that our competitors didn't mind blocking the baseline and jabbing elbows into our ribs. Missed grounders ricocheted off my shins, creating saucer-sized bruises that lasted months.

Our enthusiastic cheering section, including Denny and Fuller, stayed with us all the way, while one spectator made an ass of himself by continually yelling across the field at his embarrassed wife.

My high point came during our last double-header, when I caught one fly and one line drive to third. Our team's low point occurred our final game, when opponents batted left-handed to give us a chance.[715]

The Write Stuff lost all 18 games by more than 12 runs, but we always came back for more and walked away with a giant sportsmanship trophy. Despite my distaste for obligations outside the office, I thrived on the competition, exercise and camaraderie with other feisty *Tribune* women.

* * *

The Tribune's annual ownership statement came out October 3, showing that the average number of newspaper copies published in the preceding 12 months was 115,299 daily and 147,622 Sundays, slightly down from prior years.

[712] "ACLU Plans Annual Dinner," *The Salt Lake Tribune*, May 7, 1989.

[713] Paul Wetzel email, May 31, 2016.

[714] "Time for Utah's Public Transit to Climb Aboard Light Rail," *The Salt Lake Tribune*, October 14, 1988.

[715] VanWagoner, August 10, 2015.

---

[704] Carter, September 28, 2015.

[705] Mike Carter emails to Diane Cole Novermber 20, 2009 and December 26, 2013.

[706] "Courts Help Fuel Family Feuds," *The Salt Lake Tribune*, January 1, 1989, Page A16.

[707] Jan Thompson, "Rocky Roads May Drain Dollars; Failure of I-15 Concrete Experiment Could Cost $2.25 million," *Deseret News*, October 5, 1989.

[708] "Jordan's Tough Decision," *The Salt Lake Tribune*, October 1, 1989.

[709] Doug Robinson, "Semnani living American dream," *Deseret News,* November 11, 2001.

[710] Paul Wetzel's retirement remarks, October 2012.

[711] Paul Wetzel's undelivered retirement remarks, October 2012.

37 - Journey of a Lifetime

NCEW suddenly resurrected the Southeast Asia trip, and after rushing to get a series of inoculations, Denny and I anxiously boarded a plane for San Francisco in November. This three-week excursion became the highlight of my career.

Denny paid to go along as my spouse, or shopper extraordinaire. The dozen or so other spouses were women. I was the only female among 20-plus male editorial writers and commentators, a few of them Vietnam War veterans trying to clarify their haunting military years.

Our journey began with a briefing at the Asia Foundation in San Francisco the same day the Berlin Wall first was breached, incredibly loosening the Communist Party's grip on governments throughout Eastern Europe -- but not Vietnam. The Germanys were working on reunification, raising fears they might become an economic, if not military threat again. If he understood what was happening, my father would have been horrified. Having always lived under the cloud of the Cold War, however, I was awed by each new development.

We endured a horrendously long flight to Japan's Narita Airport before transferring to local planes headed for Bangkok and then Vietnam to sidestep the U.S. trade embargo. Bangkok was both exotic with its golden temples and chokingly polluted and gridlocked, but we were comfortable in the Intercontinental Hotel, where we talked to parrots and stowed half our useless luggage. It was too hot and muggy to wear anything but the lightest cottons.

Denny began his shopping spree, right away buying me a beautiful outfit, an antique elephant bell, wood carvings and wall hangings. His frenzy entertained our travel agent and other spouses, but I had no time for it.

We opinion writers met with Thai bureaucrats, who were concerned about porous borders permitting political outlaws to wage guerrilla war and smuggle goods and people. The prospect of the U.S. lifting its embargo against Vietnam was high on the agenda.

Our Russian Aeroflot flight to Hanoi scared me silly. As we walked down the aisle, a smelly substance spewed from vents above the seats, creating the impression we were being gassed. Our in-flight meal featured gooey rice. When I raised my camera over Hanoi, the steward sternly scolded: "No pictures!"

On November 12, we stepped into a breathtakingly beautiful countryside seemingly bombed back to the Stone Age as U.S. Gen. Curtis E. LeMay proposed during the war. My chest tightened at the sight of small-boned northern Vietnamese, some with teeth blackened by betel nut, wearing dark pajama-like clothes and bamboo conical hats while guiding water buffalo though rice paddies. Children and even some adults gathered around us with shy smiles that gave way to giggles of delight when one of our group handed them Polaroid pictures of themselves. They clutched their treasures to their bosoms while waving goodbye.

Unfortunately, the charm didn't quite eclipse my impression of the Hanoi airport lavatory, a smelly stone structure bisected by a narrow trench running to a hole in the floor. I had no idea how to proceed. I just did what I had to.

Our Vietnamese tour guide drew our attention to the Hanoi Hilton, proudly declaring John McCain its most famous resident and a friend to Vietnam. I was confused. Wasn't McCain tortured along with other American prisoners of war?

We spent our first three nights in a stark Cuban hotel on Hanoi's Red River for $100 per room. The single television channel featured Russian tractors which, we learned, tend to bog down in rice paddies. We snatched no more than five hours of sleep a night, and when I finally nodded off, each day's images swirled through my dreams.

I felt safe and unsafe, welcome and unwelcome at the same time. No matter where we went, soap was scarce, toilet paper scratchy like crepe paper. Just one stoplight hung in Hanoi's streets, and it didn't work. Few cars but many scooters and heavily laden bicycles fought for space in the city of soiled and crumbling French provincial buildings.

This was not a purely socialist system. A sort of street capitalism prevailed.

People sold pho -- beef or chicken noodle soup -- on street corners for breakfast, lunch and dinner, but we ate at fancy restaurants where we used U.S. Army-issue utensils salvaged from the war to cut through tough chicken. Heineken and Coke were staples while bottled water sold at a premium.

When I didn't have change for a $3 embroidered satin robe, the wrinkled shopkeeper motioned for us to wait. We stood around for 20 minutes, worrying he'd return with armed relatives for an ambush. Instead, he brought back two soft, dirty dollar bills that obviously had been stowed away for years.

We toured Bach Mai hospital, an open-air building bombed during the war but still in service. The stench of cesspools nauseating me as rats nosed around cots often shared by two patients. Rags served as pillows. Bandages were rinsed by hand and dried on railings between wrappings. Doctors there earned just $10 a month. Several in our group made donations on the way out, and a writer from the Midwest set up a charity upon returning to the States.

Saigon, or Ho Chi Minh City as renamed by its Communist conquerors, remained more progressive than Hanoi. Scooters and vehicles squeezed through busy streets lined by multi-story buildings.

We stayed two nights at Hotel Rex and celebrated Thanksgiving at the Moulin Rouge. Acrobats entertained us with hula hoops while we dined on "smashed potatoes" and turkey specially prepared for our holiday.

Streetwise Amerasian kids hawking gum or postcards -- in English -- pestered us outside our hotel. As the offspring of U.S. soldiers, we were told, these children were mostly outcasts, so their job prospects were limited.

At another hospital, an articulate woman doctor drew out attention to preserved fetuses deformed by the Agent Orange the American military spread over her country. Vietnam needed help, including medical supplies, to cope with the health crisis, she indicated. As it was, she noted, each pair of surgical gloves was worn repeatedly. Little did she know that the U.S. government had yet to deal with Agent Orange's impact on its own soldiers.

Most of the famous and not-so-famous Vietnamese we met were gracious and friendly.

One was Nguyen Xuan Oanh, a Harvard-educated economics adviser to the Communist government who explained Vietnam's idea of a mixed economy. Another was Nguyen Co Thach, the handsome vice premier and foreign minister who confidently sought our support for normalized relations. After all, he noted, Americans trades with China, the target behind U.S. involvement in Vietnam.

We talked to two Army officers turned publishers: Maj. Gen. Tran Cong Man and Col.

Bui Tin, who accepted South Vietnam's surrender April 30, 1975 and "liberated" ("invaded," according to U.S. officials) Cambodia January 7, 1979. Looking more like a beatnik than a soldier, Bui told us his newspapers were held back by supply shortages and edicts to avoid negative stories about the Communist government.

In Ap Bac, the site of a bloody battle January 2, 1963, former guerrilla Ngo Anh Giao told us how the Saigon government pushed villagers off their land and into the ranks of the Viet Cong. The guerrillas won battles, he explained, because the South Vietnamese Army didn't bother to hide. His take on Vietnam's political position was as clear as anyone's: Thanks to Communism, Vietnam was able to get rid of the French, who "wanted to make us slaves." Americans then helped South Vietnam's regime "put another yoke around our neck."

It was in Ap Bac that our feisty government guide, Mai, lost her cool. An obviously impoverished man shaking with anger limped up to our group, demanding to know why we'd left him behind after he'd fought for us in the war. A columnist in our group gruffly asked Mai why this man couldn't get help, and she retorted: "Why should Vietnam support him when he worked for you? He can eat if he works. My government wants me to be nice to you, I don't." She also asserted that Americans were actually fighting the Soviet Union and China in her country but didn't take troops there because they were "equally strong" while Vietnam was weak.

It was difficult to disagree.

We left the country as the Berlin Wall was crumbling, offering hope the lifting of the Iron Curtain would improve opportunities for Vietnam's 65 million people. I hoped to return someday.

NCEW group in Phnom Penh, Cambodia.

Cambodia was even more heartbreaking -- yet encouraging.

Our small plane arrived at a nearly deserted airport in the capital, Phnom Penh. We stood around a dirt patch in the hot afternoon sun waiting for a government agent to greet us. The only signs of life were two chewing women crouched on their haunches and a couple of customs officials eyeing our camera gear. Finally, a young, good-looking Cambodian pulled up on a scooter with a big smile and introduced himself as our guide, Vibol.

Nadia, our New York travel agent, scolded Vibol in French about his tardiness and lack of transportation for our group. Still smiling, he told us in broken English that he worked for the foreign ministry for now but planned to own a big travel company someday. He had a lot to learn. Or maybe we did.

We sweltered for some time longer until a big, dusty bus pulled up to take us to our hotel, the Santepeap. At $30 a night, it was overpriced. We could shower while sitting on the toilet. Our dirty water drained onto the dirt outside the hotel entrance where children and adults alike squatted at will.

Vibol made a habit of missing deadlines and collecting kickbacks from every restaurant we visited. But he had an interesting story to tell. Vibol led us through Tuol Sleng and the Killing Fields where the Khmer Rouge tortured and killed thousands of educated and wealthy Cambodians whose skulls were memorialized in a tall stupa.

During our visit, Pol Pot's followers still were trying to regain power though civil war. Grenades exploded outside our restaurant and elsewhere to show us the Vietnam-installed regime lacked control. Young soldiers wielding machine guns patrolled the streets, and we heard gunshots outside our locked-down hotel. Thanks to Vibol, who kept us drinking and dancing to live rock music at a floating restaurant past curfew one night, we spent several scary minutes with an AK-47 aimed at our driver. A pack of Marlboros finally gave us a pass.

As a teen-ager -- he was now 34 -- he had been driven from the city by the Khmer Rouge, the Maoists who killed over three million Cambodians under Pol Pot's leadership. While walking beneath heads dangling from the trees by their long hair, young Vibol scrambled to find a knife to slice off his own long locks. He learned to hide his connection to the upper class.

Vibol took us to the Killing Fields.

Dancing at floating restaurant in Phnom Penh.

For me, the tensest moment in Phnom Penh occurred in the office of Dith Monty, vice minister of foreign affairs. By then, the city's poor sanitation had sabotaged my digestive tract, and I frantically sought out the latrine. In my desperation, I mistakenly used the cistern, fouling the official's drinking water. Afterwards, I tried to push aside memories of that shameful incident with the image of Khieu Kanharith, a national assemblyman and newspaper editor who smiled broadly when I gave him a *Tribune* baseball cap. But I didn't always succeed.

While touring the streets, we noticed many hand-written signs offering English lessons. Everyone wanted to learn English so they could start businesses and make money off tourists, Vibol explained.

The morning we left Phnom Penh, my stomach still roiled. Seeing a local restaurateur bleed a 10-foot snake at breakfast didn't help. I worried while Nadia haggled with Vibol over our payment and passports. When we finally boarded three minivans for the drive back to Vietnam, we were advised not to step off the road to relieve ourselves because the war had left behind many live land mines.

Craters from U.S. bombing still scarred the countryside. Occasionally we came upon a Buddhist temple, a village of thatched huts or Cambodians carrying pigs to market on bicycles, hawking sugarcane along the Mekong or sitting astride water buffalo in the rice paddies.

The bumpy, dusty ride tortured my bursting gut. I could have kissed the ground at the border crossing. Instead, I beelined for the nearest bush, which hid me from my American companions but exposed my urgency to local field workers. I pretended not to notice.

Some of the veterans in our contingent stayed a few more days in Vietnam to see places that still haunted their nightmares, leaving just a handful of exhausted journalists for four days of scheduled meetings and side trips in Indonesia.

Reluctant to offend Indonesians with a paltry turnout, I attended every official meeting, beginning with a cocktail party at the U.S. ambassador's residence. Males in our party received batik shirts for the sultry evening. Because of my unexpected gender, I received a couple of yards of batik fabric to sew into a skirt or dress someday. That day never came.

We saw opulence next to slums in Jakarta, the capital of this Muslim nation of more than 250 million people and 13,000 islands.

Our most important meeting was with General Tre Sutrisno, commander of the Indonesian Armed Forces. As such, he essentially commanded the world's fourth most populous country and might someday succeed President Suharto, who took office after a bloody anti-Communist civil war that had killed as many as a million Indonesians. We also met with Radius Prawiro, Suharto's economic minister who refused to explain how Suharto and family became so wealthy during his presidency.

Me interviewing Gen. Sutrisno.

On an apparently slow news day, Jakarta's English-language daily, the *Indonesian Observer*, splashed a photograph of scowling, bedraggled me with smiling, youthful Gen. Sutrisno across its front page above the fold.

Scaredy-cat Denny was bolder by then. He stared down a pickpocket shadowing an oblivious *Atlanta Constitution* writer with expensive cameras slung over his shoulder. He added to his treasure trove of large, expensive souvenirs. He argued with our guide over God. One of Indonesia's basic principles of government is a belief in God, and the guide assured my heathen husband that he did, indeed, believe in God whether he knew it or not.

After a short flight on Garuda Indonesia airlines to Jogjakarta, we intrepid travelers climbed to the top of Borobudur, the world's largest Buddhist temple built in the 9th century and now towering above rice paddies and jungle as a tourist attraction. We also toured a batik sweat shop, where we bought more souvenirs before collapsing from the heat.

It would have been nice to see artsy Bali and threatened rain forests harboring endangered species, but as one of our organizers sternly reminded me, this was a political fact-finding trip, not a vacation. I mumbled something about the importance of the environment and the side trip some took to Angkor Wat, but no one listened.

Back in Bangkok, our rice-weary group stopped at McDonald's for Big Macs, fries and milkshakes. I almost threw up.

Aside from my faux pas in Cambodia, the Southeast Asia trip was so exhilarating that even homebody Denny developed a mild thirst for more travel. Once home, I devoured movies ("The Year of Living Dangerously") and books about Vietnam and Indonesia. A more mundane outcome was our shrunken appetites. We could hardly stomach American food and ate at Asian restaurants almost daily for months.

In a follow-up letter to Nguyen Quang Dy, a foreign press officer in Hanoi, I wrote:

> I was especially thankful for our exposure to some of the outlying countryside, where we met people who, despite the nation's serious economic challenges, were hard-working, open and friendly. This was very impressive given the history and political relations between the United States and Vietnam .. Your government is to be commended for its resolve to improve living conditions and to develop reasonable relations with the international community, including the United States.

38 - Writing Away the Days in 1990

The new year began with me burning myself out on a series of Southeast Asia articles for our op-ed pages. I worked long days and weekends to get the stuff done without shirking my regular responsibilities. Jim Woolf was kind enough to review the series but was brutal with his criticism. It was too long and detailed, more reporting than analysis. Too many facts at the expense of concepts.

For Cambodia, I criticized the United Nations for failing "to deal rationally" with Prime Minister Hun Sen's Communist government and instead legitimizing Pol Pot's genocidal Khmer Rouge.[716] I quoted leaders from Cambodia, Vietnam, Thailand and Indonesia on proposals for removing Vietnam from Cambodia, ending the civil war and holding democratic elections.

In an eight-part (gasp!) series on Vietnam, I defended Ho Chi Minh and blasted U.S.-backed Prime Minister Ngo Dinh Diem and his brother Nhu. I called upon the U.S. government to normalize relations with the impoverished nation that beat us in war. While conceding I may have been swayed by practiced propagandists, I pointed out that six Vietnam veterans in our group came away with similar opinions:

None exhibited any animosity, although a couple were obviously uncomfortable when confronted by the former enemy. Rather, they closed a chapter of their lives they hadn't even realized remained unfinished. They drank beer and sang Army songs together but wept alone when revisiting their abandoned bases and camps. Then they returned home to encourage their American readers to forge a new friendship with Vietnam.[717]

A couple of months after our tour, Communist Vietnam changed its constitution to soften accusations of aggression and imperialism by the United States and to permit small steps toward greater democracy and a more open economy.[718]

My columns inspired Business Editor Bob Woody to give me copies of letters he had written 22 years earlier opposing the misguided, unwinnable war.

On August 26, 1967, he wrote Utah Rep. Sherman Lloyd:

I am not now and never have been persuaded that our presence in Viet Nam is right. My sense of national vanity, purpose, need and morality does not compel Pax Americans in southeast Asia. No, we can't withdraw now. But we can stop bombing the north . . .

His February 19, 1968 letter to Utah Sen. Wallace F. Bennett went on:

My sense of national purpose, national vanity and national security does not require "victory" in Viet Nam. I don't doubt we can have physical victory -- if we really wish. But I don't think we will ever win . . . I believe the historic premises of our actions are incorrect -- that is, the preservation of "legitimate" governments, the containment of communism . . .
I have borne arms, been shot at and shelled in another war . . . I would risk that exposure again if I were persuaded my country or my world were threatened. I am not so persuaded this time. . .

Woody concluded with a plug for the vote for 18-year-olds: "Old enough to fight and die, old enough to vote!" He was both a thinker and a doer.

To the relief of my editors, I wrote little about Thailand and Indonesia. No more voluminous copy to edit and squeeze onto the page. But I did offer pieces on Vietnam and Cambodia to the Travel section, where I could include more picturesque photos. About Hanoi, I said:

My first impression, as an unseasoned traveler, was that I'd fallen into a time warp. The primitive "toilet" in the dilapidated, tiny airport provided the first clue that America had indeed bombed Vietnam back to the Stone Age.[719]

The country was poor, eager for American acceptance into world trading circles, so they showed us the best they had to offer. We enjoyed the food, which we already knew from our favorite restaurant, and we met some warm, friendly people and a few resentful ones.

My Asia series brought zealots out of the woodwork. John Whittaker, a jobless advocate for Vietnam vets hung around local bars discussing the war. Our "relationship" began with letters to the editor. On March 4, 1990, he took issue with my February 15 claim that Vietnam showed no signs of holding MIAs or their remains hostage.[720]

Whittaker contended that the Vietnamese tried to sell back 57 live prisoners of war for $4 billion in early 1981 but that President Reagan refused to negotiate or even inform the American public of the offer. He also cited former CIA Director William Casey's statement in 1986 that "the nation knows the POWs are there." Whittaker concluded: "If Diane Cole and her fellow reporters had been aware of the truth about our POWS, they might have written: 'On our recent trip to Southeast Asia, we didn't meet any of our POWs, but . . . '"

After his letter appeared, Whittaker called me repeatedly to argue the finer points of my views on Vietnam. Then he somehow slipped through *Tribune* security to invade my office at inconvenient times -- that is, when I had something more important to do. Denny at first watched from his drawing table nearby to make sure I was safe. After a couple of years, he wondered whether Whittaker and I had a thing going on.

* * *

I still produced editorials on other topics during my Asia binge. In January, for example, I advocated sending female troops into full-fledged combat as opposed to support positions that suppressed their climb up the chain of military command. "It makes no more sense to keep all women out of combat because of the inability of some to effectively fight the enemy than it does to exclude all men on account of an ill-suited few," my editorial said.[721] Given the fuzzy distinction between women's support positions and infantry combat, I called restrictions on women superfluous.

One commentary on state liquor laws called for the fine-tuning of reform legislation on Capitol Hill:

Generally, Senate Bill 141, which enjoys the support of most senators, as well as a crucial stamp of "no opposition" from Church of Jesus Christ of Latter-Day Saints leaders, would move Utahns a major step closer to meaningful liquor control.

The measure essentially would rid the state of the counterproductive use of minibottles and so-called brownbagging . . .

Utah has been odd state out with minibottles . . . Brown-bagging is another tacky anachronism.[722]

And so on.

Harry named me associate editor of the Editorial Department, a mostly meaningless title mentioned in a news story but irrelevant as to assignments and money.

Assuming the best, Lou Gladwell, an old contact from Weber State College, wrote me a note January 8:

I was news director when you visited Weber State to talk to the dean of students. I noted then what a bright and personable girl you were! And what a background you have . . . as education editor. Hooray, Diane. I am an admirer of yours.

Shauna Bona, an administrative assistant for *network*, a monthly publication on Utah women's issues, also offered congratulations:

I doubt you'll remember me from way back when you were writing about education, but I will always remember how supportive you were of me at Orem High School and then at the *Daily Utah Chronicle*. I'm glad to see you are gaining more and more power and prestige at *The Tribune*.

Although neither power nor prestige was involved, I appreciated her kind words. And I definitely remembered the quietly competent young woman.

Joan Burnside, chairman of Salt Lake Community College's Institutional Council and a member of the state school board when I covered so much conflict there, did her best to yank me from my pedestal. On January 16, she wrote a letter of "outrage" over my editorial criticizing President Orville Carnahan's junket to Russia.

The editorial must have been written without an investigation, inasmuch as the chief issue portends [that's what it said] the use of state government dollars and cites only Dr. Carnahan . . . Surely if the intent was to slander Dr. Carnahan, then the whole issue of who attended, and at what or whose expense, should be discussed. It begs the question of who or what motive was behind the . . . editorial.

Without fully understanding Burnside's complaint, I did feel kind of bad about singling out Carnahan for ridicule. I liked him and knew how insecure he was. While covering higher education, I had tired of his carping about the lack of public funding and personal prestige at his college in particular, and I disrespected his reliance on others to speak for him now. Perhaps I was unfair.

* * *

As associate editor, I started dressing up op-ed columns with larger illustrations, some sent in by former staff artist Tim Brinton, who was freelancing from California. I also expanded letters to the editor to half the op-ed page as suggested in recent seminars. Instead of reducing our month-long backlog of Forum letters as intended, however, we received more than ever, creating more work than ever.

Meantime, I went way out on a limb to widen the letters to 1 1/2 columns to facilitate reading and add variety to our pages. The big boss -- Publisher O'Brien -- did a double take. It was too drastic a change for our reliable readers. So I attempted a smaller revision. We had always published letter writers' cities of residence if they lived outside Salt Lake County, but most readers lived within the county, so I figured it would be more consistent and informative to identify their cities, too. When Fuller said we needed O'Brien's permission, I gave it up. I didn't have the energy to argue now that I had so many letters to edit.

* * *

The Tribune made a good showing in the SPJ-SDX contest that year, with several staffers taking first place: Chris Jorgensen, Mike Gorrell and Jim Woolf for spot news coverage of the Quail Creek Dam failure; Rick Egan for his photo portfolio; Tim Fitzpatrick's team for cold-fusion coverage; Paul Rolly for investigating the Mormon Church's killing of liquor legislation; Lex Hemphill for "A Night That Changed Basketball," and Cathy Free for Freestyle.[723]

I placed second with a package of three editorials, including one calling for the repatriation of Vietnamese refugees, another urging women to better prepare to support themselves, and the third suggesting a formal review of the Utah State Department of Corrections.

The repatriation editorial said:

Hypocrisy Marks U.S. Response to Vietnamese Refugee Plight

The United States' righteous indignation over the forced repatriation of Vietnamese refugees is hard to stomach.

This week, 51 of the 57,000 Vietnamese refugees living in Hong Kong detention centers were involuntarily returned to Vietnam. Speaking for President Bush, Marlin Fitzwater called the British colony's deportation. "unacceptable until conditions improve in Vietnam."

It's the U.S. position, according to U.S. State Department spokesman Richard Boucher, that Britain should "grant asylum to all those persons from Vietnam who seek it."

First of all, conditions in the camps can't be much better than those in Vietnam, where people generally have enough to eat. Access to Hong Kong jobs is limited, fostering a sense of hopelessness and dependency among refugees that hardly satisfies normal human rights standards.

Secondly, the U.S. trade embargo against Vietnam is largely responsible for driving Vietnamese -- most refugees in Hong Kong are North Vietnamese with no political justification for leaving -- from their homelands and into the crowded squalor of refugee camps. They are seeking better economic opportunities for themselves and their children, much as Mexicans do when they sneak into the United States and face deportation. The desperate conditions back home, the result of 45 years of war, cannot improve while the country is cut off from America's industrialized allies.

The United States can also claim some of the credit for keeping refugees in limbo. This country has taken in hundreds of thousands of Indochinese refugees since 1975, but it hasn't made room for hundreds of thousands of other worthy Vietnamese immigrants.

The United States has accepted 26,281 Vietnamese refugees and immigrants this year. While a significant increase over the 15,000 admitted each of the previous several years, 670,000 Vietnamese are still waiting for admission.

Major roadblocks to speedier immigration are U.S. priorities and budget-driven quotas, rather than the Vietnamese government's lack of cooperation. Highest U.S. priority goes to officers of the fallen South Vietnam regime who have spent the longest time in reeducation camps, Amerasians and their families, and families of Vietnamese-U.S. citizens. Former employees of the U.S. government have yet to make the list.

Vietnam has let nearly 250,000 residents leave the country legally since 1979 and has approved the departures of hundreds of thousands more. Although Vietnamese officials wanted all identified Amerasians resettled in the United States by the end of this year, more than 20,000 still await American paperwork. Another 90,000 households of ex-officers and soldiers from the old regime have been identified for "orderly departure," but the United States is considering only 11,000.

The United States should put its own house in order before berating other countries where desperate Vietnamese refugees have managed to find initial asylum. The first order of business should be suspension of a trade embargo that encourages the Vietnamese to seek, however fruitlessly, greener fields elsewhere.[724]

My second contest entry addressed LDS Church leaders, which must have made Gallivan cringe again. But I couldn't resist the opportunity to ride one of my favorite hobbyhorses:

Condoning Women at Work Should Benefit Utah Future

Women . . . should train themselves to make a contribution to society.

That seemingly simple, self-evident statement, made Sept. 23 by Gordon B. Hinckley, first counselor in the First Presidency of the Church of Jesus Christ of Latter-day Saints, may mean more to the majority of Utah women, their families and the state than any number of legal and social maneuvers. It could finally free women to realize their potential and improve their world.

As much or more than American women elsewhere, Utah women work outside the home. While many of those females must work to support their families, they usually do so at a much lower rate of pay than working men. A major reason is their lack of training and experience for the best jobs.

During the past several years, Utah educators, politicians and business interests have urged young women to prepare early for gainful employment. They've particularly emphasized the importance of advanced mathematics and science classes for girls, who tend to restrict their options in today's technological job market by avoiding such subjects.

But those community leaders might have been talking to a brick wall. The majority of Utah women are members of the LDS Church, and in the past, that church's leaders undoubtedly have discouraged young women from pursuing meaningful careers outside the home.

In January 1987, President Ezra Taft Benson said that mothers' and fathers' roles are clearly defined by God, and "contrary to conventional wisdom, a mother's calling is in the home, not in the marketplace."[725]

The editorial went on about President Hinckley's clarification benefitting Mormon women and even the world, but you get the idea. It felt so good to have my say about this old thorn in my side.

My third contest submission apparently persuaded legislators to order an audit of prison policy and procedures. It read, in part:

Since Gov. Norm Bangerter appointed Gary DeLand director of the State Department of Corrections in 1985 the prison has generated more than its fair share of inmate complaints, a significant number of which pose legitimate questions:

-- Is the prison's grievance procedure effective in resolving such problems as sex abuse of inmates?

-- Do inmates have reasonable access to the courts, including appropriate mailing privileges, legal advice and research and writing materials?

-- Are inmates who speak out being unfairly punished?

-- Are prisoners offered the kind of education and training that enable them to succeed once released?

-- Do prisoners receive adequate medical care, including treatment for AIDS?

-- Are certain visitation restrictions fair and valid for maintaining security?

-- Should Native American inmates have access to ceremonial sweat lodges in order to exercise their religious rights?

-- Do prison plans for double-bunking inmates satisfy federal standards of humane treatment?

Should inmates be allowed to publish a prison newspaper?[726]

This was one of several editorials I based on **Christopher Smart's** prison reporting.

It had been a harrowing year for Smart. Working from ACLU and prisoner reports, he uncovered a system that could be considered cruel and unusual -- from its lack of medical care and rehabilitation to its double-bunking of inmates in tiny cells. The ACLU was suing over the double-bunking. Smart reported sex between inmates and guards and a subsequent coverup. Apparently one prisoner's complaint was ignored because he was gay, leading administrators to conclude the sex was consensual.[727]

Smart also reported on the lack of inmate access to legal counsel. Salt Lake City lawyer Ross Anderson characterized the prison's contract with an Orem law firm to provide prisoners with legal counsel as a "ruse" to impede access to the courts.

Attorney Brian Barnard was demanding that Native American inmates be allowed a sweat lodge on prison grounds.

DeLand counterattacked with the claim a Smart story on strip searches worsened prison

safety. One inmate source, David Jolivett, was televised in a prison rampage, putting Smart's objectivity into question. Smart's beat was turned over to Paul Rolly, at least temporarily. Deland used the Jolivett "riot" to further advantage by claiming the ACLU director's comments about Jolivett's safety had set him off.

Meantime, the ACLU filed another lawsuit, this one alleging "deficient" medical and mental health care at the prison.

On December 29, 1989, I blamed most of the prison problems on Scott McAlister, whom DeLand recruited from Oregon's troubled prison system to serve as his corrections inspector general and ombudsman. McAlister resigned just before Christmas for unreported reasons.

What Smart knew but could no longer report was that McAlister had been accused of sexually harassing female employees. It fell to KTVX-TV reporter John Harrington to reveal those charges. To DeLand's chagrin, Smart returned to the beat to report the discovery of kiddie porn videos in McAlister's possession. The state wound up financing his defense and damages, but at least one bad actor left Utah's prison administration so that he could share his "expertise" with Arizona's prison system.

On March 25, 1990, another of my editorials criticized Gov. Bangerter for going "to bat for Gary DeLand, who, as his Department of Corrections director, has been playing hardball with inmates . . . and then portraying himself as an underdog to the big, bad American Civil Liberties Union." (Oh, oh. I hope the ACLU award didn't influence my opinion.) The editorial, which I submitted to AP's journalism contest in 1991, added that "no one, including criminals who rely on prison officials for health care, should have to unnecessarily writhe in pain, bleed to death or go blind for lack of medical attention. Neither should they be crammed together into cages."

Possibly partially due to that editorial, the Utah State Division of Mental Health gave me an award for "contributing to better understanding of mental illness."

In April, I accepted DeLand's invitation to tour the prison. The tough, cocky Corrections chief, a cowboy from Idaho, wanted me to see for myself what was happening instead of depending on reports from Chris Smart and ACLU Director Michele Parish-Pixler for information.

After the visit, I wrote a letter thanking DeLand for spending so much time explaining his department and philosophy. "It can't help but lead to better editorials . . . We may not always agree, but at least we'll be able to visualize the situation, imagine where you're coming from and know whom to talk to for more information if necessary."

DeLand then invited me to contact him personally with questions about the prison system. "The Department of Corrections can only benefit from increasing its openness in dealing with the press and letting the operation, facilities and staff speak for themselves," he wrote.

Clearly stoked by the attention, he asked me to tell Pat Bagley, who had recently lampooned him in an editorial cartoon, that he had shaved his beard but not his mustache. For future reference, of course.

I may have softened my attacks on DeLand or shifted my focus, but I did no about-face on him or his prison system.

My July 26, 1990 editorial blasted state policies for creating an explosion in the inmate population and state prison expenses.

> The majority [of state legislators] seems perfectly satisfied with current prison policy, practical considerations be damned . . . That policy has doubled the prison population while the crime rate has stayed the same the past decade. It has used up millions of extra dollars for new prison facilities and program expansion, leaving other Utahns, such as the poor and disabled, with insufficient state support.

In October, DeLand sent a letter thanking me for suggesting he meet with Chris Smart about his prison reporting. He attached a *San Diego Union* editorial calling for a crackdown on crime and swift punishment. "Maybe I should be running corrections in 'liberal' California rather than 'conservative' Utah," he quipped, apparently unaware of San Diego's conservative bent.

By the time ACLU lawsuits worked their way through the system in 1992, DeLand had turned over his seven-year job to his old buddy Lane McCotter, who quickly took steps to silence Chris Smart. For years, the prison had wire-tapped Smart's telephone conversations with prisoners, and McCotter gave transcripts to *Tribune* editors. Editor Will Fehr was not pleased with Smart's criticism of his editors as caught on tape, and Smart soon left *The Tribune* for the

Weekly Private Eye, which became *City Weekly*. (Fehr's replacement would rehire Smart in 2002.)

Smart's absence did not shield McCotter from controversy over a torturous prison policy that left at least one mentally ill inmate, Michael Valent, dead after spending 14 hours nude in a restraint chair. McCotter resigned under fire in 1997 and went into business with DeLand, who had become a national -- even international -- prison consultant. The U.S. Justice Department hired the pair to set up the infamous Abu Ghraib prison in Iraq, where their military replacements later tortured, raped, sodomized and murdered detainees in 2003.[728][729]

* * *

In May, Will Fehr received a letter from Richard Kendell, former associate superintendent of public instruction and then superintendent of Davis School District, commending me, Peter Scarlet and Melinda Sowerby for our coverage of the district's $40 million bond election. "The work of Diane Cole with this project was excellent."

My relationship with Davis District had come a long way since Kendell's news-averse predecessors ruled the roost.

* * *

New personal matters were unfolding that spring of 1990.

Denny lifted weights four mornings a week and studied Aikido twice a week. Lulu, who joined the National Guard, lost her New York apartment, so Denny sent her $600 for a new one. Hoever, he declined to co-sign a mortgage loan for Stormy and Winker, an affront that put us on their shit list again. Denny's dad wasn't well. His legs were swelling, and his breathing was labored. We were told his arthritis medication was to blame.

* * *

As I approached 40, the seven-year itch started irritating me again. Along with it, the "Dad Devil" gene I blamed for my negativism lowered my tolerance for everyone around me.

Even sweet receptionist Trish got on my nerves. When watering the plants on my bookcase, her spiked heels gouged the seat of the maple chair I'd salvaged from remodelers. Scowling, I said I'd do the watering from now on. "OK," she chirped. "I have time to file your clippings now." Reminding myself of the investment officer I'd detested in Los Angeles, I sourly suggested she do it when I wasn't there.

Denny's brother Jerry started dating a mellowing Dawn House after her divorce from Mike Tracy. At parties she still introduced herself as a BYU graduate but devoted less energy to questioning the Mormon Church. House was the second *Tribune* woman Jerry took to Lake Powell; Joan O'Brien the first. If he'd known that JoAnn Jacobsen noticed him when he was working in the library during college, his lineup might have included three *Tribune* women.

* * *

The character of the newsroom was changing, and a contributing factor was the 1990 retirement of the biggest character of them all, **Bob Woody**. No more "Take a number!" yelled across the newsroom. No more cigar smoke, spring rites, lizard imitations and impromptu sing-alongs.

Woody recommended his assistant of seven years, **Joe Rolando**, as his replacement. Publisher O'Brien and Editor Fehr summoned Rolando to Lamb's Restaurant, where they offered him the job, which came with a fixed salary. That is, no overtime.

After consulting his wife, co-owner of the family insurance business, Rolando told Fehr his $30,000 salary would not compensate for all the extra hours he'd have to work. Fehr offered a $25 weekly raise; Rolando asked for $125. O'Brien refused on the grounds he'd be new to his position.

So, recalling his vow as editor of the *Sun Advocate* to never again let management jerk him around, Rolando turned down the promotion and recommended **Paul Rolly** for the job. He, Steve Oberbeck and T.R. Dowell became Rolly's assistants.[730]

Rolly hit the ground running as business editor, continuing his compulsive quest for scoops. At the same time, he went around the world with bigwigs like Jon Huntsman Jr., the former gubernatorial candidate whose chemical business made billions.

In May of 1991, for instance, Huntsman took an entourage of 100 Utahns to the former Soviet Union to witness his accomplishments. In Armenia, they toured a cement plant he'd developed to replace housing that collapsed in the 1988 earthquake that killed some 25,000. At dinner, Mormon Apostles Russell Nelson and Dallin Oaks received a document officially recognizing the LDS Church in Russia. The *Deseret News* reporter was absent, so Rolly "scooped the *Deseret News* on the biggest Mormon story of the decade."[731] Six years later, Rolly's daughter went on an LDS mission there.

* * *

Attempting to write a hard-hitting editorial October 10, I attracted the publisher's unwelcome scrutiny. O'Brien carefully softened my words as follows:

My lead: The Utah Partnership for Education and Economic Development may deserve the general support of Utah government, but not its money.

His: The Utah Partnership for Education and Economic Development may deserve the general support of Utah government, but **perhaps** not its money.

Me: Established as a large advisory group a couple of years ago . . . the partnership would hardly be balanced.

Him: Established as a large advisory group **of blue-ribbon citizen volunteers** a couple of years ago . . . the partnership would hardly **seem** balanced.

Me: State agencies have no business paying the ongoing administrative costs of an organization that essentially created and controls itself.

Him: **It's questionable** state agencies should pay the ongoing administrative costs . . .

Me: Utah public officials must not risk wasting scarce tax dollars on a private agency which probably duplicates existing government efforts and whose activities it cannot control.

Him: Utah public officials must **be wary of requests to spend** scarce tax dollars on a private agency which probably duplicates existing government efforts and whose activities it cannot control. **The partnership purpose is noble, but the case for any taxpayer funding is still to be made."**

My attitude toward the partnership was influenced by the fact that James E. Moss, the former state school superintendent virtually fired for incompetence, was its leader. I also consistently railed against the use of tax dollars for activities outside government control.

O'Brien's reaction gave the partnership the aroma of a sacred cow. I stewed for days, obsessively analyzing every change and going over past news stories to justify my position. To no good purpose. I never mentioned it to O'Brien.

After all the folderol about Westminster College's bankruptcy years before, I received another thank you from President Charles H. Dick, this time for the "excellent editorial concerning Mrs. Genevieve Gore's $7 million gift" to the college. "You captured the warmth and generosity of her gift. Mrs. Gore remarked to me that your editorial was thanks enough for the gift."

Either I had been properly tamed, or the bankruptcy stories hadn't been as fatal as Gallivan had declared.

* * *

As part of our obligation to the community and journalism, *Tribune* staffers occasionally spoke to student groups and others about our role in society. I made a presentation to the annual High School Writers and Photographers Clinic at the University of Utah in November, for which DeAnn Evans, past managing editor of the *Deseret News,* claimed "the students were extremely laudatory. In fact," she continued in her thank-you note, "one of the advisers told me to get you back next year." She didn't.

* * *

That fall, NCEW asked for an essay for its quarterly *Masthead.* My contribution, titled "Woman's voice lends a different perspective," said, in part:

Woman's voice lends a different perspective

All career-minded girls (both of them) in my conservative Mormon neighborhood studied either education or nursing. Education and Mormon communities, it turns out, are good breeding grounds for editorial writers. There's always so much to complain about.

As a reporter, I could pick at the flaws in Utah schools and society and get paid for it. I could work on almost equal footing in a man's world.

Perhaps it was only logical that I would move into opinion writing, although it was my editor, not I, who first recognized the connection. I was more interested in becoming a news editor when he recommended me for a part-time writing job on the editorial pages in 1984.

I occasionally still wonder whether I'm a token in editorial. Since 1985 I have been the only woman on the Editorial Board and the only one to write and edit editorials full time.

. . . It so happens I was looking for a new challenge at a time when newspapers were being encouraged to diversify their staffs.

Even if I were one of The Tribune's conscious concessions to sex equity, rather than the best qualified candidate for the job, I think I add to the pages and to the community. I definitely lend another perspective to the discussion, even when it's sports, which I know and care practically nothing about.

Since I've been aboard, our pages have paid more attention to education, civil rights and social issues, though my male colleagues are sensitive to those subjects as well. Gun control, the environment, child care, welfare, health care, the justice system, prisons, homelessness, sex equity and the handicapped are topics I gravitate toward. Let's face it: People issues interest me most. But I've broken into such male bastions as public transportation and plain ol' politics, too. My male colleagues are slightly more concerned with business, economics and international events.

. . . I'm a married Caucasian with no children of my own, which is probably fortunate because the job is often exhausting. I don't let ideology hem me in on issues, but I'm probably more liberal than conservative. My salary, of course, is too low, but past instead of recent discrimination, on top of my community's economy, could be the culprit.

Besides sometimes influencing public opinion for the good of the community, I enjoy making the newsmakers in this state, where men generally run the show, a little uncomfortable. It's sometimes satisfaction enough to see the surprise on their faces when they discover I'm not a secretary but someone they must reckon with on their pet projects. Some never do speak directly to me during Editorial Board meetings, even when I'm the one who's asking most of the questions and the one who will be doing the writing. Yes, there's something to be said for being different. [732]

In one of my last editorials of the year, I praised an attempt by local residents to preserve a large swath of land in Sandy for a horseback-riding and hiking park. (It just so happened that our friends Terry and Nancy Hobbs Orme kept horses at their home nearby.) Dr. John Shakula, citizen chairman of the preservation effort, thanked us for taking the side of David in the struggle against Goliath (Salt Lake County planners). Regarding Commissioner Gordon E. Harmston's Forum letter, which claimed my editorial was "not factual in regard to . . . natural state," Dr. Shakula said, "You were correct, he was wrong. We have the documents to prove it."

It was always nice to be defended, even if the average reader had no idea who wrote the editorial.

* * *

Also toward the end of the year, my dad underwent prostate surgery. The procedure messed so much with his mind that he was never the same. He would wander off if left sitting on a bench in the mall for more than two minutes, later explaining that he thought we'd forgotten about him.

In the middle of all this, the United States attacked Iraq, setting off Operation Desert Storm. American officials said the action would be short and successful, but I knew better after Vietnam. It seemed that our troops had attacked without provocation -- aside from Iraq ignoring a so-called U.N. deadline to leave Kuwait. Denny worried that Lulu might be sent with the National Guard to the Middle East, but she dodged that bullet.

---

[716] Diane Cole, "World Powers Search for Keys to Cambodia Deadlock," *The Salt Lake Tribune*, January 28, 1990, p. A17.

[717] Diane Cole, "Past, Present, Future Dictate New U.S Policy on Vietnam," *The Salt Lake Tribune,* February 19, 1990, p. A23.

[718] Barbara Crossette, New York Times News Service, Feb. 27, 1989.

[719] Diane Cole, "Vietnam, Try to Heal Old Wounds," *The Salt Lake Tribune*, January 14, 1990, pT1.

[720] Diane Cole, "Vietnam Shows No Sign of MIAs," *The Salt Lake Tribune*, February 15, 1990, p. A17.

[721] "Bill to Test Females for Combat Rates Congressional Approval," *The Salt Lake Tribune,* January 6, 1990, Page A10.

[722] "Some Fine-Tuning Is Still Due for State Liquor Law Update," *The Salt Lake Tribune*, January 26, 1990, pA16.

[723] "Tribune Staff Garners 19 Journalism Awards," *The Salt Lake Tribune*, April 15, 1990.

[724] "Hypocrisy Marks U.S. Response to Vietnamese Refugee Plight," *The Salt Lake Tribune*, December 15, 1989, Page A26.

[725] "Condoning Women at Work Should Benefit Utah Future," *The Salt Lake Tribune*, October 4, 1989, Page A8.

[726] "Utah State Prison Now Needs Full Auditor General Review," *The Salt Lake Tribune*, November 6, 1989, Page A10.

[727] Linda Sillitoe, *"Friendly Fire: The ACLU in Utah,"* Chapter 6, 1996.

[728] Philip Gourevitch and Errol Morris, Standard Operating Procedure, May 14, 2008.

[729] "Abu Ghraib torture and prisoner abuse," Wikipedia.

[730] Joe Rolando email, November 30, 2015.

[731] Paul Rolly roast, August 19, 2015.

[732] Diane Cole, "Woman's voice lends a different perspective," *The Masthead*, Volume 42, No. 3, p. 10.

39 - Bull(y) Barges In, 1991

We finally learned what really ailed Denny's dad. A rare, terminal blood disease, amyloidosis, was destroying his internal organs. He was gone by January 11. My devastated husband began a prolonged period of arranging the funeral, making sense of his parents' finances and teaching his mother Marge to pay bills. She couldn't drive, either, so we -- or, thankfully, her sister Eileen -- took her shopping and to appointments from then on. It would be weeks before we got home before 10 p.m. during the week.

The response from certain co-workers was gratifying. Publishers Gallivan and O'Brien, Mark Knudsen and the River Crew graciously attended the funeral of NAC's longtime employee and sent flowers. As was customary for staff, the lengthy obituary was free. Oddly, some "friends" at work didn't acknowledge Denny's loss. Scarlet was irritated I didn't pay more attention to him right after the death.

* * *

Work duties continued unabated.

I was so aggravated by the publisher's reaction to my editorials that I let it pass when Wetzel horned in on my usual territory: state government, health and education. I explained it to Mimi:

O'Brien doesn't seem to see things as I do on much of anything. I gave up on abortion legislation, school prayer and public financing of quasi-private foundations. He never wants to take a strong stand before testing the waters -- and then it's often too late or convoluted to do any good.

Despite my discontent, I received congratulations on my first place showing in the annual SPJ-SDX contest. Congressman Bill Orton, LDS Church spokeswoman Carol L. Clark, Kennecott Corporation media relations manager Alexis Fernandez and others sent notes.

Orton's wife added a note of thanks for supporting a Child Care and Development block grant: "I appreciated that you took the time to research the issue . . . I have been very frustrated that people have been paying more attention to changes in our deer-hunting rules than money for our children!"

Regarding my editorials on health and human services legislation, Bill Walsh, director of Utah Issues, an advocacy group for low-income residents, joked: "Have you considered running for an elected office?"

When three teenagers were killed in a stampede to the stage of an AC/DC concert at the Salt Palace January 18, I editorially attacked the festival seating that allowed thousands of wild fans to congregate below the stage. Another day, I criticized Los Angeles police officers for brutally beating Rodney King. Thankfully, O'Brien didn't object.

* * *

An article from *The Hartford Courant* resurrected concerns about my health. Now I could worry about more than polluted air. In part, the story said:

If you've been thinking your job makes you sick, you may be right . . . . Sick-building syndrome, whose symptoms include headache, eye irritation and lethargy, may stem as much from job stress as from contaminants in the workplace, research suggests. Such factors as job dissatisfaction or long periods spent using video display terminals may make workers susceptible to sick building syndrome . . . Computer use and air pollutants may play a combined role in causing employee illness.[733]

A work break, preferably one that would stimulate my mind while adjusting my attitude, was overdue. The annual Knight and Nieman fellowships seemed just the ticket. Each offered a term of study, one at Stanford, the other at Harvard, for journalists from around the country. Besides prying me out of my rut, I believed, a fellowship would improve my editorials. So I applied to both.

My applications emphasized my need for time to study public policy issues so my future editorials would be better informed and more fair, credible and persuasive. I described myself as perceptive, curious, caring and audacious enough to believe I could improve society, and as having a highly developed sense of justice.

Much as I hated to ask for favors, I clenched my teeth and asked for letters of recommendation from Paul Rolly, Lex Hemphill and Vicki Varela, by then assistant state commissioner of higher education. Despite how I felt about his politics, I also requested a high-profile endorsement from Sen. Orrin Hatch. We had spoken at length about health and education policy during Editorial Board meetings, so I hoped he recognized my potential.

That was probably a mistake. Even with a strong recommendation, which was unlikely, his conservative politics might not have played well with the scholarly foundations. Regardless, I didn't even make it into the finals. Deeply disappointed, I didn't know where to turn for inspiration.

* * *

Everyone knew by the first of the year that Editor Will Fehr, my mentor, would retire in March. Many of us were seriously sorry to see him leave. Here was a man we knew well, who stayed cool under pressure and stuck up for his people. Still, there was nervous excitement about the possibility the paper might modernize. We might get more aggressive in our reporting and creative in our news display.

We got more -- or less -- than we bargained for. A bull(y) was about to barge in.

Denny's caricature of James E. Shelledy

James E. Shelledy, the 47-year-old editor of The Tribune Corporation's tiny Moscow (Idaho) *Idahonian,* was hired to replace Fehr. Accompanying him would be **Randy Frisch**, the 31-year-old publisher of the even smaller *Sparks* (Nevada) *Tribune* outside Reno -- the guy who

ran huge, inflammatory headlines. We're talking circulations of maybe 5,000, on a good day, for the *Idahonian* and *Sparks Tribune* vs. 150,000 for *The Salt Lake Tribune* Sundays.

If not promoting someone from within *The Tribune*, I wondered, why not recruit someone who knew Utah or who had worked at a paper at least as large as *The Tribune*?

When I learned that Shelledy had gone to jail in 1997 rather than reveal sources for police corruption stories, I was encouraged about the potential for investigative reporting.

Less promising was the arrogant, condescending letter of introduction he sent staffers ahead of his arrival. Attached was a a "brief (and genuine) resume," whatever that meant. He introduced himself as an editor who liked "news staffs which are competitive, motivated, creative, experienced, flexible, passionate and professional." He went on:

> I do not suffer well hidden agendas, dullness, petty office politics, clock-watching, inaccuracy, lethargy and unprofessionalism.
>
> I place a premium on energized writing that is concise and elegant, dramatic photos, graphics that explain, seductive headlines, design that enhances readership and sufficient imagination to keep the process lively and fun -- for us, as well as the reader . . .
>
> Ours is an industry in some trouble. *The Salt Lake Tribune* is no exception. We all need to attract more readers. Smart newspapers are adjusting to demographic shifts, time-strapped readers and new, broader definitions of news.
>
> Unfortunately, these realignments come at a time when revenues appear, at best, stagnant. We all will have to do better with less, which, ultimately, may be just as well. We will never succeed by outspending the competition. We will do it by out-thinking it.
>
> I feel advertising departments need to sell more creatively and surgically. Circulation staffs must reach for new heights in service and flexibility. And newsrooms, through better content, will have to entice that half of the population which isn't reading newspapers into seeing the error of its way, and we'll have to do that without alienating the half that currently makes us a part of their daily lives.

. . . It is not a voyage for the hesitant. It is, however, a mission that will inspire the committed . . . [734]

My initial reaction was incredulity. Who knew this pompous little prick, who was spouting the obvious while already putting us on the defensive? Well, non-journalist Dominic Welch did as comptroller of Tribune Corp., and apparently so did Publisher Jerry O'Brien and owner/travel writer Tom McCarthey. Welch saw Shelledy as a good teacher to his small staff in Moscow. McCarthey probably sought a family ally. O'Brien went along.

Like O'Brien, Shelledy was a graduate of Gonzaga University in Spokane and worked for the Associated Press and the *Spokesman Review*, similarities undoubtedly influential with team player O'Brien.

Unlike O'Brien, Shelledy was raised in hot, dusty Yuma, Arizona, taught in the public schools and dropped out of University of Idaho law school.[735] While his new boss shrank from confrontation, short, stout, scrappy Jay Shelledy relished it.

By the end of March, I understood that our new editor's reference to "hidden agendas" was a red herring. He was the one with hidden agendas.

His first week in the office, he took us editorial writers to lunch at the Judge Cafe, purportedly to get to know us and assure us he would never try to influence our editorial stance. He actually was testing our views on the relative value of staffers. We declined to identify under-performers, though I considered mentioning Shelledy's champion Tom McCarthey, whom I suspected of supplying Shelledy with a hit list. It would be while before he tried telling us how to do our jobs.

His first 100 days, Shelledy began diversifying the staff, a welcome change. At the same time, he started bullying supposedly stagnant staffers and creating so many new management positions -- editors -- that the newsroom teetered from being so top heavy. He was like a kid in a candy store with eyes bigger than his stomach (well, maybe not *bigger*) and enough money to buy whatever he wanted, no matter how good or bad.

His first major minority hire was Blackfoot Indian Mark Trahant, as one of four deputies in his top layer of new editors. Another was a typical white male: David Ledford, his former staffer in Moscow who would oversee news writing. Filling the female quota was Features Editor Barbi Robison, who soon would retire to make way for Judy B. Rollins to become the highest-level woman editor ever at *The Tribune*. Tom McCarthey, another white male, also gained the title of deputy, an obvious ploy to keep the owners on his side.

Then there was newsroom secretary Shirley Jones, who suddenly became administrative assistant to the triumvirate of Shelledy, Ledford and Trahant. For the first time she was asked to attend news huddles and offer opinions on stories. Barbi Robinson regarded her as a "squealer; Shelledy's rat."[736]

Shelledy interviewed all other newsroom staffers to see what role they wished to play in his new *Tribune*. In some cases, he fulfilled their dreams; in others, not so much.

The second new layer of management included four news editors. He killed two birds with one stone by picking Joan O'Brien as one of them. Besides breaking ground with a female news editor, he presumably pleased her publisher father, his boss. Tim Fitzpatrick also was chosen, again fulfilling a family legacy. The appointments of Dawn House and Judith Selby reinforced the rise of women in the ranks.

To be honest, I was jealous that other women got to edit the news when I didn't. I believed I was better suited to the job than say, intense House or lackadaisical Fitzpatrick. Yet I'd made a similar assumption about Paul Rolly, and just as he had proved me wrong, so would House. She stood up for her reporters and stood up to Shelledy when others fell short.

A third layer of managers included current white male staffers: John Keahey became business editor so Rolly could cover politics, Gerry Cunningham chief wire editor, David Noyce head of the Copy Desk and World News, and Dick Rosetta sports editor chair. Before long *Deseret News* writer Kurt Kragthorpe replaced Rosey, who was relegated to sports columnist and roving feature writer.

Jim Fisher, an academic from the Southwest, was hired to redesign *Tribune* graphics and manage the Art and Photo departments, effectively demoting Denny and Tim Kelly, who by then was chief photographer. Although Denny warned Shelledy that Fisher was "blowing smoke" about his qualifications, especially regarding his computer skills, Shelledy retorted that the decision was made. He often told underlings he'd win every argument as boss.

Denny fakes a smile with Shelledy.

Still more staff changes were enacted. Ace Fibber was rescued from the Copy Desk, where he'd sunk from the muck he'd churned up with his fake Sports award, to put out the newspaper's Front Page. Dance critic Helen Forsberg replaced Harold Schindler as arts and entertainment editor so he could resume television criticism. Ben Ling, after supervising pagination and computerizing *Tribune* archives with a system Shelledy started in Idaho, took charge of the library-turned-data center. Steve Brophy became pagination chief. Phil Miller advanced to assistant sports editor.

The new boss recruited several youngsters from his *Idahonian* home, including Tony Semerad, Sheila McCann, Sean Means and John Jordan. Columnist Michael Nakoryokov also came aboard after a past Shelledy gimmick lured him from Moscow, Russia, to Moscow, Idaho.
\

Michael Nakoryokov, left.

John Jordan, whose background was business rather than journalism, "lurked around the office like a cockroach"[737] in a white shirt, suspenders and bowtie like Shelledy's. When not flailing about in Lifestyle or on the Business Desk, he supposedly was troubleshooting computer problems. If someone asked for help, he was usually "too busy." Not too busy to flirt with our mezzanine receptionist or dwell in Shelledy's office, however.

Because the officious sycophant spent so much time with the boss, some of us assumed he was an informant. Barbi Robison, Jordan's first editor, flatly called him Stubby's [Shelledy's] spy.[738] Even if Shelledy was simply mentoring the kid as a favor to a friend or relative, the spy story stuck.

When not rearranging the staff, Shelledy was ruffling feathers with patronizing edicts and unsettling routines.

One edict applied a stricter dress code to usually laid back weekends:

> Public does come into the building, and your duties don't change. I have no problem with laid-back dress if you are just coming into the building for some specific thing [such confidence in staffers making adult decisions!] or to do an hour or two of extra work. But if you have a weekend shift, then the dress is the same as on weekdays.[739]

Another set an arbitrary, two-story-a-day quota for reporters. In my view, quotas might burn out the good people, encourage shallow reporting and pit reporters against each other when they should be sharing ideas and information to fully cover an issue.

But the quota was just the beginning of Shelledy's use of competition to motivate the troops. He also promised more pay and promotions to reporters with the most Page One stories. This sent reporters scrambling for limited space, encouraging them to hoard news tips and encroach on each other's beats. Resulting antagonism, again from my view, would undermine productivity while turning an interesting, exhilarating job into a cutthroat chore.

Offsetting his "positive" reinforcement, Shelledy tightened the vise on writers unfit for his team. Doug Parker was demoted from political editor to a humiliating assignment covering conventions and tiny, outlaying towns. Dave Jonsson was transferred from the State Capitol to pagination in the newsroom. Peter Scarlet was offered a glowing recommendation for a job elsewhere.

When Scarlet failed to leave after several months, the bully backed down. Without changing his modus operandi, Scarlet suddenly became Shelledy's greatest success story as an editor. How do you argue with someone who's always right?

Shelledy transformed newsroom routines.

Two news strategy meetings were held daily, a far cry from the days when the executive editor and city editor called all the shots. Staffers needed to be regularly evaluated and, often as not, sharply reprimanded. As seen earlier, Denny despised discipline and was run ragged with administrative tasks that kept him at work from 9 a.m. until 7:30 or so each day. No more four-day weeks. I was more apt to wait for him than vice versa.

To his credit, Shelledy successfully broke through Gallivan's if-it-ain't-broke-don't-fix-it logjam. The paper's appearance changed noticeably, with more art, color and sensational stories on the front pages.

The new editor begrudgingly permitted modest stories about 1991 winners of our business' annual writing contests. He made it clear, however, that he put little stock in such awards.

Perhaps the fact that the *Deseret News* swept the writing categories helped explain his attitude. His new staffers had yet to shine. But *The Tribune* did perform in other areas.

In the SPJ-SDX contest, yours truly won first place for editorials on Utah's debate over graduation prayer, U.S. policies regarding Manuel Noriega and Vietnam, and the preservation of Dimple Dell Park.[740] Harry Fuller took second with "Louts in Locker Room." Jeff Allred, Rick Egan, Lynn Johnson and Steve Griffin placed in photography.

Tribuners did better in the Associated Press Utah-Idaho-Spokane competition, where Shelledy had a track record as a feisty editor.[741] Vince Horiuchi placed first in spot news for a massive freeway crash, and he and Rodd Wagner took second covering the death of a fan at a rock concert run amok. Lex Hemphill won first for his coverage of new Utah Jazz contracts with John Stockton and Karl Malone, and Rick Egan won several photo awards.

Again, I won first in editorials, this time with the school prayer editorial and others on low-income day care and prison double-bunking

and medical policies. *The Tribune* scored no wins in investigative reporting, ongoing news coverage and other categories more important to Shelledy.

Here's what I wrote about school prayer:

Religious Hostility Is Relative

The current Utah debate over graduation prayers does not reflect what Mormon Apostle Dallin H. Oaks described as "a growing pattern of hostility to religion" as much as a growing hostility toward religious domination.

The conflict cannot be swept under the nearest rug, as Gov. Norm Bangerter seems to suggest.

Elder Oaks' comments, published in The Wall Street Journal *May 23, are part of his plea for Americans to retain graduation prayers. "Religion should have a place in the public life of our nation," he wrote. "To honor this principle with prayers in the graduation exercises of high school students is to honor the religious plurality of our nation and the religious liberty it was founded to protect."*

The former Utah Supreme Court justice misses an important point. Many school prayers, particularly those in Utah, do not "honor . . . plurality." Because Utahns are primarily Mormons, and because, as Elder Oaks notes, school officials cannot dictate the content of graduation prayers, most such prayers in Utah public school are Mormon-oriented prayers.

Those prayers honor one religion -- and religious conformity -- when the U.S. Constitution, as interpreted by the U.S. Supreme Court, forbids government advancement of any religion at the expense of any individual's religious freedom.

To imply, as Gov. Norm Bangerter did at his monthly KUED news conference last week, that the American Civil Liberties Union of Utah is somehow responsible for blowing this issue out of proportion is at least naive, if not insensitive to a growing share of his constituents.

More non-Mormons are moving into the state. These newcomers often are accustomed to religious diversity and are soon struck by the rather unusual dominance of one religion in both public and private life. They undoubtedly give longtime residents the confidence to finally make known their hidden resentment of denominational prayers at public functions and to demand respect for their own religious rights.

"As long as it's voluntary prayer not prescribed by government, I can't see where it ought to be offensive or in violation of the First Amendment," the governor said. "It's time to let freedom ring. Let the people decide what they want to do at the institution."

In other words, the governor would have the majority rule, even on a civil rights issue designed to protect the rights of the individual. Making prayer voluntary at a public function may work for adults, who feel confident in their personal beliefs, but it amounts to coercion when it involves students at school functions. Most students want to fit in, even if it means participating in the exercise of a religion not their own.

Even with the influx of newcomers, Utah will remain predominantly Mormon for the foreseeable future. As long as Utah's majority dismisses concerns about the separation of church and state as unimportant or misguided, the state will contend with religious hostility. [742]

Yep, I was still haranguing my fellow Utahns about religion. If compelled to sign such an opinion, I might have carried a smaller stick. After all, I was arguing with a governor and Mormon apostle I liked. And if Gallivan were still sitting in the primary publisher's seat, you can bet my spiel would have been squelched to maintain that delicate balance struck so long ago between *The Tribune* and Mormons. As it was, it felt great to finally expound on an issue so near and dear to my heart.

It also was gratifying to get support for one of my rarer international pieces, even though it again involved Southeast Asia. Here's how it went:

Look Who's Invading

As America's national interests change, it seems, so do its standards.

When Vietnam invaded Cambodia 10 years ago to eradicate Pol Pot, whose blood-thirsty Khmer Rouge were striking across Vietnam's southwest border, the United States sanctimoniously condemned the Vietnamese interventionists. (This, of course, was after the United States had immersed itself in Vietnam's internal affairs several years earlier.) Vietnam was punished with a trade embargo and international sanctions that remain in effect even today. The United States still refuses to recognize Cambodia's government because it was installed with Vietnam's support.

For all his faults, Manuel Noriega is no Pol Pot.

The two-bit dictator is suspected of stealing an election and trafficking in drugs that have infiltrated U.S. borders. He undoubtedly has violated various and sundry human rights laws while in power, and he audaciously declared war on the United States of America.

But Manuel Noriega and his henchmen are not accused of torturing and murdering more than a million of their own countrymen and trying to transport their reign of terror to neighboring lands. The danger his puny government posed to its giant neighbor more than a thousand miles to the north pales beside the Khmer Rouge's threat to Vietnam.

The United States, then, was no more justified in ousting Manuel Noriega than Vietnam was for deposing the Khmer Rouge. Probably less so. Vietnam was not merely suppressing an immoral assailant, it was stopping a genocide.

Yet the United States expects the world community to accept its reasons for invading Panama while rejecting Vietnam's explanation for intervening in Cambodia.

U.S. standards for national sovereignty have shifted with this country's own national priorities. Federal leaders have discounted Vietnam's arguments about Cambodia because it purportedly has been in America's best interests to do so. Vietnam has cost the United States a lot of money, lives and international prestige over the years, and Vietnam's struggles now make America look that much better by comparison.

Unfortunately, such fickle vindictiveness does not put the United States in a positive light. To soften its appearance as a bullying hypocrite, U.S. officials could at least concede that international sanctions against Vietnam for invading Cambodia are no longer fair or relevant. [743]

My day-care editorial began:

If children are truly a Utah priority, the state should be ensuring decent day-care services for the children who need it most. Day-care conditions for low-income children are abysmal in this state, and the 1991 Legislature isn't seriously considering improvements.[744]

* * *

Despite what it seems from my selective ramblings, my own editorials and Hurricane Jay Shelledy were not the only happenings in Salt Lake County in 1991.

In another of Utah's culturally unique episodes, Richard Worthington, 39, attacked Alta View Hospital in Sandy. The father of eight, upset with his wife's attempts to stem the tide of pregnancies with a tubal ligation, was going after the doctor with explosives and guns. Instead, he shot a nurse dead and then held nine people, including three babies, hostage for nearly 18 hours. A TV movie was made about the incident. Worthington killed himself in prison two years later.

Also that spring, an expose of a state senator's conflicts of interest gave me an I-told-you-so opportunity. Dawn House and Jim Woolf reported that Stephen Rees, a Republican from Taylorsville, sponsored and voted for legislation that gave money to his own company, the Institute for Research and Evaluation. That company paid Rees $65,000 a year to oversee reviews of abstinence-based, teen-pregnancy prevention programs.

It was a twofer for me: I'd had doubts about Rees when covering schools, and he now was called on the carpet over an old, familiar subject: sex education.

My May 7 editorial triggered Rees' demand for a retraction from O'Brien and Gallivan, who stayed involved with day-to-day decisions despite retirement. As always at the slightest hint of a lawsuit, *The Tribune* caved in.

Our lawyer Sharon E. Sonnenreich decided a technicality justified a "clarification and correction," something less than a retraction. The "clarification" conceded that reports were wrong that (1) Rees had sponsored legislation directly benefiting his company financially and that (2) his company had received direct financial benefit through any state support for abstinence programs. The key word here was "direct," as opposed to indirect, I suppose.

Shelledy, the guy who promised to stay out of Editorial's affairs, concluded that an error in the story's chart led to editorial "leaps that were too quantum." Even so, he deemed our editorial position "quite correct."

Upon publication of the clarification, Rees claimed to be exonerated and continued his fishy business as usual. He still insisted that state money for values-based sex education programs be restricted to those his institute studied.

Utah's Democratic Party threatened an ethics investigation of inappropriate use of legislative influence.[745] Citing criticism against him, Rees quit the institute in 1992 and resigned from the Senate in 1996 to accept a seat on the Utah Transit Authority Board of Directors.

On July 11, 2000, Rees died at age 53 from liver disease linked to medication taken for ulcerative colitis surgery.[746] I would hate to think I contributed to his early death, but I realize our actions as journalists can hurt people. But so can our inaction.

* * *

We still had some fun times as a staff -- like the night Jerry O'Brien threw a staff party at his estate near posh Walker Lane. While he hosted the bar and Joan ran interference, several of us skinny dipped in his pool. It was a bonding experience.

---

[733] Frances Grandy Taylor, *The Hartford Courant*, March 19, 1991.

[734] James E. Shelledy, letter to *Tribune* staff, February 5, 1991.

[735] *Moscow-Pullman Daily News*, January 28, 1991.

[736] Barbi Robison telephone interview, September 11, 2015.

[737] Gordon Harman on facebook's Tribune group. February 7, 2012.

[738] Robison, Sept. 11, 2015.

[739] Jay Shelledy, memo to all editors and managers, February 6, 1992.

[740] SPJ-SDX winners, *Salt Lake Tribune* April 15, 1991, p. B6.

[741] *Salt Lake Tribune*, June 22, 1991, p. B3.

[742] "Religious Hostility Is Relative," *The Salt Lake Tribune*, July 2, 1990, Page A8.

[743] "Look Who's Invading," *The Salt Lake Tribune,* January 1, 1990, Page A20.

[744] "Utah's Child Day-Care Services Need Greater Subsidization," *The Salt Lake Tribune*, February 4, 1991, Page A8.

[745] Bob Bernick Jr, political editor, Deseret News, June 21, 1991.

[746] Diane Urbani, Stephen Rees, Utah statesman, dies at 53," Deseret News, July 12, 2000.

40 - Rising in the Ranks

"Hey, Di, I want to talk to you about something," Rolly said to me one day. "Let's get a cup of coffee."

Rolly was more likely to confide in Dawn House than me these days, so I was surprised by the invitation. The two often were seen at D.B. Cooper's, presumably discussing new management and the latest political scandal. Aside from their mutual zest for routing out corruption, they seemed an unlikely couple. House still struggled with Mormonism, something outside Rolly's realm.

On our way to Lamb's, he dropped a bomb:

Shelledy wants me to do a column for Split Page, and I'm thinking of bringing JoAnn [Jacobsen-Wells] back from the *Deseret News* to be my partner. We would act on tips about politicians, but we'd include stuff from ordinary readers. It would be entertaining and edgy at the same time . . . along the lines of Herb Caen, Ann Landers and Ziggy.

"Oh, no!" I gasped. "You mean like Dan Valentine? You're the best investigative reporter we have, and you're going to give it up for a gossip column? You're going to join Shelledy's inner circle?! Don't do it, Paul. Please!!"

"Don't worry," he interjected. "He promised I can write a serious weekly column where I can cover a lot of the stuff I used to do on politics."

I groaned. Rolly had been unfulfilled as business editor for too long, I thought. He'd forgotten what got his journalistic juices flowing in the first place. Surely he didn't believe things would turn out like Shelledy said.

More selfishly, I didn't want our friendship to weaken and my pipeline to news tips to shrink. My editorials needed him! But I knew Rolly couldn't give up this chance for notoriety and clout over Utah power brokers.

Shelledy stood by his promise and approved JoAnn as Rolly's partner because they differed on religious, political and social issues. Years later, Rolly joked that there was another reason for his choice of partners: "I could think

of many, but when [Shelledy] said the person also had to like me, the field narrowed considerably.[747]

With Will Fehr in retirement, *The Tribune's* door reopened for JoAnn.

Rolly and Wells combined insider news nuggets with rumor, gossip, acts of kindness and mischief over a period of 13 years. They slapped people who left sprinklers on in the rain or misused public office. Their column was said to be one of the first two things people read in *The Tribune*. They read the obituaries to see who died and Rolly & Wells to see who was about to die.[748]

To show how easy it was to qualify for tax breaks, the pair started a nonprofit, the Church of Holy Rolly led by the Left Reverand Paul Rolly, and an offshore company like one associated with Salt Lake Mayor Deedee Corradini. They also registered as lobbyists, identifying the public as their client.

The duo competed in a media shootout during the NBA all-star weekend, when JoAnn made a 3-pointer and Rolly got none. They judged a polo match to raise funds for the Utah Opera Company.

Among JoAnn's pet sources and subjects were Orrin Hatch, Salt Lake City Mayor Rocky Anderson and Utah football coach Ron McBride. Rolly's favorite targets included Salt Lake County Attorney Doug Short, Salt Lake County Mayor Nancy Workman and Representatives Merrill Cook and Enid Greene.[749]

To the consternation of staffers near her cubicle, JoAnn carried on an irritating, flirtatious phone relationship with Senator Hatch that some derisively referred to as phone sex. Using her sweetest, most solicitous voice, she squeezed juicy tidbits from the senator and repaid him with morsels that kept him in the minds of constituents.

Rolly and Wells tweaked her previous employer, the *Deseret News*, at every opportunity. When the *News* was considering names for its new morning edition in 1999 and 2000, for example, Rolly and Wells beat them to the punch by registering the names with the Department of Commerce. (News management was thinking of dropping Deseret from its name because of its heavy Mormon overtones.) Another time, they published answers to a News Sunday theater quiz before the contest deadline. Milt Hollstein, my former professor and Copy Desk mentor who by then wrote a column for the News, cried foul:

In a big city with intense newspaper competition, as in the rivalry between the New York Daily News *and the* New York Post, The Tribune's *action would not have seemed out of place. Here, however, it was more a throwback to the days when rival editors not only castigated one another in their columns but also weren't above horsewhipping each other in the streets.*[750]

Not all the *News* taunts were in fun.

Upon learning the News was considering a column patterned after theirs, Rolly and Wells suggested possible names for it. Their proposal of LaVarr and LaVerne, or some such thing, set off LaVarr Webb, who had quit the News to run Mike Leavitt's gubernatorial campaign before becoming his policy deputy. Webb called JoAnn from the governor's office to complain but veered off track. "Why don't you print the latest rumor going around the Capitol -- that Rolly and Wells are fucking?" he demanded. JoAnn slammed down the phone and told Rolly, who told Shelledy. As JoAnn sat at her desk stunned, someone yelled across the newsroom: "JoAnn, Mike Leavitt on line 2." He had called to apologize.[751]

If I knew Rolly, he would never forgive Webb, who returned to the News as managing editor, for offending his "partner in crime." He could be expected to get even for years to come with snide asides and putdowns in his column.

Rolly remembered kindnesses, too. On a state-sponsored "junket" under the "guise" of economic development after the Berlin Wall came down in 1989, Utahns toured Philips, the parent of a Utah company, in Eindhoven, Netherlands. At breakfast, coffee was being served only to the Dutch on the assumption that Utahns were Mormons who avoided it. Gov. Norm Bangerter's wife Colleen tapped the waiter's arm and pointed to Rolly. "I coulda kissed her."[752]

As happens in the news business, Rolly and Wells made their share of mistakes. Once, for example, they reported that Magic Johnson sent the Utah Jazz a birthday cake for the first anniversary of the Delta Center. Magic Chemical Co. actually sent the cake.

* * *

On September 8, Shelledy announced more newsroom changes, including another layer of mid-management editors, or assistant city editors, for the 30-person City Desk.[753] **Terri Ellefsen** became deputy city editor, coordinator of three new City Desk divisions headed by young editors moving up from writing or copy

editing positions. Police reporter Rodd Wagner and music critic Anne Mathews suddenly took charge of other reporters.

Rodd Wagner

Anne Mathews

Just a year or two my junior, Ellefsen had achieved what I could not. With planning and perseverance, she broke at least part way through *The Tribune's* glass ceiling to a fairly high editor position on the news side. Here's how she did it and what she did with her new power:

I began that journey by being appointed editor of the weekly Davis County edition, but I had to find a back door into the ranks of those who worked side-by-side with the city editor. The position of the assistant city editor would bypass the silly notion that I would have to work in the unattainable NIPO [night police] position first.

That back-door opportunity came in the person of an assistant city editor who frequently called in sick [Lance Gudmundsen]. I regularly dropped by the newsroom briefly before heading out to Davis County. If Lance showed up, I continued with my Davis County duties. If he called in sick, I volunteered to fill his slot.

Over the months, it became more of a regular occurrence. I ended up filling in at least half the shifts, if not more. I was working side-by-side with City Editor Randy Peterson in my pseudo role. He was no longer having to scramble to get the daily duties done by handling the assistant editor job also. Eventually Randy decided to create a new position, that of *The Tribune's* first "assignment editor." He placed me in that position and ultimately opened up the door for further advancement.

I began a new journey. I had to change the mindset of *Tribune* editors. That, in large part, was helped by the appointment of a new editor for *The Tribune*.

Although Jay Shelledy came into the position with a roar, I soon saw that he was open to ideas of inclusivity. Once again, I had a plan. Not only had I seen an inequity with how the newsroom operated, but that inequity actually continued on the pages of the newspaper. Women and ethnic groups were being discounted as legitimate sources and material for the wire, local and sports pages. Their only home at the paper was in the Lifestyle section.

I embarked on a month and a half long journey to collect data. I plotted the number of instances women were listed on the front pages of the wire, local and sports pages. But, even more important, in what context they were portrayed when they did land on those pages. What I discovered was a disturbing trend: Women were generally portrayed in all three sections as victims while those with ethnic backgrounds often appeared on the wire and local pages as criminals.

I pulled together my findings and created a color graphic and presentation for Shelledy. That report also came with recommendations. As a result, Jay took several steps to change how the paper did business. He created a group of editors to make the decisions as to what stories appeared in the paper. Before that, the wire editor (a white guy), the executive editor (also a white guy) and the city editor (a white guy) made all the decisions on what appeared. The newly formed editor group included women and ethnic staffers. He pulled from the ranks of the writers sometimes to accomplish that goal.

Jay also invoked a new rule: The front page of the wire section and local section had to include at least one story about women and/or ethnic groups and each story had to include at least one legitimate source that was female or ethnic. To assist in that endeavor, I began meeting with community groups to obtain a list of sources we could use in our coverage. Out of those meetings came *The Tribune's* first ethnic and gender source guide.

The problem area continued to be the Sports Department. The almost all-male staff pushed back. They could not seem to find any story of value that dealt with women athletes. I began culling the wire stories to help in that matter. They slowly and reluctantly began placing women in a more prominent place in their section. I forced the issue a couple of times by writing a column featuring a female athlete. I also joined AWSM (Association of Women in Sports Media) to help in my endeavor. I felt it was critical that we hire more women sports writers. We accomplished that by obtaining a list of potential candidates. Slowly more women were added to the sports staff.[754]

Ellefsen's premeditated climb did give women a boost in the ranks of newsroom editors and enhanced their visibility on news and sports pages, but she was one of many trying to improve the treatment of women in Utah's news media during that period.

Shelledy was instrumental in the push by enabling several *Tribune* women to attend a Journalism and Women Symposium in Jackson Hole, Wyoming. We learned that nationally, women were cited as sources in only 13 percent of news stories on major newspapers and networks. Women wrote 34 percent of stories on front pages of daily newspapers, and women appeared in front-page photos 32 percent of the time.

Nancy Hobbs and I helped organize a steering committee that evaluated how women fared in Utah's news and devised a plan to address shortcomings. Others in the group were Maggie St. Claire, KSL director of public affairs; Lynne Tempest, editor of *Network*; Mary Dickson, KUED director of public information; Amy Donaldson, *Deseret News* reporter, and Ellen Fagg, a former *Deseret News* reporter.

Within a year, 26 Utah women and two male journalists, approximately two people from each local news outlet, were meeting as Women in News (WIN). Other *Tribune* participants, besides me, Hobbs and Ellefsen, were Dawn House, Kathy Kapos, Sheila McCann, Nancy Melich, Joan O'Brien, Andrea Otanez, Carol VanWagoner, Lili Wright, James Wright and Paul Wetzel.

"Our goal is two pronged," according to our press release, "to promote gender equity in news coverage and in Utah newsrooms."

We examined coverage of and by women in the *Deseret News, The Salt Lake Tribune, Ogden Standard-Examiner* and *Provo Daily Herald,* in addition to the television news stations in town. Each of us monitored a different news organization for a week to see how many times women reported stories, were used as sources and were featured in photographs and footage.

Bob Bryson reported our findings in a story December 27, 1992: "Utah's news media, much like its national counterparts, tends to ignore women as experts in stories they report." Women were more often depicted as victims, wives or entertainers than as experts to be quoted, he continued.

Hobbs was quoted: "This was the year of the woman in elections, but the stories didn't quote women. The same is true of stories about breast implants. Women were quoted as victims, but not as experts."

DeAnn Evans, a former *Deseret News* editor who by 1992 taught communication at the University of Utah, helped put the problem into perspective for Bryson: "The source of a story helps shape it and is the voice for the article. If you have all male voices, then the story is shaped only according to the male point of view."

The Bryson story noted that comparatively few women reporters wrote front-page stories or handled lead news stories on television and radio in Utah, and "to top it off, few women are represented in the ranks of newsroom management." WIN spokeswoman Maggie St. Claire, explained that women held just 10 percent of newsroom management jobs despite the strides they'd made in employment the previous 15 years.

Finally, Bryson identified Ellefsen as a point person for creating a guide of women news sources for reporters.[755]

* * *

Over time, Shelledy recruited more minorities and promoted more women to create staff diversity. Sixteen of the staffers he hired at least nominally understood more than one language. Women and minorities received more attention on the news pages.

African Americans Shinika Sykes, Samuel Autman and Karen Parker joined the staff, and Latina Andrea Otanez became an editor. Stately Sykes came from Jamaica by way of Chicago and the University of Utah to work the Copy Desk. Tall, graceful Autman moved from the Midwest to cover education. (He resented people asking if he played basketball.) Parker, the first black female undergraduate to attend the University of North Carolina at Chapel Hill,[756] left the *Los Angeles Times* for *The Tribune's* Copy Desk, where she became assistant world desk editor under Dave Noyce.

Carol VanWagoner moved beyond Newspaper in Education to community relations manager, replacing my former education colleague John Cummins, who became Reader Advocate.[757]

Shelledy simplified VanWagoner's job by scrapping *Tribune* traditions like the children's Christmas party, the adults' Christmas ball, United Way fund-raisers, Sub-for-Santa, No-Champs tennis tournaments, the Concourse d'Elegance car show, the Ski Classic and the Old-Fashioned Fourth of July at Lagoon. One PR activity survived.

"How would you and your husband like to host *The Tribune* Cruise Program?" Shelledy asked VanWagoner one day.

"No husband. Yes," was her immediate response.

Tom McCarthey ostensibly lost the freebie when appointed deputy editor.

That fall, VanWagoner invited readers to "an almost-perfect cruise" from Montreal to Puerto Rico. On Halloween, off the Atlantic Coast, the ship was caught in a huge gale. The ship's stabilizers were uncommonly retracted so it could get south faster, causing glassware to crash off the shelves. The ship's piano took off across the floor. In VanWagoner's stateroom, magnetized dresser drawers slammed in and out. The full ice bucket fell from the desktop, mixing ice with the broken goblets on the floor.

I lay in my berth, tucked a foot between the boat's side and mattress, and held on as the ship spookily careened through the storm. Several years later, I read Sebastian Junger's *New York Times* bestseller, <u>The Perfect Storm</u>. On page 300, he referred to it as the Halloween Gale. I flipped to the front of the book to check the storm's year. Yes, it was 1991, and *Tribune* cruisers experienced the wild ride![758]

Some women staffers before turn of the century: Bernie Moss, front; Donna Lou Morgan, Lori Buttars, Judy Rollins and Laurene Sowby, l-r, 2nd row; Nancy Hobbs, Helen Forsberg, Lucy Bodily, Barbi Robison, Shirley Jones, Judy Magid and Nancy Melich, l-r, back row.

Not all women benefited from Shelledy's leadership.

After declining his order for negative reviews of local artists, Ann Poore, at least according to secretary Shirley Jones, got "the biggest raise in the history of the paper" to go quietly back to the Copy Desk.[759] She frequently worked the slot, supervising copy editors and training Shinika Sykes, who earned noticeably more. While Sykes lived in a high-rise, drove a Mustang convertible and took regular trips to Chicago and Jamaica, Poore stayed in her humble home. Except the time she got gas money from her dying father to visit him in Apple Valley, California.[760]

When she asked why she made so much less than others on the desk, Shelledy claimed he could hardly pay her the same as others after she started as a secretary. It apparently made no difference, she told me, that she'd graduated with honors from the University of Utah and worked several years writing advance obituaries and reviewing art shows with George Dibble. She'd even written a politically sensitive, prominently played story -- it had required Fourth-floor approval -- about nudity and children for which she interviewed Senator Orrin Hatch.

[747] Paul Rolly and JoAnn Jacobsen-Wells, "So long to a 13-year partner," *The Salt Lake Tribune*, December 8, 2004.

[748] Jacobsen-Wells, August 2, 2015.

[749] JoAnn Jacobsen-Wells, "Rolly & Wells," *The Salt Lake Tribune*, December 1, 2011.

[750] Milton Hollstein, "Fracas Leaves Neither Paper Looking Good," *Deseret News*, July 27, 1992.

[751] JoAnn Jacobsen-Wells, August 2, 2015.

[752] Rolly roast, August 19, 2015.

[753] *The Salt Lake Tribune*, Sept. 8, 1991.

[754] Terri Ellefsen email, February 21, 2014.

[755] Robert Bryson, "Fledgling Organization Strives to put Utah Women in News," *The Salt Lake Tribune,* December 27, 1992.

[756] Wikipedia.

[757] VanWagoner, August 10, 2015.

[758] Ibid.

[759] Ann Poore email, August 2, 2015.

[760] Ibid.

41 - Reducing the Ranks

Cathy Free became one of Shelledy's early casualties.

When the fledgling boss decided *The Tribune* needed a daily Split Page columnist a la Dan Valentine, Free stepped up. After all, she had worked hard to become an award-winning columnist and even contributed stories to *People Magazine* on the side. But Shelledy already had Rolly & Wells in mind and informed Free she wasn't ready, at 29, for a daily column.[761] Free was so insulted she considered taking an offer from Spokane's *Spokesman-Review* to become a roving columnist three days a week at double her *Tribune* salary.

Then it was her husband's turn to interview with the new boss. The two chatted about guys they both knew from Idaho, including Roger Porter in Rexburg and LaMar Crosby, the gambler who'd worked with Shelledy on George Hansen's Senate campaign against Frank Church. This was a turning point for **Russell Weeks**:

I walked out of my interview knowing I had spoken to someone exactly like my battalion commander in Germany, and he was the only person I'd ever seriously entertained thoughts of killing. He was the total package: went by the book because he had no imagination, described himself as "aggressive" to barely mask that he was a bully (my battalion commander styled himself "Little Patton"), had no empathy for anyone. I walked back to City Hall, went to my office, called Cathy and said, "If you want to go to Spokane, I'm with you."

While covering Salt Lake City's Winter Olympics bid on the metro beat, Weeks had had the foresight to get Will Fehr's authorization to cover the International Olympic Committee's vote in Birmingham, England, before Fehr retired. He and Cathy had found cheap tickets (airfares were low due to passenger fears of an Iraqi war) and planned to combine his work with a vacation in Europe. They revised those plans after the Shelledy meetings.

Before leaving for England, they typed their resignations. After the IOC vote, they placed those letters in a FedEx envelope with Weeks' expense receipts. They then left the packet with a hotel clerk in Birmingham while they took a walk before heading for the train station. Weeks remembers the moment:

As we crossed the pedestrian bridge back to the hotel, we saw the FedEx truck pull out of the parking lot. I said something banal, like, "The die is cast." We had to laugh because it truly was the first day of the rest of our lives. We got our bags and headed for the train. We were very fortunate to have a path out of *The Tribune*.[762]

John Keahey saw Weeks' departure from the perspective of a Shelledy ally in the newsroom. As he tells it, Deputy Editor David Ledford ordered yet another story on the failed bid, but Weeks was in a hurry to catch a plane to Paris. Seconds after a furious Ledford slammed down the telephone "I walked into the newsroom from covering the Olympic-announcement event at the City-County Building. Ledford yelled across the newsroom, 'You're covering the Olympics, Keahey!'"[763]

Weeks remembered that part of the story differently:

I had fought with Terri Ellefsen over whether to include a couple paragraphs in the story I'd written earlier that day. I then got a call from Dave Ledford ordering me to put them in. That was probably the only time he talked to me except to call me "Little Buddy" the night Salt Lake City lost the bid.[764]

Weeks' final story dealt with the delegation's mood the morning after the vote. It excluded Salt Lake Bid Committee President Tom Welch's bitterness "because I had no plans to see him again -- ever -- and didn't want to leave a knife in his back in public." Shelledy was the one who ordered one more story, and Weeks was intimidated enough to tell him he'd see what he could do. "After thinking about it, I didn't bother with it. It's nice to know he didn't believe me."

That aside, Weeks left the Olympics story with some good memories.

Olympics reporters felt "so privileged" at the IOC convention press center to plug their TR-80s into a table that connected everyone to his or her respective newspaper, he said. "It was totally state-of-the-art then."

Tom Guinney, Tom Sieg and John Williams from Salt Lake City's Gastronomy restaurants were on hand to cater gatherings at the house leased for the Utah delegation. At one point, Weeks asked where Williams was, and Guinney quipped that he'd appear when all the work was over. "The night of the IOC vote, I saw John in one of the hotel doorways, his overcoat over his shoulders like a cape, taking it all in."

Weeks was jammed writing his story the night of the bid loss when Lisa Riley Roche from the *Deseret News* and Wendy Ogata from the *Ogden Standard-Examiner* suggested returning to the delegation house. When Weeks couldn't break away, his wife went along to interview people and bumped into a surprised Jack Gallivan. Everyone was standing around looking glum until Gov. Norm Bangerter told the bluegrass band imported from Utah to start playing. Saying, "I won't tell if you won't," the governor started dancing. "That broke the ice, and our best and brightest started to forget," Weeks said.[765]

One of Gallivan's sharpest memories of Utah's Olympics hosting efforts also came from Birmingham, where Utah lost to Japan a second time. Japan first beat out Utah in 1966.

The three-vote loss in Birmingham, announced in an auditorium with what seemed like 5,000 people, was "surreal," he recalled. First came the winner: "Good ole Japan . . . Then came the speech saying we must remember that winning is[n't] everything in the Olympics, it's the participating."[766] SLOC member Ian Cumming, a wealthy investor known for shunning the public eye, "stood up and at the top of his voice screamed out, 'Bullshit!' This left everyone aghast."

After seeing all the gifts and perks that Japan lavished on members of the International Olympic Committee, Utah's delegation understood they needed to put their schmoozing of committee members into overdrive if they ever expected to win the bid. So they did. The results of that shift is yet to come.

* * *

In Weeks' opinion, Jay Shelledy's arrival marked the end of the real newspapering tradition:

He's the only editor who ever told me the newspaper industry was dying. That may have been accurate on his part, but the internet wasn't very widespread until about 1994. That's when the Salt Lake City Library had it. He used the "dying industry" as another way to instill fear.

In his final days with *The Tribune*, Weeks witnessed "fear on the faces of reporters who needed to get in their required two stories a day" when they had nothing to offer.

I was fortunate because I had one story drop into my lap about the city firing the Animal Control Services director because he had snorted up the fees for dog licenses and would be charged for embezzlement after he was fired. That plus the Olympics stuff kept me busy.[767]

Late one night after a City Council meeting, Weeks entered the newsroom to see Randy Peterson alone in the conference room furiously redrawing page dummies. Evidently Shelledy, attending a conference in Boston, required Randy to fax him the pages and then chewed him out before forcing him to remake the pages. "The only people I'd seen abused like that were sergeants in my battalion in Germany," Weeks said. "In both cases, they were competent people ground down by insecure, fearful men."[768]

Like Weeks, Brett Prettyman, a copy clerk in 1991, also remembered Peterson bent over a desk laying out the next day's paper on 8-by-11-inch dummies. "I spent a lot of time with Randy the first year of my career, and it was his passion and dedication for the work that helped me realize I made a solid decision to become a journalist." Prettyman considered Peterson his quiet and consistent mentor.[769]

Maybe too quiet and consistent. He was the kind of guy Shelledy liked to overlook or push around. After seven years as city editor, Peterson was given responsibility for the Copy Desk and redesigning the local news section.

Free laughed when she returned from England to clean out her desk. A note in her file from Ellefsen demanded that she start writing more "twelve-inchers."

I was outta there!
I really loved my job, but the wages were low and the raises few. My salary was still based on my old copy girl salary. I was never boosted to what most other reporters were making, even after repeatedly pointing out the discrepancy.[770]

The one good thing Shelledy did, Weeks concluded, was to raise other salaries to industry scale. "I'm sure that helped a lot of people."[771]

* * *

After leaving *The Tribune,* Free worked three years for the *Spokesman-Review* and Weeks worked part time as a copy editor while getting a master's degree in English literature from Gonzaga University. The Salt Lake City Council then offered him a research and public relations job, and Free convinced *People Magazine* to give her a writing contract to cover several Western states. By 2015, Russell was still doing "interesting work -- human work" in Salt Lake City,[772] and Free had written for *People* for 34 years.

Free also had worked as a contributing editor for *Reader's Digest* magazine for five years and "crossed over to the 'dark side' to contribute a metro column ('Free Lunch') for the *Deseret News* for 12 years."[773] Her idea for taking a reader to lunch each week came from a story she did for *People* in Columbus, Ohio. Because she was allowed to write from home, she never once set foot in the *Deseret News* newsroom. "I wouldn't have fit in, and they'd have figured that out in a hurry." When the *News* shifted to values-based journalism, she quit. "It's my opinion that a newspaper should be for everyone, not select special-interest groups," she explained.[774]

Free said she will always look back on her *Tribune* days fondly:

The best part were the people and friendships made. We didn't make much money, but we had a helluva lot of fun, and I am forever grateful that I passed my initiation that first night and was made a part of the *Tribune* family.

But getting out really was the best financial decision I ever made, and career-wise, I could not be happier now. Most people probably think I sold out because *People* isn't exactly the *Wall Street Journal*. But the opportunities I have had to travel coast-to-coast and meet interesting people from all walks of life has been an incredible experience.

* * *

Joe Rolando became another Shelledy victim.

Shelledy declared in one of his many meetings that all business stories must be completed before noon to give copy editors time to focus on "the more important" stories from City Desk. Business Desk hours were changed first to 6 a.m. to 2 p.m.; then 7 a.m. to 3 p.m. Rolando argued that most business news came in between 3 and 6 p.m., at the end of most business hours. But Shelledy didn't budge, and Rolly didn't fight it.[775]

Rolando surmised that Shelledy was creating enough discomfort in the newsroom to shake out entrenched staffers he could replace with new people . . .

. . . in his image and likeness . . . Catholics say that about God's son Jesus. Rolly, who never asked me nor took any of my advice and never learned to divvy out the work, finally burned out as business editor. I thanked the good Lord I passed on that job."[776]

John Keahey, Rolly's replacement, had been burrowing in tightly with the Shelledy bunch, according to Rolando. Once appointed, the former PR guy for Mountain Fuel joked with business reporter Steve Oberbeck: "Boy, when I take over there are going to be a lot of changes. You guys just wait." Rolando didn't see the humor in it when Shelledy ordered Keahey to issue more reprimands and the good soldier zeroed in on Rolando.

With no business news to report before the 3 p.m. deadline September 12, Keahey assigned Rolando a hybrid story -- part business and mostly state legislature, which was considering a 20- to 30-year property tax exemption to lure airline manufacturer McDonnell Douglas to Salt Lake City.

Rolando was told to stay in the office and call Russ Behrmann and every legislator he could think of to determine the proposal's status. By quitting time, he had a story about the tax benefit, but no one would predict its adoption. He attached a note to his story suggesting someone check later to see if a vote was taken. Keahey edited and sent the story to the Copy Desk.

Next morning, Rolando's story appeared with Keahey's byline above his. Keahey had added the fact that House Speaker Craig Moody told an Ogden audience Utah could not afford the tax break. When Rolando walked to his desk, Keahey slipped him a written reprimand saying, in part:

I spent until 7 p.m. last night filling in the holes, getting reaction from a variety of sources and putting the issue in perspective. It's unconsionable [sic] that a reporter with your experience would not do the same. You relied on one source [Behrmann], and the story's prime element -- the property tax issue -- was buried deep in the story . . . Frankly, I expect more from you than what I got yesterday afternoon . . .[777]

Asked for specifics, Keahey said the Moody comments came from a 6 p.m. television story on a breakfast meeting of the Ogden Exchange Club. Rolando argued that he had written all the facts he had up to the "stupid 4 p.m. deadline" and added that he did not cover obscure meetings in Ogden. He pointed out that editors had trimmed some of his "perspective," including comments from the Utah Taxpayer's Association.

Contending that he had to rewrite Rolando's incomplete version, Keahey advised Rolando to accept the reprimand. Rolando was fed up:

> I had enough. I had been through this kind of unreasonableness in the newspaper business before, and I was tired of it. Shelledy's regime was particularly unreasonable, rude and arrogant.
>
> The next day, I set an appointment with an attorney in an attempt to remove that reprimand from my file. He recommended I first send a letter to the publisher.[778]

That letter noted that after 11 years at the paper, Rolando was unaware of any *Tribune* policies regarding employee files, reprimands and appeals. He wrote that he had detected "an intentional scheme" the prior 12 months, and particularly the last four months, to make his "continued employment (and others' as well) so unbearable as to, naturally, result in my termination."

"At the crux of this problem" Rolando concluded, "is Editor Jay Shelledy's insistence upon a 3:00 p.m. deadline for stories such as mine."[779]

He took the letter to the publisher the next morning, explaining that he didn't trust Shelledy to give him an objective reason for his resignation. He then delivered a copy to Shelledy with the declaration that he quit and didn't need to think about overnight. "I said I had thought about it over many nights . . ."

Looking back on it, Rolando said the reprimand actually meant little; he just wanted to

show that he wasn't going to take what the Shelledy regime was dishing out without resistance. He finished out his career in the family insurance business.

Years later, Keahey recalled that he wrote three reprimands at Shelledy's command -- one each to Rolando, Oberbeck and Bob Bryson -- before telling Shelledy's deputy David Ledford he was through with the practice unless something egregious happened.

"That was the beginning of the end for my time as business editor," he told me in a Facebook message.

Although he'd initially liked Shelledy's changes, including the hiring of strong writers like Sean Means, Sheila McCann and Tony Semerad, he regarded some of his picks as "disastrous." After three years as business editor, when Shelledy demanded more and more stories about big advertisers like ZCMI, he declined his editor's advice to resign and instead returned to reporting.

He left the job believing he'd done his best to save the jobs of reporters he'd perceived as targeted for termination. He'd welcomed Walt Schaffer, Bryson and Judy Fahys onto his business desk. Although Schaffer freaked out on him, Judy, his "proudest rescue," went on to great journalism.

Keahey was particularly critical of Ledford's decision to fabricate an anonymous source for Sheila McCann's story on fen-phen, a diet drug that damages the heart. Shelledy's response had been to support Ledford's search for another job.

Keahey felt he re-earned his credentials as a journalist when, under new management years later, he became "a pretty good news editor." But Rolando, one of his nicest and hardest-working colleagues over the years, was gone by then "and missed my conversion."

* * *

Doug Parker's fall was even harder than Rolando's.

Demoted from the primo political beat to cover conventions and towns, the demoralized newsman turned in his badge at the end of 1991. His wife Carol Sisco soon followed suit.

Parker had covered 25 years of the state legislature, half a dozen national political party conventions and three governors' administrations. He was widely regarded as competent, fair and restrained. He did his job calmly, without complaint or fanfare. His disregard for cheap shots and gratuitous conflict probably led to his downfall. He was not the young, flamboyant sort that Shelledy sought for his team.

Parker lacked other job prospects, but Sisco wrote grants for Crossroads Urban Center until landing a public affairs post at the Utah Department of Environmental Quality (DEQ) in October 1992. She got Parker a temporary writing/editing job there too, but he chose to sell books for Sam Weller's down Main Street for 18 months. Sisco recalled the day a politician walking down Main Street didn't even recognize Parker in his shorts, psychedelic tie-dye shirt, floppy hat and wild sunglasses.

A melanoma killed Parker August 17, 1995, at age 60. I blamed Shelledy for distressing Parker with his unjustified demotion, possibly causing his cancer.

The good news was that Parker and Sisco got away with ESOP shares. By 2000, Sisco was spokeswoman for the Utah Department of Human Services handling issues she'd covered for *The Tribune* for more than a decade.

* * *

The Tribune may have needed more editors in the 1970s and 80s, but a year or so into Shelledy's rule, there were almost as many chiefs as Indians to cover the news. Actually, 15 editors managed 30 reporters. Some of these appointments fed an undercurrent of discontent and disrespect among staffers.

Too many inexperienced or sluggish people had become editors while others were unfairly demoted. Making writers Rodd Wagner and Anne Mathews the equivalent of assistant city editors seemed at least premature. No matter how nice and competent on Arts and Entertainment, Helen Forsberg had drinking problems and lacked ambition.

David Ledford's enthusiasm for storytelling was turning too many stories into descriptive literature at the expense of breaking news, which often required old-fashioned, quick answers to the 5 Ws (who, what, when, where and why). Jim Fisher didn't understand the paper's new computer graphics system, and his underlings regarded him as a phony pain in the ass. By contrast, Ace Fibber was technically competent, but he lacked ethics. He should have been shown the door, not put in charge of the most important page of the newspaper.

Shirley Jones' new title presumably made her a chief too, but the main effect was to co-opt her into the Shelledy camp. In this uncharacteristic message November 15 she wrote:

Jay: A woman called and wanted me to tell you that she received very rude treatment from our woman editorial writer. She said John Cummins also was not helpful at all. She was calling regarding a letter to the editor she wanted us to run. I was able to calm her down, so she went away reasonably happy. Shirley

Cummins tersely replied: "Neither Diane nor I recall speaking to a woman caller concerning a letter to the editor in recent weeks."

Office dynamics had deteriorated. Mother Jones had morphed from staff advocate into Shelledy's good little soldier. Or a "squealing rat," as Barbi Robison put it. In the old days, Shirley would have conferred with me and Cummins before making a nasty, self-interested report to Shelledy. For all she knew, the complainer was a constant, irrational pest. Nothing pleased some letter writers.

Even upbeat Anne Wilson acknowledged that *The Tribune* climate "started going south with Jay Shelledy." She observed:

I never met a worse manager, although he did have some talent. And maybe it wasn't just him but what began to happen in the industry. It just became less fun and more work and stress. But hell, I'm still there [in 2013], so how bad could it be?[780]

I started sending out resumes for jobs at local community colleges. I wasn't sure I wanted to leave the newspaper business, but I was feeling burned out by the grindstone of the Editorial Department as the world passed me by.

The trip to Southeast Asia had strengthened my confidence and desire to travel, and one of the freebie books lying around the office -- 22 Days in France by Rich Steves and Steve Smith -- provided the itinerary for another big adventure.

Denny and I hoisted backpacks onto trains from Paris to Nice. We stayed in charming two-star hotels and discovered our favorite place, Collioure, at the end of the line.

Our broken French got us where we needed to go. In Arles, we ate fresh paella stewed on street corners and watched a bullfight in the Roman colloseum as locals danced in traditional dress. One night we nearly crawled back to our

Sarlat hotel after three pitchers of sangria. Denny's greatest thrill was standing beside Leonardo DaVinci's tomb and touring Clos Luce, the place he'd lived in Amboise. Our worse nightmare was arriving in Paris without a reservation one evening late in September, finally settling on a noisy, bug-infested flop house even worse than the Santepeap in Phnom Penh.

[780] Anne Wilson email December 31, 2013.

---

[761] Free, June 4, 2015.

[762] Weeks, June 4, 2015.

[763] John Keahey to facebook's Tribune group.

[764] Weeks, June 5, 2015.

[765] Weeks, June 4, 2015.

[766] Gallivan, May 2005.

[767] Weeks, June 4, 2015.

[768] Ibid.

[769] Brett Prettyman on facebook March 27, 2015.

[770] Free, June 4, 2015.

[771] Weeks, June 4, 2015.

[772] Free, June 4, 2015.

[773] Cathy Free, June 6, 2015.

[774] Ibid.

[775] Rolando, November 30, 2015.

[776] Ibid.

[777] Memo from John Keahy to Joe Rolando, September 13, 1991.

[778] Rolando, November 30, 2015.

[779] Memorandum from Joe Rolando to Tribune Publisher Jerry O'Brien and Editor Jay Shelledy, October 2, 1991.

42 - Desperately Seeking Inspiration in 1992

Once fully ensconced in his office, Shelledy made no pretense about keeping hands off our opinion pages. By then, he knew we had no special pull with the publisher, so he felt free to increase our workload and tell us how to do our jobs.

A Friday in early January, Dave Noyce stopped bouncing off the walls and gnawing skin from his fingers long enough to toss back the dummies (page layouts) we'd sent to the Copy Desk for our weekend pages. Shelledy followed up with this disparaging directive:

> The Copy Desk can no longer be burdened with editing or writing headlines for editorial/oped material Thursday and Friday nights because of the crush of news copy. That responsibility will have to be handled by the editorial writers on those days. Since syndicated copy is pre-edited and headlines fairly standard in the edit-page format, this ought not be an overwhelming burden for the Editorial Department. I would suggest edit writers structure their Thursdays, Fridays and Saturdays accordingly.[781]

My old pal Wally Hoffman, the cliche king, brightened my day March 1 with a letter criticizing my publisher-assigned editorial. The editorial praised Genevieve Folsom, our longtime garden editor, for creating the Civic Beautification Program that enabled the Utah desert to blossom like the rose Brigham Young foresaw when entering Salt Lake Valley.[782] Hoffman wrote:

> Dumb! dumb! dumb! Stupid! stupid! stupid! In 1989 the National Center for Health Statistics reported the life expectancy for Americans was 75.1 years (71.8 years for men and 78.5 years for women). In other words, 1.67 times the "forty-five years ago -- more than a lifetime for most Utahns." *The Tribune* asserts in its Feb. 27, 1992, editorial extolling the community service of octogenarian Genevieve Folsom, who

personally has exceeded the NCHS's allocation by at least five years and nearly double the life span assigned to "most Utahns" by *The Tribune's* editorial writers.

> I have become agonizingly aware that editing, along with just plain careful reading, has become a lost art throughout most of *The Tribune*. However, it was somewhat comforting to note a higher standard had persisted among the editorial writers. Regrettably, the virus that has contaminated the second floor has seemingly spread to the mezzanine. More's the pity.

It was no pity to me that that our department was no longer afflicted with the nitpicking and sour grapes of slide rule-wielding, calculator-packing Hoffman. It had been three years since he had ranted about throwing out the baby with the bathwater, and it would be as long as I lasted there before we did it again. In my defense, Utah's population was among the youngest in the nation because of its lopsided number of children. I still say that fewer than half of Utahns in 1992 were alive when Genevieve began her quest to beautify the state through tidy-town awards 45 years before. Hoffman obviously never quit getting my goat.

* * *

Uncontrolled hillside construction in Salt Lake County developed into one of my pet editorial topics. Despite his likable personality, liberal politics and relationship to *Tribune* staffers, County Commissioner Randy Horiuchi's ties to developers put him in my crosshairs.

His brother Vince was a reporter; his brother Wayne was Paul Rolly's best friend growing up. As an insider in Utah's Democratic Party, Randy regularly fed Rolly news tips. I reminded myself I was speaking for the common good against special interests, and by some miracle, the usually pro-business Fourth Floor went along with most of what I wrote.

* * *

Harry Fuller continued "enhancing" my mundane vocabulary and harsh tone with fancy words like "minimized" and "hospitable." When he got through with it, I hardly recognized my March 2 lead:

> *Utah lawmakers were slightly schizophrenic in their treatment of lawbreakers this past legislative session.*

They had no qualms about toughening penalties against Utahns committing crimes against individuals, but they shied from punishing traffic law violators.

Fuller changed the second sentence to: "Able to toughen penalties for committing crimes against individuals, they shied away from imposing the discipline essential to reduced traffic hazards." From my perspective, we just didn't write the same language, and the combination of the two styles in one editorial was mind blowing.

* * *

NCEW asked me to write another piece for *The Masthead*, this one about letters to the editor. So, here it goes:

Letters to the editor: who needs 'em? We do

The way our editorial staff of three dreads letter-editing duties, one might assume we detest our Public Forum. Not really.

We appreciate that letters are well-read; we even enjoy reading them ourselves, usually. Some contributors are good enough to compete for our jobs. (And, of course, some are not.)

There isn't a better public relations tool than letters to the editor. Some writers put their hearts and souls into one letter of a lifetime, then frame the printed copy and proudly present it as their "editorial." This process creates a bond between subscriber and newspaper that only a week of late deliveries could break.

Unfortunately, there's a flip side. Fail to run a writer's masterpiece (or disaster) and you weaken an avid reader's loyalty. Get a name wrong or drop a "key phrase," and you court alienation.

It's a heavy burden, especially when each of us is trying to squeeze an editorial of our own into the day.

Even so, we do our best to put as many letters into the paper as possible while limiting redundancies and rejecting the least interesting. That works out to be between five and 10 letters a day, compared to the 10 to 20 we receive.

Readers apparently prefer short letters on a variety of topics. We aim for

a 300-word maximum per letter. Since most letters are long, we have to do a lot of whittling. We sometimes have to clean up grammar, but we respect the writer's style. Public officials and professionals are well-represented in the Forum, but we also find room for less-sophisticated readers (including children) concerned about animals or school policies. Future readers, you know.

The first letters to be jettisoned lack signatures, libel someone, come from frequent writers (I limit writers to about once a month), smell of a political or special-interest letter-writing campaign, or are unintelligible diatribes. Religious sermons receive low priority.

We recently wrote more reader-friendly Forum guidelines to encourage participation, but we've found that the more letters we run or the more the Mormon Church either directly or indirectly intervenes in public policy-making, the more letters we receive. (The Tribune has become the place for Utahns to vent cultural frustrations, since the state's next largest newspaper is owned by the Mormon Church.) The more letters we receive, the more selective we can be -- but rejection wounds the writers' egos, while hanging on to letters tests readers' tolerance for stale topics.

Newspapers need letters to the editor to keep them and their communities in touch with constituents. But they also need to devote resources to the task so that someone is available to politely answer writers' inquiries and complaints and to carefully edit their copy. The Tribune has assigned one editorial writer, a public relations/editor and a typist to the task. Editing alone consumes at least 16 hours a week.

When insufficient resources are devoted to letters, they may be treated more as an irritation than a blessing, undermining potential public relations benefits.[783]

There obviously had been improvement in our letters-to-the-editor situation since the days when just one of us sent out cards to verify writer identity, edited the letters and then handled writers' calls. By 1992, the mezzanine receptionist sent out the cards, and the Reader Advocate trimmed the letters and fielded most complaints.

* * *

Shelledy also was writing for national journalism publications. In *Nieman Reports,* he expounded on changing times for newspapers. Like Serfustini before him, he stressed the need for newspapers to shift their focus away from news of record and breaking news, which was covered faster by television. Rather than simply point out problems, he said, newspapers should analyze issues and present solutions with examples of success. In his words:

> *Newspapers have moved from a medium of announcements to a medium of explanations, a medium where "beats" are the result of enterprise reporting. This change will require us to go beyond "just the fact" accounts. Our information must add perspective. Our mission must be to tell stories -- whole stories -- in compelling English.*
>
> *That reduces such things as press conferences, routine meetings and day-to-day-crime stories to lower priorities. I've told my night police reporters to ignore ordinary, late-night hold-ups at Circle K stores. (I'm convinced Circle K's exist so the rest of us don't get mugged at night. I'm further convinced, when considering stick-ups at Circle K stories, that society views such acts as fair-play turnabout.)*
>
> *. . . If we want our newspaper to be a more compelling and valuable read, we ought to do away with the terms "hard news" and "soft news" (read: news fit for the front page and news that ought to be in the "women's section"). We at* The Tribune *replaced the adjectives "hard" and "soft" with "breaking" and "non-breaking" news.*[784]

That's Shelledy. Always a pompous comedian. Who cares about Circle K victims, anyway?

I doubted readers would ever lose interest in stories about neighborhood crime, schools and local government. I also wondered how reporters could get beyond the 5Ws with in-depth analysis -- and compete with television sound bites -- while restricted to 12 inches of column space as he demanded.

Shelledy's treatise noted that *The Tribune* no longer had separate editions for early and late-breaking stories and for readers in the city or outlying areas. Finally, he predicted that "by 2010, the newsprint portion of our information flow won't even be a daily occurrence -- at least not as we know it today [1992}."

He was wrong about daily publication. *The Tribune* staff was still putting out a paper in 2018. However, internet news reporting did loom large, adding immediate online reports, including writers' blogs, to the repertoire of newspapers still in business.

* * *

In his daily "critique" one Friday in July, Shelledy announced progress on a remodel of the newsroom conference room. Opening up the pagination walls would provide a "relatively inexpensive set for cable TV newscasts planned for September."

Sure enough, that fall Jay Baltezore, a public radio reporter from Shelledy's old stomping grounds, started a daily television report of *Tribune*-gathered news. Within a year, however, that project fizzled in favor of a fledgling internet website, and Baltezore became a reporter.

The Friday memo also listed two staff changes. In another of Shelledy's greatest remediation successes (remember Peter Scarlet?), former Capitol reporter Dave Jonsson moved from part-time paginator to full-time computer assistant on the Government Desk. Shaun McCarthey, the youngest child of owners Kearns and Jane McCarthey, became a full-time copy clerk.

Shaun had worked part time when Editorial was still on the 10th floor. Without realizing he was a McCarthey, Wally Hoffman went ballistic when he set mail on, rather than beside, his computer terminal a second time. While Hoffman ranted about his stupidity, the confused kid tearfully paced the hall a few seconds before seeking solace on the Fourth Floor. Hoffman became a pussycat in Shaun's presence.

Though fond of acting in Westminster College's theater program, Shaun didn't stay in Salt Lake City. Instead, he moved to Seattle, where he became a substance-abuse counselor, married, produced movies and died at just 52. Apparently he'd enjoyed life. Like his father and brothers, he was an avid sports fan. Like his mother and brother Tom, he was infected with the travel bug. London, Australia, Thailand and Laos were his favorite places. He'd also made "pilgrimages to Abbey Road and Liverpool to honor his favorite band, the Beatles."[785]

* * *

The spring of 1992, Stormy gave birth to a love of my life, a charming, bright boy I'll call Brock. Denny and I waited at the hospital for the birth, and his yellowish (jaundiced), Jiminy Cricket countenance couldn't have been more captivating. Stormy sent him home with us frequently, particularly when she and Winker were fighting, so we bonded. He loved the night sky, pointing out the moon in his infancy. I took him to California before he turned two, an age when he could easily spout his ABCs and count. I considered him my full-fledged grandson, compensation for never having children of my own.

As wonderful as grandparenting was, it was subject to the shifting whims of my stepdaughter, and it was neither full time nor a career. I still needed inspiration and fulfillment.

So I took the GRE (Graduate Record Examination) and enrolled in the University of Utah Political Science Department. It meant staying in Utah, but with a master's degree, I might qualify for a job outside the newspaper, maybe teaching in a college or working in government. My application included my Southeast Asia series and a recommendation from Harry Fuller.

I didn't tell Fuller I might leave the paper, just that I could use the background for editorials, and he persuaded Jerry O'Brien to let me work part time as the department substitute. There was no offer to help finance my education, and I didn't suggest it.

My desk without walls.

It was tough relinquishing my precious private office. Gone were my bookshelves, car posters by Denny and personalized cartoons by Pat Bagley and Tim Brinton. When Lex Hemphill assumed my full-time slot, he filled the shelves with back editions of *The Tribune,* the *New York Times* and *Deseret News,* meticulously organized by publication dates. He lined the desk drawer with sharpened pencils and pens all pointing north. He inherited my 2020 phone extension too.

Being a student meant working twice as hard with half the sleep. Still working three days a week, sometimes more, I often did homework overnight, snatching one or two hours of sleep before racing down the hill to class and/or the office. Spring quarter, for example, I was reading one or two books and writing a class essay each week, not easy for a slow reader faced with Karl Marx, John Stuart Mill or some other political theorist or philosopher.

As one of the oldest students in my classes, I used the foulest language. Surprisingly, university students no longer spit out the f-word every other sentence. Some professors gave me a hard time, humiliating me for my apparently shallow answers. These tenured, theorizing tyrants, these sovereigns of the sabbatical, seemed pissed off that I held what they considered a dream job, and they were determined to demonstrate how little I knew. I doubted they could handle the pressures of daily deadlines.

Still, the studies soon started paying off. Medical ethics was one of my favorite subjects, so I was primed for the news that Mormon fertility doctor and geneticist Cecil Jacobson had secretly used his own sperm to impregnate patients in the beltway over three decades. His fresh sperm, he explained, was more likely than the frozen variety to cause pregnancy.

The Sperm Whale, as I called him, may have been the biological father of as many as 75 children born between 1977 and 1988. His ruse was revealed when a couple noticed their child suspiciously resembled the doctor. What a story!

None of my colleagues saw the point, but this resentful No-Mo (as Peter Scarlet called non-Mormons) pounced on the twofer -- the chance to use new academic knowledge while capitalizing on the Mormon element.

Aside from lying to patients about the donor's identity, the rotund doctor undoubtedly passed his genes to innumerable women from his Mormon ward. Given the habit of young Mormons to socialize within the same insulated community, and given the tendency of people with common characteristics to develop an attraction, it was logical to assume that the Sperm Whale's unsuspecting offspring might meet and marry at the genetic peril of their descendants. What's more, the not-so-fresh sperm of a 55-year-old was more likely to deteriorate than a younger man's, causing additional birth defects.

Lax government regulation of fertility practices permitted Sperm Whale's outrage, so I called for strict new rules.

* * *

Toward the end of the year, Shelledy sent me and Denny memos for failing to subscribe to *The Tribune*. Gotta keep those subscription rates up, after all.

Perhaps there is an error or you are unable to receive home delivery of the Tribune in your neighborhood. (You can get the Tribune only or the Tribune and D.N. for the same price.) If the records are correct and you do not wish to subscribe to the Tribune, please let me know in writing specifically what is the reason.

There was more than one error in the man's memo. First of all, *The Tribune* capitalized both T's in its name, something the big kahuna should know. Secondly, we did indeed subscribe in Summit County, not that we needed to when I re-read the newspaper page-by-bloody-page in editorial meetings. In any case, we resented being coerced into telling this upstart what we did in our private lives.

* * *

At year's end, the 153 ESOP beneficiaries received a statement showing the program's value had increased from $14.8 million to $21.1 million over 12 months. Denny and I, both vested by then, started to think there might be something to this thing after all.

---

[781] Jay Shelledy, memo to Harry Fuller and Gerry Cunningham, January 8, 1992 (1).

[782] "Blooming Like a Rose," *The Salt Lake Tribune*, February 27, 1992, p. A10.

[783] Diane Cole, "Letters to the editor: who needs 'em? We do," *The Masthead*, The Quarterly Journal of the National Conference of Editorial Writers, Volume 44, No. 1, Spring 1992, p. 7.

[784] James E. Shelledy, "Strong Editing Returns," *Nieman Reports,* Summer 1992, pp. 22-23.

[785] *The Salt Lake Tribune* obituary November 19, 2009.

43 - More Swan Songs and Sweeter Times in 1993

Jan Keller, my friend and former contact at Salt Lake City School District, needed a liver transplant to survive. I was heartsick. The Salt Lake Education Foundation, headed by former Utah Technical College President Orville D. Carnahan, whom I'd given such a bad time in editorials, sent out pleas for $125,000 in donations that would qualify her for the transplant waiting list. My $200 was a drop in the bucket, but she did receive a transplant and still is living in 2018.

* * *

Hemphill attended his first NCEW convention, and like I did my first time, he prepared a detailed report on critiques of our editorial pages. As usual, out pages were described as too gray; our editorials too long and devoid of passion. We were urged to use shorter sentences and paragraphs and to do less analysis.

"I get the feeling that editorial writing at *The Trib* is almost more a chore than a labor of love," one critic said. Another: "I have a feeling that very few people get angry about your editorials." In short, the editorials were just "too damned reasonable."

If we were boring, I believed, it was because the Fourth Floor shrank from controversy. We covered both sides of each issue to ensure fairness and avoided strong stands that might offend our publisher and friends.

The critics urged us to discard daily meetings, the "biggest time-waster." I couldn't have agreed more. Our seemingly interminable morning meetings still squandered what should have been our most productive time of day.

As with past convention reports, this one also was set aside. Instead of shorter, the daily meetings got longer.

* * *

Tribune fixtures Jerry Dunton, still a newsroom editor, and Barbi Robison, features editor, handed in their resignations.

Since my Copy Desk days, plump Dunton had been one of my trusted friends, telling me how to handle various editors and even parts of my personal life. I was glad he would have more time to explore the West he loved and

to share retirement with a nice woman, Carolyn Nielsen. But I would miss him.

Barbi made a considerable sacrifice by retiring early, at age 60, before she could make the most of ESOP. She was single with a nest egg of just $20,000, but she just couldn't stand the job under Shelledy's thumb.

"Stubby [Shelledy] and I didn't get along," she said, primarily blaming this routine:

When we would have our department meetings, Jay would rip our asses about something. Every six weeks, you could count on it. The girls [in Lifestyle] got so upset because they thought they'd been doing the right thing. I told them it was just one man's opinion. [786]

Barbi felt like Shelledy took her for granted. When Tom McCarthey became his deputy, for example, she got responsibility for his travel section on top of managing Lifestyle.

Tom McCarthey as travel editor.

McCarthey had normally used information from travel companies for his own trips, taken at advertisers' expense, and chucked out unopened freelance stories and photos by the barrel full. Believing it awful to ignore the work that went into these stories, Barbi and secretary Lucy Bodily devised a system for opening and sending rejection letters for anything Barbi couldn't use. The effort kept her at the office at least two hours late each week.

One day she found a letter referring to an expense-paid trip being set up for McCarthey as travel editor:

I was so mad! I went into Tom's office and told him, "If you think I'm going to do your work for you while you take the trips, forget it!" Five minutes later Stubby called me in laughing and said he couldn't believe that I would take on a McCarthey. I said, "I won't work for you guys for nothing." So I was fired as travel editor.[787]

Shelledy hypocrisy also stuck in Barbi's craw. Two weeks into the job, she explained, "Stubby" announced *The Tribune* would unite the east and west sides of Salt Lake City. His new deputy editors were encouraged to move into poor neighborhoods, and reporters were assigned to highlight the economic gap that needed to be bridged.

In his daily critique, Shelledy ordered staff to "pay greater attention to issues, features, people and events who live or occur west of I-15 . . . The population growth is in that area of our primary market and it represents our best opportunity for increased penetration." (Yes, he used the word penetration.)

Yet every day at the four o'clock meeting, Barbi said, Shelledy would make "terrible remarks about the west side." She finally told him he was the worst offender against efforts to unite the city. In the next four o'clock meeting, he announced that she had called it to his attention that he was the worst offender. "Everyone looked at me with surprise, but it didn't stop him. The damn little shithead!"

* * *

Shelledy also used his purported concern for westsiders as an excuse to encroach on Editorial again.

Barging into our meeting one morning, he pushed us to come down hard on Salt Lake City School District for spending more money on richer east-side students than poorer westsiders. Paul Wetzel slammed his hand on the table and declared: "That's not true!"

Shelledy's eyes widened. He then pointed at each of us in turn, shouting: "Fuck you, fuck you, fuck you!" He then stormed out, slamming the door behind him.

I was so proud of Wetzel . . . until his careful gene kicked in. He climbed the stairs to Shelledy's office to apologize for losing his cool.

* * *

After two years of Shelledy recruitment calls, brash **Lee Siegel** left the Associated Press in Los Angeles to become *Tribune* "science editor."

Some of us were leery of this outspoken "food Jew atheist," as he called himself,[788] because we suspected he snared a higher salary than longtime employees. But he was a good writer and affable, offering new blood and depth to daily coverage. He praised *The Tribune* culture for preventing him from "being driven nuts by Utahns' craziness." For awhile, he prepared a weekly science page.

One of Siegel's most exciting times at *The Tribune* was watching a tornado from newsroom windows, then huddling in the hallway before running to a Beans 'n Brew to find electricity to write a sidebar August 11, 1999. (I was lunching downtown as the sky darkened and particles of the city whipped past the windows in this rare event.)

The "science editor" concept didn't catch on and Siegel never received a promotion, so he took a University of Utah public relations job in 2000. When his animated pushiness started dominating conversations at *Tribune* retiree luncheons years later, Barbi Robinson blackballed the gatherings. "I'll never forget the last party I went to at Mike's [Korologos']," she said. "[Siegel] was going on to Shirley about his rabbits. Denny looked over at me and said, 'He IS single, you know.'"[789]

* * *

On our way to Lake Powell the September of 1993, Denny and I stopped by Scofield Reservoir to see 390 acres of forest we'd seen in the classified ads. We were searching for more peace and quiet with nature. The owner happened to be opening the gate and gave us an impromptu tour of Joe's Ridge.

We were awestruck by the awesome, panoramic view of layer after layer of mountain ridges to the west and colorful plateaus to the southeast. Hawks and vultures circled over an old growth forest of huge evergreens and quaking aspen. We mortgaged our house to snap it up.

When I came up for air from my studies on weekends, Denny and I started escaping to Joe's Ridge, where the faint howl of coyotes replaced Summit Park's incessant dog-barking and freeway roar. It was thrilling to spot deer, elk, horned toads, huge owls, woodpeckers, red tail hawks, countless smaller birds, chipmunks and wildflowers galore: columbines, scarlet gilia, sweet peas. Sego lilies (what did Vard call them?) carpeted the high point on the property in the spring.

In winter, we snapped on cross-country skis and broke trail through swaths of fresh snow decorated only by tracks of deer and snowshoe hares. Summertime, we cleared brush and fallen tree limbs for a place to pitch our tent and build a fire pit.

I kept expecting the other shoe to drop, and it did in the form of green-belt tax rules that required us to lease the land for sheep grazing and eventually stomped on our dream. But that unfortunate series of events would take years to unfold.

---

[786] Barbi Robison, September 11, 2015.

[787] Ibid.

[788] Lee Siegel email, August 3, 2015.

[789] Robison, November 13, 2015.

44 - Dominating My Days in 1994

Shelledy ordered a promotional video that presented *The Tribune* as a progressive, diverse organization. Diane Cole was the only editorial writer not to appear on camera Otherwise, the promo squeezed in as many female and minority staffers as possible: Jennifer Johnson (the only woman in Sports), Nancy Hobbs, Judy B. Rollins, Kathy Kapos Stephenson, Terry Ellefsen, Laurie Sullivan, Norma Wagner, Cherrill Crosby, Dawn House, Sheila McCann, Judge Magid, Nancy Melich, Andrea Otanez, JoAnn Jacobsen-Wells and Ann Poore. African American Verdo Thomas was there, as were Native American Mark Trahant and Japanese American Vince Horiuchi.

While focused on school, I felt left out of major new events as well as PR projects. The Salt Lake City Library hostage crisis was one. Armed with semi-automatic gun and bomb, Clifford Lynn Draper rounded up and held several people in the auditorium. One hostage, Lloyd Prescott, happened to be a heroic county sheriff who shot Draper. Though traumatic, incidents like this got adrenaline coursing as reporters rushed to get the full story. I missed the excitement of the newsroom.

Although I still had to finish my master's essay, my university classes were winding down. I was amazed, after all the times I'd threatened to quit, that I got this far.

My favorite subjects were in law, but my health policy advisor, Bob Huefner, was my best professor. With his help, I snagged an $8,000 Family Health Plan fellowship requiring my participation in seminars with Utah health-policy leaders. The process shaped my position on public health insurance policy, which became the subject of my graduate essay. A philosophy professor helped clarify my views on assisted suicide and abortion.

There had been some dark days on the way to graduation.

For the first time in my life, I'd had to hire a tutor to coach me through a class, statistics. The last day of his class, Prof. Peter Diamond publicly berated my supposed stubborn refusal to grasp political theory. He also snidely wrote on my final paper that I got more from his class than expected, given my comments in class. Without

bothering to read even to the end of my introduction, Prof. Dan McCool blithely dismissed my term paper as a "history" rather than the assigned analysis of subgovernment theory. I was aghast, believing it to be some of my best work. McCool scrawled a C-plus across the cover page, the equivalent of a D for graduate school. Another first.

While my final essay dragged on, I sent preliminary findings favoring universal health care to Republican Gov. Mike Leavitt. Deep down, I hoped it might help me get a state policy job. It didn't. At least it could have given Leavitt background for his 2005 appointment as U.S. Secretary of Health and Human Services, but given his conservative bent, he probably didn't even read it.

The 30 months I spent in school, I received no pay increase. "I'm having to pay my own tuition, plus get by on about $13,000 a year," I complained to Mimi. "Jerry O'Brien, it seems, sees a part-timer as a non-entity."

Of course it was my own idea to get a master's degree, and now that Lex Hemphill was fully ensconced in my office, I was no shoo-in for another full-time position. Our publisher was sick with kidney failure, making my situation petty by comparison.

* * *

My requested reinstatement seemed hopeless when **Jerry O'Brien** died February 15, making way for Dominic Welch, *The Tribune's* money man, to replace him.

I wrote O'Brien's sendoff, an honor yet nerve-wracking ordeal. The editorial had to be accurate and strike the right tone to please my perfectionist friend Joan, his daughter. Although she tweaked it a bit before publication, the words were mostly mine. It said, in part:

Salt Lake Tribune, Utah Lose Treasure

The Salt Lake Tribune *lost more than its publisher Tuesday, and Utah lost more than a quiet, insightful community leader.*

When Paul J.G. O'Brien died after courageously enduring an extended series of major illnesses, at age 68, the newspaper and state lost a true friend and humanitarian. He will be missed more than simple words can express.

. . . Jerry, as he wished to be known . . . was a modest man who avoided the

spotlight for himself but worked effectively behind the scenes to promote important business, community and philanthropic causes. The good he did through kindness, compassion and Christian charity is beyond measure . . .

Jerry O'Brien consistently treated others with kindness and respect . . . His first instinct was to avoid confrontation and encourage cooperation in a united community. Yet he stood his ground on important principles and goals. He adeptly used his quick, Irish wit and charm to ease others' discomfort . . .

Because of his talent for discerning and eloquently describing the positive aspects of his fellow human beings, he often authored citations recognizing contributors to local humanitarian causes. Though he might deny such a claim, he exemplified many of the traits he attributed to others: a charming personality committed to the community's best interests who did good works without regard to race, religion or stature in life; an effective but unassuming leader in campaigns to help others; a citizen supreme.

Jerry O'Brien took pride in his country, his community, his church, his newspaper, his favorite teams and, especially, his family. They, in turn, can take tremendous pride in having known him as an outstanding citizen, employer, friend, fan and father.[790]

Years after her dad's passing, Joan described him as loyal and countered my assumption that he had wrestled with alcohol. It's not for me to say so long after the fact.

The news-side obituary revealed soft-spoken, modest Jerry O'Brien had completed 35 combat missions as an armorer gunner in Europe during World War II. He had been inducted into the Spokane Softball Hall of Fame and was a Golden Gloves boxer at Gonzaga, where he was editor of the student newspaper. Before joining the Associated Press, where he became bureau chief, he worked for the *Daily Chronicle* and *The Spokesman-Review* in Spokane.

The *Deseret News* quoted Jack Gallivan: "In the death of Jerry O'Brien, Utah has lost a loving and dedicated servant; journalism a champion of the truth; and legions across the nation an irreplaceable friend."[791] O'Brien was so likable that even Thomas S. Monson, the LDS Church's representative on the Newspaper Agency board and future church leader, likened him to Jesus Christ, for goodness sake:

In the passing of Jerry O'Brien, I have lost a dear and longtime friend . . . Jerry did not seek the limelight, his service was rendered in a quiet fashion, much like the Lord Jesus Christ.[792]

O'Brien co-founded Tele-Communications Inc., Telemation and National Telefilm Associates, Inc. He sat on Republic Pictures' Board of Directors, a duty that spawned several discussions on the Editorial Board about the coloration of old black-and-white movies, yet another diversion from editorial writing.

Finally, O'Brien belonged to the Holy Cross Hospital Board of Directors. As such, he became a member of Utahns for Nonprofit Hospitals and its blue ribbon committee on health care costs.

Of course that role affected my editorials on health care, the primary emphasis of my master's degree. I continually had to tone down my criticism of insurance companies and my preference for universal health care. Even nonprofit hospitals were quite profitable for the doctors on staff, I knew, but this was not something I could clearly articulate. It was just one more Fourth Floor conflict of interest we editorial writers had to consider.

I should have counted my blessings. My challenges mounted with a changing of the guard.

* * *

Dominic Welch

Dominic Welch, a small town Carbon County native and Army veteran from the Korean conflict, graduated from Utah State University in 1957. The tall, curly headed Catholic Italian appeared on *The Tribune's* radar while working for Salt Lake City's largest public accounting firm, Haskins & Sells, where he was the only non-Mormon on a staff of 35. Two years after auditing *The Tribune* in 1962, aging *Tribune* Treasurer George Egan called him in to interview as his understudy.

"After a very uncomfortable interview with Gallivan, who needed someone to keep the books but had no respect for the [accounting] profession," Welch said, "I got the job."[793]

He was in for a shock or two.

The Tribune, with its shabby newsroom full of cigarette puffing, swearing characters, was nothing like his previous squeaky clean place of employment. Moreover, Egan wasn't ready to retire, giving Welch "virtually nothing to do" for two years.

Welch entertained himself by analyzing financial statements going back to the Kearns acquisition, reading histories about the *Tribune* family and perusing stockholder and director minutes. When he assured Egan he didn't want his job, Egan suddenly dropped everything in his lap. Over time, Welch became general manager of *The Tribune* and director/treasurer of Newspaper Agency Corp.

Welch got more than he bargained for when named publisher, too. As did we editorial writers.

For one thing, he believed a newspaper with a strong editor didn't even need a publisher:

> Ben Bradlee and all the other great editors proved that is true. In an agency arrangement like *The Tribune* had with the *News*, where the publisher has no control over production of the paper, the publisher is even more redundant. The primary responsibility of the publisher relative to the newsroom is to hire and fire the editor. My primary focus as publisher was to perform this function, and Shelledy was enough to keep me busy.[794]

Maybe if he hadn't pushed Shelledy onto Jerry O'Brien in the first place, he wouldn't have been so busy. And if he'd given Shelledy the boot early on, he could have prevented a lot of pain for the staff and even the owners. But Welch didn't recognize Shelledy's "narcissistic arrogance" at first.[795]

Welch found time to keep editorial writers on edge.

His days of sauntering into Editorial Board meetings to taunt us for wasting time were over. The gentleman with the glimmering grin from coal country still poked fun, his playful comments tumbling downstream like water in a summer creek. However, Welch became our primary time consumer. Board meetings stretched into two-hour marathons as he bantered with us or let visitors sway his opinion, leaving less time than ever to produce our pages.

Unfortunately, our new publisher took seriously his role as *The Tribune's* voice, weighing in on most of our editorials. Even worse for me were our opposing opinions on most subjects, especially taxes, health care and welfare. He perceived himself a fiscal conservative and social liberal,[796] but the liberal part was hard to detect. He was more libertarian, erring on the opposite side of government.

Asked for guidance on a topic, Welch shot from the hip, lobbing such quips as: "Let 'em get a job" or, "That guy's a horse's ass." Our job was to develop a persuasive editorial on that basis. Often I had to argue against my own principles.

Frustrating as O'Brien's gentle, laissez-faire approach could be, we learned to appreciate him leaving most writing to us while he promoted community and humanitarian causes. Only when we threatened a sacred cow like the Mormon Church did he intervene. He must have fumed in his grave when Shelledy started tweaking the church -- with Welch's tacit permission -- at the risk of resurrecting the "irrepressible conflict."

The risk was real. In 1997, Glen Snarr, the LDS Church representative on NAC's board, revolted against *Tribune* treatment of church issues. Behind the scenes, he worked to crush *Tribune* competition when the time was right.[797] But that part of the story is not yet ripe for the telling.

* * *

As I perched precariously on my part-time post in Editorial -- the publisher wasn't inclined to increase the staff to four full-time writer/editors -- Shelledy suggested I write a political column -- gratis. Since he supposedly wielded no power over the opinion pages, I didn't take the bait. Then he proposed moving me back to the newsroom.

He was reorganizing the News Desk again, this time into PODs (I can't remember what the acronym meant). Seven women, myself included, were invited to apply to edit the "communities" POD.

Instead of unilaterally picking his favorite candidate this time, Shelledy let POD reporters interview and vote for their future boss. Reluctant as I was about the process, I needed full-time work and still wanted to be a news editor. Communities dovetailed with my experience with education and my academic focus on politics, government, justice, cultural groups and feminism.

I failed Shelledy's test. Few newsroom newcomers knew me well, and I spilled my guts about religion, justice and feminism. My performance apparently underwhelmed Peggy Fletcher-Stack, the LDS religion specialist who'd been Bagley's phone buddy, and Peg McEntee from the Associated Press. So I slunk back to the mezzanine and looked elsewhere for a full-time assignment.

* * *

Tribune management began preparing its first anti-harassment policy in order to comply with state and federal law. By spring, a two-page policy forbade:

> *-- Unwelcome or unsolicited verbal, physical or sexual conduct which interferes with an employee's job performance or which creates an intimidating, hostile work environment.*
> *-- Offensive sexist, off-color or sexual remarks, jokes, slurs or propositions or comments that disparage a person or group on the basis of race, color, age, religion, sex, disability or national origin.*
> *-- Derogatory or suggestive posters, cartoons, photographs, calendars, graffiti, drawings, or gestures. Inappropriate touching, hitting, pushing or physical contact or threats to take such action.*

A board of supervisors was set up to review complaints.

This had to be earth-shattering for men on staff before the 1990s. If the Art Department pillar still existed, it would have been outlawed. Male staffers could no longer get away with suggestions to go out back and neck. There would be no more unwanted squeezes in the back hall or at the copy machine. No more racist or sexist jokes. Gay staffers could finally leave the closet without fear of reprisal.

While welcome in a way, I feared strict political correctness would have a chilling effect on office camaraderie. How would Denny communicate with women without flirting? Did he have to quit kissing Lucy on the neck and joking about his etchings? Did women have to give up Tim Kelly's comforting bear hugs?

Apparently so. A couple of years into the new policy, police reporter Norma Wagner accused Kelly of sexual harassment when he moved her by the shoulders away from a doctor he was trying to photograph. Anyone who knew Kelly was stunned. Although the review board exonerated him, his ego never recovered.

Tim Kelly gives big hugs to Carolyn Monson and Nancy Hobbs.

337

* * *

I continued to cast about for full-time employment. Salt Lake Community College offered to hire me to teach journalism and supervise the student newspaper, but I declined. The job came with a pay cut and without summers off, and the newspaper was embroiled in libel accusations and free-speech disagreements with administrators. I applied to be a consultant for the Utah State Health Policy Commission but didn't make the cut.

Shelledy came up with another opening on City Desk, this time as health policy reporter. Though a step backward on my career path, this was something I could do.

My September 6 application to Shelledy, Ledford and Fitzpatrick pointed out that I wrote most *Tribune* editorials on AIDS, Medicaid and health reform. I mentioned my role as a chief presenter in a series of health reform forums for doctors, nurses, scholars, hospital administrators and insurance representatives. I predicted which health care issues would move to the forefront in the next few years, including health care rationing, abortion, physician assisted suicide, geriatric care, cost cutting and Gov. Mike Leavitt's "Health Print" program. I also noted that Jerry O'Brien, while less than enthusiastic about reducing my work schedule for school, had assured me there would be a full-time job available when I graduated. I didn't add that I had yet to finish my essay.

This time, I made the grade. Just before I moved upstairs, however, Harry Fuller persuaded Welch to keep me in Editorial. I had to decide whether to make a change at the risk of expanding my work day and answering to someone I didn't respect. If I stayed put, I could use the confidence and background that came with my recent education to finish work faster and better, but I still would be stuck writing for someone I didn't agree with.

Shelledy's critique of September 17-19 announced that I accepted the publisher's offer to become the fourth full-time editorial writer. "Plans for her to take Cherrill Crosby's [medical writing] position on Quality of Life have evaporated."

Uneasy with my decision, I applied to replace Mark Trahant when he quit as deputy editor for news. It was a long shot after my renege, so my letter to Shelledy laid it on thick:

This is the job I've been working toward my entire journalistic career; perhaps even longer. It's a chance to return to the excitement of daily, breaking news and to teaching, something I've always hoped to do someday, while making use of my news sense, journalistic experience, local perspective and education. Teaching, you ask? I consider journalism an important form of education, not just for young journalists but for readers. What we print in the newspaper not only entertains people, it teaches readers about their government, their communities and themselves. It can inspire people to good citizenship and help improve their lives.

What makes me so sure I know what people should be reading? Experience is part of it. Experience with Utah, with *The Tribune* and with people. I've been up close to many of the kinds of challenges our readers face: divorce, domestic violence, religious and sex discrimination, step-parenting, grandparenting, chronic illnesses, higher education, home-building, etc. With 20-plus years at *The Tribune*, I have institutional memory. I may not have the specific kind of management experience your job notice implies, but as you know, schoolteachers have to know how to successfully motivate and supervise people to survive. I also was education editor at *The Tribune* for several years. Though mostly a reporting position, it required the supervision of another reporter and decisions on coverage and news play. Earlier in my career, I was make-up editor, supervising printers in the backshop. And even in editorial, which I consider a highly responsible position, I have had supervising duties as "associate editor." I'm in charge when Harry is absent, assigning topics, editing copy and making up pages when necessary. I did most of the training when Jim Woolf, Tim Fitzpatrick, Paul Wetzel and Lex Hemphill came into the department.

Why news editor in particular? Because news -- broadly defined but primarily political and social, as opposed to specialized features or subject areas -- gets me going everyday. I like variety and I like good writing. I read most of the paper (I confess that sports and recipes get short-shrift) and the wires every day, keeping track of what's covered and what's not, and how we've treated the subject. Even as an editorial writer, I search our stories for grabbing leads, logical organization, coherence and completeness. I notice if a story is redundant or leaves something out, and I have definite feelings about how stories are played. (It's the recreation of editorial writers to second-guess news editors, after all.) Meantime, I've become increasingly fascinated with the potential of the Web and frequently use it for editorial research.

I went back for my master's for a jumpstart, and I may be satisfied as an editorial writer the rest of my career at *The Tribune*, however long that may be given ESOP's performance. But as we have discussed in the past, new challenges are invigorating, and I'm ready for one. It would be nice to feel I'm progressing and making the best use of my skills and talents. I'm confident I could work well with the excellent staff you have assembled, and I would be supportive of your policies and decisions, though I couldn't help letting you know when I disagree with you. I also would enjoy helping you with your critiques if you were interested. I had doubts about replacing Joan on communities and religion, and I chose editorial over health policy reporter because the latter was more confining and less challenging for me. I've often thought, however, that the position of executive news editor could have been created just for me. Please give my candidacy serious consideration.

And even if you choose someone else, you might consider temporary exchanges with our department some time. This would let you try me out for the job without making a longterm commitment.

My latest attempt at self promotion a failure, I stayed put in Editorial.

* * *

With a shortage of desks on the mezzanine, I found myself back in the newsroom for the first time in a decade, moving from vacant seat to vacant seat to write my editorials. It was culture shock trying to concentrate while reporters yakked on the phone or among themselves. Their cynical conversations and compassion fatigue pricked my thinning skin.

Some reporters were dispassionate or downright cruel, treating tragedies like just another six inches of copy. Consider these snippets of office banter:

-- Naughty, naughty. The guy had his hands where they don't belong again.

-- How's the pervert beat lately?

-- Hey, did you hear about those videos that Alzheimer's patients watch over and over and over and think they're seeing it for the first time?

Stormy's favorite reporter told a caller: "I'm sorry, but it's not this newspaper's responsibility to write a story about every person that needs an organ transplant. Those stories are a dime a dozen." After hanging up, she deadpanned, "I meant to get her number so I can call if she dies without one."

This reminded me of the same reporter's conversation years earlier with a mother desperate for unaffordable cancer treatment for her child: "Ma'am, if we wrote a story about your child's fundraiser, everyone with a sickness would want one, and then the paper would be nothing but fundraisers."

My stepdaughters' experience with a pervert, my dad's Alzheimer's and my friend's need for a transplant apparently had undercut my sense of gallows humor.

While I understood that callousness protected journalists' softer cores, the morbid jokes were hard to stomach after so long away from the newsroom. I was grateful when a cubicle was created next to the Art Department for my filing cabinets, computer and desk. It was noisier than my old office but infinitely more pleasant than the newsroom. It even came with a view -- of the NAC reception area and a slice of sidewalk on Main Street.

* * *

After working the Government Desk's computers a couple of years, former State Capitol reporter **Dave Jonsson** finally quit, taking fond memories of *Tribune* characters[798] and a pile of ESOP credit with him. He became an information specialist for the Utah Department of Community and Economic Development, where he stayed until just before the 2002 Olympics.

Also parting company with *The Tribune* that year was **Gerry Cunningham**, who stormed out as Shelledy's managing editor. He died eight years later, at 63.

With the passing of Jerry O'Brien and the virtual demise of UPI, *The Tribune* finally welcomed Joan's boyfriend **Tom Harvey** into the fold.

* * *

Shelledy's habit of fiddling with the Editorial Department flared again one day as Harry Fuller returned to work with a head cold and lingering anesthesia from a wisdom tooth extraction. Here's what Fuller found:

> The Prince of Darkness [Shelledy] had marked up one of our page proofs [page copies for proofreading]. I sprinted up those back stairs, clutching the aforesaid page proof, found the devil's disciple in the newsroom, flung the page at him and said something like, "If you are going to work in my department, here it is" -- as I am sure startled and fascinated newsroom personnel watched -- whereupon he directed me into his sanctuary, where he threatened to have me banned permanently from the newsroom. Following further, mutually calmer discussion, exchanging views on how the paper was being run since his arrival, during which I said something like, "Well, at least you communicate more than your predecessors," we sort of agreed to co-exist. Avoided was a confrontation that might have compelled Dominic to decide the outcome.
>
> My interpretation was that medication had let me overreact to the fool, but at least I was able to call his bluff. But I doubt he ever forgot his backdown and would have schemed some way to get the better of the situation if I had not retired soon thereafter. Anyway, he never openly threatened me with getting my job, though I have no doubt he would have explored ways to do that. He did all he could to marginalize our department. I will give Dominic credit for withstanding any of those attempts if they did, in fact, occur.[799]

I remembered the confrontation differently. After Fuller flung the pages at the bully, Shelledy claimed he could have Fuller's job any day. Fuller challenged him to try, asserting that Dominic Welch, not Shelledy, controlled the Editorial Department.

Either way, I was never prouder of Fuller -- until he later apologized for losing his temper, much as Paul Wetzel had done during an earlier Shelledy incursion. As before, I felt Shelledy's authority needed to be challenged, and they wimped out. Maybe they just had more class than I did.

* * *

In December, Dominic Welch surprised staffers with a holiday letter extolling improvements in the newspaper his first year as publisher. The tone and style sounded like Shelledy.

> I don't need to tell you that 1994 is proving to be a record business year for the Tribune [no capital on "the"]. That is quite apparent from the size of our newspapers, the advertising linage, growth in circulation and control of expenses.
>
> What I do want to convey at the end of this year is a recognition of my appreciation of the continued improvement of the editorial product and the role it plays in our general success.
>
> These two intertwined factors -- revenue and content -- have made this past year exciting and satisfying for me and, hopefully, for you, as well.
>
> To that end, I am declaring a one-time special Publisher's bonus -- a newsroom staff dividend, if you will, for an exceptional year -- both in operations and content quality. Your share of this dividend, based on individual effort and time spent in the newsroom during 1994, is enclosed.

Also at the end of the year, the company adopted a "family and medical leave policy" in accordance with the Family and Medical Leave Act of 1993. For the first time, up to 12 weeks of leave would be permitted per year to care for a child, parent, spouse or even one's own health. Our newspaper would no longer discriminate against mothers -- or even fathers.

* * *

Still, not everything was roses in *The Tribune* family and mine.

TV critic Hal Schindler suffered a mild stroke which kept him off work for a week. Mark Knudsen, facing divorce, disappeared but was found two days later near death in the Tooele desert. My theory was that divorce on top of his hearing loss and pressure at work overwhelmed him, especially since he had moved to the newsroom, away from the rest of the Art Department on the mezzanine. After leaving the hospital, he stayed with us until Lulu showed up for a visit. He was a much easier houseguest than Lulu.

My brother's 12-year-old stepson Christopher, a great kid, was killed while riding his bicycle in his Ventura neighborhood. I immediately flew to California to drive my parents to the funeral. Though confused, Dad didn't say or do anything inappropriate.

About the same time, Denny's closest cousin, dentist William Green, was dying of stomach cancer, and doctors found a cyst in Stormy's eye that needed monitoring.

---

[790] "Salt Lake Tribune, Utah Lose Treasure," *The Salt Lake Tribune*, February 17, 1994, p. A18.

[791] "Tribune Publisher Jerry' O'Brien Dies at 68," *Deseret News*, February 16, 1994.

[792] Timeline, Utah Newspaper Project.

[793] Dominic Welch email, October 16, 2014.

[794] Ibid.

[795] Dominic Welch email, October 20, 2014.

[796] Welch, October 16, 2014.

[797] Utah Newspaper Project, The Quest No. 9.

[798] Jonsson, August 10, 2015.

[799] Harry Fuller email to Diane Cole. January 8, 2014.

45 - More Memo Madness and Change in 1995

When an Ogden police officer handcuffed Tom Wharton and confiscated his notebook -- he was covering the disposal of explosives after a bomb threat in January -- Shelledy got tough in his daily critique:

> An Explosive Ordinance Detail military person from Tooele Army Deport or an AFT agent (we are running this down) ripped out a page of notes. Tribune Attorney Sharon Sonnenreich will be pursuing today, upon threat of civil and criminal actions against these officers, a formal apology and return of the missing page of notes. Any government or private confiscation of notes or film or any unbecoming behavior by law enforcement officers directed specifically toward reporters or photographers will not go unanswered.

Whether the notes were returned and the apology issued, I cannot recall. But this reaction from Shelledy was a positive change from days gone by.

That is not to say Shelledy stayed on my good side.

He continued obnoxiously hyping competition and readership figures to pump up the staff. He boasted that *Tribune* circulation in March rose 2.1 percent weekdays and 1.8 percent Sundays while the *Deseret News'* "real weekday circulation fell to under 62,000 for a 3 percent decrease" over the previous March. "Most of the [*Tribune*] increase came in our primary market, but the off-the-Wasatch Front circulation rose 10 percent." The trend might be worth noting, but I wasn't going to measure my success by the church organ's struggle.

Shelledy still pitted reporters against each other for front-page bylines, creating friction and fear instead of collaboration.

After insisting that storytelling rather than breaking news was now our calling, he criticized coverage of the Lafferty death sentence April 17. "Forget narrative writing style when it is breaking news. The nut graf ought to be in the first graf," his daily critique declared.

He also reminded reporters never to use anonymous sources without his express permission. "If sources won't go on the record, then use the information as background and, if you trust it, work it into your own prose." I doubted readers would welcome unsourced "facts."

Finally, Shelledy's April 17 critique heralded the 50 prep baseball and softball games reported that day in Sports. "Most impressive." I could just see The Man sitting at his kitchen table, coffee in hand, furiously tallying each game mentioned, no matter how minor.

After earlier poo-pooing such things, Shelledy called for more 8-point obituaries and greater attention to local history. He'd apparently discovered that obits were one of the best-read parts of the newspaper and that institutional memory could be useful for fleshing out the news. Yes, he'd flushed away several longtime staffers with that kind of knowledge, but now he wanted someone for the "unofficial newsroom status of 'historian.'"

The same memo ordered more names of "common folks, as opposed to, say, politicians and Olympic officials" in the newspaper, even if it meant printing lists of students on the honor roll.

* * *

Tighter restrictions on building access were announced April 25. A four-digit code would now be required to enter the front door between 6 p.m. and 6 a.m. weekdays and 24 hours a day weekends. "Abuse of the code or defeating the door lock may result in disciplinary action," Shelledy's daily memo scolded. "It's not fair to compromise other peoples' security and make us memorize more numbers."

Woe be to the Chicago Charlies, Stephen Holbrooks and Monroe Flemings of the day.

* * *

In his usual condescending style, Shelledy spelled out the "summer dress" code in another memo:

> Some staffers are casual enough already and ought not regress further . . .
> Ground rules: There is no difference between days of the week. Weekends and holidays are no different than an ordinary Wednesday. No athletic wear, t-shirts, tank-tops, sweatshirts or shirts with messages. Dress still must be

professional (clean, appropriate, presentable.) Shorts are permissible.

I had to wonder how Shelledy would have handled columnist Dan Valentine's stiff-and-sour golf shirt.

* * *

The digital age dawned brighter for *The Salt Lake Tribune*. Shelledy announced May 9 that staffers using personal computers in the newsroom or at home "with 14,400 bod or better modems" could now use the internet through *The Tribune*.

This gave us quick access to the Library of Congress and other sources for background information, reducing the need to wade through books and past issues of the newspaper. That is, if we could figure out the new system. John Jordan, Shelledy's informant, was our facilitator, but he was unapproachable most of the time.

* * *

Shelledy again rearranged his News Desk, this time splitting up the Communities Desk I'd wanted to lead the previous year. With a vote of her peers, Peg McEntee ascended to the top of the "faith and learning" offshoot. Outgoing Deputy Editor Mark Trahant temporarily took charge of what was left of Communities. "As per normal procedure, staff will notify the editor of acceptable nominees [for a permanent editor there], " Shelledy announced in his June 3-5 critique. "Senior management will have the final choice."

Appointments outside this so-called democratic process were Dawn House, who would supervise justice and safety; Tim Fitzpatrick as editor of science and government; and Cherrill Crosby, continuing as business editor with David Clifton as an additional writer.

* * *

Another Shelledy critique recognized winners of the Utah-Idaho-Spokane Associated Press competition.

David Clifton and Lance Gudmundsen received special commendations, Clifton for reporting shooting/hostage terror at the Salt Lake City Library and Gudmundsen for a feature on Utah Transit Authority's director. Ledford's pet reporter Lili Wright, Mike Phillips and Anne Mathews received first-place accolades for a series on "People of Color." Wins went to Steve Griffin for spot sports photography and Steve Luhm for spot sports coverage of the John

Stockton-Karl Malone performance with the Utah Jazz.

"And that takes care of the journalism competition for another year, I trust," Shelledy concluded in his dismissive way. He treated the contest like a mostly meaningless but necessary pain in the ass to avoid looking bad compared to the *Deseret News*.

Our counterpart always played up its staff performance, just one more compensation for representing The Church. The *News* also paid higher salaries and offered better benefits than *The Tribune*.

* * *

Paul Rolly and Dawn House surprised me by marrying each other March 11, 1995. "It was a good luck date," House remarked. "That's the month and day Paul's parents were married. We needed a good date, with our combined families, most of whom were teenagers."[800] House had five children to Rolly's four, all raised in the Mormon Church. They were more compatible than I realized.

* * *

Salt Lake Community College complicated my life by asking me to sit on its Communications Advisory Committee. I squeezed in the monthly meetings despite my hectic life, partly because I wanted to experience a little of the decision-making I'd observed for so long as an education reporter. Perhaps I was flattered, too.

Before long, however, it became obvious that the committee had little power to make changes at the college, so my membership became an exercise in futility.

More rewarding was my return from the University of Utah to Editorial. Even before classes ended, my added knowledge and confidence made it easier to wrangle with public officials and write editorials. I didn't need to do so much research to back up my opinions, enabling me to finish my work faster.

Even Shelledy commended my editorial wrapping up the legislative session that year. His note concluded, "Tom McCarthey liked it too."

I hadn't realized McCarthey paid attention.

Health policy, environment, civil liberties, the courts, prisons, political ethics, interest groups, privatization and public policy in general eclipsed education and social welfare as my favorite editorial topics. At every opportunity, I championed tax credits and other methods to create more green space, and within a couple of years, those policies were slowly getting started. I also wrote about transportation, championing railroad safety and light-rail development.

Yet I still lambasted child-support laws, threats to civil rights in public education and tuition tax credits for private schools. I favored charter schools as an alternative to home schooling and tax-supported tuition. Merit pay for teachers never got off the ground despite my promotion of so-called "career ladders." Teacher union opposition was just too strong.

Jesse Helms, the North Carolina conservative who spewed hateful rhetoric and sponsored abusive legislation against women, homosexuals and blacks from his perch as the Senate's most ancient U.S. senator, became one of my targets. Naturally he favored school prayer, opposed abortion in all cases and resisted racial quotas. No one could hold me back when he led a travel ban on people with HIV and declared AIDS just punishment for sodomy.

There still were bumps in the road back to full-time Editorial.

Hemphill became possessive about some of my previous topics. He stewed or argued about my stance AIDS and public transportation, frustrating the hell out of me. However, I was happy to pass him the torch on Salt Lake City's Olympic bids, something I never warmed up to and he was eminently qualified to lead.

* * *

On June 17, our Front Page played it big that Jack Gallivan's decades-long campaign to attract the Winter Games bore fruit. The International Olympic Committee, meeting in Budapest, Hungary, chose Salt Lake City to host the 2002 Games. The vote occurred on a Friday, our most hectic day in Editorial, and we were obligated to rejoice on our page. I can't remember whether Hemphill did our cheering or was diverted to the news coverage, leaving me to fill the gap.

By then, Gallivan and friends had long since turned over the Olympics reins to paid campaigners and organizers. In 1991, Kennecott Corporation's chief executive officer, Frank Joklik, had become Salt Lake Bid Committee chairman and would soon lead the Salt Lake Organizing Committee (SLOC). Thomas K. Welch, a Mormon bishop, lawyer and businessman, and David Johnson, a former car salesman and sports promoter, ran the bid process before becoming president and vice president of SLOC. Our old pal Mike Korologos was their spokesman.

Welch and Johnson had learned their Birmingham lesson well. They wined and dined IOC members and provided their families with myriad gifts and privileges, from free health care and school scholarships to mountain bikes. Whether it was bribery or extortion is a matter of interpretation, but you can bet *The Tribune's* editorial heartily praised their 1995 victory in Budapest. The details of their methods would not become public until later.

* * *

Wetzel started bottling up all the juiciest topics for the week by bringing a list of his planned editorials to board meetings Mondays. He also developed an irritating habit of slamming his hand on the conference table and droning on about his extensive research. If she were there, his daughter Maryann might roll her eyes at what she called his "Mr. Know-It-All, lecture mode."[801]

I figured he was trying to make points with the new publisher, now the chief perpetrator of long board meetings. As many as four days a week, we made time for state and federal policymakers, interest groups and anyone else who wanted to bend our ears. That usually left us half a day to write editorials and make up pages.

Even so, I often enjoyed the discussions. My main strength, I thought, was to analyze and understand issues enough to see past people's official statements to their special interests. I felt respected by our visitors, if not always liked. Gov. Mike Leavitt and his deputies often directed their discussion my way. Muhammad Yunus and his local representative zeroed in on me to promote micro-loans to impoverished women as the way to end hunger in Bangladesh and elsewhere.

Steve Holbrook, the student protester and legislator who'd fallen from public grace with his 1981 solicitation arrest, became one of my favorite presenters. I admired the bearded social activist with impeccable diction, tasteful suits and shiny shoes. He hadn't let his sexual orientation and legal troubles in the straight red state of Utah keep him down. His story is worth recounting.

Holbrook founded an all-volunteer alternative radio station, KRCL 91 FM, in 1979 partly due to his chagrin over coverage of the protest movement that inspired his 1971 *Tribune* sit-in. He raised money for homeless shelters and services and, after becoming a surrogate parent for Chicago Charlie's son John C. Zahos, worked for reform of the juvenile justice system.

As an aside, Zahos became a self-proclaimed missionary who made his way into the national spotlight for trying to break into the White House compound. He died in 1999, possibly at his own hand. His Midvale gravestone identifies him as an "apostle" and includes his common salutation, "To God be the Glory."[802]

With support from Democratic Gov. Scott Matheson and Utah Social Services Director Tony Mitchell, Holbrook spurred the reorganization of Utah's Youth Corrections Program. In the early 1970s, that program primarily consisted of the State Industrial School in Ogden, a reform school that locked up as many as 400 rural truants and inner city armed robbers together. The new system devolved into 20 community-based alternative programs.

In the 1990s, Holbrook led the Coalition for Utah's Future, a group aimed at state growth issues like health, child care and homelessness. Ironically, after facing off during the *Tribune* sit-in decades earlier, Holbrook and Jack Gallivan grew to admire one another in that planning effort.[803] You might say that Holbrook no longer constituted *Tribune* clutter.

Holbrook's background, coming from Bountiful, impressed me. He entered Republican politics when growing up next door to Ivy Baker Priest, U.S. Treasurer to Dwight D. Eisenhower, and organizing Young Republican clubs at high schools throughout Utah. He was struck by social inequality, including his own LDS faith's denial of the priesthood to African Americans. Lagoon, an amusement park near his home, banned blacks from its dance floor and swimming pool.[804]

While in Hong Kong on an LDS mission, Holbrook felt like an ugly American when Vice President Lyndon Johnson flew in on Air Force 2 to buy 200 shirts amid the mind-numbing poverty.

Once back home, he joined Republican Congressman Sherman P. Lloyd's staff but was asked to leave when Medgar Evers' murder motivated him to join the local NAACP. The disappearance of three civil rights workers in Mississippi then drew him to the Mississippi Freedom Summer, a trip financed by Lagoon's owner, who had abolished restrictions on blacks. Holbrook worked in the office of Medgar Evers'

brother Charles, helping blacks register to vote. He went to jail for taking a photograph of a "Whites Only" water fountain sign. Held in a so-called hot box cell, he and his cellmate staged a hunger strike until a group of Jewish New Yorkers posted bail.[805]

* * *

The Fourth Floor's inconsistent but usually conservative political philosophy became my biggest challenge on the Editorial Page. As Dominic Welch gained confidence as publisher, he pushed harder on his positions -- and my buttons -- regarding government programs and policies. After wild discussions, I often found myself promoting views that rubbed my conscience raw.

The publisher compounded my torture by putting Randy Frisch in charge of our pages. The stunted businessman's foray into right-wing, inflammatory editorials sometimes added another hour or two to my work day as I tried to clean them up for publication.

Frisch preferred to provoke rather than persuade readers, so he didn't always ground his opinions in fact and reason. I couldn't just let his errors go, because they threatened the newspaper's reputation and my pride as a professional.

Fortunately, Frisch appreciated my extensive editing efforts more than Wetzel and Hemphill ever did. Then again, they made fewer potentially embarrassing mistakes than I did.

After retirement, Wetzel put it this way:

> If I were waterboarded and forced to say something negative about you professionally, I would admit that it annoyed me that you carpentered editorials – and everything else -- excessively on page proofs. But that's a quibble.[806]

Perhaps my obsessive editing went back to my early days tightening overwritten stories from rural stringers, letters to the editor and Common Carrier columns. I was always hyper about my own writing, trying to fix mistakes late in the printing process when I had afterthoughts. Problems popped out at me more readily on page proofs than on the computer screen, and once identified, I couldn't ignore them. My compulsiveness had to irritate writers who wanted to get home.

Despite our differences over most social programs, the publisher usually let me write what I wanted about education and religious freedom.

You can imagine my excitement, then, when a Magna elementary school showed the religious film, "Where Jesus Walked." What great fodder for filling that gaping hole on the left side of our page!

I paused when I realized that Magna's principal was Barbara Thayne, a longtime friend's sister and my brother-in-law's fiance. But I couldn't let family get in the way of an obvious, rare editorial that the publisher would approve. So I launched into an attack on educators who would endorse specific religious beliefs in public school. Luckily, Barbara took my criticism in stride.

* * *

My side of the family also played a role in my opinion writing. Specifically, I secretly wanted Dad to die, sharpening my interest in end-of-life health issues.

During my childhood, Dad had been more likely to give my brothers the back of his hand than a pat on the back, yet he had always been good to me. He was affectionate and tolerant of my escapades, even when I slammed his T-bird into a neighbor's new Olds '88. He seemed to secretly admire me for taking joy rides before I got my driver's license.

At 80, Dad could no longer feed himself, walk without help or use the toilet. Yet he was strong enough to bruise Mom as she cleaned him up while caring for him at home. In June, she'd had a heart attack and couldn't tolerate much stress.

At my insistence, Mom took Dad to a group home toward the end of the year. He panicked, triggering a stroke that ended his hostility as well his ability to walk and talk. Mom took him home, where he wailed in apparent pain night after night. On my six-week visits, I lay awake in the guest bed imagining holding a pillow over his face. I couldn't do it, but I knew he hated living this way.

At work, I weighed in on Dr. Jack Kevorkian's cavalier assisted-suicide crusade.

While favoring his aim to give people like Dad a dignified death, I feared opening the door to this ultimate solution would invite the kind of abuses and mistakes that plagued capital punishment. Rogue doctors could play God with patients; insurance companies and even families might pressure people to die early to save money. These things already were happening to a limited extent behind the scenes, and legal endorsement of Kevorkian's methods might pull out the stops.

The following editorial, which also sprang from Dad's dilemma, somehow got past our anti-social program publisher:

Shredding the Safety Net

Revolutionaries in Washington, relying on logic only seasoned politicians could appreciate, are carefully protecting Social Security from the budget ax while taking broad swipes at Medicare and Medicaid. Unless Americans soon wake up to this contradiction, they are destined to learn its consequences the hard way, when they most need government help.

Older Americans have erected an impervious shield around Social Security, extracting promises from congressional Republicans that the entitlement will be spared efforts to balance the budget. They insist they are owed the old-age benefits they bought with their payroll taxes during their working years.

Concerns about Medicare and Medicaid, government health insurance for elderly and low-income Americans, have been mild by comparison. Little protest has met recent efforts in Washington to trim spending for the two programs by as much as $400 billion over the next seven years.

Many Americans don't seem to realize that Social Security does not stand alone in reducing old-age suffering. In fact, it hardly touches some of the needs it was meant to satisfy, the most obvious being long-term care for the incapacitated.

One of an aging person's greatest worries is that the mind or body will fail, requiring help with such basic tasks as eating, taking medicine and bathing. A family, if one is available, can become impoverished trying to pay for assistance.

Medicare, health insurance available through Social Security, does not pay for long-term nursing and custodial care, which can cost $36,000 or more a year for someone with Alzheimer's disease. People who cannot afford skilled services on their own, or with Social Security payments, now turn to Medicaid once their savings are depleted.

Medicaid already pays more than half of nursing-home bills in this country. As the population ages, especially when baby boomers reach retirement, the demand for more nursing-home and home-care funds should be expected to increase.

But President Clinton and congressional Democrats already have taken steps to slow Medicaid spending, and Republicans in Congress now want to freeze the program for five years. That would cut Utah's Medicaid budget, for example, by $500 million -- 23 percent -- the next five years.

Such stringency, at a time when health-care costs continue to rise and additional people qualify for coverage, does not offer aging Americans much hope they will receive adequate assistance with chronic, debilitating illnesses.

If Congress keeps seemingly sacred Social Security benefits intact but slices gaping holes in Medicare and Medicaid, elderly Americans will be left with a shredded safety net. People who are neither well enough to care for themselves nor wealthy enough to pay for assistance will have a good chance of falling through.[807]

* * *

On October 30, Deputy Editor David Ledford issued a memo barring reporter access to the pagination system. The aim was to prevent changes in stories after they'd passed through POD and copy editors. "Henceforth, only an editor will have access to modify a story. Reporters will have to call the desk and request that changes be made."

The edict should have applied to certain editors as well.

A story quoting Robert Redford's environmental views came up short near deadline one night on Page One, Ace Fibber's responsibility. In another of his finer moments, Fibber slunk into Pagination, sat down at a paginator's screen and fabricated a Redford quote to fill the hole in his layout.

Next morning, the actor complained to the Fourth Floor that the story misstated his stance. Not only did *The Tribune* print a correction and apology, it finally issued Fibber's walking papers. Not that Fibber missed a beat. He soon was directing local sports events and writing for magazines, and he would get enough *Tribune* stock for a hillside mansion.

To his credit, Ledford also ushered in ergonomically correct work stations for the staff.

His research revealed woefully inadequate working conditions in the newsroom. Chairs were defective; desks and lighting inappropriate for video display terminals. He recommended a desk and file space for each employee so piles of files wouldn't restrict workers' feet.

"The obvious long-range solution is a new computer system and new desks," he said in a "letter to all hands" October 31. "We hope to reach that goal in 1996 or 1997."

It took a little longer than that, but eventually each writer was assigned a cubicle with a desk, file cabinet, computer terminal and four-foot high walls. Even if friendly furniture was primarily designed to shield *The Tribune* from liability for workplace injuries, it also made reporters feel better physically and emotionally. It gave them a sense of value and professionalism, something missing from my reporting days.

* * *

In November, *The Tribune's* digital version of news made its debut on the World Wide Web. The fairly modest change for us staffers became a revolution for newspapers that eventually traumatized *The Tribune* family, as we shall discuss later.

* * *

At the end of the year, the publisher announced another bonus because of the "record year for advertising and circulation revenue." There was a caveat: newsprint costs skyrocketed by $8 million and were expected to jump twice more in 1996. In his holiday letter December 22, Welch wrote:

I must warn you that 1996 will produce the greatest challenge in *The Tribune's* modern history. Increased expenses in circulation delivery and newsprint will put even greater pressures on advertising sales and expense belt-tightening. We will make every effort to avoid the more radical cost reductions most of the nation's newspapers have undertaken. But such avoidance will require your cooperation and understanding throughout the year, as well as a bumper year in revenues.

[800] Dawn House email August 27, 2015.

[801] Wetzel, October 2012.

[802] John C. Zahos obituary, *Deseret News*, March 7, 1999.

[803] Gallivan, May 2005.

[804] The Stephen Holbrook Photograph Collection, 1946-2005, background note, Utah State Historical Society, 2006

[805] Sarah Smith, "From Bountiful Utah to a Mississippi Jail," Humanists of Utah website, October 2011.

[806] Paul Wetzel email May 31, 2016.

[807] "Shredding the Safety Net," *The Salt Lake Tribune*, April 23, 1995.

46 - Catching My Stride in 1996

After four years as a part-time student, I finally finished my master's essay on the Clinton administration's failure to reform health care. Hallelujah! I told a friend how I felt about it:

My mid-life crisis helped me appreciate the small things I already had. Now I have (or assume I have, despite the red tape still to be untangled) a master's in political science, which will do absolutely nothing for my marketability. I'll probably stay at *The Tribune* writing editorials because I'd have to take a pay cut to teach or work for government in Utah, and nobody else would hire someone whose major skill is criticism. But armed with various political theories, I should be able to bullshit faster at work so I can get home earlier and play harder. That's worth something.

My shorter work days gave me more time with 3-year-old Brock, sheer joy. Stormy was divorced and employed, partially supporting herself and Brock but needing babysitters. Winker apparently had been getting high too often and returning Stormy's punches. Denny and I gladly stepped up. I got to do things with Brock I didn't get to do as a mother -- play with toys, teach language and ethics, and go to the zoo on a regular basis.

Unfortunately, Denny felt unappreciated at work, which made him less fun at home. Ot didn't help that Hairball was losing his footing and a huge snowfall snapped the logs we'd used to support a roof over our trailer in Scofield. His stress headaches returned, and his temper flared when I spent too much time reading the newspaper or too little time preparing meals. If we could have afforded it, he would have retired early.

* * *

As previously noted, I still churned out some editorials I could claim. Here's one:

Agenda for Education

It wouldn't seem like a session of the Utah Legislature without Howard Stephenson's annual attempt to privatize public education. The Draper Republican again is trying to slip his hobbyhorse into law by wrapping it in the sheep's clothing of small, inexpensive programs.

Long before joining the Legislature, the Utah Taxpayers Association executive extolled the virtues of vouchers and tuition tax credits for children attending private schools, insisting public schools need competition to improve.

Elected to the Senate, the professional tax protester busied himself with bills that would break through what he calls the "education cartel." After his first voucher legislation failed, he offered a more modest proposal: a $32,160 experiment that would subsidize the education of 20 students living in private disciplinary institutions. It, too, was rejected.

That proposal is back this year with two cosponsors -- Sens. Charles H. Stewart and Stephen J. Rees -- and a slightly higher price tag -- $50,000. Senate Bill 22 is too small to arouse stiff resistance or do much good for students, but it would set a precedent of spending public money for private education. It could open the door to other privatization schemes that would require more government regulation and divert dollars from the public schools.

In fact, Sens. Stephenson and Stewart also are trying to introduce tuition tax credits and other private school subsidies to Utah this year. Senate Bill 40 would let taxpayers claim a $100 credit for "contributions" made to the public or private schooling of each dependent. Tutoring would qualify, while books or materials promoting religious doctrine or supporting extracurricular activities would not. Senate Bill 43 would let private schools qualify for "charter school" grants.

The prospects of education privatization seem less ominous now that Utah's economy is robust and school budgets stable. But market schemes have not solved other states' education problems, and when championed by those who would discredit, micromanage or hobble public education, caution is justified.

Sens. Stephenson and Stewart helped lead the closed caucus where educators were accused of promoting homosexuality. Other Stephenson bills would require standardized tests of graduating college students, establish rules for managing local schools and permit children to drop out of school at age 14 (the latter proposal died in committee).

Public education in Utah is not above criticism and new ideas. But change should be a cooperative effort based on rational analysis of current conditions and probable consequences. Sen. Stephenson's agenda has not always made room for such deliberation.[808]

The concluding paragraph and the words "caution is justified" and "deliberation" indicate that Harry Fuller toned down this piece, but it was mostly mine. Under the old regime, I couldn't expect much of my stridency to make it into print. Waffle words would have replaced more declarative sentences.

Given his stance on taxes and public schools, I was pleasantly surprised the publisher indulged both my defense of public education and my attack on Howard Stephenson, the brains behind the Utah Taxpayers Association -- that is, anti-tax association. (Denny illustrated UTA's newsletter for years.) Even more refreshing was his support of my swipes at the local culture:

Crusade Disrupts Utah

Despite a mostly fruitful session, the 51st Utah Legislature planted moralistic seeds that, if permitted to take hold, will choke out the kind of reason and compromise that enable diverse Utahns to get along and thrive.

Championed by the ultraconservative Utah Eagle Forum, several legislators spent the 45-day session narrowing the separation between church and state. They sponsored restrictive abortion laws, a moment of silence for school prayer, state aid for private education and, most prominently, discrimination against homosexuals.

Sens. Charles Stewart and Craig Taylor, for example, proudly proclaimed it their moral duty to protect community standards -- that is, the perceived standards of a majority of Mormons they purport to represent -- by crushing clubs for homosexual high school students. Their peers indulged them by meeting in secret, devoting hours to the issue and permitting the state to intimidate and

intrude on the private lives of public school employees.

Senate Bill 246 prohibits those employees from encouraging, condoning or supporting "illegal conduct, including homosexual sex, either in their official capacity or in private if their action might "undermine the health, safety, welfare or morals of school children," undermine public confidence in the schools or disrupt normal school activities.

Depending on the response, almost any action could be construed as a violation of such broad language. Already challenged as a violation of teachers' speech, equality and privacy rights, the law is apt to cause more disruption than it prevents.

Legislators would have gone further with more time. The session ended before they could require parental permission for student participation in clubs, a measure thinly disguised to discriminate against gay and lesbian students. But moral crusaders did manage to make Utah's already strict abortion laws more restrictive.

It was a sad spectacle that produced little of substance and subtracted from time spent on growth and taxation, resolvable issues that now must be finished in special session. Even worse, it encouraged future extremism and conflict.

Extremists will interpret their victories as justification to legislate morality even more aggressively. The result may be more religious disputes like the ones over Sunday swimming-pool closure in Provo and liquor sales in Boulder.

The majority may initially prevail, but the state's growing minority will not impassively permit the enactment of sectarian values that infringe on such basic individual rights as thinking for oneself, practicing a religion of choice and being treated as equal under the law.

If Utahns are to live together congenially and prosperously, their laws must be based on values that respect residents' ,fundamental differences. To guide their lawmaking, Utah's political leaders must use moderation, compromise and constitutional principles rather than a self-righteous desire to dictate morality.[809]

Aside from the Harryisms "congenially" and "prosperously," that one was published largely as I wrote it. The next one was all mine.

Coercion in Wonderland

Some call it "Happy Valley," but Alice might argue that it's Wonderland, where up is down and confused conservatives prefer repression over freedom.

Utah County, base of operations for Utah's conservative Eagle Forum and strict constitutionalists where Provo residents cannot patronize the public pool on Sunday and Mapleton kids cannot play municipal baseball on Mondays because it conflicts with Mormon "family home evening," now has spawned another contradiction. In the name of community values, Utah County sheriff's deputies have raided movie video stores in American Fork and Lehi, confiscating more than 500 adult videos and customer lists.

The purpose of the seizure, according to Utah County Attorney Kay Bryson, is to ensure that pornography hasn't crept into the county. The customer lists, he claims, may be used to track down witnesses who can attest to the movies' content.

Never mind that some of this nation's most hallowed values -- values presumably shared by the many Utah County residents who consider themselves true Americans -- are the rights of individuals to think freely and to be secure in their homes against government intrusion.

Either the county attorney is seriously uninformed about constitutional law, or he is enforcing what he perceives to be a higher law. Either way, he is misusing his office.

No judge is going to ask video renters whether their choice of entertainment violates community standards. But the possibility that the lists may become public knowledge is an effective intimidation tactic. Members of Utah County's mainstream, conservative culture, in particular, will steer clear of any kind of video cassette that might be objectionable to their moral watchdogs.

Since fault can be found with most modern movies, whether because of vulgar language, violence or sexual suggestion, hardly anyone could feel safe from censure. The implications for

local video businesses are scary enough; the infringement on personal freedom is intolerable.

In the United States, people presumably are free to do as they please in their own homes, aside from engaging in crime. They can even watch or read what most of their neighbors would label pornography. Government is prohibited from imposing religious dogma on the populace.

As usual, the American Civil Liberties Union of Utah is one of the few entities to stand up for these principles, and it likely will be cast as the villain for doing so. Yet another irony for a community that claims to value individual liberty and the law[810]

Along with privacy rights, property rights claimed my allegiance as an editorial writer. After studying a bit of the law and getting Dominic Welch's OK, I felt confident about this argument.

Property in Jeopardy

A conservative Supreme Court could be expected to be tough on crime, but at the expense of private-property and due-process rights?

The high court's opinion on property seizures this week dangerously subordinates individual rights to government's interest in fighting crime. It unfairly punishes the innocent and fails to clarify confusing and inconsistent legal concepts.

Five of the nine justices decided that a state can take one person's property if someone else used it in a crime. In the case at hand, Michigan resident Tina Bennis lost her share of the car her husband used in an illegal sex act with a prostitute. The court majority said Mrs. Bennis had not taken "all reasonable steps" to prevent her property from being misused.

The same could be said of a landlord who "allows" a renter to perform illegal sex acts; of a car rental agency that "lets" a lessee buy drugs; of a parent whose teen-age son steals a six-pack while using the family car.

Where is this property-grabbing craze going to end? The illogical practice dates back to Old England, where the king seized ships carrying cargo on which taxes were owed. The twisted legal precedent, which held the property rather than the person accountable for debts. now has mutated into an accepted but abused form of law enforcement in the United States.

Since the war on drugs of the 1980s, it has become common for prosecutors to use civil law to seize cars, homes and cash only loosely connected to the crime. The justification is to take the profit out of the drug trade, but the property sometimes is worth far more than the drugs involved.

It is easier to prove the owner's culpability under civil law than criminal law, so government often keeps the property even when criminal charges are dropped for lack of evidence. Entire estates have been seized when a few marijuana plants were found, because the constitutional prohibition against cruel and unusual punishment does not strictly apply to civil cases.

The value of crime-connected property seized annually by U.S. governments grew from $27 million in 1985 to $531 million in 1992. And as the latest Supreme Court case shows, forfeitures have spread beyond the drug war to combat prostitution, drunk driving and other crimes.

Some legal jurisdictions accept the argument that owners were unaware their property was used in a crime; others do not. This week's ruling permits states to decide the issue. Some lower courts also say that civil property seizures illegally punish the accused twice for the same crime; the Supreme Court has yet to settle that question.

The U.S. Constitution is supposed to protect Americans from "unreasonable searches and seizures" and the taking of property without due process of law and just compensation. A majority of the U.S. Supreme Court has lost sight of these principles in the tangle of legal precedent. Now legislators in Congress and the states must restore the value of property and civil rights by writing the concepts into statute.[811]

As much as I championed individual rights, I also promoted public safety, with Welch's tacit endorsement, as seen in these editorials expressed entirely in my own words:

Lawmakers to the Rescue

Legislators have rescued Utah drivers from the cold, heavy hand of a machine. What heroes.

PhotoCop, photo-radar technology used to snag speeders in West Valley City, Layton and Sandy, came under fire at the beginning of the legislative session, and the barrage of complaints, mostly from lawmakers who like to speed, never relented. In the end, PhotoCop was stripped of much of its authority, crippling, if not killing, its usefulness.

When PhotoCop snaps a picture of speeding vehicles, citations are sent to the registered owners, who are expected to pay or identify drivers other than themselves. The system was introduced several years ago as a tool to reduce speeds in school zones, in particular, but since has expanded to higher-speed thoroughfares like Bangerter Highway.

Though law enforcement is largely a city and county responsibility, legislators justified state involvement as a matter of illegal taxation and civil rights. Despite evidence to the contrary, they castigated PhotoCop as an error-prone moneymaker that probably causes as many accidents as it prevents.

In lopsided, nonpartisan votes, both the House and Senate agreed to restrict photo radar to school zones and residential areas and to require police officers to operate the equipment. In the future, photos must be sent with each citation, and citations cannot count against driving records.

House Minority Whip Kelly C. Atkinson waxed especially eloquent in his opposition to a device he decried as violating his constitutional right to face his accusers and to avoid testifying against his spouse. He said drivers must be able to cross-examine police officers -- something they cannot do with PhotoCop -- because radar equipment is so unreliable. By challenging the technology, he noted, he has had three of seven speeding tickets dropped.

Cities now using photo radar testified that the system is an effective form of law enforcement, not taxation. Officials of West Valley City, who have the most experience with PhotoCop, say the technology increases police-force efficiency and reduces traffic accidents. Most collected revenue goes to the courts and the private company that operates the system. The fear is that the legislative restrictions will make the system cost-prohibitive.

But, as usual, state legislators know what's best for their constituents. They also know that complying with the laws they pass -- laws like speed limits in school zones -- can be painful. So in a show of contempt for both the law and local governance, they have given speeders their blessing. How unsettling.[812]

I had run into Kelly Atkinson on my education beat much earlier, when he represented bus drivers and maintenance crews in a local school district union. He had a tendency to be volatile and shoot from the hip. And, apparently, he didn't mind speeding. Did he say he got *seven* speeding tickets?

Risky Prison Contracts

The 98 Utah inmates who have not yet escaped the Dove Development Corp. sieve -- uh, jail -- soon are coming home from Texas. Their return occurs none too soon.

It's not that most Utahns want these miscreants back. But at least if the inmates are within the state, local officials can be held accountable for keeping them behind bars.

The experiment of sending 100 inmates out of state to relieve the crowding of Utah corrections facilities has failed. Though the price -- $37.70 per inmate daily, compared to $57 spent in-state -- seemed right when Utah State Prison officials struck the deal with Dove Development last year, the move has proved too costly to public safety.

With Dove's supervision, Utahns could never be sure whether the inmates were securely shut away or sneaking back home to wreak more havoc. So far, eight Utah inmates, four of them convicted murderers, have slipped away from Dove's facilities. The latest two escapes occurred Friday night.

Dove is largely culpable for the escapes and should pay with loss of business. But it should be understood that Texas law and Utah decisions helped undermine the company's success.

Utah was supposed to send prisoners least likely to cause trouble, yet most of the escapees have been violent offenders with little to lose from an escape attempt. Since Texas does not

recognize Dove escapes as violations of state law, inmates with long sentences can make a break with few repercussions.

Conveniently, new Utah State Prison beds now are available to house the 100 inmates, assuming the two latest fugitives are caught. But the system is expected to run out of space again by January, just as the 1997 session of the Utah Legislature convenes.

The Legislature must come to grips with the demand for prison space. Either more facilities must be built or better alternatives must be found. The state's bad experience in Texas should caution them against dollar-driven contracts that shield prisoners from state control and poorly protect the public.

Only prisoners who pose the least security risk should be placed outside direct state jurisdiction, and those placements must allow for strict performance standards and oversight. The state should never become so dependent on private companies or other government agencies that it cannot safely assume responsibility for Utah inmates when contractors either fail or require more room for their own lawbreakers.[813]

* * *

John Cummins retired, giving the job of Reader Advocate to Shinika Sykes, whom Shelledy hired in 1993. She almost immediately found herself in the middle of a maelstrom, defending a *Tribune* feature story about a gay couple adopting a toddler. In those days, such anomalous adoptions stirred up readers. After receiving an avalanche of spirited calls and letters on both sides of the issue, Shinika devoted her entire weekly Reader Advocate column to the controversy, concluding that the feature was tastefully written.

Other newsroom changes were under way. Judy Fahys moved from business to environment, her passion. Ledford recruited feisty Linda Fantin from Jackson, Wyoming, to cover the county beat.

Fantin became one of my best sources for editorials. Her own son Mitch, on the occasion of her 50th birthday, described her best years later: "She's always set the strongest example of hard work and compassion . . . and to boot, she's funny. Like an amazing hybrid of Hillary Clinton and Roseanne."[814] She also entered into an office romance with Phil Miller.

353

* * *

That spring, Welch sent "salary adjustment" letters to everyone in Editorial. Mine said:

> The Tribune's salary program is based on both performance and the company's salary ranges for each task. The program has been somewhat out of sync as we try to bring more equity into the ranges. However, although you and I disagree often philosophically, I want you to know that I appreciate your dedication and writing ability. Consequently, your salary will be increased to $41,327 a year, effective with our next pay period.

I might have been gratified if I hadn't sneaked a peak at Paul Wetzel's letter to see his higher salary. I was pissed. As I saw it, I was more productive and had a higher position as associate editorial page editor. I began the job years ahead of Wetzel and now held a master's degree. I suspected the publisher was rewarding Wetzel for being more agreeable. I should have taken David Beck's advice years earlier to quit comparing salaries.

* * *

Editor Shelledy apparently was feeling better about contests, because he heartily highlighted this year's AP and Society of Professional Journalists (SPJ-SDX) winners. The publisher put money where Shelledy's mouth was, giving $150 checks to first-place winners and $75 to those who placed.

The AP's highest award for public service went to Dan Harrie, Laurie Sullivan Maddox and Tony Semerad for covering Enid Greene Waldholtz's 1994 congressional campaign. The Tribune came in second place, behind The Idaho Statesman (one of Shelledy's former papers), for general excellence in content, design, writing, photography and style. Lex Hemphill took first place in editorial writing. Denny took second place in graphics for his "Utah Statehood" layout and illustrations. Semerad also was part of a team, including Ted Wilwick, Christopher Smith and Vince Horiuchi, that took first place for the general reporting entry, "Extremism in Utah."

The Utah Headliners Chapter of SPJ-SDX, headed this year by Joan O'Brien, chose my editorial, "Truth Time for Waldholtz," for its second-place award in editorials.

Honestly, I felt sorry for Enid Greene Waldholtz, Utah's third congresswoman -- and first female Republican -- even though she came off like a cold, spoiled child with limited empathy for the common person. It was tragic that a new mother with such political promise would naively enable someone -- campaign manager and husband Joe Waldholtz -- to embezzle from her wealthy father and put her in the position of violating federal campaign finance laws. I expected her quagmire to set back other women in politics.

In the same SPJ-SDX contest, Lex Hemphill placed first for an environment piece, "Go for 3 Million Acres," and Harry Fuller took third place for "Bill of Rights Peril." Jim Woolf won accolades for three of his environment, non-deadline stories; Anne Wilson took first place in the health category for her story, "Some See Ogden Surgeon as a Godsend; Others Call Him Devil with a God Complex." Sheila McCann, Semerad's significant other, placed well, as did Brent Israelsen and Rebecca Walsh, another newsroom couple. The Deseret News won its share of awards too, but The Tribune did particularly well by comparison.

* * *

Shelledy was excited about other Tribune successes. "Congratulations to the entire staff whose work the last year made us one of the half dozen fastest-growing newspapers in America -- an achievement we all prize above even Pulitzers," he wrote in the daily critique.

Of course that wouldn't stop The Tribune from touting its 1957 Pulitzer every chance it got.[815] And Shelledy happily encouraged Dawn House to seek a Pulitzer for her story on the McLellin Papers, part of the Mark Hofmann-Mormon Church forgery scandal that culminated in two murders and Hofmann's life prison sentence.

In March, Shelledy praised the Sports staff for a "successful first-ever boys/girls all-state awards banquet in which The Tribune was cheered as No.1 publication for prep sports." Gee, I wonder who was responsible for promoting prep sports? Humility was not the editor's forte.

In June, he announced that Jim Fisher, the whiz college guy who'd redesigned the newspaper while managing Photography and Art, would instead write about the media for the Business Desk. Never one to own up to a mistake, the editor cast the change in the most positive light, claiming the "formal beat" is one he'd "sought to launch since coming here."

Our compulsive bean-counter reveled in another milestone in August. "A record 132 persons attended the summer picnic Sunday, for those keeping score at home," he announced in his critique. He obviously was proud of moving the event away from Washington and Draper parks to the Cottonwood Club near his home four years earlier. I'd wager the higher numbers had a lot to do with his larger, younger staff.

The editor's annual circulation report was less effusive that fall. The *Deseret News* had surpassed our growth, increasing daily circulation 1.6 percent compared to our 1.2 percent. Sunday was even worse, with the *News* growing 1.5 percent to *The Tribune's* .3 percent. Let's not forget, he pointed out, that the national trade journal *NewsInc* had identified *The Tribune* as the "second fastest growing metro daily nationally in the 100,000-300,000 circulation category."[816]

* * *

Another Shelledy critique commended a fairly recent, unfortunate addition to the Sports Desk whom I'll call Fishy.

> Her look at what it takes to downhill ski (in the way of equipment as opposed to brains), lead of Daybreak (a news section), well done and will be appreciated by those readers interested in the sport.

Unbeknownst to her boss, Fishy had exacted a price (payola) from the ski shop she mentioned. She had picked out one of the most expensive coats on the rack in exchange for her story. Not the best example of what women can offer sports reporting.

I rarely confronted people, but when Shelledy's latest star asked for the address of our Halloween party, I flatly told her -- twice -- she wasn't invited. She and the loser she'd picked up in a Park City bar somehow found us anyway.

* * *

Sam Autman announced plans to take a reporting job with the *St. Louis Post-Dispatch*, where he hoped to find a more diverse social climate. Before leaving, he and other current and former *Tribune* education writers, including

myself, took one of the school beat's best personalities to lunch.

Doug Bates came onto my radar screen while directing Utah's reform school in Ogden. Unlike others in positions like his, he readily took phone calls from the press. When he became legal counsel and legislative liaison for the state school office, he became a major news source. It was such a breath of fresh air for a school official to treat the media with respect and to forthrightly answer our questions. He neither played cat and mouse nor complained about our stories.

After surviving with cancer much longer than predicted, Bates was nearing the end. On August 22, he wrote this note of thanks to Autman:

> Dear Sam and the rest of you, too:
> Thanks so much for the books, the kind thoughts, lunch and for a great ride over the past 17 years. Some years ago I read a comment by a prosecutor who persisted in pressing charges against mafia figures even though he usually lost. His response was, "They may beat the rap, but they'll never forget the ride."
> I don't want to forget it, and I don't want to get off. So for as long as I'm given, I hope to keep getting the hard questions, hope to give clear and honest answers, and hope to continue to be part with you in making better schools, better communities and helping you sell more newspapers so you can make more money, pay more taxes, and help keep my health insurance plan solvent.
> Sam, sorry to see you leave but better your way than my way. Good luck; call if I can help.

In response to my editorial extolling his virtues, Bates responded September 6:

> Dear Diane:
> Thank you so much for your column last Sunday. It certainly caught me by surprise, and gave me some good goals to strive for. One of my neighbors came over to tell me of an unexpected outcome -- she said that after reading your article she and her husband of some 34 years sat down and for the first time in their lives talked about their own mortality, their love for each other and planning for the unexpected. Your pen reaches hearts in ways I'm sure you'll never know. Thanks for your friendship these many years.

I cried. Had I been co-opted in my coverage of public education by having feelings for a news source? Who cared?

I received another note that day, this one from Lynn Simons from Region VIII of the U.S. Department of Education:

Dear Diane,

Thank you so much for taking time to interview Asst. Secretary Mario Moreno last week. We are so accustomed to talking with reporters who know <u>nothing</u> about education, I can't tell you how wonderful it was to talk with someone who <u>does</u>!

Please call me whenever I can help with information on federal programs.

* * *

When Shelledy announced a new mentoring program for high school students considering journalism careers, Denny and I opened our doors for a week to Migan Inez and Kerlissa Bitah, seniors at Navajo Prep in Farmington, N.M. The bright, gracious teenagers were most interested in shopping at Trolley Square and meeting Utah Jazz basketball players. As a thank-you, Kerlissa sent us a Navajo blanket on a miniature loom we still treasure. We exchanged Christmas cards for years.

* * *

I began taking estrogen to control moodiness, night sweats, and hot flashes, and within months, I found two cysts in my left breast. When my new gynecologist dismissed my concerns, my previous doctor ordered a lumpectomy. No cancer was found, and I continued hormone treatments until heavy monthly bleeding and swollen breasts outweighed the benefits. Eventually, I would give hormones another try and regret it. More on that later.

* * *

Carol Sisco and I began training for a bicycle trip to France with rides through Rose Park and up City Creek Canyon. Pedaling through Provence's vineyards and dining on savory French sauces that fall bordered on the perfect vacation. The one glitch was Carol's habit of leaving me with my pants down -- literally. When I stopped for bathroom breaks, she raced ahead, leaving me without help when I crashed and when a young motorcyclist pushed me toward the woods.

* * *

Hairball's death and work-related stress sent Denny into such a steep tailspin that his chronic fatigue flared up. Fortunately, the perfect puppy became the medicine that cured him. Loving, adorable Shimi lifted his spirits and mine.

Not even his daughters darkened our brighter mood. Stormy's payroll job allowed her to track down a good-looking, amiable guy with salary potential. Christopher didn't mind her foul mouth and liked Brock. Lulu still lived with the Gruesome Twosome at age 30 but reportedly held a job.

My brother Bill scaled another of the world's highest peak's, this one in Argentina.

But the best news of all came from an investment counselor who said Denny could retire in less than three years because of his highly appreciated ESOP. The fund had grown 50 percent in two years, pushing our joint holdings over $1 million.

ESOP was no longer just a cruel joke concocted by the company for tax and strategic purposes. It might even enable me to retire early so that I could see more of the world and try writing fiction.

The frosting on the cake was another year-end bonus based on the company's "strong financial performance." Again warning us not to count on future bonuses, Welch's holiday letter said, "A strong employee performance in 1997, like we had in 1996, is the best protection from unfavorable economic change."

---

[808] "Agenda for Education," *The Salt Lake Tribune*, February 11, 1996.

[809] "Crusade Disrupts Utah," *The Salt Lake Tribune*, March 4, 1996.

[810] "Coercion in Wonderland," *The Salt Lake Tribune*, November 14, 1996.

[811] "Property in Jeopardy," *The Salt Lake Tribune*, March 8, 1996.

[812] "Lawmakers to the Rescue," *The Salt Lake Tribune*, March 2, 1996.

[813] "Risky Prison Contracts," *The Salt Lake Tribune*, October 29, 1996.

814 Mitch Fantin on facebook, December 12, 2013.

815 "Of All Awards, Pulitzer was the Tops," *The Salt Lake Tribune*, July 24, 1988, p. T5.

816 Jay Shelledy, Critique of Tuesday's Edition, December 10, 1997.

47 - Numbers, Truth and Miracles in 1997

Under Shelledy's leadership, *The Tribune* staff had grown by 16 percent and was slightly less sexist, at least on the surface. By 1997, we had 151 employees compared to 126 a decade earlier. The gap between males and females had slightly narrowed. In 1986, 33 percent of staffers were female (40 women to 86 men) compared to 39 percent (59 to 92) in 1997. Even better, women were more likely than ever to be mid-level managers in the newsroom, not just in the Lifestyle and the Art sections.

By this time, the newspaper's paid circulation was 129,608 weekdays and 162,164 on Sundays.[817] That compares to 111,346 weekdays and 140,538 Sundays in 1988.[818]

Shelledy's April 12-14 critique identified the newspaper's favorite columnists, as chosen by "devoted" readers (vs. sometimes readers): Rolly & Wells, 41 percent; Ann Landers, 38 percent; News of the Weird, 37 percent; Editor's Sunday Column [Shelledy's], 34 percent; Tom Wharton (outdoor recreation), 32 percent; Barberi & Bell, 27 percent; Robert Kirby (religion), 24 percent; Rolly Political Report, 23 percent; Paul Fleming, 23 percent; John Youngren (media reviews), 22 percent. Shelledy added that he was second favorite behind Ann Landers among occasional readers.

It was not easy for me to admit that Shelledy had succeeded in replacing Dan Valentine and John Mooney with Rolly and Wells as *The Trib's* top personalities.

* * *

Work in my small department was especially hectic.

With the annual legislative session ending and Fuller taking vacation, the rest of us scrambled to keep up with editorials. Topping it off, Wetzel called in sick two days, and Hemphill and I essentially wrote the same editorial on a topic I'd claimed for at least a year. I was never so angry with this normally nice guy.

Making matters worse, Shinika dumped her part of the letters to the editor on me for a day so she could gather contest entries for the SPJ-SDX contest. She'd earlier alerted Hemphill to contest deadline, but since he hadn't passed the message to the rest of us, he was the sole entrant from our department. Of course he won.

* * *

By March, the Art Department also was overworked, Shelledy was snapping at Denny, and Denny was stomping around the office while staffers like me tried to work. When Knudsen left in a huff one day, Denny nearly exploded.

Shelledy had undone Denny's relationship with Knudsen by assigning the "real artist" to Sunday Arts on the second floor full time. Assuming the role of prima donna, Knudsen often left for home before his pages passed through the production process, leaving Denny to troubleshoot computer problems on deadline.

"If I'd wanted to be a computer technician, I never would have gone to art school!" Denny growled on our drive home. He was similarly sick of being a manager required to attend daily news huddles and formally evaluate his artists.

We would break the tension by singing The Animals' lyrics: "We gotta get out of this place if it's the last thing we ever do . . . there's a better life for me and you."

Shelledy was doomed as editor, Denny remarked years later, because he was an uncreative person without people skills in charge of creative people. "He went by the book, but that didn't work with us," he said. "He needed intuitive skills."[819]

* * *

Also in March, Lulu called to announce her pregnancy and impending marriage. The happy couple would be riding his motorcycle from New York to see us in August. That made about as much sense as anything else she ever told us.

After Stormy gave birth to Brock, Lulu had claimed Swamper's abuse prevented her from having babies. Now she had miraculously conceived and was going to ride across the country on the back of a motorcycle while six months pregnant.

In fact, Lulu *was* not only pregnant, she had neither job nor fiancé. Her roommate called seeking cash for letting her crash at his place. It seems her intended was an ex-con carpenter and snowplow driver with a wife in jail and three teenagers.

Swamper called Stormy, urging her to talk Lulu into an abortion. Stormy, who was getting remarried in August herself, speculated she would be raising Lulu's child within a year.

* * *

Denny and I escaped the chaos with a trip to Maui for our 20th anniversary. As we lounged on the beach, we dreamed of the newspaper being sold so we could get our hands on our ESOP money and quit work.

The wish wasn't too far-fetched. In recent Editorial Board meetings, Welch had hinted of something brewing in *The Tribune's* upper echelons. Rumors were circulating among staffers about possible buyers.

When we returned home, our neighbor greeted us with a stack of newspapers and deadpanned: "I guess you heard the news: You're now part of TCI." He pointed to a Page One story from April 22 announcing Kearns-Tribune Corporation's merger with the nation's largest cable television company, Denver-based Telecommunications, Inc.

Butterflies fluttered in my stomach (and I mocked Hoffman's cliches) as I devoured the article: *The Tribune's* $600 million worth of TCI voting stock would be traded for non-voting shares in a tax-free reorganization. (Actually, 250 shareholders held stock worth more like $650 million.[820]) I felt the rush of schussing down a freshly groomed ski slope on a clear, sunny day; the joy of gazing at a night sky pierced by red, silver and blue streamers on the Fourth of July.

The office was abuzz with the news our first day back: TCI would acquire *The Trib* to get our voting shares of TCI stock, and we needed to prepare for a distribution of the stock.

Max Knudson's follow-up in the *Deseret News* put the value of Kearns-Tribune's TCI stock at $627 million, which included *The Tribune's* smaller papers in Lewiston and Moscow, Idaho; Colfax, Washington; and Sparks, Nevada. He quoted Welch: "It's kind of a sad thing for us. It's like putting your child up for adoption . . . Only time will tell if this was the right thing, I may look back and say I was an idiot." [821]

He did, but that's for later.

Knudson also quoted DeAnn Evans, a University of Utah communications professor and former *News* editor who worried about journalistic standards now that a big corporation would own the newspaper.

Actually, the *Tribune*-TCI deal was a natural marriage for cohorts since cable television's birth. In the 1950s, Bob Magness, John W. Gallivan and the George Hatch family (owners of Ogden's *Standard-Examiner*) concocted a cable system to provide television to Elko, Nevada. That system became TCI, whose Board of Directors included Gallivan, Jerry O'Brien and, eventually, John Malone, who guided the company's phenomenal growth.

While TCI's increasingly valuable shares pumped up Kearns-Tribune's net worth, the newspaper controlled 6.9 percent of TCI's voting stock, a significant block of which was owned by employees like me. Malone stood to gain hundreds of thousands of additional voting shares, which would tip TCI's balance of power more in Malone's direction.

Even so, the merger was not Malone's idea. The crux of the deal was that Kearns-Tribune would survive and save $150 million in corporate-income taxes.

Welch and Gallivan devised the plan to "protect the *Tribune*" against the loss of advertising revenue in the digital age[822] and to protect family heirs against a huge estate-tax burden.

Gallivan, 82 by then, initially believed the merger would guarantee the newspaper's future with digital journalism through cable's faster internet connection. He also saw it as the solution to Kearns-Tribune's 40-year liquidity problem whereby heirs jeopardized the company's future by dipping into its capital to get at their wealth.[823] Now older heirs could settle their estates without breaking up the company.[824]

Another merger justification was the retrieval of company stock from shareholders outside the Kearns family like me and Denny. At ESOP's inception in the 1970s, tax attorneys predicted disaster if outsiders got pieces of the family-held company. Now the Kearns-Tribune Board of Directors meant to right that wrong.

Because ESOP became a reason for the merger, Welch told me years later, the attorneys' warning "proved partially correct in the end."[825] He was referring to the merger's tumultuous aftermath, a subject for later.

Shelledy cited yet another reason for the merger: to work Gallivan's sons John Jr. and Michael (Mickey) in as publisher and editor.[826] That was a new one on me, and I'm not sure I ever believed it.

Gallivan got cold feet before the Kearns-Tribune Board voted on the merger. "We split up over it," Welch recalled. "He just couldn't give it [*The Tribune*] up."[827]   But he was overruled.

Certain merger stipulations were of paramount importance to the Board of Directors.

One gave The Salt Lake Tribune Publishing Co. operations rights for five years. As such, Dominic Welch would remain publisher under direction of John Gallivan's son Michael J. "Micky" Gallivan and owners Philip G., Thomas K. and Sarah J. McCarthey; James P. Kearns; Robert Steiner, and A.L. Alford Jr. (owner of *The Tribune's* Idaho and Washington papers). Randy Frisch, the general manager who gave us fits in Editorial, was elevated to chief operating officer.

Another important provision preserved *The Tribune's* joint-operating agreement with the *Deseret News*.   The JOA, begun in 1952 and renewed in 1982, was set to expire in 2012. Meantime, Welch would continue as NAC president.

Finally, "should TCI wish to divest itself of *The Tribune*, the owners of the Salt Lake Tribune Publishing Co. [the management board minus Micky Gallivan] have the first right to buy it."

Years later, the devil would be found lurking within those details.

* * *

All Denny and I cared about at the moment was gaining access to ESOP, which TCI had made incredibly valuable.   After the McCarthey and James P. Kearns families, the next largest shareholder of *Tribune* stock was the employee stock plan owned by some 170 employees.[828]   Between us, Denny and I had more than 140,000 shares of TCI and Liberty Group stock. Lex Hemphill and Nancy Melich held a similar position.

We 170 ESOP participants still had to pass Go on our way to easy street, and there were roadblocks of red tape along the way.

Our Editorial Board meetings dragged on as we quizzed Welch about the merger. Has the IRS approved the deal yet? How much is the stock worth today?

At Hemphill's suggestion after attending another NCEW convention, we began setting agendas to make our meetings more manageable. When typing the agenda one day, I listed our discussion items in order of importance: 1. Stock Talk 2. Shop Talk. 3. Jock Talk. It wasn't far from the truth.

Welch played a fatherly role, patiently explaining events and advising us how to handle our good fortune.

On July 31, Denny and I submitted votes to ESOP trustee U.S. Bank & Trust Company in favor of Kearns-Tribune becoming a wholly owned subsidiary of TCI.

Max Knudson's story on the "overwhelmingly" positive vote noted that TCI's stock value had risen to $731 million.   Of 173,000 votes cast, only 614 were negative. Welch joked with Knudson that *Tribune* employees who gained the most from the sale were probably feeling invulnerable to their boss:

> *Very definitely, those who have been around awhile (and accumulated a significant number of shares) will be sticking up their noses at me. They did that before, but they had to be a little careful.*[829]

Most employees tiptoed into their new lives.   Nancy Melich splurged on two vacuums and more than doubled her annual $10 contribution to PBS.   Food Editor Donna Lou Morgan bought two lipsticks instead of one at a time. Jon Ure rejoiced at the prospect of buying romaine instead of iceberg lettuce.

Welch's nephew, Kearns-Tribune Treasurer **Tony Magann**, held our hands through the transition process to protect us from our ignorance about money. Meeting with groups of 10 or more staffers at a time, he updated us on the status of the merger and our ESOP shares. He also distributed lists of money managers and trust attorneys familiar with our situation.

Like many of us, Magann had started at *The Tribune* while in college and stayed. He worked part time for Welch between courses at the U. of U., got his master's in marketing and then ignored his uncle's advice to put it to better use.   Paralysis caused by a disastrous dive into Rockport Reservoir didn't prevent him from climbing the corporate ladder at *The Tribune*.

Because most stock shares were distributed in the 1970s, employees with the highest salaries and longest ESOP membership came out well ahead of the others. It helped that the shares of employees who quit before vesting were shared among those who stayed.

While on the job less than five years, Lee Siegel excitedly dominated our meetings with countless questions for Magann. The rest of us figured he must have negotiated a huge salary and extra shares as one of Shelledy's star recruits, but we.later learned he happily received less than 5 percent of our take. "Even though I got a small amount compared with longtime staffers, it still was significant and allowed me to make a downpayment on my home," he explained.

Magann counseled us privately about our pension and health insurance options. Denny could expect a $500 monthly pension if he retired at 55; I was looking at $300 if I quit right away. Insurance premiums would reduce the total to about $450. Thank Heaven for ESOP!

On paper, Denny and I soon would be millionaires, enabling Denny to retire at 55 on his next birthday. He had to wait until then to qualify for company-sponsored health insurance. I could safely quit at the same time if I got insurance as his spouse and took substantially equal payments from an IRA.

I feared I'd wake up from a dream, but it looked like we'd finally gotten lucky.

Fairly skipping from office to office, Denny and I shopped for lawyers and investment help. We met with Wells Fargo Wealth Management, Welch's financial adviser Rod Cushing and *The Tribune's* attorneys to prepare for the day our settlement came through.

Denny and I started scouting around for places to build a more elaborate, warmer dream home. Irrationally, we considered Idaho, Montana, Oregon, Wyoming (Bondourant) and Durango, Colorado. The rock castles, beautiful beaches, tiny art galleries and quaint cafes of Collioure, France, called to me. It was there, while walking along the sea wall as waves crashed against the rocks years earlier, that I first realized there was more to life than *The Salt Lake Tribune*. Hawaii was another attractive alternative. Each place had its downside, whether the language, cold winters or long distances from friends and family.

In the newsroom, cheers greeted each rise in TCI's stock price as staffers left on the sidelines -- those without ESOP -- grumbled about the distraction.

AT&T suddenly swallowed up TCI, making us new AT&T employees. This meant joining the conglomerate's health plan and 401K for a few brief months before leaving *The Tribune*.

Always eager to make himself the center of attention, Shelledy used his Sunday column August 3 to tell the world that TCI paid $4,087 per share of ESOP stock, creating 24 instant millionaires . . .

. . . who just moments before were paycheck-to-paycheck reporters, photographers, artists and desk editors. . . Not every employee has been around long enough to reap a seven-figure reward. But, except for a handful of people who hadn't been with the company long enough to qualify for an ESOP contribution, everyone got a windfall of some degree. Talk in the break rooms and elevators, around journalistic watering holes and in the hallways centers around investments, the stock market, mutual funds, taxes, portfolios and the like."[830]

Gee, thanks, Jay, for exposing me to the other side of journalism, the right to privacy be damned.

Denny and I were dumbfounded the jerk would alert our families, friends, acquaintances and strangers to our windfall. Other reporters, gold diggers and shysters wasted no time getting to work on us.

Investment companies came out of the woodwork with phone and mail solicitations. American Express somehow got our contact information. Family members suddenly came up with financial emergencies, such as the desperate need for a new truck to keep a job. It occurred to me that people often are killed for less money than this.

Susan Whitney of the *Deseret News* wrote a color column I might have found entertaining if I hadn't been one of Shelledy's 24.

Not until the end of his [Shelledy's] column did he get around to mentioning the millionaires...
"WHAT?" you exclaim . . .
"YES!" you shout . . .
Trying to imagine how it would feel to be a rich reporter, you are transported. No one goes into journalism for the money. "What a story!" you chortle.
. . . Seems some of the lucky ones were unhappy about Shelledy's announcement.
Their boss didn't name any names. Still, neighbors and relatives and people who had only a passing acquaintance with Tribune *employees had the relevant facts: First, everybody who'd worked there any time at all would get something. Second, those who'd worked there longest had the most stock.*
From the day Shelledy's column appeared, Tribune *employees found*

themselves being asked probing, personal, reporter-like questions. Rude questions. Such as, "Hey, are you a millionaire?"

Soon rumors are launched.

"Did you hear Rosetta bought a Cadillac?"

"I heard Woolf is going to quit and spend the next year traveling."

. . . "Did you hear how one editor saw a bunch of photographers gathered around a screen, cheering? And when she went over to see what game they were watching, it turned out they were whooping it up over a stock market report?"

. . . The Tribune employees who are your friends, who haven't even worked there 15 years, don't mind revealing the nice-but-not-thrilling facts about their Tribune/TCI stock deal. They are only getting between $10,000 and $100,000. And now they have to decide what to do with the money, they tell you, and it's kind of stressful and confusing to have to worry about it all.

They use words like "lump-sum distributions." You tell them they are not making this sound glamorous, and they laugh and refer you to their financial advisor at Smith Barney. Rod Cushing has been advising all the Tribune employees and recent retirees who now must try to decide what to do with their windfall.[831]

Well, OK, Ms. Whitney did a pretty good job of reporting. Cushing wasn't advising all *Tribune* employees, though. Just those who hired him or were considering it. What he told Ms. Whitney was that we would have to pay 45 percent of our windfall in taxes unless we were 59 1/2 or put proceeds into an IRA from which we could take substantially equal payments earlier. Even then, we were looking at a 30 percent tax bite.

Ms. Whitney figured out that most of the millionaires had worked at *The Tribune* about 30 years and called some of us (not me). Most didn't answer her "rude" questions, yet she felt they were "rich beyond insult." Jim Woolf did call her back but merely said he wasn't quite a millionaire because of his low pay in the early years and that he wasn't quitting (at least not yet).

Even so, Ms. Whitney described our dilemma fairly accurately. Especially when told one millionaire didn't want to talk to her because he had too many ex-wives to hide his money

from, and another didn't want relatives quitting work to sponge off of him.

When Ms. Whitney imagined becoming suddenly rich enough to quit and move to the south of France when faced with a crabby editor and complaining reader, one of her contacts claimed working was more fun than retirement. Must have been an idiot.

Ben Fulton of *Salt Lake City Weekly* did a story quoting Judy Rollins, a 31-year veteran who basically said her financial business was not for public consumption.

Bottom line: Was this really anybody's business? As you can see from this memoir, I decided it is now, from a vicarious and historical point-of-view. I am a reporter, after all. Maybe even a hypocrite.

On August 16, I practiced for retirement by lounging with Mimi at the teahouse Denny had built over a spring-fed pond in Summit Park.

Waiting for the ESOP deal to go through has been hell. I've lost a fair share of my work incentive, which wasn't all that strong to begin with the past couple of years.

So far I've been able to make it through the week with enough editorials, despite the dog days of summer, but I'm so antsy I can hardly stand it. Others at work are pretty excited too, especially as the stock value rises. Unfortunately, however, there are predictions of a fall within a couple of weeks -- or at least by September 10 -- and we don't have the stock certificates to dump. We're at the mercy of John Malone and the market.

It'll be interesting to see how many staffers leave early. Harry's retiring February 28, but he'll be 65 by then. Sounds like Lex will stay through the Olympics. Who knows about Paul? Sam Smith's headed out as soon as possible, which is none too soon since his health is declining. Lynn Johnson and Lance Gudmundsen will go. I wonder about Tim Kelly, since he's kind of young but hates the job. Denny and I are among the luckiest, since both of us are involved.

* * *

To my surprise, Shelledy dubbed our editorials persuasive in his Sunday column August 31. He added that Publisher Dominic Welch found our editorials informative. Too bad they couldn't also say "lively and fun to read," but at least we had entered positive territory for a change. The column went on to explain the difference between news stories and editorials, noting that an editorial does not have to be balanced or fair. "To be persuasive, however, it must be logical and reasoned in the eye of the beholder."[832]

At the same time, Harry Fuller was analyzing editorial writing in a column for NCEW's *Masthead*. A taste of it:

> *If it is conceded that the country's journalism must look to college and university education for its practitioners, and if it is further agreed that analysis, opinion, and commentary comprise an essential ingredient of American journalism, then failure to even offer college- and university-level courses conveying knowledge about history, principles, and methodology of editorializing becomes difficult to justify . . .*
>
> *Perhaps, in any event, editorial writers are actually born, not made. It does seem, when surveyed on the subject, many finding commentary work a compatible career tend to consider themselves called rather than selected. Under such circumstances, on-the-job training may be more valuable than academic preparation and so, therefore, the practical necessity of staffing and equipping higher education editorial writing courses is not compelling . . .*
>
> *Also, since communication schools and departments frequently find their presence on a college or university campus questioned because they are considered more vocational than academic, a course emphasizing research, theory, and careful knowledge-gathering, all of which commentary writing at the undergraduate level surely must cover, could help in marshaling a better self-defense.*[833]

As was his way, Fuller used complex sentences to analyze the issue from both sides, leaving readers to wonder what he was saying. I guess the gist of this and similar articles is that students received precious little training for jobs like mine.

In the same *Masthead*, former *Baltimore Sun* editorial writer Theo Lippmann Jr. reported journalism students' views of opinion pages. Female Generation Xers, he found, felt that editorial boards were directed toward old-school

readers, often using men's language and men's thought processes. "Women want 'particulars' not 'principles,'" Lippmann quoted one student saying. (No sexism there!)

Certain figures of speech went over young readers' heads, according to Lippmann. One student criticized long editorials. Still others wanted to know who was writing the editorials (to see a byline), to read editorials with strong positions and to see more lively layout.[834]

Well, Fuller and I probably wouldn't be around to see if *The Tribune's* editorial pages ever achieved such goals. Fuller would turn 65 about the same time I planned to quit. But I still wanted to make myself proud my final months on the job.

Perhaps as a token of his appreciation for our years working together, Fuller recommended me for an expense-paid, NCEW-cosponsored education seminar at Columbia University Teachers College. He wrote Gene Maeroff, director of the Hechinger Institute on Education and the Media, that I had "carried the weight of our educational coverage in this department." With my help, he put that role into perspective:

> Education is of major interest and importance to *Tribune* readers. With one of the nation's highest birth rates, Utah also has an unusually large student population. Public and higher education command the largest share of the state's public resources. Utah officials frequently wrestle with controversial issues like school prayer, school assessment, tuition tax credits, sex equity, tenure, teaching loads, teacher training and compensation.

Of the editorials submitted with my application, here's how one from April began:

> *None of the 3,500 teachers in Utah's largest public school district has been fired in two years, and no more than a handful have been fired in each of the state's other major districts.*
>
> *Utah teachers may be good but can't be that good, particularly given the random complaints of parents. Most likely, the school system's methods for weeding out poor teachers are falling short, and both administrators and teachers bear responsibility for repairing the process.*
>
> *. . . Schools are less likely to fire the dregs of the teaching ranks than to join what North Carolina education attorney*

Richard Schwartz calls "the dance of the lemons," where bad teachers transfer from school to school.

This topic played directly into the substance of the seminar -- school reform -- probably reinforcing my acceptance. Once in Manhattan in late October, though, I focused more on changes in my life than the schools'.

I spilled the beans about ESOP to several awestruck, envious participants. Their reaction, based on their prospects of working for mediocre pay another 20 years, made me feel a little guilty. I should have been more circumspect.

* * *

Back home, Terry Orme was experiencing big-time journalism as scandals surfaced on the beat he managed.

First Tom Welch resigned as president of the Salt Lake Organizing Committee after accepting a misdemeanor battery plea for fighting with his wife Alma over another woman. SLOC Chairman Frank Joklik assumed Welch's role and dumped Korologos as spokesman in favor of former TV anchor Shelley Thomas.[835] Korologos, then 61, joined Mickey Gallivan's advertising firm.[836]

Mike Carter, an AP reporter by then, was another friend affected by the shake-up. "It was an incredibly painful process to deal with Tom Welch after he got in trouble with the law for slapping his wife around," he told *American Journalism Review.*[837] He blamed Utah's religious culture and old-boy network for suppressing news of the episode for over a week in order to promote the bid and preserve Utah's image.

Another major story of the day put the powers-that-be in southeastern Utah at the center of federal investigations into illegal pot-hunting; that is, Indian pots and other ancient artifacts found on federal land. Cal Black, a former state legislator and Korologos crony, possessed a treasure trove of the collectibles, but it wasn't clear where he got them.

Ordinarily I would have been incensed about spouse abuse in Salt Lake City and the rape of state and national resources outside our annual vacation spot at Lake Powell, but there was little fire left in my belly. I let Hemphill take the lead on both scandals.

* * *

Back in the newsroom, Shelledy distributed for the staff's review *"The Tribune's* first compiled guidelines for news gathering and editing." He'd worked on the project for three years. Once published, all employees were expected to sign and return letters stating they had read their copies. Excerpts:

Following professional, ethical guidelines will reduce [mistakes and errors in judgment] and enhance credibility . . . Our stories are not predicated on favor or prejudice.

We do not financially, politically or socially enhance -- in a premeditated, direct manner -- family members, relatives, friends, colleagues or ourselves by our journalistic work.

Original freelance work for journalistic or literary outlets, print or electronic, not in competition with *The Tribune* or Utah OnLine, is permitted under the following conditions: Approval is granted in advance, the work is not done on company time, the work does not scoop *The Tribune*, and, if possible, the writer be identified with *The Salt Lake Tribune*. The editor has the final say on whether freelancing conditions have been met.

All stories/notes and photos/negatives obtained by employees of *The Tribune* while on duty are "work for hire" and are the sole property of *The Tribune*. Any reselling or marketing of such material may only be undertaken with the approval of and under conditions set by *The Tribune*.

So officious and formal. And all the while setting himself up to waffle on his own rules, as would become apparent in the brouhaha over the Elizabeth Smart case in 2003.

* * *

In November, Shelledy's daily critique announced the formal start of *The Tribune's* online project. One story would be chosen each day for additional background that didn't fit into the newspaper. Another would be . . .

. . . identified as a "chat" story over which readers can express their views . . . and one breaking story, often a wire story, will be earmarked for a 3 p.m. online update the next afternoon. These stories will be identified in the newspaper with small "Click Here" logos.

Also that day, the editor kicked off pagination training for desk staffers and editing training for paginators. I saw the move as an attempt to reduce staffing costs while blurring the line between computer operators and editors; that is, between technicians and journalists. To me, it implied that it didn't take much expertise to be a news editor.

Finally, Shelledy used the critique to sling some shit Denny's way. "If we can't do any better on full-page presentations, per Daybreak today, then we ought to stick to half pages," he wrote in reference to Denny's drawing of a gun-slinging turkey on Nancy Hobb's Thanksgiving food story.

Times like these made it nice to be a short-timer.

Shelledy occasionally commended Denny's work, like the holiday portrait he did of Karl Malone. Yet he normally reserved his graphics praise for "real artist" Mark Knudsen and political cartoonist Pat Bagley.

* * *

Calling 1997 a "tumultuous but healthy year for *The Salt Lake Tribune*," Welch distributed his third consecutive Publisher's Performance Bonus at the end of the year. "Generally, the newsroom has overcome the serious distractions resulting from our becoming a TCI subsidiary and I am appreciative of your efforts to concentrate on the news package we daily offer Utah," he wrote in his annual holiday letter.

A nice token perhaps, but after eight nail-biting months, I just wanted IRS approval of the ESOP distribution. Not even Shelledy could spoil the news in his December 19 critique:

You need to see Tony Magann today or Tuesday if you want to move immediately on distributing your ESOP stock. Do it orderly. What we don't want is a bunch of people standing around on the 4th floor. I want a paper produced today -- and a good one.

I shared the good news with Mimi:

You should have seen the hand-slapping in the office Friday of the IRS announcement. Quite a contrast to the days when people grumped that it [receipt of stock] would never become a reality, conjuring up conspiracy theories

about USBank, the McCartheys and the Fourth Floor; writing letters to Sen. Hatch to get on the IRS's case; spreading rumors.

I felt sorry for staffers who missed out on the lottery or got too little too early to quit working. Some on the sidelines said they were happy for us, but there was obvious disappointment and some resentment. When our chatter got unbearable, someone growled: "Take it outside!"

While waiting for the stock transfer, our share value doubled, clinching my decision to leave along with Denny on April Fool's Day, if not before. We were such blabbermouths we'd already old management we'd be leaving. Again, I turned to Mimi:

Thank God! Since learning of the windfall, I've found more and more about the job intolerable. As people's dreams of becoming millionaires first popped into the open and then went on hold, the office was a stress hole. Denny checked stock prices three or four times a day. When it was up, he was jubilant; when it sagged, he became despondent. It was difficult to think or talk about anything else.

Lance Gudmundsen was the first to resign, after 35 years at *The Tribune*. At 58, he left 18 months short of the 59 1/2 Shelledy arbitrarily set as the qualification for a departure cake. Shelledy further snubbed him with this terse reference in his December 30 critique: "His Features Dept. position is open to staff members who wish to apply."

Some staffers intended to shrink their schedules: Scott Rivers dropped to three days a week on the World Desk, Joan O'Brien to four days on Features. Cathy Reese took maternity leave from Features with plans to return to a 30-hour week in February. Jim Woolf accepted an eight-month international study fellowship in South America and Southeast Asia.

* * *

There were other staff changes unrelated to ESOP. Heather Ann May began a long association with the newspaper, much of it covering my old beat. Other staffers taking family leaves included Jennifer Skordas, Ryan Galbraith, Trent Nelson and Lisa Carricaburu. Men finally qualified.

Nancy Hobbs transferred back to Features from the News Desk, where she'd grown tired of Ledford's harangues and constant reworking of news stories into narratives. Her new assignment was covering food and family, a bonus to friends like me who tested area restaurants with her to review the food.

Not all was well with the staff. Having been diagnosed with hepatitis C, possibly contracted after a car accident, Ann Poore was taking heavy chemotherapy. "I was a terrible and unreliable copy editor for quite a while," she said, "but nobody on the Copy Desk understood what I was going though."[838]

I used to sit at the other end of the newsroom where I could wipe down the keyboard with alcohol pads at the end of the night without freaking anyone out. My fingers were so dry from the meds they were always bleeding, which is how the virus spreads. Yet [copy editor Jeff] Walton would insist that I sit with other staffers at the Desk. We had many a row over that. Even the Fourth Floor (Randy Frisch), which had been sympathetic, stopped being so when I came back to work . . . I just shouldn't have come back to work when I did.[839]

Still, some staffers were "absolutely incredible," about Ann's illness. Dawn House and Paul Rolly, by then a couple, sent meals to her home every Sunday. John Mooney remembered her in daily masses at the National Shrine of St. Jude, and Shirley Jones put her on LDS prayer rolls. Tom Harvey planted a garden that made her "want to live until spring to see it come up." She credited Jim Woolf and his wife with actually saving her life but wouldn't say how.

Extensive research aided by certain staffers persuaded Ann to import Ribavirin from Mexico to avoid liver failure. She sold everything of value to buy the drug, which was no longer used for AIDS but not yet approved for Hep C in the U.S., from the AIDS buyers' club later featured in the movie "Dallas Buyers Club." A University of Utah doctor agreed to monitor her treatment, and she ultimately overcame a 13 percent survival rate.

* * *

Before the year was out, Lulu called from a New York hospital. She was on the verge of giving birth. Another phone call two days later announced the arrival of eight-pound, five-ounce Willy. Mother and son had no place to go.

Just before Christmas, we picked them up from the airport. Lulu's cavernous mouth revealed a couple of brown stalactites where teeth belonged. Looking a lot like Yoda from Star Wars, red, wrinkly Willy whimpered. We held our breath to withstand the pungent odor.

She's unemployable, I thought to myself. Our dream of freedom has turned into a nightmare. Little did I know that Willy was such a sweet soul he would become my sun and stars -- for awhile.

---

[817] Joel Campbell, "Most Utah daily newspapers tally small circulation gains," *Deseret News*, May 12, 1997.

[818] The Salt Lake Tribune Ownrship Statement, October 2, 1988, p. 1.

[819] Dennis Green interview January 9, 2014.

[820] Lucinda Fleeson, "The JOA from Hell," *American Journalism Review*, March 2001.

[821] Max B. Knudson, "TCI-Tribune deal shakes Utah's newspaper scene," *Deseret News*, April 25, 1997, p. A1.

[822] Ibid.

[823] Kristen Moulton, The Associated Press, "TCI Deal Will End Era at Tribune," *The Salt Lake Tribune*, April 27, 1997, p. E1.

[824] Timeline, Utah Newspaper Project; Dominic Welch emails.

[825] Dominic Welch email October 12, 2014.

[826] James Ure, Stop the Press: How the Mormon Church Tried to Silence the Salt Lake Tribune, Chapter 21, p. 146. Ure interviewed James Shelledy September 26,2016.

[827] Dominic Welch email October 11, 2014.

From Rag to Riches & Ruin

[828]"Tribune, TCI Plan to Merge," *The Salt Lake Tribune*, April 22, 1997, p. 1.

[829] Max B. Knudson, "Vote completes S.L. Tribune-TCI merger," *Deseret News*, August 1, 1997.

[830] James E. Shelledy, "Letter From the Editor," *The Salt Lake Tribune*, August 3, 1997, pA2.

[831] Susan Whitney, "Just how are those 24 *Tribune* journalists coping with their new TCI millions?" *Deseret News*, August 31, 1997, p. A1.

[832] James E. Shelledy, "Letter From the Editor," *The Salt Lake Tribune*, August 31, 1997, p. A2.

[833] Harry Fuller, "Accrediting Council fails commentary," *The Masthead*, Summer 1997, p. 9.

[834] Theo Lippmann Jr., "Why they don't like to read editorials," *The Masthead*, Summer 1997, p. 20-21.

[835] "Korologos Resigns as SLOC's Top Spokesman," *The Salt Lake Tribune*, January 15, 1998, p. B1.

[836] "Korologos takes post with Salt Lake advertising firm," *Park Record*, July 3, 1998.

[837] Shepard, April 1999.

[838] Ann Poore email, August 3,2015.

[839] Ibid.

48 - Yearning to Be Free in 1998

"We're still waiting for the stock transfer to our accounts," I whined like a spoiled child to Mimi at the dawn of the New Year. "The promise is never fulfilled. It's taking forever!"

My tirade continued January 6:

Work? I can barely endure it. I've told everyone I'm leaving April Fool's Day, and several people are vying for my job now, including Pete Scarlet and Dawn House. Randy Right-wing Frisch will probably start writing editorials full time now that TCI sold the out-of-state papers and he has little to do.

Wetzel's been a jerk this week. I thank my lucky stars I don't have to put up with him much longer. His supercilious side is showing, and, of course, he's horning in on my territory before I'm even out the door, leaving me little to write about. Yesterday it was judicial appointments; today is was Medicare reform. Then he has the audacity to ask if he should read my page proofs "too." And he's the one who always procrastinates -- or at least *was*.

* * *

On January 8, a newsroom assistant interrupted our Editorial Board meeting with a message to call Mom; that my dad was in "very critical condition."

Mom wanted me to fly to California. I hardly felt anything until artist Rhonda Hailes-Maylett -- she'd married *Deseret News* artist Cory Maylett -- told me how sorry she was and I choked up. Even so, I finished one editorial and wrote another before leaving the office.

One apparently was so weird -- and potentially offensive to staffer Dawn House, who'd lost her brother in the Singer-Swapp showdown -- it never surfaced in print. Here it is:

Haunting Bomb Trials

Who can blame polygamists Addam Swapp and John Timothy Singer for trying for a new trial? By comparison, after all, their crime -- bombing a Kamas church and arming themselves against

police in 1988 -- is only marginally worse than animal-rights activists' firebombing of several Salt Lake County businesses, yet the activists have avoided prison.

A recent series of soft sentences and a 1995 U.S. Supreme Court ruling, it seems, have come back to haunt Utah prosecutors and the courts.

The last two years, in response to bombings at a West Jordan McDonald's restaurant, a Sandy agricultural co-op and a Murray leather crafts store, state judges have handed out relatively brief (one year to 16 months) jail terms combined with probation and restitution. Only Douglas Joshua Ellerman, accused of tossing a pipe bomb into the Utah Fur Breeders' Agricultural Cooperative, still faces federal charges that could land him in prison for up to 35 years.

Singer and Swapp so far have served nearly 10 years on federal convictions, and Swapp stands to spend another decade in federal prison on explosives and interfering charges. Both Singer and Swapp owe another 15 years to the state for manslaughter.

These members of a polygamist clan would have been treated differently if tried on all charges in state court, where bombing penalties are softer. They also might have escaped federal conviction if they'd had the benefit of the 1995 Supreme Court ruling, which says a crime must "substantially" interfere with interstate commerce to warrant federal involvement.

What happens in the Ellerman case, then, could further affect -- or be affected by -- the Singer-Swapp appeal, since federal jurisdiction in both cases is based on the claim that the bombings intruded on trade across state lines.

If Ellerman's attorney, Ron Yengich, is correct in contending that the destruction of the co-op, which buys and sells products between states, does not constitute a federal crime by Supreme Court standards, then Singer and Swapp have an even stronger argument. Contrary to the prosecution's contention in 1988, the church bombing hardly affected interstate commerce -- unless, of course, this nation officially recognizes soul-saving as a business venture.

The Singer-Swapp bombing and standoff in Summit County stirred up a lot of emotion 10 years ago -- the kind of emotion that demands stiff sentences.

But the owners of destroyed businesses also have suffered from animal-rights terrorism. If the criminals behind their loss get brief sentences, the same should be expected for those who have committed similar crimes.

Denny and I ate dinner at his mother's house before leaving for the airport that night. I feared this might not be the end of suffering for Dad and Mom; that he'd linger and rally and linger again.

In the middle of all this, I heard from Wells Fargo that my stock had transferred overnight, and I sold two-thirds of it at $28 net. Not the best possible price.

Dad lay unconscious and hooked up to IVs in acute care. His heart pounding and his gaping mouth encrusted with weepy sores, he breathed heavily through an oxygen tube. Blood poisoning was killing his kidneys.

My dysfunctional family agonized a full week over pulling the plug, but in the end, our wishes didn't matter. Refusing to "participate in starvation," Dad's doctor overrode our objections to a feeding tube. Dad died alone the night of his gastric surgery. I was left with the image of him reaching for me with a frightened, pleading look as I left his room earlier that afternoon.

Nursing a cold, I helped Mom make funeral arrangements, which included shipping Dad's body to Utah. Several of our closest *Tribune* friends attended the graveside service in Bountiful in the snow.

* * *

Back to our office drama.

Shelledy's weekend critique in late January announced Tim Kelly's impending exit. Not yet 55, Tim would be dropped from *The Tribune's* health plan. This is what the editor wrote:

Tim Kelly, who has taken more photos for *The Tribune* than all the other photographers (save Lynn Johnson) combined and who, as a young photojournalist studied under Matthew Brady [Civil War photojournalist Mathew Brady died in 1896], will be opting for early retirement, effective February 6. Additionally, Lynn Johnson, who has taken more photos for *The Tribune* than all the other photographers (save Tim Kelly) combined and who is the only photographer on staff who has experience with flash powder, will be

taking a 6- to 12-month leave of absence, starting March 1, to travel in Europe.

You may chuckle at Shelledy's hyperbolical sense of humor. I groaned. Tim was no fan of this boss who foisted Jim Fisher on the Photo Department. But at least Shelledy did acknowledge Tim's good work.

I submitted this cocky official resignation to the publisher January 30:

Despite 22-plus stimulating years at this institution, it's time to make my departure official. Thanks to *The Tribune's* effective planning and negotiating, I can now afford to take some time off work to be with Denny, who is retiring April 1.

My official date of departure will be April 4, but I will take vacation after Friday, the 13th of March. (If you're superstitious, perhaps you'll also want to remember the Ides of March as my time of exit. While you're at it, throw in April Fools' Day, too.)

I will miss my association with you and with many of the staff, but there are some other things I'd like to try, like travel and new kinds of writing.

Feel free to call on me for limited assignments, and if I'm available, I'll come running. Meantime, take good care of the paper. I'll be one of your most avid (and likely critical) readers. Thank you for the opportunity to get paid for something I truly enjoyed.

I was giving up a $750 weekly salary. I didn't expect any requests for my help in the future, and they never came.

"At least Tom McCarthey didn't act like a jerk when I told him we were leaving," I told Mimi. "He even said I'd be missed on editorials and seemed impressed that Denny had had a family member on the job since 1920."

* * *

The same day I turned in my resignation, toothless, stinky Lulu became a newsroom assistant in the Data Center, now located just a few feet from the Art and Editorial departments. Terry Ellefsen had made it happen at Denny's request. Though Lulu and I were getting along pretty well and I was grateful she had a job, I was relieved I'd soon be gone.

But an absurd comparison in Shelledy's daily critique bothered me. "[Lulu] plans to carry on the Green tradition once her father, Dennis, leaves in mid-March."

I couldn't imagine Lulu filling the shoes of her father -- or of her grandfather, for that matter. Both were reliable, productive managers for 35 years. Then again, with a little support, she might surprise us. She certainly was competent enough.

Speaking of shoes, I bought Lulu new ones, as well as a winter coat. I gave her most of my washable office attire instead of shrinkable wools. We found a dentist to clean up her mouth after Denny's cousin refused to work on her. "Don't spend a lot of money on that mouth," Bill Green warned us. "She'll just let go again. I've seen it happen a hundred times."

Denny co-signed on an apartment for Lulu and Willy downtown. Meantime, Stormy, whose attitude seemed to improve with her second marriage, announced a second pregnancy. The stage was set for more family drama ahead.

* * *

As anticipated, Shelledy's sendoff for Denny, me, Fuller and Sam Smith was insulting, even though Denny and Harry, at least, had devoted considerable time and experience to the company. Here's the "acknowledgement" we received:

> Art editor Dennis Green also has announced he will be taking early retirement as of mid-March, and Sam Smith is opting for the same as of this fall. How the Art and Photo departments will be structured following these changes remains to be seen, but several possibilities are being currently considered.
> Other early retirements include Editorial Page Editor Harry Fuller, effective March 1, and editorial writer Diane Cole, effective April 1.

A quibble about accuracy: Fuller and I were not taking early retirements. Fuller was 65, normal retirement age, and I was resigning. Even at 55, Denny would reach Kearns-Tribune's official retirement age, which entitled him to a pension and health insurance.

* * *

During our scramble for accountants and money managers, we'd learned a little about IRAs and investing. Smith Barney's Rod Cushing, who by then was managing accounts for

several staffers including Denny, was particularly helpful. I offered Mimi this technical update:

> We still don't know what we're talking about, but we've got some lingo down.
> We'd hoped to cash some of the stock out on a cost basis, but that idea turned sour at the end, so now we'll take substantially equal payments from Denny's IRA and hold onto mine for awhile. We got our trusts and IRAs set up six months ago, requiring payments for professional services even before we sniffed the dough.
> Some people intend to pay tax penalties to get money for remodeling, new cars and travel . . .

Six weeks before our departure, Denny and I still awaited the deposit of funds into our personal accounts. Meantime, we arranged for an obscenely high monthly income, by our standards, and expected to pay much more in taxes than either us had ever earned.

Denny was even more excited than I, eager to become a full-time artist and homebuilder. We contacted a realtor in Kauai about second-home property.

I was so worked up that I kept waking up at 4 a.m. and couldn't get back to sleep. My fitful nights included second thoughts. Am I really ready to quit working so young? I wondered. Is my identity so wrapped up in being a journalist and editorial writer that I'll lose myself in retirement? Will I miss the excitement of news? The influence of editorial writing? Will I get bored because I lack interests outside work -- like Denny said?

In any case, I could no longer work as an editorial writer for Dominic Welch and Randy Frisch. Our opinions just didn't jibe. And I couldn't stand working while Denny stayed home. He would get too caught up in his art and home-improvement projects to pick up groceries or make dinner, so I would be expected to feed a starving, ornery artist when I came home late from work stressed and exhausted. Eating out wouldn't be a frequent option because we lived too far from restaurants. Resentment might ruin our marriage.

* * *

Someone must have said something to Shelledy about his brusque references to certain retirements On February 12, his critique mentioned that Connie Coyne, who had moved from the Copy Desk to take over ombudsman duties from Shinika Sykes, would replace Harry Fuller, "who is retiring on that date after 36 years with *The Tribune*." He also could have said something about Connie being only the second female editorial writer at *The Tribune*.

The critique also elaborated on my leave-taking. "Editorial writer Diane Cole, who has reported stories and penned editorials for *The Tribune* for nearly 25 years, will be leaving *The Tribune* in mid-March. The publisher has not as yet decided on a replacement for her."

Another cryptic notation announced that Leah Hogsten "has been hired in the Photo Department, effective March 9, to replace Tim Kelly, who left last month."

* * *

The countdown was on. No longer worried about fallout from editors and readers, on February 22 I took out after Republican Senator Leonard Blackham, a turkey farmer from Moroni who'd said Utah needed "someone who has a great heart" to solve the state's child-care problems. "What Utah children need even more, at this point," I wrote in my Sunday editorial, "are legislators with great minds -- minds attuned to the realities of child care."[840]

Basically, I attacked Blackham for legislation that would raise to eight the number of toddlers in private homes and eliminate surprise inspections. In the process, I violated an unspoken *Tribune* rule not to criticize rural folks.

Next day, I tackled another rural lawmaker:

Big Brother Controls Land

It's a contradiction at best. Rural legislators who, by the way, are part of government yet don't like government telling them what to do, especially when it comes to land, won't let other rural Utahns decide what to do with their own private property.

Case in point: House Speaker Mel Brown, sometime dairy farmer, climbed down off his podium last week to shoot down legislation that would have helped counties conserve farm land. "We don't need a system that involves public money," he declared. "If you leave us alone and let us solve our problems by ourselves, ultimately we'll do it."

Maybe so, but not all Utahns think the solution is to sell off the last remnants of green space to developers as

farmers are doing in growing areas of the state. They can hardly afford to resist against suburban sprawl and rising property values.

And, despite Brown's assumption, not all farmers and ranchers are in his camp. Some would dearly love to preserve their farms as open space, if not for themselves, for the future of society. Problem is, their options are limited. If they're trying to retire, they may have to sell some land to live off the proceeds, and the most likely buyer is a developer, not another farmer. The market will prevail.

There also are some communities in Utah that would like to preserve green space, even if it means taxing themselves enough to buy up farm land or its development rights. Under House Bill 50, sponsored by another dairy farmer, Evan L. Olsen, R-College Ward, counties could raise sales taxes 1/8 percent to acquire conservation easements for agricultural uses.

It is not as if counties would be gobbling up vast acreage and imposing their will on taxpayers. Landowners would decide for themselves whether to sell, and voters would have to approve the tax. H.B. 50 was an attempt to let counties and farmers solve the problem of shrinking green space themselves, but with more options.

But now that Big Brother Brown has his way, neither taxpayers nor farmers will have that chance. After he watered down Olsen's measure, by trying to limit easements to 10 years and calling for a board of agriculture producers to control the process, the House unceremoniously put it to rest.

Olsen's proposal was not perfect. Communities and property owners should be able to preserve open space for more than just agriculture. Water conservation was one good idea to come from House debate. Wildlife and recreation are other values worth preserving.

But at least the farmer from College Ward understands that new ideas are not necessarily destructive of traditional interests. His legislation would have helped preserve past and current land uses for the future.[841]

My last few months on the job, I promoted green space at every opportunity (our Scofield property had something to do with that), but the Legislature was still just arguing about it in 1999.

Charter schools, which I had long advocated as an alternative to home schooling and tuition tax credits, was slowly getting started by then, but another of my favorite issues never got off the ground. The teacher union successfully buried career ladders, a form of merit pay for teachers.

* * *

When Hemphill was covering the Olympics in Nagano, he learned that Harry Fuller was retiring and Randy Frisch was ascending to Editorial Page editor. He understood then that the life he knew as an editorial writer was about to end. The icing on the cake was his return to an impenetrable office.

Because day care was closed weekends, Lulu had been bringing baby Willy to work on Saturdays and hiding him in Hemphill's nearby office in defiance of Shelledy's orders. It didn't dawn on her that someone might notice the stench of dirty diapers shut up in a small room for two days. He blew a fuse, and Lulu let me and Denny take Willy the next few weekends.

* * *

Our March 3 editorial agenda established structure and quotas for the editorial writers. Connie Coyne was assigned the Saturday shift and two editorials to write a week. Everyone else would write one weekly column along with other duties. Wetzel and Hemphill got the option of writing six or seven editorials or replacing one editorial with editing work. My replacement would either handle the Forum letters, mail and Op-ed duties -- or the letters and five or six editorials.

There would be no Editorial Page editor. Randy Frisch would manage visitors to Editorial Board meetings. Writers would work directly for the publisher on editorial positions. There would be no "hurry-up" editorials. "All editorials will be written at least one day in advance, and the publisher will be given a printed copy to review before publication."

Rules. Structure. Quotas. I was not cut out for such a system. I worked best under self-imposed goals. If we needed 14 or 15 editorials a week, I aimed to write five or six of them while doing my fair share of editing. With six or seven editorials and a column to write, it would be practically impossible to avoid

last-minute editorials -- especially if writers hoped to react quickly to breaking news events.

Requiring editorials to conform to the wacky opinions of Frisch and Welch would make the unbearable process absurd. But it gets worse. My successors were moving to tiny, windowless offices on the 8th floor, far away from humanity.

"Hallelujah!" I silently cheered. "I won't be here to slave for Frisch and Welch!" But the relief was fleeting knowing my friends were bound to suffer.

The new rules relaxed over time. Not everyone wrote a weekly column, the role of Editorial Page editor was resurrected, and someone new was hired to handle the Forum letters.

***

Two of my editorials ran my second-to-last day on the job. The first criticized home schoolers for refusing to have their children tested for academic learning;[842] the second blasted medical and defense contractors for legislation that would tie government hands and gag whistleblowers.[843]

I knew home-school radicals and government contractors would be riled, but I didn't care. I was out of there by the time home-school rabble-rouser Joyce Kinmont wrote her irritating response, which conjured up *The Tribune's* 1877 attacks on LDS Church leaders for shunning state-supported schools. "Both home and public school parents are concerned that the state is becoming far too aggressive in assuming control over families," she declared.

That day's meeting agenda began normally enough. Activist Chip Ward would talk to us about Magcorp chlorine contamination. The agenda had me editorializing against reductions in high school science requirements to accommodate LDS seminary classes, Wetzel blasting Bill Gates' highway robbery tactics, and Hemphill calling for an appeal in the case over the looting of Indian graves. Frisch had written an editorial in favor of judges campaigning only if they revealed their supporters. He planned another that would defend Budweiser as a sponsor for the 2002 Winter Olympics. I couldn't wait to put his arguments into logical order.

Last on the schedule was something different: "Friday's meeting will feature Diane Cole and Denny Green on the virtues of retirement, noon, Alta Club."

Well, I'd be damned! Welch and Frisch would make up for any slights Shelledy tossed our way.

With the Ides of March falling on the weekend, our last day at *The Tribune* was Friday the 13th, another irony for a lucky event. April Fools' Day, the same day Denny's dad retired from the newspaper, would remain our official separation date.

Farewell bonsai from the Art Department.

As expected, Shelledy unceremoniously showed Denny the door by banning fanfare for the millionaires. Shirley Jones ordered a going-away cake to be served discreetly in the Editorial Board conference room anyway. Several staffers came in for a slice. Art Department staffers pooled their resources for a bonsai going-away gift. Hemphill handed me a mock editorial n which he said:

Cole in Our Stocking

The Tribune Building on Main Street in Salt Lake City, sure to be rubble when The Big One hits, listed noticeably toward the right this morning, the first day that *The Salt Lake Tribune* published without its left-bearing anchor, Diane Cole.

Cole, the first woman ever named to *The Tribune's* editorial board (shortly after which it ceased to be called the editorial board), retired from the newspaper last week to devote her attention to her new career as a full-time capitalist.

Her departure was precipitated by an elaborate scheme hatched 20 years ago by current *Tribune* publisher Dominic Welch, who launched the company's ESOP program with the specific goal of one day transforming Cole into a Republican. He declared victory on that front last week.

Prior to the conversion, Cole had championed the liberal side of most issues, often to the consternation of the publisher. For instance, she was a strong environmentalist, especially when it came to the air space around her desk. She fought a long campaign against indoor pollution on the mezzanine, spurred by the certainty that she was being slowly and secretly poisoned by carbon monoxide.

She was a longtime defender of Utah's poor and downtrodden in her editorials, a conviction that exposed her to a number of interesting economic theories in the last several years -- such as, businesses don't pay taxes, there is no such thing as fairness, and all property tax is evil. She hadn't fully digested them by the time she left.

Cole had particular expertise in two areas on which she often wrote -- education and health care. A former teacher, she had a personal understanding of the conditions of Utah's overworked and undersupplied teachers and of the fundamental tenet of pubic education: that most kids are morons. And, by the way, she says you can take those vouchers and shove 'em.

In a move born of midlife crisis and an invasion of 143 South Main from points north, Cole returned to school in 1992 to earn a master's degree in political science. She focused her studies on health-care issues, which prepared her, upon her return to the paper, to comment on HealthPrint and to translate Cigna.

Cole's departure leaves a hollowness at the core of Utah's civic discourse. Indeed, her former Bountiful schoolmate, Senate President Lane Beattie, was reportedly going to sneak through a resolution in her honor earlier this month, but the legislative session adjourned several hours before his normal midnight filing hour.

Diane Cole will leave the fools and scoundrels of Utah's public life for others to lance. But, alas, in the emptied drawer of her desk, her ever-sharp pen was nowhere to be found. Sadly, she has taken it with her.

Welch and Frisch walked us through The Alta Club's front entrance, something I relished after so many years as a second-class citizen relegated to the elitist club's back door, where hookers had entered in the early days. Denny and I joked about wanting commemorative watches with *The Tribune's* logo.

Instead, Welch presented me with <u>Atlas Shrugged</u> by Ayn Rand to explain his politics. (Four years later, on February 7, 2002, Forum writer Shawn Hill described *Tribune* editorials as pro-big business. "I may be so lucky as to get an allusion to an Ayn Rand novel as well," he wrote.) I gave Welch a book of Molly Ivins' liberal columns. Frisch bestowed a naugahyde briefcase upon Denny, who traded it in for a shirt with a *Tribune* logo.

We left the the Tribune Building that afternoon with mostly light hearts. Having snatched it during remodeling, I took its front-door First Amendment plaque as a souvenir.

* * *

Next morning, I enjoyed a cup of coffee at home while reading two of my last two editorials in the paper. The first expounded one last time on child care; the other constituted my last hurrah.

I alluded to Utah's special Mormon culture in my criticism of relaxed child-care licensing:

> *The assertion [of the legislation] was that parents must accept responsibility for their children's care, and the underlying theme was that mothers should stay home to provide that care. But, of course, not all parents can stay home. More than half of Utah children under age 6 have their only parent or both in the work force.* [844]

I pulled out all stops for "A Parting Shot," freely using cliches, alliteration, puns and slurs that I never would have gotten past my colleagues previously:

> *As for spitting slimy chaw in public places, worst of all in squeaky clean Bountiful, where one rule is supposed to fit all,* The Tribune's *foursquare against it. But the city fathers probably bit off more than anyone can chew when they banned chewing tobacco from the gaping holes in people's heads.*
>
> *Knuckle-dragging hockey hounds have been spewing spent tobacco into the stands at the city's ice rink, a disgusting practice that more refined ice-skaters fear will tarnish the facility's image as the spot to practice world-class*

figure-skating. Some people also complain that a few mouth-breathers even project their puke onto city links, leaving sickening little surprises for more upscale clientele.

> *There should be a law, and the Bountiful City Council delivered it this week. Problem is, the new ordinance doesn't just ban the disgusting discard of used chew on the floor and links, where it offends the sensibilities of innocent bystanders. The new rule invades people's bodies -- that is, their mouths.*
>
> *No one can hold a pinch of snuff between cheek and gum without risking arrest -- or at least being ejected from the premises. Even an offender who swallows the putrid stuff or subtly slips it into a hand for proper disposal could be cited with a class C misdemeanor.*
>
> *Bountiful City fathers say they won't be heavy-handed. Jail terms and $750 fines are not expected. But why pass a law that isn't going to be enforced?*
>
> *Tobacco is under attack these days for good health reasons, but most would have to agree that chewing is less criminal than cigarette smoking, which imposes noxious fumes on others. The only person hurt by a properly stowed wad of chaw is the chewer, who comes off as a hayseed who can't wait for a case of oral cancer.*
>
> *So bounce the uncivilized slobs who don't know how to use a spittoon -- hey, if they had any class, they'd be at Symphony Hall -- but don't be too eager to dictate what people gnaw on.*
>
> *It's probably a good time to quit, before some spit-licker with a muzzle figures out the maze to Main Street . . .* [845]

That evening, Terry and Nancy Hobbs Orme hosted a party for us and Tim Kelly, who'd bailed weeks earlier. In my email invitation to staffers days earlier, I'd written:

> It will be a sad yet exhilarating day (Friday the 13th) when Denny and I bid farewell after nearly 60 collective, good and bad years at *The Tribune.* You are one of the people we will truly miss and hope you will join us in a wild evening at the Ormes' abode Saturday, March 14, beginning at 6 p.m. and perhaps spilling into the Ides of March.

That bash was a proper goodbye, complete with joke gifts. Bagley unveiled a cartoon of me saying, "I'm not sure I get it."

Photographer Rick Egan gave us a video of *Tribune* staffers. Terry and Nancy printed up calling cards for us that identified Denny as a doodler and me as a faineant. Will and Cynthia gave us a pair of walkie talkies.

Bon Voyage!

Join us in celebrating with Tim Kelly,
Denny Green and Diane Cole
as they begin new adventures

Saturday, March 14   6 p.m.
11339 S. 1700 East
(Home of Terry Orme and Nancy Hobbs)

We got cards. Barbi thanked Denny "for all your wonderful help over the years and for sharing your good sense of humor when things got tough. It helped me through many a tough time." Nancy Melich wrote: "You both have contributed immensely to the professionalism of this paper and it is our loss and our readers that you are leaving. You are both irreplaceable." She added that the new editorial rules and quotas were "such an insult" to her husband and Wetzel and "to you for all you have made of that dept."

* * *

My voice was still being heard at the newspaper the morning after the bash. One carry-over editorial picked at another old scab, the state school board's subversion of high school academics for the sake of LDS seminary. Some excerpts:

Church and school systems have become so closely wrapped together in Utah that they now depend on one another.

Some schools might become overcrowded if students didn't leave campus for seminary during the school day.

Although public schools can and should accommodate religion, they have no business promoting it by encouraging students to take LDS classes. Schools go too far when they design buildings and schedule buses and classes around seminary, as they now do in Utah. [846]

Apparently my former colleagues didn't realize how inflammatory those words were for *Tribune* readers. Maybe I was getting even for past transgressions. In any case, I was glad I didn't have to deal with their angry phone calls or the probable push-back from the LDS Church.

Two Forum letters March 31 offered a toned-down taste of their reaction. One pointed to a 1952 Supreme Court decision giving every religion the right to use released time for religious instruction. Another, from former school board member Jay Monson, contended that American students were unfairly held up to elite students in international test-score comparisons. He contended that seminary classes imparted morals and values lacking in public education.

My last editorial ran March 18. Like others during my distracted final weeks, I fell back on my easiest subject, education. This one weakly supported Utah Valley State College's bid to offer 19 more four-year programs over the next five years.

This was a capitulation for me, a consistent opponent of "institutional creep" at these former technical schools. The addition of more four-year programs was a major leap toward becoming universities, which I considered unnecessary and unaffordable in Utah. Weber State College and Southern Utah State College already had weaseled their way into university status, increasing their budgets for programs and salaries.

While noting that Utah Valley "has been chomping at the bit to become a full-fledged, four-year college while regents have tried to rein it in," I ended by encouraging the regents to consider the college's request with an open mind. [847] I had gone soft. Or maybe I just didn't care anymore now that I could afford the higher taxes the colleges would require. It also was possible this sellout wanted to teach at its satellite campus someday.

My attitude changed when I read a March 31 editorial that amounted to an about-face to my years of editorials on school spending.

It began:

> *Is Utah dead last in per-student public school spending? Next to dead last? Does it really matter? Is this figure relevant when it comes to determining education quality?*

The primary purpose of such comparisons, the author argued, had little to do with school quality and much to do about "invidious comparisons."[848]

Aha! A Scarletism! My old pal Peter Scarlet, who replaced me on the Editorial Page, was gleefully expressing the sentiments and even the phraseology of Randy Frisch.

Get a load of this paragraph:

> *About the only way Utah can reach the national average of $5,774, a golden mean that spells boredom to everyone but the residents of Garrison Keillor's Lake Woebegone, is for a European-type birthrate, combined with some healthy out-migration and tax levels that only an early 20th-century socialist could love. Until these highly unlikely things happen, Utah will have to be content with being near or at the bottom of this particular statistic. Moreover, residents should not overly concern themselves about it. It says less about educational quality than it does about demographics.*

Catchy, perhaps. Certainly harder hitting than many of my editorials. But just plain wrong and unprofessional, in my humble opinion. The idea of per-pupil spending having little effect on education quality was outrageous in the extreme.

A changing of the guard obviously had occurred overnight. My influence had become a fading memory. It was gratifying to learn, then, that my impact was not so quickly lost on everyone.

* * *

Decades after my departure, Paul Wetzel observed that I was more apt than others to challenge the status quo. "Your willingness, indeed, your compulsion to poke authority in the eye may have been your greatest gift to the page," he said. "It's what readers came to expect from *The Tribune,* in no small part because of you." He went on:

I always respected you as a colleague. I admired that you kept your own extensive clipping files and worked the phone to get information and perspective beyond what had been published in the paper.

Your return to the U. in quest of your master's in poli sci also took a lot of pluck. Ironically, your graduate degree probably hurt you financially, because *The Tribune*, to my knowledge, never rewarded or encouraged higher education. Just the opposite. I know several reporters who did not graduate because they quit the U. to work full time at *The Trib* and never finished their degrees. I didn't finally lay claim to mine until 1980.

I did find your feminist rants a bit tiresome, but you persuaded me in the end. Women do face extraordinary sexist bias. I distinctly remember one day when I was going on about how people needed to rise on their own merits. You observed, rather coldly, I thought, that I didn't realize all of the advantages from which I had benefited. That brought me up short, and it stung. But I thought a great deal about what you had said and decided you were right. That exchange was a turning point in my views and in my self-knowledge.

. . . The big picture is that I enjoyed working with you, I learned from you. Together with Lex, we three devoted ourselves to putting out the best page possible, and we sacrificed our time to that end. You set that mark.[849]

This generous assessment made me wonder whether I actually was perceptive about people. Wetzel, it seemed, was less a back-stabber than a sensitive, silent ally.

Let's face it, I was a difficult employee. I chronically criticized, complained and pushed the limits of tolerance in the community and among my supervisors. I had to be watched, restrained from going too far. Then I carped and sulked for being misunderstood and under-appreciated. I was a journalist in Salt Lake City, Utah.

840 "Both Heart, Mind Needed," *The Salt Lake Tribune*, February 22, 1998, p. AA2.

841 "Big Brother Controls Land," *The Salt Lake Tribune*, February 23, 1998, p. A10.

842 Some Children Lose," *The Salt Lake Tribune*, March 12, 1998, p. A8.

843 "Don't Ruin Fraud Tool," *The Salt Lake Tribune*, March 12, 1998, p. A8.

844 "Welcome Child Support," *The Salt Lake Tribune*, March 14, 1998, p. A10.

845 "A Parting Shot," *The Salt Lake Tribune*, March 14, 1998, p. A10.

846 "Science vs. Religion," *The Salt Lake Tribune*, March 17, 1998, p.A10.

847 "UVSC Deserves Hearing," *The Salt Lake Tribune*, March 1, 1998, p. A15.

848 "School Spending in Context," *The Salt Lake Tribune*, March 31, 1998, p. A9.

849 Paul Wetzel email, May 31, 2016.

Part IV - The Aftermath

49 - It's No Joke, April 1, 1998

On our official exit date, we lounged in paradise, a private but modest house in the jungle off Hanalei Bay on Kauai. Mimi wondered how it felt.

I've been riding a roller coaster of emotions. One minute I'm elated; the next I'm anxious. When I go to bed at night and wake up in the morning, a flush of happiness washes over me when I realize I'm free. It's the same way I first felt about Sunday mornings after confirmation, when Mom let me decide whether to stay home from church. Actually, Sunday mornings still bring on bursts of joy.

Every now and then, though, I wonder what to do to make life worthwhile -- challenging and exciting. What's my contribution? I have all the time in the world to establish a new, meaningful role for myself, but let's face it, "editorial writer" became my identity. At least that's something people might respect. An unemployed parasite? Now that's something else.

Oh, but it's wonderful to have money. I'll get used to it. How nice to go shopping and not worry about the bill. Not that I ignore prices. That habit is ingrained.

We could have afforded the Hawaiian trip without ESOP, but it would have consumed two-thirds of my annual vacation time. Now I could stay as long as I wanted.

Something was missing from this vacation. In the past, we were always so grateful to escape the stress of work and family. Now there was little stress to escape. We had to learn to appreciate a place for what it was rather than what it wasn't. It would take a while.

I was reading but hating Ayn Rand's obnoxious book. What a bunch of conservative crap! I hoped it might help me better understand Welch's thought processes. I learned that I left at the right time. I would never see government's role his way.

Of course I hadn't yet let go of *The Tribune*. I set up a shrine of memorabilia in my home office. Included were Hemphill's mock editorial, the First Amendment plaque, some writing awards and a couple of Bagley originals. I put some of my last editorials in an album.

Back home, I regularly received emails from Peter Scarlet, who had literally begged Welch for my job, even mentioning his leukemia for leverage. It hadn't hurt that he'd hobnobbed (Scarletism) with the wives of both Welch and Gallivan at social functions for years.

I felt guilty about sticking Scarlet with a mess after cleaning out only half my voluminous clipping files, so I resolved to take him to lunch. Lunches with Peter became a regular conduit to *Tribune* gossip.

Scarlet didn't let his chronic leukemia get him down. Rather, he stayed elated about his dream job, and his millions were available for medical treatment. The money also enabled him to buy a house closer to work.

Hemphill and Wetzel reportedly were frustrated by their inability to crank out editorials like Connie Coyne and Scarlet did. Hemphill could have quit given his and Nancy Melich's double dose of stock, but he wanted to work through the 2002 Winter Olympics. Meantime, he could keep his medical insurance and reduce chances of becoming a full-time caregiver to his mother-in-law. Wetzel stayed on to get his children through college and qualify for health insurance, a hard bargain for a man in his forties.

Out with the old, in with the new.

Shelledy gleefully reported in his June 21, 1998 column that ESOP, which "placed into the hands of 150 newsroom employees roughly $80 million," allowed him to infuse the staff with new blood.

The numbers guy pointed out that seven veteran staffers took early retirement, three others returned to school, two took yearlong leaves of absence and three dropped to part-time status. A couple of staffers followed significant others to the West Coast, two moved to bigger news organizations and one died. Bottom line: 18 positions -- "nearly 12 percent of the newsroom complement" -- had opened up.

"While I dislike losing experienced journalists," he claimed, "the influx of skills and experience has been impressive, and several have special talents."

The big kahuna was not through with faint praise for long-time staffers. Referring to the annual SPJ-SDX contest he typically pooh-poohed, he noted that "Lex Hemphill was chosen the best editorial writer Utah has to offer." *Tribune* photographers, the graphics staff and sports writers "were not moved to enter either the SPJ-SDX or AP competition," he wrote.

Given the shadow Shelledy cast over these contests, it was no wonder so few bothered to participate.

The only part of the column that didn't rankle me was its commendation of Utah Online, headed by Tony Semerad, as the best newspaper website the second year running. Conscientious, cooperative Semerad was one of Shelledy's best hires.

50 - Retirement Heaven with Hitches

By November 24, 1998, I had spent eight months without working for a living or writing anything worth mentioning. Instead of hurtling down the canyon dodging black ice with coffee cups squeezed between our knees, Denny and I took our time getting out of bed. No more inane staff meetings and stressful daily deadlines. No more bosses mucking up our work with inflated egos and bizarre biases. No more salary worries. The stale air of the mezzanine was only a sour memory. Denny again was the funny, loving guy I'd dated in 1976, creating whatever art he wanted and lapping up the attaboys that kept him going. He was planning the art project of a lifetime: an entire house.

It was great to pick up a novel for a change. While working, I was too burned out by researching, proofreading and writing facts all day long to read for pleasure. My first choice was Victor Hugo's three-volume Valgean edition of Les Miserables. What a wonderful writer!

Tim Kelly's wife Sharon and I started bicycling regularly and batting golf balls around Nibley, Forest Dale and other local courses. Golf no longer seemed such a ridiculous waste of precious time. Denny and Tim joined in once a week for a round at Mountain Dell or Bonneville before going to dinner together at Red Butte Cafe. The four of us also took a cruise or two together, and Tim coached our women's softball team.

I joined my neighbor's investment club and spent more time at Joe's Ridge with Brock and baby Willy, adventurous outdoorsmen.

How could this happen to a lower-middle-class American girl from the fifties who, under the constant threat of nuclear annihilation, never even expected to reach adulthood? I got lucky.

It wasn't entirely luck, of course. Someone, whether John W. Gallivan, Dominic Welch or TCI's John Malone, made some astute financial decisions. But the bottom line was that Denny and I made out like bandits because we were both at the newspaper when ESOP started, when stock distributions were largest, and then stayed there.

"We won the lottery in a state that outlaws them," I bragged to Mimi. "We're wallowing in our wealth like pigs in shit."

We still couldn't afford to a mansion in Deer Valley, but even with huge dips in the stock market -- it plunged from an all-time high just after we sold most of our TCI shares -- we were free from jobs. We could help pay for Willy's day care worry-free.

There was occasional aimlessness and regret. Though well rid of a certain Little Lord Fauntleroy editor, the dirty workplace and frustrating routines and traditions, I sometimes missed the newspaper. The Tribune was never dull. Personal difficulties were offset by the stimulating news business, which fed curiosity, uncovered problems and often led to solutions.

"If they didn't suffer," Harry Fuller said of journalists, "how could they maintain their constant search for reasons to locate and expose meanness and corruption? The old adage, misery loves company."[850]

I still met Tribune old farts and others for lunch, where we bitched about our alma mater's typos and management snafus.

Our easy money didn't guarantee health and happiness.

As 1999 dawned, my new life had become a bit of a bore. I tired of preparing three unimaginative meals a day and missed ethnic eateries like Baba Afghan, Blue Iguana, Hunan and the Sahara. Our days usually ended with the latest on the Clinton impeachment hearings, a video and a new minutes of reading.

After four years of monthly meetings, I resigned from Salt Lake Community College's Communications Advisory Committee. No longer in the news business, I had little to offer the school. My resignation letter to Davis V. Ballard March 1, 1999, recommended Tribune staffers Tony Semerad, Tim Fitzpatrick or Cheryl Crosby as my replacement.

I considered other ways of making life more meaningful. It would be noble to get directly involved in the community, perhaps volunteering with homeless adults or neglected children like Willy. Perhaps if I got involved with politics, I could improve laws and public services. I wondered whether watchdogs like Claire Geddes could use a hand hounding legislative numbskulls into working for public interests.

Unfortunately, all these options would require me to assert myself, commit to a cause and make regular trips to the valley. I wasn't ready for long-term commitments.

Nancy Hobbs and I did volunteer on Democrat Scott Howell's campaign for Orrin Hatch's Senate seat in 2000. I suggested policy issues and statements about health care to the youngsters running the campaign. My politics were left of Howell's, so his loss was barely disappointing, the overall experience less than exciting.

* * *

Denny and I found new ways to spend our days -- and to readmit drama and stress to our lives.

For one, we contacted a state forester about thinning our Scofield trees infected with mistletoe and pine beetles. I learned more than I wanted to about logging: calling for bids, identifying a grapple skidder, burning slash in the snow and meeting a logger whose wife believed mutant people-frogs monitored our every move from underground lairs.

Our stocks stagnated for a year, and I fretted about bank errors in reports to the IRS regarding the size of my annual distributions.

Willy, who was growing into a cheerful, loving little cuss despite his perpetual diarrhea, runny nose and conjunctivitis, spent many weekends with us while Lulu attended National Guard exercises. After a few months, though, Lulu started steering us away from her apartment. When Jan Keller, who lived down the hall from them, reported that Willy ran across the street naked one day, his mother nowhere to be seen, I knew something had to be done.

As I dithered about calling the Department of Family Services, Stormy stepped up. "But don't expect me ever to raise Willy if Lulu loses him!" she emphasized. Her call produced no results.

Soon "Mother" Shirley Jones called to report that Lulu was suspended for taking Willy to work again. Shelledy planned to fire her for one more infraction. "Lulu should call in sick when she can't find a babysitter," she advised. Apparently Lulu didn't listen to her any more than she did us.

Within weeks, Shirley called again, this time looking for Lulu, whose phone had been disconnected. Shelledy was lowering the boom. Lulu had not only taken Willy to work again, she had gone on a National Guard training exercise against Shelledy's orders. When reprimanded, she claimed the exercise was required by law and

threatened to have her adjutant general sue *The Tribune* for retaliation. Lulu lost her job.

Not a proud moment in the Green family tradition of newspapering.

Contending Denny and I were too busy with Willy to think about *her* children, Stormy kept her fussy second child John Deere to herself. Yet she let us take 7-year-old Brock to Hawaii's Kona Coast, where this Bill Nye the Science Guy fan eagerly explored volcano park, collected rocks and coral, constructed sand dams in the tide pools and snorkeled with colorful fish and sea turtles.

Enter the Gruesome Twosome, who flew across the country to pick over the carcass of Swamper's mother. Although she'd split her sizable estate equally among Swamper, Lulu and Stormy -- and set aside $20,000 for each grandson's college education -- Swamper wanted more. She offered each daughter $50,000 on the spot to give up the promise of $250,000 at age 40 as provided in the trust. She also had plans for the college funds.

Lulu apparently did Swamper's bidding and got her grandmother's clunky old car in the bargain. For once, Stormy took our advice and refused. By the time Swamper finished contesting the trust, it had shrunk by $200,000. Stormy eventually got enough for a downpayment on a nice house.

* * *

Denny's brother Jerry was diagnosed with multiple sclerosis. Apparently unaware of the debilitating, irreversible nature of the disease, Jerry was grateful the doctor hadn't found a tumor. As Denny sadly observed to me, a tumor could be removed. We offered financial help, but Jerry insisted he was fine and continued working six and seven days a week. His stepdaughter needed drug rehabilitation.

My 84-year-old, 90-pound, diabetic mother-in-law Marge wasn't eating or cleaning her house much anymore. Her neurotic cat, which shed, shit and sprayed all over her carpet and furniture, attacked her, puncturing holes in both hands, her arm and her foot. After several days of intravenous antibiotics, the cat struck again. When her diabetes flared, Marge wss sent into a nursing home before she moved into the same assisted-living facility where Paul Wetzel's father spent his final days with pneumonia.

My 49-year-old jobless brother Dick chased a bottle of Tylenol with beer when his credit card balance hit $40,000 and he received another job rejection. Mom found him in time, but his liver was damaged.

With an interest rate of 25 percent, Dick's debt quickly doubled. I slipped him a few bucks but decided not to lift him from his financial pit. I knew he would just borrow again, and Denny would throw a fit if he discovered my involvement. Instead, I advised Dick to declare bankruptcy before Congress cracked down on the practice. He did, undoubtedly sending my debt-averse Dad into spasms in his grave.

Denny designed himself another tattoo and got his other ear pierced. He'd started with narrow bands of Egyptian eyes of Horus on his biceps and a single earring in one of his lobes, acts that drove his mother to tears. But now he had a devil drawn between his shoulders and poked a ring through his cartilage.

* * *

As Denny's infected ear festered, my abdomen revolted against hormones I took for hyperplasia. After six months of waking in the wee hours of the morning to worry about my gut, I asked my gynecologist what she could make of the small lump near my left armpit.

On October 19, Dr. Regina Rosenthal performed a needle biopsy on the lump. I had sent Denny golfing so he wouldn't waste his day in the waiting room. Even though I threw up and slept a lot after the biopsy, I felt fine about driving back to the valley alone to get the results while Denny met with the forester in Scofield. When he called from his car, I couldn't tell him I had breast cancer. "The news is good and bad," I told him. "We'll talk about it when you get home."

After I hung up, Mom and Stormy called. Mom changed the subject. Stormy worried my cancer would divert attention from the melanoma found in her eye days earlier. She expected to spend five days in a hospital radiation unit with a plutonium chip attached to her eyeball, and she needed us to babysit.

I turned to Mimi for sympathy:

As I drove home, I thought about what a nice fall I've had (aside from all the doctor appointments). It's been a decent life . . . one I'm not ready to leave, but if I do, I have few regrets. I'm sure glad we got to retire and have time to hike and walk through Scofield and Summit Park and bicycle with Sharon and Shimi.

While later admitting he didn't know breast cancer was deadly, Denny was supportive and sweet leading up to my lumpectomy. He bought me be an authentic, classic Eames chair, something I didn't fully appreciate. I'd just wanted a comfortable leather chair to read in.

Fortunately, cancer hadn't spread to my lymph nodes, but Denny urged me to do everything short of a mastectomy to prevent a recurrence. Months of radiation and chemotherapy were added to my schedule.

Meantime, the pelvic pain that sent me to the doctor in the first place continued unabated. Afraid I might get uterine or ovarian cancer, I consulted a new gynecologist. When he diagnosed endometriosis, qualifying me for a hysterectomy, I added that surgery to my 2000 calendar.

The loss of 28 lymph nodes from my left armpit caused my arm to ache at night, creating fears of lymphedema. For six weeks, I bore my chest for young radiology technicians Monday through Friday. My left breast ballooned. "I look like an aging camel with bulges where they don't belong," I whined to Mimi.

Then my 18-week chemo sentence began. Every three weeks I was injected with poison that triggered several nights of fluish fever, nightmares and leg aches. My brain seemed more sluggish than usual.

Willy perked me up after my first chemotherapy treatment. As he raced around our house playing with toys and Denny's rock collection, he periodically paused to give us kisses. We snuggled in bed for nighttime stories, which he "read" with my glasses perched upside down on his nose. He had memorized parts of The Little Engine That Could, Basho and the Fox and Chicken Soup With Rice.

By May of 1999, I felt tired, bloated and thirsty. My bones became brittle, and my right hand and knees started to swell with arthritis. I couldn't take estrogen for what ailed me because it fed my breast cancer. In fact, I faced 10 years of estrogen suppressants.

Menopause moved in. Hot flashes became a daily – and nightly – irritant. When I sat down to eat, I practically ripped off layers of sticky clothing. Two or three times a night, I threw off the bedcovers. I became a sugar freak and packed on pounds. After carrying 145 pounds around on my 5 foot 10 inch frame for so long, I was now tipping the scales at 162., making me feel fat, old and ugly. The urge for intimacy evaporated.

Surprisingly, I didn't get overly depressed through all this, largely because of support from my *Tribune* family.

Peter Scarlet had talked to Shirley Jones about my condition, and she spread the word within hours. Many of my previous peers expressed concern.

Lifestyle columnist Judy Magid, whom I learned was treated for breast cancer seven years earlier, assured me I'd get through it. Barbi Robison called and sent cheer-up cards once a week for months. Donna Lou Morgan, enduring lung cancer herself, gave me a pep talk. Lex Hemphill and Carol Sisco invited me and Denny to dinner. Jan Keller emailed regularly.

After first ignoring my illness, Stormy started showering me with gifts, meals, love and affection, which I lapped up like a starving cat. Mom, on the other hand, became upset when Denny and I planned a vacation over Memorial Day to celebrate the end of treatment. She had planned to visit Utah to decorate Dad's grave. "I'll just have to see if I can find someplace else to stay!" she retorted. She later explained that she wasn't used to me being sick.

Bottom line: Within a year of leaving work I had a disease that may have been caused or at least aggravated by stress and hormone replacement therapy. It was a blessing not to have to work while going through surgeries, radiation and chemotherapy. When tired, I could nap. I could spend much of whatever life I had left strolling along the beach, skiing with Shimi and camping with the grandkids. Thanks to *The Tribune's* ESOP.

* * *

Life mostly returned to "normal" after my cancer scare.

Denny and I were losing a lot of money in the stock market, fueling fears I'd have to get a job. I'd fired my first investment adviser for sexism -- addressing Denny instead of me about my accounts -- and then hired Terri Ellefsen's guy at Dean Witter who blamed my losses on my busy phone.

My focus on finances made me question my principles. George W. Bush, a shill for amoral Dick Cheney, was about to be declared President on a recount of Florida's election returns, and I was worried about the stock market and tax law. What had happened to my commitment to clean air and social justice? Had wealth warped my values?

Stormy started to unravel, dominating and shouting vulgarities at her sons and nephew Willy. A counselor told her that her feelings were valid, so she assumed she was always right. Her primary quest was to cut Brock's father and extended family out of his life for good.

She recruited Denny to supervise Winker's visits with Brock, supposedly to ensure his sobriety. When that didn't get rid of him, she offered to forgive $20,000 in back child support if he would walk away from the kid permanently. The sleaze agreed.

It wasn't long before Denny and I found ourselves in the eye of the storm.

With her counselor's help, Stormy decided we'd failed to shield her from child abuse. "I would kill anyone who hurt my child that way!" she declared. "Living with you was no better than living with Swamper and [Ped O'Fiel]!"

Reminiscent of her mother at the same age, Stormy denied us access to her children. She returned birthday cards and threatened to tell the boys we didn't care about them. Since spending time with my grandsons was one of my greatest joys, she knew this separation cut deeper than anything else she could do.

Willy still raised our spirits. Lula had found work at a call center where customers didn't see her dental deficits, and Willy spent weekdays in a holding pen (lousy day care) nearby. We took him many weekends, but Lulu still kept us away from her apartment.

I finally let myself into her apartment while she was working to see what was so secret. With a sick stomach and tears in my eyes, I videotaped what I saw and went home to unload on Mimi:

We can't in good conscience leave Willy with Lulu. The apartment was even worse than I'd feared.

Garbage, dirty laundry and bugs covered the floor three layers deep in that stinking sty. Next to the bathroom sink was a waist-high pile of shitty diapers covered with fleas or some other sort of crawling insects. The same bugs were crawling around in the half-open fridge, which contained rotted sushi, curdled milk, an empty juice container and some other indescribable muck. Countless Pepsi cups. pans and plates holding leftover, rotten food were strewn about. A package of green-tinged bologna lay beside Willy's bed. No wonder Willy always has diarrhea.

I should report to Family Services or just pick Willy up from day care and leave Lulu a note telling her where to find him when she cleans up her act. Sharon says I should wait for Denny to get home, but it's hard, imagining Willy in that filth. Poor little guy!

I started this note to Lulu:

You're forcing Willy to live in squalor, in conditions not fit for a dog. He is sick all the time because he lives in filth and eats garbage. His clothes stink. He lacks socks, gloves and a hat in below-freezing temperatures.

Something drastic must be done or we will refer you and Willy to Social Services. Then we all could lose him. We will keep Willy until his home is spotless and he is provided clean clothes and nutritious meals. Then, if and when he returns to your care, we will inspect your apartment weekly to make sure he has a decent place to live.

We sincerely hope you can surmount this problem, because all of us, and especially Willy, love you and want you to succeed. It is not our first choice to raise a 3-year-old, but we will if it comes to that.

Denny and I ditched the note but picked up Willy from day care and called Lulu. "We saw your apartment, Lulu, and we're keeping Willy until his living conditions are acceptable."

Three weeks later, after Denny had filed a neglect report and consulted an attorney about temporary guardianship, Lulu called. "Willy needs to come home now," she said. "I haven't wanted to call the police, but I will if I have to."

Though hardly spick and span, her apartment was tolerable. We left Willy there with mixed emotions, worried about his future but ready for a break from the chaos. Denny decided to hold off on the guardianship petition until Lulu slacked off again.

Denny's mother Marjorie Powers Green took her last breath three weeks later, February 19, 2001, giving Denny another time-consuming, emotionally draining job. With Jerry still working full time with a disability, Denny was left to put Marge's affairs in order and ready her home for sale. Besides planning the funeral, he figured out what bills to pay and where her assets were held and cleared out 50 years of accumulation with garage sales and trips to Deseret Industries.

Count on Stormy to aggravate the situation. Not that she cared about her grandmother. She'd mocked her for years. But she let it be known to Jerry's family that Denny felt put out. She contended that Jerry's wife Barbara, as a relative newcomer to the family, shouldn't inherit Grandma's keepsakes.

As if that wasn't enough, she accused Barbara of failing as a parent and school principal. "You even had to run to your mother begging for a job!" she declared over the phone.

In fact, Barbara had recently finished a tumultuous year as principal of Brock's elementary school, where she'd doted on our grandson. When pressured to resign over a teacher conflict, she helped her aging mother manage the family business.

Denny and I felt partly to blame for Stormy's mean streak. We should have set stricter boundaries when she was younger. We didn't stand up to her then or now because it was easier to withdraw to avoid conflict.

Continuing the cowardly trend, we sought solace in a new setting. Using Denny's inheritance, we bought 10 tranquil acres outside Temecula, California. Jerry helped Denny design a Japanese-style winter house with an interior fish pond and gardens that would blur the transition between nature and our living space. The location would separate us from strife with Stormy and enable me to keep an eye on my aging mother several months of the year.

---

[850] Harry Fuller email to Diane Cole February 10, 2013.

51 - Irrepressible Conflict Resurrected in 1999

The Tribune also was mired in conflict.

After acquiring TCI, AT&T decided *The Tribune* was not a "strategic asset." With the LDS Church's consent, AT&T sold the newspaper to Dean "Dinky" Singleton, a former member of BYU's communications advisory board who now co-owned MediaNewsGroup based in Denver.

What a horrendous shock for the former owners, including Jack Gallivan and the McCartheys, who planned to buy back the family legacy they called "the gift." Their first right of refusal to purchase the newspaper was with TCI, which no longer existed.

The LDS Church had exploited a chink in *The Tribune's* armor. By using the *Deseret News* to draft a $70 million lawsuit claiming AT&T mismanaged *The Tribune,* the church had promoted the sale.[851] It was only fair, church authorities apparently assumed, after the *The Tribune* was passed to TCI without *Deseret News* approval as required by the JOA.

Later it became clear that the LDS Church wanted *The Tribune* itself, but the next best thing was to find a new owner to cut those insulting Catholics from the picture.

Still chairman of Kearns-Tribune Corporation, Gallivan tried to discuss the latest sale face-to-face with principals of the deal but was rebuffed. "It was a pretty fancy conspiracy with the Mormon Church, AT&T and MediaNews," Gallivan lamented.[852]

The McCartheys quickly sued to retrieve their "gift," but they lost a seven-year battle, which cost contestants $60 million, possibly the most expensive private legal battle in Utah history.[853]

Legal filings showed that LDS executives scurried behind the scenes to undermine Kearns-Tribune even before Jack Gallivan and Dominic Welch orchestrated the TCI merger.

As early as 1996, when trying to figure out how to boost *Deseret News* circulation and change from afternoon to morning publication, Deseret News Publishing Company Chairman Glen Snarr and Texas consultant Gary Gomm discussed acquiring *The Tribune* for the church.

Snarr felt an arrogant and untrustworthy Welch, as NAC chairman, was blocking *Deseret News* plans to publish mornings. Welch had insisted that NAC could not physically print both newspapers for morning delivery without a new press, and it was up to the *News* to pay for a new press as well as offset higher delivery costs and the loss of ad revenue.[854]

In a February 24, 1998 memo to the LDS First Presidency, Snarr and Gomm described Leo J. Hindery, Jr., then president and CEO of TCI and a director of Kearns-Tribune, as disliking the way Welch and Gallivan did business. Hindery, claiming he'd considered joining the church, reportedly told the *Tribune* officers to "knock off" bad jokes and snide remarks about Mormons.

It was hard for me to imagine Gallivan, the community peacemaker who described LDS President David O. McKay as "a very dear, great man,"[855] making insulting remarks about the church. (I cannot say the same about Welch.) Snarr later admitted in court that he'd never heard bigoted or anti-religious statements from Gallivan or Welch.[856]

Gallivan later contended that *The Tribune,* at least until Jay Shelledy's tenure, had always insisted on telling the church side of things when covering controversial Mormon subjects. In fact, in 1983 he had written a *Guide for Publishers, Editors, Writers, Reporters, Columnists, Cartoonists and all Editorial Contributions* that called for meticulous objectivity when writing about the LDS Church and cautioned against needlessly embarrassing the church or its leaders.[857]

LDS leaders were understandably offended, Gallivan acknowledged, by Shelledy's "resurrection of the Mountain Meadows Massacre" in 1998.[858]

In that instance, LDS President Gordon B. Hinckley had ordered restoration of the decaying monument marking the graves of some 140 men, women and children attacked by Mormons while crossing southern Utah from Arkansas in 1857. The restoration itself, Gallivan said, was an admission that the church had something to do with [the slaughter], and he felt *The Tribune* had covered in detail and brought closure to the episode "in a book called Lights and Shadows back in 1984, I think it was." (*The Tribune* published Lights and Shadows of

Mormonism by Josiah Gibbs in 1909. I don't know whether Gallivan was confused or there was another such reference.)

When excavators dug up victims' bones in 1998, Gallivan continued, Shelledy "discovered [the massacre] as if it had happened yesterday, and doing what he did with it would be like resurrecting the Spanish Inquisition and giving it four full pages." Shelledy gave the story more play than the moon landing or the close of World War II, the retired publisher complained.

"I was devastated when I saw that, because I knew exactly what was going to happen," he said. "I thought it was so anti-Fitzpatrick, anti-Gallivan. So unnecessary." If it were up to him, he added, he would have given the story "one solid hit inside but I sure as hell wouldn't have revived the whole Mountain Meadows Massacre, displayed it as it was displayed.[859]

At least in part, I had agreed with Shelledy on this story. A four-page spread might have been a bit much, but church officials should have expected journalists to revisit such horrendous chapters of their history.

And as Gallivan conceded, the church had "already made up its mind" -- before this massacre story went to print . . . that it should own *The Tribune.* "When we merged with TCI, they saw the opportunity to take over."

The 1998 Snarr/Gomm memo claimed Hindery wanted to circumvent the original *Tribune* owners' right to buy back the newspaper so he could sell *The Tribune* to the *Deseret News* at "market price" rather than at a premium. TCI Chairman John Malone supposedly went along with the plan (also hard to believe, given Gallivan's long relationship with Malone). The drawbacks, according to Snarr and Gomm, were that Welch couldn't be fired on a whim by TCI and the "repurchase" document was flawed.[860]

LDS authorities later informed Gallivan that Hindery came to them about buying *The Tribune,* not vice versa. Hindery reported told them in 1997 they should consider buying *The Tribune* if they didn't like NAC management.[861]

Deseret News Editor John Hughes looked forward to the church owning a combined morning paper. He intended to fire humor columnist Robert Kirby, whose "Johnny-one-note stuff is Mormon-bashing," he told Snarr. The Rolly and Wells column could continue but would need to be "cleaned up."[862]

By June 1998, the *Deseret News* expected to buy *The Tribune* from TCI for $175

million. It planned to leave *Tribune* editors in place to maintain the appearance of independence from the church, thereby addressing anti-trust and public relations concerns.[863] *News* executives did not want the church portrayed as the single news voice in the state.

Before that deal went through, however, AT&T bought TCI. Owning a newspaper was not part of AT&T's mission, so Hindery, then with AT&T Broadband, reentered the picture. This time he suggested that Tribune Publishing buy back *The Tribune* for $175 million.

But the *Deseret News* hadn't given up.

Lawsuits were threatened over the buy-back option and anti-trust issues. Orrin Hatch, as a Mormon and chairman of the Senate Judiciary Committee, told AT&T he would not object to the *News* controlling NAC. Utah Gov. Mike Leavitt, another Mormon, also discussed the matter with AT&T.[864]

In October 1999, the church was about to seal the deal to buy *The Tribune* from AT&T when AT&T fired Hindery and aborted the sale. An anonymous AT&T memo summarized the situation: "Family wants to buy assets back. NAC not transferable . . . Church will not consent because it hates family . . . Family may not have the dollars."[865]

AT&T chose a third party, an outsider who offered $200 million -- more than either the church or Tribune Publishing had agreed to pay. Dean Singleton apparently assured Snarr that MediaNews "does not allow its papers to disparage anyone or organization on religious, racial or ethical grounds." Snarr expected relief from *The Tribune's* "snide, damaging stories."[866]

MediaNews also gave the church something else it wanted: a JOA amendment granting the *Deseret News* unambiguous veto power over future sales of *The Tribune.* It simultaneously removed Tribune Publishing executives from the board and management of Newspaper Agency Corp.

During the McCarthey fight to reclaim their legacy, the Kearns-Tribune family split apart.

Philip McCarthey, as chairman of Tribune Publishing and his family's spokesman, determined to rectify Gallivan's loss of the gift that Jenny Kearns had expected to stay within the family.[867]

His father, Kearns McCarthey, initially had looked up to Jack Gallivan as a big brother, staying in the background while Jack claimed the *Tribune* limelight. As the company's largest shareholders, however, the McCartheys grew to resent being kept at arm's length on company decisions. According to Philip, an angry Kearns twice blocked Gallivan's unilateral efforts to sell the newspaper in the 1970s.[868]

The McCartheys further felt snubbed when Gallivan failed to groom Tom McCarthey to succeed him as publisher. When Gallivan put his son Mickey forward as publisher, Tom McCarthey told the *Deseret News*, his family declared, "No way, never." [869] Dominic Welch became the "compromise candidate."

The McCartheys had disagreed with Gallivan's early cable television investment as well as the later stock exchange that sent their *Tribune* stock value soaring. When the plan to buy back the newspaper failed, they cut ties to the long-time publisher. It became their quest to make *The Tribune* a McCarthey legacy, as opposed to a Kearns, Fitzpatrick or Gallivan legacy.[870] But first, Tom McCarthey told the *Deseret News*, they would have to "bring him [Gallivan] down."[871]

Gallivan saw the TCI deal much differently. He had personally negotiated the deal to fulfill his pledge to Jenny Kearns, he told the *Deseret News* in 2001. Kearns descendants would avoid a tax hit while continuing to manage the paper until buying it back in five years,[872] he noted.

But Phil McCarthey argued that there would have been no deal in the first place if it were up to the McCartheys, and they were the ones who insisted on the buy-back provision.

As the McCarthey claim for *The Tribune* foundered, new owner Dean Singleton made major management changes. Dominic Welch retired, and Randy Frisch was dropped from NAC's Board of Directors. Joseph Zerby, whom Welch had fired as NAC general manager, became NAC president. NAC bought new printing facilities so the *Deseret News* could publish mornings.

Singleton stressed that *Tribune* news and commentary would remain independent from the LDS Church, and *Deseret News* Board Chairman L. Glen Snarr said, "This should put an end once and for all to the tiresome and ludicrous allegation that the *Deseret News* or its owners seek to control the voice of the *Tribune*."[873] As was later learned, it was no rumor.

Personally, I was amazed and disgusted at Shelledy's ability to stay on as editor after bad-mouthing MediaNews Group during the ownership skirmish and then shifting allegiance. His spin naturally had him calling the shots:

> *Under the condition that the current newsroom direction and staff would stay intact, and with an understanding on a couple of other issues, I agreed to stay on should MediaNews get the Tribune.*[874]

[851] Gallivan, May 2005.

[852] Ibid.

[853] Timeline, utahnewspaperproject.org.

[854] Michael Vigh, Elizabeth Neff and Kristen Moulton, "Paper Chase," *The Salt Lake Tribune*, June 9, 2002

[855] Gallivan, May 2005.

[856] Glen Snarr memo to Leo Hindery, "The Quest No. 4," Utah Newspaper Project/Citizens for Two Voices, November 19, 1997.

[857] Ure, Chapter 24, p. 172.

[858] Gallivan, May 2005.

[859] Ibid.

[860] Vigh, Neff & Moulton, June 9, 2002.

[861] Ibid.

[862] Ibid.

[863] Ibid, Letter from R. Gary Gomm to Steven Garfinkel, senior AT&T attorney, July 7, 1999,utahnewspaperproject.org home page.

[864] Ibid.

[865] Ibid.

[866] Ibid.

[867] Spangler, June 12, 2001.

[868] Ibid.

[869] Ibid..

[870] Ibid.

[871] Ibid.

[872] Ibid.

[873] Ibid.

[874] Linda Thomson, *Deseret News*, July 4, 2002.

52 - Olympic Setbacks and Success

Toward the turn of the century, Utah attracted worldwide attention when journalists reported how far organizers went to win the opportunity to host the Winter Games. Tom Welch and Dave Johnson were being investigated for fraud and racketeering for providing special favors -- bribes -- to International Olympic Committee members deciding Utah's bid. Mitt Romney was recruited from Boston to replace Frank Joklik as SLOC president.

Staffers Terry Orme, Lex Hemphill, Mike Gorrell, Chris Smith, Linda Fantin and Lori Buttars worked in the middle of the maelstrom. Orme woke at 5 a.m. each day to see what British and American news outlets were reporting on the scandals to ensure his team stayed one step ahead.[875]

The *Tribune* team uncovered conflicts of interest among Salt Lake Organizing Committee members like Earl Holding, the Sinclair Oil tycoon given a land swap and road improvements benefiting his ski resort. In a case of graft, Holding hired the guy who was supposed to review his proposal.

The discovery that SLOC paid $10,000 a month to Tom Welch to do essentially nothing after he resigned as president created another tempest. One journalist blamed the ethical lapses on one slimy staffer (Johnson?) hiding behind a stupid philanderer (Welch?).

In 2003, a federal judge acquitted Welch and Johnson of illegally influencing IOC members for their votes. By then, ten IOC members either resigned or were expelled over the scandal.[876] Oddly, Welch received a Distingushed Service Award from the Utah Sports Hall of Fame Foundation in 2016.

The scandals, expense of building new athletic venues and decades of hype from Mr. Gallivan fed my skepticism about the 2002 Winter Games. In fact, the prospect of working during the chaos of the upcoming Olympics was just another reason Denny and I were grateful to quit when we did.

We expected a horrendous boondoggle, especially with transportation. Utah had used the international event as justification for rebuilding I-15 through Salt Lake Valley, disrupting the commute for hundreds of thousands of residents for years. As many visitors would converge on Salt Lake City during the Games, clogging traffic, and those visitors expected a big party with plenty to drink, something Utah infamously restricted.

Then within months of the Games, Islamic terrorists crashed commandeered airliners into New York City's World Trade Center, the Pentagon and a Pennsylvania field, sabotaging our nation's sense of safety. Lulu was activated to temporary Army Reserve duty to help protect the Olympics, receiving dentures in the bargain. I was not reassured. Denny and I lived just five miles from the ski jump and other venues, after all.

After considering skipping town, I bought expensive tickets to the ski jump, aerials, snowboarding and cross-country races. We could only hope to sidestep traffic snarls and terrorists in the shadow of 9/11.

Seeing spectacular opening ceremonies on TV, Denny regretted passing up the chance to be there in person.

We limited most of our driving during the 16 days to trips to competitions within Summit County. Despite immense crowds at the venues, the freeway flowed smoothly up the canyon from Salt Lake Valley to Park City, and parking was a breeze. Organized busing made the difference.

Denny and I took turns attending the Games. One sunny day my brother and I watched tireless, taut cross-country skiers swish past at Soldier Hollow in Heber City. What we didn't know then was that winners from Spain and Russia had used darbepoetin, an endurance-enhancing drug that would strip them of their medals.

Wide-eyed Brock, given a rare pass to see us, watched skiers twirl high above us in freestyle aerials at Deer Valley. He shivered by Denny's side in the stands as snowboarders performed somersaults and turns at Park City Resort. Denny and I attended the men's ski jump at Olympic Park together, mesmerized by the ability of athletes to soar with ease and grace hundreds of feet through the crisp, clear air at Kimball's Junction. Switzerland's Simon Ammann, recovering from a serious injury, captured the gold.

On the spur of the moment one afternoon downtown, we sauntered over to the medals' plaza. Denny got through heavy security despite carrying a Swiss Army knife in his pocket. We missed the awards ceremonies featuring an inordinate number of Americans to the chagrin of Russia and South Korea.

We shied away from the nightlife, which reportedly turned Salt Lake City and Park City into lively, cosmopolitan night spots with free-flowing alcohol. We had to watch the showy fireworks finale from outside the stadium.

In the end, Denny and I deemed the athletic extravaganza a grand success. I had to concede, despite my cynicism and the blemishes of bribery scandals, that Utah did an exceptional hosting job. The LDS Church welcomed the world to its headquarters by making it easy to get a beer or cocktail. I concluded that the campaign to bring the Olympic Games to Utah was one of Jack Gallivan's greatest achievements.

It was easy for me to extol the undertaking from my position as a spectator. Thanks to ESOP, I didn't work unpaid overtime for untold hours like some of my friends did. But at least one of those friends regarded this Olympics experience as the climax of his career.

* * *

Lex Hemphill simply loved the 2002 Olympics.[877] As he'd done in six previous Olympics, he covered the sports side of the Games for *The Tribune*, welcome breaks from professional basketball and editorial writing.

He prepared well in advance for the Games, taking unpaid leave in 2000 to scope out Utah's Olympic venues and a six-month paid leave in 2001 to work from home. After private offices in Editorial and at home, it was "a shock to be back in the noisy newsroom with its constant phone calls and chaos."[878]

Hemphill interviewed athletes and researched their statistics. He related their personal stories of the challenges and passion that led to superhuman feats. He also helped uncover the seamier side of the Games.

This intense, exhilarating performance allowed Hemphill to leave *The Tribune* and even journalism on the highest of notes.

* * *

As visitors dispersed from the Winter Games February 26, Mom headed for the hospital in an ambulance after another heart attack. I got through airport security in a snap on my way to fulfill my new role as the dutiful daughter of a woman in decline. I would be making many trips

between Summit Park and Temecula in the years to come.

[875] "Tribune Editorial: Editor Orme ensured that Tribune will endure," *The Salt Lake Tribune*, July 29, 2016.

[876] Lex Hemphill, "OLYMPICS; Acquittals End Bid Scandal That Dogged Winter Games," *The New York Times*, December 6, 2003.

[877] Lex Hemphill interview with Diane Cole, March 4, 2014.

[878] Ibid.

53 - Editorial Department Evolves

Peter Scarlet filled me in on *Tribune* gossip during his chemotherapy sessions and in emails. His leukemia was tolerable as long as he got to do what he loved: write editorials.

In an email in August of 2002, he reported that Dinky (Singleton) had ordered staffers to email their editorials to "this chap named Bill Long out of New Jersey, who is a corporate editor for MediaNews Group." His Olympics report is vintage Scarlet:

A week or so ago, [Long] killed an edit Paul [Wetzel] had done on the ice skating scandal and the alleged Russian mobster squaring judges. He said "this isn't going anywhere." Paul was morose for the rest of the week and wrote hardly a thing.

I did one on the going and growing concern of editing sex, violence and swear words out of movies. Long rewrote it and turned the lead into a "dialogue" in a Hollywood producer's office, something I would not have thought of doing in a million years.

Some he doesn't much trifle with. He wants only local edits. When I've mentioned national or international topics, he is quite cool to them. He can be had, though.

He e-mailed Captain Kirk [Millson] this week and told him not to do one on the census stuff and Latinos in Utah. Kirk went ahead anyway, wrote it from a "liberal" perspective in which his "conservative" take was imbedded in it. His thesis was that large-scale illegal immigration hurt Utah Latinos, helping to ensure that they cannot advance because of an ongoing influx of new illegal immigrants who are happy to work much cheaper. Long thought it was good, according to an email he later sent Kirk. Weird stuff.

Kirk said he didn't have the heart, or rather meanness, to tell Paul about how Dick Scudder interviewed Tim Fitzpatrick Monday for the editor of the Editorial Page position. It was previously arranged and Tim showed up for work dolled up. He didn't even have his ubiquitous red sneakers on. Meanwhile, Paul, who put in for it at the new owner-management's request, has never been accorded an interview, according to Kirk. Supposedly, several in the newsroom put in for the job and Long said their search was a national one.

One thing is funny. Dinky himself said run letters, even those critical of his takeover. Only falsehoods and libel are forbidden. So last week we got several anti-Dinky letters and several pro-Dinky ones. Long in our meets bashed the anti-Dinky ones as stupid and said to forget most of them. When the letters showed up in the paper a day or two later, there were two or three pro-Dinky ones and one mild anti-Dinky one there. Interesting.

* * *

Kirk Millson had moved to Editorial in 2000 from the Copy Desk, where he'd quietly toiled for 18 years, usually working nights to the detriment of his young family. Now as a respected editorial writer working days, he expected his home life and ego to improve. But he soon found himself taking editorials home at night and weekends for more research and fine-tuning. Interruptions from his son, in particular, brought out his dark side, and he started dreaming of escape. He imagined driving to the ends of the Earth -- or at least the end of the road in Panama.

He did just that -- but with his 13-year-old son -- after Dean Singleton, "who thought I was stupid," bought *The Tribune* in 2002 and "fired my two best allies [Dominic Welch and Randy Frisch], who thought I was a genius."[879]

Work obviously was miserable for Millson if it inspired such a horrendous journey, which he chronicled in a book, 9,000 Miles of Fatherhood.[880] He returned to the job, but not for long. As he told it:

My time up there [in Editorial] was weird because Randy and Dominic were obsessed with the legal fight to keep *The Trib* and were often traveling after December 2002. We ran three [editorials] a day, most days, and with just three of us working it didn't leave a whole lot of time for deep thought or research. I wrote at least seven editorials a week, and often more. Some of those probably should never have run and might have been vetoed had Randy been around, but they ran and the shit hit the fan.[881]

His favorite memory of the department involved his editorial "linking falling test scores in Salt Lake City School District with rising enrollments of kids who spoke no English."

The newsroom was so appalled they started writing a story about it. Greg Burton actually called and interviewed me. Then Dominic caught wind of it and marched down into Jay's [Shelledy] office. "Why are you writing a story about Millson?" Dominic demanded. "Because he wrote that editorial," Jay sputtered. Dominic erupted. "I write the editorials!"

What a stand-up guy. He was my hero from that day on.

* * *

After heading up *Tribune* coverage of the Winter Olympic Games, former Associated Press Bureau Chief Vern Anderson became department editor, effectively silencing the Welch regime's conservative voice.

Both Millson and Scarlet left *The Tribune* that fall. Scarlet was losing strength to leukemia; Millson was sick of being unappreciated and overworked. Malin Foster, formerly a Utah State University journalism teacher, was hired to handle the letters to the editor. A third woman -- Marilyn Karras McKinnon from the *Deseret News* -- joined the Editorial staff.

Despite Singleton's conservative bent, Anderson swerved the Editorial Page so far left that I briefly considered applying for my old job. Realistically, however, I knew I couldn't go back after five years of freedom from deadlines.

* * *

In a series of phone calls and emails, **Dominic Welch** reflected on his bittersweet years as publisher.

How did he feel about hobnobbing with community movers and shakers, one of Gallivan's greatest strengths? I asked. He responded:

I have trouble discussing my time as publisher because it is a very sensitive issue for me.

First and foremost, it was the best business assignment I ever had. I particularly enjoyed working with the Editorial Board. Although we disagreed on most issues, it was a delight to fence with bright people like you and Harry Fuller. I enjoyed most that you were willing to argue for your position because few NAC staff employees were willing to do so. I even read all the books you gave me written by that crazy Texas woman [political columnist Molly Ivins]. And I enjoyed them.

In the end, it was the highlight of my career with *The Tribune*.

Philosophically, I believed that a newspaper with a strong editor doesn't need a publisher. In an agency arrangement like *The Tribune* had with the *[Deseret] News*, where the publisher has no control over production of the paper, the publisher is even more redundant. The primary responsibility of the publisher relative to the newsroom is to hire and fire the editor. My primary focus as publisher was to perform this function. And Shelledy was enough to keep me busy.

I agree that the publisher represents the paper before the public. Gallivan was the epitome of a great publisher. He was a great speaker, a funny storyteller, a man of strong moral and ethical standards, and an all-around good guy. You had to love Jack Gallivan.

Which also means that I was a total failure as publisher. I hated public speaking and was an introvert who hated to meet new people. I [used] a terrible sharp tongue when I was offended, and I disliked working with people I didn't trust. Consequently, I did little with the public other than our advertisers. I continued to spend most of my time with the NAC, the financials and the Editorial Board.

I wasn't selected publisher because I had the talent for it. It was just another in-house political move that benefited me greatly.

When Gallivan retired in 1983, he had two trusted associates with different abilities that he could count on -- Jerry [O'Brien] and me. So he decided we should divide the management between the two of us. I was elected chief executive officer, and Jerry was selected as publisher.

I still think it was a good idea. But by the time Jerry died [in 1994], Gallivan had become convinced that only his family could manage *The Tribune*. He wasn't interested in ownership, and he never considered money issues. He just wanted to control the editorial product. He also wanted [his son] Mickey to follow me as the CEO and publisher. With me in both positions, the combination was already done, and there was no successor in line to take my place.

Mickey would have made a good *Tribune* publisher. He has most of the good traits of his father. Unfortunately, Jack never considered that the major stockholders [McCartheys] would never allow this to happen.[882]

Welch said he still believed, as he once "foolishly" told *Salt Lake City Weekly* in a quote that generated a lot of flak, that he was both "the best president and the worst publisher *The Tribune* ever had."[883]

Welch definitely was different from Jack Gallivan, and he frustrated the hell out of me for failing to see the logic and reason of my editorial opinions and for refusing to stop trucks from pumping carbon monoxide into the mezzanine. Yet he hardly failed as publisher.

Actually, it was refreshing that he wasn't so involved with the community that we had to carefully avoid stepping on his cronies' toes. The sacred cow stamp, the signal for editors to keep hands off sacrosanct copy, was no longer needed. (City Editor Randy Peterson kept it as a souvenir.[884])

Welch was less apt to protect the Mormon Church from fair criticism. "I appreciated that you didn't kiss the behinds of all the LDS running the *News* and NAC," I told him.

I agreed that Mickey Gallivan would have been a better publisher than Tom McCarthey, who lacked ambition and the work ethic. Tom's siblings Sarah and Phil might have had the intellectual capacity and motivation, but both lacked news experience. Pugnacious Phil might have lacked the temperament to work well with the staff and local community.

What's more, the McCartheys were naive advocates of Jay Shelledy, a cruel, egocentric bull in a china closet who shifted his loyalty when the McCartheys lost their grip on their legacy. It fell to *Tribune* staffers to bring him down.

[880] Kirk Millson, 9,000 Miles of Fatherhood, Plain Sight Publishing, 2014.

[881] Kirk Millson email to Diane Cole, March 2, 2014.

[882] Welch, October 16, 2014.

[883] Ibid.

[884] Randy Peterson to facebook's Tribune group February 2, 2012.

[879] Kirk Millson interview with Tom Williams on Access Utah, Utah Public Radio, May 5, 2014.

54 - Raising Sweet Willy

In a bizarre coincidence, the nation's two highest profile kidnappings of the summer of 2002 occurred within 25 miles of our two properties 725 miles apart. First, 14-year-old Elizabeth Smart disappeared from her Salt Lake City bedroom (and was hidden, we later learned, 60 miles south of Temecula). Weeks later, the battered body of 5-year-old Samantha Runnion, snatched from her yard in Stanton, California, was found off the Ortega Highway above Lake Elsinore, about 20 miles from our avocado grove. The prime suspect worked in Temecula. My fertile imagination conjured up a conspiracy by Ped O'Fiel to implicate me and Denny in these horrible, infamous crimes -- just for kicks.

Ped O'Fiel had been on my mind since the Gruesome Twosome moved to Idaho, within driving distance of Salt Lake City. Lulu had sent me into a rage by taking Willy for a visit knowing her stepfather's fetish for little boys. "I didn't leave them alone," she claimed. When Willy started reporting "dreams" no 4-year-old should imagine, I lacked the power to intervene.

It was a huge relief, then, when Lulu asked us to take care of Willy so she could "play Army." She became a logistics lieutenant stateside for Operation Desert Storm, and sweet Willy moved in with us, becoming the light of my life.

Willy was hefty 5-year-old who excelled at sports but especially enjoyed schmoozing and protecting smaller kids. At 65 pounds, he wore Size 10 clothes and could hoist himself onto the kitchen counter with ease.

His creative comments kept us entertained. He said he didn't want to lose his baby teeth because his gums would be naked. When nodding off one night, he told me not to touch him or he wouldn't be able to find his dream. Then he smacked his forehead a couple of times and said, "I can't get the right channel! All the channels in my brain are zombie channels."

When Denny spent weeks at a time at our Temecula construction site, I stayed with Willy in Summit Park, taking him to preschool and kindergarten, soccer, tee-ball, swim and ski lessons, acting classes, playdates with other kids and doctors and dentists. Bedtime stories and snuggles were mandatory.

* * *

I began chiropractic sessions for numbness in my leg and arthritis pain in my back and neck. My left arm and both legs began inflating in 2004. I'd developed lymphedema in my arm after losing so many lymphnodes in breast-cancer surgery and needed physical therapy and a compression sleeve. My legs were another story: lipoedema, cause unknown. If I didn't massage the legs and wear compression garments daily, a physical therapist warned, I could develop elephantiasis. Swell.

My new plastic-looking limbs gave Stormy a new target for insults. I should plant my "big, fat ass" in my Subaru and "march right down" with my "Barbi legs" to pick up her sons on the rare occasions she needed an overnight babysitter.

She blew a gasket and "divorced" us when I supposedly encouraged 14-year-old Brock to spend spring break with us in California. We could only hope he would survive her and find us when he needed us.

He did drop in once he got his license a couple of years later. When Stormy got wind of his whereabouts, she threatened to confiscate his cell phone and car before locking him out in the rain and reporting him as a runaway. The police had to explain the difference between running away and being abandoned.

Brock moved in with friends from school soon after that, and we got to see him more often despite moving to California full time.

* * *

Toward the end of Lt. Lulu's two-year deployment, Denny and I took her and Willy to a child psychologist to help with their reunification. As Lulu waited outside, I showed the doctor photos of her apartment so he could help prevent a repeat performance.

"Why didn't you contact the police?" he sternly asked.

"I didn't want to lose him to foster care," I stuttered.

He insisted Willy would have been placed with us, and I knew I'd blown it.

The counseling session backfired. Lulu discounted Willy's discomfort and confusion and hardly changed her habits. "Get over it," Lulu told her son. "You live with me now, and you get what you get and you don't throw a fit!"

What Willy got was more time with the Gruesome Twosome and a move across the country when Lulu, despite her lying and slovenliness, became a captain. Denny and I were devastated. We felt like we'd lost our own child.

A change of scenery helped. We established winter residency in California and joined golf leagues that jump-started our social life. We spent much of our time landscaping and adding finishing touches to our artsy California estate but took time out to visit local wineries and stroll along San Diego beaches.

Despite my earlier complaints, I missed my connection to Utah's culture, which was surprisingly less politically conservative than Temecula's. But our adjustment was easier once we got to know more people outside of journalism and Mormonism, including police and military officers, accountants and engineers.

In 2006, I flew to New England to pick up 8-year-old Willy for a summer visit. A neighbor pulled me aside to report that he spent afternoons home alone.

I asked Willy what he would do if a "susbag" (his word for a suspect/scumbag) came into the house. "I'd punch him out or stab him with Mom's Samurai sword!" He couldn't call 911, he explained, because his mom would go to jail. When I asked another question, he shook his head, covered his ears and shouted, "Blah, blah, blah, I'm not listening!"

This time I alerted local family services, but privacy laws prevented caseworkers from promising me help. When the neighbor later called to say Willy was home from school by himself, my calls and letters to the school went unanswered. I was useless.

That fall, Lulu left Willy with the Gruesome Twosome during one of her military assignments and lied to Denny about it. He told her he was through with her.

We didn't hear from Willy again until he was 12. He called to ask for bail money for his mom, who'd driven on a suspended license. "You can afford it because you live in a mansion," he told his grandpa. Denny declined his request.

About this time, Ped O'Feil's daughter called for Stormy's number. She wanted witnesses in a case of child pornography distribution against her dad. Swamper, who had exposed her own daughters and grandson to the pervert, had turned him for seeking custody of their breeding bulldogs in divorce proceedings. No kidding. Ped O'Feil was added to the national register of sex predators, and Swamper moved in with Lulu and Willy back East.

55 - ESOP's Fables

Judy B. Rollins

Longtime staffers Bob Bryson, Jon Ure, Nancy Melich and Judy B. Rollins had left *The Tribune* before the end of 1999. Judy and partner Liz Haslam moved from their ranchette in Draper to a home with a view high in Salt Lake City's Avenues district.

Others, including Randy Peterson, Tom Wharton, Paul Wetzel, Lex Hemphill, Peter Scarlet, Gordon Harman, Terry Orme, Tim Fitzpatrick, Pat Bagley, Paul Rolly, Randy Peterson and Shirley Jones, hung on longer at the paper.

Still other *Tribune* acquaintances changed places in 2000. Kathy Kapos Stephenson, for example, moved from City Desk to Features to write about food. Dawn House covered liquor control and other business matters with Tom Harvey, Joan O'Brien's husband.

Jack Gallivan's annual autumn picnic at the Pig Farm in Snyderville was a bittersweet affair after the loss of *The Tribune* and in the absence Grace Mary Gallivan. The former publisher's gracious wife, whose porcelain pig collection inspired the estate's whimsical nickname, died in June 2000 from heart failure. Peter Scarlet normally hobnobbed (Scarletism) with Mrs. Gallivan during these convivial gatherings, but now he gravitated to Dominic Welch's wife Jeanette. Gay McDonough, assisted by her brothers, husband and children, continued the tradition of hospitality, but melancholy and nostalgia were now part of the mix.

At the picnic, Judy B. Rollins told Denny about the uncrowded, out-of-the-way artist community where she and Liz spent much of their winter. His ears perked up, and before long, we were perusing property along California's central coast. A visit to sculptor Richard McDonald's gallery and studio in Carmel jump-started his return to sculpture, beginning with a bizarre object he planned to make into a fountain.

While Denny sculpted and planned his dream house, I tended grandchildren, dealt with my health and fiddled with the stock market. I bought and sold Yahoo so many times my head spun. Each time I sold, the value skyrocketed. Denny then got into the act, buying up biotech stocks, which were growing like gangbusters. He planned to pay for his million-dollar mansion with his gains. Huh!

What difference did ESOP make in the lives of other newspaper people who had lived hand-to-mouth for so long? Did they become rich jetsetters, sorry spendthrifts, saps for sticky fingered relatives and crooks grasping for their dough, or something in between?

Some longtime employees sadly missed the ESOP boat by quitting before the buy-out.

Bob Blair got no more than $150,000 worth of ESOP despite having spent 40 years on the job. More than a drop in the bucket, to be sure, but nothing like some of his younger whippersnappers.

Barbi Robison retired in 1993 with just $20,000 in savings, but she received enough to keep her going. "If not for ESOP, I would be in a poor house living on Social Security," she said.[885]

Cathy Free came up short, too. In her words:

Because I started at *The Tribune* so young. I was told that I could not be "vested" in the paper's ESOP until I was 27, or some such age. [Eligibility began at 25; participation the following year.] I lost out on thousands of dollars because of it.

Honestly, I really did get screwed financially by this newspaper. Thankfully I am now making a very good living [as a writer for *People Magazine*]. It would have been nice though, not to have to scrape by when I was giving everything I had to *The Tribune*.

Getting out was the best financial decision I ever made. And career-wise, I could not be happier.[886]

Mike Carter left *The Tribune* before being vested in ESOP. "I left before Jay Shelledy and David Ledford arrived -- and sacrificed my shot at *Tribune* millions -- and I thank my gods every day that I did."[887] He didn't like the changes he witnessed from the outside. Still, he credited *The Tribune* for the training he needed to succeed at AP and in Seattle.

Shelledy's obnoxious columns notwithstanding, no ESOP recipients were murdered for their money. A couple of unscrupulous money managers cheated naive newspaper staffers like me, some staffers squandered their wealth, and a few found money-grubbing relatives on their doorsteps. For the most part, however, the the staffers maintained fairly modest lifestyles.

Several staffers kept on working while spending portions of their ESOP funds for new cars, remodeling or to repay debts. For the first time, some invested in stocks on their own, learning firsthand the meaning of the proverb "easy come, easy go." A couple steered their lives into completely new directions.

Rod Cushing, who managed funds for nearly 75 of those staffers, offered this frank observation:

> Too many spent lots of money on their kids, contributing to the next generation of worthless assholes. Kids have to create goals, achieve their goals and learn to live independently without a lot of assistance from parents. But too many [parents] have guilt feelings about what they could not provide for them earlier in life. Once a child asks for help, it becomes easier and easier to keep asking.[888]

At least 10 of Cushing's clients continued to work past 2014, supplementing their livelihood with ESOP withdrawals that would reduce their retirement income. "I have three [clients] on strict budgets because their retirement accounts are down significantly due to extravagant lifestyles and helping kids," he reported.

About 70 percent of Cushing's *Tribune* clients bought boats, cars or more expensive homes or upgraded the ones they had, he estimated. A few bought second homes in other states like Denny and I did, though Cushing couldn't think of any who designed and built one like we did.

Six of Cushing's clients lost everything to drugs, the high life, antiques or divorce, but he wasn't aware of any family breakups directly caused by the sudden wealth. "Of those who got divorced," he said, "their marriages were broken before ESOP." And while hard feelings resulted from kids failing to repay money they borrowed, families didn't dissolve over it.

One ESOP client didn't like his money tied up in an IRA, so he closed the account and paid $400,000 in taxes. "That $400,000 would have earned a lot of income," the money manager commented. "You can't fix stupid."[889]

By 2014, 10 Cushing clients had yet to spend a nickel of their ESOP largesse, something the conservative manager admired:

> Their lifestyles did not change, and they get great comfort knowing the money will take care of them later in life. One got about $1 million and never sold one investment. That account today is worth $6.8 million.

Some specifics:

Tom Baldwin took off for San Carlos, Mexico, soon after police ordered him to put down his dog for biting someone. Sailing became his passion, but he didn't enjoy his windfall for long. He died in 2002 at age 53, possibly from a melanoma.

Guy Boulton quit the Business Desk to help billionaire Jon Huntsman write an autobiography.

Despite receiving a hefty sum, **Bob Bryson** didn't change his lifestyle much after leaving *The Tribune* in 1999 after 30 years . . . "other than I spend too much time fly-fishing, chatting with cronies or on the computer."[890] He also retained a mild interest in *The Tribune,* which had changed "to fit the variant whims of the manager [Shelledy]."[891]

Ana Daraban, who became the "Shirley Jones of *The Tribune*" after working many years in the library/morgue/data center,[892] lived on the financial edged, closely monitoring her money, before ESOP.

This single woman used her ESOP income to buy a new Honda Civic EX in 1998, get a home mortgage in 2000 and pay off her parents's second mortgage.[893] When her Honda was stolen, she replaced it with a 2012 Hyundai Accent with "all of the bells and whistles." She intended to pay off her mortgage by age 65.

"After that," she said in 2014, "I don't plan to spend too much unless I become deathly ill from some ravaging disease." She elaborated:

The ESOP money is like having a second income and has helped buy things I think are important or frivolous at times. It's been good to know that I can actually live comfortably now and in the future. And, when I retire, travel around the country. I left my money to my goddaughter who is 21 now, and some to the AIDS Foundation, Utah Symphony and Catholic Community Services.[894]

Helen Forsberg and her bar-owner husband Lou Arnold bought a bigger home before acquiring a second home in Montana. Meantime, they spent more time drinking, and Helen frequently called in sick. She retired in 2000 and died at age 60 in 201 from complications of liver failure.

Helen's obituary described a kind, broad-minded woman who loved Utah art.[895] She had generously supported gay rights and AIDS research and raised two girls -- the daughter of her husband and the daughter of her best friend Marilee Higley.

"As a mother she was loving, hilarious and determined that her daughters take hold of the world and master it," her obituary stated.[896] "She taught her girls the value of laughter, generosity and to care deeply for others in thought and action."

Helen also had served on the boards of City of Hope, RDT and Art Access, and she was a certified Hospice and Utah AIDS Foundation volunteer. As dance critic for *The Tribune,* she had written about Ballet West founder Willam Christensen passing the baton to Bruce Marks, the renovation of Capitol theatre for dance companies, and interviews with Mikhail Baryshnikov and Bill T. Jones.

Harry Fuller and his new wife Janet Goldstein bought a house in Park City, where they skied almost daily winters. They also did a lot of traveling, and Harry maintained his interest in Utah politics.

Artist **Rhonda Hailes-Maylett** used her windfall to play the stock market, creating a plump nest egg while working. Laid off during a *Tribune* downsizing in 2011, she returned to school for a master's degree in social work, hoping she might someday work with disabled adults. She also invested in quality bicycles for staying in shape.

Rhonda Hailes-Maylett

Gordon Harman bought a new, nicer house.

Lex Hemphill and **Nancy Melich** carefully weighed the relative value of money and time before leaving *The Tribune* earlier than expected. They bought a second house near Nancy's daughter in Missouri and regularly traveled to see the kids, grandkids and Lex's mother back East.

When she quit in 1999, Nancy launched a new career as literary seminar director for the Utah Shakespeare Festival in Cedar City, where she spent a few months each year.

After the 2002 Olympics ended, Lex lacked a full-time job. Kirk Millson, a tall, square-jawed conservative from the Copy Desk, had assumed his editorial duties in April 2000, and despite Shelledy's high praises, nothing else was offered. So he quit and started writing from home for *The New York Times*.

The stress of the *Times'* last-minute deadlines was hard on Lex's heart, so he opted for exercise and the kind of public service he'd missed as a journalist. He trained for the Huntsman Senior Games as a race-walker, for which he earned several medals, and spent eight years on the Sugar House Park Authority, four as president. He also joined the state Public Records Committee, serving a term as chairman.

After an eight-month leave to test retirement, photographer **Lynn Johnson** submitted his resignation. The former Mormon launched into preparations to become a deacon for the Catholic Church.

Lynn Johnson

Shirley Jones stayed at Jay Shelledy's side as long as she could, using her wealth to buy her mother a house in Arizona and take her family on cruises. She became interested in a dance host on her favorite cruiseline, but neither was willing to move, so they eventually parted company.

After finally retiring, Shirley developed health problems related to a fall from a ladder and car accidents that broke several bones, including vertebrae. Pain killers and physical therapy became her crutches, but she didn't lose her zest for life. She started dating Frank Huff, who'd done artwork for *The Tribune* before Denny became director, and she continued hosting *Tribune* gatherings until moving to assisted living in 2016.

Retireee Shirley Jones hosts Christmas party.

Kathy Kapos Stephenson was too young for the million-dollar club, but she got enough ESOP money for a retirement nest egg that gave her a sense of security while working. As Sunday Arts editor in 2018, she was one of the few longtime staffers still on the job.

Life slowed down for **Tim Kelly** after *The Tribune*. He took photos around the Great Salt Lake, watched History Channel late into the night, coached softball, golfed and traveled with Sharon, me and Denny.

Contending his conscience was clear and his heart pure, Kelly aways slept soundly and ordered cheeseburgers wherever we went. It took him 10 minutes or so to dress his burgers with evenly spaced dots of mustard before biting into his idea of filet mignon. He often was the calm for Denny's storm.

He came to Denny's aid -- as he had done when Stormy and Lulu needed rescuing from the Gruesome Twosome -- by helping haul a ton of discounted tile to California. The rental truck didn't make it up the hill to our future house, so Tim and Denny unloaded, reloaded and unloaded the tile again at dusk in the rain. What a friend.

Because Tim left before 55, he didn't qualify for company retirement and health benefits. At a cost of more than $1,000 a month, the Kellys turned to private insurers and Utah's uninsurable pool for health coverage. ESOP paid those premiums as well as even bigger health-care costs ahead.

His ESOP funds also remodeled the Kelly house and help family members obtain cars and houses of their own.

In 2006, Tim was diagnosed with Alzheimer's, which eroded his independence and retirement cache for 10 years. Sharon, disabled from a stroke just months before his death, thanked ESOP for 10 good years of retirement together and then Tim's custodial care and her medical expenses.

Ann Kilbourn, struck with multiple sclerosis in her early 20s, also used ESOP proceeds for custodial care.

Mark Knudsen, who quit not long after we did, married artist Leslie Thomas and opened a gallery in Sugar House. He showed his art at Phillips Gallery downtown. The couple bought a second home in Moab, where they spent much of their time painting and escaping Salt Lake City's suffocating inversions.[897]

Ben Ling became a stay-at-home dad in Summit Park (where Denny's brother had designed him a home in 1993), "thanks in part to ESOP and marrying a hot software engineer" from Evans and Sutherland.[898] He had left *The Trib* in '95 for a tech support job at Park City Municipal, which was closer to home and required fewer work hours. "I kept my shares in KTC [Kearns-Tribune Corp.] instead of cashing out, so that worked out really well!"

After remodeling two houses -- one in Salt Lake City and the other in Montana -- and obtaining a law degree, **Joan O'Brien** announced in 2005 that she and Tom Harvey were adopting a Chinese baby girl and naming her after Joan's mother Donna.

I never would have expected Joanieo, as I called her, to take on that responsibility at this stage in life. Tom would be in his late 60s, Joan in her late 50s by the time Donna graduated high school. But Joan wanted a family and an heir, and she became a model mother.

She also spear-headed and helped finance an effort to preserve *The Tribune's* independence from the LDS Church. More on that later.

Joan O'Brien with daughter Donna.

Terry Orme and **Nancy Hobbs**, in their early forties and not feeling financially safe enough to retire, expanded their kitchen/dining room and added a deck and hot tub to their house in Sandy. Before long, Nancy gave up her job writing food features to become a veterinary technician. Terry, appointed managing editor for news after overseeing Olympic coverage, had yet to fulfill his most important role at the paper.

Randy Peterson stayed put until normal retirement age. When he "climbed on his bike for a last ride home from work March 27, 2015,"[899] as outdoors writer Bretty Prettyman put it, Peterson had completed 42 years at *The Tribune*.

Prettyman, who was ending his own 25-year *Tribune* career to write for Trout Unlimited, told Peterson *The Salt Lake Tribune* would "never, ever, be the same. You are an amazing human, Randy."[900]

Lori Buttars noted that Peterson was the first City Desk editor she had met at *The Tribune*. "I have always valued his kind journalistic and copy editing guidance."[901]

Ann Poore got a small windfall, even though her job began at the bottom of the pay scale   years after ESOP's debut and never improved much under Shelledy's regime. "I was quite pleased until I heard what others who did what I did got," she remarked. "I got such a small amount, comparatively, that staffers I know were stunned."[902]

Still, she left *The Tribune* years before her 65th birthday.

Pepper Provenzano, World Desk editor, moved to Tucson.

His 20 years at *The Tribune* were "lean and tough years, but I loved the experience and felt so alive in that newsroom, especially as editor of the World Desk, packaging national and international news."[903]

In a 2011 letter, Provenzano thanked Jack Gallivan for changing his life:

> Your decision to award TCI Cable stocks to *Tribune* employees provided a long and unexpected series of opportunities to me and my family. Because of you, I was able to purchase our home. Because of you, our two children, Mia and Conor, were able to go to college, study abroad and take music lessons. Because of you, we provided them many more opportunities in life that otherwise would have been impossible. And because of you, I was able to create TreeUtah, the nonprofit organization responsible for the planting of more than a half million trees in cities and towns all over the Beehive State. In addition, I created TreeLink, the urban forestry resource center at TreeLink.org now reaching 100 plus countries.

At a time when so many people are falling through the cracks of our society, I think of you and remind our family and friends of a kind and gentle man, a generous and astute businessman who provided for his "family" at *The Salt Lake Tribune*.[904]

I can't helping asking: Even without ESOP, shouldn't *The Tribune* have provided the kind of wages that would have enabled employees to buy a home and send their children to college and music lessons?

Dick Rosetta, who normally spent whatever he earned, used ESOP for pay off bills on his condo and cars. Otherwise, his life didn't change much -- except for his daily calls to his stock broker to check the market. As he approached his silver birthday, he conceded:

It's better to have the money than to not have it. It has been comforting to not have financial pressures, but I truly believe I was just as happy (or carefree) before the ESOP distribution. I guess I ALWAYS knew it was going to happen, so I depended on the ol' Newspaper Employees Credit Union when I needed it.[905]

A perpetually youthful man who loved writing *Tribune* sports for 39 years, Rosey waited until after the Olympics to leave. The opportunity to carry the Olympic Torch along 1400 East between 1500 and 1700 South in February offered a satisfying segue to his retirement in June. As did his 2002 induction into the Utah Sports Hall of Fame which led to 25 years on its Board of Directors.

Also sweetening his retirement years was his annual trip to Washington, D.C., where he saw at least 17 others inducted into the National Federation of State High Schools Hall of Fame after having received the honor in 1999. Stints on the boards of the M.S. Society and Crimson Club Hall of Fame further enhanced his free time.

Peter Scarlet used a small share of his millions to move into town, a godsend once his leukemia and diabetes treatments wore him down. This lonely single gentleman surrounded himself with voluminous history books in his sparsely furnished bungalow.

But Scarlet, who relied heavily on his mother and siblings for a sense of belonging, also got a glimpse of ESOP's darker side.

Soon after the distribution of funds, Scarlet succumbed to his sister's request for a new truck to get to work. Later, she wanted more, contending that her family needed the money more than Peter did. When he failed to come through, she blocked access to their mother, who lived with her. His heart broken, Scarlet left his money to the brother who helped him keep his vehicles in mint condition over the years.

Within days of his one-year anniversary of retirement as *The Tribune's* television critic, Arts editor and historian, 69-year-old **Hal Schindler** died of a heart attack December 28, 1998. He had been one of the longest serving *Tribune* staffers, matching John Mooney's 50 years but falling two years short of Art Deck's tenure at *The Tribune* and *Salt Lake Telegram*.[906]

As sad that it was Schindler didn't get more time to enjoy his wealth and free time, at least he died pursuing his passion. When he collapsed, he was on his way to do research for a book on the Utah War. And knowing Hal, he probably wouldn't have let loose of his millions.

Several of us so-called "old farts," Schindler included, got together monthly for lunch upon release from *The Tribune*. After his funeral, we irreverently joked about him keeling over after finally picking up the tab at the last lunch, which set the skinflint back a couple hundred bucks at Thanksgiving Point.

Hal Schindler

To avoid tax penalties, artist **Sam Smith** waited until 59 1/2 to cash in his stock. His long-suffering wife had died by then, so he handed out checks to his kids, added to his antique furniture collection and embarked on a new life with his new squeeze Louise, who'd caught wind of his wealth while clerking in the credit union.

Before embarking for Sequim, Washington, Smith and Louise unexpectedly invited us to dinner at his house and then showed up late with no food. We scoured Granger for a pizza and then watched slides of Smith's Navy days. That was the last we heard from them, but word got around that his riches ran out.

I bumped into **Jon Ure** a couple of times post *Tribune*: once at the liquor store, once at the grocery store. By then, he had split with his wife and bought a sporty BMW convertible and was spending money on drugs and fast women.

He looked like hell. His teeth were rotting, his hair thinning and his gut bulging from his skin and bones. As always, though, he retained his winning, understated sense of humor. "The DEA is watching my house," he chuckled. "They don't get it that I'm the customer, not the dealer."

Lung cancer bought Ure down in 2005 at age 59.

"Jon was one of a kind, a really good reporter when he wanted to be," Anne Wilson said of him on facebook. [907]

After spending 15 years at *The Tribune* before returning to teaching, **Carol VanWagoner** "will forever thank the Kearns-McCarthey family for their generous ESOP plan. While it didn't provide enough to immediately retire, it provided an incomparable cushion that I never could have achieved working in education."[908]

Anne Wilson quit for a time, taking a job at REI sporting goods, before returning to *The Tribune* as Features Editor, a job she still enjoyed in 2014. Her husband **Con Psarras**, by then preparing to retire from a second career in broadcast news, eventually would become an adjunct communications teacher at the University of Utah.

* * *

Tom Wharton kept writing for *The Trib* well beyond ESOP's distribution.

After ovarian cancer took his wife Gayen in 2004, Wharton cruised to the Caribbean with us, the Kellys and Shirley Jones. It wouldn't be easy for him to get over the giant role Gayen played in his life, I assumed as his expansive heft nearly sank the kayak we shared on an excursion.

Gayen and Tom, their four children in tow, had written several outdoor magazine articles and books together. One book, The Southwest's Four Corners, was sold from *The Tribune's* makeshift mezzanine "store" and local bookstores.

Gayen's zeal for local causes sometimes tired me out, but her activism paid off for her community. As an environmentalist, she installed solar power in her old house and xeriscaped her yard ahead of the trends. She taught conservation to her grade-school students. As a community council member, she worked for historic preservation and established a community home for teens.

To my surprise, an NAC employee hitched her wagon to Tom soon after Gayen's passing. Yet this Wally Cleaver of the Sports Desk [909] waited until 2016, after devoting more than half a century to sports, features and even business stories, to give up his full-time gig as a journalist. As late as 2018, Tom Wharton bylines still appeared in *The Tribune*.

As with Rosey, sports reporting was integral to Wharton's identity -- money or no money. He had begun covering high school athletics in 1967, when girls' contests were still ignored or non-existent. He loved giving readers tips on places to see and eat -- places like Ray's Tavern in Green River, his hamburger heaven.

Among Wharton's most memorable assignments were the 1979 NCAA Final Four with Magic Johnson and Larry Bird in Salt Lake City, the 1993 NBA All-Star Game and several 2002 Olympic events. But his favorites were small time. One featured the basketball team fielded from two tiny high schools -- West Desert and Eskdale -- near the Nevada border. Another described the barn-raising effort to create a restroom in Kodachrome Basin without state funding.

[885] Robison, November 13, 2015.

[886] Cathy Free, June 5, 2015.

[887] Mike Carter on facebook August 27, 2015.

[888] Rod Cushing email, February 8, 2014.

[889] Ibid.

[890] Robert Bryson email, August 4, 2015.

[891] Bryson, August 4, 2015.

[892] Ana Daraban at Tim Kelly's Celebration of Life March 7, 2015.

[893] Ana Daraban email in 2014.

[894] Ibid.

[895] "Helen Forsberg, former Tribune dance critic, dies," *The Salt Lake Tribune*, April 20, 2012.

[896] "Helen Elizabeth Forsberg, 1951-2012," *The Salt Lake Tribune,* April 22, 2012.

[897] Mark Knudsen, February 25, 2014.

[898] Ben Ling email December 26, 2013.

[899] Brett Prettyman on facebook, March 27, 2015

[900] Ibid.

[901] Lori Buttars on facebook, March 27, 2015.

[902] Ann Poore, August 4, 2015.

[903] Pepper Provenzano letter to John W. Gallivan April 4, 2011.

[904] Pepper Provenzano letter to John W. Gallivan, April 4, 2011.

[905] Rosetta, August 2, 2015.

[906] Arthur C. Deck, T*he New York Times*, March 14, 1981.

[907] Anne Wilson to Tribune facebook group, February 10, 2012.

[908] VanWagoner, August 10, 2015.

[909] Paul Rolly, "Goodbye to Tribune's Tom Wharton, who took us to high school gyms, Utah's outback and more," *The Salt Lake Tribune*, March 31, 2016.

56 - Downside of Sudden Wealth

Jesse White, a name fabricated to protect his family, resembled Ringo Starr. According to his ex-wife Pauline, another alias, Jesse felt deprived and abused as a child but learned to charm his way into getting what he wanted.[910]

Jesse's Depression-era parents "could make a penny scream," Pauline told me in an email. When he realized their frugality had produced a $3 million nest egg, Jesse started taking "loans."

Pauline was hardly more than a child when she met the likable, divorced Vietnam veteran. Hanging out at D.B. Cooper's with people she recognized from bylines seemed glamorous to her, and before long she was married with children -- and swirling in the spiral of Jesse's addictions. "I tried to put on a good front," she wrote.

Jesse drank afternoons away at a downtown pub, eventually ending up in expensive rehabilitation programs and regularly falling off the wagon. He turned to dope for a high once his *Tribune* drinking buddy died from cirrhosis and his own doctor warned him of a similar fate.

Jesse wanted Pauline to attend *The Tribune's* ESOP meetings with him. "I felt weird because not many spouses were there," she said.

Everyone there was shocked to learn their share of the profits. Pauline "almost fainted."

She and Jesse quickly planned their new life. They would move to a better neighborhood, and Pauline would quit work to see their oldest child, who had addictions of her own, through high school. Except for their house payment, they'd live much the same off Jesse's salary and build up savings for retirement, when they would start enjoying their wealth.

But not all was right with the White world in 1997. Pauline's mother's silver disappeared one piece at a time. Then jewelry, including Pauline's wedding ring, went missing as Jesse pawned them. Young women at *The Tribune* started avoiding eye contact with her. Jesse claimed he was being hit on because he was so desirable and had hit it big with ESOP.

Jesse started spending a long time in a locked bathroom at home and staying away at night. "I was still blind and stupid." Pauline said. "I believed his story of constipation when he was shooting up."

That spring, Pauline crashed her car, killing her mother. In her depression, she turned over family finances to Jesse.

"This was like giving a cat its own catnip patch," she recalled.

In February 1998, when an investment officer called about supposed home renovations, Pauline discovered her $150,000 inheritance had disappeared. The Whites' savings account contained $30, and their checking account was overdrawn. Jesse had spent $320,000 in ESOP funds over seven months. "I felt I had been disemboweled," Pauline wrote. "I threw up for hours."

Realizing Jesse could take everything and leave her with the bills, Pauline got the name of a divorce attorney. "I was in shock but still thought I loved Jesse. I knew I would crumble if I needed to be mean."

While Jesse was away for a weekend, Pauline got a call from their charge-card company about some Nevada spending. She immediately closed the account. The divorce papers were served at work "because I never knew where he was."

During a year-long divorce process, the court granted each a $4,000 monthly allowance and froze the rest of the ESOP. Pauline, "still an enabler," helped set Jesse up in an apartment. Jesse bought an expensive sports car and took in three Nevada dancers, one of which he drove over to Pauline's place in his new car.

He really thought I would let him show the bimbo around my house! He also thought I would like to go for a ride with the two of them. Drug brain! My Cocker Spaniel jumped up into her lap and peed on her and the passenger seat and carpet of the car. What a good dog!

Although Jesse told family and friends Pauline divorced him because she was a lesbian, the same thing he'd told Pauline about his first wife, he defended her against his aggressive attorney in divorce meetings. On their 20th wedding anniversary, they met without their attorneys and worked out the details. She got half of what was left of ESOP.

Then their children's health insurance ended, and Pauline called Shirley Jones for an explanation. "Why would you divorce [Jesse] when he loves you so much?" Shirley wanted to know. Pauline burst into tears, and Shirley quietly asked, "It's drugs, isn't it?"

The insurance ran out because Jesse was working part time. It wasn't long before he quit altogether.

The Whites' teen-age daughter moved into Jesse's new place, where raucous parties featured strippers cavorting in the hot tub. She escaped arrest in a drug raid because small amounts of pot, acid and pills were found in Jesse's bedroom, not hers.

By this time, Jesse "looked 80 and had a horrible cough," Pauline said. He refused to see a doctor until his youngest child took him "for a ride" to ER. His cancer was Stage 4.

Jesse gave Pauline his medical power of attorney as "the only one he could trust." She was incredulous. "This is horror movie material if you ask me!" she remarked. "You cannot express your wishes and your ex is in charge of pulling the plug?"

Jesse left with a couple of last laughs. His brother described the scene at his death bed:

As [Jesse] lay dying at the University Hospital, two strippers, Dixie and Trixie, were sobbing at the end of the bed, their makeup drizzling down their cheeks. He motioned me over to the bed and said, "You know that money I got from *The Tribune*? I sure had fun spending it." I think Dix and Trix were grieving a great loss . . . his *Trib* dough.

The family stayed in intensive care while Jesse passed away in a morphine haze and the two "dancers" stripped his house of valuables.

His money gone, Pauline paid for his cremation and surreal graveside service. Beside Pauline's Mormon relatives stood Jesse's brother, a few guys from *The Tribune,* a female guns-rights activist and a handful of strippers who'd benefited from Jesse's generosity. He'd spent tens of thousands of dollars on each of their surgical enhancements.

A couple of the young woman wore tight jeans and sweaters to show off double G implants, Pauline remembered. Another wore a tight, Asian silk dress slit up to her pantyless waist, while still another showed off a body barely covered by the ruffles of a black, Spanish-style dress.

Pauline stifled giggles at the strippers' obvious attempt to shock and the Mormons' attempt to hide their shock. The two groups acted like they didn't see each other. Jesse would have loved the hilarious scene, she said.

The aftermath for Jesse's family wasn't so funny. His daughter dealt with memories of child abuse and addictions of her own. A fraudulent investment took more than half the money Pauline had left.

What did this experience do to me? I do not trust men. I date a few times and then do not see them again.

I can't blame ESOP for my lack of trust. All the things that came out so strongly in Jesse were there before the money.

He was poly-addicted: alcohol, speed-type drugs, downers to come down, sex and gambling. The money made it worse. Perhaps without it he would have sought serious help because he would have had to.

There was a positive outcome for Pauline. "I finally get to do all the outdoor things I always loved doing but Jesse hated," she said, referring to backpacking, assisting with archeological digs and rowing rafts on Class IV and V rivers.

---

910 "Pauline White" email December 15, 2013.

57 - Other *Tribune* Endings - Some Happy, Some Not

Jay Shelledy resigned May Day 2003 after 4,444 days as editor (by his obsessive calculations) over violations of the ethics guidelines he so assiduously produced and pompously presented in 1997.

Without his knowledge, his star police reporters -- Michael Vigh and Kevin Cantera -- had leaked sensational, erroneous information from the Elizabeth Smart investigation to the *National Enquirer* for $20,000.

While Elizabeth was held captive in California as a homeless religious zealot's "wife," the *Enquirer* reported July 2, 2002 that her father Ed and uncles Tom and David were part of a homosexual sex ring. Apparently Vigh and Cantera had relied on police reports to speculate that a member of this so-called ring was involved in the kidnap.

"Pity the fools," Tom Smart thought at the time. "One thing I was really sure of is that it wasn't me.[911]

Denny and I, who knew Tom as a *Deseret News* photographer, also were damned sure it wasn't him.

Vigh and Cantera had sold rumors from the police probe to the *Enquirer* nine days after the kidnapping in 2002. Shelledy claimed he didn't learn about the indiscretion until April 17, 2003, nine months later. He waited another 10 days to disclose it in his weekly column.

Coming across as unrepentant and proud, Shelledy wrote that Vigh and Cantera had "led the way on the Smart story and were recognized by most outside media as the most knowledgeable in the reportorial litter." He had encouraged the pair to participate in television interviews, and he now contended their leaks were neither illegal nor unethical but "akin to drinking water out of a toilet bowl -- dumb, distasteful and, when observed, embarrassing."[912]

The *Enquirer's* claim that his reporters were its sources was "baloney," he declared.[913]

Shelledy's reaction, an embarrassment itself, was *almost* understandable. As a young journalist, he had gone to jail rather than reveal a white supremacist as his news source. As editor, he had cultivated Vigh and Cantera as a

hard-hitting team he referred to as Vightera, much like *Washington Post* Editor Ben Bradlee did with "Woodstein" in the Watergate saga.[914] Within days of Elizabeth Smart's disappearance, the duo was introduced on television as the Bob Woodward and Carol Bernstein of Salt Lake City.

"They not only weren't Woodward or Bernstein," Tom Smart told the *American Journalism Review*, "but they didn't have Ben Bradlee either . . . Ben Bradlee could have saved their ass."

When Deputy News Editor Vern Anderson questioned Vightera's sources at the height of the Smart story, Shelledy told him to back off and urged the pair to stay out front on it. He ran the two "to a degree that I had not experienced at the newspaper,"[915] Anderson said. When Shelledy ordered Anderson to keep hands off their "abortion" identifying Tom Smart as the family member under investigation, Andersen walked out.

Vightera offered to resign and reveal their sources once the *Deseret News* reported their $20,000 deal with the *Enquirer* and the Smart family threatened to sue. Shelledy simply slapped them on the wrist for failing to get his permission for the arrangement. He removed them from the ongoing Smart story and barred them from freelancing for a year.

Cantera told Kelly McBride of the Poynter Institute that Shelledy had given him carte blanche to talk to other media outlets. "We never had to get specific permission."[916]

The *Tribune* newsroom went ballistic over the obvious breach of ethics. Reporter Christopher Smart, Elizabeth Smart's relative, said the staff looked like a "lynch mob."

Staffers were enraged that Vightera's checkbook journalism -- and the editor's tolerance of it -- harmed the Smart family and undermined *Tribune* credibility. Some were also upset that another writer, who was put on probation without bylines for a year for plagiarizing an online encyclopedia, received harsher treatment for a milder infraction.

Forty-three writers and editors signed a published apology demanding that Vigh, Cantera and Shelledy be held accountable. Their statement, as published in the newspaper, read in part:

Editor James E. Shelledy initially characterized the reporters' conduct as a violation of the newspaper's freelancing policy and labeled it "distasteful." We believe it goes beyond that. We believe what they did violates the basic tenets of journalism . . . We are committed to the highest standards of integrity and, to the extent our credibility has been damaged, we will work to repair it.[917]

Shelledy undoubtedly regretted standing behind his stars when he learned that Cantera had described *Tribune* editors as "lightweights" unlikely to scoop the *Enquirer* on details of the Smart case.[918] Regardless, he claimed in a later column that he fired Vightera for selling the *Enquirer* more than background material.[919] He apparently was more incensed about his reporters lying to him and damaging *The Tribune's* reputation than violating journalistic standards and undermining the Smart case.

Tribune Publisher Dean Singleton described this episode as the worst in his newspaper career.

"When I heard the full facts of the story, I felt like I was going to vomit," Singleton said in an interview from Seattle, where he attended a meeting of the Newspaper Association of America. "I'm hurt by this, angered by it and embarrassed by it. And we will do whatever it takes to win back the community's trust."[920]

The MediaNews magnate flew to Salt Lake City to personally apologize to the Smart family, meet with the staff and accept Shelledy's resignation.[921]

Shelledy said he was tired and *The Tribune* needed new direction after his 12 yeas at the helm. "It will take a new editor to bring an end to the newsroom contention over what will forever be known as the *Enquirer* affair."[922]

Some *Tribune* staffers shed tears as they bade the boss farewell; others breathed a big sigh of relief.

Reader Advocate Connie Coyne's column that week noted that *The Tribune* had lost a portion of the trust and credibility its staff spent decades building. She wrote:

Monday in the Tribune *newsroom was like the inside of a hornets' nest after some fool whacked it . . . We are sorry for the damage done by former reporters, because they forgot their ideals. The Smart family -- already wounded by a terrible crime -- suffered again through the actions of two people who used to sit next to us. We are sorry.*

Rachel Smolkin of *American Journalism Review* put a positive spin on the Shelledy era, describing him as a "bearish 60-year-old . . .

widely credited with energizing and elevating *The Tribune*" by replacing staffers and hiring Jim Fisher to modernize the paper's layout, art and design . . . He displayed willingness, even zest, for taking on sacrosanct government and religious institutions, including the Mormon Church.[923]

There is more than one way to skin a cat.

Yes, Shelledy replaced a lot of long-time staffers, including valuable Doug Parker and Joe Rolando. Jim Fisher was not his best hire. Some might conclude the editor delighted in antagonizing the Mormon Church to the detriment of the newspaper's future independence.

Managing Editor Tim Fitzpatrick helped set the record straight with Ms. Smolkin. "Jay can be and often was a nasty and arrogant boss," he said, explaining that he could be stubborn and capricious, a micromanager who created a star system and undermined his editors by going directly to reporters.

In remarks written but undelivered at his own retirement years later, Paul Wetzel blamed Shelledy for weakening *The Tribune's* sense of "family togetherness:"

He gave the old Tribune *the shaking it needed, producing innovations that included outstanding Faith and Outdoors sections, aggressive reporting and trenchant local columns. He recruited new talent. Unfortunately, he also was a mercurial egomaniac who delighted in keeping everyone off balance. Bligh and Ahab had nothing on Jay, and like them, he lost his ship through his own folly.*[924]"

From my perspective, Shelledy diminished big, often admirable ideas for a better *Tribune* by being small. His obsession with his own image took priority over the the success of his staffers. His disloyalty -- shifting allegiance when his superiors were losing the tug-of-war for *The Tribune* -- set a bad example for employees. By then, of course, he'd already undermined staff loyalty and cohesion by pitting employees against each other.

The ultimate irony of this episode came when the LDS Church wished Shelledy well. "While we had our differences," LDS Spokesman Bruce Olsen said, "we enjoyed a cordial and constructive relationship."[925] Had church authorities so soon forgotten who was behind those stories so embarrasing to their institution -- or had Shelledy defected to their side?

In any case, Singleton replaced Shelledy with *The Tribune's* first female editor before the smoke cleared from the newsroom. Nancy Conway, a longtime trusted colleague who led Singleton's ANG Newspaper Group in Northern California, crashed through the newspaper's glass ceiling. At last!

Shelledy brazenly moved to Louisiana State University to teach mass communication ethics, of all things. Yes, he knew about ethics -- from the underside of the issue. But the hypocrisy doesn't end there. He was the one who often repeated the old slur, "If you can't, teach."

And speaking of teaching, Shelledy's protege Jim Fisher became a popular journalism instructor at the University of Utah -- before being accused of sexism and moving on.

* * *

"Gentle Jack" Schroeder died November 6, 2002 at age 79. Our sports writer/mentor had covered the Olympics in Munich and lived to see the Winter Olympics in Salt Lake City. He spent his last days in St. Joseph's Villa, a nursing home, and was buried in a Ute baseball cap signed by winning football coach Ron McBride, who had visited him at his deathbed.[926] Schroeder left no survivors.

Except us, his friends.

Dick Rosetta expressed the loss many of us shared.

> I will miss "Gentle Jack." As I am sure many will. As I held his hand at the Villa the other day after our luncheon, I told him thanks for the memories and thanks for being a great teacher. I also told him that when I am inducted into the Utah Sports Hall of Fame next Thursday, I will make mention of the guidance he provided that ultimately paved the path into the hall. I also told him I loved him, which, I speculate, is all that Jack really wanted from life from us all. The unanswered questions? Perhaps it is best -- as Lynn [Johnson] suggested -- that they go into eternity with Gentle Jack. I just know he is in a more peaceful place where they don't ask questions.[927]

With retired photographer Lynn "the Bishop" (Scarletism) Johnson executing his wishes, Schroeder threw one last *Tribune* party, a rousing wake. Finishing off the liquor left from previous bashes, celebrants got sick one last time at Jack's expense. I missed it, but Bob Woody assured me it was:

> " . . . one of the best parties ever at the House that Jack Built orchestrated by the Deacon [Lynn] Johnson and Mother Jones and assorted friends. It was a love and laughter fest with attendees from all the generations that have ever known Jack. No bitching. No fist fights. No back-stabbing. No grousing. No mean mocker. Jack was there! We just kind of felt he was out in the kitchen fetching up some more chicken legs.
>
> The morning mass was without melancholy. Deacon Johnson did the honors for the homily. The music was elegantly simple -- a cantor with the most hauntingly beautiful voices I've ever heard. A class happening. We all left Jack's loving each other very much and very grateful for the times we had had together.[928]

Johnson described the event, attended (and bar-tended) by his two children, as the best time in his life.

* * *

Food Editor **Donna Lou Morgan** died October 14, 2003 at age 75 from lung cancer. She neither smoked nor drank alcohol, but she toiled in that polluted newsroom off and on for 34 years, inhaling second-hand smoke all the while.

Myrlene Korologos, the "admiral" of our River Crew, also died from lung cancer August 18 of the same year at age 65. Although a heavy smoker, her habit reportedly did not cause her illness.

Our group of 10 would never be the same without Merky's outstanding organizational skills and soothing, smoky voice. Her husband Mike would not have her by his side for a momentous milestone in his life.

* * *

In 2004, Mike Gorrell wrote about **Mike Korologos'** rise as the son of Greek immigrants to the Summer Olympics in Athens, where he advised the American College of Greece, headquarters of the U.S. Olympic Team.

The story told of Korologos' lifelong love for the Olympics, his two-year stint as spokesman for Salt Lake City's 2002 Games and his elation at carrying the Olympic torch in St. George. It recounted how Korologos met Olympics promoter Tom Welch in the early 1990s while writing a freelance piece for Delta Air

Lines' magazine about Salt Lake City's 1998 Olympic bid. And how Welch later persuaded Evans Advertising to lend Korologos' public relations skills to the bid committee.

Korologos' contacts, availability and language skills put him in good stead to become attache to the Greek Olympic Committee in SLOC after Welch's resignation.

Like all good Greek kids, Gorrell reported, the Korologos boys took Greek classes each day after public school let out. "A lot of the Greek grammar books had stories and drawings of the Olympics," Korologos told him. "I got Olympics into my blood."[929]

But Korologos' Greek was rusty. When Greece's IOC member Lambis Nikolaou asked for a hairdresser for his wife, Korologos suggested a place where she could get her brains fixed. Nikolaou told him he was the only Greek he knew whose "Greek is greek to me."

Korologos concluded:

> This [advisory role for the Athens Games] sort of closes the circle for me, takes me back to the third grade at Greek school. The Opening Ceremony probably will choke me all up, being there with the pomp and pageantry and nearly 3,000 years of history. Look how beautiful they made the Salt Lake Games -- and we don't have the history they do. Who says you can't go home again?

* * *

JoAnn Jacobsen-Wells retired in 2004 in order to qualify for *Tribune* health insurance before that perquisite ended. Her early retreat gave her time to teach at Brighton High School, where she supervised the cheerleading squad two years and became teacher of the year. After that, she returned to Africa for humanitarian work.

JoAnn's departing column dubbed her previous 13 years the highlight of her newspaper career. "Who wouldn't want to write a column that attracted an average of three hate-mail letters a day and turned some of Utah's highest elected officials into valued confidential sources.?"[930] she joked. Remember phone sex with Orrin Hatch?

* * *

After 68 years on Main Street, *The Salt Lake Tribune* moved to Kem Gardner's new Gateway development on westside Salt Lake City in 2005. Jack Gallivan was disgusted with the change,[931] a loss I would have shared if still working for newspaper.

A nostalgic Tom Wharton said it might take awhile to adjust to the sterile new newsroom.[932] Ironically, given the shrinking staff and newspaper, Editor Nancy Conway said the new offices provided more efficient work space that would allow for growth.

One quick visit reminded me of the mezzanine. Each staffer had a filing cabinet, desk, telephone, computer terminal and cubicle with half-panels -- an improvement over the cramped clumps of dirty desks I'd known in the noisy newsroom. Pat Bagley had fashioned full walls for himself, an indication he may have hated the close quarters of the 10th floor as much as I did when we worked side-by-side.

According to Denny, the new office lacked character and left him cold. He vowed never to return.

I could have adjusted to Gateway offices, although I would have missed being in the heart of Downtown. In fact, the good ol' days in the Tribune Building were not that great. My nostalgic colleagues seemed to forget the filth, messiness, dimness, battered furniture and general din of the cramped old newsroom. The remodeled version was more orderly but still crowded and polluted. We were lucky to have moved to the spacious mezzanine.

* * *

During dinner at Shirley "Mother" Jones' house that fall, Paul Rolly remarked that the "old *Tribune*," the one we knew early in our careers, was the newspaper's heyday. He cited the time he, Bruce Bartley and I attended the afternoon showing of "Deep Throat" after the first reel was confiscated. Yes, those were good times.

* * *

The Pig Farm picnic that year was smaller than usual. At 91, **Jack Gallivan** joked about having had "every surgery available except a hysterectomy." Barbara Woody confided that Bob had experienced a heart attack scare. "I rushed to the bathroom to comb my hair and put on some makeup while Bob called 911."

Woody made it to Mike Korologos' 70th birthday at Cinegrill in January 2007. When I showed him pictures of our new house, he sent me this note:

> I first thought I was looking at a wing of the Getty Museum. Then I thought of your parties and the wife of a staffer crashing through the window

during a frenzied dance. Or maybe a copy boy.

An impressive facade.

I saw such a kitchen at the Imperial Palace in Taiwan. Beautiful! Did you guys hand-wrought it?

We look forward to touching the textures.

That was a hell of a party for Mike [Korologos]. It brought the best of the *Tribune* generations together. You know, it wasn't all bad, was it?

Love, B&B

After her years as Reader Advocate, **Shinika Sykes** covered higher education for the newspaper. In a story on the University of Utah one day, she allegedly plagiarized its student newspaper, *The Daily Utah Chronicle*. More than a decade after joining the staff, Shinika was fired in August 2006.

* * *

Multiple sclerosis finally took **Ann Kilbourn** March 9, 2008 at age 55.[933] She'd lived with the disease for 35 years, 20 of them as a *Tribune* staffer.

Ann Kilbourn

Ann had infused her unusual feature stories -- about subjects like tattoo art -- with wit and whimsy, a reflection of the wacky sense of humor she carried with her even while wobbling across the newsroom with a cane, often assisted by artist friend Mark Knudsen.

In 1981, the M.S. Society named Kilbourn its Champion of the Year, and in 1988, she received the Governor's Trophy for "achievement, determination and example in encouraging the employment of people with disabilities."[934]

When bedridden, Ann often called up Tim Kelly to come by to lift her or run an errand.

* * *

By 2009, bankers had thrashed the country's mortgage market and my personal finances. My UBS Financial broker had invested in Lehman Brothers just before it went belly up, gutting monthly income. With our California mortgage gobbling half of Denny's income, we decided to pay it off with proceeds from the sale of Summit Park and Scofield real estate, which we'd hoped to pass on to our grandsons. Location, taxes and zoning obstacles made Joe's Ridge an especially impractical asset.

We spent the summer clearing, cleaning and repairing our Utah properties so we could get out of the woods, both literally and figuratively. By fall, we'd unloaded some of our favorite belongings.

I hated losing the huge, 1930s veneer desk I'd snagged from NAC for $5 and the antique stove Denny refurbished. It was painful letting go of Denny's drawings and paintings at a pick-a-picture potluck we held for friends and family, but our new house had more windows than wall space for art.

Both Utah properties sold sell the spring of 2010. We had to part with Denny's stained-glass windows and the doors and bannisters -- some from the houses of Brigham Young's lesser wives -- we'd rescued from the wrecking ball. We gave up the house Denny and Jerry built from scratch. Our retreat from Utah was complete.

* * *

Jerry Dunton drew his last breath in 2009. A substantial crowd of family, fellow history buffs and *Tribune* colleagues attended his August funeral.

Despite suffering his first heart attack in his 40s, enduring open-heart surgery in 2002, dealing with a short fuse and packing on too many pounds, Dunton had survived for 75 years. The younger of this single father's two sons, Robert, had become commander of the 1457th Engineer Battalion and other combat units of the Utah Army National Guard and given him a grandson, achievements that made Dunton extremely proud.

After retiring, Dunton and Schindler had become immersed in Utah Westerners, meeting regularly over coffee to hash over details of the past and visiting historic sites around the region. Now both were part of that history themselves.

* * *

Peter Scarlet also "pegged out," as he would have put it, about 3 a.m. December 23, 2009 at home. His chronic leukemia and subsequent diabetes did him in at age 61.

In the *Tribune* obituary, editorial writer Kirk Millson noted that Scarlet had spent his entire career at *The Tribune*, the last four on the Editorial Board, "where he delighted in rhetorically slaughtering the sacred cows of the political left."[935] Scarlet was "born a few hundred years too late," Millson wrote. "He was cheerful and garrulous, gentle and caring. A pillar of integrity who was fiercely loyal to his friends, Peter lived by an old-school values system that seemed out of place in modern society."

Eileen Rencher, the state education spokeswoman who had become Scarlet's best friend and confidante, discovered his body when stopping to get him up for chemotherapy. Her advanced Parkinson's Disease aside, Eileen planned his funeral and asked me to speak.

Denny and I drove to Summit Park, where we were greeted by a frozen drain that flooded our office and guest room and reinforced our plan to sell the house.

Among Scarlet's pallbearers were *Tribune* friends Tim Fitzpatrick, Denny, Millson, Paul Wetzel, Paul Rolly and Ann Poore. Though I strayed slightly from my script, here is my eulogy for him:

Our friend Peter was a paradox. He was introverted and sensitive to the point where he would withdraw into a corner if ignored and seemingly carry on a conversation with himself, yet he was so garrulous (his word) that his editors at *The Salt Lake Tribune* had to threaten him with reprimands. It was his habit to get into the office in the wee hours of the morning, bang out a few stories or thoughts and then chat away the rest of the day while others tried to work. Despite the Troll's (another Peter word) best efforts to dislodge him as unproductive, Peter became that editor's "greatest success" and went on to obtain his dream job as an editorial writer. With a little push and direction, Peter came through.

Peter would toss multi-syllable words into the same pot with colloquialisms like "pegged out," the expression he would use to describe what he did that cold day nearly a fortnight (another Peter word) ago when he took his leave of us all. He loved guns and the desert yet withdrew from physical activity and conflict and was personally kind and gentle. He talked about European battlefields as if he were there but never saw the real thing. He had a vivid imagination but an unimaginative diet of burgers and spaghetti. He was always glad to have others pick up the tab. He lived simply and modestly but wore Brooks Brothers shirts and gave generously to Habitat for Humanity. His idea of entertainment was to accompany a friend to the doctor and chat in the waiting room.

Pete often said himself that he was born 100 years -- or was it 200 -- too late. One of his proudest achievements was finally finishing his history degree in his 40s at the University of Utah, where he loved to hobnob with his favorite professor, Bobby Goldberg. He was an encyclopedia of anecdotes about not only historical figures but also characters at the newspaper (I wish he were here now for reference) and in the community he rarely left. Consider this recent message he wrote me about Eileen Rencher's two dogs, Princess and Max: "The Princess is half the size of Max, and, I happily told Eileen, is directly associated with the Magna Mater (Cybele) and is as fabled in times past as the she wolf that suckled Romulus and Remus." I can hear his chuckle even now.

Peter could recall the magnificent and the mundane about local church leaders (he had been a troublemaker as a Boy Scout and deacon in the Mormon Church), educators and his acquaintances and relatives, including his favorite aunt who raised several children while managing to earn a law degree. He had a nickname for everyone who meant anything to him, including himself, whom he referred to as his adoptive father's "booby prize" -- undoubtedly a double entendre. In fact, his biological father died before Peter's birth, so his mother's second husband got both wife and child at once.

As for others in his sphere, there were Countess Ava (Shirley Jones), Sister Faust (Sherri Clark), Princess Aurora (Dawn House), Captain Kirk (Millson), Petrushka (Ann Poore),

Archbishop (Lynn Johnson), Cardinal (Jack Schroeder), Daethen (Terri Ellefsen), the Austrian (Art Deck), the Troll (Jay Shelledy) and Sluggo (Mike Cassidy's name for Mike Korologos, who hired Peter and Cassidy as copy boys about the same time), the Man from Trenton (David Ledford), Dominus (Dominic Welch), Nan (Anne Wilson), Bookie Buns (me), Sistie Ugler . . . well, you get the idea.

Peter-the-Paradox never married and he rarely moped (another Peter word) about it or the illness that eventually took him out. Still, he suffered greatly from a split in his immediate family that kept him from his mother before she died. Meantime, he cultivated companionships with women -- and men -- that lasted a lifetime, and he was pleased to have them listen to his tales of woe over lunch, visit him in the hospital or sit through a chemotherapy session by his side. As one of them, Jan Keller put it, "He had many mothers." In addition to herself, there were Shirley Jones, Sherri Clark, Lucille Stoddard and Eileen Rencher.

Peter's relationship with Eileen Rencher was especially precious to him these past few years, months and weeks, with him helping her through tough times and she taking him to the doctor and simply holding his hand for one of the last hours of his life. Eileen surely gave Peter a sense of belonging and love that he so desired.

Peter was like a brother to me, one who only asked to chat once in awhile. He tended to repeat himself, a habit that could drive me to distraction and caused me to quit listening. If you did answer him, you were guaranteed a drawn-out story. But what sibling hasn't driven another to distraction? He was the memory I so often lack. I wish I could remember now some of the stories he would tell. He could make me laugh. And though our politics were almost diametric opposites, he could bat out an editorial in a matter of minutes (yes, they needed heavy editing), and more than once and to the surprise of many, I used his ideas.

Like a good soldier, Peter was honest and loyal to the extreme. He was often the first to extend condolences to others who lost a loved one. Funerals were important to him as a place to express his affection for those who had departed. He had suffered so many losses himself, from his parents to three of his brothers, that he knew grief and the importance of people showing their love and sympathy. He would be honored and delighted to see the many people who came here to pay their respects today.

As former *Tribune* artist Mark Knudsen put it, "Peter was an eccentric and lovable presence. Completely original. I will miss him." So will we all.

Peter Scarlet entered the ground in South Jordan City Cemetery inside a plain pine box as requested.

Assisting Eileen at the gravesite was a Goth-looking Scottish woman in her 50s who wore a diamond stud in one nostril and purple-tinged, black hair with cropped bangs. When she introduced herself, I recognized a character from one of Scarlet's favorite ironies.

Eileen's caregiver was the widow of Grant Robertson, the man who had invested and lost Eileen's fortune in a pyramid scheme. The couple had met online less than four years earlier. Robertson had shot himself in a parking lot outside KSL's broadcast studio -- not far from Eileen's condominium -- a few months before Scarlet's demise.

At Scarlet's wake at the Rollys that afternoon, I boldly asked Mrs. Robertson why her husband's life insurance policy paid off in a suicide. She matter-of-factly explained that he'd bought three million-dollar policies more than five years before, the limit for the suicide clause. With the money, she'd been able to repay his investors. Grant's only way out of his money pit -- he was paying out $26,000 a month to investors -- was to kill himself.

I will always miss Peter, especially on his September birthday, which we regularly celebrated with lunch in the city. He visited my Temecula house once, happy to go with me to my Mom's doctor appointment. Even though he got deathly sick driving back to Utah alone, he raved about the trip as a highlight of his life.

* * *

Robert H. Woody, *The Tribune's* long-time business editor, died April 21, 2010 at 84. Those of us who knew him would miss the impish antics that masked his deep thinking.

During two decades of retirement, Woody had hiked through Europe and taken continuing education classes at the University of Utah. His widow Barbara donated his letters to the 10th Mountain Museum in Denver. His obituary suggested donations to Doctors without Borders and Amnesty International.

"It was a wonderful experience being a wife of a newsman," Barbara remarked in 2014. "It allowed so many avenues of exploration."[936]

His long-time assistant Joe Rolando kept a picture of Woody typing like a madman at his messy desk -- above his own desk in his den. Rolando felt "very blessed to have worked with him," maintaining that the two had never spoken a harsh word to each other, perhaps because he, having worked for a fast-paced, informal weekly newspaper, "fit perfectly with Woody's unique style." He added:

> I have often thought of him as a 1960s-style Humanist. He was confident that individual responsibility would save the environment, conquer and reduce disease and achieve racial and gender equality. He also believed in capitalism, but not at the expense of those less fortunate, hardly an endorsement for most of the dyed-in-the-wool conservatives he interviewed every day for business stories.[937]

Fond memories of Woody stayed with Rolando into his own retirement because of the thoughtful way he appreciated people, he said. "Woody's frenzied self-indulgence about his work stayed at the office," he said. "At home, he painstakingly wrote letters – many in calligraphy -- to those who meant the most to him. I was among those fortunate enough to have received them."

Rolando sent Woody a fountain pen inscribed with his name for retirement. Woody sent this pithy response in October 1990:

> Dear Joe,
> I cannot tell you how much I was touched by your gift and sentiments.
> As I said, if I have longer rather than shorter years, it will be because of you.
> You backed me a hundred thousand times. And you cut your own swath at the same time.
> Our years were pleasant even under utmost stress. I remember no anger. And for that I am grateful.
> You not only backed me but you bailed us all out from time to time.
> Joe, you are a hell of a good man and you have a lot of good friends out there. That includes me.

Best, Bob

Vintage Woody.[938]

* * *

A blood disorder ended the life of **David Beck** May 17, 2010 in St. Petersburg, Florida, where he'd retired.

At age 41, the sardonic journalist I knew had settled down with a widowed journalist with three children, grandchildren and dogs in Santa Cruz, California. That family called him "Papa Davey," and his stepson even adopted his last name.[939]

I was incredulous at this transformation of a seemingly confirmed bachelor. His obit, written by wife Judy Neuman, noted that Beck was known for his dry wit, voluminous knowledge of history, music, film and books, as well as his culinary abilities. She further described him as a Chicago White Sox fan who hated the New York Yankees, bad drivers and prejudiced people.

I could have added that he smacked his lips when eating and showed little patience for poor restaurant service.

* * *

Another of my longtime favorites, **Will Fehr**, died in November 2010 of heart failure at 84, my mother's age.

While still on the job, he'd had a blood clot in his leg, so I suppose he was lucky to enjoy as much retirement as he did. Denny and I seen Fehr occasionally at Mountain Dell Golf Course, where he took oxygen to compensate for the high altitude's effect on his heart.

I regretted missing Fehr's funeral. Even while my boss, he was my friend. Denny and I had attended a couple of his Christmas parties high in the Avenues, where he and Cynthia enjoyed a spectacular city view. Cynthia had practically given us her watercolor of the Tribune building on the "beautified" Main Street, where widened, tree-lined sidewalks were devoid of people.

Even now, whenever I consider a new investment, I remember Fehr's advice: "Cole, buy a few good, dividend-paying stocks, hold onto them and reinvest the dividends."

* * *

Jack Fenton died of a staph infection in 2011 at age 78. Not one to stand on ceremony, according to his wife Pat, no public services were held. But his obituary suggested contributions be made to Habitat for Humanity, the Humane

Society of Utah or KUER Radio. Jack's ashes were interred at the Utah Veteran's Cemetery and Memorial Park at Camp Williams.

* * *

John W. Gallivan later in life.

Jack Gallivan died October 4, 2012 at age 97. It was the first autumn for many years that *Tribune* veterans failed to gather at his Pig Farm for a BBQ beneath the splendor of the mountainside's changing colors. We would never again be regaled with this mirthful man's generous hospitality and detailed accounts of an intoxicating life, whether it involved a glass of whiskey or the reason he grew a beard his final years.

Jack, as we eventually called him, had achieved great things in nearly 40 years as publisher of the *Tribune* and president of Kearns-Tribune Corp. But his legacy extended beyond that.

Salt Lake City Mayor Deedee Corradini made an apt observation at the dedication of the Gallivan Center downtown. For seven decades, she said, "Jack Gallivan has been our community's conscience, cheerleader, visionary, perspective, common sense counselor, humorist and friend."[940]

The obituary written by his family described Jack as a champion of "the Utah Community."[941] He campaigned for the Salt Palace and downtown art center and pioneered broadcast and cable television. He promoted urban renewal, city-county consolidation, liquor-by-the-drink, light rail, the Central Utah Project, the Winter Olympics bid and the Newspaper Preservation Act of 1970. One of his last legacies was the crusade against homelessness which produced nearly 700 transitional apartments in Salt Lake County.

This was the man whom the Salt Lake Area Chamber of Commerce named "Giant in Our City" in 1981 and the David Eccles School of Business added to its Hall of Fame. He had been a trustee of Westminster College as well as chairman of the board of University Hospital for more than a decade.

Jack Gallivan's mission was to take care of people, his obituary said. Loving mankind unconditionally was "as natural to him as the beat of his own great heart."[942]

One example of that, according to Mike Korologos, was his constant concern for "the individuals who worked at *The Salt Lake Tribune*."[943]

"I dare say I would be about $2 million less rich if not for this man and his vision of the future, where he didn't have to buy newsprint," Gordon Harman, *Tribune* director of information technology, told me.[944]

By then my own frustration with Gallivan's boosterism, which translated into interference with *Tribune* reporting and commentary, had mellowed. His community involvement had prevented us from aggressively and even fairly covering certain important issues, including foibles of the Mormon Church and culture.

But overall Jack was a great human being. I hope I helped him just a little to achieve some of his goals, even if my part depended on his leadership and indulgence.

I was pleasantly surprised to learn that late in life Gallivan had joined the Damned Old Democrats, an informal group that met Fridays at the Alta Club for lunch. Fellow DODs included Harry Fuller, Walker Wallace, Ed Firmage, Jack, Champ and Mickey Gallivan, Pat Shea and Bob Huefner, the University of Utah adviser I'd admired as a master's student.

I had never known for sure where he stood politically. The Kearns family was Republican, yet Gallivan's son Champ had worked for the Kennedys. My ability to slip subversive ideas into so many editorials should have given me a clue.

It broke my heart that this wonderful, compassionate character spent his declining years believing he'd ruined his legacy by failing to keep *The Tribune* in the Kearns family.

"I was hired to succeed [Fitzpatrick] in maintaining *The Tribune*, the Kearns family ownership, for the rest of my days, so my mission in life is destroyed, frustrated," he told Paul Rolly and Dawn House in an interview at his home in May 2005. He reiterated that concession to staffers attending the last couple of picnics at his Pig Farm.[945] So sad.

* * *

On Halloween of 2012, my assumed rival **Paul Wetzel** wrapped up nearly 39 years at *The Tribune*, 22 of them writing editorials full time. He left with mixed feelings:

I thought the date of my retirement a lovely symbol. During those years, I wrote about 4,000 editorials. My finest hours came on September 11, 2001, and in 2010 when I explained to readers how and why the Affordable Care Act would work.[946]

In retirement remarks, Wetzel told his colleagues:

I've observed and sometimes written about interesting things. The Teton Dam break (June 5, 1976), Maurice Abravanel's retirement [as Utah Symphony conductor], the building of Symphony Hall, the Kojian affair [Abravanel's successor had an affair with a female Mormon missionary and was fired], Ramses II, Leonardo's drawings, Bernstein conducting the Vienna Philharmonic in Mahler, countless elections and the endless follies at the Legislature, the fall of the Soviet Union, Clinton's impeachment, 9/11, the wars in Iraq and Afghanistan, the advent of Obamacare.

I figure I have written hundreds of music reviews and some 4,000 editorials for *The Tribune* . . .

From the beginning, the people who are *The Tribune* have been my joy. Eccentric people, talented people, mentally ill people, intense people, relaxed people, amusing people, brilliant people, but all of them people who care deeply about the word and pictures and the news and their community. I can't imagine any other business would have been as interesting or as fun.

. . . You have amused and entertained me, sometimes frustrated me, often inspired me, but most importantly, you have been my best friends.[947]

Paul Wetzel near retirement.

In a speech prepared for but not delivered his last day, Wetzel noted some high and low points of his commentary career:

I had the Editorial Page on the right side of conscience as the war criminal George W. Bush blundered into Iraq, on the right side of conscience, that is, until my publisher ordered us to steer a course for the darkness. Not resigning on that day is my greatest professional regret.

I didn't resign, and today I'm retiring. Lance Gudmundsen famously told a story of an old *Tribune* wire editor who, on the occasion of his retirement, was asked to say a few words. "Every day was a God-damned nightmare," he told his astonished colleagues. I've always loved that story because it embodies the crusty cynicism of old newspapermen. But as my high school principal told me a couple of years before I joined *The Tribune*, cynics are disappointed idealists.[948]

One last feminist rant, Paul: Where do *newspaperwomen* fit into this picture?

* * *

Harry Fuller visited *The Tribune's* Gateway offices for the first time after Wetzel's departure. As he tells it:

> I left deeply depressed. The editorial writers are huddled in a cavelike niche -- four cubicle stations each no larger than a desk would contain, no light except that provided by their computer monitors, although the page editor has a large personal office across a narrow hall at least allowing a window view.
>
> No replacement was made nor likely will be after Paul retired, so the department has reverted to three people including the editor who, reputably, writes hardly anything. Consequently, the published editorial space usually consists of one too-long, locally written editorial, supplemented at the bottom by one reprinted from another newspaper, which is what we used to do for our third editorial on Saturdays. It's really a dismal situation but, amazingly, the remaining writers don't seem to realize the depth to which their situation has fallen, huddled as they are in their dark daily toil. Hell, we had more space and light in our 10th floor location. I was told they often gather in Paul's otherwise unused, dimly illuminated cubicle to eat their meager lunch.
>
> We can probably be assured the current department staffers aren't spending time outside the U.S. [NCEW fact-finding junkets], much less outside the office. In effect, two writers doing research, even relying on Google, answering phone calls, conducting personal and phone interviews, selecting and editing columns, doing make-up, then electronically justifying it, proofreading and actually writing editorials does not etch a picture that includes much extended traveling.
>
> It's clearly the end of an era. Be reassured that you newspapered when that meant something and you were valued for what you did. And you did it well. I am increasingly proud of what we achieved, the four of us, and what we meant to the daily paper's result. I can confidently tell you, from what I have heard recently, that Mr. Gallivan felt the same way.
>
> I ran into Ed Oberbeck on leaving the building and, answering a question, he said working at the new location is "terrible," although a pleasant irony for him is that he now works alongside his brother Steve, laying out pages for the business section. The former make-up department was discontinued so that, now, each news section does their own page make-up, including the editorial department, just the three of them, or maybe two since no one seems to know what the editor does. If not for computerization, or maybe because of it, it all sounds God-awful primitive.
>
> Remember make-up guy Ron Bowman? Ed said he quit before he could be laid off and now works managing a deli section at a Walmart, or some similar place. As I said, the entire experience depressed me. I could hardly wait to get home and fortify my equilibrium with a stiff drink.
>
> The worst irony in this: Shelledy's politicking to diminish the Editorial Department seems to have prevailed in the end.
>
> All in all, give me the good old days. And if that makes me sound like a geezer, so be it. [949]

While Fuller had regarded technology, especially when used to make up pages, as just one more chore, I had appreciated its benefits. My last few years on the job, efficient paginators like Ron Bowman, Ed Oberbeck and Steve Brophy put our pages together electronically, often coping with copy that didn't fit our layouts. Working with these technicians on corrections was easier than dealing with backshop printers of the good ol' days.

I would have loved to have access to Google and other online archives when researching topics. My voluminous news-clip file would have been unnecessary, saving me countless hours of busywork. Plus, I would have had many sources to choose from. Fuller disagreed:

> Try as I might, I am unable to share your enthusiasm for online sources such as Google. It's probably my persistent computer illiteracy, but it takes me almost as long to locate what I'm researching online as it did to peruse printed material. At least I didn't have to first eliminate all the intrusive advertising before then slogging around cyberspace until finding the link that actually provides what I'm looking for. Using the various search engines daily, most of the day, would probably make such work easier. [950]

A year later, Fuller reported, even fewer in-house editorials appeared on the Opinion Page. On April 21, 2014, there were "just two overly long" editorials, and both were from other publications.[951]

How I would have liked to substitute an outside editorial for our own occasionally! Doing so regularly, however, surely reduced *The Tribune's* political influence over local issues.

All the years we'd worked together, Fuller had struck me as politically conservative. In retirement, however, his emails became increasingly liberal. When I told him so, he responded:

> Shhhh . . . Don't blow my cover. Mostly, I seldom considered myself in any political corner, although I'll concede my views generally tended toward the liberal. Another reason why you could slip your ideas into always well-reasoned and well-written editorials, once you got the hang of it.
>
> I consider my definition of "liberal" a proud label, meaning the willingness and ability to be open-minded in considering available information for ultimately arriving at the most convincing position.

That's when he revealed he'd become a Damned Old Democrat with the Gallivans. That's one way to endure a Republican-dominated political climate.

* * *

After 18 years as a couple, **Linda Fantin** and **Phil Miller** made their marriage official on Christmas Eve 2013 in a 1,000-year-old castle, Diocletian's Palace, in the Julian Alps of Slovenia.[952] Miller had not only made a spunky, attractive journalist his wife, he had landed his dream job: traveling throughout the country covering major-league baseball for the Minneapolis *Star-Tribune.*

When Miller left *The Tribune,* he had proudly identified himself as "old *Tribune.*" Wetzel later expounded on that description, saying Miller was:

> . . . among a distinguished few who left *The Tribune* for greater glory in the wider world because the management here was too near-sighted and cheap to hold on to his considerable talent, even when he gave them the chance. I am not among those distinguished few.[953]

* * *

Denny's brother **Jerry Green** died of an apparent heart attack August 18, 2014. The day of his funeral, his wife Barbara repeatedly asked where "that nice man" was and then relived the horror of his death. We understood too late how much help the couple needed.

Gallivan's son-in-law **Edward McDonough,** whom I knew as Judge Caruthers, died November 27, 2014 from lung disease.

By the time **Tim Kelly** died January 8, 2015, our good times together had faded with his memory. Despite his advanced dementia, however, he said his trademark "too-da-loo" as I left his assisted-living facility for the last time.

Brain cancer took **Dominic Welch's** life February 15, 2017 at age 84. Another sad passing of a strong *Tribune* personality, the originator of the ESOP that freed us staffers from our paycheck-to-paycheck lives.

Welch had told me once that he maintained voluminous *Tribune* files that would remain private until his death. They had yet to be released in 2018.

Not a month after Dominic died, a car crash killed his nephew **Tony Magann,** who had facilitated our transition to ESOP.

Shirley Jones died October 23, 2017 in assisted-living. People who'd worked with her at *The Tribune* flooded a group facebook site with loving memories of Mother Jones. Here latter years, she'd lamented the loss of the "old *Tribune:*"

> I was there almost 40 years, and I enjoyed every minute of it. It was hard when they closed the door."[954]

Dick Rosetta, Tom Wharton, Pat Bagley, Paul Wetzel, Terry Orme and Nancy Hobbs, l-r.

911 Smokin, August/September 2003.

912 Associated Press, May 1, 2003.

913 Rachel Smolkin, "Salt Lake Blues, *American Journalism Review*, August/September 2003.

914 Ibid.

915 Ibid.

916 Kelly McBride, Poynter Institute, May 1, 2003, March 2, 2003.

917 A Statement From Tribune Staffers, *The Salt Lake Tribune*, April 30, 2003.

918 Smolkin, August/September 2003.

919 James E. Shelledy, "Reporters Fired Over Smart Case Story," *The Salt Lake Tribune,* April 30, 2003.

920 Glen Worchol, "Publisher Vows to Rebuild Trust," *The Salt Lake Tribune*, April 30, 2003.

921 Ibid.

922 C.G. Wallace, Associated Press, April 30, 2003.

923 Rachel Smolkin, *American Journalism Review*, August/September 2003.

924 Paul Wetzel, 2012.

925 Lucinda Dillon Kinkead, "Trib editor quits amid Enquirer imbroglio," *Deseret News*, May 2, 2003.

926 Paul Rolly, "One last ode to Ron McBride, a humanitarian coach," *The Salt Lake Tribune*, November 16, 2011.

927 Rosetta, November 7, 2002.

928 Bob Woody email to Diane Cole November 15, 2002.

929 Mike Gorrell, "Utahn lends an assist to Athens," *The Salt Lake Tribune*, August 5, 2004, p. C1.

930 Rolly & Wells, December 31, 2004.

931 Heather May and Glen Warchol, "Tribune packs up for move from Main to Gateway," *The Salt Lake Tribune,* May 6, 2005.

932 Jason Bergreen, "In With the New: Tribune embraces its Gateway home," *The Salt Lake Tribune*, May 16, 2005.

933 Ann Kilbourn obituary, *The Salt Lake Tribune*, March 12, 2008.

934 Ibid.

935 Peter Scarlet obituary, *The Salt Lake Tribune,* December 27, 2009.

936 Barbara Woody email to Diane Cole, February 3, 2014.

937 Joe Rolando email, April 2017.

938 Ibid.

939 David Lawrence Beck obituary, *Tampa Bay Times*, May 21, 2010.

940 John William Gallivan, A Gentle Irish Man, *The Salt Lake Tribune*, October 4-5, 2012.

941 Ibid.

942 Ibid.

943 Paul Rolly, "Jack Gallivan, longtime Tribune publisher, dies at 97, *The Salt Lake Tribune*, October 4, 2012.

944 Gordon Harman, October 9, 2015.

945 Jack Gallivan comments at 25-year employee picnics in Snyderville.

946 Wetzel email, March 27, 2016.

[947] Wetzel retirement remarks, October 2012.

[948] Wetzel undelivered retirement remarks, October 2012.

[949] Harry Fuller emails February 7-10, 2013.

[950] Harry Fuller email February 10, 2013.

[951] Harry Fuller email April 21, 2014.

[952] Linda Fantin facebook entry December 26, 2013.

[953] Paul Wetzel thoughts upon retirement, sent via email March 27, 2016.

[954] Shirley Jones phone conversation November 14, 2014.

58 - *Deseret News* Moves In for the Kill

In January 2010, MediaNews filed for Chapter 11 bankruptcy, setting up *The Tribune* for another ownership change. Within a year, Alden Global Capital, a New York hedge fund, acquired *The Tribune* and began selling off assets and laying off staffers to boost profits.

The hedge fund quickly sold *Tribune* printing presses and warehouses to Deseret News Publishing Co. and, in 2013, secretly renegotiated terms of the two newspapers' joint operating agreement (JOA). The *News* began choking its old rival/partner to death.

NAC, the jointly owned production, advertising and delivery operation of the *Tribune* and *Deseret News,* had become MediaOne of Utah. Revised terms of the JOA gave the *Deseret News* a majority on MediaOne's Board of Directors and hiked its share of profits from 42 percent to 70 percent.

Even the prior 58-42 percent split had failed to reflect how much more readership -- 60 percent vs. 40 percent of combined circulation -- and advertising revenue *The Tribune* generated than the Mormon paper. Now the division was even more lopsided in the church's favor and cut *Tribune* income in half.

The Tribune could not maintain the status quo under such circumstances, according to **Terry Orme**, who became editor/publisher October 1, 2013 when Editor Nancy Conway and Publisher Dean Singleton left the scene.[955] It was now Orme's job to slash expenses to salvage the newspaper.

While facing a second round of layoffs after slicing the staff by 20 percent in September 2013, [956] Orme doubted the newspaper could survive another year. His remaining employees worked under constant fear of losing their jobs.

MediaNews Group, *The Tribune's* parent company, intended to retain digital news (sltrib.com) and back away from print.[957] But according to Orme, the digital format's ads and subscriber fees simply could not finance the news staff the way print ads did.

This situation rang a bell for Mike Korologos. As far back as 1958, his journalism

professor Neff Smart, former publisher of the *Orem-Geneva Times,* predicted that technology -- in the form of cable-linked pay television as the internet was not yet imagined -- would revolutionize news gathering and dissemination.[958] In the current case, Utah journalism would be gravely impaired.

In casual discussions of *The Tribune's* dire circumstances, Joan O'Brien half-seriously suggested that ESOP recipients pool their money to buy the newspaper. Even if we wanted to, the *Deseret News* would never let that happen as long as the JOA let it veto potential buyers. That power not only blocked the McCartheys in 1999, it could prevent other interested Utahns from intervening now.

Orme's grim warning spawned my first opinion column to *The Tribune* since my departure. This is what it said:

> When I quit writing editorials for The Salt Lake Tribune *in 1998, I thought I was through imposing my opinions on Utah. I can no longer sit silently while the community I loved lets its most fundamental, hard-fought freedoms vanish.*
>
> *Since 1871,* The Tribune *has offset the power of The Church of Jesus Christ of Latter-day Saints to control Utah territory. The church repeatedly tried to extinguish that independent voice, but from the start, more Utahns, including Mormons, read* The Tribune *than the church-owned Deseret News. They realized that a free press — the open exchange of ideas — is vital to Americans' ability to control their leaders, their institutions and their own lives.*
>
> *When the cost of publishing two major newspapers threatened their viability 61 years ago,* Tribune *and* Deseret News *officers agreed, with U.S. Department of Justice approval, to keep news departments separate while combining advertising, printing and delivery. That joint operating agreement (JOA) has been uneasy, with* The Tribune *generating most of the revenue and readership while each paper held veto power over potential purchasers of the other. Profits have been split 58-42 percent to reflect* The Tribune's *primary contribution.*
>
> Tribune *news reports embarrassing to the LDS Church periodically caused friction, conflict that undoubtedly influenced the sale of* The Tribune *to*

MediaNews Group, a non-Utah group, in 2000. The final coup now awaits federal approval.

The LDS Church, through Deseret News Publishing, has designed JOA amendments that reverse the profit split, leaving The Tribune 30 percent of profits for a news staff already severely reduced by financial cutbacks. Unlike the Deseret News, The Tribune has no wealthy church for financial infusions but now must make a profit for investors to stay afloat.

Yes, newspapers are dying or changing form across the country, but The Tribune's news staff has been operational despite the trend. Its demise would not only be tragic but downright dangerous to individual freedom in Utah, which essentially is a theocracy run by the LDS Church. If the Deseret News is allowed to swallow up, squeeze out or co-opt The Tribune, there will be no other viable alternative voice for Utahns, no check on the church's power over the state. The LDS Church also dominates Utah's broadcast news media through Bonneville International.

In deciding whether the proposed JOA amendments satisfy terms of the Newspaper Preservation Act, the Justice Department's antitrust lawyers must understand that the outcome will affect the average Utahn's First Amendment speech and religion rights. Moreover, it is imperative for Utahns to start shouting from the mountain peaks of Mt. Olympus to ensure this newspaper — and alternate voices — endure in their state.

Editorial independence in Utah may be of scant concern to The Tribune's parent company, MediaNews Group, and the management company, Digital First Media, that has accepted both the JOA amendments and a cash settlement to relinquish control of the newspapers' printing, distribution and advertising.

That is understandable. MediaNews and Digital First Media are not owned and operated locally but must make profits for Alden Global Capital, an international hedge fund. These investors don't necessarily live in a state dominated by one church.

And what do I care, now that I'm a Californian, what happens in Utah? Because for most of my life, Utah was my home and The Tribune my refuge. Because I was a non-Mormon in a Mormon land where I didn't belong until I realized The Tribune was there to stick up for me and thousands like me. Because I treasure the First Amendment.[959]

My reference to the LDS theocracy predictably stirred up certain readers. Paul Sharp of Salt Lake City submitted a letter to the editor that said:

> Tribune ex-writer Diane Cole whines about the First Amendment and "refuge" from control by the Mormon Church. What nonsense.
> The LDS Church is as fundamental a protector of freedom as exists. There is hardly a more compelling Mormon doctrine than agency -- freedom of choice -- and none defend it more.
> Might this kind of paranoia die the death it deserves? Dare we hope that one day the Tribune will grow up to become a real newspaper and cease sponsoring slanted, anti-Mormon bigotry and ignorance?[960]

Mr. Sharp and I obviously had different concepts of freedom. After living beneath the umbrella of the Mormon Church my entire life, I didn't feel free to do what I believed about marriage, religion, women on the job and countless matters of conscience.

And I was hardly the first to criticize Mormon rule. In his swan song from the U.S. Senate in 1905, for instance, Republican Thomas Kearns called the Mormon Church a "monarchy" ruling Utah politics.[961]

The newspaper was still publishing a year after Orme's prediction. However, he'd had to eliminate eight more staffers in April 2014, and he declared no more.

"We are feeling very badly for our old friend Terry, who has had to be the hatchet man for the ogres who own the paper and is clearly torn up about it all," wrote Lex Hemphill in an email April 13.

* * *

Joan O'Brien took up the cause to rescue The Tribune.

After using her legal training to dig into court records from the late 1990s, this former staffer -- whose father had been publisher and husband still worked as an editor --- led the charge for an antitrust suit against both Kearns-Tribune and Deseret News Publishing over JOA revisions. Documents from the McCartheys' 1999 lawsuit provided chilling evidence that the LDS Church attempted to wrest *The Tribune* from Kearns-Tribune Corp. without appearing to violate federal laws against news monopolies.

Joan O'Brien led effort to save T*ribune*.

Joan spent a chunk of her own money and raised more to hire an attorney. She organized Utah Newspaper Project, also known as Citizens for Two Voices, which held demonstrations and other gatherings to build public support for *Tribune* independence from the church. Besides Joan, the board included longtime reporter Patty Henetz, Gallivan's grandson Ted McDonough, Harry Fuller and his wife Janet.

Nearly 16,000 people, including me and Denny, signed a petition urging the U.S. Department of Justice to review the revised JOA. Conflict averse though he was, Joan's father would have been proud.

In June, chemicals magnate and philanthropist Jon M. Huntsman Sr., a former general authority of the LDS Church, confirmed his interest in buying *The Tribune*. "We should never have any political or religious organization filter our news,[962]" he declared. The Justice Department put sales talks on hold while considering the antitrust petition.

Life went on at the newspaper, where Orme and Co. were generating ideas to keep it afloat.

* * *

As a publicity stunt to pump up circulation, *The Tribune* sponsored a public roasting of **Paul Rolly**, by then in his 42nd year of journalism, primarily at *The Tribune,* and his 24th year as a columnist. After Joann Jacobsen-Wells retired in 2004, Rolly continued a column on his own four days a week, never missing a day for illness or vacation. He even filed a column from his hospital bed when treated for pneumonia.[963]

Held at the Gallivan Center downtown August 19, 2015, the event gave Rolly a chance to revive cleaned-up versions of his favorite tales -- that is, without his usual cursing and tangled asides.

He made no bones about his liberal bent and his disdain for a government "junket in the guise" of economic development. He admitted his compulsion to even the score with anyone who messed with him, as House Speaker Marty Stephens did in 1999.

Rolly got roasted.

As the story goes, Gov. Mike Leavitt had announced plans to run for a third term, jeopardizing the Republican legislator's plan to replace him. "If you're a Republican in Utah, you have designs on becoming governor," Rolly told his audience. "If you're a Democrat, you run for Salt Lake City mayor."[964]

While Leavitt was aboard the USS Salt Lake City at the bottom of the Pacific Ocean outside San Diego, Rolly continued, Stephens attempted a coup by lining up votes for the Republican Party nomination. Leavitt got wind of it and, hoping to nip it in the bud, directed Press Secretary Vicki Varela to call Rolly with the tip. Rolly called Stephens for confirmation and refused a request to hold the story. So the speaker called Channel 4's Chris Vanocur to announce he was running for governor, and the story ran before Rolly's column came out the next morning.

"I was miffed he would scoop me on my own story," Rolly said, "so I purposely didn't call Marty for his side on stories" for weeks after that. After being ignored for so long, Stephens set up a breakfast meeting at Lamb's to smooth the muckraker's ruffled feathers. While eating, Rolly asked Stevens to confirm, off the record, the reason a Republican caucus over redistricting didn't adjourn before two Democrats had to leave for a Jewish observance.

"If it was a Monday night [LDS family home evening]," Rolly informed listeners, "they would have adjourned early."

Stephens said he'd never betray the caucus, but as long as Rolly already knew what went on, he'd confirm it. Meantime, several caucus members saw the two together at Lamb's, leaving them to assume, when they read the column the next day, that Stephens was the source. The icing on the cake? "No one watches Channel 4, so I had my scoop anyway."

Vintage Rolly.

Illustrating the power of the press, Rolly recalled the time Gov. Leavitt and Varela cooked up a PR scheme to fly Michael Jordan, "one of the richest men in America," to southern Utah to golf at state expense when the Utah Jazz hosted the NBA All-Star game. That item appeared in the Rolly & Wells column alongside another in which the state claimed it didn't have the resources to rescue a wild horse stranded on a cliff. The state somehow scraped up the resources to save the horse, and thereafter Leavitt and Varela measured issues with the potential for bad press by a "Michael Jordan Meter."

Rolly's favorite column that never made it into print concerned a widow who sued the State of Utah for negligence in her husband's death. Her husband had been driving up I-80 in Parleys Canyon one evening when his car skidded on ice and mounted the median before slamming into a bridge abutment. The roadway had been repaved so many times that it no longer had the curvature to prevent such accidents.

The appeals court overturned a $250,000 judgment against the state on grounds of government immunity. When Rolly learned Attorney General Jan Graham planned to sue the widow for $40,000 in attorney's fees, he called her office for a comment. The attorney general backed down, and the column was discarded.

"That kinda shows the power of the press," Rolly commented.

Senator Jim Dabakis, a gay Democrat championing the survival of The Tribune's independent voice, praised Rolly for "changing our community for the good." JoAnn Jacobsen-Wells joked that Senator Orrin Hatch promised to retire if Rolly would.

Tongue in cheek, Gayle Ruzicka of the ultra-conservative Eagle Forum expressed surprise that the columnist had a beautiful wife [Dawn House] and nine children between them. "I've never thought about Paul being human," she told the audience. "I thought he lived in a dark room of The Tribune where they threw him raw meat once in awhile."

Ruzicka described the time Rolly called to confirm she was Pat Buchanan's campaign manager when he ran for President. "No," she said, and offered the name and number of the actual campaign manager. "Much to my surprise, I found I really was the campaign manager," she said. "Either that, or he didn't want to rewrite his column. When you write fiction, you don't have to write the truth."[965] (I have to wonder whether critics like Ruzicka have considered that journalists are humans capable of mistakes.)

Calling him "the stick that beats me," House Speaker Greg Hughes also attacked Rolly's accuracy, claiming his first rule of journalism is "not to be in the room you're reporting on." He accused Rolly of fact-checking only with [former Republican legislator] "David Irvine and some Democrat that hates my guts."

Hughes ribbed 69-year-old Rolly about being past his prime, joking that if he was a household name, it was in senior living centers. He added that Rolly actually was a household name in the Hughes household, where they would say, "That's bull Rolly, you're full of Rolly, Rolly just hit the fan."

The House speaker then "kidded" that Rolly drank on the job. There was the time, he said, when a beer thief punched Rolly in the face at a convenience store where Rolly clerked. "Did he want a beer or did he want your beer? The man's . . . liquored up when he writes those things!" he asserted. (Who was he kidding?)

State Senator Curt Bramble also roasted Rolly, but in a lighter vein.

> Roasts are about coming up with vicious, outright lies, zingers, one-liners with no respect for the target that tears them down for a laugh at their expense . . . that's not me. I needed an expert. So I called the one person I know capable of doing all those things, and Paul, thanks for taking my call.

Bramble teased that Rolly harbored an inferiority complex, lacked a soul, held a low opinion of others and focused on minutiae.

> Paul tackles the really big issues. That's why my Senate buddies always scour the paper to see if they have any unpaid parking tickets or there's another story about those pesky legislative license plates.

The senator joked that Rolly was known to ask lawmakers in the afternoon to be a second source on a tip they gave him that morning. He said Rolly practiced what he preached about the environment by recycling his columns. He went on:

> Hypocrisy? How about Paul's championship of transparency: the use of anonymous sources. Progressive? What about *The Tribune's* hedge-fund ownership, use of coal for electricity, huge use of ink, annual destruction of 250 million trees, low wages and use of child labor [for delivery]?

Finally, Bramble described Rolly as an old school, hard-nosed investigator who would sink his teeth into the bad guys and never let go . . . perhaps like J. Edgar Hoover. In the end, he commended Rolly for being the conscientious conscience of Utah and the Legislature. "He reminds us that what we do is to represent the people."[966]

For that last characteristic, Rolly could be proud. He also deserved praise for his calm response to aspersions cast upon his integrity and accuracy. There was a time when insecurity would have triggered an angry retort rather than relaxed chuckles to such biting remarks.

We journalists needed a thick skin. After all, we slung arrows daily and bought ink by the barrel, obligating us to accept our share of criticism. Constant deadlines led to mistakes requiring correction.

* * *

Careful management by **Terry Orme**, pressure from Joan O'Brien's legal campaign and support from staffers and readers propped up *The Tribune* for three years beyond its predicted collapse. Then on May 31, 2016, Jon Huntsman's son Paul purchased the paper from New-York-based Digital First Media, apparently with the LDS Church's blessing.

Hallelujah! The newspaper would survive, and staffers should gain better health and retirement benefits along with job security. Layoffs should end.

Clearly, staff cutbacks had been deep. As of May 26, 2016, the newspaper employed 83 reporters, editors and photographers[967] compared to 178 in 2006, 151 during Shelledy's regime in 1997 and 126 a decade before that.

Assured ongoing *Tribune* independence and a more reasonable revenue split between *The Tribune* and *Deseret News*, Utah Newspaper Project dropped its two-year-old federal lawsuit.[968] *The Tribune* would receive 40 percent of JOA profits instead of the 30 percent adopted in 2013. The LDS Church would relinquish veto power over *Tribune* ownership.

According to *The Tribune's* May 26 story, Jon Huntsman Sr. pledged to:

> . . . *preserve the newspaper's journalistic independence, uninfluenced by outside interference and guided by* "*what is best for our community, without biases. . . . Put away your thoughts that the family will make [the paper] an organ for the LDS Church or the Republican Party . . . We're not going to tell you what to write*" *as long as it's the truth from reliable sources.*[969]

I wondered whether the family's patriarch had embraced a free press since his run for governor in 1988, when he balked at reporters' questions about his business and years as special assistant to President Nixon. I also doubted a devout Mormon could stand by while *The Tribune* wrote stories embarrassing to the LDS Church.

* * *

Terry Orme became an early loser in the Huntsman deal.

Paul Huntsman immediately assumed his publisher title, leaving Orme as editor until July 29, 2016, when he gave Orme's job to **Jennifer Napier-Pearce,** an Orme protege relatively new to newspapers. Like Huntsman, this wife of a Supreme Court justice happened to be LDS.

Even so, Napier-Pearce was regarded by many as a good choice, and I appreciated the appointment of a second female editor. Yet Orme deserved better treatment.

Orme had been a selfless, respected leader who listened to his employees[970] and deeply felt the pain of letting them go. He steered *The Tribune* through perilous cost-cutting and graciously agreed to stay on as a consultant until the end of 2016 to see ongoing legal issues through.

On April 10, 2017 *The Tribune* received its second Pulitzer Prize -- 60 years after the first -- for its investigation of the way Utah colleges handled rape cases. Most editors and reporters of the series were women, a huge leap forward from my days on City Desk.

As publisher, Terry Orme had pushed that story forward, but he was no longer on hand to bask in the glory of journalism's top prize. He was volunteering as a citizenship teacher of refugees and immigrants at Horizonte, an alternative school in Salt Lake City.

Later that year, *The Tribune* hired a second full-time editorial writer, another woman. More than 30 of the people I'd known on staff still worked there, among them columnist Paul Rolly, cartoonist Pat Bagley, editors Tim Fitzpatrick and David Noyce; news editors and writers Dan Harrie, Tom Harvey, Mike Gorrell, Stephen Hunt, Christopher Smart, Sean Means and Peggy Fletcher-Stack; sports editors and writers Joe Baird, Jay Drew and Kurt Kragthorpe; photographers Rich Egan, Steve Griffin and Al Hartmann; feature writers Catherine Reese Newton and Kathy Kapos Stephenson; copy editors Mark Hansen, Ed Oberbeck and Michael Nakoryakov, and office staff Ana Daraban, Gordon Harman and Chris McDonald. Tony Semerad and Sheila McCann were on hand to remind me that Jay Shelledy actually did hire some great people. Semerad now was newsroom editor -- the slot Will Fehr filled on my first visit to the newsroom in 1972. Semerad's wife Sheila held Keith Otteson's old position as managing editor.

Unfortunately, Joan O'Brien's easy-going, ethical husband Tom Harvey quit by the end of the year over differences with the new management. An ominous signal of trouble ahead.

By mid-2018, I hardly recognized *The Salt Lake Tribune.*

Mark Knudsen put the issue into perspective May 14, 2018: "When you see a headline in *The Tribune* that just says, 'The Church,' it's not really *The Tribune* anymore."

This dismal situation gets worse.

Due to steep losses in circulation and revenue, *The Tribune* quit publishing local news sections Mondays, Tuesdays, Thursdays and Saturdays and lopped off another third of the staff. Just 60 people were spared, including cartoonist Pat Bagley, four editors (Tim Fitzpatrick, Sheila McCann and David Noyce among them), three copy editors (Michael Nakoryakov was one), 14 news writers (Tony Semerad and Dan Harrie were the two I knew), five arts and living staffers (Kathy Stephenson, Sean Means and Catherine Reese Newston were holdovers from my era), nine in sports (I knew only Joe Baird), six photographers (Rick Egan from my time), six digital employees and a few columnists. Friends Ana Daraban and Chris McDonald stayed on the payroll as support staff.

Paul Rolly voluntarily retired at age 70, but several of my former colleagues were among the 34 sent packing. Mike Gorrell was notified by email his services were no longer needed. Gordon Harman, Chris Smart, Steve Hunt and Al Hartmann also went home.

The last straw, for me, was a partnership that would put *Tribune* reporters on KSTU Fox 13 and Fox bylines in *The Tribune.* *Tribune* credibility and identity as a local watchdog had vanished. That chapter in my life was over.

---

[955] Terry Orme conversation, October 5, 2013.

[956] Tribune Editors, "News release: Trib changes leadership, reduces staff by nearly 20 percent," *The Salt Lake Tribune,* September 12, 2013.

957 Tony Semerad and Tom Harvey, "Tribune owners betting heavily on digital future, documents show," *The Salt Lake Tribune*, October 25, 2013. Tom Harvey, "Tribune sells interest in printing plant to rival," *The Salt Lake Tribune*, October 21, 2014.

958 Mike Korologos, March 25, 2015.

959 Diane Cole, "Utah needs a financially secure Tribune," *The Salt Lake Tribune*, November 30, 2013, p. A19.

960 Paul Sharp, "Anti-Mormon bigotry," *The Salt Lake Tribune,* December 5, 2013, p. A14.

961 Malmquist, pp. 239-241.

962 Tony Semerad, "Huntsman: Buy The Tribune? Maybe, but any sale is on hold," *The Salt Lake Tribune*, June 6, 2014.

963 Terry Orme, "I knew Paul Rolly before he was a household name," *The Salt Lake Tribune*, August 14, 2015.

964 Rolly roast, Gallivan Center, August 19, 2015.

965 Gayle Ruzicka at Rolly Roast, August 19, 2015.

966 Curt Bramble at Rolly Roast, August 19, 2015.

967 Semerad, May 26, 2016.

968 Tony Semerad, "Salt Lake Tribune sale to Huntsman is done; new deal ups paper's profit share," *The Salt Lake Tribune*, May 31, 2016.

969 Tony Semerad, "Huntsman expects to cinch Tribune purchase next week, will keep current top editor in place," *The Salt Lake Tribune*, May 26, 2016.

970 Tribune Editorial, July 29, 2016.

59 - Tying Up Loose Ends

After five years in assisted living, the last one involving hospice, my 92-year-old mother wasted away on liquids and morphine in 2016. Witnessing her physical and mental decline was heartbreaking and exhausting; her starvation horrifying. Thanks to ESOP, I was able to serve as her guardian her fading years -- years I otherwise would have worked in Salt Lake City.

If I had stayed in the news business, I would have pontificated on the overwhelming challenges facing Americans at the end of life. In 2018, health-care reform is more important than ever as Alzheimer's and other chronic diseases rob growing numbers of seniors of their comfort, independence and security.

Grandson Brock accepted a robotics job close enough to spend occasional weekends with us -- compensation for losing touch with him for a decade and his brother and cousin even longer. John Deere never did reconnect; Willy visited but withdrew when we failed to supplement tuition at a college as expensive as Harvard. Another topic worth analysis: Why can colleges and banks bury penniless students so deeply in debt?

I quit consulting Mimi regularly as I golfed, wrote and tended my garden. Denny worked in our aging avocado grove and sculpted. After 40 years together, Denny still made me laugh. If he received short shrift in these pages, it's because I relied heavily on journals used as my sounding board during times of trouble.

Reviewing these pages as an older woman, it seems such a shame I wasted so much effort wallowing in self-incrimination, doubt and worry my working years. But deadlines applied horrendous pressure, and I could not guess how well Denny and I would come out of it. Even now I have nightmares that might qualify as post-traumatic stress. Yet I can finally concede that I did a decent job at *The Tribune*. So did my peers.

Most Utah journalists the last quarter of the 20th century were intelligent, honorable professionals. Integrity -- accuracy, honesty, sensitivity and fairness -- was the code for 99 percent of them. Some could be lazy, arrogant or sloppy, stealing other writers' words or causing unfortunate mistakes, public ridicule and heartache. A couple of acquaintances sneaked phony stories into print as a joke that backfired. But I remember only one who lied outright and another who extorted favors. Overall, the news people I knew served Utah and the First Amendment well. I am proud to have served with them, and I wish they all could have come out of it as well as or better than I did.

Acknowledgments

Many friends and acquaintances contributed to this book with their anecdotes, details, analysis or editing skills.

Thanks to my elder colleagues who still live to tell their tales, including Mike Korologos, Bob Blair, Barbi Robison, Harry Fuller, Dick Rosetta, and to others who have passed on, including Dominic Welch, Bob Woody and Jack Gallivan. Among other peers (or their spouses) who faithfully provided memories are Ben Ling, Mike Carter, John Keahey, Ann Poore, Mike Gorrell, Joe Rolando, Mark Knudsen, Nancy Melich, Lex Hemphill, Paul Wetzel, Brian Nutting, Paul Rolly, George Raine, Dennis Green, JoAnn Jacobsen-Wells, Dave Jonsson, Robert Bryson, Barbara Woody, James Ure, Lori Ure, Terri Ellefsen Swain, Kirk Millson, Cathy Free, Russell Weeks, Carol Sisco, Robert Triptow, Janice Keller, Anne Wilson, Con Psarras, Kathy Kapos Stephenson, Carol VanWagoner, Pepper Provenzano, Ana Daraban and Tom Wharton. Gordon Harman not only gave up memories, he passed along copies of employee badges he found during *The Tribune's* move to Gateway. Many of the photographs came from the files of Dennis Green and Tim Kelly. Rod Cushing provided vital substance to the ESOP tales.

Thanks to Max Zimmer, another grownup Bountiful child who knows the paralyzing impact of writer's block, I finally got this writing job done. Barbara Tolle and Dennis Green provided invaluable advice and editing while reading my rough drafts. Thanks to David Edgerton for steering me toward self-publishing on Amazon. It also helped immensely to have a friendly writing program that allows quick references to dictionaries and other resources, such as Google and Wikipedia. I relied on *Deseret News'* archives for many of my facts because *Tribune* archives were less accessible.

Without Mimi, my journal, my memory would have been a jumble of incidents without context or a timeline. Unfortunately, Mimi was my sounding board when hurt, frustrated or angry, so this memoir focuses more on the negative than the positive. That's too bad, because my *Tribune* years were enjoyable overall, and my husband kept me going -- and still does -- with his love, support and wonderful sense of humor. That doesn't come across well enough in the book.

While I contacted many people to sharpen my memory and add depth to the period I worked at *The Salt Lake Tribune,* this memoir is selective to those people and things I knew. I consciously chose not to "interview" those I knew only in passing or as antagonists. Jay Shelledy and Walt Schaffer stand out in that group. Some of my closest friends declined to participate in this crowd-sourced project, so there is less about them than I would have liked.